Survey Research in Corporate Finance
Bridging the Gap between Theory and Practice

Financial Management Association
Survey and Synthesis Series

Survey Research in Corporate Finance

Bridging the Gap between Theory and Practice

H. Kent Baker
Kogod School of Business, American University

J. Clay Singleton
Crummer Graduate School of Business, Rollins College

E. Theodore Veit
Crummer Graduate School of Business, Rollins College

OXFORD
UNIVERSITY PRESS

2011

OXFORD
UNIVERSITY PRESS

Oxford University Press, Inc., publishes works that further
Oxford University's objective of excellence
in research, scholarship, and education.

Oxford   New York
Auckland   Cape Town   Dar es Salaam   Hong Kong   Karachi
Kuala Lumpur   Madrid   Melbourne   Mexico City   Nairobi
New Delhi   Shanghai   Taipei   Toronto

With offices in
Argentina   Austria   Brazil   Chile   Czech Republic   France   Greece
Guatemala   Hungary   Italy   Japan   Poland   Portugal   Singapore
South Korea   Switzerland   Thailand   Turkey   Ukraine   Vietnam

Library of Congress Cataloging-in-Publication Data

Baker, H. Kent (Harold Kent), 1944–
  Survey research in corporate finance : bridging the gap between theory
and practice / H. Kent Baker, J. Clay Singleton, E. Theodore Veit.
      p. cm. – (Financial Management Association survey and synthesis series)
  Includes bibliographical references and index.
  ISBN 978-0-19-534037-2 (cloth : alk. paper) 1. Corporations—Finance.
2. Finance—Research. I. Singleton, J. Clay, 1947- II. Veit, E. Theodore. III. Title.
HG4014.B35 2011
  658.15'50723—dc22   2009053093

1 3 5 7 9 8 6 4 2
Printed in the United States of America
on acid-free paper

Contents

Acknowledgments

This book would not have been possible without the outstanding work of numerous survey researchers who have investigated many areas in corporate finance during more than half a century. The book benefited substantially from the capable editorial assistance of Linda A. Baker and Meghan Nesmith, who carefully reviewed the chapters and made many helpful suggestions. We thank our talented publishing team at Oxford University Press including Catherine Rae, Michael List, Susan Dodson, John Erganian, Kiran Kumar, and many others. H. Kent Baker acknowledges the support provided by the Kogod School of Business at American University, especially Dean Richard Durand and Senior Associate Dean Kathy Getz. Finally, The authors dedicate this book to their wives: Linda A. Baker, Kathleen M. Singleton, and Marcia R. Veit.

Survey Research in Corporate Finance

Bridging the Gap between Theory and Practice

Survey Research in Corporate Finance: An Overview

In theory, there is no difference between theory and practice.
But, in practice, there is.

Jan L. A. van de Snepscheut

An Allegory

In an imaginative allegory, Percival (1993) relates a story about a frog pond having several inhabitants: turtles, tadpoles, and frogs. Those who ruled the frog pond believed that tadpoles should receive training in frog-pond school to become successful frogs. Traditionally, turtles did most of the teaching, except for a few "frogs in residence" who gave special lectures. Most turtles in different frog-pond schools taught the same frog-pond theory that assumed "rational" behavior. The turtles told the tadpoles that they needed to learn what frogs *should* do, not what frogs *actually* do, because this "normative" approach would teach tadpoles how to think.

The tadpoles repeatedly pointed out to the turtles that frogs often did not behave the way the theory said they should; that is, the facts did not fit the theory. Although this was a source of puzzlement, the turtles said that they knew best. They pointed out that over the years, many eminent turtles had developed and empirically tested numerous theories. When the tadpoles asked why the turtles did not ask the frogs why they did what they did, the turtles simply scoffed at this naïve question. Such an approach would be unscientific. Furthermore, frogs would not be able to rationally explain their behavior. Thus, if the turtles could not fully understand frog behavior, how could frogs possibly understand it? According to the turtles, the moral of the story is that we should not let what appear to be facts cause us to deviate from our commitment to sound theory.

As Weaver (1993) points out, this story calls attention to some of the broad gaps between practitioners (frogs) and academics (turtles). Everything works in theory but not necessarily in practice. As a way of bridging the gap between financial theory and practice, Weaver recommends that academics survey practitioners, practitioners participate in such surveys, and journal editors publish the results. This recommendation offers at least two potential benefits. First, evidence from properly designed and executed surveys could be useful in empirically validating conceptual hypotheses and the relative usefulness of various theories. Second, a continuing dialogue between academics and practitioners could be helpful in designing research agendas, courses, and programs. In short, finance practice can contribute to finance theory and vice versa. Following Weaver's suggestion could result in a win-win situation.

Role of Survey Research in Finance

Because corporate finance is a multifaceted discipline, there is no one right way to test hypotheses that confront researchers. Finance academics, however, often take two broad paths—theoretical and empirical—to better understand research issues. As Ramirez, Waldman, and Lasser (1991, p. 17) state, "A major aim of both theoretical and empirical financial research should be to aid the financial decision-maker." Unfortunately, some turtles may be more concerned with the elegance and sophistication of their theories, models, and statistical techniques than with actually helping decision makers. As Harold S. Geneen, the American business executive, reportedly remarked, "You cannot run a business, or anything else, on a theory."

Some research is theoretical, such as that conducted by the eminent turtles in the allegory. Normative financial theories and conceptual frameworks can produce knowledge that helps develop practice. For example, practitioners have generally adopted some advances in finance, such as the use of discounted cash flow methods in capital budgeting and the use of a weighted average cost of capital as a hurdle rate, developed in the academic realm. Thus, those exposed to normative theories may learn to become successful analysts, managers, and executives despite the fact that current practitioners do not always behave the way these theories say they should. Other research is empirical. As Aggarwal (1993) notes, all theory should be subject to empirical tests. When a normative theory is inconsistent with relevant empirical evidence, researchers should consider revising the theory.

Researchers use primary data and secondary data to test theories. Primary data are new data collected by the researcher for the purpose of the project, using such methods as direct observation, interviews, and surveys. Primary data can be expensive and difficult to acquire. Secondary data have been previously collected by someone else, possibly for some other purpose. To understand the world and test theories, financial researchers typically rely on secondary data available from numerous financial databases. Empirical studies in finance tend to be based on large samples of financial observations. Although these large samples can offer cross-sectional variations and the statistical power to analyze these variations, they have limited ability to deal with non-quantifiable issues.

In this book, our interest focuses on survey research, which involves soliciting self-reported information from people about themselves, their opinions, and their activities. The main goal of survey research is to allow researchers to generalize about a large population by studying a small portion of that population. By measuring groups of people that form a microcosm of large populations, surveys gain their inferential power, although they rarely achieve perfection on this dimension.

Rea and Parker (2005) note that survey research applications cut across many institutional and disciplinary boundaries. Although survey research has derived considerable credibility from its widespread acceptance, such acceptance appears greater in some business disciplines than in others. For example, casual observation suggests that academics in management and marketing appear to embrace survey methodology to a greater extent than those in finance. If this observation is correct, those using this research technique in finance follow a less well-trodden path than that used by researchers in some other business disciplines. Graham (2004, p. 40) observes relative to the finance discipline:

> Survey research is by no means the standard academic approach these days; in fact it's sometimes looked down on in academic circles as "unscientific". The common attitude is that managers and investors can do very different things than what they say they do—and even if they do what they say, their real reasons for doing things can be different from the ones they cite.

As Graham (2004) notes, survey research has its skeptics. Yet, all empirical research also suffers from design flaws. Thus, survey research is not unlike other forms of financial research in that in some cases, there are only imperfect solutions to design problems. As Groves, Fowler, Couper, Lepkowski, Singer, and Tourangeau (2004, p. 34) note, "A survey is no better than the worst aspect of its design and execution." Researchers conducting surveys need the knowledge to make appropriate trade-off decisions and to understand how these decisions affect the final results. If properly designed and executed, a survey can accomplish its goals. In conducting empirical research, Bruner (2002, p. 50) notes, "The task must be to look for patterns of confirmation across approaches and studies much like one sees an image in a mosaic of stones."

According to Pinsonneault and Kraemer (1993), survey research has three distinct characteristics. First, the purpose of the survey is to produce quantitative descriptions of some aspects of the studied population. Second, the main approach used to collect data is to ask people structured and predefined questions. Third, researchers typically collect data about a fraction of the study population in such a way as to be able to generalize the findings to the population. Thus, survey research may be the most appropriate method if the researcher needs information that is unavailable elsewhere and wants to generalize the findings to a larger population.

Purpose of the Book

This book has three primary objectives. The first objective is to provide financial researchers with a useful overview of survey methodology. Our intent here is not to address the details of how to gather survey data because this type of information is available from many other sources. Instead, we offer some general guidance about the fundamentals of survey methodology associated with design, collection, processing, and analysis of survey data.

Our second and main objective is to synthesize the major streams or clusters of survey research in corporate finance. What do we know from survey research in finance about how practitioners make decisions about such matters as capital budgeting, determining a firm's cost of capital, managing a firm's capital structure, making policy decisions regarding the payment of dividends, and managing risk? A synthesis can provide useful information about the gap between theory and practice and about how the size of the gap has changed over time. Our synthesis concentrates on academic survey research that is relevant to decision makers. Those same practitioners may also pay attention to surveys reported in trade press publications such as *CFO Magazine,* but we exclude such publications from our analysis.

The third objective is to provide a valuable resource and guide for those interested in conducting and reading survey research in finance. Presenting a synthesis of the types of studies conducted thus far may act as a starting point for future survey research in corporate finance.

Perspectives on Survey Research

Numerous views exist on the role of survey research in corporate finance. To gain a better perspective of these opinions, we survey and report the key findings of three groups: finance academics, finance journal editors, and finance practitioners. For example, we investigate what these disparate groups see as strengths and limitations of survey findings, how survey research can be improved, and the topics financial researchers should be studying with the help of survey research.

Views of Finance Academics

In March 2008, we sent a one-page mail survey with a return envelope to 635 members of the Financial Management Association who indicate a primary or secondary interest in corporate finance. The objective of the survey was to learn the opinions of finance professors about survey research in finance. Respondents returned a total of 154 completed surveys, a response rate of 24.3 percent. Because an important part of the survey asks about the level of training of academics in the use of survey research, we limit the analysis to only those 144 respondents having a doctorate degree or those having completed all degree requirements toward their doctorate except for dissertation completion.

Table 1.1 displays a summary of the responses to the first nine survey questions, which seek to learn how respondents view survey research and how they perceive finance professors who conduct survey research. These questions ask respondents to indicate their level of agreement or disagreement using a five-point scale, where strongly agree = 2, agree = 1, no opinion = 0, disagree = –1, and strongly disagree = –2. The last column of Table 1.1 indicates the weighted average response for each statement, where a weighted average response between 1.0 and 2.0 suggests an average response between strongly agree and agree, a weighted average response between 0.0 and 1.0 suggests an average response closer to agree than disagree, and so forth. We list the statements in declining order of agreement and discuss them in that order.

As Table 1.1 shows, the majority of the respondents express agreement with the first seven statements (hereafter S*x*). The statement generating the most agreement (S1), with a weighted average of 1.24 of a possible 2.00, is "survey research in finance has produced data unavailable from other sources." Here, 87.5 percent of respondents indicate agreement with the statement. The level of agreement drops to 82.7 percent for the next statement (S2): "survey research has helped bridge the gap between theory and practice in finance." Respondents also generally agree that "survey research has made a valuable contribution to the finance literature" (S5). The results show that 82.5 percent of the respondents agree that "the publication of survey results has revealed important insights about finance issues" (S4). A majority of respondents also agree that "I use the results of survey research in finance in my teaching" (S6) and "survey responses have suggested new avenues for further research in finance" (S3). However, a relatively high percentage of respondents (21.5 percent) offer "no opinion" for S3. Although a majority of respondents agree that "I find published survey research in finance useful in my own research" (S7), 19.6 percent of respondents disagree with this statement.

TABLE 1.1 Responses of finance academics to statements about personal views of survey research

This table provides responses from finance academics on their personal views on six statements involving survey research. Percentages may not add to 100 due to rounding.

Statement (S)	N	Strongly agree +2	Agree +1	No opinion 0	Disagree −1	Strongly disagree −2	Weighted average
				%			
1. Survey research in finance has produced data unavailable from other sources.	144	39.6	47.9	9.0	3.5	0.0	1.24
2. Survey research has helped bridge the gap between theory and practice in finance.	144	28.5	54.2	9.7	5.6	2.1	1.01
5. Survey research has made a valuable contribution to the finance literature.	144	28.5	52.8	9.0	7.6	2.1	0.98
4. The publication of survey results has revealed important insights about finance issues.	143	23.1	59.4	8.4	9.1	0.0	0.97
6. I use the results of survey research in finance in my teaching.	144	29.9	44.4	12.5	11.1	2.1	0.89
3. Survey responses have suggested new avenues for further research in finance.	144	21.5	50.0	21.5	6.3	0.7	0.85
7. I find published survey research in finance useful in my own research.	143	16.8	40.6	17.5	19.6	5.6	0.43
8. Finance professors in general believe survey research makes a valuable contribution to the finance literature.	144	4.9	31.3	33.3	23.6	6.9	0.03
9. Academic bias against publishing survey research in finance has discouraged me from pursuing this research methodology.	142	10.6	19.7	38.7	21.8	9.2	0.01

Table 1.1 shows that respondents are fairly evenly split in their views about the remaining two statements (S8 and S9): "finance professors in general believe survey research makes a valuable contribution to the finance literature" and "academic bias against publishing survey research in finance has discouraged me from pursuing this research methodology." A large percentage of respondents offer no opinion on these two statements—33.3 percent and 38.7 percent, respectively.

In summary, the responses to S1 through S7 provide strong evidence that the respondents believe that survey research in finance has many positive attributes. Yet, they have more mixed views about how finance professors generally view the contribution of survey research to the finance literature and whether a bias exists against publishing survey research in finance. While some respondents avoid conducting survey research because of the perceived bias (real or imagined) against survey research in finance, this view represents a minority of respondents.

Table 1.2 shows the results for four questions (S10 to S13) about the respondents' personal experience with and knowledge of survey research. The results indicate that 26.6 percent and 19.1 percent of respondents have published a survey-type article in an academic journal (S10) or a practitioner journal (S11), respectively. These percentages appear high, given the relatively low percentage of total articles in finance that employ survey methodology. However, our results may contain non-response bias if those more interested or versed in survey

TABLE 1.2 Responses to questions about personal experience with and knowledge of survey research

This table provides responses from finance academics to four questions involving the respondents' personal experience with and knowledge of survey research.

Statement (S)		Yes	No	
	N	%	%	
10. Have you ever published an article using survey research in an academic journal?	143	26.6	73.4	
11. Have you ever published an article using survey research in a practitioner journal?	141	19.1	80.9	
12. I studied survey research methodology in my highest degree program.	144	31.3	68.8	
		Low %	Moderate %	High %
13. What is your level of expertise about survey research methodology?	141	51.8	38.3	9.9

research methods responded to our survey. Less than a third (31.3 percent) of the respondents indicate that they studied survey research methodologies in their doctoral programs (S12). When asked about their level of expertise regarding survey research methodology, the majority (51.8 percent) indicate that their expertise in survey research methodology is low, while only 9.9 percent indicate their knowledge of survey methodology is high. Not surprisingly, the low level of expertise is consistent with the small number of respondents indicating they studied survey research methodology in their doctoral programs.

In the survey questionnaire, item 14 asks respondents to select from three different descriptions of the level of importance of survey research in finance literature. Alternatively, respondents can provide an open-ended response. As Table 1.3 shows, the majority of respondents (62.2 percent) believe that "survey research should play a complementary role to other types of original research" (14b). Only 15.4 percent of the respondents indicate that survey research should be considered equal to other types of original research (14a), whereas 21.0 percent indicate that survey research has a limited role relative to other types of original research. These responses suggest that finance academics participating in the survey, on average, believe that survey research plays a useful role in finance literature, although a somewhat inferior role to other types of research.

Table 1.4 presents the responses to a question about future survey research. Specifically, the questionnaire asks respondents, "What finance issue would benefit most from future survey research?" The responses to this question suggest

TABLE 1.3 Responses to a question about the importance of survey research in finance literature

This table shows the responses from 143 finance academics on their views concerning the importance of survey research in the finance literature.

14. Which of the following statements best describes your view of the importance of survey research in the finance literature?	%
a. Survey research should be considered equal to other types of original research.	15.4
b. Survey research should play a complementary role to other types of original research.	62.2
c. Survey research has a limited role relative to other types of original research.	21.0
d. The role of survey research should be as follows: (responses appear below)[a]	1.4
Total	100.0

[a](1) Observation and documentation of practice. (2) To find out what managers think and do or say they do.

TABLE 1.4 Finance issues that would most benefit from future survey research

This table shows the responses from finance academics on their views about corporate finance topics that would most benefit from future survey research. This table does not list responses that were too general to classify or related to topics other than corporate finance.

Topic	Number of responses
Corporate governance	10
Capital budgeting	10
Risk measurement and management	9
Behavioral finance	8
Capital structure and financing	7
Dividend policy	6
Theory versus practice	5
Hedging and swaps	4
Mergers and acquisitions	3
Working capital management	2
Privately held firms; investor/entrepreneur interactions	1
Project management	1
Issues related to boards of directors	1
Nonprofit financial management	1
Value of firm reputation with non-shareholders and stakeholders	1
The usefulness of academic finance programs to practitioners	1
Small business finance and financial management	1
Ethics in financial decision making	1
Value-based management	1
Use of economic value added analysis	1

that finance professors have an interest in learning about various subjects through survey research. The most interest appears to be in surveying practitioners about corporate governance, capital budgeting, risk measurement and management, behavioral finance, and capital structure and financing. While some of these topics of interest are likely to change over time, some topics on the list have already been the subject of survey research for many years and are likely to be of continuing interest in the future. In addition to the issues indicated in Table 1.4, respondents identify another 24 topics, some of which are too general to classify (e.g., "perceptions of managers") or lack specificity (e.g., investments).

In summary, this survey of finance academics suggests strong agreement that survey research in finance has produced data unavailable from other sources, has helped bridge the gap between theory and practice, and has made valuable contributions to the finance literature. The majority report not studying research methodology in their highest degree program and view their level of expertise about survey research methodology as low. The majority also indicate that survey research should play a complementary role to other types of original research. In addition, they suggest numerous corporate finance areas that could benefit from future survey research such as corporate governance and capital budgeting.

Views of Finance Journal Editors

Because journal editors play a critical role in the publication process, knowing their views and the policies of the journals, if any, regarding survey research is important. Two studies specifically address the issue of how finance journal editors view survey research.

To gain some insight about how editors of "core" and "non-core" finance journals, as initially identified by Cooley and Heck (2005), view survey research, Baker and Mukherjee (2007) survey 50 editors by using an e-mail survey. Compared with the 35 non-core finance journals, the 15 core journals such as the *Journal of Finance, Journal of Financial Economics,* and *Journal of Financial and Quantitative Analysis* are typically more established journals with higher citation-impact factors. An impact factor is a proxy for the relative importance of a journal within its field, with journals having higher impact factors viewed as more important than those with lower ones.

Based on a 50 percent response rate, Baker and Mukherjee (2007) report the following key findings. First, none of the 25 editors reports having an established policy for the publication of survey-based research. Most responding editors (about 82 percent) indicate that the review process for survey-based manuscripts is the same as for other types of research. Only a few editors (about 9 percent) report screening such manuscripts more rigorously than other manuscripts before they go through the review process. None indicates discouraging the submission of survey-based manuscripts.

Baker and Mukherjee (2007) also ask editors to indicate their views on the role survey-based research should play in the finance literature. The respondents are evenly split on whether survey-based research "should be considered equal" (43.5 percent) or "should play a complementary role" (43.5 percent) to other types of original research. Several editors (13.0 percent) believe survey-based research has "a limited (or no) role."

When asked about the strengths and weaknesses of survey-based research, the responding editors indicate the major strengths of surveys as producing data unavailable from other sources (30.4 percent), suggesting new avenues for future research (26.8 percent), and providing the only way to answer a research question (23.2 percent). The respondents perceive that the greatest weaknesses of survey research are the difficulty of generalizing the results (27.7 percent);

non-response bias (25.9 percent); and the problem of dealing with adverse selection problems, because those who take the time to respond may not be the best respondents (22.4 percent).

Using an open-ended question, Baker and Mukherjee (2007) ask the editors to indicate up to three finance issues that would benefit most from survey-based research. The most frequently cited issue is investment decisions and practices (25.0 percent), followed by behavioral finance (21.5 percent) and risk management (14.3 percent).

To determine the extent to which finance journals publish survey-based articles, Baker and Mukherjee (2007) examine 49 finance journals, identify 180 survey research articles published during the period 1985 through 2005, and classify these articles by general topic area. This count includes only articles by researchers who collect data directly from the subjects under study. Core journals publishing the most survey-based articles include *Financial Management, Journal of Business Finance and Accounting,* and *Financial Review.* Among the non-core finance journals, those publishing the most survey-based articles over the study period are the *Financial Services Review, Journal of Financial Education,* and *Quarterly Review of Economics and Finance.*

Baker and Mukherjee (2007) report that the average number of survey research articles published per year over the 21-year period for the core and non-core journals is 0.276 and 0.213, respectively. The most common finance discipline, representing almost 33 percent of the published survey articles, is financial management, especially in the areas of capital budgeting, cost of capital, and dividend policy. The next most common finance areas are investments/portfolio management and financial markets/institutions, with about 13 percent and 12 percent, respectively, of the survey articles.

The number of published survey-based articles represents only a small percentage of the thousands of articles published in the journals reviewed. Although about 63 percent of these finance journals published at least one survey-based article during this period, a substantial percentage rarely publish survey-based articles, if ever. Baker and Mukherjee (2007, p. 21) note, "The reason for the infrequent publication of survey papers may have more to do with the quality of the research than to any bias against the survey method."

We supplement the Baker and Mukherjee (2007) study by surveying editors of 58 finance journals. Our sample overlaps with the sample of journals used by Baker and Mukherjee (2007) but also includes other business journals publishing finance articles such as the *Journal of Business Research* and the *Quarterly Journal of Finance and Accounting.* By using SurveyMonkey's Web site, which can be found at http://www.surveymonkey.com, we contacted editors in mid-April 2008, followed by a second survey sent to non-respondents two weeks later. These multiple contacts resulted in responses from 29 editors, representing a 50 percent response rate. The respondents' journals represent a cross-section of core and non-core finance journals. Although we took the normal precautions to reduce non-response bias including keeping the survey short, guaranteeing confidentiality, and using multiple contacts, such bias may still exist. Given the high response rate, we believe the overall responses are at a minimum suggestive of the views of finance editors.

The survey consists of five key questions. In response to the question, "Does your journal have a policy on publishing articles using survey research?" 82.8 percent of the 29 responding finance editors indicate no, 13.8 percent yes, and 3.4 percent "don't know." When asked to explain their journal's policy, one editor comments that the journal uses the "same standards as for all other research"; another says the policy is to "consider survey-based research providing findings appropriate to financial education," while a third editor notes that "only in very rare cases would we publish surveys." In the Baker and Mukherjee (2007) survey, none of the responding editors indicates having a policy of publishing articles using survey research. Thus, in both studies, finance editors typically report that their journals do not have explicit policies involving survey-based research.

When asked, "During the past three years, about what percentage of the articles published in your journal use survey research?" the 28 responding editors indicate the following: none (28.6 percent), up to 5 percent (35.7 percent), 5 percent up to 10 percent (17.9 percent), 10 percent and greater (3.6 percent), and don't know (14.3 percent). These responses are consistent with the non-survey evidence provided by Baker and Mukherjee (2007) that the publication of survey-based articles appears to be an infrequent occurrence in finance journals. In fact, they estimate that the percentage of survey-based articles in relation to the total number of articles published in each journal ranged from 0 percent to less than 4 percent.

A third question asked the editors, "What attributes would make a survey-based paper potentially worthy of publication in your journal?" Excluding two editors who indicate that survey-based papers do not fit their journals, an analysis of the remaining 26 responses suggests the attributes cluster into two broad areas: originality and rigor.

The most common attribute cited, mentioned by about 65 percent of the respondents, is the originality of the research; that is, editors look for surveys providing new findings or useful insights that make a unique contribution to the literature and are of interest to their readers. For example, one editor looks for "originality. (1) Answering questions that have not been asked before; (2) examining old issues from a different perspective; (3) asking questions about why practitioners do something instead of what they do." Another editor remarks that survey research should offer "original insights and provide evidence that cannot be normally gathered using available data bases." A third editor wants survey-based research to provide a "new contribution to the literature/insight into an unresolved phenomenon," and a forth wants surveys to provide "new findings that could help steer academic research and/or inform practitioners."

Another attribute necessary for a survey-based paper to merit publication, mentioned by about 35 percent of responding editors, involves the rigor of the research methodology; that is, there should be a well-structured research question as well as sound empirical methods and analysis. In addition, a survey needs to be the best way to get the data needed to address the research question. For instance, one editor looks for a "meaningful question, adequate sample size, mitigation of selection biases in response," while another wants a "rigorous survey design, appropriate method of analysis, interesting and important topic." A third editor expects a survey-based paper to be of "great depth, well-written, noteworthy authors." Another respondent suggests that a survey "used in conjunction with other financial data" may enhance the rigor of the research design.

The fourth question asks, "From the perspective of your journal, what finance-related issues would benefit most from survey-based research?" Although 21 editors provide usable responses, the number of finance-related issues is 31 because some respondents mention more than one issue. Table 1.5 shows the distribution of specific responses but excludes general comments such as "many" and "almost all finance fields." As Table 1.5 indicates, the area receiving the most responses is managerial perspectives and practices about corporate investment, financing, dividends, and risk management. Other major areas are investor behavior and attitudes toward risk, followed by financial education and literacy. Not surprisingly, the finance issues that journal editors report as benefiting most from survey-based research are highly consistent with those reported by Baker and Mukherjee (2007), which may partly reflect the overlap of editors responding to both surveys.

TABLE 1.5 Responses by finance journal editors on finance-related issues benefiting most from survey-based research

This table presents 31 usable responses from 21 finance journal editors about what finance-related issues would benefit most from survey-based research. Some editors list more than one issue.

Issues	%
Managerial perspectives and practices about corporate investment, financing, risk management, real options, and dividends	35.5
Investor behavior and attitudes toward risk	29.0
Financial education and literacy	12.9
Behavioral finance	6.5
Other (corporate governance, project finance, credit decisions, alternative measure of expectations, and assumptions for building theoretical models)	16.1
Total	100.0

The final question asks editors to make additional comments about survey-based research in finance. The following are representative and unedited comments from these editors.

- "Survey based research can play a major role in developing theories on why they do the things they do. Two examples are—dividend adjustment process and pecking order theory. This line of research can also test the validity of theories by focusing on how practice differs from theory and why. We can learn a lot from practitioners. When the survey research focuses on the same issues over and over (example, capital budgeting surveys), it loses its power and makes practitioners leery of its purpose. The result is practitioners are turned off."
- "Although survey research (except as conducted by the 'superstars') has fallen into disfavor in top journals, it's an important medium for understanding the decision processes followed by—and possible behavioral biases of—financial managers."
- "The biggest issues revolve around potential selection biases when only some survey participants respond to the survey."
- "I find survey research usually very helpful, but I am cautious about sample selection bias and low response rates."
- "I suspect that there are many problems, e.g., non-response bias, which are just ignored."
- "It has a place but finance data are so good it's limited."

Concluding Observations

Based on the Baker and Mukherjee (2007) survey and ours, several observations emerge. First, the responding finance journal editors generally appear to be receptive to survey-based research, especially if such manuscripts possess the attributes of originality and rigor. In practice, these qualities are no different from papers based on any other research methods that are published in high-quality journals. For some journals, the appropriateness of using survey-based data may neither be obvious, as evidenced by the paucity of such articles in these journals, nor the typical approach used, given the plethora of financial databases available to researchers. As one editor remarks, "Given the orientation of our journal, I would be hard-pressed to see a fit for survey-based papers in our journal. That's not to say that the research isn't worthwhile, but it's just not a fit for us." Thus, those engaging in survey-based research should make sure that their paper represents an appropriate fit for a specific publication outlet.

Second, responding editors typically acknowledge that survey-based research can be of value, especially when a survey is the best way to get the data or the only way to answer a research question. For example, finance areas identified by editors as benefiting from survey-based research include examining managerial perspectives and practices as well as investor behavior and attitudes toward risk.

As one editor notes, "Since the electronic databases have been so thoroughly mined, I believe that new and interesting data from surveys needs to continue to make its way into finance research." Although survey researchers in finance may follow a less well-trodden path than those using other approaches to research, their work should not be viewed as "unscientific" if they follow a set of theories and principles that offer a unified perspective on the design, conduct, and evaluation of surveys.

Views of Finance Practitioners

The purpose of our survey of practitioners is to determine the extent to which these financial executives find the results of survey research informative. The questions also differentiate between academic and professional surveys to determine whether the respondents find one source more helpful than the other. We make this distinction in part because we think that academic financial professionals may largely ignore academic research.

In the summer of 2008, we surveyed the chief financial officers (CFOs) of all companies included in the Russell 1000 Index as of May 2008. The Russell 1000 Index measures the performance of the large-cap segment of the U.S. equity universe. It is a subset of the Russell 3000 Index and includes approximately 1,000 of the largest companies based on a combination of their market cap and current index membership. The Russell 1000 represents about 92 percent of the market value of the U.S. equity market. We sent the surveys in an envelope containing a signed personal letter from one of the researchers on university letterhead and a prepaid business reply postcard. The letter sent to each CFO stated the following:

> For purposes of this study, survey research is a method used to gather information about opinions, attitudes, and behavior from a sample of individuals through questionnaires and interviews. Such research appears in both academic journals and professional/trade publications. Examples of trade publications include *CFO Magazine, Business Week,* the *Economist,* and *Fortune.* Some typical academic journals are the *Journal of Applied Corporate Finance, Financial Services Review, Journal of Fixed Income,* and *Financial Management.*

The postcard contained the following three yes/no questions:

1. Have you ever found survey research on corporate finance, published in academic journals, helpful to you in your position as a corporate financial officer?
2. Have you ever found survey research on corporate finance, published in professional/trade publications, helpful to you in your position as a corporate finance officer?

3. Academics sometimes survey financial professionals, soliciting their opinion or asking about company practices. Have you ever found the results of these surveys helpful to you in your position as a corporate finance officer?

Although the third question overlaps with the other two, we inserted it to directly test the respondents' attitudes toward academic surveys and to provide a check on the consistency of the answers. We promised the recipients anonymity but also offered them the opportunity to receive a summary of the results if they provided their e-mail address.

We received 108 responses, resulting in a 10.8 percent response rate. This response rate is low but compares favorably with some recent surveys of CFOs such as Graham and Harvey (2001) and Brav, Graham, Harvey, and Michaely (2005), whose surveys of CFOs obtained response rates of 9 percent and 16 percent, respectively. About 5 percent of our mailing was returned because the CFO was no longer at the company's address. This apparently high turnover in CFOs is not surprising.

Table 1.6 shows the responses to the three yes/no questions (hereafter Q*x*). The table shows that the respondents find surveys published in professional

TABLE 1.6 Responses by finance practitioners on whether survey research has been helpful in their position

This table presents the results from 82 survey respondents to three "yes/no" questions involving whether survey research has been helpful in their current position as a corporate financial officer. To calculate the mean, yes is coded as 1 and no as 0.

Question	Yes %	No %	Mean %	Standard deviation
1. Have you ever found survey research on corporate finance, published in academic journals, helpful to you in your position as a corporate financial officer?	51	49	0.509	0.502
2. Have you ever found survey research on corporate finance, published in professional/trade publications, helpful to you in your position as a corporate finance officer?	75	25	0.759	0.430
3. Academics sometimes survey financial professionals, soliciting their opinion or asking about company practices. Have you ever found the results of these surveys helpful to you in your position as a corporate finance officer?	55	53	0.507	0.502

journals (Q2) more helpful than those published in academic journals (Q1) by a wide margin. Of the 82 survey participants, 75 percent respond yes to the question about professional journals, while only 51 percent respond similarly to the question about academic journals. The responses to Q3 about academic surveys are virtually identical to responses to the first question about survey research published in academic journals, lending credence to consistency in the responses. These results suggest that the responding CFOs find survey results valuable. While these CFOs prefer the publications oriented toward their professional responsibilities, they are aware of and apparently read some of the academic publications because they find them useful.

To compute the mean response for each question, we code yes as 1 and no as 0. These mean values are all statistically significantly different from zero beyond the 0.001 level. The Pearson correlation between answers to these two questions is 0.40, indicating the respondents see a difference between the helpfulness of surveys based on where they are published.

Organization of the Book

The remainder of the book consists of eight chapters, which we briefly discuss next. Chapter 2 discusses conducting survey research, and Chapters 3 through 8 examine topics in corporate finance that offer a substantial body of survey-based studies. Chapter 9 provides a discussion of the current state of the art of survey research in corporate finance. It also addresses the question, "Do theory and practice actually meet?"

Chapter 2: Conducting Survey Research

This chapter provides some guidelines and insights on how to conduct effective survey projects in finance, especially self-administered surveys. It places more emphasis on a few practical and technical aspects of scientific sample survey research than the conceptual and theoretical aspects. Although we draw heavily upon our experience as survey researchers, we attempt to provide a balanced view of the attributes and limitations of survey research. The chapter devotes attention to discussing each stage of the survey process.

Chapter 3: Capital Budgeting

This chapter synthesizes the findings of many frequently cited survey studies regarding the methods used to evaluate capital budgeting projects. It examines survey studies that focus on the methods used by U.S., non-U.S., and multinational firms. Many studies look at the popularity of specific discounted cash flow (DCF) methods, such as net present value (NPV) and international rate of return (IRR), versus the popularity of non-DCF methods, such as payback period and accounting rate of return. Trends away from non-DCF methods and toward the use of DCF methods are apparent from the studies discussed.

This chapter also looks at survey studies asking firms if they consider risk differences in capital budgeting projects, and if so, what methods they use to measure project risk. Do they use sensitivity analysis, scenario analysis, simulation, covariance of project returns with firm returns, or other some method to measure project risk? An extension of this line of questioning involves asking how firms that measure project-risk differences reflect those differences in the evaluation process; that is, do they increase the required payback period or the required rate of return, do they reduce the size of the expected cash flows, do they simply reject risky projects, or do they use other methods or a combination of methods?

Another line of questioning asks firms if they engage in capital rationing, and if so, why. Do they use capital rationing because of debt limits imposed by internal management, debt limits imposed by outside agreement, a desire to maintain specified earnings per share (EPS) or price/earnings (P/E), or for some other reason? Still other studies investigate what firms use as a hurdle rate when evaluating projects; that is, do they use the weighted average cost of capital (WACC), the cost of debt, the cost of equity, the cost of financing a particular project, or some other hurdle rate?

This chapter also provides a synthesis of the survey literature on the use of postaudits. The purpose of postaudits is to mitigate the potential challenges associated with evaluating, adopting, and implementing capital budgeting projects, including both unintentional and intentional errors in forecasting project cash flows. Several studies of U.S. and non-U.S. firms ask survey participants if they use postaudits, and some studies explore the use of postaudits in greater detail. Finally, this chapter briefly examines survey research addressing issues such as cash flow forecasting, the use of real options, the impact of firm goals on capital budgeting, and how firms deal with future inflation in capital budgeting analysis.

Chapter 4: Cost of Capital

A common theme of corporate finance survey studies involves how firms determine the cost of capital and related topics. Researchers studying cost-of-capital topics have conducted surveys using samples of U.S. firms, non-U.S. firms, and multinational firms. This chapter reviews many of the most frequently referenced survey studies. A central line of survey questions asks how firms weight capital components to estimate their cost of capital. While some firms use the theoretically correct target capital structure, many others use book-value weights based on the current balance sheet, market-value weights based on the current capital structure, weights reflecting the financing being used to finance the projects, and other methods. Related to this theme are surveys asking how firms estimate their cost of debt and equity and if they adjust the cost of debt and/or equity for taxes. For firms that use the capital asset pricing model (CAPM) to estimate their cost of equity capital, how do they select input values for the model?

Chapter 4 also reveals answers to other important cost of capital questions such as how frequently firms estimate their cost of capital, what the numerical value of each firm's WACC is, and whether firms use multiple hurdle rates. Still other surveys ask how firms estimate their divisional cost of capital, whether firms believe disclosure affects their cost of capital, and how firms use their WACC in applications other than capital budgeting.

Chapter 5: Capital Structure and Financing Decisions

The purpose of this chapter is to review the survey research that tests the connections between normative theories of capital structure and corporate practice. The theoretical capital structure models addressed include (1) static trade-off, (2) pecking order, (3) signaling, (4) agency cost, and (5) neutral mutation. Because most of the survey research reviewed in this chapter investigates more than one of the five models, we arrange the survey discussions chronologically to provide order and perspective. This chapter traces the results of the most important surveys and summarizes where the literature stands today on the extent to which managerial practice follows the theoretical models.

Chapter 6: Dividends and Dividend Policy

Although corporate payout policy is one of the most researched areas in the finance literature, the question of why firms pay dividends and why investors want them remains one of the important unsolved puzzles in finance. The purpose of this chapter is to review and synthesize the dividend literature primarily using survey methodology and to chronicle how perspectives on corporate dividend policy have changed over time. The chapter documents the perceptions of corporate managers and those of institutional and individual investors about dividend policy. Chapter 6 also investigates several key questions. For example, why do some firms pay dividends and some investors prefer them? Do managers perceive that their firm's dividend policy creates value for shareholders? What factors influence a firm's dividend payout pattern? Do managers' views align with theoretical explanations for why firms pay or do not pay dividends? By focusing on those studies that attempt to describe dividend policy in practice, this chapter shows how survey research contributes to resolving the dividend puzzle and to our understanding of dividend policy.

Chapter 7: Share Repurchases, Special Dividends, Stock Splits, and Stock Dividends

In addition to distributing capital to shareholders by means of cash dividends, some firms use share repurchases and special dividends. While the practice of repurchasing shares has increased dramatically in the United States in the past several decades, the practice of paying special dividends has declined during that same period. This chapter provides a synthesis of the theories and empirical findings of share repurchases and special dividends focusing on survey-based evidence. Some firms also split their stock and pay stock dividends. These decisions involve the costly process of altering the number of shares in a publicly traded company. The chapter examines the perceptions of managers involving these other methods of distribution and whether such actions affect firm value.

Chapter 8: Risk Management and Derivatives

Under the perfect market and complete information assumptions of Modigliani and Miller (1958), investors can costlessly diversify or use homemade hedging so that hedging by the firm cannot enhance firm value. Researchers, therefore, have focused on how exceptions to perfect capital markets and complete information can enable firms to employ hedging to reduce firm volatility and add value. These imperfections include taxes, bankruptcy, agency costs, economies of scale, the cost of external funds, and information advantage. Much survey research in corporate finance focuses on how firms use derivatives to take advantage of these imperfections.

One way to investigate the use of derivatives is to examine each theoretical market imperfection from the perspective of its empirical implications. For example, the tax and bankruptcy arguments suggest that small firms should hedge more of their exposure than large firms. The economies of scale argument proposes that large firms should hedge more risk than small firms. The agency cost argument proposes that leveraged firms should use more derivatives than unlevered firms. The cost of external funds theory suggests that firms with heavy research and development expenditures should be active derivatives users.

This chapter on risk management and derivatives reviews the survey research that investigates these research questions. In addition to addressing survey research of U.S. firms, Chapter 8 also reviews survey research of non-U.S. firms and compares the findings to the results from U.S. firms.

Chapter 9: State of the Art: Do Theory and Practice Actually Meet?

Chapter 9 brings together all the pieces of this book on survey research in corporate finance. This chapter begins by discussing the importance of theory in conducting research and the importance and usefulness of both normative and positive models. The chapter also highlights the strengths and weaknesses of empirical research and survey research. Strong evidence supports the assertion that the academic and practitioner communities alike benefit from both types of research. However, only direct methods such as survey research can investigate how financial managers and others view theory. Survey research complements other forms of empirical research by exploring the relationship between theory and practice. By using survey methods, researchers can ask financial executives whether they are pursuing goals that theory suggests they should pursue. Survey research provides a means of identifying whether gaps exist between theory and practice, which is a focal point of this book.

This chapter reviews the key findings of past survey research in corporate finance. Specifically, Chapter 9 summarizes the major academic survey research findings about how firms conduct capital budgeting analysis, estimate the cost of capital, manage their capital structure, set dividend policy, elect to repurchase stock, pay special dividends, initiate stock splits, pay stock dividends, and manage risk with derivative securities. The chapter concludes with some thoughts on the past and future role of survey research in finance.

Final Thoughts

Our review of the corporate finance survey literature finds substantial support for a continued or even an enhanced role of survey research. We reach this conclusion because of documented past contributions of survey research and because our surveys of finance academics, finance journal editors, and finance practitioners suggest that survey research will continue be a part of the finance literature.

As with other methodologies, survey research has limitations and weaknesses. Yet, with proper planning and execution, survey researchers can overcome some of these weaknesses and provide meaningful results. As the following chapter shows, methods are available for mitigating these limitations, which in turn can lead to reliable and valid survey results. We are confident that additional methods and techniques will be developed in the future to further refine survey research to make it even more rigorous and useful. We believe the outlook for survey research in finance is bright, and we hope that this book contributes to its advancement.

References

Aggarwal, Raj. 1993. "Theory and Practice in Finance Education: Or Why We Shouldn't Just Ask Them." *Financial Practice and Education* 3:2, 15–18.

Baker, H. Kent, and Tarun K. Mukherjee. 2007. "Survey Research in Finance: Views from Journal Editors." *International Journal of Managerial Finance* 3:1, 11–25.

Brav, Alon, John R. Graham, Campbell R. Harvey, and Roni Michaely. 2005. "Payout Policy in the 21st Century." *Journal of Financial Economics* 77:3, 483–527.

Bruner, Robert F. 2002. "Does M&A Pay? A Survey of Evidence from the Decision-Maker." *Journal of Applied Finance* 12:1, 48–68.

Cooley, Philip L., and Jean L. Heck. 2005. "Prolific Authors in the Finance Literature: A Half Century of Contributions." *Journal of Financial Literature* 1:1, 46–69.

Graham, John R. 2004. "Roundtable on Corporate Disclosure." *Journal of Applied Corporate Finance* 16:4, 338–362.

Graham, John R., and Campbell R. Harvey. 2001. "The Theory and Practice of Corporate Finance: Evidence from the Field." *Journal of Financial Economics* 61:2–3, 187–243.

Groves, Robert M., Floyd J. Fowler Jr., Mick P. Couper, James M. Lepkowski, Eleanor Singer, and R. Tourangeau. 2004. *Survey Methodology*. Hoboken, NJ: John Wiley & Sons.

Modigliani, Franco, and Merton H. Miller. 1958. "The Cost of Capital, Corporate Finance, and the Theory of Investment." *American Economic Review* 48:3, 261–297.

Percival, John. 1993. "Why Don't We Just Ask Them?" *Financial Practice and Education* 3:3, 9.

Pinsonneault, Alain, and Kenneth L. Kraemer. 1993. "Survey Research Methodology in Management Information Systems: An Assessment." *Journal of Management Information Systems* 10:2, 75–105.

Ramirez, Gabriel G., David A. Waldman, and Dennis J. Lasser. 1991. "Research Needs in Corporate Finance: Perspectives from Financial Managers." *Financial Management* 20:2, 17–29.

Rea, Louis M., and Richard A. Parker. 2005. *Designing and Conducting Survey Research*, 3rd ed. San Francisco: Josey-Bass.

Weaver, Samuel C. 1993. "Why Don't We Just Ask Them?" *Financial Practice and Education* 3:3, 11–13.

2

Conducting Survey Research

> Few survey undertakings are as difficult as defining, sampling, contacting, and obtaining responses to self-administered questionnaires from businesses and other organizations.
>
> Don Dillman (2007, p. 323)

Introduction

Because financial researchers need answers to important questions, they have an unquenchable thirst for information. Over the past several decades, they have sought to explain the attitudes, beliefs, and behaviors of corporate managers, investors, and other participants in financial markets by using a variety of research methods. As Alreck and Settle (2004) note, answers to research questions must meet several criteria; they must be accurate, reliable, and valid. If done properly, survey research data can not only meet these criteria but also be the most effective and dependable way to get information to answer pressing research questions.

There are two broad categories of data: primary and secondary data. Most "traditional" empirical research in finance relies on the analysis of secondary data such as stock prices and financial and accounting data. Secondary data already exist. In many instances, such data may satisfy the research requirements of the study at hand. By using commercial databases and services such as Compustat, Global Vantage, CRSP, Thomson One, Datastream, SDC Platinum, I/B/E/S, and Wharton Research Data Services (WRDS), researchers can conduct large-sample studies. When the data depict how people operate, researchers typically must collect primary data firsthand and directly from those under study for a specific purpose. For example, researchers may want to acquire information from executives or other decision makers about their personal backgrounds (descriptive), how they think and act (behavioral), or the beliefs and opinions they hold (attitudinal). As Neuhauser (2007) notes, the increasing interest in behavioral finance has led to increased usage of the survey method in recent years. Other primary data collection options include laboratory experiments, fieldwork, and in-depth interviews. These approaches play an important role, especially in the areas of experimental finance and economics.

The main purpose of this chapter is to provide some guidelines and insights on how to design and conduct credible academic survey research. Although the chapter focuses on self-administered questionnaires and not survey interviews, this emphasis is not intended to imply that such interviews cannot be a highly useful means of data collection. The chapter also describes the survey research process. Given its brevity, the chapter provides an overview of survey research, not a comprehensive treatment of the subject. The chapter should be of interest to those who collect, analyze, or read about survey data.

Because survey research is an approach that cuts across many boundaries and disciplines, the same basic survey tools, skills, and activities apply regardless of the purpose or topics of the survey project. Although many sources provide in-depth discussion of survey methodology, such as Alreck and Settle (2004), Brace (2004), Rea and Parker (2005), Dillman (2007), and Fowler (2008), certain nuances exist in conducting survey research in finance and reporting its findings.

While this chapter emphasizes practical and applied aspects of survey research in finance, it also considers conceptual and theoretical aspects when they support a broader understanding of the subject matter. The execution of high-quality surveys requires more than merely following step-by-step instructions and relying on opinions. Over the past several decades, a set of theories and principles has evolved that offers a unified perspective on designing, conducting, and evaluating surveys. In other words, a science based on experimental and other research findings underlies this discipline. The field arising from this research domain is often called *survey methodology*. Although a review of this extensive body of research findings is beyond the limited scope of this chapter, other sources are available. For example, the Wiley Series in Survey Methodology offers several dozen books that cover topics of current research and practical interests in survey methodology and sampling. In particular, Groves, Fowler, Couper, Lepkowski, Singer, and Tourangeau (2004) provide an extensive review of research evidence to help guide those who conduct or read survey research.

Conducting a credible survey requires a process perspective and often a team approach, given the knowledge and skills needed. Various authors view the steps in the survey research process somewhat differently. For example, Kasunic (2005) proposes a seven-stage process: (1) identify the research objectives, (2) identify and characterize the target audience, (3) design the sampling plan, (4) design and write the questionnaire, (5) pilot test the questionnaire, (6) distribute the questionnaire, and (7) analyze the results and write a report.

Others organize the elements of the survey process in a different way. For example, Czaja and Blair (1996) view this process as consisting of six stages: (1) planning and development of the survey, (2) pretest, (3) final survey design and planning, (4) implementation of survey and data collection, (5) data coding and data file construction, and (6) research and analysis of data. Rea and Parker (2005) consider a finer breakdown and identify 11 stages of the survey research process: (1) identifying the focus of the study and method of research, (2) determining the research schedule and budget, (3) establishing an information base, (4) determining the sampling frame, (5) determining the sample size and sample selection procedures, (6) designing the survey instrument, (7) pretesting the survey instrument, (8) selecting and training interviewers, (9) implementing the survey, (10) coding the completed questionnaires and computerizing the data, and (11) analyzing the data and preparing the final report.

Regardless of the classification scheme, these stages represent a system of interlocking activities of which some are sequential and some parallel. As Figure 2.1 illustrates, the survey process involves both forward and backward linkages; that is, the steps in the survey process are not necessarily sequential, and some can overlap. For example, researchers often make decisions about data collection before designing and selecting a sample or constructing the questionnaire, because data collection is typically the most expensive and time-consuming aspect of the survey project.

A key to conducting a credible survey is to develop and execute an effective plan. Perhaps the most common planning error is to underestimate the time and skills needed to conduct a well-designed survey. Researchers also often fail to incorporate quality along the way. To achieve a quality product, the researcher must check every step of the process. For example, the researcher must devise ways to minimize survey biases and errors. Taking shortcuts, such as failing to pretest the questionnaire, failing to follow up on nonrespondents, and having inadequate quality controls, can invalidate the results and badly mislead users.

Survey answers are of interest because of their relationship to something they are supposed to measure. A measure should be both reliable and valid. *Validity* refers to the degree to which a study accurately reflects or assesses the specific concept that the researcher wants to measure. Both external and internal validity are of concern to researchers. External validity typically refers to the extent to which the results of a study are generalizable, whereas internal validity refers to the rigor in which the researcher conducts the study. In a valid study, the answers correspond to what they are intended to measure. No systematic bias exists because the survey is free of extraneous factors that systematically push or pull the results in one particular direction. The effects of sampling and many other factors may bias the results of a survey. Further bias can be introduced when

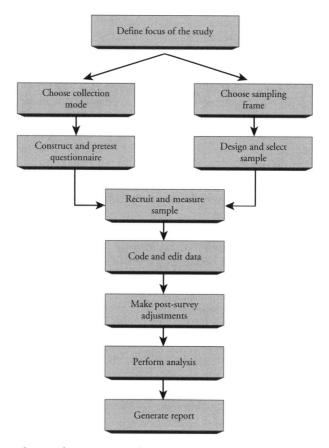

FIGURE 2.1 Steps in the survey research process.
Source: Adapted from Groves and colleagues (2004, 47).

designing questions, recording and processing findings, and even reporting the survey results.

Reliability refers to the consistency of the measurement. Good questions are reliable when they provide consistent measures in comparable situations. A survey with high reliability implies a low level of random error. In short, having some data may not be better than having no data. If the data are invalid, this can lead to false conclusions and wrong decisions. Such data are likely to be no more reliable than simply guessing what the survey outcomes would be. Thus, in the world of research, the following adage applies: no information is better than bad information.

Surveys tend to be weak on validity and strong on reliability. The artificiality of the survey format can put a strain on validity because people's attitudes, beliefs, and behaviors may be difficult to measure. Reliability tends to be a cleaner matter because survey research presents all subjects with a standardized stimulus (e.g., questions), which helps to eliminate unreliability in the researcher's observations. Thus, devoting careful attention to such factors as question wording and questionnaire format and content can reduce unreliability. Litwin (1995), Groves et al. (2004), and Alreck and Settle (2004) discuss the importance and measurement of validity and reliability.

The remainder of this chapter has the following organization. The next section provides an introduction to survey research and discusses the strengths and limitations of surveys. This section is followed by four sections that discuss components of the survey research process: (1) planning and designing the survey, (2) designing and developing the survey instrument, (3) collecting and processing the data, and (4) interpreting and reporting the results. Woven throughout the discussion of these four stages is commentary regarding how choices can affect the reliability of the data and the validity of the results. The final section provides a summary and conclusions.

What Is a Survey?

Survey research is a method for collecting data to gain insight about people and their thoughts and behaviors. As previously discussed, a survey is only one of several approaches used to gather primary data. A *survey* is a data-gathering and analysis approach in which respondents answer questions or respond to statements that are developed in advance. Surveys fall into two broad categories: self-administered questionnaires (mail-out and online) and interviews (in person and telephone). With a self-administered questionnaire, people record their own answers. With a survey interview, the interviewer asks questions from a prepared questionnaire, either in person or over the telephone, and records the answers. Brace (2004) and Rea and Parker (2005) provide a comparison of different data collection methods in survey research and elaborate on the strengths and limitations of each method.

Pinsonneault and Kraemer (1993) and Groves et al. (2004) identify several characteristics that distinguish surveys from other data-gathering approaches. First, the purpose of the survey is to produce quantitative descriptors of some aspects of the studied population. Second, the main approach used to collect data is to ask subjects structured and predefined questions. Every individual is asked the same questions in more or less the same way. Consequently, using standardized procedures permits obtaining comparable information for everyone taking the survey, which in turn allows for meaningful analysis. Third, surveys gather information from only a subset of a population of interest—a sample—in such a way as to be able to generalize findings to the larger population. Well-designed and organized surveys gain inferential power from their ability to systematically obtain information from a relatively small group forming a microcosm of a large population.

Survey Benefits

Researchers often initiate a survey when they are confronted with an information need and the existing data are insufficient. In fact, the main point of conducting a survey is to get information that is otherwise unavailable. Thus, the survey approach can provide unique information that complements the results obtained from traditional large-sample analysis. Such analysis offers, among other benefits, statistical power, cross-sectional variation, and small-sample clinical studies, which provide results for a specific sample. As Graham and Harvey (2001) note, large-sample studies often have weaknesses related to variable specification and the inability to ask qualitative questions. Thus, survey research offers a balance between these two approaches.

Finance surveys offer several other advantages over methods that use secondary data. In some instances, surveys can provide information unavailable from other sources, such as attitudes, beliefs, and behaviors. For example, Graham and Harvey (2001) conduct a survey-based study of chief financial officers (CFOs) to determine current practices involving cost of capital, capital budgeting, and capital structure within their firms. Baker, Veit, and Powell (2001) survey CFOs of NASDAQ firms to determine factors influencing dividend policy decisions. Baker, Powell, and Veit (2003) survey CFOs to determine why their firms use open-market repurchases. These examples illustrate that survey research is the most appropriate method because the target respondent population is accessible, and the research requires personal, self-reported data.

Surveys also offer considerable versatility and flexibility. Surveys are versatile because they permit specifying variables and asking a wide variety of questions. For example, sample survey research can be applied to any facet of descriptive data, behavioral patterns, and attitudinal information about societal preferences and opinions. The flexibility of surveys stems from the availability of several mechanisms to deliver the survey, such as self-administered and interviewer-administered surveys. For example, studies by Gitman and Forrester (1977) on capital budgeting and by Pinegar and Wilbricht (1989) on capital structure rely on mail surveys, while Lintner (1956), in his path-breaking analysis of dividend policy, uses personal interviews. In these situations, the data collection methods that the authors use are the most appropriate approaches, given the object of each study.

Survey research also provides a direct way for outsiders to understand how companies operate. It provides researchers with an opportunity to ask qualitative questions with specific responses. This attribute can help overcome some of the difficulties of variables and/or model specification inherent in quantitative research. For example, Dhanani (2005) notes that if dividend policy is prompted by more than a single factor, quantitative studies may be unable to distinguish between the individual-specific effects. Surveys, in contrast, can go directly to the financial executives in charge of dividend policy to discover the factors they consider.

In some situations, mixed-mode surveys (i.e., those using different modes of data collection) may be appropriate. Recent examples of mixed-mode surveys in finance include Brounen, de Jong, and Koedijk (2004), who use a third party to gather responses by mail, fax, telephone, and the Internet, and Brav, Graham, Harvey, and Michaely (2005), who employ both a paper questionnaire and one-on-one interviews with top executives. Benefits of mixed-mode surveys are that they provide an opportunity to compensate for the weaknesses of each survey method, offer possibilities for improving response rates, and reduce nonresponse bias and coverage errors. Additionally, a mixed-mode survey can be particularly useful when one mode, such as interviews, confirms the results of another mode, such as a self-administered questionnaire. Yet, using a mixed-mode survey raises many challenging issues including the possibility of producing different results for each mode. Dillman (2007) discusses the potential consequences of using mixed-mode surveys and describes a way of minimizing mode differences called "unimode construction," which assures that respondents have a common mental stimulus, regardless of the survey mode.

Another benefit of survey research is that it enables the researcher to choose the volume of data to collect and the degree of complexity depending on the scope of information requirements and resource availability. For example, Graham and Harvey (2001) conduct a comprehensive study in corporate finance consisting of more than 100 questions. They can have a comprehensive survey partly because it represents a joint effort between the Financial Executives Institute (FEI) and Duke University, and the financial executives surveyed are accustomed to receiving quarterly surveys. Another benefit of well-structured surveys is that they generate standardized data that are amenable to quantification, computerization, and statistical analysis. Finally, survey research can help bridge the gap between theory and practice, as shown in surveys by Trahan and Gitman (1995), Graham and Harvey (2001), and Brounen, de Jong, and Koedijk (2004), among others.

Survey Limitations

Despite their positive attributes, surveys have disadvantages and limitations. For example, respondents may not be representative of the population. Failure to follow strict procedures when defining which participants are studied and how they are selected can compromise the ability to generalize for a population by leading to errors and biases. Further, survey data may be superficial because designing questions that go into great detail can be difficult, if not impossible. Surveys measure attitudes, beliefs, and behaviors, not actual actions.

Additionally, respondents may be unwilling to answer sensitive questions. As Alreck and Settle (2004, p. 9) note, "Survey responses are not definitive and precisely indicative because respondents' answers are merely stand-ins for actual conditions or actions." Information obtained from self-reported sources may not be the undiluted truth because respondents may answer differently than if they were unaware of the researcher's interest in them. Thus, surveys rarely achieve perfection in making inferences about a large population from a sample (see, for example, Kish 1995; Lohr 1999; Chaudhuri and Stenger 2005; Scheaffer, Mendenhall, and Ott 2005). A final limitation of survey research is that it can be expensive.

Although surveys are a popular, suitable, and acknowledged research tool in many disciplines, some express lingering doubts about finance surveys. Although Aggarwal (1993) notes that much value exists in assessing the state of practice in finance by surveying practicing executives, he cautions against relying too heavily on managerial views without a proper underpinning in theory. He presents five reasons researchers interested in understanding the forces underlying financial practice should remain skeptical of information obtained through surveys. First, financial executives may be reluctant to divulge their reasoning and other details about their strategies and actions. Second, financial executives may not be fully aware of all the reasons for their firm's strategies and actions. Third, researchers may be unable to gain access to a representative number of executives to obtain reliable and representative information on financial practices. Fourth, the changing nature of financial systems and techniques requires frequent updating of surveys to understand current practice. Finally, suitable interpretation of empirical evidence requires the application of an appropriate theoretical or conceptual framework.

More recently, Graham (2004, p. 40) notes: "Survey research is by no means the standard academic approach these days; in fact it's sometimes looked down on in academic circles as 'unscientific.' The common attitude is that managers and investors can do very different things than what they say they do—and even if they do what they say, their real reasons for doing things can be different from the ones they cite." Based on their survey of finance journal editors, Baker and Mukherjee (2007) conclude that these editors believe survey-based research has a place in financial research when such research is done to the same standards as other types of research.

Given the benefits and limitations of survey methods, researchers should treat survey results as another body of evidence. Because each research method has its own strengths and weaknesses, using different approaches may provide a richer and more complete view of an issue than relying on a single approach. As with other research methods, the value of survey research depends on the care and expertise that go into the work and the amount of resources devoted to it.

Planning and Designing the Survey

The planning and designing stage of the survey consists of several steps: identifying the research objectives, identifying and characterizing the target audience, and designing the sampling plan.

Identify the Research Objectives

The first step of the planning and designing stage is to identify the objectives of the investigation. Establishing objectives requires a statement of the issue under study and of how the survey will answer questions about the issue. If the survey has a sponsor, one of the sponsor's roles is to describe the information needed to address specific issues. If there is no sponsor, the researcher has several means available to identify the key issues to be addressed, which in turn leads to developing the objectives. For example, relevant theory and the state of previous research can help the researcher identify the objectives. Thus, familiarity with the pertinent literature can help frame the research objectives by identifying what information is available from nonsurvey sources and whether any surveys have already been conducted on this topic. From our experience, researchers conducting survey research often attempt to determine whether specific finance theories are used in practice. For example, Baker, Powell, and Veit (2003) indicate that the primary objective of their survey is to determine which reasons for share repurchases cited by managers support the major theoretical explanations.

Conducting in-depth interviews of subject matter with experts can also be useful in identifying the key issues to investigate. When conducting these in-depth interviews, the researcher may work from a list of topics and possible questions, but the interview tends to be free-flowing. During the course of the interview, unanticipated issues might arise that the researcher may need to address in the study.

Another information-gathering technique is a focus group. This approach involves a moderator guiding a semistructured discussion among a small group of individuals who have some knowledge of or interest in the issues associated with the research study. This group can provide useful background information on issues necessary for developing the questionnaire and in formulating specific research questions and hypotheses. Rea and Parker (2005) provide a discussion of the role of focus groups in the survey research process. Based on our review of surveys conducted in finance, using focus groups to gather information to develop objectives for the study is a rare occurrence.

The objectives of the survey should present a set of reasonable expectations and should be as specific, clear-cut, and unambiguous as possible. A survey is unlikely to provide answers to all questions involving a complex problem or issue. This is especially true for those conducting an initial or exploratory survey on a specific topic or problem. For instance, Lintner's (1956) path-breaking survey is an example of an interview survey with a limited focus that paved the way for many other dividend studies. As Figure 2.1 shows, defining the study's focus helps in making decisions about the format for data collection and the sample.

Identify and Characterize the Population

Identifying and characterizing the population involves specifying the population to be surveyed, followed by identifying the sample unit and sample frame. The initial *population* consists of those people or elements possessing the knowledge and information sought by the survey. The researcher needs to analyze the characteristics of the population, which can be helpful in choosing the method of surveying and in developing questionnaire items that respondents can interpret. The *sample unit,* which is the smallest entity that will provide a response, is often a person such as a CFO or investor, but it could be an individual company, organization, institution, or other sample unit. The researcher wants to gather the perspectives of this sample unit about some research issue or question. The *sample frame* is a list of all the sample units in the population to be surveyed. The researcher draws a sample from this list. For example, Farrelly and Baker (1989) identify their initial population as institutional investors who are members of the Financial Analysts Federation (FAF). Because there are many types of institutional investors, they define the sample unit as security analysts and portfolio managers who are FAF members. The sample frame consists of several thousand FAF members meeting this criterion. From this sample frame, the FAF used a random-sort system to identify 503 names for a mailing list.

In finance, the basis for identifying the initial population is often theory driven. Occasionally, the target audience results from some type of event or action that the researcher is investigating. Frequently occurring events, such as firms paying a regular dividend or repurchasing shares, may lead to large initial sample sizes using short (recent) time periods. For example, Baker, Powell, and Veit (2003) identify an initial sample of 642 U.S. firms that enacted an open-market share repurchase between January 1998 and September 1999. Other types of events, such as reverse stock splits or specially designated dividends, occur less frequently and may require a longer sample period to obtain a sufficiently large initial population. For instance, Baker, Mukherjee, and Powell (2005) survey firms that issued specially designated dividends from 1994 to 2001, and after excluding multiple events and firms that no longer existed, they obtain an initial population of 343 individual firms.

While extending the time period may allow a larger initial population for an event-based survey, it also increases the probability that those involved in the event decision may no longer work for that firm or may not remember the reasons for enacting the past event. Thus, in these retrospective surveys, the respondent should not be forced to report events that have occurred too long ago to be remembered accurately. Including less-recent events also increases the likelihood that respondents' views or opinions about issues related to the event may have changed due to more recently published information or a change in the firm or economic environment. In summary, the researcher should generally avoid asking questions that tax the respondent's memory.

Non-event-based surveys often attempt to learn the views or perceptions of a sample of people about various topics. The basis for the initial population for these surveys may be geography, listing on an exchange, membership in an organization, or inclusion in a certain public or proprietary database. For example, Graham and Harvey (2001) identify an initial sample of approximately 4,440 firms by including all *Fortune* 500 firms and firms with membership in the FEI for their broad-based survey of current finance practices.

Design the Sampling Plan

The next step is to design the sampling plan, which involves determining how to select the sample size and the individuals to participate in the survey. These considerations affect the adequacy of the sample and, where possible, should be based on theory. Haphazardly choosing a sample may severely compromise the ability to make inferences about the population and the precision and confidence that the researcher can express about the finding. Thus, using well-established principles to select a representative sample is critical. Scheuren (2004) notes that the factors affecting the type of sample used include the objectives and scope of the survey, the applicable theory, the available time frames, the time and cost involved, the method of data collection, the subject matter, and the kind of respondent needed. A goal of this step is to select a sample that is an approximate microcosm of the population.

Of particular concern in designing the sample is controlling for sampling error. Sampling error occurs when those in the sample are not perfectly representative of the population as a whole. Whenever any sample is less than the entire population, some sampling error will exist. Increasing the proportion of the population included in the sample results in smaller sampling error. Although sampling error is random error, it affects both the validity and reliability of the data. Thus, as sampling error increases, the validity and reliability of the sample data decreases. Sampling error also increases as the variation among individual members of the population increases. Therefore, the greater the population variance is, the larger the sample size must be to attain a given level of reliability. Alreck and Settle (2004) discuss in greater detail how to control sampling error.

In selecting the sample, the researcher should also decide on the type of survey design—cross-sectional or longitudinal. With a cross-sectional design, the researcher collects data at one point in time from a sample selected to describe a larger population. Corporate finance surveys tend to use a cross-sectional design. With a longitudinal design, the researcher studies the same general population (trend), the same specific population (cohort), or the same sample (panel) at different points in time. For example, in a capital budgeting study, Gitman and Maxwell (1987) use a population similar to that studied by Gitman and Forrester (1977) to identify any changes occurring between the two studies. In their study of cost of capital techniques, Gitman and Vandenberg (2000) compare their results to an earlier study by Gitman and Mercurio (1982) that uses the same survey instrument. Baker and Powell (2000) provide longitudinal comparisons between 1983 and 1997 on the determinants of dividend policy from firms listed on the New York Stock Exchange (NYSE). In a study of corporate finance practices, Brounen et al. (2004, p. 73) asks exactly the same questions as Graham and Harvey (2001) in order "to facilitate a fair comparison of both sets of survey results."

Several procedures are available for selecting a sample, including probability sampling (random, systematic, stratified, and cluster) and nonprobability sampling (convenience, judgment, and self-selecting). In probability samples, all members of the population have an equal chance of being selected, and the selection of each sample participant is independent of the selection of other participants. Conducting probability sampling requires extensive knowledge of the composition and size of the population. Some form of random sampling is generally desirable to reduce bias. Deviation from using probability samples results in less legitimate and accurate statistical analysis. Generalizing the survey findings to a larger population requires a probability sample. Having a perfect probability sample, however, is highly unlikely if not impossible. Various sources provide in-depth discussions of survey sampling (see Kish 1995; Sampath 2001; Knottnerus 2003; Chaudhuri and Stenger 2005).

In nonprobability sampling, the probability of selecting a specific respondent as part of the sample is unknown. For example, distributing questionnaires to participants at a finance conference would be an example of a nonprobability sample. Using nonprobability samples is acceptable when the survey findings are considered unique to those participating in the survey. Using such an approach is unacceptable if a researcher is simply unwilling to devote the resources to drawing a true probability sample. A chief shortcoming of nonprobability samples is that they do not enable generalizing survey data with a known degree of accuracy.

With a fixed level of funding, several research strategies are possible. Two approaches lean in opposite directions: collect a large amount of data from a small sample or obtain a small amount of data from a large sample. The choice of the appropriate strategy often hinges on the information requirements and level of confidence in the data. For example, Bruner, Eades, Harris, and Higgins (1998) examine how some of the most financially sophisticated companies and financial advisers estimate capital costs relative to financial theory. Because the amount of data needed from each respondent was large and the necessary level of confidence was high, the authors chose a relatively small sample consisting of the most senior financial officer from 27 highly regarded corporations and 10 leading financial advisers. In finance, survey researchers often take a middle ground approach and obtain a moderate amount of data (say, from a several-page survey) using a moderate sample size (say, several hundred to a thousand participants).

Determining the appropriate sample size is a function of the precision and confidence level desired, as well as the population size. Although statistical approaches are available for the computation of a specific sample size, they may be of little value in practice because of their restrictive assumptions. Determining the sample size needed to make generalizations about the entire population is by no means clear-cut. In practice, most finance surveys probably do not require a precise sample size. However, a trade-off exists between the benefits of greater accuracy and the additional time and cost associated with larger samples. Judgment plays an important role in making an intelligent choice involving sample size. One way to gain higher reliability, lower sampling error, and greater confidence is by spending more money and expending more time and effort on selecting a representative sample. Still, selecting a sample and getting a good response rate are not necessarily the same. Alreck and Settle (2004), Groves et al. (2004), Kasunic (2005), and Rea and Parker (2005) provide guidance in using appropriate sample selection procedures and in determining the sample size.

Researchers face many choices and challenges regarding sampling. As Alreck and Settle (2004, p. 84) note, "While there are scientific principles and statistical procedures associated with sampling, the task of designing a sample, choosing a sample size, and selecting respondents remains largely an art." Ultimately, designing survey samples requires not only expertise but also sound judgment. However, defining and validating good judgment is a difficult task.

Designing and Developing the Survey Instrument

Although all stages of the survey research process are important, the survey instrument—usually a questionnaire—is the core of the survey project. The task of designing and developing the questionnaire can be a detailed and time-consuming process. Designing the survey questionnaire involves addressing such issues as the method of delivering the instruction, as well as its length, structure and organization, and page design and format.

Questions serve as a measure of the respondents' attitudes, beliefs, and behaviors. When designing questions, the researcher should make sure that the questions are both reliable and valid (Fowler 2008). One step toward ensuring a consistent measurement and hence a reliable instrument is to ask each respondent in a sample the same set of questions. Also, each question should have the same meaning to all respondents. If not, the answers may differ simply because of ambiguous terms or concepts in the question. Finally, respondents should have the same perception of what constitutes an adequate answer for the question. As discussed shortly, perhaps the simplest way to accomplish this task is to provide respondents with a list of acceptable answers by using closed-ended questions.

In designing and developing the survey instrument, the researcher should also take steps to improve the validity. When asking a factual question, respondents often report information with less-than-perfect accuracy for several reasons: (1) they do not know the information, (2) they cannot recall it, (3) they do not understand the question, or (4) they do not want to report the answer. To combat these problems, the researcher should ask questions about which respondents know the answers and that relate to a period that the respondents can recall, are clear and unambiguous, and do not relate to sensitive issues, where possible. If the questions are subjective questions, improving the validity of subjective measures involves making the questions as reliable as possible, offering many categories of responses, and asking multiple questions with different question forms.

The following discussion examines four steps in designing and writing the questionnaire: (1) determining the questions to ask; (2) selecting the question structure, response format, and specific wording; (3) determining the questionnaire length, question sequence, and questionnaire layout; and (4) developing ancillary documents. In practice, constructing a questionnaire is a skill refined over time by knowledge and experience. Some principles and practices for constructing self- and interviewer-administered survey questions are generally similar.

Determining the Questions to Ask

Before writing survey questions, the researcher must gather preliminary information about key issues of the survey. The questions should follow from the study's objectives, a topic already discussed as the first step in the survey planning and designing stage. Having clearly written objectives avoids overlooking important issues and wasting time asking respondents useless questions. Thus, the place to start in designing a questionnaire is with the data collection objectives.

The four main types of survey questions ask people about their attributes, attitudes, beliefs, and behaviors. Attribute questions generally ask for information involving personal (e.g., position, education, and years of experience) or demographic characteristics (principal nature of the business and organization size). For example, in a study of corporate finance practices, Graham and Harvey (2001) collect demographic information about the sample firms. In their study of how corporate managers view dividend policy, Baker, Saadi, Dutta, and

Gandhi (2007) ask six attribute questions to provide a profile of the respondents and their firms. Researchers often collect this type of information to explore if respondents differ in their attitudes, beliefs, and behaviors based on various attributes. For instance, Baker, Dutta, and Saadi (2009) test whether perceptions about dividend policy differ between managers of financial and nonfinancial firms.

Attitude questions ask respondents about their personal outlook and orientation or how they feel about something, whereas belief questions are opinion questions asking respondents about what they think of an issue. For example, Baker and Smith (2006) survey managers about the level of importance they believe their firm attaches to each of 16 determinants of dividend policy. When asking attitude or belief questions, a good idea is to ask multiple questions about a single concept and then create a scale by combining these questions. This approach also allows the researcher to examine the consistency of responses. For example, de Jong, van Dijk, and Veld (2003) ask multiple questions on the same topic when surveying managers of Canadian firms about their dividend and share repurchase policies to test for consistency of responses.

Behavioral questions ask respondents to indicate what they have done in the past or what they are doing at the present. Such questions tend to be factual in nature. For example, in their study of open-market repurchases, Baker, Powell, and Veit (2003) ask managers to indicate the primary method used by their firm to accomplish their last stock repurchase and the primary source of funds used to finance the repurchase.

This step results in a list of questions representing the information to be sought from the survey. If there are numerous questions, the researcher should prioritize the questions to identify those to eliminate if the questionnaire becomes too lengthy. As discussed later, pretesting can help refine the overall length and quality of the survey instrument.

Selecting the Question Structure, Response Format, and Specific Wording

After identifying the key issues or research questions, the researcher can prepare a draft questionnaire. The researcher must rewrite the research questions so that they can be quantitatively measured and are understandable to potential respondents.

Question Structure

Question structure refers to the type of response behavior that is being asked of the respondent. The two main categories for survey questions are structured and unstructured. With structured questions, also called closed-ended or forced-choice questions, the researcher asks a question and provides a fixed list of answer choices from which the respondent selects one or more as indicative of the best possible answer. Unstructured or open-ended questions do not list answer choices for the respondent. Thus, respondents can answer in their own words. As Brace (2004) notes, a questionnaire that measures behavior is likely to consist primarily of closed questions, whereas one exploring attitudes is likely to have a higher proportion of open-ended questions. The researcher can also use a hybrid structure, which is a partially closed-ended question that allows the respondents to write an answer if the options provided are unsuitable. For example, a hybrid question may have an "other" response, which asks the respondent to provide an answer in the space provided.

In surveying CFOs about their views on initial public offerings, Brau, Ryan, and DeGraw (2006) use both types of question formats. Their closed-ended questions consist of responses using a five-point agree/disagree scale and three-point questions (yes, no, and don't know). They also use open-ended questions for cross-validation.

Survey researchers often prefer to use structured questions because of their advantages. Rea and Parker (2005) discuss the various pros and cons of closed-ended and open-ended questions. One advantage of closed-ended questions is that they provide a uniform set of alternative answers that facilitates comparisons among respondents. Thus, the set of answers is known beforehand, which can lead to greater reliability. Another advantage of having a fixed list of response possibilities is that it makes the question clearer to the respondent. Additionally, closed-ended questions are often a better way to address sensitive issues because they provide an acceptable range of alternative answers instead of asking someone to provide specifics on an issue that the respondent may view as particularly personal. Fixed responses are also less burdensome and time consuming to the respondent because they do not have to construct a response. Thus, using fixed-alternative questions may increase the response rate. Finally, the structured-question format makes precoding possible and allows direct entry of responses into the computer for data processing. *Precoding* refers to assigning code values to the categories of structured questions. For example, in a study of why companies use open-market repurchases, Baker, Powell, and Veit (2003) use a five-point scale to measure the respondents' level of agreement or disagreement with various statements, which they precode as follows: -2 = strongly disagree, -1 = disagree, 0 = no opinion, $+1$ = agree, and $+2$ = agree strongly.

Using closed-ended questions has several potential drawbacks. For example, such questions may not permit subtle distinctions among respondents. To address this drawback, researchers sometimes insert another alternative in the fixed-response format: "other (please specify)." Although this alternative represents a compromise between closed- and open-ended response formats, the researcher should carefully control this option and base this decision on evidence obtained during the pretest of the survey instrument. The simplicity and ease of response may also increase the chances of inadvertent errors in answering the questions.

Using open-ended questions might provide interesting information, but they should be used sparingly in survey instruments for several reasons. For example, open-ended questions often result in irrelevant information and require a greater degree of communicative skills from respondents. Additionally, such questions necessitate some degree of interpretation and data standardization for analysis. Thus, open-ended questions lead to qualitative responses, which can be difficult to generalize. Filtering and categorization can alter the original intention of the respondent, which is a threat to validity. In mail-out questionnaires, Rea and Parker (2005) note that respondents are more likely to avoid questions requiring an original written response than those with fixed answers.

Despite these limitations, open-ended questions may be useful in giving respondents an opportunity to add comments and in conducting exploratory surveys. Such questions may also be valuable as a follow-up to a fixed-answer question as a means of getting more information or as a venting question at the end of the questionnaire; that is, the researcher may ask respondents to add any information, comments, or opinions pertaining to the subject matter of the questionnaire but not addressed in it. For example, in their e-mail survey of journal editors, Baker and Mukherjee (2007) ask editors to make additional comments about their views on survey-based research in finance. This was helpful in clarifying some of their responses to closed-ended statements.

Response Format

When using structured questions, researchers choose the categories or response choices to be offered to respondents. Such questions are called categorical items because all responses fall into a particular category. Therefore, answers to structured questions are usually a choice of position within some category or along some continuous spectrum. Response options should reflect the concepts being measured and fit with the question wording.

Alreck and Settle (2004) present three principles to observe when choosing the categories for a specific item: (1) the list must be all-inclusive, (2) the categories must be mutually exclusive, and (3) more variance in meaning should exist between categories than within them. The *all-inclusive principle* indicates that the list should include every possible response. Some structured questions may include an "other" category for responses that do not fit into any of the specified categories. The *mutually exclusive principle* indicates that no answer should fit into more than one category. The final principle involves the size and number of categories. The answers should cluster into categories on a meaningful basis. The number of categories has a lower limit of two and an upper limit of about six or eight for any one question. Choosing more narrow categories is generally preferable to using too few because the researcher can always later combine categories but cannot split them after data collection.

The researcher must carefully choose the range of categories or scale increments. Coding the scales with numbers is efficient and practical because it facilitates data entry and analysis. Additionally, using numeric scales helps to ensure accuracy, reliability, and validity. Alreck and Settle (2004), Brace (2004), Kasunic (2005), and Rea and Parker (2005) provide a discussion of creating item scales, including scale data types (nominal, ordinal, interval, and ratio).

Although many different types of itemized rating scales exist, a common conventional scale type used in finance surveys is the Likert scale (see, for example, Baker, Powell, and Veit 2003; Baker, Mukherjee, and Powell 2005; Baker et al. 2007; Baker, Dutta, and Saadi 2009; Brau, Ryan, and DeGraw 2006). As an attitudinal rating scale, the Likert scale states the issue or opinion and often asks for the respondent's view on the level of importance or degree of agreement or disagreement. Responses to each statement can be given scores, say, from 1 to 5, negative to positive, or −2 to +2. For example, to determine the importance that Canadian managers place on factors determining their firm's dividend policy, Baker et al. (2007) use a four-point scale, where 0 = no importance, 1 = low importance, 2 = moderate importance, and 3 = high importance. Sometimes, the scale is odd-numbered or centered on zero, with a middle value labeled as undecided, neutral, don't know, or doesn't apply, which is a scale value of zero. For example, a five-point Likert scale may appear as follows: −2 = disagree strongly, −1 = disagree, 0 = neutral, +1 = agree, and +2 = agree strongly. Examples of other finance surveys using Likert scales are Pruitt and Gitman (1991), who use a seven-point scale, and Baker, Mukherjee, and Paskelian (2006), who use a five-point scale. Although not a unique attribute, the use of Likert scales enables a researcher to calculate means and standard deviations for each statement because these scales use interval data.

Likert scales have both advantages and disadvantages. Advantages of this type of scale include flexibility, economy, ease of composition, and the ability to obtain a summated value or score. A Likert scale is economical because it provides answers in the form of coded data that are comparable and can readily be manipulated. Typically, the researcher uses the Likert scale for several items to obtain inherent economy. When using Likert scales, however, the researcher should be aware of several issues.

Brace (2004) identifies four interrelated issues of which questionnaire writers should be aware when using Likert scales: the order effect, acquiescence, central tendency, and pattern answering. First, an order effect or bias may result from how the question presents the response codes. A type of order bias tends to exist to the left of a self-completion scale. The order of the response alternatives can also affect the distribution of responses. For example, Dillman and Tarnai (1991) find that respondents are more likely to use the negative end of the scale when listing the alternatives from poor to excellent rather than the other way around. Second, according to the acquiescence effect, respondents have a tendency to agree rather than disagree with statements. Third, the central tendency effect indicates that respondents are reluctant to use extreme positions. When using the Likert scale, the researcher must be reasonably certain that a high percentage of respondents will not select only a neutral value. Finally, respondents may fall into a routine of pattern answering.

Similar to the Likert scale in format is the verbal frequency scale. Instead of strength of agreement, the verbal frequency scale typically uses four or five words to indicate how often the respondent has undertaken an action: 1 = always, 2 = often, 3 = sometimes, 4 = rarely, and 5 = never. Sometimes, frequency scales are in reverse order to that shown. For example, Graham and Harvey (2001) measure how frequently CFOs use different capital budgeting and cost of capital techniques on a scale of 0 to 4 (0 meaning never, 4 meaning always). Using a verbal frequency scale for several items, not just one or two, produces efficiencies. The verbal frequency scale offers the advantages of ease of assessment and response by those being surveyed. Because verbal frequency scale data are ordinal values, this type of scale has the disadvantage of limiting precision. Thus, using a verbal frequency scale is appropriate when respondents are unable or unwilling to provide exact percentages.

Another type of attitudinal rating scale is a semantic differential scale, which is a bipolar rating scale. Unlike the Likert scale, the semantic differential scale places polar opposite statements at the two ends of the scale, such as important and unimportant. Respondents then indicate with which dimension they most agree by placing a mark along the scale. An advantage of this scale is that no need exists to semantically identify each of the scale points, avoiding any bias toward agreeing with a statement because the respondent must consider both ends of the scale.

Question Wording

The questionnaire should be written from the respondent's perspective, not from that of the researcher. Wording understandable to the researcher may be unsuitable for respondents. Information derived from the target audience analysis discussed earlier is indispensable when designing and writing the survey instrument because it can help the researcher word questions so that respondents can understand them. Thus, the wording should strive to reduce any guesswork for the respondent when providing requested information.

Question phrasing is of critical importance because the meaning of a question can go beyond the literal interpretation of the words. Small changes in wording, which appear to be equivalent or innocuous, can produce very different results. The manner in which a question is asked can strongly affect the results of a survey. If a respondent misinterprets an item from the questionnaire, the data obtained through the survey will be erroneous and misleading. Hence, a bad question equals bad data. As Alreck and Settle (2004) note, question wording can introduce systematic bias, random bias, or both. Even questions expressed with focus, brevity, and clarity may jeopardize validity and reliability.

According to Groves et al. (2004), survey questions should meet three distinct standards: (1) content standards (are the questions asking for the right information?); (2) cognitive standards (can respondents understand the questions as intended and answer them without undue difficulty?); and (3) usability standards (can the questions be administered easily under field conditions?). These standards imply that each question should focus on a single, specific issue or topic. Additionally, questions should be expressed as simply and clearly as possible so that every respondent interprets the question in the same way. This requires keeping each question brief, making use of appropriate wording, and using simple instead of compound sentences to avoid ambiguity. Many sources provide specific guidelines for writing questions (e.g., Brace 2004; Groves et al. 2004; Alreck and Settle 2004; Rea and Parker 2005; Kasunic 2005; Dillman 2007).

Books on questionnaire design frequently offer a list of question-wording admonitions such as avoid being vague, use simple words, and avoid bias. Although these lists are well intended, they cannot be considered absolute principles. Therefore, the researcher should exhibit considerable discretion when applying various guidelines because survey questions are not written in the abstract. Instead, questions should focus on issues involving a specific population. Any set of guidelines, regardless of how comprehensive, cannot cover every situation. Yet, such suggestions as avoiding negatives and biased terms or suggestions as well as asking two questions in one (also called compound or double-barreled questions) represent useful advice.

As Fowler (1995, p. 78) notes, "A good survey instrument must be custom made to address a specific set of research goals." Nonetheless, Fowler suggests the following general rules for designing good survey instruments:

- Ask people about their firsthand experiences: what they have done, their current situations, and their feelings and perceptions.
- Ask one question at a time.
- Word a question so that every respondent is answering the same question.
- Specify the number of responses to be given to questions for which more than one answer is possible.
- Design survey instruments to make the tasks of reading questions, following instructions, and recording answers as easy as possible for interviewers and respondents.

Determining the Questionnaire Length, Question Sequence, and Questionnaire Layout

This section discusses three important aspects of developing a questionnaire: length, question sequence, and layout.

Questionnaire Length

Determining the length of the questionnaire requires balance. The researcher wants to include enough questions to make the survey relevant but not too many so as to affect the completion rate and response quality. Bogen (1996) and Galesic and Bosnjak (2009) find that questionnaire length can have a negative effect on the response rate. Prioritizing questions as must know, useful to know, and nice to know provides a helpful means of identifying which questions are possible candidates to discard if the questionnaire becomes too long. Questions that may be dropped include those that are unlikely to be analyzed and those that ask for information that is available from other sources.

There are several ways to lessen the negative impact of questionnaire length on response. For example, the researcher can offer incentives such as promising to provide respondents with a copy or summary of the survey's results, appealing to philanthropy, or offering some type of financial reward or prize. Groves et al. (2004) note that offering an extrinsic benefit for participation increases cooperation rates. For example, cash incentives tend to be more powerful than in-kind incentives of similar value. A review of finance surveys included in this book reveals that relatively few academic finance surveys offer financial incentives to encourage participation beyond offering a summary of the survey results.

Questionnaire Organization

Self-administered questionnaires usually contain three parts: an introduction, a body, and a conclusion. The first part of the questionnaire introduces the survey to the respondents and sets the stage for what follows. Alreck and Settle (2004, p. 147) stress the importance of the introduction as follows:

> If the survey is introduced properly, the response rate will be increased and the reliability and validity of the survey will be enhanced. If it's done poorly, refusal and non-response will increase data collection time and expense. Error and bias will result and the reliability and validity of the data will be diminished.

The introduction includes nonquestion text such as the survey title, instructions, and definitions. Instructions typically apply to a set of items or questions. The researcher should provide more elaborate instructions when using more complex scaling techniques and when dealing with less sophisticated respondents. Instructions involving scales should be clear and complete enough to be sufficient for the least sophisticated respondents. For example, instructions should indicate what items or statements to rate, the standard to use to judge the items or answer the questions, how to use the scale, and how to record the responses (such as by a check mark, number, or circle). As a general guideline, erring on the side of providing more thorough instructions is better than being too brief. Although the researcher should strive to use words easily understood by the target audience, some finance terms may not have a universal definition. In such cases, the term may be defined as part of the introduction or as part of the question.

The body of the questionnaire contains questions often called *demographic* and *substantive*. Demographic or biographic questions are fact based, and respondents can typically answer them quickly and easily. For example, demographic questions could include such areas as education, age, income, or position. Substantive questions address the survey objectives. The questions should generally be grouped by topic or subject matter, which avoids skipping around on the part of the respondent from topic to topic. A questionnaire containing several sections or subjects may require transitional statements. If the questionnaire contains questions of a sensitive nature, these questions should be positioned toward the end of the questionnaire. Thus, when respondents encounter such questions, they may feel vested in completing the questionnaire, and the likelihood of answering these questions may increase. Demographic or biographic questions that measure the attributes or characteristics of the respondents should also be placed near the end of the questionnaire.

In the conclusion of the questionnaire, the researcher typically thanks respondents for their time and cooperation. The conclusion may also contain administrative information such as a reminder on how to return the questionnaire, a serial identifier or number to enable distinguishing between respondents, and an identifier to distinguish between different versions of the same questionnaire. Alreck and Settle (2004), Rea and Parker (2005), and Dillman (2007) provide useful guidance in constructing the questionnaire.

Question Order

Poor sequencing can confuse respondents, bias their responses, and affect the quality of the research effort. Moreover, the answers may change when varying the order of items. Dillman (2007) discusses sources of order effects in self-administered questionnaires. One way to control for order bias is to keep the list of questions fairly short. Another method of controlling order bias is to vary the order of items from one subsample to the next. For example, Brav et al. (2005) use two different versions of their survey questionnaire, with the ordering reversed on the nondemographic questions because of their concern that the respondents might burn out as they respond to questions with many subparts. Graham and Harvey (2001) also employ different survey versions in which they interchange two sets of questions to investigate whether an order bias exists that affects the response rate. They want to see if a higher proportion of respondents answer questions that appear at the beginning of either version of the survey. Alreck and Settle (2004) point out that the order or sequence in which survey questions are listed may affect the response and induce order bias due to initiation (i.e., initiation requires that respondents learn how to handle the response task), routine, and fatigue.

Dillman (2007) suggests the following as guidelines for developing a well-ordered self-administered questionnaire. First, the researcher should pay particular attention to initial questions because they can affect not only the response rate but also answers to subsequent questions. The first question is especially critical to determining whether respondents continue a self-administered questionnaire. Once respondents begin answering the survey, they are unlikely to terminate prematurely. Thus, early questions should meet four criteria: (1) apply to everyone, (2) be relatively easy to answer, (3) be sufficiently engaging to encourage respondents to continue, and (4) be germane to the key focus of the study (connectedness). Although demographic questions often meet the first two criteria, they are not particularly interesting and do not meet the fourth criterion of connectedness between the respondent and the survey purpose as understood by that person. Thus, Dillman suggests that a questionnaire should seldom begin with demographic questions.

Second, the topics and questions should be grouped in a general way from most salient to least salient to the respondent, such as by creating questionnaire sections and using distinct headings (where appropriate) to separate questions having similar component parts. Grouping questions together that deal with the same topic makes the task of answering the questionnaire easier for respondents. Common ways of grouping items are by topic, scaling technique, or both. Grouping related questions from most to least salient is also advisable. Typically, survey questions should follow a logical sequence and a relatively uniform format to reduce the potential of format-related biases and to help respondents expeditiously answer the questionnaire.

Third, as previously mentioned, questions dealing with delicate or sensitive issues should appear near the end of the questionnaire. Placing sensitive or objectionable questions early in the questionnaire may lead to early termination, while placing them near the end increases the likelihood that respondents will not see them until they have become vested in answering the questionnaire. One way to deal with sensitive questions is to conduct reliability checks by asking the same question in a different manner and placing it in a different location within the survey instrument. For example, Baker, Veit, and Powell (2003) conduct a study to investigate the practice of firms repurchasing fewer shares than announced. Because some of the questions relate to the possible existence of unethical behavior, Baker et al. list these questions near the end of the questionnaire.

Questionnaire Layout

The layout of the questionnaire page depends on whether the questions are mailed to respondents (or sent as attachments in e-mail) or whether they appear on Internet-based surveys. Although the guidelines for developing paper-based questionnaires also apply to Web-based questionnaires, designing and developing the latter requires additional design and computer programming skills. Therefore, this subsection focuses on the layout of paper-based questionnaires.

Kasunic (2005), among others, provides guidelines to consider when laying out a questionnaire.

- Keep answer choices in a straight, neat column.
- Break the questionnaire into logical sections where possible.
- Have clear skip patterns for contingency questions.
- Make judicious use of white space to improve the visual appearance.
- Avoid splitting a question across two pages.
- Use the right-hand edge of the paper for answer choices.
- Limit the use of types of fonts and font sizes.
- Use boldface, italics, and different font colors sparingly.
- Avoid using all caps.
- Use at least a 10-point type size for easy reading.
- Include page numbers.
- Include the title of the survey as the header or footer of each page except the title page.

In summary, the questionnaire format should be visually attractive and nicely reproduced. Internet survey tools such as SurveyMonkey typically do this automatically.

Developing Ancillary Documents

In addition to the questionnaire instrument, several ancillary documents are needed to support the survey. For paper-based questionnaires, these ancillaries often include (1) a prenotification letter or e-mail; (2) a questionnaire cover letter; (3) a mailing and response envelope (when using a mail survey); (4) a reminder letter, postcard, or e-mail; and (5) a thank-you letter, postcard, or e-mail. Each mailing piece should be consistent in quality.

A prenotification letter indicates the purpose of the survey and requests the cooperation of the recipient. This letter should arrive several days before the questionnaire. Using a prenotification letter by mail adds to the postage cost of a survey. Research evidence is mixed regarding the effectiveness of a prenotification letter on increasing response rates (Chiu and Brennan 1990; Yammarino, Skinner, and Childers 1991; Wright 1995). From our own experience, however, using a prenotification letter is generally worth the additional cost.

The purpose of the cover letter is to explain the project and gain cooperation of the recipient. The one-page letter should use a conventional business-letter-style format and be written on quality stationery from a university, sponsor, or other organization. Other important elements of a cover letter include showing respect for the recipient's time and effort and avoiding begging. The cover letter accompanying the initial questionnaire typically should generally consist of the following parts: (1) date; (2) name and inside address; (3) the request; (4) reason for selecting the recipient; (5) purpose and importance of the survey; (6) promise of anonymity or confidentiality; (7) an explanation of how the results will be used; (8) encouragement and/or incentives to participate; (9) estimated time needed to complete the questionnaire; (10) deadline for completing the questionnaire; (11) person to contact to answer questions, including a phone number or e-mail address; and (12) a real signature in contrasting ink. When no preexisting relation exists between the sender and receiver and the gender is known, salutations such as "Dear Mr. Martin" are appropriate and may lead to a higher response rate. For some financial surveys, name lists (names and addresses) may be available from such sources as the sponsor, Standard & Poors' Research Insight, and Hoovers (http://www.hoovers.com). Alreck and Settle (2004) and Dillman (2007) provide more detailed guidelines for writing cover letters.

For the typical mailed questionnaire, the mailing envelope should be a standard number 10 business envelope with nothing printed on the back. The front should contain only the name and address, the return address (often with the university or business logo), and a stamp or metered postage. Typing names and addresses directly onto envelopes is typically preferable to using labels because of the more personal appearance. Doing this may increase the response rate. The return envelope should have real stamps affixed and be smaller than the mailing envelope. For example, if the mailing envelope is a number 10, the return envelope should be a number 9 so that it will fit inside the mailing envelope without folding. Using real first-class postage makes the correspondence more personal, reduces the likelihood that the recipient will discard the questionnaire, and may therefore positively affect the response rate.

A reminder letter, postcard, or e-mail can be sent to nonrespondents. This communication, which should be brief and to the point, may have a positive effect on the response rate. For example, Kaplowitz, Hadlock, and Levine (2004) find that a reminder mail notification had a positive effect on the response rate for a Web survey application compared to a treatment in which respondents only received an e-mail containing a link to the Web survey. Reminder mail notifications, however, did not produce higher response rates to the Web survey for respondents who had received a prenotice.

Evaluating the Questionnaire

Having taken the steps just discussed, the questionnaire is still not in final form or ready for distribution. After constructing a self-administered questionnaire, which often requires numerous revisions, the researcher should obtain feedback on the survey instrument. Pretesting enables the researcher to assess such critical factors as questionnaire clarity, comprehensiveness, and acceptability. The importance of empirical verification through testing cannot be understated because pretesting can help identify questionnaire problems. Based on the experience of the pretest, the researcher can fine-tune the questionnaire for use in the actual survey process.

Pretesting is a broad term that incorporates various methods or combinations of methods. Pretesting is the best way to discover how surveys and procedures work under realistic conditions. Presser, Couper, Lessler, Martin, Martin, Rothgeb, and Singer (2004) discuss methods for testing and evaluating survey questions. As Scheuren (2004) notes, these pretesting techniques consist of two major categories: prefield and field. The researcher may use prefield techniques such as respondent focus groups and intensive (cognitive) interviews during the preliminary stages of questionnaire development.

Although focus groups typically help define the topics and the research questions, they may also evaluate questions. As Fowler (1995) notes, focus-group discussion can contribute both to examining the assumptions behind the reality about which people will be asked and to evaluating how people understand terms or concepts used in the survey instrument. For example, Brav et al. (2005) use CFO focus-group participants to help refine and clarify their survey instrument on dividend policy. In short, focus groups can provide useful input to the design of survey questions. From our experience, however, few published surveys in finance use focus groups to evaluate the questionnaire.

Another prefield approach also generally used early in the questionnaire development cycle is to conduct intensive one-on-one (cognitive) interviews. With "think aloud" interviews, the researcher uses probes or other procedures to discover how the respondents understood the questions and arrived at their answers, as well as their ability to use the scales. A limitation of cognitive testing concerns the ability to generalize the results.

Field techniques include expert reviews, field or pilot pretests, and split-ballot experiments, among others. Expert reviews entail using both subject-matter experts and questionnaire-design experts. These experts examine the questionnaire to ensure that it collects the information needed to meet the objectives of the survey. In addition, they review such matters as question wording, structure, sequencing, and instructions to respondents. This method is relatively inexpensive and easy to carry out but is only as good as the experts. For example, in an international study of ethics in the investment profession involving eight countries, Baker, Veit, and Murphy (1995) have investment professionals from each country review the questionnaire and suggest changes. In their study of the theory and practice of corporate finance, Graham and Harvey (2001) circulate a draft survey to a group of prominent academics for feedback. Brav et al. (2008) solicit feedback from academics on the initial version of the survey involving the managerial response to the May 2003 dividend tax cut.

Another field approach to evaluating the survey instrument is a field or pilot pretest, which involves a small-scale implementation of the draft questionnaire. The basic requirement for pretest respondents is that they are members of the study's actual target population. Pilot tests can expose problems or weaknesses in the questions, questionnaire layout, process, and technology (when using a

Web-based questionnaire). For example, pretesting can enable identifying poorly worded questions, high rates of missing data, and inconsistencies with other questions. Pretesting can also provide information about the variance of responses. Thus, the pretest is an effective way of fine-tuning the questions for use in the actual survey process by assessing such critical factors as the clarity, comprehensiveness, and acceptability of the questionnaire. In a study of how institutional investors view corporate dividend policy, Farrelly and Baker (1989) pretest the questionnaire among 18 security analysts and portfolio managers. Baker (1992) uses a telephone pilot study to obtain feedback about a preliminary questionnaire designed to determine why NYSE-listed firms also list their shares on the London, Frankfurt, and Tokyo stock exchanges. A drawback of field pretests is that they lack flexibility to probe and understand the types of problems that respondents face.

A final field approach is to compare different versions of the instrument or procedures using split-ballot experiments. Using this approach, different portions of the pretest sample receive questions with different wording, order, and so on. Although split-ballot experiments can identify whether differences exist, they cannot resolve the issue of which version produces better data.

Graham and Harvey (2001) and Brav et al. (2005) use one or more of the following methods to evaluate their draft questionnaires. They circulate a draft survey to a group of academics for feedback and revise the survey based on their suggestions. They also obtain the advice of marketing-research experts on the survey design and execution. As a result of this feedback, they change the format of the questions and overall survey design. Using the penultimate version of the survey, they have executive master of business administration students and financial executives complete the survey and provide feedback. Based on this and other feedback, they make final changes to the wording of some questions and delete others.

These methods are useful in determining whether questions meet the content, cognitive, and usability standards discussed earlier for survey questions. Applying these techniques may help to reveal serious errors or oversights affecting the survey responses. Regardless of the methods employed, the researcher should revise the survey instrument as necessary. Fowler (1995) and Groves et al. (2004) provide a detailed discussion of presurvey evaluation of questions.

Collecting and Processing the Data

Having thoroughly tested the questionnaire, the researcher can now distribute or provide Internet access to it. Implementing the survey instrument and processing the data are critical phases of the research process. Regardless of the type of data collection (mail or Internet), a major concern should be to ensure the privacy and minimize the inconvenience of potential respondents.

When distributing the questionnaire, several factors are important to consider. For example, the researcher must take precautions to control distribution of the questionnaire form in order to avoid multiple submissions by the same individual or by an unauthorized individual. For paper-based questionnaires, each questionnaire distributed should have a unique identifier. Having this identifier enables keeping track of respondents and avoids sending needless reminders to those who have already responded to the survey. For Web-based versions of questionnaires, the researcher can control access by providing a unique PIN or username/password combination. Another consideration is the duration of the response window, which is the period between the time the questionnaire is distributed and the deadline for completing the questionnaire. Although no fixed rule exists, allowing three to five weeks is sufficient in most cases.

Collecting the Data

During the past several decades, the most common modes of collecting data were mail, telephone, and in-person methods. Factors influencing the decision about which of these methods of data collection to use include the specific information needs, the accessibility of the sample population, the budget available for the study, and time constraints (research schedule) involved for completing the project. In practice, the survey administrator must decide how to deliver the questionnaire early on in the design process.

Each method of data collection has its own strengths and weaknesses. For example, in terms of data collection costs, self-completion surveys, such as mail and online surveys, are less expensive than interviewer-administered surveys, such as one-on-one visits and telephone interviews. Thus, the sample size for a given budget tends to be greater for self-administered versus interviewer-administered surveys. By contrast, the data quality is usually higher for interviewer-administered versus self-completion surveys. Considerable variation also exists in the time required to collect data with mail surveys, requiring more time than telephone interviews. Rea and Parker (2005) provide an in-depth discussion of the advantages and disadvantages of different data collection methods such as mail-out, Web-based, telephone, and in-person interviews.

Today, a multitude of data collection methods exist. As Dillman (2007, p. 495) notes, "The major development of the twenty-first century, so far, is recognition that the use of all survey modes continues, and none seem likely to disappear." An important advancement in collecting survey data is the development of self-administered electronic survey methods such as e-mail and Web surveys. These methods have the potential for bringing about efficiencies by practically eliminating paper, postage, and data-entry costs and by overcoming international boundaries.

Several methods are available for online data collection. The least sophisticated approach is to send a questionnaire in a plain text e-mail message. Advantages of this method include simplicity and universality. Neither producing the questionnaire nor responding to it requires much technical ability.

Also, respondents can read plain text e-mail questionnaires with any e-mail program. Although this approach lends itself to short, informal surveys of a limited number of potential respondents, it suffers from serious formatting and processing problems. Another way to collect survey data via the Internet is by sending e-mail questionnaire attachments in, for example, Microsoft Word. Using this approach requires that recipients have the appropriate word processing program. Alreck and Settle (2004) and Dillman (2007) provide an in-depth discussion of surveys using the Internet. Sheehan (2001) provides a review of e-mail response rates.

Using Web-based surveys to collect data can be superior to either e-mail questionnaires or attachments. Web-based surveys range from simple to highly sophisticated and provide capabilities beyond those available from other types of self-administered questionnaires. Although researchers should use Web-based surveys judiciously, the advantages of this method include lower data collection costs, the ability to conduct surveys more quickly, and fewer data-handling problems. Web survey software and services are available and affordable. For example, companies such as SPSS (http://www.spss.com) provide question-building and data-entry programs, while others such as SurveyMonkey (http://www.surveymonkey.com), Zoomerang (http://www.zoomerang.com), Infopoll (http://www.infopoll.com), and iResearch (http://www.iresearch.com) provide services to help create online questionnaires. Kaplowitz, Hadlock, and Levine (2004) find that a Web-based survey application achieved a comparable response rate to a hard copy mail questionnaire when both were preceded by an advance surface mail notification.

Despite the attractiveness of e-mail and Web-based surveys in being less costly and more efficient, postal mail surveys remain popular among financial researchers. Rea and Parker (2005) note that mail surveys offer many of the same advantages as Web-based surveys. For example, both types of surveys can be completed at the convenience of respondents, involve virtually no time constraints on respondents, provide anonymity and/or confidentiality, and can use visual images and complex questions. A major shortcoming of mail questionnaires is the relatively high percentage of nonresponse. Low response rates increase the likelihood of nonresponse bias, which reduces the survey's validity. Questionnaire design is only one determinant of response. Other factors affecting the response rate include sponsorship, multiple contacts, the content of letters, personalization, appearance of envelopes, incentives, interest of the respondent, and other attributes of the communication process.

Improving Response Rates

Dillman (2007, p. 149), a leading authority on mail and Internet surveys, makes the following observation of response rates:

> The questionnaire is only one element of a well-done survey. Moreover, no matter how well constructed or easy to complete, it is *not* the main

determinant of response to mail or other self-administered surveys. Implementation procedures have a much greater influence on response rates. Multiple contacts, the contents of letters, appearance of envelopes, incentives, personalization, sponsorship and how it is explained, and other attributes of the communication process have significantly greater collective capability for influencing response rates than does questionnaire design.

Dillman (2007) describes five requisite elements for achieving high response rates using mail surveys: (1) a respondent friendly questionnaire; (2) up to five contacts with the questionnaire recipient (a prenotice letter, questionnaire, thank-you postcard, replacement questionnaire, and final contact); (3) return envelopes with real first-class stamps; (4) personalization of correspondence; and (5) a token prepaid financial incentive. Each of the five different components constituting the typical mail survey can affect the response rate.

Several books (e.g., Goyder 1987; Groves et al. 2002) and numerous articles in academic and practitioner journals examine methods to increase response rates. Groves et al. (2004) provide a brief review of this research evidence. For example, previous experimental research on how to improve mail survey response is unanimous on the influence of multiple contacts being more effective than any other technique (e.g., Goyder 1985; Dillman 1991). As Groves et al. report, research evidence also shows that the longer the data collection period, the higher the likelihood that all persons will be made aware of the survey request. Additionally, response propensities increase when the sponsor of the survey has some connection to the target population. Research indicates that an advance letter can generate higher rates of cooperation than for surveying with no such prenotification (Traugott, Groves, and Lepkowski 1987). Singer, Van Hoewyk, and Maher (2000), however, report a contrary finding about prenotification. Baker, Veit, and Murphy (1995) use prenotification from a sponsor connected to the target audience, a financial incentive, and multiple mailings to achieve a 74.9 percent response rate.

Another way to influence the generally low response rates for mail surveys is to use inducements or incentives to respond. These inducements or incentives do not have to be of great value but instead represent a token of appreciation or a goodwill gesture. Inducements take many forms including small financial incentives (e.g., cash and pens), drawings or sweepstakes, and reports of results. A strong case exists for including a modest cash incentive with the survey (e.g., James and Bolstein 1990, 1992; Church 1993) but not for sending postpayments of any kind, including lotteries and prizes (e.g., James and Bolstein, 1992). Some studies such as Singer (2002) report diminishing returns as the amount of the cash incentive rises. Using inducements, such as drawings or reports of results, requires respondents to reveal their identity. As Dillman (2007) notes, providing incentives is consistent with social exchange theory, which asserts that actions of individuals are motivated by the return these actions are expected to bring from others. Examples of including incentives in corporate finance surveys include Graham and Harvey (2001), who offer an advance copy of the results to interested parties to encourage executives to respond, and Brav et al. (2005), who offer two randomly selected $500 cash rewards to respondents from the mass e-mailing.

Another factor that may affect the response rate is the timing of the mailing. A lower response rate is likely to result from a mailing during a holiday or when respondents are particularly busy and pressed for time. Such periods may introduce bias and decrease the validity of the survey. According to Alreck and Settle (2004), response rates are likely to increase if recipients of business organizations receive the questionnaire during the middle of the month rather than at the beginning or end of the month.

Processing the Data

The researcher must compile the questionnaire data and transform it for interpretation and analysis. Web-based questionnaires offer the benefits of ease in processing the data because the task is automated. Using a paper-based version of the questionnaire requires coding the data and organizing the data into a spreadsheet or database. The remaining portion of this subsection deals with paper-based questionnaires.

While the data collection is underway, the researcher can prepare the processing system and test the computer programs to be used for data analysis. Data processing begins upon receipt of the first completed questionnaires. The first tasks in handling returned questionnaires are to open the surveys as they are returned, record the date of receipt, and assign a unique identification number if not already assigned. The researcher may have already numbered each survey or return envelope before sending them out. As discussed shortly, the purpose of consecutively numbering the completed questionnaires is to compare early and later returns during analysis. Next, the researcher reviews or sight-edits each questionnaire to determine its acceptability for processing and makes corrections and notations. Respondents are likely to fail to complete some individual items. If only a few missing items exist, the questionnaire is typically usable. If large portions of the questionnaire are incomplete, discarding the questionnaire from further processing is an appropriate option.

The third step involves postcoding for those responses that do not have a precode, such as open-ended questions and "other, please specify" response categories. If the questionnaire contains mainly structured questions, most of the precoding has already occurred. The researcher should also maintain an orderly codebook containing code lists for each question. After the data have been recorded, sight-edited, and postcoded, the fourth step is to enter the survey data into a spreadsheet or database program and to cross-check for accuracy. The fifth step is to edit the data to make sure that they are acceptable for analysis. Editing the computer data files involves checking the records to make sure that they conform to the format and that the variable values are within range. For example, if a Likert scale contains five values (−2, −1, 0, +1, and +2), the coded data should correspond to the values within this range.

The final steps involve data processing, statistical analysis, and data recoding. The main objectives of data processing are to summarize the data into information and to perform statistical analysis in order to make inferences about the entire population based on the survey sample. Analyzing the data involves conducting appropriate statistical analyses to shed light on the research questions being studied by using statistical significance tests, measures of central tendency, determinations of variability, and regression and correlation analysis, among others. Statistical analysis software such as SPSS greatly facilitates the task of processing data and revealing meaningful patterns or relationships contained in the data. In some instances, the researcher may want to recode the data to provide more meaningful categories. For example, continuous items with many values may be recoded into fewer but larger categories.

Testing for Nonresponse Bias, Interpreting, and Reporting the Results

The final stage of the survey process involves testing for nonresponse bias, interpreting the data, and documenting the findings.

Testing for Nonresponse Bias

Because interpretation of survey data presents some limitations, the researcher should first address major limitations such as nonresponse bias to ensure the representativeness of the sample. Nonresponse bias occurs when a substantial number of people in the survey sample fail to respond to the questionnaire or to an item in the questionnaire. Nonresponse bias may also occur when respondents have different characteristics from nonrespondents or the population. Hence, nonresponse bias makes the sample less representative of the population. Nonresponse is almost inevitable for most surveys because some members of the sample will refuse to participate despite reasonable efforts by the survey administrator. Because nonresponse bias is likely to be high and its potential effect severe for self-administered online and mail surveys, the researcher should exert considerable effort to minimize this bias.

Nonresponse bias can harm the quality of survey statistics and render a survey's results questionable. Therefore, the researcher should endeavor to increase response rates through such means as using multiple modes of data collection, repeated contacts, long data collection periods, advance letters, trusted sponsors, short questionnaires, guarantees of confidentiality, personalization, incentives, and persuasion letters for initial refusals. As previously mentioned, Groves et al. (2004) discuss various studies supporting the effectiveness of these techniques in increasing response rates. Numerous finance studies incorporate such approaches in an attempt to increase the response rate and to reduce nonresponse bias. For example, Graham and Harvey (2001) use multiple modes of data collection, multiple and personalized contacts, and a third-party vendor to preserve anonymity. Baker, Powell, and Veit (2003) use repeated contacts, while Baker, Veit, and Murphy (1995) use prenotification, a trusted sponsor, a financial incentive, and multiple mailings.

Nonresponse bias poses a potentially serious limitation when using direct mail and online surveys because of their typically low response rate. Notable exceptions include a 74.9 percent response rate obtained by Baker, Veit, and Murphy (1995) of investment professionals from eight countries outside North America; a 44.5 percent response rate achieved by Brau, Ryan, and DeGraw (2006) of CFOs; and a 34 percent response rate achieved by both Block (1999) of Chartered Financial Analysts (CFAs) and Kringman, Shaw, and Womack (2001) of initial public offering (IPO) firms that switch underwriters. Using a mail survey of 700 CFOs, Trahan and Gitman (1995) obtain a 12 percent response rate. Graham and Harvey (2001) attain a response rate of about 9 percent, while Brav et al. (2005) get a 16 percent response rate. As the remaining chapters show, there appears to be a trend toward lower response rates in finance surveys, especially mail surveys.

Several methods are available for investigating whether nonresponse bias might affect the survey results. One approach, suggested by Wallace and Mellor (1988), compares the responses from surveys returned on time (first mailing) with those who respond late (second mailing). The assumption underlying this approach is that those not responding on time can be viewed as a sample from the nonresponse group in the sense that they did not return the survey until the researcher made further attempts to contact them. Thus, if the responses for these two groups of firms are similar, nonresponse bias is unlikely to be a major problem. Various tests such as t-tests or chi-square tests can be used to determine whether any differences exist. For example, Graham and Harvey (2001) test whether the mean response for the early respondents (first mailing) differ from the mean for the late respondents. They also perform multivariate chi-square tests to test for differences between the early and late responses for each set of subquestions. Other corporate finance surveys using Wallace and Mellor's approach include Baker, Powell, and Veit (2003) and Baker et al. (2007).

A second approach, recommended by Moore and Reichert (1983), investigates for possible nonresponse bias by comparing characteristics of responding firms to those of nonresponding firms or to the population at large. For example, Baker, Powell, and Veit (2003) use t-tests to determine whether differences exist in total assets, net sales, total debt to total capital, dividend yield, and price-to-book ratio between responding and nonresponding firms. Graham and Harvey (2001) perform chi-square tests to determine whether the responses represent industry groupings in the same proportion as that found in the FEI population. They also perform Monte Carlo simulations to determine the representativeness of their sample. Brav et al. (2005) use parametric *t*-tests and nonparametric Wilcoxon tests to see whether significant differences exist between their sample and the population. For example, to test for the representativeness of surveyed public firms, they examine sales, debt-to-assets, dividend yield, earnings per share, credit rating, and book-to-market.

Interpreting the Data

The interpretation phase involves describing the data distributions and measuring item iterations. To make sense of large volumes of data, researchers often use graphical displays (charts and graphs) and tables. For example, Graham and Harvey (2001); Brounen, de Jong, and Koedijk (2004); Dong, Robinson, and Veld (2004); and Brav et al. (2008) use either vertical or horizontal bar charts as well as tables. Although survey studies in corporate finance sometimes portray their data using some form of graphical presentation, the most common form of displaying data is a table. According to Kasunic (2005, p. 94), "In general, tables are better than graphs for giving precise, structured numeric information, whereas graphs are better for indicating trends and making broad comparisons or showing relationships." This observation may be true for academic finance journals but may not be the case for practitioner-oriented finance journals or magazines.

Documenting the Findings

The final step in the survey process is to write the report. Various formats exist for preparing a final report, depending on the intended audience. Thus, before writing the report, the researcher should conduct an audience analysis. This analysis entails determining the primary and secondary audience, their level of knowledge about the topic and research methodology, and what they should understand from reading the report. This analysis will help to identify the appropriate level of detail to include and how to organize the report. A key point is to write for the readers of the report.

Although report organization may differ, key components generally consist of the following: (1) title page; (2) abstract or executive summary; (3) introduction (purpose, scope, and hypotheses, if applicable); (4) literature review; (5) research method (sample selection, survey procedure and limitations, and data analysis); (6) results; (7) conclusions and recommendations; (8) references; and (9) appendix (e.g., a copy of the survey instrument). From our experience, including a copy of the questionnaire is an especially important part of the document.

Summary and Conclusions

Survey research can be a useful technique for gathering data. Researchers conduct surveys because this research method is often the only way to get the information needed. Nonetheless, results of surveys should be interpreted with some caution because of potential biases and measurement problems that are often associated with survey data. For example, surveys measure beliefs or perceptions and may not represent the reality in the field.

Although survey researchers in finance follow a different path than others, their goal is no less important—to understand or to predict human behavior or conditions. Survey research occupies a special position between large-sample analysis and clinical studies. When coupled with other empirical and theoretical studies, survey research can help bridge the gap between theory and practice. This chapter has outlined and briefly discussed the steps necessary to conduct effective surveys in finance.

References

Aggarwal, Raj. 1993. "Theory and Practice in Finance Education: Or Why We Shouldn't Just Ask Them." *Financial Practice and Education* 3:2, 15–18.

Alreck, Pamela L., and Robert B. Settle. 2004. *The Survey Research Handbook*, 3rd ed. New York: McGraw-Hill/Irwin.

Baker, H. Kent. 1992. "Why US Companies List on the London, Frankfurt and Tokyo Stock Exchanges." *Journal of International Securities Markets* 6:3, 219–227.

Baker, H. Kent, Shantanu Dutta, and Samir Saadi. 2009. "Impact of Financial and Multinational Operations on Manager Perceptions of Dividends." *Global Finance Journal* 19:2, 171–186.

Baker, H. Kent, and Tarun K. Mukherjee. 2007. "Survey Research in Finance: Views from Journal Editors." *International Journal of Managerial Finance* 3:1, 11–25.

Baker, H. Kent, Tarun K. Mukherjee, and Ohannes George Paskelian. 2006. "How Norwegian Managers View Dividend Policy." *Global Finance Journal* 17:1, 155–176.

Baker, H. Kent, Tarun K. Mukherjee, and Gary E. Powell. 2005. "Distributing Excess Cash: The Role of Specially Designated Dividends." *Financial Services Review* 14:2, 111–131.

Baker, H. Kent, and Gary E. Powell. 2000. "Determinants of Corporate Dividend Policy: A Survey of NYSE Firms." *Financial Practice and Education* 10:1, 29–40.

Baker, H. Kent, Gary E. Powell, and E. Theodore Veit. 2003. "Why Companies Use Open-Market Repurchases: A Managerial Perspective." *Quarterly Review of Economics and Finance* 43:3, 483–504.

Baker, H. Kent, Samir Saadi, Shantanu Dutta, and Devinder Gandhi. 2007. "The Perception of Dividends by Canadian Managers: New Survey Evidence." *International Journal of Managerial Finance* 3:1, 70–91.

Baker, H. Kent, and David M. Smith. 2006. "In Search of a Residual Dividend Policy." *Review of Financial Economics* 15:1, 1–18.

Baker, H. Kent, E. Theodore Veit, and Michael R. Murphy. 1995. *Ethics in the Investment Profession: An International Survey.* Charlottesville, VA: Research Foundation of the Institute of Chartered Financial Analysts.

Baker, H. Kent, E. Theodore Veit, and Gary E. Powell. 2001. "Factors Influencing Dividend Policy Decisions of Nasdaq Firms." *Financial Review* 36:3, 19–37.

Block, Stanley B. 1999. "A Study of Financial Analysts: Practice and Theory." *Financial Analysts Journal* 55:4, 86–95.

Bogen, Karen. 1996. "The Effect of Questionnaire Length on Response Rates: A Review of the Literature." Washington, DC: U.S. Bureau of the Census. Available at http://www.census.gov/srd/papers/pdf/kb9601.pdf.

Brace, Ian. 2004. Questionnaire Design: How to Plan, Structure and Write Survey Material for Effective Market Research. London: Kogan Page.

Brau, James C., Patricia A. Ryan, and Irv DeGraw. 2006. "Initial Public Offerings: CFO Perceptions." *Financial Review* 41:4, 483–511.

Brav, Alon, John R. Graham, Campbell R. Harvey, and Roni Michaely. 2005. "Payout Policy in the 21st Century." *Journal of Financial Economics* 77:3, 483–527.

———. 2008. "Managerial Response to the May 2003 Dividend Tax Cut." *Financial Management* 37:4, 611–624.

Brounen, Dirk, Abe de Jong, and Kees Koedijk. 2004. "Corporate Finance in Europe: Confronting Theory with Practice." *Financial Management* 33:4, 71–101.

Bruner, Robert F., Kenneth M. Eades, Robert S. Harris, and Robert C. Higgins. 1998. "Best Practices in Estimating the Cost of Capital: Survey and Synthesis." *Financial Management* 8:1, 13–28.

Chaudhuri, Arijit, and Horst Stenger. 2005. *Survey Sampling: Theory and Methods*, 2nd ed. Boca Raton, FL: Chapman & Hall/CRZ.

Chiu, Irene, and Mike Brennan. 1990. "The Effectiveness of Some Techniques for Improving Mail Survey Response Rates: A Meta-Analysis." *Marketing Bulletin* 1, 13–18.

Church, Allan H. 1993. "Estimating the Effect of Incentives on Mail Survey Response Rates: A Meta-Analysis." *Public Opinion Quarterly* 57:1, 62–79.

Czaja, Ronald, and Johnny Blair. 1996. *Designing Surveys: A Guide to Decisions and Procedures.* Thousand Oaks, CA: Pine Forge Press.

de Jong, Abe, Ronald van Dijk, and Chris Veld. 2003. "The Dividend and Share Repurchase Policies of Canadian Firms: Empirical Evidence Based on an Alternative Research Design." *International Review of Financial Analysis* 12:4, 349–377.

Dhanani, Alpa. 2005. "Corporate Dividend Policy: The Views of British Financial Managers." *Journal of Business Finance and Accounting* 32:3–8, 1625–1672.

Dillman, Don A. 1991. "The Design and Administration of Mail Surveys." *Annual Review of Sociology* 17, 225–249.

———. 2007. *Mail and Internet Surveys: The Tailored Design Method*, 2nd ed. Hoboken, NJ: John Wiley & Sons.

Dillman, Don A., and John Tarnai. 1991. "Mode Effects of Cognitively Designed Recall Questions: A Comparison of Answers to Telephone and Mail Surveys."

In Paul N. Biemer, Robert M. Groves, Lars E. Lyberg, Nancy A. Mathiowetz, and Seymour Sudman (eds.), *Measurement Errors in Surveys,* 367–393. New York: John Wiley & Sons.

Dong, Ming, Chris Robinson, and Chris Veld. 2005. "Why Individual Investors Want Dividends." *Journal of Corporate Finance* 12:1, 121–158.

Farrelly, Gail. E., and H. Kent Baker. 1989. "Corporate Dividends: Views of Institutional Investors." *Akron Business and Economic Review* 20:2, 89–100.

Fowler, Floyd J. Jr. 1995. *Improving Survey Questions: Design and Evaluation.* Thousand Oaks, CA: Sage Publications.

———. 2008. *Survey Research Methods*, 4th ed. Thousand Oaks, CA: Sage Publications.

Galesic, Mitra, and Michael Bosnjak. 2009. "Effects of Questionnaire Length on Participation and Indicators of Response Quality in a Web Survey." *Public Opinion Quarterly* 73:2, 349–360.

Gitman, Lawrence J., and John R. Forrester Jr. 1977. "A Survey of Capital Budgeting Techniques Used by Major U.S. Firms." *Financial Management* 6:3, 66–71.

Gitman, Lawrence J., and Charles E. Maxwell. 1987. "A Longitudinal Comparison of Capital Budgeting Techniques Used by Major U.S. Firms: 1986 versus 1976." *Journal of Applied Business Research* 3:1, 41–50.

Gitman, Lawrence J., and Vincent A. Mercurio. 1982. "Cost of Capital Techniques Used by Major U.S. Firms: Survey and Analysis of Fortune's 1000." *Financial Management* 11:4, 21–29.

Gitman, Lawrence J., and Pieter A. Vandenberg. 2000. "Cost of Capital Techniques Used by Major U.S. Firms: 1997 vs. 1980." *Financial Practice and Education* 10:2, 53–68.

Goyder, John. 1985. "Race-to-Face Interviews and Mail Questionnaires: The Net Difference in Response Rate." *Public Opinion Quarterly* 49:2, 234–252.

———. 1987. The Silent Minority: Nonrespondents on Sample Surveys. Boulder, CO: Westview Press.

Graham, John R. 2004. "Roundtable on Corporate Disclosure." *Journal of Applied Corporate Finance* 16:4, 338–362.

Graham, John R., and Campbell R. Harvey. 2001. "The Theory and Practice of Corporate Finance: Evidence from the Field." *Journal of Financial Economics* 61:2–3, 187–243.

Groves, Robert M., Don A. Dillman, John L. Eltinge, and Roderick J. A. Little (eds.). 2002. *Survey Nonresponse.* New York: John Wiley & Sons.

Groves, Robert M., Floyd J. Fowler Jr., Mick P. Couper, James M. Lepkowski, Eleanor Singer, and Roger Tourangeau. 2004. *Survey Methodology.* Hoboken, NJ: Wiley-Interscience.

James, Jeannine M., and Richard Bolstein. 1990. "The Effect of Monetary Incentives and Follow-Up Mailings on the Response Rate and Response Quality in Mail Surveys." *Public Opinion Quarterly* 54:3, 346–361.

———. 1992. "Large Monetary Incentives and Their Effect on Mail Survey Response Rates." *Public Opinion Quarterly* 56:4, 442–453.

Kaplowitz, Michael D., Timothy D. Hadlock, and Ralph Levine. 2004. "A Comparison of Web and Mail Survey Response Rates." *Public Opinion Quarterly* 68:1, 94–101.

Kasunic, Mark. 2005. *Designing an Effective Survey.* Pittsburgh, PA: Carnegie Mellon University and the Software Engineering Institute.

Kish, Leslie. 1995. *Survey Sampling.* Hoboken: NJ: Wiley-Interscience.

Knottnerus, Paul. 2003. *Survey Sampling Theory.* New York: Springer-Verlag.

Kringman, Laurie, Wayne H. Shaw, and Kent L. Womack. 2001. "Why Do Firms Switch Underwriters?" *Journal of Financial Economics* 60:2–3, 245–284.

Lintner, John. 1956. "Distribution of Incomes of Corporations among Dividends, Retained Earnings, and Taxes." *American Economic Review* 46:2, 97–113.

Litwin, Mark S. 1995. *How to Measure Reliability and Validity.* Thousand Oaks, CA: Sage Publications.

Lohr, Sharon L. 1999. *Sampling: Design and Analysis.* Pacific Grove, CA: Duxbury Press.

Moore, James S., and Alan K. Reichert. 1983. "An Analysis of the Financial Management Techniques Currently Employed by Large U.S. Corporations." *Journal of Business Finance and Accounting* 10:4, 623–645.

Neuhauser, Karyn L. 2007. "Survey Research in Finance." *International Journal of Managerial Finance* 3:1, 5–10.

Pinegar, J. Michael, and Lisa Wilbricht. 1989. "What Managers Think of Capital Structure Theory: A Survey." *Financial Management* 18:4, 82–91.

Pinsonneault, Alain, and Kenneth L. Kraemer. 1993. "Survey Research Methodology in Management Information Systems: An Assessment." *Journal of Management Information Systems* 10:2, 75–105.

Presser, Stanley, Mick P. Couper, Judith T. Lessler, Elizabeth Martin, Jean Martin, Jennifer M. Rothgeb, and Eleanor Singer. 2004. "Methods for Testing and Evaluating Survey Questions." *Public Opinion Quarterly* 68:1, 109–130.

Pruitt, Stephen W., and Lawrence J. Gitman. 1991. "The Interactions between the Investment, Financing, and Dividend Decisions of Major U.S. Firms." *Financial Review* 26:3, 409–430.

Rea, Louis M., and Richard A. Parker. 2005. *Designing and Conducting Survey Research: A Comprehensive Guide*, 3rd edition. San Francisco: Jossey-Bass.

Sampath, S. 2001. *Sampling Theory and Methods.* New Delhi: Narosa Publishing House.

Scheaffer, Richard L. III, William Mendenhall, and R. Lyman Ott. 2005. *Elementary Survey Sampling.* Pacific Grove, CA: Duxbury Press.

Scheuren, Fritz. 2004. *What is a Survey?* Available at http://www.amstat.org/sections/srms/pamphlet.pdf.

Sheehan, Kim. 2001. "E-mail Survey Response Rates: A Review." *Journal of Computer-Mediate Communication* 6:2. Available at http://jcmc.indiana.edu/vol6/issue2/.

Singer, Eleanor. 2002. "The Use of Incentives to Reduce Nonresponse in Household Surveys." In Robert M. Groves, Don A. Dillman, John L. Eltinge, and Roderick J. A. Little (eds.), *Survey Nonresponse,* 163–177. New York: John Wiley & Sons.

Singer, Eleanor, John Van Hoewyk, and Mary P. Maher. 2000. "Experiments with Incentives in Telephone Surveys." *Public Opinion Quarterly* 64:2, 171–188.

Trahan, Emery A., and Lawrence J. Gitman. 1995. "Bridging the Theory-Practice Gap in Corporate Finance: A Survey of Chief Financial Officers." *Quarterly Review of Economics and Finance* 35:1, 73–87.

Traugott, Michael W., Robert M. Groves, and James M. Lepkowski. 1987. "Using Dual Frame Designs to Reduce Nonresponse in Telephone Surveys." *Public Opinion Quarterly* 51:4, 369–374.

Wallace, R. S. O., and C. J. Mellor. 1988. "Nonresponse Bias in Mail Accounting Surveys: A Pedagogical Note." *British Accounting Review* 20:2, 131–139.

Wright, Malcolm. 1995. "The Effect of Pre-Notification on Mail Survey Response Rates: An Experimental Result." *Marketing Bulletin* 6:3, 59–64.

Yammarino, Francis J., Steven J. Skinner, and Terry L. Childers. 1991. "Understanding Mail Survey Response Behavior: A Meta-Analysis." *Public Opinion Quarterly* 55:4, 613–639.

∞ 3

Capital Budgeting

> Chains of habit are too light to be felt until they are too heavy
> to be broken.
>
> Warren Buffett

Introduction

Capital budgeting refers to the process that managers use to make decisions about whether long-term investments or capital expenditures are worth pursuing by their organizations. The basic notion is that managers use capital raised by the firm, usually long-term funds, to invest in assets that will enable the firm to generate cash flows for several years into the future. Typical investments include new or replacement machinery, plants, products, and research and development (R&D) projects. Capital budgeting involves perhaps the most important challenge facing management: finding or creating investment projects whose benefits exceed costs. This function, known as the *investment decision,* involves allocating funds over time to increase shareholder wealth. For most companies, the investment decision is among the most important made by managers.

Allocating funds among alternative investment opportunities is crucial to a firm's success. Sound capital investment decisions can improve cash flows and lead to higher stock prices, thereby enhancing shareholder wealth. This is particularly important in the face of limited investment funds, an area of capital budgeting known as *capital rationing.* Many capital investment projects involve large expenditures that may have a direct impact on a firm's performance and future direction. Because capital investment decisions often involve committing large amounts of funds for lengthy periods, they are also typically difficult or costly to reverse. Making the right capital budgeting decisions is essential to achieving the goal of maximizing shareholder wealth because errors in capital budgeting can affect the firm over the long term.

Not surprisingly, the corporate finance area receiving the most attention by survey researchers is capital budgeting, as evidenced by the more than 100 published survey studies in this area. Scott and Petty (1984), Mukherjee (1987), and Burns and Walker (2009) provide reviews of the capital budgeting survey literature. Early studies by Miller (1960), Istvan (1961), and Christy (1966) represent groundbreaking work that began to shed light on this topic. Other classic surveys on capital budgeting include Klammer (1972); Fremgen (1973); Gitman and Forrester (1977); Petty, Scott, and Bird (1975); Schall, Sundem, and Geijsbeek (1978); and Gitman and Maxwell (1987). A more recent study by Graham and Harvey (2001) continues the work of measuring the gap between theory and practice in the capital budgeting area. As the following discussion suggests, closing this gap has taken many years. Although Warren Buffett's words quoted at the beginning of this chapter refer more to the difficulty of breaking investing habits, his words appear to apply equally to capital budgeting.

Of the four stages of the capital budgeting process—identification, development, selection, and control—Burns and Walker (2009) note that the selection stage is the most investigated by survey researchers, especially identifying analytical methods or techniques used by businesses compared to those proposed in the finance literature. Of the four stages, the selection stage is arguably the most involved. Other capital budgeting surveys focus on such topics as evaluating and adjusting for project risk, using capital rationing, identifying appropriate hurdle rates, and conducting postaudits. In addition, some surveys examine how firms estimate cash flows and deal with inflation.

This chapter focuses the discussion of survey research on capital budgeting related to these major topics: (1) project evaluation methods, (2) risk evaluation and adjustment, (3) capital rationing, (4) hurdle rates, (5) postaudits, and (6) other capital budgeting topics. These topics represent the central issues addressed in capital budgeting survey research. The goal of this chapter is to synthesize the important contributions to the survey literature on capital budgeting in order to explore the gap between theory and practice. Selecting among the large number of capital budgeting survey studies requires establishing criteria for inclusion in this review. In general, the surveys focus on large firms involving more than a single industry and are published in mainline academic journals.

Comparing the results of two or more survey studies requires caution when the population and sample sizes differ; when the questions asked are not worded identically or appear in a different order; and when selection bias, time-period bias, or other biases exist in selecting one or more studies to analyze. Despite these potential limitations, the following discussion attempts to synthesize the results of different studies over time.

Project Evaluation Methods

Since the 1940s, academics have been describing how to evaluate potential capital budgeting projects. The following is a brief synopsis of the theory describing various evaluation methods.

Theory: Project Evaluation

Many capital budgeting methods are available for evaluating project proposals. The academic literature contends that discounted cash flow (DCF) methods of evaluating potential capital budgeting projects, such as net present value (NPV) and internal rate of return (IRR), are superior to non-discounted cash flow methods, such as payback period (PB), and methods using accounting income, such as the accounting rate of return (ARR). The central argument in favor of DCF methods concerns the need to consider the time value of money: projects taking longer to realize positive cash flow are less desirable. Most introductory corporate finance textbooks rely on simple logic to convince its readers of the benefits of DCF methods. These textbooks usually do not mention the one necessary assumption—that the market for the firm's stock must be informationally efficient such that the stock's price reflects the firm's economically relevant financial decisions and not extraneous or cosmetic factors. An early book by Terborgh (1949) describes several dozen rules proposed for evaluating capital budgeting projects. Some he refers to as theoretical orphans, and some he suggests "border on superstition" (p. 271). By the mid-1960s, textbook authors such as Quirin (1967) describe most of the capital budgeting methods we know today, such as IRR, NPV, PB, and ARR.

A project's IRR is the return generated based on the amount of the initial outlay and the amount and timing of the subsequent cash inflows. When an independent project's IRR exceeds the required rate of return or hurdle rate on the project, the standard decision rule is to accept the project. Because calculating the IRR assumes reinvestment of the cash flows at the project's IRR, this can lead to ranking mutually exclusive projects in a manner that results in suboptimal decisions. An alternative measure, the modified internal rate of return, avoids this reinvestment-rate assumption. Most researchers believe that a more reasonable reinvestment assumption is that firms can reinvest realized cash flows at the firm's weighted average cost of capital (WACC); that is, when a project generates positive cash flows, the firm can use those funds to repurchase the firm's outstanding common stock and repay the firm's debt in proportions equal to those reflected in the firm's WACC. This repurchase of stock and repayment of debt means that the firm will forgo paying its WACC on those cash flows. This reinvestment at a rate equal to the firm's WACC is considered more reasonable than assuming a firm's managers can reinvest the project cash flows at the same rate of return generated by the project.

A project's NPV is the present value of the project's cash inflows less the present value of its cash outflows. In theory, NPV represents the change in the value of the firm (in today's dollars) if the firm adopts the project. Increasing the value of the firm is consistent with the stated goal of maximizing shareholder wealth that most firms espouse. Thus, projects that promise to increase the value of the firm are worth accepting. Further, managers prefer projects that enhance the value of the firm by the greatest amount. Therefore, finance theory views NPV as superior to IRR when evaluating mutually exclusive projects (projects that compete for adoption such that the firm may adopt one but not both projects) or under conditions of capital rationing (when a firm limits its expenditure on projects to fewer than all acceptable projects).

Other DCF methods include the profitability index (PI) and the discounted payback period (DPB). While the PI is similar to NPV, some managers prefer it to NPV because of its interpretation: the PI is the present value of the project's cash inflow per dollar of initial investment. Thus, the PI represents the return per dollar of investment and permits ranking projects on a relative basis. However, the PI suffers from the same limitations as IRR in that this method can lead to suboptimal decisions for mutually exclusive projects. This can occur when the competing projects are of different sizes. For example, assume Project A has a very high PI (return per dollar invested) compared with Project B. However, if Project B is substantially larger, its adoption may add more value to the firm.

The DPB also incorporates discounted cash flows into the evaluation process. It measures the time between project adoption and the firm's recovery of its initial outlay using discounted cash flows (cash flows in today's dollars). The standard rule is to view projects with shorter recovery periods as less risky and therefore more attractive. While focusing on project risk, DPB ignores cash flows expected after reaching the payback period. Thus, DPB ignores total project profitability and can result in suboptimal decisions for mutually exclusive projects.

Despite the theoretical soundness of DCF methods, studies show that non-discounted methods remain popular among managers. Part of the popularity of the payback period (PB) method is its simplicity and focus on risk. While other methods also reflect risk, the PB method, like the DPB method, measures the length of time needed for a firm to recover its initial outlay; the shorter the recovery period, the less risky and more desirable the project. Unlike the DPB method, the PB method uses undiscounted cash flows; like the DPB method, the PB method ignores all cash flows beyond the payback period, meaning it ignores total project return. The deficiencies of the PB method include failing to consider the time value of money and, as mentioned, ignoring cash flows beyond the payback period.

The accounting rate of return (ARR) method also boasts simplicity. Calculating the ARR involves dividing the average annual incremental accounting profit generated by a project by the average investment in the project. Two weaknesses of this method are its failure to consider the time value of money and its use of accounting profits generated by a project instead of cash flows. Because firms cannot necessarily spend and invest accounting profits, most scholars prefer evaluating projects based on incremental cash flow. For these reasons, financial experts typically suggest evaluating projects using other methods.

Practice: Project Evaluation Methods

While the prior section described the theory surrounding the use of various project evaluation methods, the current section provides a synopsis of what survey research reveals about the use of these methods in practice. This section groups studies based on their focus: U.S. firms, multinational firms, non-U.S. firms, and small firms.

U.S. Firms

Because space limitations prevent the discussion of the results of all capital budgeting survey studies, this section highlights some frequently cited survey studies that examine the use of various capital budgeting techniques. The following provides a discussion of the most frequently referenced capital budgeting survey studies.

Miller (1960) provides one of the earliest survey studies involving capital budgeting. He sends questionnaires to 200 firms selected from two sources: the *Manual of Excellently Managed Companies* published by the American Institute of Management and a list of the 500 largest companies published by *Fortune* magazine. The 200 firms selected are diverse in terms of industry and geographic location. While much of Miller's study focuses on how firms use the measure "return on investment," it also provides some insight about capital budgeting. Of the 127 responding firms, 91 percent indicate they evaluate capital budgeting projects using a quantitative measure. Only 30 percent of respondents report using a DCF method (see Table 3.1).

In another early study, Istvan (1961) reports the results of interviews with top-ranking executives of forty-eight major corporations. The participating firms account for nearly 25 percent of total capital expenditures in 1959 according to figures by the Department of Commerce. Only 10 percent of the responding firms use time-adjusted rates of return, including both IRR and NPV. Istvan (1961, p. 51) concludes that "the results of the research indicate that the general failure of businessmen to employ sound economic theory in their evaluation of capital expenditures can be laid to an inability to understand the concepts and/ or promulgate an understanding throughout the various strata of the firm, rather than to excessive costs of implementation."

Christy (1966) uses a mail survey of publicly held firms in 10 industries characterized by a high level of uncertainty. Of 243 questionnaires mailed to firms

TABLE 3.1 Use of discounted cash flow methods to evaluate capital budgeting projects: U.S. firms

This table shows the percentage of U.S. firms using discounted cash flow (DCF) methods to evaluate capital budgeting projects as indicated by various survey studies. These methods generally include IRR, NPV, and PI, but may also include the discounted payback method in some cases. In addition to indicating the author or authors of each study, we also indicate the year published. A number of studies may understate the percent of firms using DCF methods because of the wording of the question, as indicated by the notes in the right-hand column.

Author(s)	Year published	Population/Sample	Percentage of firms
Miller	1960	"Well-managed" *Fortune* 500 firms ($n = 127$)	30
Istvan	1961	Major corporations ($n = 48$)	10
Pflomn	1963	U.S. manufacturing firms ($n = 346$)	n/a
Christy	1966	Large firms/select industries/Standard & Poor's Stock Guide ($n = 108$)	14
Robichek and McDonald	1966	*Fortune* 500 manufacturing firms ($n = 163$)	47
Mao	1970	Medium-size and large firms noted for efficient management ($n = 8$)	75
Klammer	1972	Select large manufacturing firms/Compustat ($n = 184$)	57
Fremgen	1973	Firms in select industries/Dun & Bradstreet ($n = 177$)	76
Petty, Scott, and Bird	1975	*Fortune* 500 firms ($n = 109$)	58[a]
Gitman and Forrester	1977	*Forbes* firms with large capital expenditures ($n = 103$)	74[b]
Schall, Sundem, and Geijsbeek	1978	Select large firms/Compustat ($n = 189$)	86
Kim and Farragher	1981	*Fortune* 1000 firms ($n = 200$)	68[b]
Moore and Reichert	1983	*Fortune* 500 firms ($n = 298$)	86[c]
Gitman and Maxwell	1987	*Forbes* 1000 firms with growth characteristics ($n = 109$)	72[b]

(Continued)

TABLE 3.1 (cont'd) Use of discounted cash flow methods to evaluate capital budgeting projects: U.S. firms

Author(s)	Year published	Population/Sample	Percentage of firms
Reichert, Moore, and Byler	1988	*Fortune* 500 firms (*n* = 313)	90[c]
Klammer, Koch, and Wilner	1991	Select large industrial firms from Compustat (*n* = 100)	95
Bierman	1993	Largest 100 *Fortune* 500 industrial firms (*n* = 74)	99
Gilbert and Reichert	1995	Firms listed in *Fortune* magazine directory (*n* = 151)	91[c]
Burns and Walker	1997	*Fortune* 500 firms (*n* = 141)	84[d]
Graham and Harvey	2002	Medium-size and large firms/members of the Financial Executives Institute (*n* = 392)	76[e]

[a]May understate the use, as this is the percentage of firms using DCF methods as the primary tool for "new product lines" only.
[b]May understate the use, as this is the percentage of firms using DCF methods as the "primary tool."
[c]May understate the use, as this is the percentage of responding firms that use IRR or NPV "frequently."
[d]May understate the use, as this is the percentage of firms using the IRR method, ignoring other DCF methods.
[e]May understate the use, as this is the percentage of firms using IRR "always or almost always," ignoring other DCF methods.

listed in the Standard & Poor's Stock Guide, respondents returned 108 completed questionnaires. The results show that 11 percent of responding firms do not use any quantitative project evaluation methods, and just 14 percent of firms report using DCF methods.

Robichek and McDonald (1966) mail questionnaires to *Fortune* 500 manufacturing firms and receive replies from 163. They find that 47 percent of responding firms use DCF methods. Mao (1970) interviews eight firms selected for their efficiency of management practices. As a result of the small sample size, he does not make any statistical generalizations about how businesses make decisions. However, he notes that because he chose the companies included in the study for their management efficiency, the study indicates how progressive managers currently practice capital budgeting. While Mao discovers that 75 percent of surveyed firms use DCF methods, he concludes that "this study confirms the prevalence of the payback period and accounting profit criteria in practice" (359).

As finance theory and business education advanced over the years, surveys became a common tool to determine which capital budgeting techniques practitioners use. Klammer (1972) reports the findings of a survey of 369 large firms with sizable and continuing capital expenditures. He draws the sample from the 1969 Compustat listing of manufacturing firms having 15 or more firms in the same Standard Industrial Classification (SIC) group and five firms in the same SIC sub-classification as well as substantial capital expenditures. The survey results show that 57 percent of participants report using DCF methods.

Fremgen (1973) surveys 177 firms randomly selected from the 1969 edition of *Dun and Bradstreet's Reference Book of Corporate Managements*. He excludes financial institutions from the sample. Fremgen discovers that 76 percent of respondents use DCF methods.

Using a mail survey of all firms listed in the 1971 *Fortune* 500, Petty, Scott, and Bird (1975) receive 109 usable responses. They gather information on the evaluation methods employed for new and existing product lines and find that 58 percent of responding firms use DCF techniques.

Gitman and Forrester (1977) receive completed questionnaires from 103 of the 268 firms they contact. They select firms to survey from two lists in *Forbes*. One list reflects the 600 firms experiencing the most rapid stock price growth during the period 1971 through 1976; the other lists the 500 firms having the largest dollar capital expenditures in 1969. They find that 66 percent of respondents use DCF methods.

Using Compustat, Schall, Sundem, and Geijsbeek (1978) identify 407 firms with large or moderate plant assets and large or moderate annual capital expenditures. They receive responses from managers at 189 firms, of which 86 percent use DCF methods to evaluate capital budgeting projects. This is the highest percentage found as of that date.

Kim and Farragher (1981) send questionnaires to the chief financial officers (CFOs) of all *Fortune* 1000 firms and receive 200 usable responses. They discover that 86 percent of surveyed firms use DCF methods to evaluate capital budgeting projects. Comparing their findings to earlier studies, Kim and Farragher conclude that there is a trend toward the use of DCF methods. They also conclude that at the time of their study, large firms have had enough time to begin using theoretically preferred methods, and they expect the trend to continue at a more rapid pace in the future.

The Moore and Reichert (1983) survey of *Fortune* 500 firms also finds a trend toward greater use of DCF methods. They document that 86 percent of the 298 firms surveyed make frequent use of NPV or IRR. They also report two statistically significant relationships between firm size and the use of different methods; that is, a positive relationship exists between the use of IRR and firm size, and a negative relationship exists between the use of the PB method and firm size.

Gitman and Maxwell (1987) study a population similar to that studied by Gitman and Forrester (1977) to identify any changes occurring between the two studies. Gitman and Maxwell send 333 questionnaires to firms listed in *Forbes* that have high stock price increases and high growth of fixed assets as determined using Compustat. They learn that the percentage of responding firms using DCF methods increased from 66 percent in the Gitman and Forrester study to 72 percent in the current study. Because it is one of the few longitudinal studies on the topic of capital budgeting, there are several more references to the Gitman and Maxwell study throughout this chapter.

Klammer, Koch, and Wilner (1991) send questionnaires to the CFOs of 484 large industrial firms, including the firms that responded to the earlier study by Klammer and Walker (1984). Klammer, Koch, and Wilner find that while the use of DCF methods is very common for evaluating expansion of new operations (87 percent) and expansion of existing operations (86 percent), a smaller percentage of firms use DCF methods to evaluate other types of projects such as replacement (60 percent), foreign operations (79 percent), and social expenditures (16 percent). Still, about 95 percent of firms use DCF methods to evaluate at least one type of project.

In a survey of the 100 largest *Fortune* 500 industrial firms, Bierman (1993) receives usable responses from 74 firms. Regarding the use of DCF methods, he reports that 99 percent of responding firms use either NPV or IRR as the primary or secondary method of project evaluation.

Gilbert and Reichert (1995) send surveys to the CFOs of all firms listed in the *Fortune* 500 and receive usable responses from 151 firms. They discover that 91 percent of responding firms use DCF methods to evaluate projects. The authors compare their results to the results of similar surveys from 1980 and 1985 and conclude that large U.S. firms are more widely using modern analytical models and techniques taught in colleges.

Two years later, Burns and Walker (1997) also send surveys to the CFOs of each *Fortune* 500 industrial firm and receive 180 responses. They find that only 4 percent of firms rely on just one method to evaluate projects. Of the remaining firms, 23 percent of firms use two methods, 49 percent use three methods, 19 percent use four methods, and just 4 percent use more than four methods.

A more recent study by Graham and Harvey (2001) reports the results of a survey on capital budgeting, cost of capital, and capital structure practices of business managers. They use a mail survey to contact all CFOs in the 1998 *Fortune* 500 and a fax survey to contact the 4,440 member firms associated with the Financial Executives Institute (FEI). Both medium-size and large firms participated, and 392 firms completed surveys. One finding is that 76 percent of the responding firms use DCF methods.

Table 3.1 summarizes the findings of many studies about the use of DCF methods. We again caution the reader about comparing the responses of two or more surveys when the studies use different populations, samples, and question wording. Yet, a trend appears to exist as the values in the fourth column (the percent of firms using DCF methods) begin at 30 percent and 10 percent in the Miller (1960) and Istvan (1961) studies, respectively, and increase through the Graham and Harvey (2001) study. Additionally, several studies, including the most recent three, may understate the percentage of firms using DCF methods because of the wording of the question relative to the wording of the questions in earlier studies (see the Table 3.1 notes).

Two of the four capital budgeting synthesis studies reviewed note the apparent trend in the use of DCF methods suggested by survey studies over time. Scott and Petty (1984, p. 119), who provide a synthesis of capital budgeting studies during the period 1960 through 1978, conclude that "corporate managements are gradually coming to use more sophisticated and theoretically sound approaches in their capital budgeting analyses" Similarly, Kim and Ulferts (1996, p. 83), who review capital budgeting studies conducted from 1980 through 1993, state that "efforts over the last 40 years have established only one point: discounted cash-flow techniques have become more popular."

Tables 3.2 and 3.3 are similar in that they report findings about the use of various capital budgeting evaluation techniques by surveyed U.S. firms. Table 3.2 presents the results of studies showing the percentage of respondents that use various evaluation techniques as the *primary* evaluation method. Table 3.3 indicates the percentage of respondents using various evaluation techniques, but not necessarily as the *primary* method used.

According to Miller (1960), the two most popular capital budgeting methods are the payback period and return on total assets based on the original cost of the asset, selected by 52 percent and 46 percent of respondents, respectively. About 12 percent of respondents report using return on total assets based on the original cost less current liabilities, where current liabilities are considered to be a

TABLE 3.2 Primary capital budgeting evaluation techniques: U.S. firms

This table shows the percentage of U.S. firms using various capital budgeting evaluation techniques as their *primary technique*. Key: PB = payback period, ARR = accounting rate of return, PI = profitability index, IRR = internal rate of return, and NPV = net present value. Two studies ask for the "most important" method used rather than the "primary" method used as indicated in the notes. This table differs from Table 3.3 which asks about all methods used, not just the primary method used.

Author(s)	Year published	Percentage of firms using each method					
		PB	ARR	PI	IRR	NPV	Other
Miller	1960	Results discussed in text.					
Istvan	1961	27	50	n/a	10	n/a	12
Pflomn	1963	Results discussed in text.					
Klammer	1972	26	29	n/a	22	21	2
Fremgen[a]	1973	14	22	1	38	4	5
Petty, Scott, and Bird[a]	1975	11	31	2	41	15	0
Gitman and Forrester	1977	9	25	3	54	10	0
Kim and Farragher	1981	12	8	0	49	19	0
Gitman and Maxwell	1987	1	14	7	48	24	6

[a]Question asked for the "most important" method used.

source of free financing. Almost 30 percent report using DCF methods, and 7 percent use other methods.

Istvan (1961) discovers that the "great majority" of firms studied properly estimate the "dollar advantage of a proposal" (net excess of incremental inflows over incremental outflows per unit of time) but are weak in measuring the acceptability of projects. He identifies the relative use of five measures of acceptability: payback period method (27 percent); simple rate of return calculated as annual advantage/investment (50 percent); IRR (10 percent); and two methods classified in Table 3.2 as "other": necessity-postponability of the project based on management judgment (8 percent) and the MAPI formula (4 percent) as described by Terborgh (1958).

Pflomn (1963) documents the practices of 346 U.S. manufacturing firms in a report published by the National Industrial Conference Board. The report addresses such issues as the popularity of various evaluation methods, the discount rates used by firms, and the use of postaudits. Although Pflomn does not report percentages, he does report that the most common method used to evaluate projects is the payback period method, while return on investment (undiscounted) also shows wide usage. Pflomn also reports that the most widely used of the more sophisticated techniques is the IRR method.

Table 3.2 illustrates how firms moved toward more heavy reliance on IRR and NPV from the 1960s to the 1970s (see Klammer 1972; Fremgen 1973; Petty, Scott, and Bird 1975; Gitman and Forrester 1977). By the mid-1980s, the use of DCF methods clearly dominates other methods. The study by Gitman and Maxwell (1987) indicates that a combined total of 72 percent of respondents use either IRR or NPV as the primary method, and just 15 percent of firms use PB or ARR as the primary method. Despite differences among the various studies, a trend clearly exists toward using DCF methods.

Table 3.3 shows a similar trend using responses to somewhat different questions. Here, the surveys ask respondents to identify "all methods used" or some variation of that theme (Table 3.2 reports only the primary method used). Despite the difference in the nature of the questions, Table 3.3 suggests a similar

TABLE 3.3 Capital budgeting evaluation techniques used: U.S. firms

This table shows the percentage of U.S. firms using various capital budgeting evaluation techniques (not necessarily just the primary technique) as indicated by various survey studies. Survey participants can indicate more than one method. Key: PB = payback period, ARR = accounting rate of return, PI = profitability index, IRR = internal rate of return, and NPV = net present value. The notes indicate the precise wording when the survey questions asked respondents to indicate something other than all methods used.

Author(s)	Year published	Percentage of firms using each method				
		PB	ARR	PI	IRR	NPV
Christy	1966	51	43	n/a	14[a]	
Robichek and McDonald	1966	65	47	n/a	25	31
Fremgen[b]	1973	87	49	6	71	20
Schall, Sundem, and Geijsbeek[b]	1978	74	58	n/a	65	56
Moore and Reichert[c]	1983	80	59	n/a	66	68
Reichert, Moore, and Byler[c]	1988	76	59	n/a	n/a	83
Bierman[d]	1993	84	50	n/a	99	85
Gilbert and Reichert[c]	1995	63	46	n/a	82	85
Burns and Walker[b]	1997	73	21	10	84	73
Graham and Harvey[c]	2002	57	20	12	76	75

[a]The 14 percent is divided in unknown proportions between IRR and NPV.
[b]Question asked for methods used.
[c]Question asked for "frequently used" methods.
[d]Question asked for "primary" and "secondary" methods.
[c]Question asked for methods that are "always" or "almost always" used.

trend toward using DCF methods (IRR and NPV) and moving away from non-DCF methods (PB and ARR). These findings also suggest increased use of the profitability index (PI) as an evaluation tool. The early study by Christy (1966) indicates the popularity of the payback period and accounting rate of return. A later study by Robichek and McDonald (1966) finds more frequent use of DCF methods. Schall, Sundem, and Geijsbeek (1978, p. 286) conclude that "there is slight evidence within the sample that the level of sophistication in capital budgeting methods is positively related to the size of the firm's capital budget and negatively related to the firm's beta value." In referring to the use of modern management techniques such as NPV and IRR, Moore and Reichert (1983, p. 64) report that "it is the larger firms which can most readily afford and effectively employ these relatively expensive and highly specialized financial techniques." Finally, Graham and Harvey (2001) investigate the tendencies of firms with different characteristics to use different capital budgeting methods and arrive at the following conclusions:

- Large firms and firms run by chief executive officers (CEOs) that have master of business administration (MBA) degrees are more likely to use the NPV method.
- Highly leveraged firms, firms that pay dividends, and public firms are more likely to use NPV and IRR.
- Small firms, firms with CEOs without MBA degrees, firms with CEOs over age 59, and firms with long-tenured CEOs are more likely to use the payback method.

Multinational Firms

Table 3.4 shows responses to five studies focusing on capital budgeting methods used by multinational U.S. firms. We address these studies separately because they focus on a specific type of firm. The period covered by these studies begins with Oblak and Helm (1980) and ends with Shao and Shao (1996). The studies by Oblak and Helm (1980); Stanley and Block (1984); Kim, Crick, and Farragher (1984); and Brunwasser and McGowan (1989) survey multinational corporations (MNCs) at the headquarters level. The study by Shao and Shao reports the findings of a survey of foreign subsidiaries of U.S. multinational firms.

Oblak and Helm (1980) send surveys to 226 *Fortune* 500 firms that operate wholly owned subsidiaries in more than 11 foreign countries as indicated in the *Directory of Corporate Affiliations*. They conclude from the 58 responses that MNCs conduct a more detailed analysis of their foreign projects than their domestic projects.

Stanley and Block (1984) send surveys to 339 *Fortune* 1000 firms that operate in five or more countries outside the United States, and they receive 121 responses. The authors (p. 48) conclude that there is evidence of sophistication in capital budgeting by multinational firms as indicated "by the fact that the

TABLE 3.4 Primary capital budgeting evaluation techniques: U.S. multinational firms

This table shows the percentage of U.S. multinational firms using various capital budgeting evaluation techniques as the primary method. The study by Shao and Shao (1996) is the only one listed that gathers responses from foreign subsidiaries of U.S. firms rather than from the headquarters firm. Key: PB = payback period, ARR = accounting rate of return, IRR = internal rate of return, and NPV = net present value.

Author(s)	Year published	Population/Sample	Percentage of firms using each method				
			PB	ARR	IRR	NPV	Other
Oblak and Helm	1980	*Fortune* 500 multinational firms (*n* = 59)	10	14	60	14	2
Stanley and Block	1984	Multinational industrial firms in *Fortune* magazine (*n* = 121)	5	11	65	17	3
Kim, Crick, and Farragher	1984	*Fortune* 500 U.S. firms (*n* = 186)	12	14	62	9	3
Brunwasser and McGowan[a]	1989	*Fortune* 500 multinational firms (*n* = 29)	24	13	27	22	14[b]
Shao and Shao	1996	Foreign subsidiaries of U.S.-based multinational manufacturing firms/*Fortune* magazine (*n* = 188)	26	15	40	15	3

[a]Percentages were calculated by combining the responses for the use of each technique for domestic and foreign projects.

[b]"Freely remittable net present value" received 10 percent of responses, and profitability index received 4 percent.

internal rate of return is the primary method of evaluation for 65 percent of the respondents." They further observe that larger firms tend to use more advanced techniques than smaller firms.

Kim, Crick, and Farragher (1984) send questionnaires to the 500 largest U.S. and non-U.S. firms, generating responses from 186 U.S. firms and 127 non-U.S. firms. They find that among the U.S. multinational firms, IRR dominates as the primary method (62 percent). Among non-U.S. multinational firms, their evidence shows that the most common primary method is IRR (34 percent) and the second-most common primary method is payback period (31 percent). (Note: Table 3.4 does not show these results.) Kim, Crick, and Farragher report several other findings. First, 95 percent of U.S. multinational firms and 81 percent of non-U.S. multinational firms use the same methods to evaluate foreign and domestic projects. Second, the use of DCF methods by multinationals has increased since the time of Stonehill and Nathanson's (1968) study 17 years earlier. Third, comparing the project evaluation methods used by non-U.S. multinationals to those used by U.S. multinational firms leads Kim, Crick, and Farragher (p. 214) to conclude that "U.S. companies use more sophisticated capital budgeting procedures than their non-U.S. counterparts."

Brunwasser and McGowan (1989) send surveys to the 108 multinational firms in the *Fortune* 500 that derive more than half their sales from manufacturing or mining. From the 29 responses received, the authors (p. 28) conclude that "approximately 90 percent [of responding firms] use a discounted cash flow technique as the primary method for evaluating both domestic and foreign projects," and "the internal rate of return continues to be the most popular primary method, while net present value methods have replaced payback as the most popular secondary method."

Shao and Shao (1996) survey foreign subsidiaries of U.S. multinational firms. While the previous surveys of multinational firms suggest a trend away from PB and ARR and toward DCF methods, the survey of subsidiaries implies greater emphasis on non-DCF methods in foreign subsidiaries of U.S. multinational firms. Shao and Shao (p. 53) conclude "that actual use of sophisticated capital budgeting by foreign managers was not as widespread as expected by theorists."

Non-U.S. Firms

Table 3.5 shows the responses to seven surveys of non-U.S. firms. Again recognizing that differences exist in populations surveyed and question wording, there are still some relevant comparisons to be made. These studies ask respondents to indicate all capital budgeting methods used or the methods used that are either "important or fairly important" or "always used or almost always used."

The Pike studies (1983a, 1996) of firms in the United Kingdom use essentially the same firms in both studies, thus providing a relatively pure time-series comparison. The 1983 study involves 208 of the 300 largest U.K. firms, with

TABLE 3.5 Capital budgeting evaluation techniques: Non-U.S. firms

This table shows the percentage of non-U.S. firms using various capital budgeting evaluation techniques. The surveys ask respondents to indicate all that apply. The studies by Brounen et al. (2004) and Baker et al. (2009) include more methods than the other studies and ask firms to indicate methods used "always" or "almost always." Key: PB = payback period, DPB = discounted payback period, ARR = accounting rate of return, PI = profitability index, IRR = internal rate of return, and NPV = net present value.

Author(s)	Year published	Population/Sample	Percentage of firms using each method			
			PB	ARR	IRR	NPV
Pike	1983a	208 largest U.K. manufacturing and retail firms ($n = 150$)	79	51	54	38
Sangster	1993	Large Scottish firms listed in *Jordan's Scotland's Top 500 Companies* ($n = 94$)	78	31	58	48
Pike	1996	140 U.K. respondents to the Pike 1983a study ($n = 100$)	94	50	81	74
Kester, Chang, Echanis, Haikal, Isa, Skully, Tsui, and Wang	1999	Firms listed on various Asian stock exchanges				
		Australia ($n = 57$)	93	73	96	96
		Hong Kong ($n = 29$)	100	80	86	88
		Indonesia ($n = 16$)	81	56	94	94
		Malaysia ($n = 35$)	94	69	89	91
		The Philippines ($n = 35$)	100	78	94	81
		Singapore ($n = 54$)	98	80	88	86
Arnold and Hatzopoulos	2000	Large, midsize, and small U.K. firms listed in the *Times* 1000				
		Small firms ($n = 34$)	71	62	76	62
		Medium-size firms ($n = 24$)	75	50	83	79
		Large firms ($n = 38$)	66	55	84	97

(Continued)

TABLE 3.5 (cont'd) Capital budgeting evaluation techniques: Non-U.S. firms

Author(s)	Year published	Population/Sample	Percentage of firms using each method					
			Percentage of firms indicating each method is used "always" or "almost always"					
			PB	DPB	ARR	PI	IRR	NPV
Brounen, de Jong, and Koedijk	2004	European firms/employees ≥ 25/Amadeus data set of Bureau Van Dijk						
		United Kingdom (n = 68)	69	25	38	16	53	47
		The Netherlands (n = 52)	65	25	25	8	56	70
		Germany (n = 132)	50	31	32	16	42	48
		France (n = 61)	51	11	16	38	44	35
Baker, Dutta, and Saadi[a]	2009	762 Canadian firms on the Toronto Stock Exchange with select information available from Stock Guide database (n = 214)	67	25	40	11	68	75

[a]Not reported here are responses of adjusted present value (17 percent), modified IRR (12 percent), and real options (10 percent).

150 responses received. Pike seeks responses from those same firms in the later study and receives 99 responses (he adds one more response to reach 100). The results of these two studies suggest that while the frequency of use of ARR remains basically unchanged at about 50 percent and the use of PB increases moderately (from 79 percent to 94 percent), the frequency of use of two DCF methods (IRR and NPV) increases greatly during the period between the two studies. The employment of IRR increased from 38 percent of firms to 74 percent, while the application of NPV increased from 54 percent to 81 percent. Pike (1996, p. 89) also concludes that "firm size is still significantly associated with the degree of use for DCF methods [larger firms are more likely to use DCF] but not for payback." Additionally, Pike (1996, pp. 89-90) notes that the increased use of DCF methods by large firms has increased to the point where "the gap between theory and practice is trivial."

Sangster (1993) sends surveys to the 491 largest Scottish firms listed in *Jordan's Scotland's Top 500 Companies* and receives 94 usable responses. He concludes that payback is the most popular method, followed by IRR, NPV, and ARR. He also notes that DCF techniques are almost as widely used as payback and may be more popular than payback in companies using more than one of the four methods. He indicates that DCF techniques appear to be gaining in popularity. Finally, Sangster finds no evidence of an association between firm size and the use of DCF methods, which he attributes to more frequent use of DCF methods by small firms. He suggests this finding may result from the growth of information technology and better management education. Sangster (p. 328) also concludes that "whatever the cause, it is clear that there has been a . . . move towards greater use of the more sophisticated techniques."

Table 3.5 also shows the usage of various methods to evaluate capital budgeting projects by firms located in different countries. Kester, Chang, Echanis, Haikal, Isa, Skully, Tsui, and Wang (1999) send questionnaires to executives at 1,732 firms listed on six different Asia-Pacific stock exchanges. Their findings show that firms in each country use many different evaluation methods, but most rely more heavily on DCF versus non-DCF methods. For example, at least 94 percent of surveyed firms in Australia and Indonesia use IRR and NPV. Hong Kong and the Philippines are an exception because 100 percent of the responding firms in each country use a combination of the payback period and other methods. Kester et al. (p. 32)conclude that "executives from the surveyed countries consider DCF techniques such as NPV and IRR to be more important than non-DCF techniques for evaluating and ranking capital investment projects." Thus, the practices of companies in the surveyed countries of the Asia-Pacific region are similar to their Western counterparts.

The study of U.K. firms by Arnold and Hatzopoulos (2000) reports the findings from surveys sent to 100 large firms, 100 medium-size firms, and 100 small firms, where all firms are selected from the *Times* 1000. They receive responses from 38 large firms, 24 medium-size firms, and 34 small firms. The data presented in Table 3.5 suggest that larger firms are more likely to use DCF methods than non-DCF methods. Arnold and Hatzopoulos conclude that only a small number of firms do not use DCF methods. They also suggest that over time, firms have not replaced one method with another but instead use a broader array of methods.

Brounen, de Jong, and Koedijk (2004) survey firms in the United Kingdom, the Netherlands, Germany, and France and ask the same questions as the Graham and Harvey (2001) survey to facilitate comparisons. They identify firms from the Amadeus data set of Bureau Van Dijk and send questionnaires to all firms with 25 or more employees. Brounen, de Jong, and Koedijk (p. 73) state their "goal is to select 2,000 firms in the U.K., Germany, and France, and 500 firms in the Netherlands." To create their sample, they begin with all public firms and add private firms. They receive 313 responses. The authors report the methods used always or almost always by firms to evaluate capital budgeting projects in the four different Western European countries. The data presented in Table 3.5 suggest that firms tend to use multiple project evaluation methods. Only firms in the Netherlands indicate that they use a DCF method (NPV) most frequently. Firms in the United Kingdom, Germany, and France (especially smaller firms) most commonly use the payback period method. The authors also discover that larger firms are more likely to use the NPV method and that smaller firms are more likely to use payback. In comparing the results of their study to Graham and Harvey (2001), Brounen, de Jong, and Koedijk (p. 100) conclude that "the gap between science and practice appears to be rather constant across borders."

Baker, Dutta, and Saadi (2009) send surveys to 762 Canadian firms that are listed on the Toronto Stock Exchange and have select data available from the Stock Guide database. They receive 214 usable responses from primarily manufacturing firms (44 percent), retail and wholesale firms (24 percent), and mining firms (14 percent). They discover 84 percent of responding firms use DCF methods: 58 percent as the primary method and 26 percent as the secondary method. The methods used often or always are NPV (75 percent), IRR (68 percent), PB (67 percent), and ARR (40 percent). As other authors before them, Baker, Dutta, and Saadi report that larger firms are more likely to use DCF methods. They also find that firms with CEOs who have MBA degrees are more likely to use DCF methods when evaluating certain types of projects (expansion of operations, project replacement, project abandonment, and foreign operations). Baker, Dutta, and Saadi find that while firm size and CEO education are not related to the use of NPV, larger firms appear to be more likely to use IRR. They report a decline in the use of the payback period and note the popularity of the payback period among firms managed by CEOs who do not have MBA degrees. Overall, the findings suggest that the majority of large Canadian firms employ capital budgeting methods that are consistent with finance theory.

Small Firms

Although their results are not presented in a table, Danielson and Scott (2006) examine small U.S. firms (between one and 250 employees) using data collected for the National Federation of Independent Business Research Foundation by the Gallup Organization. With a sample drawn from Dun & Bradstreet and using 792 observations, they discover that only 12 percent of respondents use DCF methods exclusively. The most common method used is "gut feel" (26 percent), followed by PB (19 percent) and ARR (14 percent). Another 11 percent of respondents indicate they use a combination of methods. Not surprisingly, Danielson and Scott conclude that small firms use much less sophisticated methods than recommended by finance theory. They attribute this finding to several factors, including (1) owners of small businesses frequently lack college educations; (2) small businesses may have incomplete management teams; (3) small businesses do not operate in perfect capital markets, which may mean capital budgeting theory does not apply; and (4) small businesses have limited access to capital due to firm size and longevity.

Binder and Chaput (1996) use the results of some 30 survey studies to see if certain previously undiscovered yet rational factors affect the use of DCF techniques. They hypothesize that a trade-off between the costs and benefits of each capital budgeting evaluation technique affects the use of the different methods. Among their findings is that as uncertainty increases, firms use more non-DCF methods. They find a positive relationship between the use of DCF methods and both the AAA bond yield (due to the greater time value of money) and the availability of managers with MBA degrees (suggesting greater knowledge). Their evidence also shows that the use of DCF methods is negatively related to uncertainty, suggesting that when cash flows are more difficult to forecast, firms use DCF methods less frequently. Binder and Chaput (p. 253) conclude, "Overall, the evidence is consistent with the hypothesis that firms do a cost-benefit calculation when determining which capital budgeting rule(s) to employ, as opposed to the argument that the use of certain capital budgeting methods is evidence of bad judgment." They also argue that their findings suggest future surveys should not simply ask what methods are used but also how firms use them.

Summary of Project Evaluation Methods

Finance theory suggests firms should employ DCF methods to evaluate capital budgeting projects. Survey studies of U.S. firms conducted in the 1960s suggest that the majority of firms do not use DCF methods. Rather, methods such as PB and ARR tend to dominate. Moving forward to the early 1970s, studies provide evidence that a simple majority of larger firms now use DCF methods, but frequently these methods are not the primary methods employed. During the late

1970s and 1980s, studies begin to reveal greater influence of DCF methods in capital budgeting analysis. More recent studies of U.S. firms suggest that while firms still use the PB and ARR (often as secondary methods), DCF methods dominate among medium-size and large firms.

Some early studies note an apparent relationship between the size of a firm's capital budget and its use of DCF methods. More recent studies identify relationships in which large firms and firms run by CEOs that have MBA degrees are more likely to employ the NPV method. Survey studies also document relationships in which small firms, firms run by CEOs who do not have MBA degrees, firms with CEOs over age 59, and firms with long-tenured CEOs are more likely to use the PB method.

Studies surveying multinational firms find that even in the early 1980s, DCF methods dominate as the primary methods being employed, although non-DCF methods such as PB and ARR remain popular. One study reports that U.S. MNCs use DCF methods more than non-U.S. MNCs. A study of small U.S. domestic firms concludes that these firms use much less sophisticated methods than those recommended by finance theory.

Similar to their counterparts in the United States, surveys of U.K. firms reveal a transition over time from using PB and other non-discounted methods to using DCF methods, especially IRR and NPV. Entering the twenty-first century, survey results reveal the widespread use among U.K. firms of multiple methods. In the United Kingdom, the use of DCF methods now exceeds that of non-DCF methods by firms of all sizes, although larger firms tend to use DCF methods more frequently than smaller firms. A study of Asia-Pacific firms and another study of select European firms also indicate the use of multiple methods.

A study of Canadian firms also finds that firms commonly use multiple methods, with NPV, IRR, and PB emerging as the most common tools. Canadian firms have experienced a decline in the use of the payback period method, which firms managed by CEOs who do not have MBA degrees use more often.

Risk Evaluation and Adjustment

Evaluating projects that are expected to increase firm risk can pose a dilemma for managers. The theory describing how managers should measure project risk and adjust project evaluation to reflect risk differences are the subjects of the current section.

Theory: Risk Evaluation and Project Adjustment

Much of the following discussion of risk in capital budgeting emanates from the important theoretical work of Tobin (1958), Markowitz (1959), Sharpe (1963,

1964), Lintner (1963, 1964, 1965a, 1965b), and Gordon (1964). In finance, analysts frequently measure project risk using probability distributions to define the variability of future returns. When evaluating capital budgeting projects that will not change the risk of the firm, finance theory indicates that firms should require a minimum return equal to the firm's WACC (e.g., Ehrhardt 1994). A firm's WACC is the cost of funds needed to finance capital projects, so generating a return that covers those costs is a logical requirement. Additionally, as a project generates cash flow, the firm can reinvest those cash flows at the firm's WACC by using the cash flow to retire debt early or repurchase common equity in proportions equal to the firm's target capital structure. Thus, the firm will forgo incurring the WACC on those funds in the future. However, if a firm adopts a project that increases or decreases firm risk, the firm's WACC will increase or decrease accordingly. Thus, if a firm evaluates a project that will increase its cost of capital, it should require a higher return on the project.

The finance literature describes several methods for evaluating total project risk (e.g., Brigham and Ehrhardt 2008; Ross, Westerfield, and Jaffe 2008). This section focuses on three: sensitivity analysis, scenario analysis, and Monte Carlo simulation. Sensitivity analysis involves identifying key variables that are likely to affect the return on a project. For example, deviation of unit sales from the forecasted level affects a project's NPV. Sensitivity analysis involves changing key input variables one at a time to determine how sensitive a project's NPV is to deviations from the expected values of the input variables. Analysts consider projects with more sensitive NPVs to be more risky. Analysts often consider sensitivity analysis as a relatively basic means of measuring risk because it only indicates the variability of the outcome if certain key variables differ from their expected values. It does not consider the likely size or probability of the deviations of the key variables from their expected values.

Scenario analysis also involves identifying key variables that are likely to affect the return on a project (e.g., NPV). However, instead of altering each variable one at a time, the analyst can alter several variables simultaneously. A common form of scenario analysis involves developing three scenarios: worst, most likely, and best case. An analyst may base possible values and their probabilities on observed relative frequency of their occurrence in the past, subjective evaluation, or a priori reasoning. The sum of the probabilities of all three scenarios equals 1.0 or 100 percent. Based on the resulting probability distribution of NPVs, the analyst can calculate the expected value, expected standard deviation, and expected coefficient of variation of the outcomes, where higher coefficients of variation suggest greater relative project risk. Scenario analysis requires more analysis and forecasting than sensitivity analysis. If done properly, the result may provide a more complete picture of the potential return distribution.

A third tool for measuring risk is Monte Carlo simulation. This method involves creating probability distributions that describe the possible values of each key input variable that affects a project's NPV. The analyst then randomly selects a value for each variable from each probability distribution. Given the randomly generated input values, the analyst enters the values into the algorithm for determining the project's NPV. After repeating this process thousands of times, the analyst can use the results to construct a probability distribution of outcomes. From these data, the analyst can measure the expected NPV as well as the standard deviation and coefficient of variation of the NPV. The latter two measures suggest the level of project risk in a stand-alone context.

These three risk-measuring tools—sensitivity analysis, scenario analysis, and Monte Carlo simulation—are all measures of total risk. Finance theory suggests that total project risk may not be the most appropriate measure to consider when determining the required rate of return on a project. Instead, firms can be viewed as portfolios of projects, making the contribution of a project to the risk of the firm (called within-firm risk) a more appropriate risk measure. Theory suggests that if a firm is publicly traded so that stockholders can efficiently diversify their portfolios, the project's systematic risk, as measured by beta, may be the most appropriate risk measure. Because the total risk of a project may be more easily estimated than within-firm risk or systematic risk and because of high correlations between each pair of risk measures, many firms use total risk as a proxy for within-firm or systematic risk.

After measuring project risk, finance theory suggests several methods for adjusting project evaluation to directly reflect different risk levels (e.g., Brigham and Ehrhardt 2008; Ross, Westerfield, and Jaffe 2008). Theory suggests that adopting projects that increase the risk of a firm will result in a higher WACC for the firm. Thus, the firm will need to earn a higher return on the project to cover the financing costs. Therefore, firms should adjust the required rate of return on projects that will change the firm's risk. This method of adjusting the required return or hurdle rate on a project is the risk-adjusted discount rate method (RADR).

A second method of adjusting project evaluation to reflect risk differences is the certainty-equivalent (CE) method. Instead of adjusting the discount rate (required rate of return on a project) to reflect risk differences, this method involves adjusting each cash flow to reflect the level of uncertainty in the cash flow. For assured cash flows, the certainty-equivalent coefficient is 1.0. For cash flows with greater uncertainty, the certainty-equivalent cash flow is lower than 1.0. The analyst adjusts the uncertain cash flow to a certainty-equivalent cash flow so that a rational person would not recognize a difference between the expected uncertain cash flow and the certainty-equivalent cash flow. Thus, cash flows with greater uncertainty have certainty-equivalent cash flows that are much smaller. Once the cash flows have been changed to reflect certainty-equivalent cash flow, firms should apply a hurdle rate equal to the risk-free rate to find the risk-adjusted NPV.

Practice: Risk Evaluation and Project Adjustment

The current section synthesizes the results of survey research focusing on how managers evaluate project risk and adjust the analysis of projects to reflect risk differences. The discussion that follows groups studies based on their focus: U.S. firms, non-U.S. firms, and multinational firms.

U.S. Firms

Table 3.6 lists 15 frequently referenced survey studies of U.S. firms that ask participants about their views on project risk differences in capital budgeting. In the early study by Robichek and McDonald (1966), just 15 percent of survey participants respond affirmatively when asked "Does your company have a formal system to allow for differential riskiness or uncertainty in the future profitability of proposed projects?" Several years later, Klammer (1972) and Fremgen (1973) find that the majority of surveyed managers consider the risk of projects when evaluating them for possible adoption. While differences in population, sample, time period, and other factors may explain the large increase in proportion of firms considering risk, the small number considering risk in the Robichek and McDonald study may result from use of the qualifying words "formal system" in the question.

Petry (1975) sends questionnaires to the largest 400 of the *Fortune* 500 firms plus the *Fortune* 50 firms in each of the following categories: retailing, transportation, and utilities. Regarding the discrimination of projects based on different levels of risk, Petry (p. 64) finds that 71 percent of "industrial and retail corporations explicitly accounted for risk in making capital budgeting decisions." Later studies such as Gitman and Maxwell (1987) report that an even higher percentage of participating firms (76 percent) consider risk differences when evaluating capital budgeting projects. Still later, Payne, Heath, and Gale (1999) randomly select 852 U.S. firms and 588 Canadian firms from Compustat and receive responses from 90 U.S. firms and 65 Canadian firms. They find that 86 percent of responding U.S. firms report differentiating projects based on risk level compared to 83 percent for Canadian firms.

In addition to the risk measures discussed in the literature, managers use additional means to measure the risk of capital budgeting projects (e.g., Gitman and Vandenberg 2000; Schall, Sundem, and Geijsbeek 1978). Some of these methods include the length of the payback period, the size of the project (the larger the required investment in a project, the greater the risk to the firm), the track record of the division recommending the project, the track record of the individual recommending the project, subjective risk evaluation, and the probability of economic loss. Table 3.7 lists the responses of U.S. firms to questions about the methods they use to evaluate project risk. According to Petty, Scott, and Bird (1975), the most common risk measure is the project's payback

TABLE 3.6 Considering differences in the risk of capital budgeting projects: U.S. firms

This table shows the percentage of U.S. firms responding positively to a question about whether they consider risk differences of individual capital budgeting projects when evaluating those projects for possible adoption. The table also provides Information about the population and sample of each study. Studies listed here showing "N/A" instead of a percentage appear in Table 3.7 indicating how they adjust for project risk.

Author(s)	Year published	Population/Sample	Firms considering project risk (%)
Robichek and McDonald	1966	*Fortune* 500 manufacturing firms ($n = 163$)	15
Klammer	1972	Select large manufacturing firms/Compustat ($n = 184$)	61
Fremgen	1973	Firms in select industries/Dun & Bradstreet ($n = 177$)	67
Petty, Scott, and Bird	1975	*Fortune* 500 firms ($n = 109$)	n/a
Petry	1975	Top *Fortune*-listed firms in select industries ($n = 284$)	71
Brigham	1975	Select executives who completed a particular university program (large firms/not randomly selected; $n = 33$)	52
Gitman and Forrester	1977	*Forbes* firms with large capital expenditures ($n = 103$)	71
Schall, Sundem, and Geijsbeek	1978	Select large firms/Compustat ($n = 189$)	95
Kim and Farragher	1981	*Fortune* 1000 firms ($n = 200$)	n/a
Gitman and Mercurio	1982	*Fortune* 1000 firms ($n = 177$)	67
Kim, Crick, and Farragher	1984	*Fortune* 500 U.S. firms ($n = 186$)	91
Gitman and Maxwell	1987	*Forbes* 1000 firms with growth characteristics ($n = 109$)	76
Klammer, Koch, and Wilner	1991	Select large industrial firms from Compustat ($n = 100$)	70
Payne, Heath, and Gale[a]	1999	Random from Compustat/U.S. firms ($n = 90$)	86
Gitman and Vandenberg	2000	*Fortune* 1000 firms ($n = 111$)	n/a

[a] Statistics are for U.S. firms only. Survey results from Canadian firms are reported in a separate table.

TABLE 3.7 Methods used to evaluate project risk: U.S. firms

This table shows the percentage of U.S. firms that report using various methods to measure the risk of capital budgeting projects. The findings of the different studies are difficult to compare because different studies provide a different array of possible answers. However, the use of various methods by firms in Gitman and Mercurio (1982) and Gitman and Vandenberg, which used similar samples and questions, suggests little change.

Author(s)	Year published	Percentage of firms using each method										
		Sensitivity analysis	Simulation techniques	Probability distribution of cash flows	Covariance with firm returns	Payback period	Based on project size	Division's track record	Track record of person suggesting project	Evaluate risk subjectively	Probability of loss	Other
Petty, Scott, and Bird[a]	1975	n/a	27	31[b]	n/a	61	n/a	n/a	n/a	n/a	n/a	n/a
Schall, Sundem, and Geijsbeek	1978	n/a	n/a	23	4	n/a	n/a	n/a	n/a	73	11	15
Kim and Farragher	1981	23	10	n/a	n/a	n/a	n/a	n/a	n/a	n/a	n/a	n/a
Gitman and Mercurio[c]	1982	n/a	n/a	n/a	55	59	76	45	31	n/a	n/a	n/a
Klammer, Koch, and Wilner	1991	57	n/a	12	1	n/a	n/a	n/a	n/a	n/a	n/a	2
Gitman and Vandenberg[c]	2000	n/a	n/a	n/a	57	56	76	44	29	n/a	n/a	n/a

[a] Responses show the percentage of participants indicating they use these methods "frequently" or "always."

[b] The wording used in this study is "measure expected variation in returns."

[c] Reflects the percentage of the respondents indicating the method is "important" or "very important."

period, which 61 percent of respondents report using. The authors describe the second-most commonly used risk measure, which 31 percent of the respondents report using, as "expected variation of returns," which we classify here as a probability distribution of cash flows. The final tool for evaluating risk addressed in this study is simulation analysis, which 27 percent of the respondents report using. Petty, Scott, and Bird also identify the use of CE and RADR, which are discussed later as methods of incorporating risk in the evaluation process rather than a means of measuring risk.

Schall, Sundem, and Geijsbeek (1978) find the most common method of measuring project risk is subjective evaluation (73 percent), followed by constructing a probability distribution of project cash flows (23 percent), identifying the probability of a loss (11 percent), and evaluating the covariance of a project's cash flow with cash flows of other projects (4 percent). "Other" received 15 percent of responses. Kim and Farragher (1981) find sensitivity analysis to be the most popular method of measuring project risk (23 percent), followed by simulation analysis (10 percent). Gitman and Mercurio's (1982) survey results show that project size is the most common measure of risk (76 percent), followed by payback period (59 percent), covariance of project returns with returns on the firm's other projects (55 percent), the track record of the division presenting the project (45 percent), and the track record of the person presenting the project (31 percent).

Other studies report different findings. For example, evidence by Klammer, Koch, and Wilner (1991) documents that 57 percent of respondents report using sensitivity analysis to measure risk, 12 percent develop probability distributions of outcomes, and just 1 percent measure covariance of the project with other projects. In their replication of Gitman and Mercurio (1982), Gitman and Vandenberg (2000) find that the percentage of respondents describing each method as important or very important is somewhat similar. Yet, they conclude more firms in the recent study specifically differentiate project risk than in the earlier study. Gitman and Vandenberg (p. 67) also note that "project size, the relationship of project returns to the firm's other projects, and the project's payback period remain the most important factors in assessing project risk."

Firms that differentiate the risk of capital budgeting projects need a method to reflect the different risk levels in project evaluation. Table 3.8 shows the responses of U.S. firms to questions about methods used to adjust for capital budgeting project risk. In most studies, regardless of the study year, adjusting the discount rate is the most common or one of the most common methods for adjusting for project risk in the evaluation process. For those studies in which adjusting the discount rate is not the most common method, adjusting cash flows is the preferred method. The use of these two methods is consistent with finance theory. A somewhat less popular but still fairly common method involves requiring a shorter payback period.

The data presented in Table 3.8 reveal no clear trends over time in the use of different methods to adjust for project risk. The fact that most surveys provide

TABLE 3.8 Methods used to adjust for project risk: U.S. firms

This table shows the percentage of U.S. firms using various methods to adjust project evaluation for project risk. The table suggests that adjusting the project discount rate and adjusting project cash flows are common in the 1970s and remain the most important methods in more recent periods.

Author(s)	Year published	Percentage of firms using each method					
		Adjust discount rate	Require shorter PB	Adjust cash flows	Adjust cash flows and discount rate	Consider subjectively	Other
Klammer	1972	21[a]	10[a]	n/a	n/a	n/a	n/a
Fremgen	1973	54	40	32	n/a	29	8
Petty, Scott, and Bird[b]	1975	37	n/a	8	n/a	n/a	n/a
Petry	1975	30	14	47[c]	n/a	n/a	9
Gitman and Forrester	1977	43	13	46[d]	n/a	n/a	n/a
Schall, Sundem, and Geijsbeek	1978	64[c]	32	n/a	n/a	n/a	n/a
Kim and Farragher	1981	19	14	3	n/a	n/a	3
Gitman and Mercurio	1982	32	n/a	39	20	n/a	9
Kim, Crick, and Farragher	1984	14	16	11	n/a	n/a	50[f]
Gitman and Maxwell	1987	44	9	42[d]	n/a	n/a	n/a
Klammer, Koch, and Wilner	1991	40	19	n/a	n/a	n/a	n/a
Payne, Heath, and Gale[g]	1999	47	14	33	n/a	n/a	9
Gitman and Vandenberg	2000	39	n/a	32	21	n/a	8

[a]These responses are to a question about the risk analysis techniques used. We report them here as methods used to adjust for project risk.

[b]Responses show the percentage of participants using these methods "frequently" or "always."

[c]Includes adjusting cash flows subjectively and on a probabilistic basis.

[d]Includes the certainty-equivalent method and subjective adjustment of cash flows.

[e]While 64 percent of respondents indicate they raise the required rate of return to reflect project risk, another 16 percent say they raise the discount rate in computing present value. Because respondents can reply to more than one method, this 16 percent may be included in the 64 percent that indicate they adjust the discount rate.

[f]Methods include "adjust accounting rate of return," "borrow funds locally," and "insure risk where possible."

[g]Statistics are for U.S. firms only. Table 3-9 reports survey results of Canadian firms.

different alternative answers to survey questions may account for much of the variation in observed frequencies. Of course, differences in the characteristics of the samples are also likely to contribute to the varying results.

In the Gitman and Forrester (1977) and Gitman and Vandenberg (2000) studies, adjusting project cash flows *and* the discount rate is a method used by 20 percent and 21 percent of responding firms, respectively. If these firms are adjusting cash flows downward and discount rate upward to reflect higher risk (it is not clear if they are), they are doing so without support of finance theory. Finally, Fremgen (1973) indicates that 29 percent of the respondents consider risk subjectively when evaluating projects.

Non-U.S. Studies

Some non-U.S. studies ask managers about how their firms evaluate risk. Again, the wording of the questions and the alternative answers available to respondents differ among the studies. Table 3.9 summarizes responses to surveys published from 1983 through 2009. Recall that the two Pike studies (1983a, 1996) are unique in that most of the firms that participate in the earlier study also participate in the later study. A comparison of the two studies reveals a marked increase in the percentage of respondents using sensitivity analysis (from 38 percent to 88 percent) and probability analysis (from 12 percent to 48 percent).

The study of firms in six Asian countries conducted by Kester et al. (1999) suggests the widespread use of finance theory techniques. The risk measurement tool used most frequently by firms in Australia, Hong Kong, and Malaysia is sensitivity analysis (100 percent, 100 percent, and 83 percent, respectively), followed by scenario analysis (96 percent, 100 percent, and 80 percent, respectively). For firms in the other three participating Asian countries (Indonesia, the Philippines, and Singapore), the most commonly used tool to measure risk is scenario analysis (94 percent, 97 percent, and 90 percent, respectively), followed by sensitivity analysis (88 percent, 94 percent, and 79 percent, respectively). Firms in all six countries indicate frequent use of decision trees, ranging from 35 percent of respondents from the Philippines to 58 percent of Hong Kong respondents. Only 9 percent of respondents in Malaysia indicate the use of simulation techniques, but firms from the other surveyed countries indicate more frequent use, ranging from 24 percent for Malaysian firms to 38 percent of Australian firms.

Payne, Heath, and Gale (1999) show that a roughly equal percentage of Canadian firms use sensitivity analysis, quantify risk based on personal experience, and quantify risk based on other firms' experience (60 percent, 63 percent, and 60 percent, respectively). Arnold and Hatzopoulos (2000) find that 85 percent of U.K. firms participating in their study use sensitivity analysis and scenario analysis, while 31 percent use probability analysis.

Baker, Dutta, and Saadi (2009) document that 84 percent of responding Canadian firms differentiate the risk of capital budgeting projects. The authors

TABLE 3.9 Methods used to evaluate project risk: Non-U.S. firms

This table shows the percentage of non-U.S. firms that report using various methods to measure the risk of capital budgeting projects. The findings of the different studies are difficult to compare because different studies use a different array of possible answers and different populations. The use of sensitivity analysis and scenario analysis appears to be among the most popular methods for firms in the United Kingdom and Asian countries.

Author(s)	Year published	Population/Sample	Percentage of firms using each method								
			Sensitivity analysis	Scenario analysis	Simulation	Sensitivity and scenario analysis	Probability analysis	Decision trees	Quantify based on personal experience	Quantify based on other firms' experience	Other
Pike	1983a	208 largest U.K. manufacturing and retailing firms (n = 150)	38	n/a	n/a	n/a	12	n/a	n/a	n/a	4
Pike	1996	140 U.K. respondents to the Pike 1983a study (n = 100)	88	n/a	n/a	n/a	48	n/a	n/a	n/a	20[a]
Kester, Chang, Echanis, Haikal, Isa, Skully, Tsui, and Wang	1999	Firms listed on Asian stock exchanges									
		Australia (n = 57)	100	96	38	n/a	n/a	44	n/a	n/a	2
		Hong Kong (n = 29)	100	100	35	n/a	n/a	58	n/a	n/a	4
		Indonesia (n = 16)	88	94	25	n/a	n/a	50	n/a	n/a	n/a
		Malaysia (n = 35)	83	80	9	n/a	n/a	37	n/a	n/a	n/a
		The Philippines (n = 35)	94	97	24	n/a	n/a	33	n/a	n/a	n/a
		Singapore (n = 54)	79	90	35	n/a	n/a	46	n/a	n/a	n/a

(Continued)

TABLE 3.9 (cont'd) Methods used to evaluate project risk: Non-U.S. firms

Author(s)	Year published	Population/Sample	Percentage of firms using each method								
			Sensitivity analysis	Scenario analysis	Simulation	Sensitivity and scenario analysis	Probability analysis	Decision trees	Quantify based on personal experience	Quantify based on other firms' experience	Other
Payne, Heath, and Gale[b]	1999	588 Canadian firms randomly selected from Compustat (n = 65)	60	n/a	n/a	n/a	n/a	n/a	63	60	11
Arnold and Hatzopoulos	2000	300 U.K. firms taken from the *Times* 1000 (n = 96)	n/a	n/a	13	85	31	n/a	n/a	n/a	6[c]
Baker, Dutta, and Saadi	2009	762 Canadian firms on the Toronto Stock Exchange with select information available from Stock Guide database (n = 214)	74	32[d]	13	n/a	n/a	n/a	77[e]	n/a	17

[a]Percent of firms using beta analysis.
[b]This table reports only Canadian firms used in the study.
[c]Includes 3 percent using beta analysis.
[d]Actual response is "scenario analysis/decision trees."
[e]Actual response is "judgment."

report that firms managed by CEOs with MBA degrees are more likely to do so. While 83 percent of firms that differentiate risk measure project risk individually, 16 percent of respondents group projects into classes based on risk. Classifying firms into risk groups is more pronounced for small firms and firms with CEOs that do not have MBA degrees. The majority of firms use both judgment (77 percent) and sensitivity analysis (74 percent) as a means of measuring project risk. Other popular tools for measuring risk include scenario analysis/decision trees (32 percent) and simulation analysis (13 percent).

Table 3.10 displays the responses for non-U.S. studies (U.K. firms in three studies, Canadian firms in two studies, and firms from a variety of countries in still another study) to questions about how these firms adjust project evaluation to reflect project risk. These responses are similar to those of U.S. firms in that the most common method of adjusting for project risk is altering the discount rate. Compared to U.S. firms, non-U.S. firms use a shorter required payback period more frequently (compare Table 3.8 to Table 3.10). Comparing the responses of U.S. firms to non-U.S. firms in the Payne, Heath, and Gale (1999) study (Table 3.8 and Table 3.10) shows that non-U.S. firms differ only slightly regarding the adjustment of the discount rate and adjustment of cash flows. However, similar to Kim, Crick, and Farragher (1984), non-U.S. firms in Payne, Heath, and Gale (1999) appear to require shorter payback periods as a means of adjusting for risk more frequently than U.S. firms. Baker, Dutta, and Saadi (2009) find that firms managed by CEOs with MBA degrees are more likely to adjust the discount rate or cash flows to reflect risk, while firms managed by CEOs without MBA degrees are likely to adjust both the discount rate and cash flows.

As indicated earlier, Brounen, de Jong, and Koedijk (2004) survey firms in the United Kingdom, the Netherlands, Germany, and France and compare their results with the Graham and Harvey (2001) study of U.S. firms. Both studies present detailed information about altering discount rates and cash flows to adjust for various possible sources of project risk (e.g., business-cycle risk and unexpected inflation). Table 3.11 summarizes some of these results. Both studies suggest that firms do not generally consider specific risk factors such as business-cycle risk when evaluating individual projects. For those firms that do consider specific risk factors, the two most common sources of risk considered are interest rate risk and currency risk. Of course, the nature of the firms' operations influences the importance of these various factors to project risk. For example, firms adopting foreign projects are more likely to consider the foreign exchange risk of projects. The most notable results from Table 3.11 are the relatively high percentage of U.K. firms that consider foreign exchange risk when adjusting for project risk compared to firms in the other countries and the relatively low percentage of U.S. firms and firms from the Netherlands that consider interest rate risk when adjusting for project risk relative to firms in the other countries.

TABLE 3.10 Methods used to adjust for capital budgeting project risk: Non-U.S. firms

This table shows the percentage of non-U.S. firms that report using various methods to adjust project evaluation for project risk. This table suggests that U.K., Canadian, and other non-U.S. firms use methods similar to those used by U.S. firms (e.g. adjusting the project discount rate and adjusting project cash flows).

Author(s)	Year published	Population/Sample	Percentage of firms using each method				
			Adjust the discount rate	Require shorter payback period	Adjust cash flows	Consider subjectively	Other
Pike	1983a	208 largest U.K. manufacturing and retailing firms (n = 150)	36	30	n/a	n/a	n/a
Kim, Crick, and Farragher	1984	Non-U.S. Fortune 500 firms (n = 127)	8	21	4	n/a	67[a]
Pike	1996	140 U.K. respondents to the Pike 1983a study (n = 100)	65	60	n/a	n/a	n/a
Payne, Heath, and Gale	1999	588 Canadian firms randomly selected from Compustat (n = 65)	49	28	35	n/a	6
Arnold and Hatzopoulos	2000	300 U.K. firms taken from the Times 1000 (n = 96)	52	20	n/a	46	n/a
Baker, Dutta, and Saadi	2009	762 Canadian firms on the Toronto Stock Exchange with select information available from Stock Guide database (n = 214)	28	9	1[b]		

[a]Major methods include adjust the accounting rate of return (30 percent), borrow funds locally (20 percent), and insure the risk (10 percent).
[b]Actual response is "use certainty equivalents."

TABLE 3.11 Adjusting the discount rate and/or cash flow of capital projects based on perceived interest rate or foreign exchange risk

This table shows the percentage of U.S. firms and firms in select European countries that report adjusting the discount rate and/or cash flows for two specific sources of risk: interest rate risk and foreign exchange risk. The table suggests that European firms generally report making more adjustments for interest rate risk and foreign exchange risk than U.S. firms. Note: when the surveys were sent to European countries, the Euro had been in existence for less than one year.

Country[a]	Percentage of firms adjusting for each risk	
	Interest rate risk	Foreign exchange risk
United States	48.7	44.9
United Kingdom	75.8	62.5
The Netherlands	49.0	50.0
Germany	63.8	51.3
France	71.4	41.8

[a]Graham and Harvey (2001) provide the results for U.S. firms, and Brounen, de Jong, and Koedijk (2004) provide the results for European firms.

Multinational Firms

Although most studies of multinational firms do not address the question of how firms measure project risk, several studies look at how multinational firms adjust project evaluation to reflect risk differences. An early study by Stonehill and Nathanson (1968) divides a sample of multinational firms into two groups—U.S. multinationals and foreign multinationals—and considers how those groups evaluate the risks of foreign projects. We combine two of Stonehill and Nathanson's categories ("vary required rate of return on investment" and "adjust cost of capital in present value analysis") into one category called "adjust the discount rate." As Table 3.12 shows, 50 percent of Stonehill and Nathanson's respondents from foreign multinationals adjust the discount rate for the risk of foreign projects. This is the most common method used by this sample of foreign multinational firms at the time of the study. Another 27 percent of foreign multinationals consider the risk of foreign projects subjectively, and 9 percent borrow funds locally. For U.S. multinational firms, the two most common methods of adjusting for the risk of foreign projects is to consider risk subjectively (44 percent) and adjust the discount rate (33 percent). Other methods used include insuring against risk (8 percent), borrowing funds locally (5 percent), and requiring a shorter payback period (6 percent).

Although data from the Baker and Beardsley (1973) study do not appear in Table 3.12, their findings are important. They survey 134 U.S. multinational firms about the risks involved in investing in foreign capital budgeting projects

TABLE 3.12 Methods used to adjust for project risk by U.S. and non-U.S. multinational firms: Domestic projects versus foreign projects

This table shows the percentage of U.S. and non-U.S. multinational firms that report using different methods to adjust for risk in the evaluation of domestic projects and foreign projects. Stonehill and Nathanson (1968) and Kim, Crick, and Farragher (1984) study the evaluation of foreign projects by U.S. and non-U.S. firms separately. Oblak and Helm (1980) examine the evaluation of only foreign projects by U.S. multinationals and Brunwasser and McGowan (1989) investigate the evaluation of foreign and domestic projects by U.S. multinational firms. The chapter narrative discusses the results of Stanley and Block (1984) and Shao and Shao (1996).

Author(s)	Year published	Population/Sample	Adjust the discount rate	Require shorter payback period	Adjust cash flows	Adjust cash flow and discount rate	Adjust required accounting rate of return	Insure risk when possible	Borrow funds locally	Consider subjectively	Other
Stonehill and Nathanson[a]	1968	Fortune 500 U.S. firms (n = 92; evaluating foreign projects)	33[b]	6	n/a	n/a	n/a	8	5	41	4
		Fortune's 200 largest non-U.S. firms (n = 18; evaluating foreign projects)	50[b]	0	n/a	n/a	n/a	0	9	27	14
Oblak and Helm	1980	Fortune 500 U.S. multinational firms (n = 59; evaluating foreign projects)	14	13	7	n/a	19	9	22	n/a	5
Kim, Crick, and Farragher	1984	Fortune 500 U.S. firms (n = 186; evaluating foreign projects)	14	16	11	n/a	10	13	22	n/a	5
		Fortune 500 largest non-U.S. firms (n = 127; evaluating foreign projects)	8	21	4	n/a	30	10	20	n/a	2

Stanley and Block	1984	Multinational industrial firms/*Fortune* 1000 largest firms (n = 188; evaluating foreign and domestic projects)	Results discussed in text.			n/a		n/a	n/a	22
Brunwasser and McGowan	1989	*Fortune* 500 U.S. multinational firms (n = 29; evaluating foreign projects)	24	n/a	22	22	n/a	n/a	n/a	22
		Fortune 500 U.S. multinational firms (n = 29; evaluating domestic projects)	30	n/a	21	21	n/a	n/a	n/a	21
Shao and Shao	1996	Foreign subsidiaries of U.S. multinational firms (n = 188; evaluating foreign and domestic projects)	Results discussed in text.							

[a] Responses are to the question, "How do you make a distinction between foreign and domestic investment alternatives?"

[b] This is the sum of the responses for "varied required rate of return on investment" and "adjust cost of capital in a present value analysis."

and how firms evaluate these risks, with a focus on the financial risk related to foreign projects. Baker and Beardsley (p. 39) note, "Although all firms indicated an awareness of the increased risk and uncertainty attributed to foreign investments, no consistent pattern emerged whereby these factors were analyzed on a quantitative basis." Only 49 percent of participating firms add a premium to the return they require on foreign investments. Baker and Beardsley comment that this could be because the firms use some other method of risk adjustment, such as altering the forecasted cash flows.

In a survey of U.S. multinational firms, Oblak and Helm (1980) question which risk-adjustment methods are used when evaluating foreign projects. While the responses differ from those in the Stonehill and Nathanson (1968) study, there are many similarities to the responses of U.S. firms reported by Kim, Crick, and Farragher (1984). The greatest difference is in the use of an adjusted accounting rate of return. Compared to Kim, Crick, and Farragher, Oblak and Helm report more extensive use of this method by U.S. multinational firms: 19 percent versus 10 percent, respectively. Given the time difference between the two studies, this may indicate movement away from non-discounted cash flow methods.

Brunwasser and McGowan (1989) also survey U.S. multinational firms but ask firms to respond about risk adjustment for domestic projects and foreign projects to see if differences exist between the two. While they find few differences, Brunwasser and McGowan (p. 28) conclude: "Two-thirds of the MNCs adjust the discount rate or the project cash flows, or both, in adjusting for foreign project risk. In addition, there appears to be little difference in how MNCs adjust for risk in foreign versus domestic projects."

As with Stonehill and Nathanson (1968), Kim, Crick, and Farragher (1984) divide their sample into two groups: U.S. multinational firms and non-U.S. multinational firms. Their evidence shows that the method used most frequently by non-U.S. MNCs to modify their analysis of projects based on risk is to adjust the required accounting rate of return (30 percent). This method is much less popular with U.S. firms (10 percent). No single method stands out for U.S. firms, with a fairly even division among borrowing money locally to reduce risk (22 percent), requiring a shorter payback period (16 percent), adjusting the discount rate (14 percent), and insuring against the risk when possible (13 percent).

Although the results do not appear in Table 3.12, Shao and Shao (1996) also study risk analysis related to capital budgeting by U.S. multinational firms. Unlike most surveys of multinational firms, they survey the foreign subsidiaries of U.S.-based multinational firms using multinational firms identified in the July 1991 issue of *Forbes*. Of the 532 subsidiaries surveyed worldwide, 188 subsidiaries located in 43 different countries agreed to participate. The highest number of responses comes from subsidiaries in Canada (22), England (19), and Australia (11). The questions concern the techniques subsidiaries use for all projects, domestic and foreign.

Shao and Shao (1996) ask participating foreign subsidiaries of U.S.-based multinational firms to rate the use of seven different risk assessment methods as most important = 1 to least important = 5. The most important methods and their average importance value are sensitivity analysis (2.02), followed by subjective determination (2.81) and computer simulation (3.10). The least important methods are coefficient of variation (3.84) and decision trees (3.82). Shao and Shao use the same scaling system to determine the most important methods used to adjust for project risk. The most important methods are to subjectively adjust cash flows (2.91), followed by adjust the payback period (2.97), no adjustment (3.21), adjust the accounting rate of return (3.45), use a risk-adjusted discount rate (3.62), and use certainty-equivalent cash flows (4.04). Shao and Shao (p. 49) conclude that "sophisticated risk-adjustment techniques were not used as often as expected." This finding suggests a substantial gap exists between theory and practice for foreign subsidiaries of U.S. multinational firms. Further, Shao and Shao (p. 49) comment, "When risk adjustment and risk assessment procedures were used, subsidiaries exposed to high political and financial risk used more sophisticated capital budgeting techniques." Additionally, when firms use a risk-adjustment procedure, (p. 51) "subsidiaries subjected to high degrees of financial leverage, high cost of capital requirements, and high total asset investment levels used more sophisticated capital budgeting techniques."

Stanley and Block (1984) survey 339 multinational *Fortune*-listed firms that operate in five or more countries outside the United States as reported in the *Directory of American Firms Operating in Foreign Countries.* Of the 121 responding firms, they learn that 62 percent adjust project evaluation for risk. About 55 percent of the respondents indicate differences between their risk analysis of domestic and foreign projects. The finding that 45 percent of the respondents make no distinction between the risk of domestic and foreign projects is similar to the finding of Baker and Beardsley (1973). Stanley and Block conclude that firms using advanced project evaluation methods are more likely to analyze the risk of projects.

Summary of Risk Evaluation and Project Adjustment

Finance theory indicates that firms should consider risk differences of projects being evaluated for possible adoption. Despite the finding by Robichek and McDonald (1966) that only 15 percent of firms consider risk differences of capital projects, just nine years later, Petry (1975) reports that 71 percent of responding firms consider risk differences. Over time, different studies discover that the importance of different tools for measuring project risk has changed. For example, Petty, Scott, and Bird (1975) indicate that 61 percent of firms use the payback period as a measure of risk; Schall, Sundem, and Geijsbeek (1978) report that the majority of firms evaluate risk subjectively; Gitman and Mercurio (1982) and Gitman and Vandenberg (2000) report the majority of firms base project risk on the size of the project; and Klammer et al. (1991) discover the majority of firms use sensitivity analysis to measure project risk.

Once firms have measured project risk, they use a variety of methods to adjust for the risk in project evaluation. Finance theory suggests firms can either adjust the discount rate or adjust the cash flows (the latter is a component of the certainty-equivalent method). Of the 13 studies listed in Table 3.8, either a majority or a plurality of respondents in nine of the studies indicate adjusting the discount rate is the most widely used method of adjusting for project risk. This is true of the earliest study listed in the table (Klammer 1972) and the most recent study (Gitman and Vandenberg 2000).

Survey studies indicating how non-U.S. firms measure project risk report a preference for using sensitivity analysis and/or scenario analysis. Both of Pike's studies (1983a, 1996) reveal a plurality of respondents use sensitivity analysis. Kester et al. (1999) discover that many Asia-Pacific firms use multiple methods, with sensitivity analysis and scenario analysis employed by a majority of firms. Two survey studies of Canadian firms (Arnold and Hatzopoulos 2000; Baker, Dutta, and Saadi 2009) similarly report that a majority of firms use both judgment and sensitivity analysis. Baker, Dutta, and Saadi also find that firms managed by CEOs with MBA degrees are more likely to differentiate project risk. Consistent with finance theory, a plurality of survey participants in the same studies of non-U.S. firms adjust for differences in project risk by changing the discount rate. Baker, Dutta, and Saadi (2009) discover that Canadian firms managed by CEOs with MBA degrees are more likely to adjust either the discount rate or cash flows to reflect risk, while firms managed by CEOs without MBA degrees are more likely to adjust both the discount rate and cash flows.

Capital Rationing

Some firms elect not to adopt all capital budgeting projects that have positive NPVs. The sections that follow discuss the theory behind capital rationing and provide a synopsis of important survey research on the subject.

Theory: Capital Rationing

An optimal capital budget is one in which a firm adopts all independent positive-NPV projects. This budget is optimal because each positive-NPV project the firm adopts is expected to increase the value of the firm after considering all costs (including financing costs). Although finance theory specifies that capital rationing should not exist, there are four primary reasons firms may limit the number of projects they adopt or the dollar amount of their capital budget. One reason is management reluctance to issue external financing because of its higher cost (Thakor 1990). Related to this is the argument that managers will forgo marginally acceptable projects to maintain reserve-borrowing capacity for higher-NPV projects that may be found later (Myers 1984). If the latter theory is correct, capital rationing should be inversely related to reserve-borrowing capacity. A second reason for capital rationing is to control for biased forecasts (Antle and Eppen 1985; Hirshleifer 1993). This theory suggests that junior managers are likely to provide forecasts biased in favor of adopting projects. By only adopting projects that promise the highest returns, those projects are likely to be successful even if the cash flow forecasts are biased. The third reason argues that risk-averse managers reject even positive risk-adjusted NPV projects when the downside risk is great (Bierman and Smidt 1993). The fourth possible reason for capital rationing involves limiting project adoptions due to a lack of qualified personnel to manage projects (Brigham and Ehrhardt 2008).

Practice: Capital Rationing

The following synopsis of survey studies related to capital rationing places the studies into one of two groups: U.S. firms and non-U.S. firms.

U.S. Firms

Several survey studies contain questions about the application of capital rationing. Table 3.13 shows the responses of U.S. firms to the question of whether they employ capital rationing. The earliest study indicated is Robichek and McDonald (1966), who learn that 80 percent of respondents set financial limits on their capital budgets. Later, Fremgen (1973) finds that 73 percent of responding firms sometimes employ capital rationing. Studies by Petty, Scott, and Bird (1975), Gitman and Forrester (1977), and Gitman and Maxwell (1987) all use different wording to ask if respondents use capital rationing. The results suggest a further decline in the use of capital rationing. Gitman and Maxwell (p. 46) conclude that the most likely reason for the decline in capital rationing is "that management has established planning models of sufficient sophistication to pre-select the projects that will pass through the process, thereby also eliminating the need for competitive decisions."

Mukherjee and Hingorani (1999) send questionnaires to all CFOs of *Fortune* 500 firms and receive 102 usable responses. They find that 64 percent of respondents employ capital rationing. Their study is devoted to the topic of capital rationing, and more of their findings are discussed shortly.

In the studies by Gitman and Mercurio (1982) and Gitman and Vandenberg (2000), respondents are asked to indicate to the nearest 10 percent how often their firm has more acceptable projects than funds available to invest. The weighted average percentage in the latter study is 40 percent, compared to 66 percent in the earlier study. Gitman and Vandenberg (p. 64) conclude that this reported reduction in capital rationing "may suggest that firms have consciously moved toward the theoretical equilibrium where capital rationing does not exist."

Of course, differences in observed responses between the earliest study and the most recent study may not be evidence of a trend in the use of capital rationing. As discussed earlier, differences in responses may reflect differences in question

TABLE 3.13 Use of capital rationing by U.S. firms

This table shows the percentage of U.S firms that report using or sometimes using capital rationing. Because surveys often ask different questions, the table presents the findings in three different columns: percentage of firms regularly using capital rationing, percentage of firms sometimes using capital rationing, and percent of time firms use capital rationing. The results could suggest there has been a reduction in the use of capital rationing.

Author(s)	Year published	Population/Sample	Percentage of firms regularly using capital rationing	Percentage of firms sometimes using capital rationing	Percent of time firms using capital rationing[a]
Robichek and McDonald	1966	*Fortune* 500 manufacturing firms (n = 163)	80	n/a	n/a
Fremgen	1973	Firms in select industries/Dun & Bradstreet (n = 177)	64	73	n/a
Petty, Scott, and Bird	1975	*Fortune* 500 firms (n = 109)	58	n/a	n/a
Gitman and Forrester	1977	*Forbes* firms with large capital expenditures (n = 103)	52	n/a	n/a
Gitman and Mercurio	1982	*Fortune* 1000 firms (n = 177)	n/a	n/a	66
Gitman and Maxwell	1987	*Forbes* 1000 firms with high growth (n = 109)	40	n/a	n/a
Mukherjee and Hingorani	1999	*Fortune* 500 firms (n = 102)	n/a	64	n/a
Gitman and Vandenberg	2000	*Fortune* 1000 firms (n = 111)	n/a	n/a	40

[a]Respondents indicated to the nearest 10 percent the percentage of time their firm has more acceptable projects than available funds. The percentage in the table is the weighted average.

wording and the use of different populations and samples. Also, the state of the economy at the time of a survey may affect the use of capital rationing stemming from such causes as the availability of external financing.

Several survey studies ask managers why their firms use capital rationing. Table 3.14 summarizes the results of five such studies published between 1973 and 2000. In all studies appearing in the table, the primary reason offered for capital rationing is a limit placed on debt financing by the management of the unit. An alternative answer is a limit on debt financing imposed by management at a higher level than the unit. The data suggest a decline in the importance of debt limitations imposed by outside agreement and a corresponding increase in the importance of maintaining target earnings per share or ratio of price to earnings. Gitman and Vandenberg (2000, p. 66) suggest the increased importance of earnings per share (EPS) and the price-earnings ratio (P/E) on capital rationing reflects "the greater market focus that occurred during this period."

Mukherjee and Hingorani (1999) report that 82 percent of firms that employ capital rationing say they make that decision internally, not externally; that is, external lenders do not impose capital rationing on the firms. The survey then asks participants to indicate their level of agreement with five different statements designed to identify the reasons for internal capital rationing. The five-point scale employed ranges from –2 = strongly disagree to +2 = strongly agree and 0 = no opinion. The statement generating the highest level of agreement, with a score of 0.88, is "capital rationing is more severe when senior managers cannot trust project forecasts and when the project's downside risk is large." This supports the risk-aversion theory of capital rationing. The statement generating the second-highest level of agreement, with a score of 0.78, is "firms impose capital rationing and avoid low-NPV projects in order to preserve borrowing capacity to finance potentially high-NPV projects in the near future." This statement supports the reserve-borrowing capacity theory. The statement generating the third-highest level of agreement, with a score of 0.66, is "capital rationing is used to discourage biased cash flow forecasts." This statement supports the theory about controlling estimation bias. Respondents reject the statement that "capital rationing is more severe when managers have job mobility than when managers are bound to firms," which received a score of –0.48. This refutes the theory that capital rationing is related to job mobility.

Mukherjee and Hingorani report six key findings based on these results and other responses gathered in their comprehensive study of capital rationing. Their first finding states that the primary reason for capital rationing is a reluctance to issue external financing. Second, respondents tend to agree with the notion that firms impose capital rationing to avoid accepting projects with high downside risk and to discourage optimistic forecast bias from middle managers. Third, the ceiling on funds available to adopt capital projects is far from rigid in that firms lower the ceiling to avoid adopting low-NPV projects or raising external funds and raise the ceiling to permit adopting high-NPV projects. Fourth, to make a

TABLE 3.14 Reasons for capital rationing cited by U.S. firms

This table shows the percentage of U.S. firms that give various reasons for using capital rationing. This table suggests that debt limits imposed by internal management remain the leading reason for the use of capital rationing. While some other reasons vary over time, maintaining a target EPS or P/E ratio shows some consistency.

Author(s)	Year published	Population/Sample	Percentage of firms indicating each reason							
			Debt limit imposed by outside agreement	Debt limit imposed by external management[a]	Debt limit imposed by internal management[b]	Restriction-related to dividend payments	Maintain a target EPS or P/E[c]	Limit on stock issuance	Inadequate CFO[d] to finance investments	Other
Fremgen[e]	1973	Firms in select industries/Dun & Bradstreet (n = 177)	41	36	67	29	21	15	3	8
Gitman and Forrester	1977	Forbes firms with large capital expenditures (n = 103)	11	3	69	2	15	n/a	n/a	n/a
Gitman and Mercurio[e]	1982	Fortune 1000 firms (n = 177)	17	4	61	2	11	n/a	n/a	11
Gitman and Maxwell	1987	Forbes 1000 firms with high growth (n = 109)	6	7	46	21	21	n/a	n/a	n/a
Mukherjee and Hingorani	1999	Fortune 500 firms (n = 65)	Results discussed in text.							
Gitman and Vandenberg[e]	2000	Fortune 1000 firms (n = 111)	9	4	59	1	23	n/a	n/a	19

[a] External management refers to a higher authority outside the reporting organization, such as corporate management when the reporting firm is a division or subsidiary.
[b] Internal management refers to the management of the firm, or the management of the division or subsidiary when the reporting firm is a division or subsidiary.
[c] This may imply reluctance to issue additional shares of common stock.
[d] CFO refers to cash flow from operations.
[e] Multiple responses are permitted.

decision under capital rationing, most firms rank projects according to IRR or PI and select the combination that maximizes NPV. Fifth, most firms disagree with the statement that capital rationing should not exist in an efficient capital market. Finally, of the firms facing capital rationing, 83 percent disagree with the notion that capital rationing is inconsistent with maximizing firm value.

Non-U.S. Firms

Table 3.15 summarizes the findings of several surveys of non-U.S. firms related to capital rationing. Scapens and Sale (1981) send questionnaires to 744 *Times* 1000 firms (excluding subsidiaries of overseas firms) and all *Fortune* 500 firms. They report only on the responses of divisionalized firms in each country, which total 211 in the United Kingdom and 205 in the United States. In response to a question about why these firms place capital expenditure ceilings on projects, the most common reason is that investment decisions are important for the whole group and require central control (indicated by 93 percent of both U.S.

TABLE 3.15 Use of capital rationing by non-U.S. firms

This table shows the responses of non-U.S. firms to questions about the use of capital rationing. Few studies provide definitive data on this topic. Arnold and Hatzopoulos (2000) suggest that about half of surveyed U.K. firms use capital rationing. While Kester et al. (1999) divide Asian countries into those in which less than half the firms use capital rationing and those in which more than half of the firms use capital rationing, they do not reveal how far above or below 50 percent each country actually is. The chapter narrative discusses the results of several studies.

Author(s)	Year published	Population/Sample	Percentage of firms
Scapens and Sale	1981	Divisionalized firms in the *Times* 1000 (United Kingdom; n = 300)	Results discussed in text.
		Divisionalized firms in the *Fortune* 500 (United States; n = 205)	Results discussed in text.
Pike	1983b	Largest U.K. industrial companies (n = 126)	Results discussed in text.
Kester, Chang, Echanis, Haikal, Isa, Skully, Tsui, and Wang[a]	1999	Firms on various Asian stock exchanges (n = 226)	
		Australia, Hong Kong, Malaysia, and Singapore	< 50
		Indonesia and the Philippines	> 50
Arnold and Hatzopoulos[b]	2000	300 U.K. firms taken from the *Times* 1000 (n = 96)	49

[a]Authors do not report percentages, only "less than half" and "more than half."
[b]This is the composite of large, medium-size, and small firms.

and U.K. managers). The second-most common reason, reported by 32 percent of U.S. firms and 36 percent of U.K. firms, is that management wants to control the areas of activity and mix of products. The third-most popular reason is that management wants to control cash when funds are low (15 percent for U.S. firms and 21 percent for U.K. firms).

Another early survey study of capital rationing by Pike (1983b) asks U.K. firms to indicate the importance of certain constraints on their firm's investment program (the results do not appear in Table 3.15). The constraint ranked as being most important is the lack of profitable investment opportunities (19.8 percent), followed by an unwillingness to increase the level of borrowing (19.0 percent). The remaining three constraints, in declining order, are general economic uncertainty (18.7 percent), lack of available capital (8.7 percent), and lack of trained managers capable of implementing investment opportunities (7.4 percent).

Kester et al. (1999) report that less than half of surveyed firms in Australia, Hong Kong, Malaysia, and Singapore use capital rationing, while more than half of surveyed firms in Indonesia and the Philippines use capital rationing. Arnold and Hatzopoulos (2000) find that 39 percent of surveyed U.K. firms use capital rationing. None of these results differ markedly from the responses given by U.S. firms to similar questions.

Summary of Capital Rationing

Several survey studies ask about the employment of capital rationing, which finance theory suggests should not be used. Early studies of U.S. firms by Robichek and McDonald (1966); Fremgen (1973); Petty, Scott, and Bird (1975); and Gitman and Forrester (1977) find that more than half of respondents employ capital rationing. More recent studies by Gitman and Maxwell (1987) and Gitman and Vandenberg (2000) indicate a decline in the use of capital rationing. When researchers ask U.S. firms why they employ capital rationing, the most popular response is that internal management imposes a debt limit that restricts capital expenditures.

Studies of capital rationing activities of non-U.S. firms find little difference from the activities of U.S. firms. Kester et al. (1999) report that less than half of surveyed firms in Australia, Hong Kong, Malaysia, and Singapore use capital rationing, while more than half of surveyed firms in Indonesia and the Philippines use capital rationing. Meanwhile, Arnold and Hatzopoulos (2000) find that 39 percent of surveyed U.K. firms use capital rationing.

Hurdle Rates

Hurdle rates are minimum rates of return firms require on projects in order to adopt the projects. The next section discusses how finance theory suggests firms determine hurdle rates.

Theory: Hurdle Rates Used in Capital Budgeting

Using DCF methods to evaluate capital budgeting projects requires the use of a required rate of return or hurdle rate. For example, after calculating a project's IRR, it must be compared to the return required on the project to make a decision to accept or reject the project. Similarly, an analyst needs a required rate of return to use as a discount rate to calculate the NPV of a project. Finance theory suggests that if a project will not alter the risk of the firm, the firm needs to earn a minimum return equal to the financing costs associated with investing in capital projects. Assuming a firm will use both debt and equity in proportions that reflect the firm's target capital structure, the firm will need to earn its WACC in order for the project to add value to the firm. A firm's WACC is the sum of the weight of each component of capital in the target capital structure multiplied by the after-tax cost of each component. The after-tax cost of each component is the cost of raising those funds in the next period.

Finance theory states that the hurdle rate should not be the actual cost of financing the project. Because the cost of equity is higher than the cost of debt, projects that are to be financed with equity would need to promise a higher return than projects that are to be financed with debt. As a result, using the cost of the source of financing as the hurdle rate would add an element of randomness to capital budgeting analysis. Also, using less expensive debt financing for one project may force the firm to use more expensive equity to evaluate a future project. However, using the firm's WACC as a discount rate to evaluate all projects that do not affect firm risk spreads the high cost of equity over all projects adopted, which should result in more rational capital budget decisions.

Adopting high-risk projects can increase a firm's risk. If so, the firm's WACC should also rise, as providers of financing demand higher returns for the higher risk they are taking. Therefore, finance literature suggests using a risk-adjusted discount rate or hurdle when evaluating projects that alter the risk of the firm (e.g., Brigham and Ehrhardt 2008; Ross, Westerfield, and Jaffe 2008). Firms have many tools available with which to measure risk. Once measured, analysts can adjust either the project cash flows using the certainty-equivalent method or the hurdle rate to reflect different levels of risk.

Practice: Hurdle Rates Used in Capital Budgeting

This section presents a synopsis of survey studies indicating how firms determine hurdle rates in practice. This section groups studies based on their focus: U.S. firms, non-U.S. firms, and multinational firms.

U.S. Firms

In an early survey study of U.S. industrial firms, Pflomn (1963) concludes that the most common "yardsticks" for judging capital expenditures include a maximum payback period, the current average company return on investment, the average return on investment for the industry, and the current cost of borrowing. He finds that firms less commonly employ their cost of capital adjusted upward as a profit goal. According to Pflomn (p. 41), executives using "the cost of capital concept warn that it should not be confused with a profit goal, or minimum acceptable rate of return. It must be adjusted upward to compensate for the fact that not all capital projects are cost saving or profit producing and that some will fail." He also notes that some firms make additional adjustments to recognize differences in project risk.

Christy (1966) finds that only 13 percent of surveyed firms agree with the notion that investing in all projects promising a return greater than the firm's cost of capital is sensible. He attributes this to managers believing that firms need to be compensated for the risk of capital projects. While Christy attributes the return premium to project risk, one interpretation of his discussion of the "optimistic" nature of managers is that they require a higher return on projects in an effort to overcome forecasting bias.

Brigham (1975) surveys the managers of 33 "quite large" U.S. firms. The sample is not random, as the respondents all participated in one or more university programs focusing on capital budgeting issues. Brigham finds that 48 percent of firms using hurdle rates use the same rate for all projects, while 7 percent vary hurdle rates according to project risk (see Table 3.16). Another 11 percent of responding firms vary hurdle rates based on the type of project (e.g., replacement, expansion, etc.), and 34 percent use different rates for different organizational units (subsidiaries, divisions, product lines, domestic versus overseas). His results also show that 61 percent of the responding firms use a form of WACC as a hurdle rate.

The study by Petty, Scott, and Bird (1975) finds that 40 percent of respondents indicate the minimum return on projects is a "management determined target rate of return." The second-most frequent response is WACC (30 percent), followed by the cost of the specific source of funds (17 percent) and the firm's historical rate of return (11 percent). The fact that 40 percent of respondents indicate that the rate is determined by management ignores the fact that management may employ the WACC or other return in making that determination.

Two studies published 21 years apart ask survey participants to indicate what discount rate their firms use to evaluate projects. In both cases, respondents could indicate more than one discount rate. Schall, Sundem, and Geijsbeek(1978) find the most commonly used cutoff rate is the WACC (46 percent), followed by a measure based on past experience (20 percent), the cost of debt (17 percent), and a rate based on expected dividend payout and growth rate (17 percent). The more recent study by Payne, Heath, and Gale (1999) shows even greater use of the WACC (64 percent), the cost of debt (38 percent), the cost of equity (29 percent), and the risk-free rate plus a risk premium (23 percent).

Gitman and Mercurio (1982) learn that 17 percent of survey respondents use the cost of the specific source of project financing as a hurdle rate, which they

TABLE 3.16 Hurdle rates used to evaluate capital budgeting projects: U.S. firms

This table shows the percentage of U.S. firms that report using various hurdle rates to evaluate capital budgeting projects. The results suggest that using the weighted average cost of capital (WACC) has remained the most popular hurdle rate between 1975 and 2003.

Author(s)	Year published	Population/Sample	Percentage of Firms Using Each Cutoff Rate								
			Cost of debt	Cost of equity	WACC	Cost of financing project	Measure based on past experience	Premium over risk-free rate	Expected growth and dividend payout	Desired firm growth rate	Other
Pflomn	1963	U.S. manufacturing firms (n = 346)	Results discussed in text.								
Christy	1966	Large publicly traded firms in select industries listed in Standard & Poor's Stock Guide (n = 108)	Results discussed in text.								
Brigham	1975	Select executives who completed a particular university program (large firms/not randomly selected; n = 33)	n/a	n/a	61	n/a	10	n/a	n/a	n/a	29
Petty, Scott, and Bird	1975	Fortune 500 firms (n = 109)	n/a	n/a	30	17	n/a	n/a	n/a	n/a	40[a]
Schall, Sundem, and Geijsbeek[b]	1978	Compustat firms with either large net plant assets or large capital expenditures, or moderate size of both (n = 189)	17	9	46	n/a	20	8	17	n/a	16

(Continued)

TABLE 3.16 (cont'd) Hurdle rates used to evaluate capital budgeting projects: U.S. firms

Author(s)	Year published	Population/Sample	Percentage of Firms Using Each Cutoff Rate								
			Cost of debt	Cost of equity	WACC	Cost of financing project	Measure based on past experience	Premium over risk-free rate	Expected growth and dividend payout	Desired firm growth rate	Other
Gitman and Mercurio	1982	Fortune 1000 firms (n = 177)	n/a	n/a	83	17	n/a	n/a	n/a	n/a	n/a
Bierman	1993	Largest 100 Fortune 500 industrial firms (n = 74)	n/a	n/a	93	n/a	n/a	n/a	n/a	n/a	n/a
Payne, Heath, and Gale[c]	1999	U.S. firms listed in Compustat (n = 90)	38	29	64	13[d]	20	23	n/a	n/a	7
Gitman and Vandenberg	2000	Fortune 1000 firms (n = 111)	n/a	n/a	92	8	n/a	n/a	n/a	n/a	n/a
Block	2003	Fortune 1000 firms (n = 298)	n/a	6	85	n/a	n/a	n/a	n/a	5	3

[a] Responses are to "management determined."
[b] Participants are to indicate all methods used.
[c] Responses are only from the U.S. firms participating in the study.
[d] Actual wording is "depends upon project financing."

note is counter to finance theory. A later study by Gitman and Vandenberg (2000), using a similar sample and identical questions, finds the percentage of respondents using the cost of the source of project financing as a hurdle rate declined to 8 percent from 17 percent. They also note that the percentage of firms using WACC as a hurdle rate increased from the time of the Brigham (1975) study to both the time of the Gitman and Mercurio (1982) and Gitman and Vandenberg (2000) studies. These findings suggest that the practices of U.S. firms regarding the use of discount rates are becoming more consistent with finance theory.

Poterba and Summers (1995) use a questionnaire to survey CEOs of *Fortune* 1000 companies about hurdle rates. Based on 228 usable responses, they find that most firms use more than a single hurdle rate. They also learn that some managers distinguish between the cost of capital and hurdle rates as a way to adjust for biased estimates of projects' profitability.

Bruner et al. (1998) conduct a telephone survey of 27 prestigious CFOs and 10 leading financial advisors. They find that WACC is the dominant discount rate and that firms tend to use market value weights instead of book value weights. Additionally, they discover that the capital asset pricing model is the dominant equity model and that firms base the after-tax debt cost on marginal tax rates, not average rates.

Finally, Block (2003) discovers that 85 percent of firms surveyed use the WACC as a hurdle rate, while less than 50 percent of firms use a divisional cost of capital. Another 6 percent of respondents use the cost of equity capital as a hurdle rate, 5 percent use the desired growth rate of the firm, and 3 percent use other methods such as a desired return on stockholders' equity and the industry average return.

Non-U.S. Firms

Table 3.17 presents the results of several survey studies of non-U.S. firms that collect information about the use of hurdle rates. Of the six Asia-Pacific countries studied by Kester et al. (1999), Australian firms appear to operate closest to the manner suggested by finance theory when selecting hurdle rates; that is, only 14 percent of responding Australian firms report using the cost of the source of financing the project as a project's hurdle rate. The remaining respondents indicate that they use either the WACC (48 percent) or a risk-adjusted discount rate for projects (38 percent). Respondents from Hong Kong appear to operate furthest from the view suggested by finance theory. About 57 percent of responding Hong Kong firms report using the cost of financing a project as the project's hurdle rate, 24 percent use the firm's WACC, and 19 percent use a risk-adjusted discount rate. The survey results of firms from other countries participating in the Kester et al. study tend to fall between these two extremes.

The study by Payne, Heath, and Gale (1999) reports the use of hurdle rates by both U.S. and Canadian firms. Table 3.17 contains the findings for Canadian

TABLE 3.17 Hurdle rates used to evaluate capital budgeting projects: Non-U.S firms

This table shows the percentage of non-U.S. firms that report using various hurdle rates to evaluate capital budgeting projects. This table suggests that, while Canadian and U.K. firms primarily use the WACC (like U.S. firms - see Table 3.16), most Asian firms report primarily using the cost of financing each project as the hurdle rate.

Author(s)	Year published	Population/Sample	Percentage of firms using each cutoff rate						
			Cost of debt	Cost of equity	WACC	Cost of financing project	Risk-adjusted discount rate	Previous experience	Other
Kester, Chang, Echanis, Haikal, Isa, Skully, Tsui, and Wang	1999	Firms listed on several Asian stock exchanges							
		Australia (n = 57)	n/a	n/a	48	14	38	n/a	n/a
		Hong Kong (n = 29)	n/a	n/a	24	57	19	n/a	n/a
		Indonesia (n = 16)	n/a	n/a	29	43	29	n/a	n/a
		Malaysia (n = 35)	n/a	n/a	29	47	24	n/a	n/a
		The Philippines (n = 35)	n/a	n/a	16	32	52	n/a	n/a
		Singapore (n = 54)	n/a	n/a	11	51	38	n/a	n/a
Payne, Heath, and Gale[a]	1999	Canadian firms listed in Compustat (n = 65)	34	29	46	17[b]	n/a	35	26
Arnold and Hatzopoulos[c]	2000	300 UK firms taken from the Times 1000 (n = 96)	11	8	54	n/a	n/a	n/a	18
Baker, Dutta, and Saadi	2009	762 Canadian firms on the Toronto Stock Exchange with select information available from Stock Guide database (n = 214)	n/a	n/a	64	38	37	44	25

[a]Respondents are asked to check all that apply.
[b]Actual response is "depends on project financing."
[c]Responses are a composite of small, medium-size, and large firms.

firms, and Table 3.16 presents the findings for U.S. firms. Although 34 percent of the Canadian firms report using the cost of debt and 29 percent report using the cost of equity, an even larger proportion of firms report using the WACC (46 percent). Although the figures reported by Payne, Heath, and Gale for both U.S. and Canadian firms are similar regarding the use of the cost of debt and cost of equity as a hurdle rate, the percentage of U.S. firms using the WACC is considerably higher (64 percent versus 46 percent). Another important difference between the responses of Canadian firms and U.S. firms shown in this study is the difference in the use of cutoff rates based on previous experience (35 percent and 20 percent, respectively).

Table 3.17 also contains the results of the Arnold and Hatzopoulos (2000) survey of small, medium-size, and large firms in the United Kingdom. More than half of responding firms (54 percent) report using the WACC as a hurdle rate, but relatively few respondents report using the cost of debt (11 percent) or the cost of equity (8 percent). The authors do not offer alternative responses such as the cost of financing the project or a risk-adjusted discount rate, but they note that U.K. firms have moved in the direction of using more theoretically correct required rates of return.

Baker, Dutta, and Saadi (2009) learn that 64 percent of responding Canadian firms report using WACC either often or always to evaluate capital budgeting projects, and larger firms are more likely to do so. This is a greater percentage than found in other non-U.S. firms but lower than the percentage of U.S. firms that report using WACC in studies by Bierman (1993) and Gitman and Vandenberg (2000). Baker, Dutta, and Saadi report that other hurdle rates used by Canadian firms often or always reflect management's experience (44 percent) and the cost of the specific funds used to finance the project (38 percent).

Multinational Firms

Table 3.18 presents the results of two surveys that focus on multinational firms. The first study conducted by Oblak and Helm (1980) reports the responses of U.S. multinational firms regarding the use of different hurdle rates. The majority of firms (54 percent) indicate using the WACC, with the cost of equity next most common (25 percent), followed by the cost of debt (13 percent). The study conducted by Kim, Crick, and Farragher (1984) surveys both U.S. and non-U.S. multinational firms. Although the responses of the U.S. multinational firms are highly similar to those reported by Oblak and Helm, the responses of the non-U.S. multinational firms differ in several respects. Most notable is the lower percentage of non-U.S. multinational firms using the WACC as a hurdle rate (41 percent) and the higher percentage using hurdle rates based on previous experience (17 percent). The less frequent use of WACC as a hurdle rate by non-U.S. multinational firms is consistent with the earlier findings that a higher percentage of U.S. firms generally use WACC as a hurdle rate.

TABLE 3.18 Hurdle rates used to evaluate capital budgeting projects: Multinational corporations

This table shows the percentage of MNCs that report using various hurdle rates to evaluate capital budgeting projects. The table suggests that MNCs uses the firm's WACC more than any other hurdle rate. This is true for both U.S.-MNCs and non-U.S. MNCs. The results of the study by Kim, Crick, and Farragher (1984) suggest the primary difference between the hurdle rates used by U.S. and non-U.S. MNCs is that more non-U.S. firms use measures based on past experience than U.S. MNCs.

Author(s)	Year published	Population/Sample	Percentage of firms using each cutoff rate				
			Cost of debt	Cost of equity	WACC	Measure based on past experience	Other
Oblak and Helm[a]	1980	*Fortune* 500 U.S. multinational firms ($n = 59$)	13	25	54	5	3
Kim, Crick, and Farragher[a]	1984	*Fortune* 500 U.S. firms ($n = 186$)	19	22	48	3	8
		Fortune 500 non-U.S. firms ($n = 127$)	15	17	41	17	10

[a]Respondents could indicate more than one method.

Summary of Hurdle Rates Used in Capital Budgeting

Finance theory suggests the hurdle rates for capital projects should be the firm's WACC if the project will not affect the firm's risk and a risk-adjusted discount rate if the project will affect firm risk. An early survey study by Pflomn (1963) finds that the hurdle rates used by participating firms deviate from theory in that the most common hurdle rates are the current average company return on investment, the average return on investment for the industry, and the current cost of borrowing. Most survey studies ranging from the early study by Brigham (1975) to the more recent study by Block (2003) find that a majority of firms indicate WACC is the most common hurdle rate employed. This suggests that U.S. firms participating in survey studies continue to select hurdle rates in a manner consistent with finance theory.

For non-U.S. firms, the results are mixed. Kester et al. (1999) find that the majority of Australian firms surveyed report using the WACC, but a majority or plurality of firms in Hong Kong, Indonesia, Malaysia, the Philippines, and Singapore use the cost of financing the project under consideration. Studies of Canadian firms conducted by Payne, Heath, and Gale (1999) and Baker, Dutta, and Saadi (2009) indicate that a majority of firms report using the WACC, which is also true of U.K. firms as reported by Arnold and Hatzopoulos (2000). Baker, Dutta, and Saadi (2009) also find that larger firms are more likely to employ WACC as a discount rate than smaller firms. Surveys focusing on the activities of multinational firms also find that either a majority or a plurality of responding firms employ WACC as a cutoff rate (Oblak and Helm 1980; Kim, Crick, and Farragher 1984).

Postaudits

If a firm's forecast of input variables used in capital budgeting are inaccurate, conducting postaudits can identify the sources of the forecasting errors. Managers and analysts can use this information to improve forecasts and the implementation of future capital budgeting projects.

Theory: Postaudits in Capital Budgeting

Potential challenges associated with evaluating, adopting, and implementing capital budgeting projects include unintentional errors in forecasting project cash flows, possible intentional bias in forecasting cash flows (units and unit managers may need to compete for investment funds), and ineffective and/or inefficient implementation of adopted projects. One tool to help reduce problems emanating from these and other challenges is to postaudit adopted projects. Gordon and Myers (1991) and Smith (1994) classify the possible benefits of the postaudit into four categories.

1. *Managerial learning:* By following the project from its initial proposal until project termination, managers can learn which activities lead to successful versus unsuccessful projects.
2. *Reduced forecast bias:* When forecasted project cash flows differ substantially from actual cash flows, the firm needs to learn why. Perhaps the forecasts contained biases that managers can avoid in the future. Also, when managers know that projects are subject to a postaudit, they are less likely to knowingly inflate cash flow forecasts.
3. *Reduced risk management:* Some managers may have a bias against adopting risky projects because an unsuccessful project can result in the loss of their jobs. Postauditing potential investments may reveal a tendency for managers to avoid risky yet beneficial projects.
4. *Identification of abandonment timing:* Managers can become committed to projects they recommended. As a result, they may experience a bias against abandoning a project. They may also feel that their reputation is in jeopardy if the firm abandons a project before the scheduled termination date. Having independent parties conduct the audit is likely to mitigate an emotional bias.

Some firms have informal postaudit procedures that they implement on an ad hoc basis. However, the finance literature suggests establishing a formal capital budgeting system that involves comparing actual cash flows to forecasted cash flows, performing postaudits regularly, and making abandonment decisions based on the present value of expected cash flows of the abandonment value (Gordon and Pinches 1984; Gordon and Myers 1991; Myers, Gordon, and Hamer 1991).

Practice: Postaudits in Capital Budgeting

The following is a synopsis of survey research regarding capital budgeting postaudits. The discussion is divided into two sections: surveys of U.S. firms and surveys of non-U.S. firms.

U.S. Firms

Table 3.19 presents the results of several survey studies that ask firms if they conduct a postaudit of capital budgeting projects. In an early study, Pflomn (1963) notes that most firms have some type of postcompletion audits to determine if they realized forecasted benefits. He indicates that some of these efforts are "spasmodic" with inconclusive results, but other firms use thorough postaudits for important projects. Surprisingly, early studies show as much as or greater application of postauditing procedures than in more recent studies. Klammer (1972) and Scapens and Sale (1981) find that 88 percent and 84 percent of survey participants, respectively, employ some sort of postaudit procedure. Gitman and Mercurio (1982) ask about the use of "formal" follow-up procedures and learn that 56 percent of firms do so, while another 32 percent use informal follow-up procedures. The total percentage of firms using formal or informal follow-up procedures is 88 percent, consistent with the earlier studies.

Pohlman, Santiago, and Markel (1988) send a questionnaire to the CFOs of 498 *Fortune* 500 firms and receive usable responses from 232 firms. The authors focus their questions about postauditing on cash flow estimates made by large firms. Their evidence shows that about 75 percent of participating firms compare their actual cash flows with forecasted cash flows. Of those who make such comparisons, all make comparisons of operating cash flows, 95 percent make comparisons of initial investment outlays, and 68 percent make comparisons of salvage values.

Gordon and Myers (1991) send surveys to 690 large U.S. industrial firms (excluding utilities and transportation firms) and receive 282 responses, representing a 40.9 percent response rate. They find that 76 percent of the respondents to their survey indicate their firms conduct postaudits of capital projects, but a much smaller proportion of firms use what the authors consider to be "adequate" postaudit procedures. They define adequate postaudit procedures to include (1) an ongoing feedback process, (2) use of risk-adjusted DCF analysis to assess potential abandonment, and (3) documentation of procedures and policies. Gordon and Myers report that only 25 percent of the respondents conduct postaudits using adequate procedures. Using data from the same survey supplemented with data from the Financial Accounting Standards Board Data Bank, Myers, Gordon, and Hamer (1991) examine whether adopting sophisticated postaudit procedures is associated with improved firm performance. Based on a matched-pair experimental design, their empirical evidence provides support for this argument.

Klammer, Koch, and Wilner (1991) discover that 86 percent of respondents postaudit major projects, while Cooper, Cornick, and Redmon (1992, p. 22) discover that 80 percent of respondents have a "review mechanism which could be used to change future evaluation procedures." The latter study is based on 102 responses to a survey of *Fortune* 500 firms.

Smith (1994) identifies 72 *Fortune* 500 firms that did not make CEO changes in the past five years and that do not compensate their CEO on a substantially fixed or substantially variable basis. She then interviews 67 of those firms about their postaudit process. The other five firms declined to be interviewed. Smith learns that 76 percent of survey participants perform investment postauditing at some level, while the remaining 24 percent have no formal procedures. She further notes that these results are consistent with those of Gordon and Myers (1991). Smith (p. 136) concludes that her findings show that "in this sample of

TABLE 3.19 Use of postaudits of capital budgeting projects by U.S. firms

This table shows the percentage of U.S. firms that report conducting post audits of their capital budgeting projects. Because the question wording among surveys differs, the table includes the approximate wording. Comparing the findings of the Gitman and Mercurio (1982) to those of the Gitman and Vandenberg (2000), which uses similar questions and samples, suggests a decline in the use of formal post audits.

Author(s)	Year published	Population/Sample	Approximate question wording	Percentage of firms
Pflomn	1963	U.S. manufacturing firms (n = 346)	Results discussed in text.	n/a
Klammer	1972	Select large manufacturing firms/Compustat (n = 184)	Postaudit major projects?	88
Scapens and Sale[a]	1981	Divisional firms in the Fortune 500 (n = 227)	Postaudit projects?	84
Gitman and Mercurio	1982	Fortune 1000 firms (n = 177)	Formal follow-up procedure?	56
			Informal or ad hoc follow-up?	32
Pohlman, Santiago, and Markel	1988	Fortune 500 firms (n = 232)	Results discussed in text.	n/a
Gordon and Myers; Myers, Gordon, and Hamer	1991	690 large U.S. industrial firms, excluding utilities and transportation (n = 282)	Conduct postaudits (all types)?	76
			Use "adequate" postaudit procedures?[b]	25
Klammer, Koch and Wilner	1991	Select large industrial firms from Compustat (n = 100)	Postaudit major projects?	86
Cooper, Cornick, and Redmon	1992	Fortune 500 firms (n = 102)	Review adopted projects?	80
Smith	1994	Select Fortune 500 firms (n = 67)	Postaudit at some level?	76
Gitman and Vandenberg	2000	Fortune 1000 firms (n = 111)	Formal follow-up procedure?	47
			Informal follow-up procedure?	33

[a]Responses of U.S. firms participating in a study of both U.S. and U.K. firms.
[b]The authors define "adequate postaudit procedures" as including ongoing feedback, use of discounted cash flow project evaluation methods, and documentation of postaudit policies and procedures.

large industrial firms, most do not use sophisticated capital investment post auditing," and the few firms that do so generate on average "substantially higher long-run excess returns."

Gitman and Vandenberg (2000) replicate the earlier study by Gitman and Mercurio (1982) and find that fewer firms in the later study have formal postaudit procedures than in the earlier study (47 percent versus 56 percent, respectively). Gitman and Vandenberg (p. 66) suggest that the "decline could possibly be the result of the firm's use of better decision methods up front." About the same proportion of firms employ informal or ad hoc postaudit procedures in the 2000 study as in the 1982 study (33 percent).

Non-U.S. Firms

Table 3.20 presents the results of several surveys of non-U.S. firms that provide insights into postauditing. Scapens and Sale (1981) survey divisionalized U.K. firms and report that only 36 percent of respondents postaudit capital budgeting projects. As Table 3.19 shows, this compares to 84 percent of divisionalized U.S. firms participating in the same study. Scapens and Sale conclude that "the widespread use of post-completion audits in the US indicates that they have general applicability and could be more widely adopted in the UK" (p. 411).

Pike (1983a) finds that 48 percent of surveyed U.K. firms postaudit major capital projects. In a later study using a similar sample, Pike (1996) reports that the employment of postaudit procedures had increased to 72 percent of surveyed firms. Arnold and Hatzopoulos (2000) also ask survey participants if they postaudit major capital expenditures. About 87 percent of the respondents indicate that they always do (28 percent) or sometimes do (59 percent). These figures are the composite responses for large, medium-size, and small firms participating in the survey.

Summary of Postaudits in Capital Budgeting

Academics teach that there are many advantages associated with postauditing capital budgeting projects. Most surveys of U.S. firms find that the majority of respondents report using postaudits. This includes early studies by Klammer (1972) and Scapens and Sale (1981) and later studies by Smith (1994) and Gitman and Vandenberg (2000). Some studies look more deeply into the subject by asking if the postaudits are formal or informal or if they qualify as adequate according to certain stated criteria. For example, Gordon and Myers (1991) find that 76 percent of respondents conduct postaudits but just 25 percent of respondents conduct adequate postaudits meeting certain stated criteria. Gitman and Vandenberg (2000) find that survey respondents decreased the use of formal postaudits since Gitman and Mercurio (1982) conducted their survey. Gitman and Vandenberg suggest the decrease in the use of formal postaudits may reflect better decision methods used at the time the decisions are first made.

TABLE 3.20 Use of postaudits of capital budgeting projects by non-U.S. firms

This table shows the percentage of non-U.S. firms that report using post audits of their capital budgeting projects. All four studies in the table report the responses of U.K. firms. There appears to be a trend towards greater use of post audits in the United Kingdom compared to a possible decrease in the use of post audits in the U.S. (see Table 3.19).

Author(s)	Year published	Population/Sample	Approximate question wording	Percentage of firms
Scapens and Sale[a]	1981	Divisional firms in the *Times* 1000 (United Kingdom; *n*=300)	Postaudit projects?	36
Pike	1983a	Large U.K. manufacturing and retail firms (*n* = 150)	Postaudit major projects?	48
Pike	1996	140 U.K. respondents to the Pike 1983a study (*n* = 100)	Postaudit major projects?	72
Arnold and Hatzopoulos	2000	300 U.K. firms taken from the *Times* 1000 (*n* = 96)	Always or sometimes audit major expenditures?	87[b]

[a]Results of U.K. firms participating in a study of both U.S. and U.K. firms.
[b]Represents the composite of small, medium-size, and large firms. More small firms indicate they always audit major expenditures than medium-size or large firms.

Early studies of U.K. firms by Scapens and Sale (1981) and Pike (1983a) reveal that less than half of survey respondents conduct postaudits. Later studies of U.K. firms by Pike (1996) and Arnold and Hatzopoulos (2000) suggest a trend toward greater use of postaudits, as the percentage of firms indicating they postaudit projects increases to 72 percent and 87 percent, respectively.

Other Capital Budgeting Topics

Some survey research in capital budgeting has received less attention than the topics discussed thus far. The following section provides a brief synopsis of studies addressing some of these tangential topics.

Cash Flow Forecasting and Forecasting Accuracy

Finance theory indicates that capital budgeting projects should be evaluated based on the incremental cash flow generated by the projects (e.g., Brigham and Ehrhardt 2008; Ross, Westerfield, and Jaffe 2008). Some use the term free cash flow (FCF) to specify the cash flow available for distribution to the firm's creditors and stockholders. While there are several different ways to describe the calculation of FCF, one common formula is as follows:

$$FCF = IO + CFO + NOWC + SV, \qquad (1)$$

where IO = initial outlay for the project,
  CFO = cash flow from operations generated by the project,
  NOWC = net operating working capital, and
  SV = salvage value.

While a common belief is that most firms fully recognize the cash flows associated with the initial outlay and salvage value, there is some concern that practitioners measure periodic benefits in terms of accounting profits rather than FCF. Using accounting profits ignores such factors as the difference between depreciation for accounting purposes and depreciation for tax purposes, the fact that accounting profits deduct interest expense while cash flow does not, and the fact that accounting profit ignores any incremental investment in working capital. Because some firms may use accounting profit or other accounting measures to evaluate capital budgeting projects, several surveys ask managers about the measures they use.

This section also looks at surveys revealing additional information about project forecasting. One line of questioning asks managers how they view the accuracy of forecasts of project cash flows or other measures of project benefit. A related line of questioning seeks to find out if firms have established procedures to ensure consistency of forecasts from project to project.

Recall that Kim, Crick, and Farragher (1984) send questionnaires to U.S. and non-U.S. multinational firms. One question asks survey participants how they measure potential benefits from foreign projects. More than 59 percent of U.S. firms and 63 percent of non-U.S. firms say they measure benefits in terms of cash flow. Kim, Crick, and Farragher conclude that this finding is consistent with finance theory and an improvement over the findings of Stonehill and Nathanson (1968), who report that only 48 percent of surveyed firms measure the benefits from projects in terms of cash flow.

Pruitt and Gitman (1987) send surveys focusing on cash flow forecasting biases to *Fortune* 500 firms and receive 121 usable responses. Following is a paraphrased list of statements about capital budgeting forecast biases from that study and the percentage of respondents indicating general agreement with the statements.

- Revenue forecasts are typically overstated (79 percent).
- Revenue overstatement is intentional (37 percent).
- Revenue overstatement is due to lack of forecasting experience (36 percent).
- Cost forecasts are typically understated (43 percent).
- Cost understatement is intentional (27 percent).
- Cost understatement is due to lack of forecasting experience (35 percent).
- Research and development people typically underestimate R&D costs (55 percent).
- Marketing people typically overestimate sales (87 percent).
- Decision makers consider forecasts to be optimistic and adjust them accordingly (59 percent).
- Postaudits show forecasts to be more optimistic than actual values (76 percent).
- The actual profitability of accepted projects is typically higher than forecasted (7 percent).
- Management has much confidence in the profitability projections of most capital budgeting proposals (50 percent).

The study by Pohlman, Santiago, and Markel (1988) also focuses on cash flow forecasting for capital budgeting analysis. They find that firms with higher risk are more likely to follow systematic approaches to forecasting project cash flows. Further, firms following systematic approaches to cash flow forecasting tend to achieve greater accuracy in those forecasts. The following provides a brief summary of additional key findings (the percentages represent the percentage of respondents).

- Sixty-seven percent have someone in the firm who is responsible for coordinating and supervising cash flow estimation. Capital-intensive firms and highly leveraged firms are more likely to have such a person.

- Eighty-five percent have standard procedures for estimating taxes, depreciation, investment tax credit, and salvage values.
- Sixty-six percent require the use of a standard model for cash flow forecasting.
- Seventy-eight percent have standard forms or worksheets for reporting cash flow and other investment information.
- Fifty-six percent use single-dollar estimates, 8 percent use a range of estimates, and 36 percent use both.

Lazaridis (2006) surveys firms in Greece and Cyprus, asking questions similar to those asked in the Pohlman, Santiago, and Markel (1988) study. Lazaridis sends questionnaires to 800 larger firms from each area of Greece and 120 selected enterprises from the Republic of Cyprus and receives replies from 573 Greek firms and 112 Cypriot firms. While the respondents are among the larger firms in Greece and Cyprus, the average firm size is small when compared with the firms responding to the Pohlman, Santiago, and Markel study. Following is a brief summary of Lazaridis's key findings.

- Seventy-seven percent of Greek firms and 92 percent of Cypriot firms have someone in the firm who is responsible for coordinating and supervising cash flow estimation.
- Thirty-eight percent of Greek firms and 36 percent of Cypriot firms have standard procedures for estimating taxes, depreciation, and salvage values.
- Eight percent of Greek firms and 13 percent of Cypriote firms require the use of a standard model for cash flow forecasting.
- Twenty-four percent of Greek firms and 19 percent of Cypriote firms have standard forms to collect cash flow data and other investment information.

Petry and Sprow (1993) ask survey participants how they estimate the residual value of assets, an important element in forecasting project cash flows. Table 3.21 shows how firms classified into three industry groups determine those values. For real estate assets (land and buildings), the most common estimate by industrial/retail firms is the depreciated value of the assets, which the authors note contrasts with finance theory, as real estate generally tends to appreciate in value over time. For non-real-estate assets, the highest percentages of respondents in all three industry groups indicate the use of the expected market value of the assets, which is consistent with finance theory.

Chadwell-Hatfield et al. (1996/1997) randomly select 393 U.S. manufacturing firms to survey, using Compact Disclosure to identify firms. They receive 118 usable responses. They ask survey participants to indicate the percentage of projects for which they use various income or cash flow measures to evaluate projects. The authors find that the most common measure is operating income and report that 49 percent of respondents indicate they use operating income to evaluate 81 to 100 percent of proposed projects. Only 8 percent of respondents

TABLE 3.21 Residual value of capital investments

This table indicates the percentage of respondents that report using various methods to estimate the residual value of capital investments, divided into real estate and other capital projects. The table suggests that the method used depends upon the type of industry and the type of asset.

	Percentage of firms using each method		
Real estate	Industrial/ Retail	Financial/ Services	Utilities
Same as depreciated value	32	16	14
Cost plus anticipated inflation	9	24	21
Depreciated value plus anticipated inflation	13	8	21
Cost plus past average real estate inflation	10	16	7
Cost plus expected real estate inflation	18	12	21
Miscellaneous	18	24	17
Other capital projects			
Same as depreciated value	25	14	18
Expected market value	28	43	35
Zero	19	29	9
Higher than depreciated value	11	4	27
Lower than depreciated value	7	4	9
Miscellaneous	9	7	3

Source: Petry and Sprow (1993, 368).

do not use operating income at all to evaluate projects. The second-most common measure is cash flow, which 35 percent of respondents say they use to evaluate 81 to 100 percent of projects and just 11 percent say they do not use at all. Cash flow from operations is tied with earnings after taxes as the next most common measure of project benefits, with 32 percent of respondents using both measures to evaluate 81 to 100 percent of projects. Free cash flow is the least popular measure and is used by 24 percent of firms to evaluate 81 to 100 percent of their projects. Chadwell-Hatfield et al. note that their findings suggest that many firms use accounting income projections to evaluate capital budgeting projects despite the fact that finance theory specifies the use of cash flow measures. They also note that their results conflict with those of Schall, Sundem, and Geijsbeek(1978), who report that 62 percent of firms in their sample use cash flow estimates.

Danielson and Scott's (2006) survey of small businesses discovers that 74 percent of responding firms consider tax implications and less than 70 percent of responding firms forecast cash flows when making investment decisions. The authors also discover that many small businesses do not have formal planning systems to aid in capital budgeting decisions.

In summary, most published research appears to find that the majority of surveyed U.S. firms measure project benefits in terms of cash flow (Kim, Crick, and Farragher 1984; Schall, Sundem, and Geijsbeek 1978). Danielson and Scott (2006) also find this to be true of small U.S. firms. However, Chadwell-Hatfield et al. (1996/1997) report that U.S. firms use operating income more frequently than cash flow as a measure of project benefits. In terms of forecasting accuracy, the majority of managers believe their analysts overstate revenue when evaluating projects, but they do not believe that cost forecasts are under- or overstated (Pruitt and Gitman 1987). Pohlman, Santiago, and Markel (1988) discover that firms with higher risk are more likely to follow systematic approaches to forecasting project cash flows, and firms following systematic approaches to cash flow forecasting tend to achieve greater accuracy in their forecasts.

Use of Real Options

Since Myers (1977) first described the concept of real options, this topic has generated much interest among finance academics. The concept recognizes that some capital budgeting projects offer advantages not offered by other projects. These advantages can involve flexibility, growth options, staged investment options, entry and exit options, abandonment options, and the right to defer outlays. If managers can accurately value such options, analysts may discover that a project's true value exceeds its traditionally calculated NPV.

Graham and Harvey (2001) report that just 27 percent of U.S. survey participants say they either always or almost always incorporate the real options of a project when evaluating it. Ryan and Ryan (2002) discover that only 1.6 percent of survey participants in a U.S. study report using real options either always or often as a supplementary capital budgeting tool. In fact, survey participants rank real options last among 13 possible supplementary tools. Similar to Graham and Harvey (2001), Brounen, de Jong, and Koedijk (2004) find that 27 percent of surveyed firms in France, Germany, the Netherlands, and the United Kingdom use real options always or almost always in deciding which projects to pursue. Baker, Dutta, and Saadi (2009) find that just 10 percent of the Canadian firms surveyed use real options often or always when evaluating projects. Not surprisingly, the authors find that larger firms tend to use real options more frequently than smaller firms. However, somewhat surprising is the fact that firms managed by CEOs who have MBA degrees appear less likely to use real options.

Block (2007) surveys top-ranking officers of *Fortune* 1000 companies to see if they use real options to complement traditional analysis. Out of 279 respondents, 40 (14.3 percent) indicate that their firms currently use real options. Of these respondents, the most common users of real options are in technology, energy, utilities, health care, and manufacturing industries. Block finds a significant relationship between industry classification and the use of real options. Triantis and Borison (2001), who interview 39 executives of large companies in seven different industries, also find a tendency among those who use real options to represent certain industries. Block concludes that firms using real options come from industries where sophisticated analysis is the norm. His survey identifies four major reasons for not using real options: (1) top management support is lacking, (2) discounted cash flow is already a proven method, (3) real options require too much sophistication, and (4) real options encourage excessive risk taking.

When Baker, Dutta, and Saadi (2009) ask firms that employ real options why they do so, the three most popular responses are as follows: real options provide a management tool to help form a strategic vision, real options incorporate managerial flexibility into the analysis, and real options provide a way of thinking about uncertainty and its effect on valuation. Baker, Dutta, and Saadi also ask survey participants who use real options which options they value most frequently, and they receive the following responses: growth (85 percent), the right to defer outlays (80 percent), flexibility of output or input mixes (77 percent), abandonment option (69 percent), staged investment (67 percent), and entry and exit (51 percent). Baker, Dutta, and Saadi also ask firms not using real options why they do not use them. By far, the most common response was lack of expertise or knowledge, given by 78 percent of survey participants.

In summary, the results of the studies discussed here suggest that practitioners in the United States, Europe, and Canada have not generally embraced the employment of real options. This could be a result of business schools not doing an adequate job of teaching how to use these tools or because managers find real options difficult to employ or not useful in real-world applications.

Firm Goals and Capital Budgeting

Finance theory generally identifies the primary goal of management as maximizing shareholder wealth or maximizing the value of the firm (e.g., Brigham and Ehrhardt 2008; Ross, Westerfield, and Jaffe 2008). Both descriptions recognize that when shareholders invest in a firm's common stock, they assume risk with the goal of increasing their wealth. The stockholders elect members to the firm's board of directors who, in turn, hire managers to achieve the goals of the stockholders. Success in enhancing the wealth of stockholders is measured by the total return, which reflects a combination of stock price appreciation and the receipt of cash dividends. Because most of the return realized by stockholders comes from stock price appreciation, some firms describe their goal as stock price appreciation. Generally, firms have other stated goals as well, such as creating a healthy work environment for employees, enhancing the welfare of the community, improving the environment, and so forth. Finance theory suggests that these secondary goals cannot supplant the primary goal of shareholder wealth enhancement because of the duty of the firm's board of directors and managers to the firm's owners—the stockholders (e.g., Brigham and Ehrhardt 2008; Ross, Westerfield, and Jaffe 2008). Unless the stockholders provide explicit instructions to the board of directors to focus the primary goal on other constituencies, the board and managers must make decisions that benefit stockholders.

The goals pursued by managers are important to the capital budgeting framework. If managers of publicly traded firms strive to maximize shareholder wealth, finance theory suggests that they should measure project benefits in terms of cash flow generated and project risk in terms of systematic risk and that they should evaluate projects using DCF methods (preferably NPV). If managers focus on different goals, then other measures of project benefits (e.g., accounting profit), other risk measures, and other project evaluation methods may be more suitable.

Several studies investigate firm goals as they relate to capital budgeting. Robichek and McDonald (1966) permit respondents to select from six different objectives. They note that the one listed objective associated with maximizing firm value is to increase the firm's stock price. This objective ranked last among the choices, behind such objectives as increasing the level of future profits, increasing the level of return on stockholders' capital, and increasing the level of future EPS. Robichek and McDonald attribute the low rating given to increasing the stock price to the fact that the other choices listed are easier to identify and control. According to a survey by Petty, Scott, and Bird (1975) of U.S. firms, several objectives rank higher than the maximization of the stock price, including maximizing the percentage return on asset investment and achieving a target growth rate of earnings per share. The authors do not seem to believe these responses indicate deviation of firm goals from the maximization of shareholder wealth. Rather, they conclude (p. 160) that "executives appear to favor objectives that can be translated into explicitly measurable goals."

Stanley and Block's (1984) survey of U.S. multinational firms finds the primary financial objective of surveyed firms is to maximize return on equity (29 percent), followed by maximizing growth in earnings per share (26 percent) and maximizing the value of securities (22 percent). The remaining 23 percent is divided among stabilizing performance, insuring availability of funds, maximizing sales growth, maximizing return on sales, and "other." The authors note that respondents may be thinking about operational objectives as opposed to overall corporate goals in responding to the question. Stanley and Block note that no relationship exists between the selection of a primary goal and either firm size or the ratio of foreign sales to total sales.

Grinyer, Sinclair, and Ibrahim (1999) survey the 300 largest U.K. firms as identified in the *Times* 1000 and generate 88 usable responses. When asked which interests managers should primarily serve, the responses are as follows: stockholders (38 percent), the corporation as an organization (27 percent), and stockholders and the corporation (26 percent). Other responses include employees (5 percent), management (1 percent), and various combinations of stockholders, the corporation, employees, and management (8 percent). Grinyer, Sinclair, and Ibrahim(p. 20) conclude that "it appears that respondents did not perceive themselves as being subject to effective constraints that compelled them to maximize the wealth of stockholders. This suggests that, if true, systematic risk, which is of interest to diversified stockholders, may not be the appropriate risk measure for capital budgeting analysis."

Finally, Brounen, de Jong, and Koedijk (2004) find that maximization of shareholder wealth is one of the top priorities for firms in the United Kingdom and the Netherlands. For French and German firms participating in the survey, "maximizing shareholder wealth" is well below such goals as "maximizing profits;" "maximizing sustainable growth;" "market position, service, quality;" "cost control, productivity, and efficiency;" "continuity;" and "optimizing leverage." The authors learn that firms participating in their survey that have the goal of maximizing shareholder wealth are more likely to use DCF methods when conducting capital budgeting analysis than firms with other goals.

In summary, the goals pursued by managers are important to the capital budgeting framework. If managers of publicly traded firms strive to maximize shareholder wealth, finance theory suggests that they should measure the potential benefit of projects in terms of cash flow generated, measure project risk in terms of systematic risk, and evaluate projects using DCF methods. Early studies of U.S. firms by Robichek and McDonald (1966) and Petty, Scott, and Bird (1975) discover that the goal of stock price maximization is ranked lower than other goals such as increasing the level of future profits, increasing the level of future EPS, and enhancing return on assets (ROA). Similarly, Stanley and Block (1984) find that maximizing return on equity (ROE) and EPS are the most important objectives of U.S. multinational firms. Grinyer, Sinclair, and Ibrahim (1999) find that managers of U.K. firms indicate that they primarily serve stockholders (38 percent) but that serving the corporation as an organization is also very important (27 percent). Finally, Brounen, de Jong, and Koedijk (2004) find that maximizing shareholder wealth is one of the top priorities for firms in the United Kingdom and the Netherlands. For French and German firms, maximizing shareholder wealth is well below such goals as maximizing profits, maximizing sustainable growth, and several other possible goals.

Inflation in Capital Budgeting Analysis

Finance theory suggests that firms using DCF methods to evaluate capital budgeting projects should use the firm's WACC as a hurdle rate for projects that will not affect the risk of the firm (e.g., Brigham and Ehrhardt 2008; Ross, Westerfield, and Jaffe 2008). Additionally, there are two different ways firms can estimate WACC: based on nominal rates that reflect current market conditions or based on real rates in which inflation premiums are removed. If a firm uses a market-based WACC, the rate reflects future inflation as determined by the market-place. Applying that market-based WACC to constant dollars rather than dollars that also reflect expected future inflation will result in an NPV that is lower than its true value. To adequately incorporate inflation in the analysis of capital budgeting projects, firms have two choices. The first is to apply a market-based WACC to forecasted future cash flows that also reflect expected future inflation. The other is to use a real WACC where the analyst has removed expected inflation from the cost of debt and equity and apply that real WACC to constant-value cash flows (cash flows unadjusted for inflation). Most view the first method as more practical.

Pike (1983a, 1996) surveys the same firms at different times to see if the firms have changed how they deal with inflation when evaluating capital budgeting projects. He finds in the earlier study that 50 percent of responding U.K. firms report always reflecting inflation in their analysis of capital budgeting projects, while 96 percent of firms do so in the later study. Pike also reports the percentage of firms using different inflation-adjustment methods in both studies. The methods and the percentage of firms in the 1983 and 1996 studies that use these methods include specifying cash flow in constant prices and applying the real rate of return (39 percent and 70 percent), adjusting for estimated changes in the general level of inflation (39 percent and 58 percent), specifying different inflation rates for different costs (33 percent and 53 percent), and considering inflation during risk analysis or at the sensitivity analysis stage (16 percent and 39 percent).

Arnold and Hatzopoulos (2000) also look at how small, medium-size, and large U.K. firms deal with expected inflation in capital budgeting. They discover that 13 percent of all respondents report making no adjustments for inflation (although just 3 percent of large firms do so); 42 percent specify cash flow in constant prices and apply a real rate of return; 39 percent express all cash flows in inflated price terms and discount at the market rate of return (55 percent for large firms); and 17 percent consider inflation during the risk analysis or sensitivity stage. Arnold and Hatzopoulos note that 24 years earlier, Carsberg and Hope (1976) report finding that only 15 percent of surveyed U.K. firms applied a market-determined rate to inflated cash flows. Based on this, Arnold and Hatzopoulos (p. 614) conclude that "there has been a significant bridging of the theory-practice gap in the treatment of inflation over the past two decades."

Hendricks (1983) sends a survey focusing on the inflationary aspects of capital budgeting to the 300 largest industrial firms in the *Fortune* 500 and receives 193 usable responses. He finds that 50 percent of responding firms say they specifically adjust forecasted cash flows to reflect anticipated inflation when analyzing capital budgeting projects. Firms with larger annual capital budgets and firms that use DCF methods are more likely to make adjustments for inflation. Of the firms that make adjustments for inflation, 96 percent adjust material costs, 93 percent modify wage costs, 92 percent change capital outlays scheduled for future years, 89 percent adjust revenues, 55 percent alter salvage values, and 51 percent adjust the terminal value of working capital.

In a recent study, Lazaridis (2006) considers how firms in Greece and Cyprus deal with inflation in capital budgeting. He finds that respondents from 29 percent of Greek firms and 45 percent of firms from Cyprus report not adjusting capital budgeting cash flows for inflation and notes that this is far less than for the U.S. firms reported by Hendricks (1983). Lazaridis also notes that the inflationary environment in Greek and Cyprus at the time of his study was different from the inflationary environment in the United States at the time of the Hendricks (1983) study. The approach most reported by Greek and Cypriot firms is the "gross profit per unit approach" (36 percent and 26 percent, respectively), followed by the "real cash flow approach" (24 percent and 23 percent, respectively).

In summary, studies of U.K. firms by Pike (1983a, 1996) find that the proportion of firms reflecting inflation in their analysis of capital budgeting projects increased between the two studies from 50 percent to 96 percent of responding firms, although not all firms adjust for inflation in a manner consistent with finance literature. Arnold and Hatzopoulos (2000) also discover that a minority of firms report adjusting for inflation in a manner consistent with finance theory; that is, just 39 percent of responding firms express all cash flows in inflated price terms and discount at the market rate of return. Of the large firms, 55 percent report adjusting for inflation in this manner. For U.S. firms, Hendricks (1983) discovers that 50 percent of firms say they adjust forecasted cash flows to reflect anticipated inflation and discount those cash flows using a market rate of return. He also finds that firms with larger annual capital budgets and firms that use DCF methods are more likely to properly adjust for inflation.

Summary and Conclusions

For about half a century, surveys of managers regarding the methods used in capital budgeting have helped reflect and monitor the gap between theory and practice. Despite differences in populations, samples, question wording, respondent bias, and other factors that may explain differences in findings, survey studies in capital budgeting have done much to inform academics and practitioners about the state of the discipline. Studies involving the choices of analytical methods and techniques used indicate a trend toward greater use of DCF methods for project evaluation by U.S. firms, non-U.S. firms, and multinational firms.

Regarding risk differences of capital budgeting projects, early studies discover that less than half of responding firms consider risk differences of capital projects. Later studies of U.S. firms document that more than half of firms consider risk differences. Over time, various studies find the importance of different tools for measuring project risk has changed. While early studies report the payback period to be the most popular tool to measure risk, later studies find subjective judgment, project size, and the use of sensitivity analysis to be more frequently used tools for measuring project risk. When evaluating projects with different amounts of risk, most survey studies discover that either a majority or a plurality of respondents adjust the discount rate used to evaluate the project. This is consistent with finance theory.

Although finance theory suggests capital rationing is inconsistent with maximizing firm value, early studies disclose that more than half of U.S. firms employ capital rationing. Later studies suggest a decline in the use of capital rationing. When asked why they employ capital rationing, the most popular response for U.S. firms is that internal management imposes a debt limit that restricts capital expenditures. Studies of capital rationing activities conducted by non-U.S. firms report little difference from the activities of U.S. firms.

Studies suggest a majority or plurality of firms from the following countries use WACC as a hurdle rate as opposed to less theoretically sound measures: the United States, Canada, the United Kingdom, and Australia. Studies of multinational firms also find that a majority report using WACC as a hurdle rate. However, the majority (or plurality) of firms in Hong Kong, Indonesia, Malaysia, the Philippines, and Singapore report using the cost of financing the project under consideration.

Regarding the postauditing of capital budgeting projects, early survey research finds that many firms used this technique as far back as the early 1970s. Somewhat surprising is the fact that some studies report that firms may be moving away from the use of postaudits.

Most published survey research finds that the majority of surveyed U.S. firms (both large and small) measure project benefits in terms of cash flows. Regarding forecasting accuracy, the majority of managers responding to surveys believe revenue is frequently overstated, but the majority do not believe that cost forecasts are frequently under- or overstated. One study finds firms with higher risk are more likely to follow systematic approaches to forecasting project cash flows, and those same firms tend to achieve greater accuracy in their forecasts. Regarding the use of real options in capital budgeting, a majority of practitioners responding to surveys in the United States, Europe, and Canada report not using this tool.

Theory suggests that firms with the goal of shareholder wealth maximization are more likely to conduct capital budgeting in a manner consistent with finance theory. Some surveys of U.S. firms find that the goal of stock price maximization is ranked lower than such goals as increasing the level of future profits, increasing the level of future EPS, enhancing ROA, and maximizing ROE. One study of the goals of non-U.S. firms reports that maximizing shareholder wealth is one of the top priorities for firms in the United Kingdom and the Netherlands, while

French and German firms focus on such goals as maximizing profits and maximizing sustainable growth.

Some survey studies focus on how firms adjust capital budgeting analysis for expected inflation. Findings suggest that half of U.S. firms specifically adjust forecasted cash flows to reflect anticipated inflation. Also, firms with larger annual capital budgets and firms that use DCF methods are more likely to make adjustments for inflation. Studies of U.K. firms document that the proportion of firms reflecting inflation in their analysis of capital budgeting projects increased from 50 percent in an early study to 96 percent in a later study, although not all U.K. firms make the adjustments in a manner consistent with finance literature.

What lies ahead for capital budgeting surveys? In their review of the capital budgeting survey literature from 1984 through 2008, Burns and Walker (2009) note that survey researchers have addressed some of the neglected areas involving the identification, development, and control stages of the capital budgeting process. Still, these researchers have focused much of their attention on the selection stage, with its emphasis on project evaluation techniques. Burns and Walker (p. 89) conclude, "As a result, there are many opportunities that still await surveyors to deeply delve into the capital budgeting process by re-focusing their efforts towards the neglected stages." For example, these authors identify the decision support system as a promising area of survey research. Evidence presented in this chapter is consistent with this view involving the future of capital budgeting surveys. Thus, further focus on general capital budgeting surveys that examine the analysis and selection of capital budgeting proposals is unlikely to contribute much to the existing body of knowledge.

References

Antle, Rick, and Gary D. Eppen. 1985. "Capital Rationing and Organizational Slack in Capital Budgeting." *Management Science* 31:2, 163–175.

Arnold, Glen C., and Panos D. Hatzopoulos. 2000. "The Theory-Practice Gap in Capital Budgeting: Evidence from the United Kingdom." *Journal of Business Finance and Accounting* 27:5–6, 603–626.

Baker, H. Kent, Shantanu Dutta, and Samir Saadi. 2009. "Corporate Finance Practices in Canada: Where Do We Stand?" Working Paper, University of Ontario Institute of Technology and Queen's University.

Baker, James C., and Laurence J. Beardsley. 1973. "Multinational Companies' Use of Risk Evaluation and Profit Measurement for Capital Budgeting Decisions." *Journal of Business Finance* 5:1, 38–43.

Bierman, Harold. 1993. "Capital Budgeting in 1992: A Survey." *Financial Management Letters* 22:3, 24.

Bierman, Harold Jr., and Seymour Smidt. 1993. *The Capital Budgeting Decision.* New York: Macmillan Publishing Company.

Binder, John J., and J. Scott Chaput. 1996. "A Positive Analysis of Corporate Capital Budgeting Practices." *Review of Quantitative Finance and Accounting* 6:3, 245–257.

Block, Stanley. 2003. "Divisional Cost of Capital: A Study of Its Use by Major U.S. Firms." *Engineering Economist* 48:4, 345–362.

———. 2007. "Are 'Real Options' Actually Used in the Real World?" *Engineering Economist* 52:3, 255–268.

Brigham, Eugene F. 1975. "Hurdle Rate for Screening Capital Expenditure Proposals." *Financial Management* 4:3, 17–26.

Brigham, Eugene F., and Michael C. Ehrhardt. 2008. *Financial Management: Theory and Practice*, 12th ed. Mason, Ohio: Thomson South-Western.

Brounen, Dirk, Abe de Jong, and Kees Koedijk. 2004. "Corporate Finance in Europe: Confronting Theory with Practice." *Financial Management* 33:4, 71–101.

Bruner, Robert F., Kenneth M. Eades, Robert S. Harris, and Robert C. Higgins. 1998. "Best Practices in Estimating the Cost of Capital: Survey and Synthesis." *Financial Practice and Education* 8:1, 13–28.

Brunwasser, Harold J., and Carl McGowan. 1989. "The Evaluation of International Capital Investment Decisions by United States Domiciled Multinationals: A Survey of Current Practice." *American Business Review* 7:1, 23–29.

Burns, Richard M., and Joe Walker. 1997. "Capital Budgeting Techniques among the Fortune 500: A Rationale Approach." *Managerial Finance* 23:9, 3–15.

———. 2009. "Capital Budgeting Surveys: The Future Is Now." *Journal of Applied Finance* 19:1–2, 78–90.

Carsberg, Bryan, and Anthony Hope. 1976. *Business Investment Decisions under Inflation: Theory and Practice*. London: Institute of Chartered Accountants.

Chadwell-Hatfield, Patricia, Bernard Goitein, Philip Horvath, and Allen Webster. 1996/1997. "Financial Criteria, Capital Budgeting Techniques, and Risk Analysis of Manufacturing Firms." *Journal of Applied Business Research* 13:1, 95–104.

Christy, George A. 1966. *Capital Budgeting: Current Practices and Their Efficiency*. Eugene: Bureau of Business and Economic Research, University of Oregon.

Cooper, William D., Michael F. Cornick, and Alonzo Redmon. 1992. "Capital Budgeting: A 1990 Study of Fortune 500 Company Practices." *Journal of Applied Business Research* 8:3, 20–23.

Danielson, Morris G., and Jonathan A. Scott. 2006. "The Capital Budgeting Decisions of Small Businesses." *Journal of Applied Finance* 16:2, 45–55.

Ehrhardt, Michael C. 1994. *The Search for Value: Measuring the Company's Cost of Capital*. Boston: Oxford University Press.

Fremgen, James M. 1973. "Capital Budgeting Practices: A Survey." *Management Accounting* 54:11, 19–25.

Gilbert, Erika, and Alan Reichert. 1995. "The Practice of Financial Management among Large United States Corporations." *Financial Practice and Education* 5:1, 16–23.

Gitman, Lawrence J., and John R. Forrester Jr. 1977. "A Survey of Capital Budgeting Techniques Used by Major U.S. Firms." *Financial Management* 6:3, 66–71.

Gitman, Lawrence J., and Charles E. Maxwell. 1987. "A Longitudinal Comparison of Capital Budgeting Techniques Used by Major U.S. Firms: 1986 versus 1976." *Journal of Applied Business Research* 3:1, 41–50.

Gitman, Lawrence J., and Vincent A. Mercurio. 1982. "Cost of Capital Techniques Used by Major U.S. Firms: Survey and Analysis of Fortune's 1000." *Financial Management* 11:4, 21–30.

Gitman, Lawrence J., and Pieter A. Vandenberg. 2000. "Cost of Capital Techniques Used by Major U.S. Firms: 1997 vs. 1980." *Financial Practice and Education* 10:2, 53–68.

Gordon, Lawrence A., and Mary D. Myers. 1991. "Postauditing Capital Projects: Are You in Step with the Competition?" *Management Accounting* 72:7, 39–42.

Gordon, Lawrence A., and George E. Pinches. 1984. *Improving Capital Budgeting: A Decisions Support System Approach.* Reading, MA: Addison-Wesley.

Gordon, Myron J. 1964. "Security and Investment: Theory and Evidence." *Journal of Finance* 19:4, 607–618.

Graham, John R., and Campbell R. Harvey. 2001. "The Theory and Practice of Corporate Finance: Evidence from the Field." *Journal of Financial Economics* 60:2–3, 187–243.

Grinyer, John R., C. Donald Sinclair, and Daing Nasir Ibrahim. 1999. "Management Objectives in Capital Budgeting." *Financial Practice and Education* 9:2, 12–22.

Hendricks, James A. 1983. "Capital Budgeting Practices Including Inflation Adjustments: A Survey." *Managerial Planning* 31:4, 22–28.

Hirshleifer, David. 1993. "Managerial Reputation and Corporate Investment Decisions." *Financial Management* 22:2, 145–160.

Istvan, Donald F. 1961. "The Economic Evaluation of Capital Expenditures." *Journal of Business* 34:1, 45–51.

Kester, George W., Rosita P. Chang, Erlinda S. Echanis, Shalahuddin Haikal, Mansor Md. Isa, Michael T. Skully, Kai-Chong Tsui, and Chi-Jeng Wang. 1999. "Capital Budgeting Practices in the Asia-Pacific Region: Australia, Hong Kong, Indonesia, Malaysia, Philippines and Singapore." *Financial Practice and Education* 9:1, 25–33.

Kim, Suk H., Trevor Crick, and Edward J. Farragher. 1984. "Foreign Capital Budgeting Practices Used by the U.S. and Non-U.S. Multinational Companies." *Engineering Economist* 29:3, 2–10.

Kim, Suk H., and Edward J. Farragher. 1981. "Current Capital Budgeting Practices." *Management Accounting* 62:12, 26–30.

Kim, Suk H., and Gregory Ulferts. 1996. "A Summary of Multinational Capital Budgeting Studies." *Managerial Finance* 22:1, 75–85.

Klammer, Thomas. 1972. "Empirical Evidence of the Adoption of Sophisticated Capital Budgeting Techniques." *Journal of Business* 45:3, 387–398.

Klammer, Thomas, Bruce Koch, and Neil Wilner. 1991. "Capital Budgeting Practices: A Survey of Corporate Use." *Journal of Management Accounting Research* 4:1, 113–130.

Klammer, Thomas, and Michael C. Walker. 1984. "The Continuing Increase in the Use of Sophisticated Capital Budgeting Techniques." *California Management Review* 27:1, 137–148.

Lazaridis, Ioannis T. 2006. "Cash Flow Estimation Practices in Mediterranean Countries." *Managerial Finance* 22:8, 625–633.

Lintner, John. 1963. "The Cost of Capital and Optimal Financing of Corporate Growth." *Journal of Finance* 18:2, 292–310.

———. 1964. "Optimal Dividends and Corporate Growth under Uncertainty." *Quarterly Journal of Economics* 78:1, 49–95.

———. 1965a. "Security Prices, Risk, and Maximal Gains from Diversification." *Journal of Finance* 20:4, 587–616.

————. 1965b. "The Valuation of Risk Assets and the Selection of Risky Investments in Stock Portfolios and Capital Budgets." *Review of Economics and Statistics* 47:1, 13–37.

Mao, James C. T. 1970. "Survey of Capital Budgeting: Theory and Practice." *Journal of Finance* 25:2, 349–360.

Markowitz, Harry M. 1959. *Portfolio Selection.* New York: John Wiley & Sons.

Miller, James H. 1960. "A Glimpse at Practice in Calculating and Using Return on Investment." *National Association of Accountants Bulletin* 41:10, 65–77.

Moore, James S., and Alan K. Reichert. 1983. "An Analysis of the Financial Management Techniques Currently Employed by Large U.S. Corporations." *Journal of Business Finance and Accounting* 10:4, 623–645.

Mukherjee, Tarun K. 1987. "Capital-Budgeting Surveys: The Past and the Future." *Review of Business and Economic Research* 22:2, 37–59.

Mukherjee, Tarun K., and Vineeta L. Hingorani. 1999. "Capital-Rationing Decisions of Fortune 500 Firms: A Survey." *Financial Practice and Education* 9:1, 7–15.

Myers, Mary D., Lawrence A. Gordon, and Michelle M. Hamer. 1991. "Post-Auditing Capital Assets and Firm Performance: An Empirical Investigation." *Managerial and Decision Economics* 12:4, 317–327.

Myers, Stewart C. 1977. "Determinants of Corporate Borrowing." *Journal of Financial Economics* 5:2, 147–175.

————. 1984. "The Capital Structure Puzzle." *Journal of Finance* 39:3, 575–592.

Oblak, David J., and Roy J. Helm Jr. 1980. "Survey and Analysis of Capital Budgeting Methods Used by Multinationals." *Financial Management* 9:4, 37–41.

Payne, Janet D., Will Carrington Heath, and Lewis R. Gale. 1999. "Comparative Financial Practice in the US and Canada: Capital Budgeting and Risk Assessment Techniques." *Financial Practice and Education* 9:1, 16–24.

Petry, Glenn H. 1975. "Effective Use of Capital Budgeting Tools." *Business Horizons* 18:5, 57–65.

Petry, Glenn H., and James Sprow. 1993. "The Theory and Practice of Finance in the 1990s." *Quarterly Review of Economics and Finance* 33:4, 359–381.

Petty, J. William, David F. Scott Jr., and Monroe M. Bird. 1975. "The Capital Expenditure Decision-Making Process of Large Corporations." *Engineering Economist* 20:3, 159–172.

Pflomn, Norman. P. 1963. *Managing Capital Expenditures.* New York: National Industrial Conference Board.

Pike, Richard H. 1983a. "A Review of Recent Trends in Formal Capital Budgeting Processes." *Accounting and Business Research* 13:51, 201–203.

————. 1983b. "The Capital Budgeting Behaviour and Corporate Characteristics of Capital Constrained Firms." *Journal of Business Finance and Accounting* 10:4, 663–665.

————. 1996. "A Longitudinal Survey on Capital Budgeting Practices." *Journal of Business Finance and Accounting* 23:1, 79–88.

Pohlman, Randolph A., Emmanuel S. Santiago, and F. Lynn Markel. 1988. "Cash Flow Estimation Practices of Large Firms." *Financial Management* 17:2, 71–79.

Poterba, James M., and Lawrence H. Summers. 1995. "A CEO Survey of U.S. Companies' Time Horizons and Hurdle Rates." *Sloan Management Review* 37:1, 43–53.

Pruitt, Stephen W., and Lawrence J. Gitman. 1987. "Capital Budgeting Forecast Biases: Evidence from the Fortune 500." *Financial Management* 16:1, 46–51.

Quirin, G. David. 1967. *The Capital Expenditure Decision*. Homewood, IL: Richard D. Irwin.

Robichek, Alexander A., and John G. McDonald. 1966. "Financial Management in Transition, Long Range Planning Service." Report no. 268. Menlo Park, CA: Stanford Research Institute.

Ross, Stephen A., Randolph W. Westerfield, and Jeffrey F. Jaffe. 2008. *Corporate Finance*, 8th ed. New York: McGraw-Hill Higher Education.

Ryan, Patricia A., and Glenn P. Ryan. 2002. "Capital Budgeting Practices of the Fortune 1000: How Have Things Changed?" *Journal of Business and Management* 8:4, 355–364.

Sangster, Alan. 1993. "Capital Investment Appraisal Techniques: A Survey of Current Usage." *Journal of Business Finance and Accounting* 20:3, 307–313.

Scapens, Robert W., and J. Timothy Sale. 1981. "Performance Measurement and Formal Capital Expenditure Controls in Divisionalized Companies." *Journal of Business Finance and Accounting* 8:3, 389–419.

Schall, Lawrence D., Gary L. Sundem, and William R. Geijsbeek Jr. 1978. "Survey and Analysis of Capital Budgeting Methods." *Journal of Finance* 33:1, 281–287.

Scott, David F. Jr., and J. William Petty II. 1984. "Capital Budgeting Practices in Large American Firms: A Retrospective Analysis and Synthesis." *Financial Review* 19:1, 111–123.

Shao, Lawrence Peter, and Alan T. Shao. 1996. "Risk Analysis and Capital Budgeting Techniques of U.S. Multinational Enterprises." *Managerial Finance* 22:1, 41–57.

Sharpe, William F. 1963. "A Simplified Model for Portfolio Analysis." *Management Science* 9:2, 277–293.

———. 1964. "Capital Asset Prices: A Theory of Market Equilibrium under Conditions of Uncertainty." *Journal of Finance* 19:3, 425–442.

Smith, Kimberly J. 1994. "Postauditing Capital Investments." *Financial Practice and Education* 4:1, 129–137.

Stanley, Majorie T., and Stanley B. Block. 1984. "A Survey of Multinational Capital Budgeting." *Financial Review* 19:1, 36–54.

Stonehill, Arthur, and Leonard Nathanson. 1968. "Capital Budgeting and the Multinational Corporation." *California Management Review* 10:4, 39–52.

Terborgh, George. 1949. *Dynamic Equipment Policy*. New York: McGraw-Hill.

———. 1958. *Business Investment Policy*. Washington, DC: Machinery and Allied Products Institute.

Thakor, Anjan V. 1990. "Investment Myopia and the Internal Organization of Capital Allocation Decisions." *Journal of Law, Economics, and Organization* 6:1, 129–154.

Tobin, J. 1958. "Liquidity Preferences as Behavior toward Risk." *Review of Economic Studies* 25:2, 65–86.

Triantis, Alex, and Adam Borison. 2001. "Real Options: State of Practice." *Journal of Applied Corporate Finance* 14:2, 8–24.

4

Cost of Capital

The more you explain it, the more I don't understand it.
Mark Twain

Introduction

The term *cost of capital* refers to the cost of a firm's long-term sources of financing. Because most firms use a variety of long-term financing sources such as bonds, preferred stock, and common equity, firms may view their cost of capital as the weighted average of the cost of each source of capital, where the weights reflect the firm's target or market-value-weighted capital structure. Finance textbooks have described the process of calculating a firm's cost of capital in this manner for many years (e.g., Bierman and Smidt 1966; Brigham and Ehrhardt 2008). Thus, most financial experts view the term cost of capital as synonymous with the term *weighted average cost of capital* (WACC). In this chapter, the terms cost of capital and WACC are used interchangeably.

Firms may need to estimate their cost of capital for many reasons. The most common reason is for use as the hurdle rate in evaluating capital budgeting projects that are unlikely to alter the risk of the firm. Firms also use the cost of capital in making the abandonment decision, which is analytically related to the capital budgeting decision; that is, firms must consider the opportunity cost of having funds invested in a project relative to the cash flows generated by the project. Frequently, the economic life of a project (i.e., the life that will maximize the project's net present value and, therefore, firm value) may be shorter than the physical life of the assets related to the project. Managers and outside investors also use the cost of capital to value firms using the free cash flow to financing (FCFF) approach. This popular valuation method involves forecasting a firm's future FCFF and discounting it to present value, using the firm's cost of capital as a discount rate. Many firms also use the cost of capital as a benchmark for compensation plans. Such firms frequently determine bonuses to be paid based on whether the firm generates a return on invested capital that exceeds the firm's cost of capital. Finally, managers determine their target capital structure by seeking a capital structure that minimizes the firm's cost of capital.

This chapter reviews the theory of how firms should estimate and use their cost of debt, equity, and overall cost of capital. It then discusses the findings of major survey studies indicating how firms claim they actually estimate and use these values. Where possible, the chapter identifies relationships between the methods employed by firms and firm characteristics, as well as any trends appearing in the use of different methods. As discussed in Chapter 3, some experts expect that larger firms and firms with chief financial officers (CFOs) having master of business administration (MBA) degrees are more likely to conform to finance theory in conducting capital budgeting and estimating the cost of capital. Many of these same experts expect to find a trend toward employment of the theoretically correct cost of capital methods. These expectations are intuitively appealing. First, larger firms are more likely to employ specialists familiar with theoretically correct capital budgeting and cost-of-capital methods. Second, because the theoretically correct methods are generally taught in MBA programs, those having completed such programs are more likely to employ such methods. Finally, because business schools throughout the world now teach theoretically correct methods, the employment of these methods is expected to become the norm.

Fewer survey studies have focused on how firms determine their cost of capital than on how firms conduct capital budgeting. However, many survey studies about capital budgeting ask questions related to the cost of capital. Our discussion of survey research in capital budgeting (Chapter 3) addresses the question about what hurdle rates (discount rates) firms use to evaluate capital budgeting projects. Because these rates include such values as the firm's cost of debt, the firm's cost of equity, the cost of financing the project, and so forth, they are discussed in the previous chapter rather than here, despite the clear overlap between the two subjects.

Among the early survey studies focusing on how firms estimate the cost of capital are studies conducted by Brigham (1975), Gitman and Mercurio (1982), Poterba and Summers (1995), and Bruner, Eades, Harris, and Higgins (1998). More recent studies focusing on cost of capital techniques include studies conducted by Gitman and Vandenberg (2000) and Block (2003). Many survey studies focusing on the general topic of capital budgeting also provide useful information about how firms estimate their cost of capital. These studies go back as far as Pflomn (1963); Christy (1966); Schall, Sundem, and Geijsbeek

(1978); Bierman (1993); and Petry and Sprow (1993). Two important studies look at broad issues of corporate finance and touch on vital cost of capital issues: Graham and Harvey (2001), who survey U.S. managers, and Brounen, de Jong, and Koedijk (2004), who survey European managers. Meanwhile, Arnold and Hatzopoulos (2000) examine cost of capital issues in the United Kingdom, and Kester, Chang, Echanis, Haikal, Isa, Skully, Tsui, and Wang (1999) investigate cost of capital issues in the Asia-Pacific Region. Finally, some studies focus on closely related topics such as the use of divisional costs of capital (Block 2003). This chapter highlights the survey studies just mentioned and others that help bridge the gap between theory and practice regarding the use and calculation of cost of capital.

As in other chapters in this book, this chapter will look at survey studies conducted at different times using different populations, samples, and question wording. Thus, the reader should be aware that the results of one study may not be directly comparable to the results of another study. Despite these obvious limitations, this chapter attempts to synthesize the numerous studies in this area.

In an early study, Pflomn (1963) documents the practices of 346 U.S. manufacturing firms for publication by the National Industrial Conference Board. The exact method of data collection and date of collection are unknown. Without stating percentages, Pflomn reports that firms use several different criteria to establish the minimum rate of return on projects, including, but not limited to, the current average company return on investment, the return on investment in other companies, the average return on investment for the industry, the average rate of return for individual plants or divisions, the overall cost of capital, and the current cost of borrowing. He also reports learning that many surveyed managers believe one or more of the following: (1) there is no cost associated with retained earnings financing, (2) the cost of equity is approximately equal to a firm's ratio of earnings to price, and (3) firms must add an additional increment to the cost of capital because some projects will fail and others must make up for that failure. Pflomn also notes that some projects are more risky than others, so firms need to generate a higher return on more risky projects. Pflomn (p. 40) states that "a few companies claim that the only realistic standard is one based on the over-all cost of capital."

Christy (1966) mailed questionnaires to the 243 publicly held firms listed in Standard & Poor's Stock Guide classified in the following industries: chemicals, plastics, electrical equipment and parts, radio and television, machinery, drugs, cosmetics, office equipment, business forms, and electrical products. Christy received 108 responses, a 44 percent response rate. One question asks respondents to identify the statement that best matches their view of the cost of capital. Most respondents express views that are inconsistent with finance theory. The largest proportion of respondents (32 percent) indicate that the cost of capital is the rate of return needed on investments to avoid a decline in earnings per share.

Another 26 percent view the cost of capital as a weighted average of (1) the current yield on the company's debt obligations reduced by tax savings and (2) the current earnings-to-price ratio of the company's common stock. Eighteen percent of respondents say the cost of capital is the cost of additional borrowed capital reduced by the tax savings. Just 6 percent of respondents identify the cost of capital as the rate of return required on investments that prevents the stock price from declining, which Christy identifies as the generally accepted theoretically correct definition. The remaining respondents give varying descriptions, although one firm, described by Christy as an "eminent company," indicates that they do not use the cost of capital notion. Christy (p. 23) concludes that even in companies that are fairly large, "cost of capital practice lags prevailing theory by a number of years."

Theory: Weighting Schemes Used to Calculate WACC

Finance theory specifies that the weights used to calculate WACC should reflect a firm's target capital structure, which is the capital structure that will maximize the value of the firm and minimize the firm's WACC (e.g., Brigham and Ehrhardt 2008). Clearly, the weights used to calculate WACC should not be book-value weights appearing on the firm's balance sheet, unless, by coincidence, they also happen to be the capital structure weights that maximize the firm's stock price. Book-value weights of debt and equity ignore current market conditions. If a firm issued debt last year and interest rates have since risen, the book value of debt continues to reflect the cost of debt at the time of issue. Similarly, using the weight of equity on a firm's balance sheet ignores the current market value of equity.

Some experts advocate using market-value weights based on the number of shares of common stock, the market price per share, and the market value of a firm's outstanding debt. While this is clearly better than using book-value weights, the capital structure calculated in this way may still deviate from the firm's target capital structure. This can happen because firms regularly deviate from their target capital structure to avoid raising every dollar of capital in the target proportions. To do so would be a financial burden on the firm due to high flotation costs as firms raise small amounts of capital more frequently. Also, using market-value weights based on the current capital structure ignores the fact that a firm's target capital structure can change over time as the firm changes and as market conditions vary. In conclusion, firm managers should decide on a firm's target capital structure and employ those weights to calculate the firm's WACC.

Furthermore, a firm should not base the weights on the financing sources used to finance the specific project or projects under consideration (e.g., Ross, Westerfield, and Jaffe 2008); that is, if a firm will use only debt this quarter to finance projects, it should not use 100 percent as the weight of debt to calculate the WACC. Using debt to raise funds now will eventually lead to raising equity funds in the future to bring the capital structure closer to the target structure. The firm should allocate the higher cost of equity over all projects, not just the projects adopted during a quarter when the firm actually utilizes equity as a source of financing. To do otherwise will lead to suboptimal decisions.

Practice: Weighting Schemes Used to Calculate WACC

The following sections synthesize the findings of key survey studies about weighting schemes used to calculate WACC. Each section focuses on studies of different populations: U.S. firms, non-U.S. firms, and multinational firms.

Studies of U.S. Firms

Panel A of Table 4.1 shows the responses of U.S. firms to questions about the weighting schemes employed by managers when estimating their firms' cost of capital. These studies are listed in chronological order for ease in comparing the results of the studies over time. Gitman and Mercurio (1982) report responses from 177 of the 1,000 questionnaires sent to *Fortune* 1000 firms in 1980. The authors identify a response bias in that larger firms are more likely to respond to the survey than smaller firms. Despite that limitation, the results show that 42 percent of all respondents use their firm's target capital structure as weights as suggested by finance theory. Other weights employed include current market-value weights (29 percent), the cost of the specific source of financing (17 percent), and book-value weights (16 percent). The authors observe that smaller firms are more likely than larger firms to use the cost of the specific source of financing. Consistent with finance theory, Gitman and Mercurio also find that most respondents use all sources of capital (except current liabilities) to calculate the WACC. However, a significant proportion of responding firms (although less than half) exclude some long-term sources of capital from the calculation of WACC. The authors note that this differs from finance theory.

Some 11 years after the Gitman and Mercurio (1982) study, Petry and Sprow (1993) report the responses to similar questions from 500 randomly selected firms among the 1990 *Business Week* 1000 firms. The authors describe this population as being comparable to the *Fortune* 1000 firms used by Gitman and Mercurio. Petry and Sprow report their findings using groups classified by industry types: industrial and retail, financial and services, and utilities.

The 151 responses provide different results from the Gitman and Mercurio (1982) study regarding the application of various weighting schemes. Petry and Sprow (1993) find that for respondents operating in financial and service industries, the most popular response is target capital structure weights (29 percent),

TABLE 4.1 Weighting schemes used to calculate the cost of capital

This table shows how firms respond to questions about the weighting schemes they employ to calculate the cost of capital. Panel A indicates the responses of U.S. firms and Panel B reports the responses of U.K. and Canadian firms. Finance theory advocates the use of target capital structure weights, which are popular with some groups of respondents but not all.

Author(s)	Year published	Population/Sample	Percentage of firms					
			Cost of specific financing source	Book-value weights	Current market-value weights	Book-value of debt and market-value of equity	Target capital structure weights	Some other weighting scheme
A. U.S. firms								
Gitman and Mercurio[a]	1982	*Fortune* 1000 firms (*n* = 177)	17	16	29	n/a	42	1
Petry and Sprow	1993	*Business Week* 1000 firms						
		Industrial/Retail (*n* = 91)	n/a	27	21	20	25	7
		Financial/Services (*n* = 26)	n/a	25	21	17	29	8
		Utilities (*n* = 34)	n/a	46	11	16	22	5
Bruner, Eades, Harris, and Higgins[a,c]	1998	U.S. firms listed in *Creating World-Class Financial Management: Strategies of 50 Leading Companies* (1992; *n* = 27)[b]	n/a	15	59	n/a	52	n/a
Gitman and Vandenberg[a]	2000	*Fortune* 1000 firms (*n* = 111)	8	20	34	n/a	50	2

B. U.K. firms

Arnold and Hatzopoulos	2000	Large, midsize, and small U.K. firms listed in the *Times* 1000					
		Small (n = 34)	n/a	37	44	n/a	19	n/a
		Midsize (n = 24)	n/a	26	47	n/a	26	n/a
		Large (n = 38)	n/a	19	42	n/a	39	n/a
		Composite (n = 96)	n/a	26	44	n/a	30	n/a
Baker, Dutta, and Saadi	2009	762 Canadian firms on the Toronto Stock Exchange with select information available from Stock Guide database (n = 214)	n/a	n/a	58	18	23	n/a

[a]Multiple responses are permitted.

[b]This publication identifies firms "selected by their peers as being among those with the best financial management. Firms were chosen for excellence in strategic financial risk management, tax and accounting, performance evaluation and other areas of financial management. . . . The companies included were those mentioned the greatest number of times by their peers."

[c]One question asks "target vs. current debt/equity," with 52 percent saying target and 15 percent selecting current debt/equity (33 percent respond "n/a" or "uncertain"). A second question asks "market vs. book weights?" with 15 percent indicating book and 59 percent indicating market-value weights (26 percent respond "n/a" or "uncertain").

followed by book-value weights (25 percent). For firms in industrial and retail industries, the most common response is book-value weights (27 percent), followed by target capital structure weights (25 percent). For utility firms, the most common response is also book-value weights (46 percent), followed by target capital structure weights (22 percent). Of special note is that Petry and Sprow specified that respondents could only indicate one weighting scheme used to calculate WACC, unlike Gitman and Mercurio, who permitted multiple responses. Also, the Petry and Sprow study provides more alternative responses than the Gitman and Mercurio study.

Despite these differences, Petry and Sprow (1993) surprisingly report that 11 years after the Gitman and Mercurio (1982) study, a smaller percentage of participating firms use theoretically correct target capital structure weights. Petry and Sprow (p. 371) suggest that "if executives expect future financing to be in the same proportions as current book, then this response [use of current book values] would be in accordance with financial theory." The greater deviation from finance theory found by Petry and Sprow compared to Gitman and Mercurio may result from differences in the population, sample, and/or question wording.

The study published by Bruner et. al (1998) surveys 27 "best-practice firms" that are identified by peer firms as having good financial management practices. When asked if they use target weights or current debt/equity weights, 52 percent of the firms indicate the use of target capital structure weights and 15 percent indicate employment of current debt/equity weights. When asked if the weights they use are based on market value or book value, 59 percent specify market value and 15 percent indicate book value. The authors conclude (p. 15) that "WACC is the dominant discount rate used in discounted cash flow analysis" and "weights are based on market not book value mixes of debt and equity."

Gitman and Vandenberg (2000) conduct a survey similar to that of Gitman and Mercurio (1982). They use identical questions (and add two new questions) and a somewhat similar population (*Fortune* 1000 firms, with 111 usable responses). However, just 41 percent of responding firms in the earlier study indicated their principal activity is manufacturing compared to 94 percent of responding firms in the later study. Compared to the 1982 study, the 2000 study finds a higher percentage of respondents use target capital structure weights (50 percent versus 42 percent), market-value weights (34 percent versus 29 percent), and book-value weights (20 percent versus 16 percent). Conversely, a lower percentage of respondents report using weights based on the specific source of financing (8 percent versus 17 percent).

Consistent with Gitman and Mercurio (1982), Gitman and Vandenberg (2000) find that firms generally include all long-term sources of financing in their WACC calculation. Also consistent with finance theory (e.g., Brigham and Ehrhardt 2008), participating firms tend to exclude current liabilities from this calculation. Inconsistent with finance theory, the authors find that a large number but less than half of responding firms exclude some long-term sources of financing from the calculation of WACC. They report that 35 percent of respondents with capital leases exclude the leases in the calculation of WACC and 21 percent of firms with preferred stock outstanding exclude this source from the WACC calculation.

Studies of Non-U.S. Firms

The Arnold and Hatzopoulos (2000) study of capital budgeting in the United Kingdom involves a survey of 100 large, 100 midsize, and 100 small firms selected from the 1996 *Times* 1000. The authors receive usable responses from 96 firms (38 large firms, 24 mid-size firms, and 34 small firms). The responses show that 54 percent of all surveyed firms use a WACC to appraise major capital investments (61 percent of large firms, 63 percent of midsize firms, and 41 percent of small firms). For firms that use a WACC, Panel B of Table 4.1 shows responses to a question about how they determine the weights they use. The responses show that the current market value of debt and equity is the most used weight for each size group. While the use of target capital structure weights is the second-most common weighting scheme for large firms, target weights are the third-most common weighting scheme for small firms and are tied with book-value weights for midsize firms.

Baker, Dutta, and Saadi (2009) send surveys to 762 Canadian firms that (1) are listed on the Toronto Stock Exchange and (2) have select data available from the Stock-Guide database. They receive 214 usable responses from primarily manufacturing firms (44 percent of total responses), retail and wholesale firms (24 percent), and mining firms (14 percent). They find that the majority of participating firms employ market-value weights (58 percent) to calculate WACC. The next most common weighting scheme is the use of theoretically correct target capital structure weights (23 percent), followed by book-value weights (18 percent). Baker, Dutta, and Saadi report that smaller firms and firms managed by CEOs who do not have MBA degrees are more likely to use market-value weights. Comparing the results of the Baker, Dutta, and Saadi study to the Gitman and Vandenberg (2000) study of U.S. firms suggests that U.S. firms are more likely to employ the theoretically correct target capital structure as weights.

Studies of Multinational Firms

Several studies look specifically at whether multinational firms calculate their WACC the same way when evaluating domestic projects as when they evaluate foreign projects. An early study by Stonehill and Nathanson (1968) reports the findings from a survey of 92 U.S. and 18 foreign multinational firms (Table 4.2). The authors ask firms that calculate the cost of capital if they use a different rate

TABLE 4.2 Discount-rate differences on foreign and domestic projects: Multinational firms

This table displays responses to questions about the use of different discount rates for foreign versus domestic projects. Respondents could respond to more than one answer.

Author	Year published	Population/Sample	Percentage of firms				
			No difference	Project cost of capital	Parent cost of capital	Subsidiary or divisional cost of capital	Other
Stonehill and Nathanson	1968	219 U.S firms and 100 foreign firms from *Fortune's* list of 500 largest U.S. firms and 200 largest foreign firms (*n* = 93 U.S. and 18 foreign)					
		U.S. multinational firms	42	21	n/a	11	28
		Non-U.S. multinational firms	44	22	n/a	11	22
Stanley and Block	1984	339 U.S. multinational firms listed in *Fortune* 1000 (*n* = 121)	68	32	49	n/a	

for domestic projects than for foreign projects. Of the U.S. firms, 69 percent say they use the same rate for both compared with just 47 percent of foreign firms. Of the U.S. and non-U.S. multinational firms that employ different rates for domestic and foreign projects, 45 percent and 0 percent, respectively, use a local cost of capital; 18 percent and 11 percent vary the cost of capital subjectively; 33 percent and 9 percent use the local prime rate; and 18 percent and 44 percent use the cost of funds being used to finance the project. The response "other" accounted for 9 percent of U.S. firms and 11 percent of foreign firms.

Stanley and Block (1984) send questionnaires to 339 U.S. multinational firms and receive responses from 121 firms (Table 4.2). They begin with the 1,000 largest U.S. firms from *Fortune* magazine and then identify those firms operating in more than four countries outside the United States based on the *Directory of American Firms Operating in Foreign Countries*. They find that 88 percent of responding firms employ WACC to evaluate capital budgeting projects and 12 percent do not. Thirty-two percent of responding firms use a different method to calculate the cost of capital when evaluating domestic projects than for foreign projects, while 68 percent use the same cost of capital. Thirty-two percent of respondents use a project cost of capital and 49 percent employ the parent cost of capital, while some firms use both (they did not specify a percentage). Just 34 percent of respondents say they adjust for expected foreign exchange rate changes when they calculate the cost of debt denominated in a foreign currency. Stanley and Block report that 21 percent of respondents report a lower cost of capital in foreign markets than in domestic markets, while 40 percent report higher costs. Another 39 percent of the respondents report similar costs.

Summary of Studies about Weighting Schemes Used to Calculate WACC

The study by Gitman and Mercurio (1982) indicates that the most common weighting scheme employed by respondents is the theoretically correct target capital structure. As one might expect, the authors find that smaller firms are more likely than larger firms to report using an incorrect method such as the cost of the source of project financing. Although all sources of long-term financing should be used in the calculation of WACC, Gitman and Mercurio find that a significant number of surveyed firms, although less than half, exclude some long-term sources of financing. Bruner et al. (1998) find that the majority of best-practice firms participating in their study use the theoretically correct target capital structure weights. The study by Gitman and Vandenberg (2000) finds results consistent with the Gitman and Mercurio (1982) study, but the results suggest a trend toward even greater use of the theoretically correct target capital structure weights and away from using weights reflecting the sources used to finance the project under consideration. Also consistent with finance theory, firms generally include all long-term sources in their calculation of WACC and exclude current liabilities. Inconsistent with finance theory, a large number of firms, although less than half, continue to exclude some long-term sources such as capital leases and preferred stock from the calculation of WACC. The study of firms in the United Kingdom by Arnold and Hatzopoulos (2000) reports the use of market-value weights most frequently, followed by target capital structure weights. These findings apply to firms of all sizes. For large U.K. firms, target capital structure weights are the second-most common weights used. In conclusion, the expected trends and relationships appear to exist for U.S. firms, while U.K. firms appear to be somewhat behind U.S. firms in terms of the weighting schemes used to calculate WACC.

Theory: Estimating the Cost of Debt

Finance theory suggests that firms using long-term debt as a future source of financing should identify and use the after-tax cost of that debt in calculating WACC. This concept has been taught in universities for many years (e.g., Bierman and Smidt 1966; Brigham and Ehrhardt 2008). As discussed earlier, this cost of debt is the cost of raising new long-term debt funds, not the cost of debt already on the firm's balance sheet. The relevant cost of debt to the firm should also reflect the fact that interest expense is tax deductible so that the after-tax cost of debt is lower than the before-tax cost of debt. Firms can convert the before-tax cost of debt (r_{db}) to an after-tax cost of debt (r_{da}) as follows:

$$r_{da} = r_{db}(1 - T), \tag{1}$$

where T is the firm's marginal tax rate.

In the United States, neither preferred nor common stock requires a tax adjustment because firms pay dividends from after-tax profits; that is, dividends do not represent a tax-deductible expense.

Practice: Estimating the Cost of Debt

The discussion that follows summarizes the findings of key survey research about estimating a firm's cost of debt. The two sections focus on studies of U.S. and non-U.S. firms, respectively.

Studies of U.S. Firms

Few survey studies ask respondents about their estimation of the cost of debt. However, the Gitman and Mercurio (1982) study of *Fortune* 1000 firms asks several questions in this regard. Panel A of Table 4.3 shows that 66 percent of responding firms estimate their cost of debt based on the firm's current market-based cost. This compares with the 34 percent who use their firm's historical contractual cost of debt (the cost of debt already on the firm's balance sheet). The authors also ask respondents to indicate which sources of financing they tax-adjust when estimating their cost of capital (the results do not appear in Table 4.3). Forty percent of respondents indicate they tax-adjust the cost of debt, and 40 percent indicate they tax-adjust the cost of capital leases. Another 17 percent indicate they tax-adjust the cost of common stock and 5 percent tax-adjust the cost of preferred stock. Less than 50 percent indicate that they tax-adjust the cost of all components of capital. The authors note the deviation of these responses from finance theory and suggest that the responses may reflect ambiguity in the question.

The Bruner et al. (1998) study finds somewhat similar results in their survey of best-practice firms. While a substantially lower percentage of survey respondents (52 percent) indicate the use of current market-based costs of debt to estimate WACC, a slightly smaller percentage (37 percent) use historical con-tractual costs. Other possible responses of "uncertain" and "n/a" received a com-bined 11 percent of responses. When asked what tax rate they use to convert the before-tax cost of debt to an after-tax cost, 52 percent of respondents indicate they apply a marginal or statutory rate and 37 percent apply a historical average tax rate.

As discussed earlier, Gitman and Vandenberg (2000) replicate the earlier Gitman and Mercurio (1982) study to reveal changes that have occurred since the earlier study. Regarding the calculation of the cost of debt, Gitman and Vandenberg find little difference between the responses of the two studies; that is, 69 percent of respondents say they use current market-based costs versus 66 percent in the earlier study, and 32 percent say they use historical contractual costs versus 34 percent in the earlier study. Gitman and Vandenberg also ask about the tax adjustment of various sources of capital. The results are again similar to the 1982 study in that the majority of respondents indicate they do not tax-adjust all sources of capital. Rather, 43 percent tax-adjust the cost of debt (versus 40 percent in the 1982 study), 32 percent tax-adjust capital leases (versus 30 percent in the earlier study), 11 percent tax-adjust preferred stock (versus 5 percent in the earlier study), and 14 percent tax-adjust common stock (versus 17 percent in the earlier study). Gitman and Vandenberg (pp. 56-57) note that "what is clear from this study is that more respondents tax-adjust debt costs than any other component cost and very few tax-adjust equity costs."

Studies of Non-U.S. Firms

The results of one survey of non-U.S. firms are of interest here (see Panel B of Table 4.3). McLaney et al. (2004) send questionnaires to the 1,292 U.K. firms listed on the U.K. Stock Exchange for which Datastream financial database

TABLE 4.3 Estimating the cost of debt: U.S. and non-U.S. firms

This table shows the responses to questions about how firms estimate the cost of debt financing. All four surveys presented here show the majority or plurality of firms estimate the cost of debt based on the current market-based costs, which is consistent with finance theory. Less than half of survey respondents utilize their historical contractual cost of debt in calculating WACC.

Author(s)	Year published	Population/Sample	Percentage of firms		
			Current market-based cost	Historical contractual cost	Uncertain
A. U.S. firms					
Gitman and Mercurio	1982	*Fortune* 1000 firms (*n* = 177))	66	34	n/a
Bruner, Eades, Harris, and Higgins	1998	U.S. firms listed in *Creating World-Class Financial Management: Strategies of 50 Leading Companies* (1992; *n* = 27)[a]	52	37	11
Gitman & Vandenberg	2000	*Fortune* 1000 firms (*n* = 111)	69	32	n/a
B. Non-U.S. firms					
McLaney, Pointon, Thomas, and Tucker	2004	1,292 U.K. firms listed on the U.K. Stock Exchange for which Datastream reports accounting data (*n* = 193)	41	40	n/a

[a]This publication identifies firms "selected by their peers as being among those with the best financial management. Firms were chosen for excellence in strategic financial risk management, tax and accounting, performance evaluation and other areas of financial management. . . . The companies included were those that were mentioned the greatest number of times by their peers."

reports accounting data. From the 193 usable responses, the authors find that 40 percent of firms estimate their cost of debt using the book value, which they interpret as the rate on the debt currently on the balance sheet. The authors note that this is likely to lead to an inappropriate cost of capital. An almost equal proportion of responding firms (41 percent) indicate they use the market value of debt, which the authors suggest involves using current market rates of debt—a theoretically correct course of action.

Summary of Studies about Estimating the Cost of Debt

Gitman and Mercurio (1982) find that consistent with finance theory, most firms studied (66 percent) estimate the cost of debt based on current market conditions as opposed to basing it on the historical cost of debt. While finance theory suggests tax-adjusting the cost of debt, less than half of surveyed firms (40 percent) do so. Although finance theory indicates firms should not tax-adjust the cost of common equity, 17 percent of respondents do so. The study of best-practice firms conducted by Bruner et al. (1998) finds just 52 percent of firms use a market-based cost of debt. The study by Gitman and Vandenberg (2000) finds results more consistent with the Gitman and Mercurio (1982) study. In fact, their results suggest a slight increase in the percentage of respondents using the theoretically correct market-based cost of debt to calculate WACC. Gitman and Vandenberg (2000) find that fewer than half of participating firms (43 percent) comply with finance theory by tax-adjusting the cost of debt. Consistent with finance theory, their evidence shows that few firms tax-adjust the cost of common equity (14 percent). Evidence from U.K. firms reported by McLaney et al. (2004) suggests that less than half of responding U.K. firms report using the market-value cost of debt (41 percent), while a similar proportion (40 percent) use the book-value cost of debt. One might conclude from these findings that U.S. firms generally use theoretically sound methods to estimate their before-tax cost of debt and that the trend may continue. However, there remains much work to do in educating managers to tax-adjust the cost of debt and not the cost of equity.

Theory: Estimating the Cost of Equity

Like the cost of debt, the cost of equity for WACC estimation purposes is the cost of raising incremental funds, not the cost of equity already on the balance sheet. For both retained earnings and newly issued common stock, the cost of equity can be viewed as the return investors require on their equity investments. If stockholders earn less than the required return, they will sell the stock, causing the stock price to decline. Therefore, the cost of equity represents the return stockholders must earn on their investments to prevent the price of the stock from declining. The only difference between the cost of retained earnings and the cost of issuing new common stock is that firms incur flotation costs when they issue common stock. These flotation costs increase the cost of new common stock above the cost of retained earnings.

The cost of the equity financing raised in the past may not reflect current market conditions; that is, if a firm issued equity financing last year but the market price of the stock has risen, the higher stock price may reflect lower investor-required returns and a lower cost of equity capital. Because WACC is forward-looking, it should reflect the cost of raising funds in the current environment.

There are several different theoretically sound methods of estimating the cost of retained earnings (r_e), given that their assumptions are met. One common method is the dividend discount model in which an analyst begins with the expected dividend yield and then adds the expected future growth rate of the dividend.

$$r_e = \frac{D_1}{P_0} + g,$$

(2)

where D_1 = expected dividend payment at the end of year 1;

P_0 = current market price of the stock, which is assumed to be in equilibrium;

D_1/P_0 = expected dividend yield; and

g = expected growth rate of the dividend, which is assumed to be constant to infinity.

This model calls for using the current stock price, the forecasted dividend in the next period (D_1), and the expected dividend growth rate. Forecasting the growth rate can be done by using analysts' forecasts, by basing it on past growth rates, or by using a model like the earnings retention model (Ehrhardt 1994).

A second model indicated by Ehrhardt (1994) for estimating a firm's cost of retained earnings is the capital asset pricing model (CAPM). This model assumes investors hold efficiently diversified portfolios. Because such portfolios eliminate unsystematic risk, investors require compensation only for the systematic risk of assets they hold.

$$r_e = r_{RF} + b_i(k_M - r_{RF}),$$

(3)

where r_{RF} = risk-free rate of return,

b_i = the systematic risk of the firm's common stock as measured by beta, and

k_M = expected return on the market portfolio.

Other methods of estimating a firm's cost of equity include the bond-yield-plus-risk-premium model, the earnings/price approach, and multifactor models. The bond-yield-plus-risk-premium approach is described in many finance textbooks such as Brigham and Ehrhardt (2008). This method recognizes that investors require a higher return on a firm's equity investments than on the firm's fixed-income securities. If a firm can identify the additional return that investors require on the firm's equity above the return they require on the firm's debt (the risk premium), adding this premium to the yield to maturity on the firm's long-term debt leads to an estimate of the firm's cost of equity. The earnings/price approach defines the cost of equity as the ratio of a firm's earnings per share divided by the stock price. While not used today, this model was very popular in the 1960s and 1970s. Multifactor models (some based on arbitrage pricing theory, or APT) involve finding stockholders' required rate of return based on more than one independent variable, unlike CAPM, which considers just one independent variable, beta (Ehrhardt 1994, p. 83–93).

The cost of issuing new common stock exceeds a firm's cost of retained earnings because issuing new shares of common stock involves flotation costs. The dividend discount model described in the preceding text for estimating the cost of a firm's retained earnings can be adjusted to estimate the cost of issuing new common stock. We describe this in equation (4), which is identical to equation (2), except the current stock price is reduced by flotation costs (Ehrhardt 1994, pp. 136–139).

$$r_e = \frac{D_1}{P_0(1-F)} + g,$$

(4)

where F = flotation costs as a percentage of the market price of the stock.

Although this approach frequently appears in textbooks, this treatment for dealing with flotation costs is flawed. When using equation (4), flotation costs increase r_e and WACC by a fixed percentage that remains a factor for the life of the project; that is, future cash flows from the project are discounted at the higher WACC to determine the project's net present value. However, the flotation costs are not an ongoing expense for the firm. Instead, flotation costs are cash outflows occurring at the initiation of a project and affect only the project's initial cash outlay. Therefore, a more appropriate method of reflecting flotation costs in capital budgeting analysis is to include this dollar cost in the initial outlay of the project. An analyst can calculate the flotation cost of the project in dollars and use it to increase the initial cash outlay of the project. The firm then uses its WACC that reflects the firm's cost of retained earnings to discount future cash flows.

Practice: Estimating the Cost of Equity

The sections that follow summarize the results of key survey studies investigating how firms estimate their cost of equity. The two sections consider studies of U.S. and non-U.S. firms, respectively.

Studies of U.S. Firms

Numerous survey studies ask how firms estimate their cost of equity capital. In an early study, Pflomn (1963, p. 40) notes, "Some companies believe that expenditures made from retained earnings incur no capital cost" (Pflomn offers no percentages). He also points out that there is a cost of retained earnings because by retaining earnings, a firm acquires new equity capital just as if it had sold new shares of common stock. This concept is recognized in the literature as early as 1963.

Petty, Scott, and Bird (1975) send questionnaires to the controller of each *Fortune* 500 firm and receive responses from 109 firms. One question the authors ask survey participants is how they determine their firm's cost of equity. The authors describe the responses as mixed: 31 percent of responses "offered little or no meaning," 30 percent indicate earnings models (presumably the earnings-price ratio), and 30 percent indicate dividend models. The most common dividend model they describe is "dividend yield plus growth rate." Petty, Scott, and Bird note considerable differences in the "level of sophistication" of the methods in use.

As one might expect, different surveys list different possible answers for respondents to select. Table 4.4 presents the results of five studies of U.S. firms that address cost of equity issues. The study of *Fortune* 1000 firms conducted by Gitman and Mercurio (1982) asks how firms estimate the cost of equity. The most common response is "return required by investors" (36 percent). While this response does not shed light on how firms determine what return investors require, it does suggest the theoretically correct notion that a firm's cost of retained earnings is the return investors require on the firm's common stock. The second-most common response is more specific about the method employed—namely, "current dividend yield plus an estimate of growth" (26 percent), which is a variation of the dividend discount model. This is followed by "market return adjusted for risk" (23 percent), which may be interpreted as CAPM. Two other methods receiving responses are earnings-price ratio (16 percent) and "cost of debt plus a risk premium" (13 percent). Only a small percentage of respondents indicate "historical dividend yield plus estimate of growth" (3 percent), which is another dividend discount model, and "dividend yield estimate only" (2 percent).

Gitman and Mercurio (1982, p. 24) conclude, "A bit surprising is the fact that a number of respondents use approaches not reflecting future expectations, but rather relying solely upon the firm's past behavior to estimate equity cost." They report that only 16 percent of responding firms recognize the higher cost of issuing new common stock in their cost of equity calculations. Clearly, this is inconsistent with finance theory, which identifies a difference due to flotation costs.

Petry and Sprow (1993) ask a similar question but offer different alternative answers. Recall that Petry and Sprow survey a sample of *Business Week* 1000 firms and group respondents into broad categories based on industry. For firms in the industrial/retail and financial/services sectors, the most common method of estimating the cost of equity (41 percent of firms in both groups) is the CAPM. Gitman and Mercurio (1982) did not offer CAPM as a response, although they listed an answer that could be interpreted as CAPM—specifically, "market return adjusted for risk."

Petry and Sprow (1993) find the second-most common method used by firms in the industrial/retail and financial/services sectors is the "bond rate + equity risk premium" (29 percent for industrial/retail and 33 percent for financial/services). Ranked third is the earnings-price ratio (14 percent and 22 percent, respectively), followed by a dividend discount model (dividend yield plus estimated growth). For firms classified as utilities, the most common method is the dividend discount model (62 percent), followed by the CAPM (50 percent), "debt yield + equity risk premium" (47 percent), and earnings-price ratio (21 percent). Firms classified as utilities indicate greater use of "miscellaneous" methods to estimate the cost of equity than the other two groups. The miscellaneous methods emphasize comparable companies or are methods mandated by regulatory authorities.

Bruner et al. (1998) ask respondents how they estimate the cost of equity. The fact that firms participating in this study are best-practice firms may explain the high percentage of firms indicating they use CAPM (81 percent). Later, we discuss other findings from this study regarding the application of CAPM.

Recall that Gitman and Vandenberg (2000) designed their study to emulate the Gitman and Mercurio (1982) study in terms of population, sample, and questions in order to reveal changes over time. One difference between the two studies is that the latter lists more possible responses to the question about how firms calculate the cost of equity. Specifically, the 2000 study added responses of "CAPM," "arbitrage pricing theory," (APT) and "other." As in the earlier study, the 2000 study finds that the most common method of estimating the cost of equity is "investors' required return" (70 percent versus 36 percent in the 1982 study), followed by CAPM (65 percent). Other responses include "cost of debt plus a risk premium for equity" (17 percent) and "market return adjusted for risk" (14 percent). Just 1 percent of respondents report using APT to estimate investor-required returns. Finally, Gitman and Vandenberg find that the percentage of firms differentiating between the cost of retained earnings and the cost of issuing new common stock is just 11 percent, down from 16 percent in the 1982 study by Gitman and Mercurio.

Graham and Harvey (2001) also ask survey participants how they estimate their cost of equity. Their population includes members of the Financial Executives Institute who work for both small and large firms. Graham and Harvey define large firms as those having annual sales greater than $1 billion. They ask survey participants if their firms calculate the cost of equity, and if so, how. Just 64 percent of respondents indicate they explicitly estimate their cost

TABLE 4.4 Methods used to estimate the cost of equity: U.S. firms

This table shows how U.S. firms respond to questions about how they estimate their cost of equity capital. Three of the responses are variations of dividend discount models (DDM) and are labeled as such. Finance theory suggests a firm's cost of equity is the return stockholders require on their investments in the firm's common equity. Several answers can be interpreted as indicating just that. One of the most common methods of determining the return stockholder require on equity is to use the CAPM, which is a very popular response in all surveys where that response is listed.

| Author(s) | Year published | Population | Percentage of firms | | | | | | | | | | | | |
| | | | Investors' required return 'Whatever our investors tell us they require' | Variations of the DDM | | | | | | Market return adjusted for risk | Capital asset pricing model CAPM | Multibeta CAPM (arbitrage pricing theory) | Other | Don't calculate cost of equity |
				Average historical return on the stock	Historical dividend yield plus estimated growth	Current dividend yield plus estimated growth	Dividend yield estimate only	Cost of debt plus premium for equity	Earnings-price ratio					
Gitman and Mercurio[b]	1982	Fortune 1000 firms (n = 177)	36	n/a	3	26	2	13	16	23	n/a	n/a	n/a	n/a
Petry and Sprow[b]	1993	Business Week 1000 firms (n = 151)												
		Industrial/Retail	n/a	n/a	n/a	9	n/a	28	14	n/a	41	n/a	14[c]	17
		Financial/Services	n/a	n/a	n/a	11	n/a	33	22	n/a	41	n/a	32[c]	19
		Utilities	n/a	n/a	n/a	62	n/a	47	21	n/a	50	n/a	21[c]	3

Study	Year	Sample												
Bruner, Eades, Harris, and Higgins	1998	U.S. firms listed in *Creating World-Class Financial Management: Strategies of 50 Leading Companies* (1992; n = 27)[d]	n/a	n/a	n/a	n/a	n/a	n/a	n/a	n/a	n/a	81	n/a	n/a n/a
Gitman and Vandenberg[b]	2000	*Fortune* 1000 firms (n = 111)	70	n/a	n/a	5	9	0	17	3	14	65	1	5 n/a
Graham and Harvey[b,c]	2001	Medium-size and large firms/members of the Financial Executives Institute (n = 392)	n/a	14	39	n/a	16	n/a	n/a	n/a	73	34	7	n/a

[a]Gitman and Vandenberg (2000) note that the two studies do not give a definition of "return required by investors," so the findings may suffer from ambiguity. However, on page 57, they conclude that "it is clear respondents considered this term to be a synonym for CAPM."

[b]Multiple responses are permitted.

[c]Reflects the percentage of responses for "miscellaneous" and "bank short-term rate + equity and maturity risk premium."

[d]This publication identifies firms "selected by their peers as being among those with the best financial management. Firms were chosen for excellence in strategic financial risk management, tax and accounting, performance evaluation and other areas of financial management. . . . The companies included were those mentioned the greatest number of times by their peers."

[e]Responses of "always use" or "almost always use."

of equity. For those firms, the method receiving the highest percentage of responses for always or almost always use is the CAPM (73 percent), and the second-most frequent response is the average historical return on the stock (39 percent). The third-most popular method is CAPM with extra risk factors (34 percent), classified in Table 4.4 as APT, and the fourth-most popular method is to use the dividend discount model (dividend yield plus the growth rate). Sixteen percent of respondents say they apply the dividend discount model method always or almost always. Two other listed methods for estimating cost of equity are "whatever our investors tell us they require" (14 percent) and "[the return] required by regulators" (7 percent). Graham and Harvey find that firms with the following characteristics are more likely to estimate the cost of equity using CAPM: large firms, public firms, firms with low leverage, firms with small management ownership, and firms with CEOs that have MBA degrees. The authors note that less use of CAPM by smaller firms is consistent with the notion that estimating the beta of small firms is more difficult than for large firms. Meanwhile, the authors find that small firms are more likely to determine the cost of equity based on whatever their investors tell them they require. This may be explained by the notion that the owners of small firms are more likely to directly influence firm policy.

Studies of Non-U.S. Firms

Table 4.5 presents the results of several studies showing how a variety of non-U.S. firms estimate their cost of equity. The study by Kester et al. (1999) reports the findings of a survey of Asia-Pacific firms listed on Asian stock exchanges. They send questionnaires to all firms listed on the following stock exchanges (the integers represent the number of responding firms from each exchange): Australian Stock Exchange (57), Stock Exchange of Hong Kong (29), Jakarta Stock Exchange (16), Kuala Lumpur Stock Exchange (35), Philippine Stock Exchange (35), and Stock Exchange of Singapore (54). Regarding how firms estimate their cost of equity, the survey provides just four possible responses, and respondents may indicate all that apply.

The findings show that only Australian firms indicate that CAPM (73 percent) is the most popular means of estimating the cost of equity. Other methods employed by Australian firms are the dividend yield plus growth rate method (16 percent) and the cost of debt plus risk premium method (11 percent). The relative popularity of these three methods among firms from Indonesia and the Philippines is exactly the opposite of Australia; that is, the CAPM is the least used method by Indonesian and Philippine firms (0 percent and 24 percent, respectively), the dividend yield plus growth rate is the second-least used method (33 percent and 35 percent, respectively), and the most popular method is the cost of debt plus risk premium (53 percent and 59 percent, respectively).

TABLE 4.5 Methods used to estimate the cost of equity: Non-U.S. firms

This table shows responses to questions about how non-U.S. firms estimate their cost of equity. The table suggests that a dividend discount model (current dividend yield plus estimated growth) is the most popular method among Asian firms (except Australia) and CAPM is the most popular method among European firms surveyed.

Author(s)	Year published	Population/Sample	Percentage of firms							
			Whatever our investors tell us they require	Average historical return on the stock	Current dividend yield plus estimated growth	Cost of debt plus premium for equity	Capital asset pricing model	Multibeta CAPM (arbitrage pricing theory)	By regulatory decisions	Other
Kester, Chang, Echanis, Haikal, Ids, Skully, Tsui, and Wang[a]	1999	Firms on various Asian stock exchanges								
		Australia (n = 57)	n/a	n/a	16	11	73	n/a	n/a	4
		Hong Kong (n = 29)	n/a	n/a	54	23	27	n/a	n/a	4
		Indonesia (n = 16)	n/a	n/a	33	53	0	n/a	n/a	13
		Malaysia (n = 35)	n/a	n/a	50	38	6	n/a	n/a	6
		The Philippines (n = 35)	n/a	n/a	35	59	24	n/a	n/a	0
		Singapore (n = 54)	n/a	n/a	43	43	17	n/a	n/a	9
Arnold and Hatzopoulos	2000	Large, midsize, and small U.K. firms listed in the Times 1000	Results discussed in text.							

(Continued)

TABLE 4.5 (cont'd) Methods used to estimate the cost of equity: Non-U.S. firms

Author(s)	Year published	Population/Sample	Percentage of firms							
			Whatever our investors tell us they require	Average historical return on the stock	Current dividend yield plus estimated growth	Cost of debt plus premium for equity	Capital asset pricing model	Multibeta CAPM (arbitrage pricing theory)	By regulatory decisions	Other
Brounen, Jong, and Koekijk[a,b]	2004	European firms with 25 or more employees/Amadeus data set of Bureau Van Kijk								
		United Kingdom (n = 68)	19	31	10[c]	n/a	47	27	16	n/a
		The Netherlands (n = 52)	45	31	11[c]	n/a	56	15	4	n/a
		Germany (n = 132)	39	18	10[c]	n/a	34	16	0	n/a
		France (n = 61)	34	27	10[c]	n/a	45	30	16	n/a
Baker, Dutta, and Saadi[a,d]	2009	762 Canadian firms on the Toronto Stock Exchange with select information available from Stock Guide database (n = 214)	20	n/a	13	52	37	7	6	53[e]

[a]Multiple responses are permitted.
[b]Responses of "always" or "almost always" use.
[c]Actual response is "backed out of discounted dividend/earnings model, e.g. Price = Div/(cost of cap – growth)."
[d]Responses of "often" or "always."
[e]Includes earnings-price ratio (22 percent), average historical return on common stock adjusted for risk (14 percent), and accounting return on equity (18 percent).

For firms in Hong Kong and Malaysia, the order of popularity of the three methods is different again, with the dividend yield plus growth rate the most popular (54 percent and 50 percent, respectively). The second-most popular method for Hong Kong firms is CAPM (27 percent), followed by the cost of debt plus risk premium (23 percent). For Malaysian firms, the second-most popular method is the debt yield plus risk premium method (38 percent), followed by CAPM (6 percent). Firms in the remaining country, Singapore, employ the dividend yield plus growth rate and debt yield plus risk premium about equally (43 percent), while CAPM is the least popular method (9 percent). Perhaps the most important observation from this study is that Asia-Pacific firms participating in this study employ theoretically correct methods to a large extent. However, the authors did not list theoretically incorrect methods in the survey, and 13 percent of Indonesian firms and 9 percent of Singaporean firms indicate they use "other" methods, which may be theoretically incorrect.

Arnold and Hatzopoulos (2000) ask U.K. firms to choose from two alternatives when calculating their WACC: (1) using the CAPM for equity and the market rate of return on debt capital or (2) using some method other than CAPM with the cost of debt derived from current market interest rates. The application of CAPM appears to be the only differentiation because the debt components of the two alternatives can be interpreted as being identical. The results indicate that 50 percent of small firms, 68 percent of midsize firms, and 79 percent of large firms use CAPM. This evidence suggests that the application of the CAPM is popular among all sizes of U.K. firms that participated in this study.

Another study addressing how non-U.S. firms estimate their cost of equity comes from Brounen, de Jong, and Koedijk (2004). The authors survey firms having 25 or more employees in the United Kingdom, the Netherlands, Germany, and France. They send questionnaires to about 6,500 firms and receive 313 usable responses (68 from the United Kingdom, 52 from the Netherlands, 132 from Germany, and 61 from France). Their questions are identical to those asked by Graham and Harvey (2001) in order to facilitate a comparison of responses to those from U.S. firms. When asked if firms explicitly calculate their cost of equity, the response is yes for 74 percent of U.K. firms, 60 percent of the Netherlands firms, 59 percent of French firms, and 53 percent of German firms. This compares to 64 percent of U.S. firms in the Graham and Harvey study.

In follow-up questions, participants could identify more than one method employed to estimate the cost of equity. Table 4.5 presents the percentage of respondents indicating they always or almost always use each method. The percentage of firms indicating "whatever our investors tell us they require" ranges from 19 percent for U.K. firms to 45 percent for firms in the Netherlands. In fact, this is the most common response for German firms (39 percent) and the second-most common for firms in France and the Netherlands (34 percent and 45 percent, respectively). The usage by all four European countries exceeds the usage by U.S. firms as reported in the Graham and Harvey study (14 percent).

Brounen, de Jong, and Koedijk (2004) find that private firms are more likely to respond "whatever our investors tell us they require" and public firms are more likely to favor the application of beta, which the authors describe as rational given the lack of availability of betas for private firms. In the United Kingdom, the Netherlands, Germany, and France, the most common method of estimating the cost of equity capital (other than "whatever our investors tell us they require") is the CAPM, indicated by 47 percent, 56 percent, 34 percent, and 45 percent of firms, respectively. Despite the popularity of CAPM, these percentages are still below the percentage for U.S. firms (73 percent). For firms in all four European countries, the next most popular method used to estimate the cost of equity is the historical return on common stock. This is reported by firms in the United Kingdom, the Netherlands, Germany, and France as being used always or almost always by 31 percent, 31 percent, 18 percent, and 27 percent of respondents, respectively. According to Graham and Harvey (2001), 39 percent of U.S. firms use this method. Between 10 percent and 11 percent of firms in each of the four countries indicate they back the cost of equity out of the dividend discount model compared to 16 percent of U.S. firms.

Brunen, de Jong, and Koedijk (2004) find a positive relationship between the application of CAPM to estimate the cost of equity and the stated goal of maximization of shareholder wealth, as opposed to other goals such as "maximizing profits," "maximizing sustainable growth," "market position, service, quality," "cost control, productivity, and efficiency," "continuity," and "optimizing leverage." They also find that firms with the following characteristics are more likely to employ CAPM: larger firms, exchange-listed firms, and firms where the CEO has a long tenure with the firm.

A study of U.K. firms by McLaney et al. (2004) finds that 47 percent of responding firms utilize CAPM to estimate the cost of equity. This percentage is well below the 79 percent of large U.K. firms using CAPM reported by Arnold and Hatzopoulos (2000). McLaney et al. also report that 28 percent of responding firms employ a version of the dividend discount model and 27 percent employ an earnings yield model such as the price-to-earnings ratio.

Baker, Dutta, and Saadi (2009) find that 75 percent of responding Canadian firms estimate their cost of equity capital and that larger firms and firms managed by CEOs with MBA degrees are more likely to be in this group. The authors ask the firms that estimate their cost of equity what methods they use, and they report the percentage of firms employing different methods either often or always. Baker, Dutta, and Saadi find that the most popular response is "judgment" (60 percent), followed by cost of debt plus equity risk premium (52 percent), CAPM (37 percent), earnings-price ratios (22 percent), and "whatever our investors tell us they require" (20 percent). Dividend growth models and multifactor asset pricing models are used often or always by just 13 percent and 7 percent of respondents, respectively. These results contrast with the results of the Brounen, de Jong, and Koedijk (2004) study of European firms, as those firms tend to use the cost of debt plus an equity premium more frequently and use CAPM and multifactor asset pricing models less frequently.

Summary of Studies about Estimating the Cost of Equity

An early study of U.S. firms by Petty, Scott, and Bird (1975) finds that just one-third of respondents employ theoretically sound methods to estimate the cost of equity. Gitman and Mercurio (1982) find that the majority of survey participants use theoretically correct methods. Petry and Sprow (1993) also find that most responding firms use theoretically correct methods, and Gitman and Vandenberg (2000) later provide evidence that a trend continues toward even greater use of theoretically correct methods to estimate the cost of equity.

In 2001, Graham and Harvey survey both small and large firms and report that just 64 percent of respondents indicate they explicitly estimate their cost of equity. They find that firms with the following characteristics (as well as others) are more likely to use CAPM to measure the cost of equity: large firms, public firms, and firms with CEOs who have MBA degrees. Meanwhile, the authors find that small firms are more likely to determine the cost of equity based on whatever their investors tell them they require, which may be explained by the notion that the owners of small firms are more likely to directly influence firm policy.

Several studies of non-U.S. firms provide evidence about estimating the cost of equity. Kester et al. (1999) find that most surveyed firms in the Asia-Pacific region use theoretically correct methods to estimate the cost of equity. However, their findings suggest that most firms in the Asia-Pacific countries surveyed (with the possible exception of Australia) have some progress to make before they utilize these methods to the same extent as U.S. firms. Brounen, de Jong, and Koedijk (2004) find that firms in the United Kingdom, the Netherlands, Germany, and France commonly employ theoretically correct methods to estimate the cost of equity. Their findings suggest that firms from these countries have generally adopted theoretically correct methods for estimating their cost of equity. McLaney et al. (2004) study U.K. firms and find substantial deviation from finance theory in the use of methods for estimating cost of equity.

Theory: Use of Multiple Hurdle Rates

Finance theory suggests that firms should not use a single hurdle rate for all projects. The basic notion is that the higher the risk of the project, the higher the hurdle rate should be (Ehrhardt 1994). The rationale for this is that adopting projects equally as risky as the firm is unlikely to increase firm risk. If firm risk remains unchanged, the firm's cost of capital also will remain unchanged (other conditions being equal). Under these circumstances, employing the firm's cost of capital as a hurdle rate is appropriate. However, if a firm adopts projects that are likely to increase firm risk, the firm's sources of capital are likely to increase the return they require on their investment in the firm. When investors require higher returns, the firm's cost of capital rises assuming other conditions remain unchanged.

Firms can employ sensitivity analysis, scenario analysis, and Monte Carlo simulation to evaluate the total risk of a project. This may be appropriate when total risk is the relevant risk to investors or when the firm is unable to measure other types of project risk such as within-firm risk and systematic risk. When systematic risk is the most relevant risk, firms can measure the systematic risk of a project using such techniques as the pure-play approach or the multiple-regression approach (e.g., Ehrhardt 1994). Firms can also attempt to evaluate within-firm risk, which involves measuring or estimating the covariance of project returns with the firm's current returns.

Regardless of which type of risk is most relevant, some projects are likely to increase firm risk or lower firm risk. If a firm operates with two divisions and each division has a different level of risk, finance theory suggests the firm should establish divisional costs of capital to utilize as discount rates for projects being evaluated by each division. Further, if a high-risk division is considering a project that is more risky than the division itself (i.e., adopting the project is likely to increase the division's risk), the firm should use a hurdle rate that is higher than the division's cost of capital. Ehrhardt (1994, p. 120) states

> there is no simple guideline for determining the number of different costs of capital you [a firm] need. You may have multiple divisions that compete in the same line of business; it makes sense to use the same cost of capital for each of these divisions. On the other hand, you may have a single division that competes in more than one line of business; in this case you might want multiple costs of capital for different projects within this division.

Practice: The Use of Multiple Hurdle Rates

The following sections synthesize the findings of key survey research about the use of multiple hurdle rates in capital budgeting. The two sections discuss surveys of U.S. and non-U.S. firms, respectively.

Studies of U.S. Firms

While finance theory tends to address the need for multiple hurdle rates in terms of differences in the risk of individual projects and differences in the risk of corporate divisions, there are clearly other means of identifying risk differences.

For example, a firm with subsidiaries that are not under corporate control may be viewed as more risky than subsidiaries or divisions that are under corporate control. Similarly, a division with several different product lines may assign different costs of capital to each product line. Firms may regard capital projects involving the replacement of equipment as less risky than projects involving expansion into new markets or product lines. Finally, firms may consider foreign projects as being more risky than domestic projects because of the addition of currency risk, political risk, and other risks not associated with domestic projects.

In the Christy (1966) study discussed earlier, the author finds that just 13 percent of respondents think firms should adopt all capital projects that exceed the firm's cost of capital. Christy suggests that unforeseen problems can cause a project to be less profitable than estimated due to overly optimistic forecasts, early obsolescence of the product being considered, unexpected competition, and so forth. Therefore, the author argues that firms desiring a 10 percent long-run return on a project must require a 15 percent or 20 percent return on projects. According to Christie (p. 24), this extra 5 percent or 10 percent is a risk allowance such that "acceptable projects must promise to return the cost of capital plus a risk premium."

Table 4.6 presents findings from survey studies of U.S. firms beginning with Brigham (1975), who surveys the managers of 33 "quite large" firms. The sample is not random, and the respondents have participated in university programs that focus on capital budgeting issues. The survey asks participants how their firms make various capital budgeting decisions. Brigham finds that when survey participants are asked about the hurdle rates used in capital budgeting (multiple responses were permitted), 48 percent of respondents indicate they employ one rate for all projects. The next most popular response is the application of different rates for different subsidiaries, divisions, product lines, and domestic versus overseas projects (45 percent). Thirty-five percent of respondents indicate they employ different rates for different types of investments (replacement, expansion, etc.) and 23 percent report they vary the hurdle rate based on the risk of the specific project. Brigham observes that although the responses suggest many firms fail to perform as theory suggests, every firm indicates that judgment is very important in making capital budgeting decisions; that is, some projects that fail discounted cash flow (DCF) analysis may be accepted, while others that pass DCF analysis may be rejected if projected cash flows are considered risky. Therefore, Brigham (1975, p. 39) states that "implicitly, but in an unspecified manner, differential hurdle rates are being applied."

When Brigham (1975) asks respondents if their company has trended toward greater emphasis on quantitative factors rather than qualitative factors in making capital budgeting decisions in recent years, 92 percent reply affirmatively. In fact, 96 percent indicate they are likely to move "toward more quantification of project risk," 50 percent say they are likely to move "toward greater use of

TABLE 4.6 Use of multiple hurdle rates: U.S. firms

This table shows responses to questions about the hurdle rates used for projects with different risk. While finance theory suggests that firms use risk-adjusted discount rates, the responses of U.S. firms are clearly mixed. However, data in the last column suggests that the majority of U.S. firms select hurdle rates consistent with this theory.

Author(s)	Year published	Population/Sample	One rate for all projects	Different rates for different subsidiaries, divisions, product lines, or foreign projects	Different rates for different types of investments[a]	Based on project risk
Brigham[b]	1975	Select executives who completed a university program (large firms/not randomly selected; $n = 33$)	48	45	35	23
Ross	1986	Large firms in select industries/not selected randomly ($n = 12$)	Results discussed in text.			
Gitman and Mercurio	1982	*Fortune* 1000 firms ($n = 177$)	33	n/a	10[c]	60
Bierman[b]	1993	Largest 100 *Fortune* 500 industrial firms ($n = 74$)	n/a	35[d]	n/a	72[e]
Bruner, Eades, Harris, and Higgins	1998	U.S. firms listed in *Creating World-Class Financial Management: Strategies of 50 Leading Companies* (1992; $n = 27$)	41	n/a	n/a	59[f]

Gitman and Vandenberg	2000	Fortune 1000 firms (n = 111)	23	n/a	16[c]	61
Graham and Harvey	2001	Medium-size and large firms/members of the Financial Executives Institute (n = 392)	Results discussed in text.			
Block	2003	Fortune 1000 firms (n = 298)	53	47[g]	n/a	n/a

[a]Project types include replacement, expansion, new products, and so forth.
[b]Participants can indicate more than one.
[c]Actual response is "group projects into risk classes."
[d]Actual response is "based on the division's risk."
[e]Actual response is "based on the risk or nature of the project."
[f]This is the total responses of yes and "sometimes" to the question about whether the firm adjusts its cost of capital to reflect project risk.
[g]This is the percentage of respondents indicating they require different returns on projects "for different divisions, subsidiaries or projects."

multiple hurdle rates," and 50 percent indicate they are likely to move "toward more frequent revisions of hurdle rates." Among his conclusions, Brigham (p. 25) suggests that "sophisticated techniques for quantifying risk analysis are . . . gaining ground." He also notes that the firms in his sample are large and relatively sophisticated, so inferences cannot be made about the practices of industrial firms generally and certainly not for small firms. As Brigham notes, although most firms use cost of capital methods that are inconsistent with the academic literature, there is movement in the right (theoretically correct) direction.

Ross (1986) surveys 12 large manufacturing firms that account for about one-third of the combined sales of industries in which they operate: steel, paper, and aluminum. He finds that the hurdle rate employed by all 12 firms to evaluate large projects is close to the corporate cost of capital. However, only 33 percent of firms use the same rate for small projects, while the remaining 67 percent of firms use a higher rate for both small and medium-size projects. When asked to specify the rates employed for projects of different sizes, just six firms provided the rates for small and midsize projects. For small projects, the range is 35 percent to 60 percent, and for midsize projects, the range is 25 percent to 40 percent. Ross finds that firms conducting thorough analysis of their smaller projects tend to be firms that employ the same discount rate for all projects.

Both the Gitman and Mercurio (1982) and the Gitman and Vandenberg (2000) studies ask respondents about risk-classification procedures for projects. The most common response in the two studies is "individually measure project risk" (60 percent and 61 percent, respectively), followed by "do not specifically differentiate project risk" (33 percent and 23 percent, respectively). The fewest responses are for "group projects into risk classes," which is classified in Table 4.6 as "differentiate rates for different types of investments." This answer receives just 10 percent and 16 percent of responses, respectively. Gitman and Vandenberg note that finding 23 percent of respondents that do not differentiate the risk of projects is consistent with the findings of Bruner et al. (1998). Gitman and Vandenberg (p. 60) conclude that "clearly, most firms appear to differentiate project risk. Those firms that do consider risk differences most often do so on a project-by-project basis, rather than on a group basis"

Bierman (1993) surveys the largest 100 *Fortune* 500 industrial firms. When asked what discount rates they employ, respondents could designate more than one rate, and on average, each respondent identified two discount rates. Of the respondents, 93 percent indicate they use a WACC. About 72 percent of responding firms say they select a discount rate "based on the risk or the nature of the project," which includes such classifications as whether the project is for replacement or expansion. Another 35 percent of respondents indicate they apply a hurdle rate that is "based on the division's risk."

Bruner et al. (1998) offer survey respondents three possible answers to a question about whether they adjust their cost of capital to reflect individual project risk. To this question, 26 percent respond yes and 33 percent respond "sometimes."

The remaining 41 percent indicate that they do not adjust the cost of capital to reflect individual project risk. The authors also find that 48 percent of respondents distinguish between strategic and operational projects.

Poterba and Summers (1995) send surveys to the CEOs of *Fortune* 1000 firms and receive 228 usable responses. They report finding that the average difference between the lowest and highest discount rates used by surveyed firms is 11.2 percent. Based on responses to an open-ended question about the types of projects to which firms apply the lower and higher rates leads the authors to conclude that firms apply the lower rates for such reasons as defending market share and strategic decisions like entering new markets, similar to the finding of Bruner et al. (1998). Poterba and Summers also find a relationship between the background of the CEOs and hurdle rates such that CEOs with finance backgrounds have hurdle rates that are 150 to 200 basis points higher than those with other backgrounds. They also find no relationship between traditional proxies for risk (e.g., beta) and the hurdle rates used by the firms in the study.

Block (2003) surveys the top financial officers of *Fortune* magazine's listing of the 1,000 largest U.S. firms and receives responses from 298 firms. When asked if they require different rates of return "for different divisions, subsidiaries or projects," 53 percent indicate they do not. Block (p. 350) concludes that "in spite of much progress by corporate management in regard to capital budgeting procedures in general, a similar pattern is not evident for the topic of divisional cost of capital." Block also investigates how firms view the risk of foreign projects relative to domestic projects. He notes that while some people argue that foreign projects expose firms to greater political risk and exchange rate risk, among other risks (e.g., Shaked 1986), others argue that the portfolio effect generated by adopting foreign projects actually reduces firm risk (e.g., Shapiro 1983). Of the participants in the Block study, 78 percent say the hurdle rate should be higher for foreign investments, 13 percent say it should be lower, and 9 percent offer no opinion. Block finds that firms with high ratios of fixed to total assets and high levels of revenue are more likely to employ divisional costs of capital. Block (p. 350) writes that "one can only surmise that when firms become increasingly dependent on large, permanent asset acquisitions, the depth of analysis increases."

As a follow-up question, Block (2003) asks the 139 firms that use divisional costs of capital what the primary consideration is for determining the divisional cost of capital. The question lists three possible variables and asks respondents to rank each in terms of its level of importance (first, second, or third). The variable receiving the highest number of responses as being most important is "risk" (87 percent), followed by "strategic importance of the division" (13 percent) and "division's ability to raise its own capital" (0 percent).

When Graham and Harvey (2001) ask, "How frequently would your company use the following discount rates when evaluating a new project in an overseas market?" 59 percent say they always or almost always use "the discount rate for the entire company." Another 51 percent either always or almost always use a "risk-matched discount rate for this particular project (considering both country and industry)." Thirty-five percent of respondents report using "the discount rate for the overseas market (country discount rate)," while another 16 percent indicate using "a divisional discount rate (if the project line of business matches a domestic division)." Finally, 10 percent of respondents employ "a different discount rate for each component cash flow that has a different risk characteristic (e.g., apply different discount rates to depreciation versus operating cash flows)." Graham and Harvey note that firms could logically adjust the cash flows for risk to avoid adjusting the discount rate for risk. However, they find firms not adjusting cash flows for foreign exchange risk are also less likely to adjust the discount rate for the risk for overseas projects. They find that firms with the following characteristics are more likely to utilize a company-wide discount rate for overseas projects: growth firms, small firms, firms with foreign exposure, and firms with short-tenured CEOs.

Surveys of Non-U.S. Firms

When Kester et al. (1999) survey Asia-Pacific firms about capital budgeting practices, they ask managers which approaches they use "to determine the minimum acceptable rate of return to evaluate proposed capital investments." The most frequent response of Australian firms is a single discount rate (WACC) for all projects (48 percent). Respondents from four countries identify the cost of the specific source of capital used to finance the project as being the most utilized rate. Those countries include Hong Kong (57 percent), Indonesia (43 percent), Malaysia (47 percent), and Singapore (51 percent). Survey participants from the Philippines indicate the most common discount rate is based on the risk of the project (52 percent). Table 4.7 presents the response percentages for each country for each approach to WACC selection.

Kester et al. (1999) also ask respondents who employ multiple risk-adjusted discount rates how they determine those rates for projects (the results are not in the table). The authors offer respondents three brief descriptions of methods and ask them to select the one that best describes their own method. The most common method used by managers in every country (Australia, 62 percent; Hong Kong, 50 percent; Indonesia, 100 percent; Malaysia, 63 percent; the Philippines, 50 percent; and Singapore, 85 percent) is to classify projects into different risk classes based on the type of project (such as replacement and expansion), then apply risk-adjusted discount rates centered on the firm's average cost of capital. This approach is consistent with finance theory. For firms in Malaysia and Singapore, the second-most common method (25 percent and 15 percent, respectively) is a two-step process in which divisions are assigned divisional costs of capital. Within each division, managers utilize the divisional cost of capital for average-risk projects, a discount rate higher than the divisional

TABLE 4.7 Use of multiple hurdle rates: Non-U.S. firms

This table shows responses to questions about the hurdle rates used for projects with different risk. While finance theory suggests that firms use risk-adjusted discount rates, the responses of non-U.S. firms indicate that the majority of firms in just one surveyed country use a rate based on project risk: the Philippines.

Author(s)	Year published	Population/Sample	One rate for all projects	Based on project risk	Cost of specific source of project financing
Kester, Chang, Echanis, Haikal, Ids, Skully, Tsui, and Wang	1999	Firms on various Asian stock exchanges			
		Australia ($n = 57$)	48	38	14
		Hong Kong ($n = 29$)	24	19	57
		Indonesia ($n = 16$)	29	29	43
		Malaysia ($n = 35$)	29	24	47
		The Philippines ($n = 35$)	16	52	32
		Singapore ($n = 54$)	11	38	51

cost of capital for higher-risk projects, and a rate lower than the firm's divisional cost of capital for lower-risk projects. This method is tied as the second-most popular method employed by firms in Hong Kong (25 percent). The third method listed is using the CAPM to determine the discount rate for projects. This method ranks second for Australian firms and is tied for second for Hong Kong (24 percent and 25 percent, respectively). Some respondents from Australia, Malaysia, and the Philippines indicate they use "other methods," which are not described (10 percent, 13 percent, and 29 percent, respectively).

Grinyer, Sinclair, and Ibrahim (1999) send questionnaires to the largest 300 firms (by sales) in the United Kingdom as listed in the U.K. *Times* 1000. They use the 88 responses received to test five hypotheses about capital budgeting. One hypothesis is "A majority of managers of large quoted corporations will, when evaluating capital projects, emphasize the consideration of total risk rather than the systematic risk borne by diversified stockholders." Finance theory suggests that for large publicly traded firms, stockholders should diversify their portfolios, eliminating diversifiable risk and leaving only systematic risk in their portfolios (e.g., Brigham and Ehrhardt 2008). If so, stockholders should only expect to be compensated for the systematic risk of their investments. Because the systematic risk of adopted projects can change the systematic risk of the adopting firm, firms should require higher returns on capital budgeting projects based on the amount of each project's systematic risk, not their total risk.

When asked about the types of project risk for which firms adjust their discount rate, 80 percent agree or strongly agree they adjust for individual project risk (total risk). This compares with 49 percent who agree that they adjust for corporation portfolio risk (within-firm risk) and 31 percent who adjust for diversified stockholders' risk (systematic risk). While many respondents adjust for more than one type of risk, the results permit the authors to reject the null hypothesis that when managers evaluate capital projects, they place the same or less emphasis on total risk than on systematic risk.

Summary of Studies about the Use of Multiple Hurdle Rates

Although finance theory indicates that firms should determine hurdle rates based on project risk, Brigham (1975) finds that 48 percent of respondents indicate they employ one rate for all projects and just 23 percent vary the hurdle rate based on the project risk. He concludes that most firms use cost of capital methods that are inconsistent with academic literature. However, his findings also suggest movement in the right direction. The studies by Gitman and Mercurio (1982) and Gitman and Vandenberg (2000) show that the percentage of survey participants considering the risk of individual projects is roughly 60 percent. Still, about one-third of firms in the 1982 study and one-fourth of firms in the 2000 study indicate they do not differentiate project risk.

Bierman (1993) reports that 75 percent of respondents say they select discount rates based on the risk or nature of the project, while Bruner et al. (1998) find that 59 percent of survey respondents adjust the cost of capital always or sometimes to reflect project risk. Block (2003) finds that 53 percent of responding firms require different rates of return for different divisions, subsidiaries, or projects.

When Graham and Harvey (2001) ask both large and small firms how frequently they use the firm's overall discount rate to evaluate projects for the entire company, 59 percent say they always or almost always use it. Another 51 percent either always or almost always use a risk-matched discount for each project. The low percentage of firms basing discount rates on project risk likely reflects the large number of small firms participating in the study.

Several studies of non-U.S. firms also look at this topic. Kester et al. (1999) find that 48 percent of Australian firms use a single discount rate for all projects, while 38 percent use risk-adjusted discount rates. They also find that the most popular hurdle rate used by firms from Hong Kong, Indonesia, Malaysia, and Singapore is the cost of the specific capital used to finance the project. Firms from the Philippines indicate the most common discount rate is based on the risk of the project. The evidence suggests that Asia-Pacific firms are behind U.S. firms in the adoption of theoretically correct methods of determining hurdle rates.

Theory: Frequency of WACC Calculation

The cost of capital reflects a firm's target capital structure and the marginal cost of raising new capital from each source in the target capital structure. Clearly, firms do not change their target capital structure frequently. However, when they do change their target structure, this change must be reflected in a revised WACC.

While target capital structures do not change often, conditions in the financial markets change constantly; that is, when market interest rates change, a firm's cost of debt, preferred stock, and common equity are also likely to change. Similarly, changes in firm growth, stock prices, dividend payments, risk, investor attitudes toward risk, tax rates, underwriting costs, and other factors can all change the cost of one or more components of capital.

Because firms should evaluate potential capital budgeting projects based on the cost of raising new capital, they should estimate their cost of capital each time they evaluate new projects. Those firms considering projects on an annual basis, semiannual basis, or quarterly basis should estimate their cost of capital annually, semiannually, or quarterly to match the length of time between project-evaluating episodes. Likewise, firms that continuously evaluate capital budgeting projects should continuously estimate their WACC.

Practice: Frequency of WACC Calculation

The following synopsis of survey research related to the frequency of WACC calculation is divided into two subsections: surveys of U.S and non-U.S. firms, respectively.

Surveys of U.S. Firms

Table 4.8 shows the results of five survey studies asking respondents how frequently they estimate their cost of capital. In the earliest study, Brigham (1975) offers respondents four mutually exclusive answers, with the most popular response being "less than annually" (39 percent), followed by "depends on conditions" (32 percent; we classify this in Table 4.8 as "when conditions warrant change"). Another 16 percent of respondents indicate they change their hurdle rates more than once a year and 13 percent specify they change annually. Brigham (p. 20) observes that "firms revise hurdle rates less frequently than one might expect."

The study by Gitman and Mercurio (1982) offers answers similar to those in the Brigham (1975) study but adds one more: "each time a project is evaluated." In the Gitman and Mercurio study, the answer receiving the greatest proportion of responses by far is "when conditions warrant change" (50 percent). In declining order of popularity, the other responses are annually (22 percent), "less than annually" (13 percent), "each time a major project is evaluated" (11 percent), and "more than annually" (4 percent). Gitman and Mercurio (p. 27) conclude that "since the revision of the cost of capital seems appropriate when capital market conditions change, the majority of respondents seem to behave as might be expected."

Bruner et al. (1998) offer respondents answers that also differ somewhat from those offered by the other studies. They find the most popular response regarding the frequency of WACC calculations is "annually" (37 percent). For comparison purposes, Table 4.8 shows the responses to three different answers (monthly [4 percent], quarterly [19 percent], and semiannually [11 percent]) combined into the category called "more than annually," which receives a total of 34 percent of responses. Only 19 percent of survey participants selected the response "infrequently," while the response "continually/every investment" (classified here as "when conditions warrant change") received just 7 percent of responses. Bruner et al. (p. 25) conclude from their findings that "only large material changes in costs may be fed into more formal project evaluation systems."

Recall that the Gitman and Vandenberg (2000) study emulates that of Gitman and Mercurio (1982) to investigate changes over time. Gitman and Vandenberg find similar response frequencies for all possible responses, with the highest percentage response for "when conditions warrant change" (49 percent). The largest decline in frequency is for "less than annually" (9 percent in the current study versus 13 percent in the earlier study). Gitman and Vandenberg conclude that the data suggest respondents now recalculate their WACC more frequently than in the 1980s. They attribute this to more frequent shifts in long-term interest rates in the later years, which affect the cost of WACC components.

Surveys of Non-U.S. Firms

The final study listed in Table 4.8 is the study of U.K. firms conducted by McLaney et al. (2004). They find the majority of responding firms (54 percent) reassess the cost of capital annually, while another 25 percent indicate either monthly, quarterly, or semiannually. The remaining 9 percent of firms indicate reassessment when conditions change (e.g., when long-term interest rates change) or each time the firm evaluates a major project.

Summary of Studies about the Frequency of WACC Calculation

Finance theory suggests that firms reevaluate their WACC whenever they consider capital budgeting projects and there have been changes in market conditions.

TABLE 4.8 Cost of capital estimation frequency

This table shows responses to questions about the frequency with which firms determine their cost of capital. Finance theory suggests estimating the cost of capital each time a firm evaluates new projects, or when market conditions cause the cost of capital to change. Depending on the firm's operating cycle, this could mean annually, more than annually, etc.

Author(s)	Year published	Population/Sample	Percentage of firms					
			Annually	More than annually	Less than annually	When conditions warrant change	Each time a major project is evaluated	Infrequently
Brigham	1975	Select executives who completed a university program (large firms/not randomly selected; $n = 33$)	13	16	39	32	n/a	n/a
Gitman and Mercurio	1982	Fortune 1000 firms ($n = 177$)	22	4	13	50	11	n/a
Bruner, Eades, Harris, and Higgins	1998	U.S. firms listed in Creating World-Class Financial Management: Strategies of 50 Leading Companies (1992; $n = 27$)[a]	37	34[b]	n/a	7[c]	n/a	19
Gitman and Vandenberg	2000	Fortune 1000 firms ($n = 111$)	27	5	9	49	10	n/a
McLaney, Pointon, Thomas, and Tucker	2004	Firms listed on U.K. Stock Exchange for which accounting data are available on Datastream ($n = 193$)	54	25[b]	n/a	3[d]	6	n/a

[a]This publication identifies firms "selected by their peers as being among those with the best financial management. Firms were chosen for excellence in strategic financial risk management, tax and accounting, performance evaluation and other areas of financial management. . . . The companies included were those that were mentioned the greatest number of times by their peers."

[b]The responses of monthly, quarterly, and semiannually are combined.

[c]The actual response is "continually/every investment."

[d]The actual response is "when long-term rates change."

Brigham (1975) finds the most common response by survey respondents to questions about the frequency of WACC calculation is "less than annually" (39 percent), suggesting that firms may recalculate their WACC less frequently than theory suggests. Gitman and Mercurio (1982) find the most frequent response by a wide margin is "when conditions warrant change," suggesting that the actions of most responding firms are consistent with finance theory. Bruner et al. (1998) find the most common response to a similar question is "annually" (37 percent). "When conditions warrant change" receives just 7 percent of responses.

Gitman and Vandenberg (2000) find the frequency of responses to the question about the frequency of WACC calculation to be similar to those found by Gitman and Mercurio (1982). The most frequent response is for "when conditions warrant change." The largest decline in frequency from the Gitman and Mercurio study is for "less than annually." Both suggest increased consistency with finance theory.

A study of U.K. firms conducted by McLaney et al. (2004) finds that most respondents reassess the cost of capital annually (54 percent), while 25 percent of respondents indicate they do so either monthly, quarterly, or semiannually. This may be consistent with finance theory, provided the firms employ a capital budgeting cycle that involves evaluating projects once annually.

Miscellaneous Cost of Capital Topics: Numerical Values of WACC

The remainder of this chapter discusses some cost-of-capital topics that receive only minor attention in survey studies. The next two sections focus on survey studies about the numerical value of WACC. The first section focuses on surveys of U.S. firms while the second deals with surveys of non-U.S. firms.

Studies of U.S. Firms

Various survey studies ask respondents to indicate the numerical value of their current WACC. Unfortunately, the format of the alternative responses provided by the authors varies from survey to survey, making comparisons difficult. Petry (1975) is one of the earlier surveys collecting this information. He surveys the CFO of the following firms: *Fortune* 50 retailing firms, *Fortune* 50 transportation firms, *Fortune* 50 utility firms, and the top 400 *Fortune* 500 industrial firms. Petry receives 284 responses, a 52 percent response rate. The survey asks respondents for the "cutoff of minimum investment return rates," and the findings for the industrial and retail firms are presented in Panel A of Table 4.9. The numbers reported represent the cost of capital on an after-tax basis. Petry reports an average minimum after-tax rate of 12.8 percent for all surveyed firms and observes that the firms with lower cutoff rates seem to be labor intensive, while those with higher cutoff rates seem to be capital intensive. Petry (p. 64) offers that "this information suggests that risk is somewhat related to the minimum investment rate required."

Schall, Sundem, and Geijsbeek (1978) send questionnaires to 424 firms listed in Compustat that have either (1) net plant assets greater than $200 million, (2) more than $20 million of capital expenditures, or (3) net plant assets greater than $150 million and more than $10 million of capital expenditures. The authors receive 189 responses. One question asks survey respondents to indicate the numerical value of their cost of capital. In reporting the results, the authors group the values in one-percent ranges as indicated in Table 4.9. The average after-tax cost of capital is 11.4 percent, somewhat lower than the average minimum after-tax rate (12.8 percent) reported by Petry (1975). Neither the Schall, Sundem, and Geijsbeek (1978) study nor the Petry (1975) study reveal the year in which the authors gathered the study data. However, the 20-year Treasury bond rate was 8.37 percent one year before publication of the Petry study and 7.73 percent one year before publication of the Schall, Sundem, and Geijsbeek study. This may explain the differences found in the average cost of capital for firms in the two studies.

Panel B of Table 4.9 presents the results of the Gitman and Forrester (1977) and the Gitman and Maxwell (1987) studies together because the later study attempts to emulate the former in terms of population and question wording. Gitman and Forrester send questionnaires to 268 firms that appear on two *Forbes* lists. One list reflects the 600 firms experiencing the most rapid stock-price growth from 1971 to 1976, and the other list includes the 500 firms having the largest dollar capital expenditures during 1969. They receive 103 usable responses. The Gitman and Maxwell survey identifies a similar sample using updated lists and sends questionnaires to 333 firms, receiving 109 usable responses. The idea is to observe any differences that may have occurred during the intervening 10 years. Casual observation of the results suggests little difference between the responses for the two studies. Gitman and Maxwell (pp. 45-46) note that long-term government bond rates are about the same at the time the two different surveys were taken, "hence one can expect little difference in the cost of capital for firms. Indeed, data presented . . . show very little change in the cost of capital."

Scapens and Sale (1981) survey the *Fortune* 500 firms receiving usable replies from 227 firms. They also survey U.K. firms (some of those findings are discussed later in this chapter). Their study focuses on divisionalized firms. While the study does not report the distribution of responses for the actual hurdle rates employed by firms, the average hurdle rates applied to projects by U.S. firms is 17.1 percent. This rate is higher than the average rates reported by Petry (1975) and Schall, Sundem, and Geijsbeek (1978), which were 11.4 percent and 12.8 percent, respectively. As a benchmark, the rate on 20-year Treasury bonds at the time Scapens and Sale mailed their questionnaires was 10.65 percent, substantially higher than the same rate one year before the publishing of the other two studies.

One of the questions Poterba and Summers (1995) ask *Fortune* 1000 firms concerns the hurdle rates applied to capital budgeting projects. While some of the responses are in nominal terms and others in real terms, the authors converted the nominal rates to real rates by subtracting 5 percent, which they describe as consistent with the predominant thinking at the time they collected the survey data. Poterba and Summers find the average real discount rate utilized by respondents is 12.2 percent. They describe this rate as being above the historical real rate of return in the United States on either equity or debt. They suggest that some managers may establish hurdle rates higher than the firm's cost of capital in order to adjust for overly optimistic projections of project cash flows. This is similar to the argument presented by Christy (1966).

Panel B of Table 4.9 presents the results of the Gitman and Mercurio (1982) and Gitman and Vandenberg (2000) studies together. Recall that the later study attempts to emulate the earlier study in terms of the population and question wording. In this case, the surveys ask respondents to identify their actual overall cost of capital from an array of 12 choices, each with a two-percentage-point range. There is a clear difference between the responses to this question at the two different points in time. The most frequent response to this question in the earlier study is 15 to 17 percent, and for the later study, 9 percent to 11 percent. By weighting the midpoint of each cost of capital range by the proportion of responses, the authors find the weighted mean rate of 14.3 percent for the earlier study and 11.5 percent for the later study. Gitman and Vandenberg (p. 58) conclude that the difference in the cost of capital figures results from "the known decline in interest rates reflected in the U.S. government bond rates" (the rate at the time of the first study was 12.4 percent versus 7.1 percent at the time of the second study). Gitman and Vandenberg (p. 58) also state that the differences in cost of capital may also be "attributable to a general shift in the average responding firms' risk as well as the risk preferences of investors in the economy."

Surveys of Non-U.S. Firms

Recall that Scapens and Sale (1981) survey both U.S. and U.K. firms. For the U.K. portion of the study, they send surveys to 744 firms in the *Times* 1000 (the authors exclude subsidiaries of overseas firms) and receive 300 usable responses. They find that the average hurdle rates U.K. firms apply to projects is 18.5 percent. This rate is higher than the 17.1 percent rate for U.S. firms found in the same study. In another study, Pike (1983) asks the 208 largest U.K manufacturing and retailing firms to select the hurdle-rate range that applies to them. Of the 150 usable responses received, the most popular response is a hurdle-rate range of 15 percent to 19 percent. Pike notes that this is consistent with the findings of Scapens and Sale (1981).

TABLE 4.9 Numerical value of the cost of capital or cutoff rate: U.S. firms

This table shows responses to questions about the current numerical cost of capital of participating firms. Panel A shows the results from two early independent studies during the 1970s. Panel B shows the results of related studies. The Gitman and Forrester (1977) and the Gitman and Maxwell (1987) studies use identical questions and similar samples and generate similar results. The Gitman and Mercurio (1982) and Gitman and Vandenberg (2000) studies also use identical questions and similar samples; however the results suggest lower costs of capital in the later study.

A. Unrelated studies

Authors	Year published	Population/Sample	Cost of capital or cutoff rate (industrial and retail firms only)					Cost of capital						Cost of capital (continued)				
			10 %	12 %	15 %	20 %	Other	7.0 to 7.9 %	8.0 to 8.9 %	9.0 to 9.9 %	10.0 to 10.9 %	11.0 to 11.9 %	12.0 to 12.9 %	13.0 to 13.9 %	14.0 to 14.9 %	15.0 to 15.9 %	16.0 to 16.9 %	17.0 % +
Petry	1975	Top *Fortune*-listed firms in select industries (n = 284)	41	14	25	8	12											
Schall, Sundem, and Geijsbeek	1978	Select large firms/ Compustat (n = 189)						4	4	3	43	6	16					
Schall, Sundem, and Geijsbeek														0	7	12	3	1

(Continued)

TABLE 4.9 (cont'd) Numerical value of the cost of capital or cutoff rate: U.S. firms

B. Related studies

			Cost of capital					
			< 5 %	5 to 10 %	10 to 15 %	15 to 20 %	20 to 25 %	> 25 %
Gitman and Forrester	1977	*Forbes* firms with large capital expenditures/rapid stock-price growth (n = 103)	0	9.5	60	23	7	0
Gitman and Maxwell	1987	*Forbes* firms with large capital expenditures/rapid stock-price growth (n = 109)	1	9.4	62	22	5	1

			Cost of capital					
			< 5 %	5 to 7 %	7 to 9 %	9 to 11 %	11 to 13 %	13 to 15 %
Gitman and Mercurio	1982	*Fortune* 1000 firms (n = 177)	1.7	0.6	3.4	10.1	20.9	21.5
Gitman and Vandenberg	2000	*Fortune* 1000 firms (n = 111)	0.0	9.0	5.5	43.6	28.2	14.5

	Cost of capital (continued)					
	15 to 17 %	17 to 19 %	19 to 21 %	21 to 23 %	23 to 25 %	> 25 %
Gitman and Mercurio	22.6	12.3	4.0	0.6	0.6	1.7
Gitman and Vandenberg	2.6	2.7	0.9	0.0	0.0	0.0

Arnold and Hatzopoulos (2000) survey U.K firms of varying size and ask respondents to select from a list of possible ranges the "cutoff points used to evaluate the viability of major capital investments." For firms of all sizes, the most frequent response is 11 to 15 percent, and the second-most frequent response is 16 to 20 percent (see Table 4.10). Although the results are not as precise as in the Gitman and Vandenberg (2000) study (which specifies two-percent intervals versus the five-percent intervals specified by Arnold and Hatzopoulos), the results are generally consistent with the U.S. study. Arnold and Hatzopoulos reveal that they took the survey when the risk-free rate of return was "about 7 percent," which is similar to the rate on U.S. government bonds at the time of the Gitman and Vandenberg study. The modal range in the Arnold and Hatzopoulos study for large firms is 11 to 15 percent compared to the modal range for the Gitman and Vandenberg study of 9 to 11 percent.

McLaney et al. (2004) also survey U.K firms to find their overall cost of capital. Table 4.10 shows the percentage of respondents indicating a cost of capital within various ranges. Surprisingly, about 7 percent of respondents indicate a cost of capital of 0.1 percent to 5 percent. Meanwhile, 42 percent of respondents indicate a cost of capital between 5.1 percent and 10 percent, and another 47 percent indicate a range of 10.1 percent to 15 percent. Just 4 percent of respondents indicate a value exceeding 15 percent. After analyzing the data, the authors conclude that 10 percent is a reasonable estimate of the after-tax cost of capital for U.K. firms participating in the survey. When the authors mailed the survey, the yield on 20-year British government bonds was about 7.0 percent.

Drawing conclusions from studies about the numerical value of firms' cost of capital is difficult. Several studies suggest a positive relationship between market rates of interest and the cost of capital, which is intuitively appealing. Studies of U.K. firms fail to reveal meaningful differences between the rates used by U.K. firms and U.S. firms.

Selection of Values of CAPM Variables

There is little agreement among academics or practitioners regarding the numerical values that should be used in the CAPM. Should the risk-free rate be the rate on Treasury bills or Treasury bonds? What should analysts use as the expected return on the market? How should an analyst determine a firm's beta coefficient? For firms using CAPM to estimate the cost of equity capital for capital budgeting purposes, these are important questions. One survey study seeks answers to these questions.

As discussed earlier, Bruner et al. (1998) find that 81 percent of surveyed best-practice firms say they employ CAPM to estimate their firms' cost of equity. As Panel A of Table 4.11 shows, the two most popular factors used to represent the risk-free rate are the rate on 10-year Treasury securities (33 percent) and the rate

TABLE 4.10 Numerical value of the cost of capital or cutoff rate: U.K. firms

This table shows responses of U.K. firms to questions about the cutoff point or cost of capital used to evaluate capital investments. The modal rate for each size firm in the Arnold and Hatzopoulos (2000) study is 11 percent to 15 percent while the modal rate for firms participating in the McLaney et al. (2004) study is similar at 10.1 percent to 15.0 percent.

Author(s)	Year published	Population/Sample	Percentage of firms with cutoff points used to evaluate major capital investments within each range					
			0 to 10 %	11 to 15 %	16 to 20 %	21 to 30 %	> 30 %	Blank
Arnold and Hatzopoulos	2000	Large, midsize, and small U.K. firms listed in the *Times* 1000						
		Small (*n* = 34)	9	41	15	15	3	18
		Midsize (*n* = 24)	8	46	24	4	0	17
		Large (*n* = 38)	21	39	26	8	0	5
		Composite (*n* = 96)	14	42	22	9	1	12

			Percentage of firms with cost of capital in each range			
			0.1 to 5 %	5.1 to 10 %	10.1 to 15 %	> 15 %
McLaney, Pointon, Thomas, and Tucker	2004	Firms listed on U.K. Stock Exchange for which accounting data are available on Datastream (*n* = 193)	7	42	47	4

on Treasury securities with maturities between 10-years and 30-years (33 percent). Panel B of the same table shows that more than half of survey participants obtain their firm's beta from published sources (52 percent) and another 30 percent calculate their own betas. Finally, Panel C of Table 4.11 shows the most popular source of the market-risk premium is a fixed rate of 5.0 percent to 6.5 percent. Other popular sources of the risk premium include estimates from financial advisors (15 percent) and a fixed rate of 4.0 percent to 4.5 percent

TABLE 4.11 Sources of factor values used in the capital asset pricing model

This table shows responses to questions about how firms estimate the factor values used to estimate the cost of equity capital using the CAPM.

A. Selection of a risk-free rate	Percentage of respondents
90-day T-bills	4
3- to 7-year Treasuries	7
10-year Treasuries	33
20-year Treasuries	4
10- to 30-year Treasuries	33
Other	4
n/a	15
B. Source of beta factor	
Published sources	52
Financial advisor's estimate	4
Self-calculated	30
n/a	15
C. Market-risk premium	
Fixed rate of 4.0 to 4.5 percent	11
Fixed rate of 5.0 to 6.0 percent	37
Geometric mean of historical premium	4
Arithmetic mean of historical premium	4
Average of historical and implied premium	4
Financial advisor's estimate	15
Premium over treasuries	7
Value line estimate	4
n/a	15

Source: Bruner et al. (1998, Exhibit 2, pp. 17–19).

(11 percent). Regarding selection of a market-risk premium, Bruner et al. (p. 22) conclude that "few respondents specifically cited use of any forward-looking method to supplement or replace reading the tea leaves of past returns." They also conclude (p. 27) that "best-practice companies can expect to estimate their WACC with an accuracy of no more than plus or minus 100 to 150 basis points."

Divisional Betas

Several early theoretical studies investigate the notion of using divisional costs of capital to account for risk differences in the divisions of multidivisional firms (Gordon and Halpern 1974; Fuller and Kerr 1981; Gup and Norwood 1982). The theory suggests that multidivisional firms may have some divisions that are more risky than others. Therefore, the adoption of projects equally risky as a high-risk division will increase firm risk. Consequently, each division should be assigned its own cost of capital (hurdle rate) based on the risk of the division.

Block (2003) asks firms that use divisional risk as a means of determining divisional costs of capital how they determine divisional risk. Table 4.12 shows that the most common source of divisional risk is subjective assignment by management based on the perceived risk of the division (65 percent). The three objective methods receive far fewer responses: "the beta of a company in the same line of business" (the pure-play method; 17 percent); "the average beta of the entire industry the division is in" (12 percent); and using nonmarket information "such as the variability of the division's earnings compared to the variability of the firm's overall earnings" (6 percent).

Slope of the Marginal Cost of Capital Line

Finance theory suggests that when firms raise substantial capital in a short time, their marginal cost of capital (MCC) increases (e.g., Brigham and Ehrhardt 2008). The increase results because issuing more and more debt leads to increasing risks to creditors and higher lender-required rates of return. The higher required returns translate into higher financing costs for the issuing firm. Also, firms generally prefer to raise needed equity capital internally through the retention of earnings. However, if a firm needs more equity capital than can be provided by retained earnings, it must issue new shares of common stock. Because issuing new common stock involves flotation costs, which include such costs as underwriting fees and issuance discount, a firm's cost of equity increases if it must issue new common stock. Therefore, when a firm first begins to raise capital, it can employ inexpensive debt and retained earnings at relatively low costs. At some point, the cost of additional increments of debt financing begins to

TABLE 4.12 Estimating divisional betas

This table shows responses to a question asking how firms using risk as the primary determinant of divisional cost of capital measure divisional risk. The results show a strong preference for using a subjective risk measure.

Risk measure	Percentage of firms
An objective measure such as the beta of a public company in the same line of business	16.5
An objective measure such as the average beta of the entire industry the division is in	12.4
An objective measure, not market related, such as the variability of the division's earnings compared to overall corporate earnings	5.8
A subjective measure such as top management's view of the perceived risk generally associated with the division	65.3

Source: Block (2003, p. 353).

increase, causing the firm's WACC to increase. Eventually, the cost of equity also increases, resulting in a further increase in WACC. The term *marginal cost of capital* refers to the cost of an additional dollar of capital. Firms should recognize the MCC schedule as a rising step function as firms raise larger and larger amounts of capital (see Figure 4.1). Because of the rising MCC, adopting projects that require raising investment capital beyond a breakpoint in the MCC line means a firm must generate a higher return on the project to be economically feasible; that is, a firm must require a higher return on projects that increase the firm's WACC.

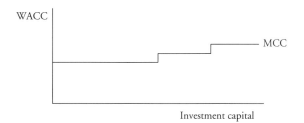

FIGURE 4.1 Marginal cost of capital schedule.

This figure shows that as a firm raises additional increments of investment capital (the horizontal scale), the firm's weighted average cost of capital, or WACC (the vertical scale), increases, as shown by the rising marginal cost of capital (MCC) line.

Brigham (1975) asks firms if their hurdle rate reflects the amount of capital they plan to raise. In other words, do firms recognize an increasing MCC function? More than half of the responding firms (55 percent) respond yes, while the remaining firms (45 percent) indicate they do not. Brigham states (p. 21) that "some of the companies have simply never thought in a formal way of the relationship between funds raised and capital budgeting hurdle rates."

A much later study by Gitman and Vandenberg (2000) finds that almost 90 percent of respondents indicate they utilize just one cost of capital regardless of the amount of financing needed to adopt all projects. Gitman and Vanderberg (p. 64) note, "This suggests that most respondents face a flat weighted marginal cost of capital function."

Gitman and Mercurio (1982) and Gitman and Vandenberg (2000) also ask survey participants if they distinguish between the cost of retained earnings and the cost of issuing new common stock. In the 1982 study, the authors find that just 16 percent of respondents differentiate between the costs of the two equity components. The later study by Gitman and Vandenberg finds this percentage had declined to 11 percent. Gitman and Vandenberg (p. 57) note that "this finding implies that most firms calculate only one cost of equity capital: not differentiating the cost of existing equity from the cost of new common stock equity."

Cost of Capital Applications

Finance theory suggests there are a variety of applications of the cost of capital (e.g., Brigham and Ehrhardt 2008), the most obvious being to evaluate capital budgeting projects for potential adoption. A second application, which is closely related to the capital budgeting decision, is the project abandonment decision. Both decisions involve consideration of the time value of money and the opportunity cost of having funds invested in projects. To enhance firm value, firms should abandon projects at the time when the net present value (NPV) of the project is at its highest value (at the end of the project's economic life). That may be well before the end of the physical life of the asset(s) associated with the project. A third application of a firm's cost of capital is to estimate the value of the firm using the free cash flow (FCF) approach. This popular valuation method involves forecasting a firm's future FCF and discounting it to present value using the firm's cost of capital as a discount rate. Other recognized applications of a firm's WACC are as a benchmark for compensation plans and as a guide to help determine a firm's target capital structure.

Finance theory indicates that firms should not employ the cost of capital to evaluate leases or make bond-refunding decisions. Leases and bonds are forms of debt financing. As such, decisions about leases and bond refunding should be based on the firm's cost of debt, not the firm's WACC.

The surveys by Gitman and Mercurio (1982) and Gitman and Vandenberg (2000) both ask respondents about applications of the cost of capital. In each study, respondents are offered five potential uses (see Table 4.13). Clearly, the most common use in both studies is to evaluate new projects, and the percentage of respondents applying it in that manner increased modestly from 93 percent in the earlier study to 97 percent in the later study. The second-most common application in the later survey is to estimate the firm's value. The percentage of respondents using the cost of capital for this purpose increased greatly from the earlier study (44 percent) to the later study (79 percent). The third-most common application in the later study is to evaluate the "abandonment of existing projects." Once again, the percentage of firms using this application increases from 45 percent in the earlier study to 72 percent in the later study. These three applications are consistent with finance theory. The two remaining applications are not consistent with finance theory, and one of them increased in popularity: making bond-refunding decisions. The use of WACC for this purpose increases from 35 percent to 46 percent of responding firms. The other application—leasing decisions—decreases modestly in popularity from 64 percent to 60 percent. Responses to a related question show the most common discount rate employed by firms in making the leasing and bond-refunding decisions is the after-tax cost of debt. The percentage of firms indicating use of the after-tax cost of debt for lease-purchase decisions increased from 39 percent in the 1982 study to 61 percent in the 2000 study. Meanwhile, the percentage of respondents indicating use of the after-tax cost of debt for bond-refunding decisions increased from 38 percent in the earlier study to 50 percent in the later study. Gitman and Vandenberg (2000, p. 64) conclude that "it appears that the cost of capital is

TABLE 4.13 Cost of capital applications: U.S. firms

This table shows the percent of firms that apply the cost of capital to different situations. The 1982 study is by Gitman and Mercurio and the 2000 study is by Gitman and Vandenberg.

Application	Percentage of respondents	
	1982 study	2000 study
New projects	93	97
Abandonment of existing projects	45	72
Leasing decisions	64	60
Bond refunding decisions	35	46
Estimating the firm's value	44	79

Source: Gitman and Vandenberg (2000, p. 65).

used primarily for new project decisions, whereas the after-tax cost of debt is used for the financing decisions concerned with lease-purchase and bond-refunding."

Related to this is a finding by Bruner et al. (1998). When they ask survey participants if they employ the cost of capital to do more than analyze investment projects, the authors find that 51 percent of respondents respond in the affirmative. Bruner et al. do not ask follow-up questions that would indicate the other uses.

Does Greater Disclosure Lead to a Lower Cost of Capital?

Another line of survey research concerns the views of financial managers about a hypothesized relationship between a firm's cost of capital and its disclosure of financial information. Theory suggests that when firms reveal more information about themselves, it reduces information asymmetry between the firm and the stock market. There are two different theories about how such disclosure may reduce the cost of capital. One theory, suggested by Klein and Bawa (1976), Barry and Brown (1985), Coles and Loewenstein (1988), Handa and Linn (1993), and others, proposes that when firms reveal more information about their circumstances and condition, analysts can forecast the firm's future cash flows with less uncertainty. Less uncertainty means less risk, a lower required return on the firm's equity, and a reduced cost of capital. The second theory, proposed by Demsetz (1968), Copeland and Galai (1983), Glosten and Milgrom (1985), Amihud and Mendelson (1986), and others, suggests that investors expect reduced losses from trading with those who have superior information about the firm because others are less likely to have superior information. Again, the perceived lower risk leads to lower required rates of return, lower cost of equity, and lower cost of capital. Armitage and Marston (2008) note that most empirical studies indicate a negative relationship between the level of disclosure and the cost of equity, although some studies do not support this relationship (e.g., Botosan 1997; Botosan and Plumlee 2002). Several survey studies seek to ask financial executives their view of the hypothesized relationship.

Two recent survey studies reveal managers' opinions about the theory that greater disclosure leads to a lower cost of capital. Graham, Harvey, and Rajgopal (2005) e-mail surveys to 3,174 members of an organization of financial executives (the authors did not name the organization or the distribution date). In a secondary effort, they also solicit responses from the same group by distributing hard copies of the survey to executives attending the Forum on Corporate Finance at the University of Illinois and at the University of Washington CFO Forum (the dates are not provided). Between these two efforts, the authors receive 267 responses, a response rate of 8.4 percent. They also ask attendees at a November 2003 conference of financial executives to complete the survey (the authors do not reveal the conference name). Of the approximately 670 attendees, 134 completed the survey. One survey question involves listing several statements and asking respondents if the statements describe their firm's motives for voluntarily communicating financial information. Of the 11 statements, "reduces our cost of capital" is ranked 10th in terms of the percentage of respondents either agreeing or strongly agreeing with the statement. These results suggest that reducing the cost of capital is not seen by respondents as an important reason for increasing disclosure. The statements showing the most participant agreement are "promotes a reputation for transparent/accurate reporting" and "reduces the 'information risk' that investors assign to our stock." It can be argued, however, that reducing information risk leads to a lower cost of capital, but that is apparently not the focus of managers when they increase disclosure.

Armitage and Marston (2008) interview 16 senior executives at varied U.K. firms. The interviewees represent a wide variety of industries and include nine finance directors, four former finance directors, and three investor relations (IR) professionals. The authors note that all IR professionals have one or more credentials in accounting, banking, investment analysis, or other finance/accounting areas. Thirteen participating firms are among the 300 largest in the United Kingdom. Armitage and Marston find that most participants do not believe there is a strong link between the amount of disclosure and the cost of equity and just 25 percent believe that disclosure reduces the cost of capital. The authors conclude that the evidence from U.K. managers is consistent with the Graham, Harvey, and Rajgopal (2005) findings of U.S. managers suggesting that the primary motive for voluntary disclosure is not to reduce the cost of capital. However, Armitage and Marston (2008) also find that 56 percent of survey participants believe providing more information reduces the cost of debt.

Summary and Conclusions

A review of survey research over the past 40-plus years regarding the estimation and utilization of the cost of capital clearly suggests a reduction in the gap between theory and practice. Trends are toward (1) using target capital structure weights, (2) estimating the cost of debt based on current market costs, (3) estimating the cost of equity based on forward-looking data and the use of dividend discount models, (4) using CAPM and APT, (5) basing hurdle rates on project risk, (6) changing cost of capital estimates when market and firm conditions change, and (7) applying the cost of capital to more than just the evaluation of investment projects.

Narrowing the gap between theory and practice is good for managers because it means firms are making decisions that lead to the maximization of shareholder wealth. The fact that the gap is narrowing is good for academics because it demonstrates a level of success in an important goal: educating people about how to evaluate financial situations and make good financial decisions. The fact that a gap between theory and practice continues to exist is also good for academics because it means there is more work to be done.

References

Amihud, Yakov, and Haim Mendelson. 1986. "Asset Pricing and the Bid-Ask Spread." *Journal of Financial Economics* 17:2, 223–249.

Armitage, Seth, and Claire Marston. 2008. "Corporate Disclosure, Cost of Capital and Reputation: Evidence From Finance Directors." *British Accounting Review* 40:4, 314–336.

Arnold, Glen C., and Panos D. Hatzopoulos. 2000. "The Theory-Practice Gap in Capital Budgeting: Evidence from the United Kingdom." *Journal of Business Finance and Accounting* 27:5–6, 603–626.

Baker, H. Kent, Shantanu Dutta, and Samir Saadi. 2009. "Corporate Finance Practices in Canada: Where Do We Stand?" Working Paper, University of Ontario Institute of Technology and Queen's University.

Barry, Christopher B., and Stephen J. Brown. 1985. "Differential Information and Security Market Equilibrium." *Journal of Financial and Quantitative Analysis* 20:4, 407–422.

Bierman, Harold Jr. 1993. "Capital Budgeting in 1992: A Survey." *Financial Management* 22:3, 24.

Bierman, Harold Jr., and Seymour Smidt. 1966. *The Capital Budgeting Decision*. New York: MacMillan Publishing Company.

Block, Stanley. 2003. "Divisional Cost of Capital: A Study of Its Use by Major U.S. Firms." *Engineering Economist* 48:4, 345–362.

Botosan, Christine A. 1997. "Disclosure Level and the Cost of Equity Capital." *Accounting Review* 72:3, 323–349.

Botosan, Christine A., and Marlene A. Plumlee. 2002. "A Re-Examination of Disclosure Level and the Expected Cost of Equity Capital." *Journal of Accounting Research* 40:1, 21–40.

Brigham, Eugene F. 1975. "Hurdle Rate for Screening Capital Expenditure Proposals." *Financial Management* 4:3, 17–26.

Brigham, Eugene F., and Michael C. Ehrhardt. 2008. *Financial Management: Theory and Practice*, 12th ed. Mason, Ohio: Thomson South-Western.

Brounen, Dirk, Abe de Jong, and Kees Koedijk. 2004. "Corporate Finance in Europe: Confronting Theory with Practice." *Financial Management* 33:4, 71–101.

Bruner, Robert F., Kenneth M. Eades, Robert S. Harris, and Robert C. Higgins. 1998. "Best Practices in Estimating the Cost of Capital: Survey and Synthesis." *Financial Practice and Education* 8:1, 13–28.

Christy, George A. 1966. *Capital Budgeting: Current Practices and Their Efficiency*. Eugene: Bureau of Business and Economic Research, University of Oregon.

Coles, Jeffrey L., and Uri Loewenstein. 1988. "Equilibrium Pricing and Portfolio Composition in the Presence of Uncertain Parameters." *Journal of Financial Economics* 22:2, 279–303.

Copeland, Thomas E., and Dan Galai. 1983. "Information Effects on the Bid-Ask Spread." *Journal of Finance* 38:5, 1457–1469.

Demsetz, Harold. 1968. "The Cost of Transacting." *Quarterly Journal of Economics* 82:1, 33–53.

Ehrhardt, Michael C. 1994. *The Search for Value: Measuring the Company's Cost of Capital.* Boston, MA: Oxford University Press.

Fuller, Russell J., and Halbert S. Kerr. 1981. "Estimating the Divisional Cost of Capital: An Analysis of the Pure-Play Technique." *Journal of Finance* 36:5, 997–1009.

Gitman, Lawrence J., and John R. Forrester Jr. 1977. "A Survey of Capital Budgeting Techniques Used by Major U.S. Firms." *Financial Management* 6:3, 66–71.

Gitman, Lawrence J., and Charles E. Maxwell. 1987. "A Longitudinal Comparison of Capital Budgeting Techniques Used by Major U.S. Firms: 1986 versus 1976." *Journal of Applied Business Research* 3:1, 41–50.

Gitman, Lawrence J., and Vincent A. Mercurio. 1982. "Cost of Capital Techniques Used by Major U.S. Firms: Survey and Analysis of Fortune's 1000." *Financial Management* 11:4, 21–30.

Gitman, Lawrence J., and Pieter A. Vandenberg. 2000. "Cost of Capital Techniques Used by Major U.S. Firms: 1997 vs. 1980." *Financial Practice and Education* 10:2, 53–68.

Glosten, Lawrence R., and Paul R. Milgrom. 1985. "Bid Ask and Transaction Prices in a Specialist Market with Heterogeneously Informed Traders." *Journal of Financial Economics* 14:1, 71–100.

Gordon, Myron J., and Paul J. Halpern. 1974. "Cost of Capital for a Division of a Firm." *Journal of Finance* 29:4, 1153–1161.

Graham, John R., and Campbell R. Harvey. 2001. "The Theory and Practice of Corporate Finance: Evidence from the Field." *Journal of Financial Economics* 60:2–3, 187–243.

Graham, John R., Campbell R. Harvey, and Shiva Rajgopal. 2005. "The Economic Implications of Corporate Financial Reporting." *Journal of Accounting and Economics* 40:1–3, 3–73.

Grinyer, John R., C. Donald Sinclair, and Daing Nasir Ibrahim. 1999. "Management Objectives in Capital Budgeting." *Financial Practice and Education* 9:2, 12–22.

Gup, Benton E., and Samuel W. Norwood III. 1982. "Divisional Cost of Capital: A Practical Approach." *Financial Management* 11:1, 20–24.

Handa, Puneet, and Scott C. Linn. 1993. "Arbitrage Pricing with Estimation Risk." *Journal of Financial Economics* 28:1, 81–100.

Kester, George W., Rosita P. Chang, Erlinda S. Echanis, Shalahuddin Haikal, Mansor Md. Isa, Michael T. Skully, Kai-Chong Tsui, and Chi-Jeng Wang. 1999. "Capital Budgeting Practices in the Asia-Pacific Region: Australia, Hong Kong, Indonesia, Malaysia, Philippines and Singapore." *Financial Practice and Education* 9:1, 25–33.

Klein, Roger W., and Vijay S. Bawa. 1976. "The Effect of Estimation Risk on Optimal Portfolio Choice." *Journal of Financial Economics* 3:3, 215–231.

McLaney, Edward, John Pointon, Melanie Thomas, and Jon Tucker. 2004. "Practitioners' Perspective on the UK Cost of Capital." *European Journal of Finance* 10:2, 123–138.

Petry, Glenn H. 1975. "Effective Use of Capital Budgeting Tools." *Business Horizons* 18:5, 57–65.

Petry, Glenn H., and James Sprow. 1993. "The Theory and Practice of Finance in the 1990s." *Quarterly Review of Economics and Finance* 33:4, 359–381.

Petty, J. William, David F. Scott Jr., and Monroe M. Bird. 1975. "The Capital Expenditure Decision-Making Process of Large Corporations." *Engineering Economist* 20:3, 159–172.

Pflomn, Norman P. 1963. *Managing Capital Expenditures.* New York: National Industrial Conference Board.

Pike, Richard H. 1983. "A Review of Recent Trends in Formal Capital Budgeting Processes." *Accounting and Business Research* 13:51, 201–209.

Poterba, James M., and Lawrence Summers. 1995. "A CEO Survey of U.S. Companies' Time Horizon and Hurdle Rates." *Sloan Management Review* 37:1, 43–53.

Ross, Marc. 1986. "Perspectives on Capital Budgeting: Capital Budgeting Practices of Twelve Large Manufacturers." *Financial Management* 15:4, 15–18.

Ross, Stephen A., Randolph W. Westerfield, and Jeffrey F. Jaffe. 2008. *Corporate Finance,* 7th ed. New York: McGraw-Hill Higher Education.

Scapens, Robert W., and J. Timothy Sale. 1981. "Performance Measurement and Formal Capital Expenditure Controls in Divisionalized Companies." *Journal of Business Finance and Accounting* 8:3, 389–419.

Schall, Lawrence D., Gary L. Sundem, and William R. Geijsbeek Jr. 1978. "Survey and Analysis of Capital Budgeting Methods." *Journal of Finance* 33:1, 281–287.

Shaked, Israel. 1986. "Are Multinational Corporations Safer?" *Journal of International Business Studies* 26:1, 83–101.

Shapiro, Alan C. 1983. "International Capital Budgeting." *Midland Journal of Corporate Finance* 1:1, 26–45.

Stanley, Majorie T., and Stanley B. Block. 1984. "A Survey of Multinational Capital Budgeting." *Financial Review* 19:1, 36–54.

Stonehill, Arthur, and Leonard Nathanson. 1968. "Capital Budgeting and the Multinational Corporation." *California Management Review* 10:4, 39–52.

Capital Structure and Financing Decisions

> Given the complexities of the real-world setting, actual [capital structure] decision procedures are inevitably heuristic, judgmental, imitative and groping even where, as with so much of what passes for capital budgeting, they wear the superficial trappings of hard-nosed maximization.
>
> Merton Miller (1977, p. 272)

Introduction

The long-term liabilities and shareholders' equity accounts on a firm's balance sheet constitute its capital structure. These accounts record how a firm finances its assets through a combination of debt, preferred stock, retained earnings, and common equity. In most countries, debt enjoys a tax subsidy, lowering its cost. The percentage of debt in capital structures, however, varies widely across companies and industries. Explaining this variation and determining whether a firm can enhance its value by changing its capital structure are two concerns that dominate theoretical research in capital structure.

Most theories of capital structure are normative because they use rational economic models to describe how firms should establish and adjust their capital structures. This chapter identifies five theoretical capital structure models: (1) static trade-off, (2) pecking order, (3) signaling, (4) agency cost, and (5) neutral mutation. The purpose of this chapter is to review the survey research that tests the connections between these normative theories and corporate practice.

Unlike other topics in this book, capital structure theories almost outnumber the related studies using survey research. Also unlike other topics, the surveys reviewed demonstrate little consensus around any of the five capital structure theories. Instead, we find support, not always recognized by researchers, for a financial planning rule-of-thumb approach to the practice of managing capital structure. Respondents often cite this approach either explicitly or implicitly in more than thirty years of survey research. Despite this consistency, some survey researchers do not believe the rule-of-thumb approach should explain capital structure practice, even though Miller (1977) suggests that heuristics are the dominant real-world decision rule.

Because most of the survey research reviewed in this chapter investigates more than one of the five models, organizing such research around each model is impractical. Instead, the surveys are ordered chronologically to provide order and perspective. This chapter traces the results of the most important surveys and summarizes where the literature stands today on the extent to which managerial practice follows the theoretical models.

Theories of Capital Structure

One of the potential disconnects between capital structure models and corporate practice is that all the models originate in the famous irrelevance theory of Modigliani and Miller (1958; hereafter MM). This theory, often called the "nothing matters" proposition, holds that a firm's capital structure does not affect its value if markets have perfect information and there are no taxes or bankruptcy costs. The intention of MM was not to use this elegant argument to explain real-world behavior. Rather, their purpose was to show the necessary yet minimally sufficient assumptions that render capital structure irrelevant to the value of the firm. This approach helped later researchers focus on the effect of relaxing these unrealistic assumptions. Despite extensive theoretical capital structure literature that has explored the effects of more realistic assumptions, the irrelevance tag may lull corporate executives into believing that capital structure does not matter.

Academic researchers continue to pay homage to MM when building models that assume capital structure does affect a firm's value. Although the purpose of this chapter is not to review the derivation of capital structure models, the chapter organizes the five theories into groups to provide a foundation for interpreting some of the survey research that investigates the relevance of capital structure theory in the corporate world. Myers (1984) is responsible for labeling the first two groups.

Static Trade-Off Models

Static trade-off models assume that each firm has a value-maximizing optimal capital structure that minimizes its overall weighted average cost of capital (WACC).

Because the after-tax cost of debt is usually less expensive than equity, firms will add debt up to the point where the risk of bankruptcy raises the WACC. This model comes directly from MM, who point out that firms will favor debt as a source of financing when it enjoys a tax shield. In the presence of bankruptcy costs, MM note that firms should be concerned about having too much debt. In static trade-off models, companies use capital market transactions to maintain their optimal capital structure in the face of market imperfections such as bankruptcy, income taxes, and debt tax shields.

Fischer, Heinkel, and Zechner (1989) provide a variation of this theory by modeling capital structure choice with transaction costs. In their model, capital structure is dynamic rather than strictly static because transaction costs discourage firms from rebalancing when they depart from their target capital structure. Still, their approach is classified as a static trade-off model because capital structures vary around a target, subject to the cost of rebalancing. The static trade-off model has been a longtime staple of successful corporate finance textbook authors such as VanHorne (2001), Brigham and Ehrhardt (2008), and Brealey, Myers, and Allan (2008).

Pecking-Order Models

Pecking-order models assert that when managers possess valuable insider information, they should have a preference for internal over external capital because the market is unlikely to underprice internal equity. According to Myers and Majluf (1984), managers who have private information about their company's prospects should exhaust internal sources before raising external capital, first with straight and convertible debt and then with equity. Researchers commonly refer to these models as asymmetric information models because of the difference in information between corporate insiders and outsiders.

Berger, Espinosa-Vega, Frame, and Miller (2005) investigate this model empirically by collecting data on bank loans. However, bank loans, unlike bonds, are short-term debt, so Berger et al. did not test the pecking-order theory against a broader definition of capital structure. Their findings indicate that low-relative-risk firms seem to adopt debt structures that could reduce information asymmetry, while high-relative-risk firms do not. These results are inconsistent with the pecking-order hypothesis. Despite these negative findings, the pecking-order model remains important because survey evidence suggests that some firms may use this approach.

Signaling Models

Signaling models, developed by Miller and Rock (1985), are similar to the pecking-order models in that they invoke information asymmetries; their motivation, however, differs dramatically. In signaling models, potential investors grow accustomed to management presenting news about the company's prospects in the most flattering light. As a consequence, investors discount every management report, even when it is truthful, which in turn raises the firm's cost of capital above what it otherwise would be. Management, therefore, has an incentive to convey credible information to the market about the firm's positive net present value projects. One way of providing a credible signal is to fund these projects with new capital. Theoretically, management will not issue more stock and dilute its ownership stake to finance a new project unless it believes the project will be profitable. Managements, therefore, should view capital structure changes as a way to communicate with the market and overcome their inherent credibility problem.

In these models, internal funding still dominates all external sources. Companies do not have a preference among external sources because the act of financing externally signals an unavailability of internal financing. As discussed in Chapter 6, most of the theoretical and empirical development of signaling models involves signaling with dividends. Even so, signaling is one of the prominent capital structure theories.

Agency Cost Models

Jensen and Meckling (1976) assume that agency costs are widespread in non-owner-managed firms. These costs arise because management has an incentive to invest in perks, such as a Learjet or expensive office decorations, which benefit management without increasing shareholder wealth. When the firm partially finances its assets with debt, it must pay out cash in the form of interest and principal that it might otherwise use to fund management perquisites. By substituting debt for external equity, the firm also increases the managers' stake in the financial outcome, bringing the interest of both managers and the remaining shareholders closer together. Therefore, management can maximize firm value by issuing both debt and equity and can thereby minimize agency costs.

The agency cost theory says that firms subject to agency costs should maintain capital structures that have both debt and equity, but these models say little about the proportions or preferences for specific instruments. Extensions of this model can be found in Barnea, Haugen, and Senbet (1980), who argue that exchanging short-term for long-term debt can reduce agency costs in the presence of information asymmetry, and in Chang (1992), who shows that the optimal capital structure contains less debt when leverage and employee-compensation contracts are jointly determined.

Neutral Mutation Models

In responding to critics of the MM model, Miller (1977) suggests that theoretical models will never match executive practice because no one can measure whether a firm's value is maximized by its capital structure. Instead, Miller states that executives understandably rely on "heuristic, rule-of-thumb, intuitve kinds of decision making" (p. 272). According to Miller, these rules persist because they are benign "neutral mutations" that "serve no function, but do no harm, [and] can persist indefinitely" (p. 273).

Survey research has not extensively tested the neutral mutation model, because some researchers such as Kamath (1997) have misinterpreted Miller's hypothesis as implying that financial decisions are only habits, and few executives will respond to a survey that suggests their decisions are driven by custom rather than concrete analysis. On the contrary, Miller (1977) suggests that neutral mutations are remnants of a previous environment in which they had survival value. By the same Darwinian logic, rules of thumb persist as long as they are appropriate to the environment, with variations wide enough to allow the organism to adapt to cyclical changes. In evolutionary terms, the only time that rules of thumb face serious challenges is when the environment undergoes a structural change. Neutral mutation financial models, therefore, are more an explanation than a model. Despite their lack of theoretical elegance, Miller's financial rules of thumb are an important explanation for firm behavior.

In their synthesis of capital structure theory, Chaplinsky and Harris (1998) suggest that capital structure theories deserve a "new synthesis" and should be viewed as a trade-off between the benefits of leverage, the deductibilty of interest, and the costs of bankruptcy, supplemented by the recognition that markets charge a risk premium for information asymmetry and agency costs. According to Chaplinsky and Harris, every firm has an optimal capital structure that goes beyond "a narrow decision about the level of debt [to] a broad look at the firm, its products, its markets and its governance" (p. 11). Like many academic researchers, they do not discuss rules of thumb as an explanation for capital structure practice. This chapter will focus on what survey research shows about management's perspective on the capital structure decisions it makes and also on relating that perspective to all five of the capital structure theories.

Empirical Support of Capital Structure Theories

A relationship between stock prices and capital structure changes is to be expected, as informational efficiencies in the market encourage appropriate monitoring by investors of capital structure and price securities. Three empirical studies confirm the connection between capital structure and stock prices. First, Smith (1986) documents how a firm's stock price responds to changes in leverage. Second, Asquith and Mullins (1986) report that the market reacts negatively to changes in capital structure that dilute shareholders' equity. Finally, Cheung and Ng (1992) summarize previous research that confirms the informationally efficient market assertion that changes in firm value track changes in capital structure. Without such empirical support, MM would be correct that capital structure really is irrelevant.

Pioneering Research: The Early Years (Pre-1985)

Stonehill, Beekhuisen, Wright, Remmers, Toy, Pares, Shapiro, Egan, and Bates (1986) survey capital structure decisions during the period from 1972 to 1973. This survey provides a comparison across five countries: France, Japan, the Netherlands, Norway, and the United States. The authors' intent is to help financial executives better understand the challenges of managing the capital structure of foreign subsidiaries operating in countries with different financial regulations, customs, and social contracts. According to Stonehill et al. (1986), their objective is to explain "the financial structure norms and determinants in various companies and why they differ from one another" (p. 28). Stonehill et al. purport that problems arise whether the foreign subsidiary adopts the debt ratio of the parent company or conforms to local norms.

In 1972, Stonehill et al. (1986) conducted in-person interviews with executives of eighty-seven manufacturing firms in France, Japan, the Netherlands, Norway, and the United States. In the sample, Japanese companies constitute 23 percent (twenty companies); French 9 percent (eight companies); Dutch, 15 percent (thirteen companies); Norweigen, 30 percent (twenty-six companies); and United States, 23 percent (twenty companies). In the interviews, they ask respondents about their firms' capital structure decisions between 1966 and 1970. The researchers also inquire about the firm's financial objective, the determinants of the firm's debt ratio, and how the firm measures its total debt as a percentage of total assets. Although administration of this survey occurred after MM and before the development of the other four capital structure theories, the results can be interpreted in light of those theories.

Stonehill et al.'s (1986) discussion of the survey results contains a facinating picture of the state of capital markets in the 1960s and 1970s. For example, the authors caution that the U.S. firms surveyed might favor borrowing in foreign markets because the Bretton Woods fixed exchange rate system was in effect until 1971. They also cite a lack of foreign direct investment by countries other than the United States as a defining feature of the global economy. Even with these anachronisms, the survey responses suggest the respondents' attitudes toward capital structure theories that, for the most part, were not yet articulated.

Stonehill et al. (1986) first ask about financial goals. The interviewers pose a fill-in-the-blank question—namely, "The financial objective of your firm is . . .," followed by nine prescribed choices and an open response. The survey results show that the executives overwhelmingly choose maximize earnings growth as the financial objective, defined either in total (France, Japan, and the Netherlands), as earnings before interest and tax (EBIT; Norway), or as per share (United States) by a margin of almost two to one. The authors explain that in every country but the United States, the concept of per share or a shareholder perspective is almost unknown. According to Stonehill et al. "most financial executives favor goals which benefit the firm as an independent entity and enable management to maintain flexibility and control" (p. 32). This attitude is closer to a rule of thumb than to any of the formal theories.

Stonehill et al. (1986) then turn to debt ratio determinants. The interviewers pose fifteen prescribed determinants plus one open-ended determinant of the firm's debt ratio. The survey asks respondents to rank these according to their relative importance to the actual determination of their firm's debt ratio during the period from 1966 to 1970. Managing financial risk is the most often cited reason for capital structure policy, ranking first in the Netherlands, Norway, and the United States; third in Japan; seventh in France; and first overall (Stonehill et al. 1986, p.38). This ranking might imply that the respondents use a static trade-off approach, as this theory cites the risk-reward of increasing debt to lower the cost of capital without risking bankruptcy. Furthermore, the following two prescribed responses having to do with the cost of capital received low rankings:

"Our firm measures its weighted average cost of capital after taxes. We add debt to our capital structure until we think it has an adverse effect on our common stock price" (ranked thirteenth of sixteen overall).
"Given the level of our net operating income before taxes and financial charges, our debt ratio is relatively high (low) because of the favorable (unfavorable) influence of debt leverage on after-tax earnings per share" (ranked ninth of sixteen overall).

The authors point out that when they offer the prepared response "Our debt ratio is relatively high because of the tax advantage of debt. We borrow all we can because debt is the least expensive source of funds," it does no better than second place in the Netherlands, fourth place in France and Japan, fifth place in the United States, seventh place in Norway, and third place overall. Based on these low rankings, Stonehill et al. (1986) conclude that respondents are not following the static trade-off theory.

When asked to define their leverage measure, the respondents use either total debt at book value divided by total assets at book value (45 percent) or total debt at book value divided by total equity at book value (38 percent). Respondents avoid the choices involving market values. The almost exclusive focus on book measures of leverage reinforces the overall conclusion from this study: financial managers do not think about market forces as they would if they followed any of the capital structure theories, but more in terms of rules of thumb.

Scott and Johnson (1982) conducted a survey of *Fortune* 1000 firms in 1979. In this survey, they ask chief financial officers (CFOs) fourteen questions about whether they believe their firms have an optimal capital structure and whether that belief incorporates the cost of bankruptcy. They receive 212 responses, resulting in a 21.2 percent response rate. To maintain confidentiality, they coded the responses to distinguish between large firms (top half by sales) and small firms (bottom half by sales).

Scott and Johnson state that the purpose of their study is to "provide insight into the financing policies of large American corporations" (1982, p. 51). They explore the extent to which these large firms use the static trade-off theory to manage their capital structure by using four questions about optimum capital structure. Scott and Johnson state the following:

> By constructing a series of questions we hoped to ascertain if the financial executives subscribe to or reject the traditional "u-shaped" or "saucer-shaped" average cost of capital curve. This four-question approach to gathering opinions on the shape of the cost of capital curve is certainly indirect. We do not believe, however, that it is devious—at least not intentionally so. A direct question to the executives on the relationship between leverage use and the shape of the cost of capital curve was not asked in order to avoid financial jargon more familiar to academics than practioners. (p. 54)

Table 5.1 shows the responses. These uniformly high responses lead Scott and Johnson to observe, "It was clearly evident that the participating executives

TABLE 5.1 Optimal capital structure survey questions and responses about the role of capital structure

This table shows the frequency of responses to four yes-no questions soliciting CFO's opinions regarding their firm's capital structure. The purpose of this table is to display the uniformly positive responses to these questions which suggest the respondents believe in an optimal capital structure, in turn supporting the static trade-off theory. All but five of the 212 responding firms answered these questions

Question	Frequency	
	Yes (%)	No (%)
Does your firm believe that there is a functional relationship between its capital costs and the amount of debt which it utilizes in its financial structure?	92	8
Does your firm believe that the use of a "proper" amount of debt in its capitalization (as opposed to none, or too much) will result in a lower overall cost of capital to the corporation?	92	8
Does your firm believe that the use of an excessive amount of debt will eventually result in an increase in the yield (cost) of debt faced by your company?	97	3
Does your firm believe that the use of an excessive amount of debt will eventually result in the market price of your common stock being adversely affected?	90	10

subscribe to the concept of an optimal capital structure. Further, they believe the prudent use of debt can lower the firm's overall cost of capital and that debt-use [*sic*] can affect common stock price" (1982, p. 57). These responses appear to support the static trade-off approach to capital structure management. Of course, researchers had not yet developed the alternative theories.

Further evidence for the static trade-off theory can be found in the responses to two other questions in Scott and Johnson's (1982) survey about target debt ratios and the cost of bankruptcy. Of the respondents, 89 percent say they have a target debt ratio, with 64 percent of these ratios falling in the range of 26 to 30 percent, which Scott and Johnson indicate demonstrates that corporations actively set debt ratios as part of capital structure management. Responses to the question, "Does your firm believe that there is some *maximum* amount of debt financing that should not be surpassed? (i.e., does your firm subscribe to the concept of a corporate debt capacity?)" results in a positive response from 87 percent of respondents. While this question does not mention bankruptcy costs, the respondents almost surely link a limited debt capacity with the penalty for exceeding that capacity. For these two questions, at least, the respondents appear to be following a static trade-off approach.

When Scott and Johnson (1982) explore the differences between the large and small firms, the support for the static trade-off theory weakens. Large and small firm responses differ in two ways: in how small firms measure debt capacity and in how they use agency debt ratings. If these firms had been using a static trade-off approach, they would not have used book values to measure leverage and debt agency ratings would not have dictated their leverage.

While 89 percent of the whole sample reports measuring leverage, 36 percent of the large firms and 50 percent of small firms use book values to compute their debt ratios. The Stonehill et al. (1986) survey demonstrates a similar focus on book values. Using book values to define leverage is more consistent with a rule of thumb than with the static trade-off theory. Furthermore, 21 percent of the large firms report that they measure their debt capacity by whatever it takes to maintain their debt rating, while only 6 percent of the small firms do so. Scott and Johnson quote one large firm respondent as saying, "Our debt capacity is limited by our desire to maintain an AAA rating" (1982, p. 56). Debt ratings are an external factor, so this response suggests more of the large-firm executives acknowledge the importance of capital markets. Even so, relying on an external agency to establish debt capacity would be more like a rule of thumb than recognizing the trade-off between the advantages of debt and the cost of bankruptcy, as the static trade-off theory requires. Less than 20 percent of the whole sample of firms rely on debt-rating agencies, so even if the other firms are sensitive to market forces, it is far from a unamious opinion. In sum, the differences between large and small firms reveal that many firms do not think about market forces, indicating less-than-complete support for the static trade-off theory.

Scott and Johnson (1982, pp.56–57) summarize their results as follows:

1. "Firms use target financial leverage ratios as an input to making financial decisions."
2. "It was clearly evident that the participating executives subscribe to the concept of an optimal capital structure. Further, they believe the prudent use of debt can lower a firm's overall cost of capital."
3. "The participating financial executives overtly accept the concept of corporate debt capacity."

Taken at face value, these results support the static trade-off theory of capital structure. While Scott and Johnson (1982) did not design the questions with any of the other theories in mind, there seems to be little evidence of respondents using the pecking-order theory. The authors find that 87 percent of the firms say their management establishes their target debt ratios and that external influences, such as security analysts and trade creditors, have almost no effect. If management is concerned about information asymmetry or signaling, they would rate the importance of these external audiences far more highly, so support for the pecking-order theory is weak.

Confounding Factors: The Middle Years (1985 to 2000)

Pinegar and Wilbricht (1989) and Norton (1991) conducted complementary surveys on capital structure that build on the work done by Scott and Johnson (1982). In a survey of the CFOs of *Fortune* 500 firms conducted in 1986, Pinegar and Wilbricht obtain a 35 percent response rate; however, since their research design did not require the responding firms to identify themselves, they could not provide a measure of response bias by industry or size. As discussed in Chapter 2, anonymity is a common feature of survey research, designed to increase response rates. *Fortune* 500 firms are successful and among the largest in the market, meaning this survey also could not explore differences based on size or financial condition. Pinegar and Wilbricht point out that their sample is homogeneous to the extent that it excludes utilities and financials.

The Pinegar and Wilbricht (1989) survey investigates whether managers seem to follow the pecking-order, signaling, or static trade-off capital structure theory. Because Pinegar and Wilbricht were conducting the survey shortly after the enactment of the Tax Reform Act of 1986, they inquire about whether managers consider taxes when setting capital structure policy. The Tax Reform Act, the second of the two "Reagan tax cuts," decreased individual income taxes and increased corporate tax rates. The authors hypothesize that to the extent managers adapt their capital structures to reflect changes in their or their shareholders' tax situation, large, successful firms should have more flexibility to change their capital structures in response to changes in taxes than small firms. Further, Pinegar and Wilbricht expect that because of diffused ownership in large firms, managers would want to lower agency costs. Their large-firm sample biases their results in favor of managers reporting they have a target capital structure. Despite this bias, the survey finds that almost 70 percent of the respondents appear to be using a pecking-order model. When asked about raising capital, these managers rank internal equity as their first choice and external equity as their last choice by a margin of 84 percent to 40 percent, respectively. Managers choose straight debt over convertible debt, while common outranks preferred stock. Based on this analysis, Pinegar and Wilbricht suggest that a large percentage of their sample might use a pecking-order model.

Pinegar and Wilbricht (1989) also want to determine whether managers use capital structure as a way to signal investors about their firm's prospects. To probe this aspect, they ask respondents whether they view the market for their common stock as efficient. About half of the respondents reply that the market fairly prices their stock more than 80 percent of the time. Only 10 percent respond that their market misprices their stock more than 50 percent of the time. Regardless of opinion, few respondents see their capital structure as affecting their firm's stock price. The authors interpret these results as providing little support for managers sending deliberate signals of firm value through capital structure.

In reviewing the pecking-order, signaling, and static trade-off models, Pinegar and Wilbricht (1989) conclude that static trade-off models received the least support from their respondents. Although the Tax Reform Act of 1986 was a frequent presence in the news at the time of the survey, the responses indicate little concern over the tax implications of capital structure decisions. The authors report that their sample demonstrates a general disinclination toward any formal capital structure theory. To the contrary, the respondents appear to use financial planning principles. By financial planning principles, the authors mean that the respondents use rules of thumb to adjust debt and equity rather than explicitly maintaining a static capital structure, using a pecking order to determine which security to issue, or signaling about inside information. When asked about the prevalence of financial planning by using the question, "Please indicate the relative importance of the following considerations in governing your firm's financing decisions," the respondents rank seven considerations as shown in Table 5.2.

Table 5.2 demonstrates that financial planning considerations, such as maintaining financial flexibility and long-term survivability, are ranked higher than debt ratings and comparability with other firms.

In Table 5.3, Pinegar and Wilbricht (1989) contrast the scores in Table 5.2 with the scores the respondents award to eleven considerations associated with capital structure theories.

Pinegar and Wilbricht (1989) point out that in Table 5.2, five of the seven financial planning considerations score 3.99 or above and outrank all but one of

TABLE 5.2 Financial planning considerations: Responses to questions about whether firms use financial planning heuristics in capital structure decisions

This table shows the means calculated from the respondents' choices to the question: "Please indicate the relative importance of the following considerations in governing your firm's financing decisions". The means use the scale from the original survey which says: "on a scale of 1 to 5 where 1 = unimportant and 5 = important". The seven responses offered are shown below in the rows of the table and are designed to elicit which of the financial planning responses the respondents favor. This table suggests that the respondents favor flexibility and survivability over debt ratings and comparability.

Consideration	Mean response
Maintaining financial flexibility	4.55
Ensuring long-term survivability	4.55
Maintaining a predictable source of funds	4.05
Maximizing security prices	3.99
Maintaining financial independence	3.99
Maintaining a high debt rating	3.56
Maintaining comparability with other firms in the industry	2.47

TABLE 5.3 Capital structure decisions: Respondents' ranking of theoretical rationales for their capital structure decisions

This table shows the means calculated from the respondents' choices to the question: "Please indicate the relative importance of the following considerations in governing your firm's financing decisions." The means use the scale from the original survey which says: "On a scale of 1 to 5 where 1 = Unimportant and 5 = Important." The eleven responses offered are shown below and are designed to elicit which of the capital structure theories the respondents favor. The purpose of this table is to compare the generally lower mean scores awarded to these theoretical considerations to the generally higher mean scores awarded the financial planning considerations in Table 5.2.

Consideration	Mean response
Projected cash flow from asset to be financed	4.41
Avoid dilution of common stockholders' claims	3.94
Risk of asset to be financed	3.91
Restrictive covenants on senior securities	3.62
Avoid mispricing of securities to be issued	3.60
Corporate tax rate	3.52
Voting control	3.24
Depreciation and other non-debt tax shields	3.05
Correcting mispricing of outstanding securities	2.66
Personal tax rates of debt and equity holders	2.14
Bankruptcy costs	1.58

the eleven considerations that should be important under one or more of the theoretical models in Table 5.3. Pinegar and Wilbricht also note that the three top-scoring theoretical considerations—"projected cash flow from asset to be financed," "avoid dilution of common stockholders' claims," and "risk of asset to be financed" (p. 87)—could just as easily be interpreted as supporting a financial planning perspective rather than evidence of signaling, especially in light of the managers' consensus that capital structure decisions are not related to stock price.

Pinegar and Wilbricht suggest that capital structure may not be as simple as any of the formal theoretical models suppose: "The findings strongly suggest that corporate managers evaluate investment and financing decisions simultaneously. Hence, these decisions are not independent and security price reactions to capital structure changes may reflect a revision in market expectations of the firm's operating performance" (1989, pp. 85–86). Furthermore, Pinegar and Wilbricht note that "multiple factors bear on the financing choice, and several financing alternatives may be considered simultaneously. Perhaps such complexities explain why managers are guided more by planning principles than by the implied precision of our theoretical models" (p. 88).

This survey suggests that managers are more likely to use a pecking order than a target debt-equity mix in making capital structure decisions. Respondents do not believe their stock prices are associated with capital structure, so they are unlikely to consider signaling. Finally, financial rules of thumb appear to be more prevalent than any of the capital structure models.

The Norton (1991) study uses the same target audience (CFOs of *Fortune* 500 companies) and time frame (1984). This study is an ideal companion to Pinegar and Wilbricht (1989) because it looks for sources of heterogeneity in the responses, which is difficult to do while maintaining anonymity. The response rate of 21 percent is lower than Pinegar and Wilbricht's 35 percent but large enough to warrant reasonable inferences.

Norton (1991) investigates the degree of heterogeneity through both factor and cluster analysis. Although the author admits that these techniques do not offer robust tests for statistical significance, he asserts that they can shed light on financial theory.

Norton (1991) uses principal components analysis to reduce the dimensionality of the survey responses. When a data set has fewer underlying causal factors than the number of variables, principal components uses a mathematical algorithm to extract the underlying causal structure that best explains the variability in the data. When applied to survey data, principal components analysis assumes that some of the survey questions elicit the same underlying attitudes and beliefs. The extracted components are assumed to match these attitudes and beliefs. The number of components is always the same as the number of questions, but the researcher also assumes that the smaller number of underlying attitudes and beliefs can be associated with a reduced set of components. The identity of the components is not obvious because they are not identical to the original questions.

Norton's (1991) survey consists of twenty-seven questions about the theoretical motivations for capital structure policy. He uses principal components analysis to identify the nine most important components. In the language of principal components, the managers' responses to the twenty-seven questions are loaded (or weighted) on these components, giving each a distinct mix of responses. The author labels these components as "factors" and interprets these factors through their response weights. For example, the question responses that are highly weighted toward factor 1 all have to do with the market as a whole. Therefore, Norton labels this factor as "capital market is the firm's primary concern." This factor explains 14.8 percent of the variance in the responses and is weighted by the question responses shown in Table 5.4.

Norton (1991) interprets this factor as indicating that managers focus on the broad capital markets instead of catering to clienteles or market segments. His original Table 2, adapted in this chapter as Table 5.5 with information from his Table 1, shows all nine factors, which together explain 66.7 percent of the variance in the responses.

According to Norton (1991), factors 1 (the capital market is a firm's primary concern rather than clienteles or certain market segments), 5 (information asymmetries may have little impact on capital structure decisions), and 7 (active management) taken together suggest that managers adopt a marketwide view and do not use a pecking-order model that would acknowledge information asymmetries. These results differ from Pinegar and Wilbricht (1989), who find that pecking-order models are the most consistent with their respondents' choices.

Finding factors 2 (agency costs may be of little importance to the firms), 4 (signaling is not done or may not be important to the firms), and 5 (information asymmetries may have little impact on capital structure decisions) suggests that agency costs are not important. Factors 6 (tangible factors affect financing decisions), 7 (active management), 8 (management wishes to maintain flexibility), and 9 (labor market constraints on management) collectively indicate that rules of thumb may be important considerations. These results are consistent with Pinegar and Wilbricht (1989) and Scott and Johnson (1982).

Finally, these respondents consider taxes (factor 3), unlike those in Pinegar and Wilbricht (1989), who report that taxes rank tenth of the eleven theoretical considerations. Norton hypothesizes that management's "beliefs and preferences" (rules of thumb) have a greater effect on a firm's financing decisions than do any of the theoretical explanations (1991, p. 437).

Cluster analysis provides a different perspective on the responses. This technique defines the distance between each manager's responses to all the questions in multidimensional space and then assigns them to clusters such that the intracluster distance is minimized and the intercluster distance is maximized. This technique classifies the firms into groups based on their managers' responses.

TABLE 5.4 Questions and associated weights: How each question loads on factor 1

This table displays how the responses to Norton's (1991) twenty-five questions are weighted on factor one, which the author interprets as: "capital structure is the firm's primary concern." Each factor extracted from the responses explains a portion of the variability among responses. This factor explains 14.8 percent, the highest among all nine factors displayed in Norton (1991). The purpose of this table is to illustrate how the responses are loaded on (or attracted to) this factor—both positively and negatively.

Question	Weight	Question	Weight
Private placements at least 75% of the time	68	Debt sends an unfavorable signal	17
Private placements offer a satisfactory information exchange	64	Private placements offer higher prices than public issues	12
Clientele versus market	64	Private placements offer less-restrictive covenants	21
Income bonds not used due to poor connotation	−49	Debt used to lower costs	1
Insured debt	−3	Investors' tax views	−4
If D/E = 0, attitude would differ toward profits	−22	Lower D/E if firm was more R&D dependent	13
Income bonds are an attractive hybrid financing tool	29	Financing costs set by market	−13
		Play yield curve	−10
Stock price falls when debt is issued	28	Suggest restrictive covenants	23
Decrease debt if interest no longer deductible	12	Callable bonds	−49
Tax-loss carry-forwards	0	Bankruptcy and jobs	9
Common stock sends an unfavorable signal	0		

Source: Adapted from Norton (1991, pp. 434–435).

The cluster analysis results suggest the responses contain three identifiable clusters of three, fifty-seven, and thirty-eight firms. Norton (1991) discards the first cluster as too small and focuses his analysis on the other two. These clusters reveal a potentially confounding factor. The first cluster shares responses that are contrary to the theoretical models: no belief in optimal capital structure, pecking order, signaling, or agency costs. Norton hypothesizes that these firms are successful and well managed and probably meet their financing needs with internally generated funds. He observes that these firms do not consider taxes

TABLE 5.5 Factor analysis results interpretation of the nine most important factors produced by factor analysis

This table combines information from two tables in Norton (1991) that report the results of his factor analysis. The purpose of this table is to summarize the factors identified by the author and the percentage of the overall variance each factor explains. These nine factors together explain 66.7 percent of the response variance.

Factor	Variance explained (%)	Interpretation
1	14.8	The capital market is a firm's primary concern, rather than "clienteles" or certain market segments
2	9.5	Agency costs may be of little importance to the firms
3	8.3	Taxes affect capital structure decisions
4	7.6	Signaling is not done or may not be important to the firms
5	6.0	Information asymmetries may have little impact on capital structure decisions
6	5.5	Tangible factors affect financing decisions
7	5.5	Active management
8	5.2	Management wishes to maintain flexibility
9	4.4	Labor-market constraints on management

Source: Adapted from Norton (1991, pp. 434, 435, and 438).

from their investors' viewpoints and do not cite bankruptcy costs as a capital structure consideration.

The firms in the second cluster are more inclined to respond in terms of financing alternatives, which indicates they follow a pecking-order model, and are more concerned about their investors' taxes. Norton (1991) suggests these firms in the second cluster might be less financially successful and might have a higher cost of capital than those in the first group. Norton concludes that "the capital structure decision process may differ among the responding firms" (p. 442). If capital structure decisions among firms depend on their relative financial health, then decisions within a firm should also vary over time. Norton implies this possibility when he says, "Thus, as managers face different situations over the life cycle of the firm, their incentives, motivations, and expectations may affect their capital structure decisions" (p. 444).

Norton's (1991) hypothesis that capital structure decisions depend on the firm's stage in its life cycle is a much more complex concept of firm dynamics than the transactions costs model of Fischer, Heinkel, and Zechner (1989). At the same time, a life-cycle model would result in inevitable complications and would require either a longitudinal survey or a research design that utilizes a variety of firms with identified financial characteristics. Norton's study design did not allow him to pursue this hypothesis.

Although neither the Pinegar and Wilbricht (1989) nor the Norton (1991) study provides solid support for any of the capital structure models, both provide related explanations for the failure to find empirical support for the theories of capital structure. The studies pose three related challenges for capital structure theories. First, Pinegar and Wilbricht argue that rather than separating the investment and financing decisions as financial theory would suggest, perhaps financial executives think about raising capital on a project-by-project basis. Solving the simultaneous problems of choosing a project and deciding how to finance it might lead executives to rely on financial planning rules of thumb rather than closely reasoned capital structure theories. Second, an implication of Norton's study is that a firm's financial condition affects its capital structure decisions. Third, although these two studies survey only large firms, both mention the possibility that firm size could be a confounding factor.

A subsequent survey by Kamath (1997) uses Pinegar and Wilbricht's (1989) questions with a different sample. This survey indirectly tests the rule-of-thumb approach. Kamath surveyed the CFOs of almost 700 firms listed on the New York Stock Exchange as of December 31, 1998, and received a 21 percent response rate. His sample excludes *Fortune* 500 industrial firms, financials, and real estate investment trusts (REITs). The questions are slight modifications of six of the Pinegar and Wilbricht questions plus six questions from the Gitman and Mercurio (1982) survey of cost of capital techniques, reviewed in Chapter 6. Kamath's purpose was to gather information on managerial views and practices with respect to capital structure by the largest retailers, utilities, transportation companies, and others and to extend the Pinegar and Wilbricht sample by including second-tier industrial firms. Kamath also posed a question about adhering to industry norms as a way of testing Miller's (1977) neutral mutation hypothesis.

The reponses to Kamath's questions about the objectives of capital structure policy indicate a split between static trade-off and pecking order. In raising new funds, 65 percent of the respondents say they follow the pecking-order model, while 35 percent maintain a target capital structure. These results confirm the findings of Pinegar and Wilbricht (1989) as well as Scott and Johnson (1982). When asked about planning principles, the respondents rank financial flexibility and ensuring long-term survivability as the most important. These results confirm that these firms use rules of thumb to determine their capital structure. This survey reveals more about these rules of thumb than Kamath may recognize.

Kamath (1997) interprets Miller's (1977) neutral mutation hypothesis as implying that habit drives financing decisions. As mentioned previously in this chapter, that was almost surely not Miller's intent. Nevertheless, this research is important because of what it inadvertently reveals about rules of thumb. To test the influence of habit on capital structure, Kamath asks managers if maintaining comparability with the industry is important. Kamath admits that this question is a distant cousin of habituation. Even so, the responses do not support the hypothesis that financing decisions are a product of habit. When divided into firms that identify themselves as static trade-off and pecking-order firms, the static firms rate their industry debt ratio as somewhat more important in guiding their capital structure decisions. Unfortunately, Kamath does not disclose enough information to allow readers to reach a judgment about the statistical significance of this difference. He does note that all respondents rank the following statement as least important: "Overall, for practical purposes, this financial planning principle [maintaining comparability with other firms in one's industry] is viewed to be as relatively unimportant as the objective of minimizing the probability of being acquired." Therefore, Kamath's results do not support the hypothesis that capital structures are decided by habit.

Yet, these findings provide some support for a financial-planning-based rule-of-thumb approach. Kamath (1997) reports the results of respondents' opinions about the relative importance of eight financial planning principles. Table 5.6 displays these results.

TABLE 5.6 The importance of financial planning principles: Responses to the inquiry, "Indicate the relative importance of the following considerations in governing your firm's financing decisions"

According to the authors: "Means are calculated by assigning values of 1 through 5 for rankings from 'unimportnat' to 'important,' respectively, and multiplying each value by the fraction of responses within each rank. A value of 0 is assigned when a factor is not ranked" (Kalmath, p. 339). In other words, the higher the mean, the more often that principle is highly ranked by the respondents. The purpose of this table is to show that financial planning principles, like financial flexibility and long-term survivability, not normally associated with any of the capital structure theories, receive high scores.

Planning principle by order of importance	Mean
Maintaining financial flexibility	4.43
Ensuring long-term survivability	4.37
Maximizing security prices	3.93
Maintaining a predictable source of funds	3.78
Maintaining financial independence	3.63
Maintaining a high debt rating	3.36
Maintaining comparability with other firms in the industry	2.61
Minimizing the probability of being acquired	2.58

Source: Abridged from Table 2 in Kamath (1997, p. 339).

While his interest in these results centers on their implications for the neutral mutation hypothesis, Kamath observes that the "ability to maintain financial flexibility and to ensure long-term survivability are rated as the two most important financial planning principles" (p. 338). He does not acknowledge the extent to which these results support a rules-of-thumb approach suggested by Pinegar and Wilbricht (1989) and Scott and Johnson (1982).

From the viewpoint of the potentially confounding issues raised by Pinegar and Wilbricht (1989) and Norton (1991), Kamath's (1997) research could not address the question of firm size, industry, or life cycle because his anonymous survey did not identify respondents. Even though the firms identify themselves as static trade-off and pecking-order firms, Kamath often fails to partition his sample between these firms. When he does divide the sample, as in the case of the question, "Given an attractive new growth opportunity that could not be taken without departing from your target capital structure or financing hierarchy, cutting the dividend, or selling off other assets, what action is your firm most likely to take?" the responses from both static trade-off and pecking-order firms are very similar. For example, 67.3 percent of the forty-nine firms that indicate they pursue a static target capital structure and 72 percent of the ninety-three firms that follow a pecking-order strategy select the response "deviate from the target capital structure or financing hierarchy."

When Kamath (1997) asks for respondents' views on the determinants of their firm's debt ratio, the results are inconsistent with empirical studies of debt ratios. For example, Table 5.7 presents the possible responses and their mean scores to the question, "In your opinion, the debt ratio of your firm depends on . . ."

TABLE 5.7 Debt ratio determinants: Responses to survey question about how firms determine debt ratios

According to the author: "Means are calculated by assigning values of 1 through 5 for ranking from 'disagee' to 'agree,' respectively, and by multiplying each value by the fraction of responses within each rank. A value of 0 is assigned when a statement is not ranked." (Kamath 1997, p. 349). In other words, the higher the mean, the more often that principle is highly ranked by the respondents. The purpose of this table is to show that debt ratios do not have a common determination, unlike the results expected when theory governs capital structure choices.

Response	Mean
Past profits	3.19
Average debt ratio in your industry	2.99
Past growth	2.93
Degree of diversification achieved by your firm	2.56
Past dividend payout	2.51

Source: Summarized from Table 6 in Kamath (1997, p. 349).

The questions shown in the table are all designed to elicit responses consistent with theory. Kamath (1997) concludes that because no theory emerges as a clear favorite, none of the capital structure theories explain these responses. The two least popular alternatives, diversification and past dividends, are suggested by researchers (Barton, Hill, and Sundaram 1989; Jahera and Lloyd 1991) who proposed that, in theory, firms with homogeneous product lines should have lower debt ratios than heterogeneous firms. According to Baskin (1989), finding no strong relation between debt ratios and past dividends is inconsistent with the theory that high dividend payouts and high debt ratios should be related. The responses to the question about industry averages suggest that while few firms would consciously position themselves as an outlier, managers do not set debt ratios in relation to the firm's industry norms.

Kamath's (1997) survey suggests that financial managers see both the static and pecking-order models as viable decision models for determining and managing capital structure. This evidence confirms the results of Scott and Johnson (1982), Pinegar and Wilbricht (1989), and Norton (1991). Kamath indirectly tests his interpretation of the neutral mutation hypothesis and finds no support. He does not explicitly test the signaling and agency cost models. Despite the suggestions of earlier authors like Pinegar and Wilbricht (1989), Scott and Johnson (1982) and Norton (1991), this study's design does not allow for an investigation of the effects of firm size, industry, or life-cycle stage and does not examine how firms treat their capital structure over time. The results do, however, support the rule-of-thumb approach as being the most popular among financial executives.

Much of the theoretical research conducted in the decade after the publication of these three studies does not substantially advance our understanding of how firms make capital structure decisions. Despite the need for empirical verification, none of these theoretical studies used survey research to test their hypotheses. This chapter does not review these studies, as they are theoretical and, despite their inventiveness, do not find support in surveys of practitioners.

A Comprehensive Survey: 2001

The landmark survey by Graham and Harvey (2001) is both robust and representative. In this study, the authors send out more than 4,000 surveys to CFOs in the United States and Canada and receive about 400 replies. The surveys ask detailed questions about capital budgeting, cost of capital, and capital structure. The responses cover both large and small firms, with 26 percent of the sample having less than $100 million in sales and 42 percent having more than $1 billion in sales. Capital structures vary, with one-third of the sample carrying less than 20 percent debt in their capital structure, one-third with debt ratios between 20 percent and 40 percent, and the final third having debt that constitutes more than 40 percent of capital. The sample has sufficient variation to shed light on numerous corporate finance questions and to be representative of the population.

The results concern many extant theories of corporate finance. Graham and Harvey conclude, "Our survey of the practice of corporate finance is both reassuring and puzzling" (2001, p. 232). The fact that respondents use theories such as the capital asset pricing model (CAPM) and practices such as net present value that academics endorse is reassuring. Yet, the fact that Graham and Harvey find evidence that "financial executives [are] much less likely to follow the academically prescribed factors and theories when determining capital structure" (p. 233) is a much more difficult result to explain.

According to Graham and Harvey (2001), the two most important determining factors in debt issuance are financial flexibility and credit ratings. When asked, "What factors affect how you choose the appropriate amount of debt for your firm?" the prepared responses rank as shown in Table 5.8.

Table 5.8 also displays the responses to the authors' question about debt policy. If the respondents follow the bankruptcy theory, the response "the potential costs of bankruptcy, near bankruptcy or financial distress" should be awarded a high rank. Instead, the financial planning principle, financial flexibility, is the most highly ranked response.

Graham and Harvey (2001) are hard-pressed to find evidence in these results that the respondents follow any of the capital structure theories. They express some support for the static trade-off capital structure theory because 34 percent of firms report having a tight target debt ratio, 37 percent have a flexible ratio, and only 19 percent have no target. This conclusion is supported by the results that demonstrate the importance of firm size: 55 percent of large firms have some sort of target debt ratio compared with only 36 percent of small firms. The evidence that these executives report about not considering bankruptcy costs (ranked seventh of fourteen) or their shareholders' personal taxes (ranked eleventh of fourteen) when determining their capital structure weakens the case for the static trade-off theory.

These results also provide only weak support for the Fischer, Heinkel, and Zechner (1989) proposal that transactions costs restrict a firm's ability to adjust to their target debt ratio. Although the respondents recognize transactions costs (ranked fifth of fourteen), when asked, "What other factors affect your firm's debt policy?" the respondents rank "We delay issuing debt because of transactions costs and fees" fifth out of eight choices, with a mean score of 1.04 out of a possible 4.0. Graham and Harvey consider this a more direct test of the Fischer, Heinkel, and Zechner (1989) proprosal and conclude "the support for the transactions cost hypothesis is weak" (2001, p. 215).

As Table 5.8 shows, financial flexibility is the top-ranked factor in determining leverage. While some might interpret this result as being consistent with a pecking-order approach, Graham and Harvey (2001) do not find support for that theory when they cross-tabulate these responses with stock issuance; that is,

TABLE 5.8 Factors affecting the appropriate amount of debt: Chief financial officers' responses to 14 factors affecting the appropriate amount of debt in their firm's capital structure, ranked by their mean score

This table displays the responses to the question: "What factors affect how you choose the appropriate amount of debt for your firm." The offered responses are shown as rows in the table along with their relative rank and mean score. The mean scores are calculated from the responses which are based on a scale where: "Respondents are asked to rate on a scale of 0 (not important) to 4 (very important)," Graham and Harvey (2001, pp. 212-213). The purpose of this table is to demonstrate that, contrary to theory, respondents appear to be favoring financial planning rules-of-thumb, like financial flexibility, over theoretical considerations, like the costs of bankruptcy.

Factor	Rank	Mean score
Financial flexibility (we restrict debt so we have enough internal funds available to pursue new projects when they come along)	1	2.59
Our credit rating (as assigned by rating agencies)	2	2.46
Volatility of our earnings and cash flows	3	2.32
The tax advantage of interest deductibility	4	2.07
Transactions cost and fees for issuing debt	5	1.95
Debt levels of other firms in our industry	6	1.49
The potential costs of bankruptcy, near bankruptcy, or financial distress	7	1.24
We limit our debt so that customers/suppliers are not worried about our firm going out of business	8	1.24
We restrict our borrowing so that profits from new/future projects can be captured fully by shareholders and do not have to be paid out as interest to debtholders	9	1.01
We try to have enough debt so that we are not an attractive takeover target	10	0.73
The personal tax cost our investors face when they receive interest income	11	0.68
If we issue debt, our competitors know that we are very unlikely to reduce our output	12	0.40
To ensure upper management works hard and efficiently, we issue sufficient debt to make sure that a large portion of our cash flow is committed to interest payments	13	0.33
A high debt ratio helps us bargain for concessions from our employees	14	0.16

Source: Summarized from Table 6 in Graham and Harvey (2001, pp. 212-213).

in the pecking-order approach, firms avoid using external equity when they have asymmetric information that leads them to believe the market undervalues their stock. Although survey respondents report that their firm's stock is undervalued and that undervaluation is the most important factor in the decision to issue stock, large, dividend-paying companies are more likely to cite undervaluation. Under the pecking-order hypothesis, undervaluation should be more important for small firms that do not pay a dividend and have greater information asymmetry.

With the exception of the static trade-off theory, the extant capital structure theories and their variations find little support. Among these discredited hypotheses are signaling, transactions costs, underinvestment costs, asset substitution, bargaining with employees, free cash flow, and product market considerations.

While Graham and Harvey (2001) find that capital structure policies vary with firm size, they do not directly investigate Norton's (1991) conjecture that the stage of the company's life cycle might affect its capital structure. They also do not consider Pinegar and Wilbricht's (1989) rule-of-thumb interpretation of the importance of financial flexibility. In fact, Graham and Harvey state in a footnote, "Like us, [Pinegar and Wilbricht] find that flexibility is the most important factor affecting financing decisions, and that bankruptcy costs and personal tax considerations are among the least important. Our analysis, examining a broader cross-section of theoretical hypotheses and using information on firm and executive characteristics, shows that the relative importance of these factors is robust to a more general survey design" (p. 218). Despite this striking similarity, Graham and Harvey do not classify financial flexibility as supportive of any of the capital structure theories, leaving the reader to wonder why respondents consistently rank it as the most important.

Instead, Graham and Harvey conclude,

Perhaps the relatively weak support for many capital structure theories indicates that it is time to critically reevaluate the assumptions and implications of these mainline theories. Alternatively, perhaps the theories are valid descriptions of what firms should do—but corporations ignore the theoretical advice. One explanation for this last possibility is that business schools might be better at teaching capital budgeting and the cost of capital [where the techniques are widely used] than teaching capital structure. (2001, p. 233)

Summary of the U.S. Evidence

The main goals of capital structure theory are to explain the variation in debt ratios across companies and to determine whether a firm can enhance its value by changing its capital structure. Setting the neutral mutation explanation aside for the moment, the theories that purport to explain capital structure practices (static trade-off, pecking order, signaling, and agency cost) all employ rational economic theory to determine how firms should behave.

Despite their elegance and academic appeal, none of these theories finds unqualified support from survey research. Several studies including Scott and Johnson (1982), Kamath (1997), and Graham and Harvey (2001) find some support for the static trade-off theory. Yet, Kamath (1997), Pinegar and Wilbricht (1989), and Graham and Harvey (2001) find support for the pecking-order theory. Evidence by Stonehill et al. (1986) as well as Kamath and Graham and Harvey contradicts this support. Graham and Harvey summarize their ambiguous findings by saying, "We find moderate support that firms follow the trade-off theory and target their debt ratio. Other results . . . are generally consistent with the pecking-order view. However, the evidence in favor of these theories does not hold up as well under close scrutiny" (pp. 232–233). None of the studies reviewed in this chapter finds any evidence that firms use signaling or consider agency cost as a way of managing capital structure.

There is consistent support across all surveys that managers use rules of thumb as guidelines to determine a firm's capital structure. Research shows that managers determine their firm's capital structure policy, use book values to measure leverage, and allow bond-rating agencies to establish debt capacity. Managers tell researchers that security prices and security analysts have little influence on their capital structure decisions. This widespread support for rules of thumb suggests that the state of our understanding of how firms determine capital structure today is much the same as it was in 1990. Current capital structure theories do not adequately explain capital structure decisions in practice. A period of low interest rates and loose credit standards from 2000 through 2007, however, provides an opportunity to witness changes in capital structures and can perhaps provide an insight into capital structure policy in practice.

Evidence from Stock Repurchases: An Opportunistic Explanation

As discussed in Chapters 2 and 3, survey research faces many challenges. The most vital for this discussion is the potential difference between how managers respond to surveys and how they act in practice. This section reviews some empirical evidence on how managers in the United States reacted when interest rates stayed historically low for a long period.

The decision to repurchase stock changes a firm's capital structure. Whether companies account for the transaction using the cost method (which produces a contra-equity account, typically called treasury stock) or the par-value method (in which the repurchased shares are extinguished), the firm reduces shareholders' equity and the debt-equity ratio increases. Traditionally, firms use excess cash to fund repurchases. Chapter 7 provides a detailed discussion of stock repurchases.

Firms repurchased their own stock at a phenomenal rate between 2003 and 2007, in some cases issuing debt instead of drawing down cash. The attendant changes in capital structure may provide an empirical clue to these executives' motivations. Stock-repurchase payouts during this period exceeded the dividend payout for the first time in history. Figure 5.1 shows that the average cash value of stock repurchases as a percentage of earnings soared for both small (Panel A) and large (Panel B) companies from 2002 through 2007.

One possible explanation for the dramatic increase in stock repurchases is low interest rates. Companies may have borrowed and used the proceeds to repurchase their own stock. Figure 5.2 shows the increase in book leverage (book value of debt divided by book value of equity) for the same U.S. companies compared to the Fed's discount rate. The upward trend in leverage could be, for large companies, a result of exchanging debt for equity when interest rates were low.

Figure 5.2 shows the average leverage increases between 2002 and 2006 for large firms. Small firms did not experience as large of an increase in their leverage. Figure 5.2 also shows how the interest rate (U.S. Federal Reserve discount rate) began falling in 2001 and rebounded through 2006. While association is not evidence of causation, the popularity of stock repurchases ended at about the same time as the financial crisis led to tightened credit standards for corporate borrowers in 2007. Executives may have been opportunistic in exchanging cheap debt for more expensive equity, suggesting they care about capital structure to the extent that it affects their weighted average cost of capital.

As further discussed in Chapter 7, Brav, Graham, Harvey, and Michaely (2005) report the results of a survey on payout policy that they administered in 2002. In discussing the possible motivations for repurchases, Brav et al. comment, "Companies are likely to repurchase when good investments are hard to find, when their stock's float is adequate, and when they wish to offset option dilution" (p. 485). When surveyed about priorities, managers report that they allocate money to repurchases after exhausting investment opportunities and that they would *pay down* debt if they reduced repurchases. Brav et al. do not ask survey recipients about the circumstances under which they would issue debt to maintain or increase repurchases, which is apparently what many companies did as interest rates fell in the years after the survey was conducted. Given the extraordinary credit markets in the years following the survey, the finding that neither the researchers nor the respondents considered the possibility of changing the capital structure by funding stock repurchases with debt is not surprising.

In survey research, timing is highly important. Without the experience of an extended period of low rates that, in hindsight, were symptomatic of the dislocations in the bond market, the executives might not have believed that they would issue debt to systematically repurchase shares on such a massive scale.

The lesson here is that executives may not always do what they say they might when presented with a hypothetical situation. Just as Graham, Harvey,

Panel A, Small Firms

S&P 600 Companies Cash Payout
as a % of Income Before Extraordinary Items

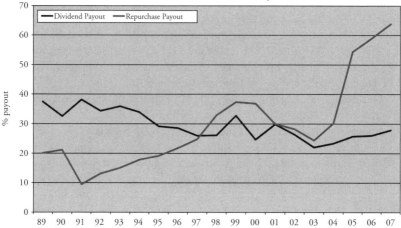

Panel B, Large Firms

S&P 500 Companies Cash Payout
as a % of Income Before Extraordinary Items

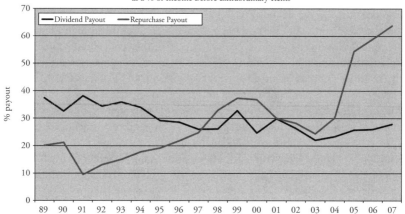

FIGURE 5.1 Stock repurchases and dividends as a percent of earnings before extraordinary items, 1989 to 2007

Panel *A,* small firms, shows how the cash payout ratio changes between 1989 and 2007 for small (Standard & Poor's [S&P] 600) firms in the United States. Panel *B,* large firms, shows how the cash payout ratio changes between 1989 and 2007 for large (S&P 500) firms in the United States. For both *A* and *B,* the increase in repurchase payout as a percentage of income starts to increase between 2003 and 2004 and reaches a peak in 2007. The dividend payout, however, increases only slightly over this time period. The purpose of both figures is to suggest that repurchases are more widely used, starting between 2003 and 2004 for both large and small firms.

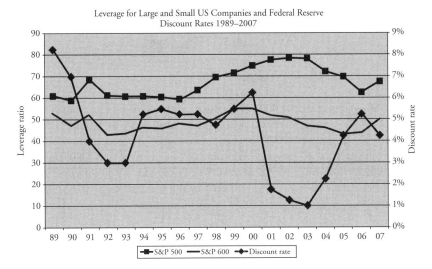

FIGURE 5.2 Leverage for large and small U.S. companies

This figure shows how leverage (book debt divided by book equity) changes between 1989 and 2007 for both large (Standard and Poor's [S&P] 500) and small (S&P 600) companies. These ratios (left-hand scale) are superimposed on a graph of the discount rate (right-hand scale). The U.S. Federal Reserve discount rate drops between 2000 and 2001 and rebounds between 2004 and 2006. Leverage rises for large companies between 2001 and 2004 and starts to decline in 2004. Leverage for small firms is mostly unchanged. The purpose of this figure is to track changes in leverage and to suggest that these changes, for large firms at least, coincide with low interest rates and the increase in share repurchases shown in Figure 5.1.

and Rajgopal (2006) find that executives are willing to sacrifice economic value for the sake of appearances, financial executives may contradict their response to Brav et al. (2005) when they increase their debt to repurchase shares. The survey literature on stock repurchases suggests that using repurchases to change capital structure has only recently become a major motive.

This protracted episode of low interest rates suggests capital market conditions may influence capital structure decisions. Corporations could lower their overall cost of capital by issuing bonds to lower their cost of debt and by substituting cheap debt for more expensive equity. Executives should exploit an inexpensive source of capital when the opportunity presents itself. If companies manage their capital structure opportunistically, then determining which capital structure theory applies is more difficult. Looking at share repurchases and capital structure changes alone cannot reveal *why* companies change their capital structure, as there are many motives for repurchasing stock. Now that this episode is over, conducting another survey that asks managers to recall their motives for altering their capital structures would reveal the extent to which capital structure decisions are opportunistic.

Evidence from Non-U.S. Firms

One advantage of financial theory is that its principles should apply regardless of the company's domicile. Unfortunately, institutional arrangements often vary by country, making cross-border comparisons difficult. As Stonehill et al. (1986) point out, the interpretation of ownership through equity and the rights of lenders differ from country to country. Much of the research on capital structure took place before the spread of International Financial Reporting Standards (IFRS). Thus, accounting standards at that time were sufficiently diverse to suggest that empirical research based on reported leverage would be difficult to interpret. Some researchers, therefore, investigate the determinants of capital structure through surveys. While this approach is not as susceptible to accounting incompatibilities as other types of empirical research, it does have its challenges. Ironically, if Graham, Harvey, and Rajgopal(2006) are correct that managers make decisions based more on appearances than economics, ignoring the accounting differences between countries may mean overlooking important factors in determining capital structure.

Logic suggests that different legal systems might also affect managers' leverage decisions. La Porta, Lopez-de-Silanes, Shleifer, and Vishny (1997), for example, point out that common-law legal systems should provide more investor protection than civil-law systems. The purpose of their empirical research is to assess the ability of firms in different legal environments to raise external finance through either debt or equity. They predict that countries with better legal protections should have more external finance in the form of both higher-valued and broader capital markets. Their rationale is that entrepreneurs are more willing to finance externally in countries with better legal property-rights protection.

La Porta et al. (1997) use marketwide variables such as market capitalization, the number of listed firms, and the frequency of initial public offerings. They also gather data that ranges from macroeconomic (e.g., gross domestic product [GDP] growth, debt to GDP) to corporate governance (e.g., one-share-one-vote) to WorldScope accounting measures (e.g., market capitalization to sales, market capitalization to cash flow). While the authors' macrovariables are largely free of reporting bias, they normalize their accounting variables for differences in accounting terminology but not for accounting standards. Their evidence suggests that companies in common-law countries with better investor protection are more willing to engage in external financing, resulting in both broader and higher-valued capital markets. Their results confirm that legal systems are a factor in capital structure decisions. Although the authors do not frame their research around the various capital structure theories, one interpretation of these results potentially favors a pecking order in the sense that companies domiciled in countries with poor protection against expropriation use less public financing and vice versa.

Another thread of this research argues that capital market effectiveness matters as much if not more than the legal system. Demirgüç-Kunt and Maksimovic (1999), for example, argue that a well-functioning legal, regulatory, and administrative system can overcome a less favorable legal system. In countries with better-developed administrative systems, more companies issue long-term debt. Using firm-level accounting data and indexes of economic development and legal systems, Demirgüç-Kunt and Maksimovic find

> systematic differences in the use of long-term debt between developed and developing countries and small and large firms. We find strong evidence that large firms in countries with effective legal systems have more long-term debt relative to assets, and their debt is of longer maturity. Large firms in countries with effective legal systems have lower short-term liabilities, suggesting that such firms are substituting long-term debt for short-term debt. For small firms, evidence of a relation between the effectiveness of the legal system and the ratio of long-term debt to assets is weaker. (p. 332)

Because a country's legal system and institutional arrangements explain much of the variation in the use of long-term debt, Demirgüç-Kunt and Maksimovic argue that firms' capital structures will reflect both the nature and effectiveness of the country's legal system. Here again, these results favor the pecking-order theory because firms either finance internally or externally, depending on the structure and effectiveness of their domestic legal system.

Survey research has addressed the question of capital structure in countries other than the United States. For example, Bancel and Mittoo (2004) survey companies in sixteen European countries to determine the factors that influence their capital structure decisions. Although highly similar to the questionnaire of Graham and Harvey (2001), Bancel and Mittoo modify or add several questions to enhance the cross-country comparison. The authors conduct their survey in late 2001 and early 2002. Their sample of 720 European firms results in a 12 percent response rate (eighty-seven firms). Of their sample, 45 percent of firms are from French civil- (or code-) law countries and 21 percent are from English common- (or case-) law countries; the sample also includes countries that use the German (19 percent) and Scandinavian (15 percent) legal systems.

The purpose of the Bancel and Mittoo (2004) study is to examine whether similar factors drive European and American managers' views on capital structure. They also study the sensitivity of different determinants of capital structure to the country's institutional and legal environment. They address two major questions through their survey: (1) What role does the legal system play in determining capital structure? and (2) Which of the capital structure theories are most consistent with their respondents' views?

In the capital structure theory debate, Bancel and Mittoo (2004) find that 75 percent of surveyed firms report having a target debt-to-equity ratio. Table 5.9 reports their responses to the question, "What factors affect how you choose the appropriate amount of debt for your firm?"

Bancel and Mittoo use the results in this table to point out that several of the top-ranked factors reflect the static trade-off model; namely, the tax deductibility of interest (3), volatility of earnings (4), concerns about financial stability

TABLE 5.9 Target capital structure: Respondents' ranking of factors affecting their target amount of debt

This table displays the results of Bancel and Mittoo's (2004) question: "What factors affect how you choose the appropriate amount of debt for your firm." The offered responses as well as resulting rank and mean scores are shown. Mean scores are based on a rating scale of 0 (not important) to 4 (very important). The authors say that 3 is associated with important and 4 with very important but further details of the scale are not reported by the authors. One purpose of this table is to show that the factor ranked first, financial flexibility, is more consistent with a financial planning view of capital structure than with any of the theories. The other purpose is to show how the remaining responses rank in comparison.

Factor	Rank	Mean score
Financial flexibility	1	3.39
Our credit rating	2	2.78
The tax deductibility of interest	3	2.59
Volatility of our earnings and cash flows	4	2.33
We limit our debt so that customers/suppliers are not worried about our financial stability	5	1.97
Transactions cost and fees for issuing debt	6	1.94
Debt levels of other firms in our industry	7	1.84
The potential costs of bankruptcy or near bankruptcy	8	1.76
Personal tax cost our investors face when they receive interest income	9	0.96
We try to have enough debt so that we are not an attractive target	10	0.85
To ensure upper management works hard and efficiently	11	0.73
If we issue debt, our competitors know that we are unlikely to reduce our output	12	0.44
A high debt ratio helps us bargain for concessions from our employees	13	0.27

Source: Adapted from Bancel and Mittoo's Table 3 (2004, p. 113).

(6), and the costs of bankruptcy (8). The authors do not comment on the possibility that the top-ranked factor, financial flexibility, is more characteristic of a rule-of-thumb or financial planning approach.

Table 5.10 shows the responses to the question, "Has your firm seriously considered issuing common stock? If yes, what factors affect your firm's decisions about issuing common stock?"

TABLE 5.10 Target capital structure: Respondents' ranking of factors affecting their target amount of stock

This table displays the responses to Bancel and Mittoo's (2004) question: "Has your firm seriously considered issuing common stock? If yes, what factors affect your firm's decisions about issuing common stock?" The offered responses as well as resulting rank and mean scores are shown. Mean scores are based on a rating scale of 0 (not important) to 4 (very important). The authors say that 3 is associated with important and 4 with very important but further details of the scale are not reported by the authors. The purpose of this table is to differentiate between the various capital structure theories. For example, the static tradeoff model receives some support because a target debt-equity ratio ranks second among all responses.

Factor	Rank	Mean score
Earnings per share dilution	1	2.72
Maintaining a target debt-to-equity ratio	2	2.67
If our stock price has recently risen, the price at which we can issue is "high"	3	2.61
The amount by which our stock is undervalued or overvalued by the market	4	2.44
Providing shares to employee stock option plan	5	2.07
Whether our recent profits have been sufficient to fund our activities	6	1.94
Using a similar debt-equity ratio as is used by other firms in our industry	7	1.85
Diluting the holdings of certain shareholders	8	1.67
Stock is our "least risky" source of funds	9	1.50
In case of paying a target by shares, the ability to use the pooling of interest method	10	1.15
Issuing stock gives a better impression of our firm's prospects than using debt	11	1.15
The capital gains tax rates faced by our investors (relative to tax rates on dividends)	12	0.98
Inability to obtain funds using other sources	13	0.93
Common stock is our cheapest source of funds	14	0.67

Source: Adapted from Bancel and Mittoo's Table 4 (2004, p. 116).

Table 5.10 shows that maintaining a target debt-to-equity ratio ranks second, again consistent with a static trade-off model. Bancel and Mittoo (2004) observe that contrary to the pecking-order theory, issuing equity is associated with insufficient profits (ranked sixth) rather than with an inability to obtain funds from other sources (ranked last). The results also do not support signaling, as issuing stock to give a better impression of the firm ranks tenth.

In the legal system debate, their survey responses favor the LaPorta et al. (1997) position, as executives view debt more favorably in countries where the legal environment provides better creditor protection. Their cross-border results are not wholly homogeneous. Bancel and Mittoo (2004) find support for the financial flexibility factor differs between civil-law and common-law systems. They also discover that managers' concerns about the potential cost of bankruptcy are significantly different across systems, despite similarities between the quality of German and Scandinavian systems. The authors advise that better specification of potentially contradictory firm- and country-specific factors beyond the scope of their survey are needed to sort out the implications of these results.

Bancel and Mittoo (2004) conclude that their evidence provides some support for the trade-off theory but less support for the pecking-order and agency theories. They note that few firms use debt when recent profits are insufficient to support the firm's activities as predicted by pecking order. Respondents consider factors relating to the agency costs such as motivating managers to work hard or borrowing short-term to reduce the chance that the firm will undertake risky projects as unimportant. Bancel and Mittoo conclude by stating, "Overall our results support that most firms determine their optimal capital structure by trading off factors such as tax advantage of debt, bankruptcy costs, agency costs, and accessibility to external financing" (p. 131).

Bancel and Mittoo (2004) compare their results from European managers with the attitudes of American managers, drawing on Graham and Harvey's (2001) survey data to conclude that determinants of capital structure are similar between U.S. and European firms. Most importantly, they find that respondents from both groups of firms rate financial flexibility and credit rating as the most important factors in determining the appropriate amount of debt.

While Bancel and Mittoo's (2004) survey results justify their conclusions about the relative popularity of the static trade-off model among both European and U.S. respondents, they ignore the support these same results provide for financial planning. Financial flexibility ranks first in both U.S. and European samples. In addition, diluting earnings per share and a relatively high stock price rank first and third, respectively, in the European sample and first and fourth, respectively, in the U.S. sample. These strong preferences for a rule-of-thumb approach are inconsistent with any of the capital structure theories.

Brounen, de Jong, and Koedijk (2006) also replicate the Graham and Harvey (2001) study in other countries. Their survey consists of a sample of 6,500 firms from the United Kingdom, the Netherlands, Germany, and France. They receive 313 responses (a 5 percent response rate), with Germany (132) providing the most responses, followed by the United Kingdom (68), France (61), and the Netherlands (52). Their sample appears representative in firm size and industry and includes both public and private firms. Their capital structure questions exactly match those of Graham and Harvey (2001), and they extend Bancel and Mittoo's (2004) research by including questions about capital budgeting and cost of capital.

Over two-thirds of the British, Dutch, and German firms report a target debt ratio. In France, that proportion is less than one-third. When asked, "What factors affect how you chose the appropriate amount of debt for your firm?" the top-three ranked responses are identical to Bancel and Mittoo (2004), as shown in Table 5.9, and Graham and Harvey (2001), as shown in Table 5.8: financial flexibility, credit rating, and earnings volatility. Table 5.11 shows these results compared to Brounen, de Jong, and Koedijk's (2006) results. The first finding from this comparison is that the cross-national variation is almost nonexistent.

The second conclusion obtained from Table 5.11 is that financial flexibility ranks first in every country, while credit rating ranks second in every country except the United Kingdom and the Netherlands, and earnings volatility ranks no less than fourth. The results of Graham and Harvey (2001), Bancel and Mittoo (2004), and Brounen, de Jong, and Koedijk (2006) confirm that contemporary managers agree on the importance of these factors regardless of their firm's domicile.

TABLE 5.11 Cross-country capital structure factors: Respondents' ranking of factors affecting their debt issuance decisions

This table compares the results of pan-European, United States, and individual country surveys. In each survey questions are asked about the factors affecting the decision to issue debt. The purposes of this table are to show that there is little international variation and that financial flexibility—the primary indicator of a rule-of-thumb approach—ranks first in every area surveyed.

Factor	United Kingdom	The Netherlands	Germany	France	Europe	United States
Financial flexibility	1	1	1	1	1	1
Credit rating	6	4	2	2	2	2
Volatility of earnings	2	2	3	4	4	3

Source: European results adapted from Bancel and Mittoo (2004), and U.S. results adapted from Graham and Harvey (2001). The other country results are adapted from Brounen, de Jong and Koedijk, Table 2 (2006, p. 1415).

Brounen, de Jong, and Koedijk (2006) find support for the static trade-off model in the high percentage of firms that report a target debt ratio and the importance of tax benefits (ranked third by every country in their sample except Germany, where it ranks fifth) and bankruptcy costs (ranked seventh in the United Kingdom, fifth in the Netherlands, ninth in Germany, and eighth in France).

Support for the pecking order model is less robust. Brounen et al. (2006) note that financial flexibility could be considered evidence of a pecking order model, but the French and U.K. firms with a target debt ratio also value financial flexibility, thereby contradicting the model. They note that Graham and Harvey (2001) use size as an instrumental variable in analyzing their results for a pecking order. Large, dividend paying firms should place less importance on flexibility because they have less information asymmetry. In fact, the results of Graham and Harvey and Brounen et al. convey opposing results, with financial flexibility valued more by large, dividend paying firms than by small firms.

Indications that firms use capital structure as a signaling device are even harder to find. In response to, "What other factors affect your firm's debt policy?" the respondents rank "using debt gives our investors a better impression of our firm's prospects than issuing stock" below 1.0 on average (0 being the lowest score) in every country except France (1.06). These scores are lower than the Bancel and Mittoo (2004) survey, where the response received 1.55, and about the same as Graham and Harvey (2001), where it received 0.96. Brounen et al. (2006) conclude that the firms in their sample do not actively signal information about their corporate prospects and value through their capital structure policy.

Brounen et al. (2006) view agency costs to be at the heart of capital structure literature. Even so, they find very limited support for this interpretation of capital structure choice. Answering the same question as above – other factors affecting the appropriate amount of debt – the respondents give low scores to the response, "We restrict our borrowing so that profits from new/future projects can be captured fully by shareholders and do not have to be paid out as interest to debtholders." This response ranks eighth among fourteen possible responses in the United Kingdom and ninth in the Netherlands.

Brounen et al. (2006) confirm the finding that managers cite financial flexibility as the factor most influential in their capital structure decisions. They conclude that, of all the possible explanations, the static trade-off theory receives the most support. Financial flexibility is important but the pecking-order theory does not appear to be the driving force. They also document strong resemblances in capital structure policies among the four European countries and with the United States. Similar to other researchers, while their results suggest that their respondents highly value financial flexibility, these authors do not consider the possibility that rules of thumb guide their respondents' capital structure decisions. On the other hand, they provide more supporting evidence that the desire for financial flexibility transcends national and institutional boundaries.

Beattie, Goodacre, and Thomson (2006) surveyed finance directors of 831 U.K. firms in the summer of 2000 and received 198 responses (a response rate of 24 percent). The sample appears to be representative of the population. The purpose of this study is to report on a comprehensive survey of the corporate-financing decision-making process in U.K. companies to enable a comparison between practice and extant theories of capital structure. Results suggest that international differences may be unimportant in the debate over which capital structure is most popular and that in fact, managers may be opportunistic in selecting which capital structure theory to follow.

Beattie, Goodacre, and Thomson (2006) find that half the respondents report that they have a target debt level, indicating support for the static trade-off model, while 60 percent state that they use a financing hierarchy consistent with the pecking-order model. In addition, 32 percent of respondents report following both models, while 22 percent indicate using neither. Among the respondents who follow a pecking-order model, "A company issues debt when recent profits are not sufficient to fund activities" is ranked thirteenth out of seventeen possible responses to a question about how their respondents determined their capital structures—a response that is inconsistent with a pecking order of financial alternatives.

Beattie, Goodacre, and Thomson (2006) suggest that managers may actually follow both models, with the immediate choice of whether to issue debt or equity depending on the relative costs. They reference Pinegar and Wilbricht's (1989) survey results on the topic of market efficiency, but they do not acknowledge that their relative cost suggestion is similar to Pinegar and Wilbricht's rule-of-thumb explanation for capital structure choice. Their relative cost approach, however, is consistent with the hypothesis that capital structure decisions may be opportunistic, depending on market conditions, like during the protracted low interest rate environment between 2000 and 2003.

Beattie, Goodacre, and Thomson (2006) acknowledge that studies by Graham and Harvey (2001) and Brounen, de Jong, and Koedijk (2006) find financial flexibility to be the most important determinant. Even so, they do not offer their respondents the opportunity to select financial flexibility as a determinant of capital structure. In response to the question about the relative importance of various factors in choosing the appropriate amount of total debt, respondents rank "ensuring the long term survivability of the company" first. The authors argue that this factor is similar to financial flexibility. Although the statements may be similar, they are not equivalent. Perhaps Beattie, Goodacre, and Thomson see an actual similarity or believe the responses are similar because they are both ranked first. In another section devoted to size differences, Beattie, Goodacre, and Thomson use the term "financial flexibility," saying that the larger companies in their sample are more likely to maintain spare borrowing capacity, "consistent with larger companies maintaining financial flexibility to reduce the need to raise external funds" (p. 1425). Because the authors do not allow their respondents to choose financial flexibility as important and because they interpret financial flexibility differently than other survey researchers, the implications of these authors' results for the importance of financial flexibility for their respondents are unclear.

On the subject of size variations, Beattie, Goodacre, and Thomson (2006) note that larger companies are statstically more likely to follow a static trade-off approach and to maintain spare borrowing capacity. Yet, preference for a pecking order of financing options is invariant to firm size in their results. The authors observe far fewer size-related differences than the other recent surveys such as Graham and Harvey (2001) and Brounen, de Jong, and Koedijk (2006), perhaps as a result of their focus on listed companies rather than the mix of private and public companies in the other studies' samples. Thus, size does not appear to be an important determinant in capital structure policy for this sample of firms.

When summarizing their findings relative to the various theories, Beattie, Goodacre, and Thomson (2006) report mixed support for the various capital structure theories. Respondents do not consider the static trade-off or pecking-order theories mutually exclusive, and a substantial proportion of firms follow either both or neither approach. Despite these findings, these authors conclude that their results broadly support both Graham and Harvey (2001) and Brounen, de Jong, and Koedijk (2006). They suggest that capital structure decisions may be idiosyncratic and note that researchers should seek a better understanding of the diversity and complexity of firms' capital structure decisions rather than simply describing the associations between capital structure outcomes and firm-specific characteristics for the average firm. The same could be said for surveys that try to associate capital structure decisions with a simplistic, static, and theoretical view of the firm.

Armitage and Marston (2008) provide a tangentially related survey that examines the connection between managerial attitudes toward disclosure of financial information and their firm's cost of capital. Their research consists of interviews with sixteen executives from firms located in the United Kingdom: nine are current finance directors, four had served as finance directors, and three are directors of investor relations. They conducted the interviews between November 2005 and June 2006. The companies are representative of large, listed U.K. companies.

This research relates to capital structure in that it investigates how managers perceive their role in influencing the cost of capital. According to the signaling theory explanation, managers convey information to the market about their company's true prospects through their capital structure decisions. In this survey, the managers report that they do not believe disclosure would affect the cost of capital. Armitage and Marston (2008) surmise that most managers believe their disclosure is adequate and further disclosure would bring few benefits and some additional costs. The importance of this research is that managers do not see signaling as a motive for disclosure; therefore, signaling neither does nor should influence capital structure decisions.

Burton, Helliar, and Power (2005) investigate the attitudes of managers in the United Kingdom toward seasoned equity offerings (SEOs) and these offerings' relationship to capital structure. In the United Kingdom, companies sell equity through offering rights or directly to institutional investors. After conducting a few intensive interviews, Burton, Helliar, and Power survey 452 London-listed firms undertaking SEOs between December 1998 and September 2001. The 63 responses represent a response rate of about 14 percent. The institutional details of stock sales differ markedly from the United States, but the relevant point is that the responses suggest the motives for these sales are heterogeneous with issue costs, shareholder structure, and issue size being indistinguishable. Similar to their American and European counterparts, managers appear to value flexibility.

Researchers frame survey evidence from countries outside the United States differently than domestic research because they must contend with the effects of international differences. In fact, cross-border comparisons appear to play a minor role in explaining capital structure policies. Table 5.12 summarizes the implications of four such surveys.

This table demonstrates that evidence of these capital structure theories is as weak outside the United States as it is within the United States. While the static trade-off and pecking-order theories receive some support, signaling does not, especially in light of the specific test applied by Armitage and Marston (2008). The evidence for agency costs is somewhat stronger, but it is still weak.

TABLE 5.12 Capital structure theories outside the United States: Support for the four capital structure theories in survey research conducted outside the United States

This table is compiled from the survey results that tested any of the four theories: static tradeoff, pecking order, agency costs, and signaling, from the four international surveys shown in the first column under Researchers. The purpose of this table is to display the lack of support for any of the four theories in the research conducted outside the United States.

Researchers	Static trade-off	Pecking order	Agency costs	Signaling
Bancel and Mittoo (2004)	Some	Little	Little	Not tested
Brounen, de Jong, and Koedijk (2006)	Yes	Some	No	No
Beattie, Goodacre, and Thomson (2006)	Some	Some	Not tested	Not tested
Armitage and Marston (2008)	Not tested	Not tested	Not tested	No

Financial flexibility, financial planning, and rules of thumb, however, appear internationally to be consistent with the U.S. results. European survey respondents rank financial flexibility and debt rating above all other responses as that which assists them in making their capital structure decisions Bancel and Mittoo (2004); Brounen, de Jong, and Koedijk (2004), (2006); and Beattie, Goodacre, and Thomson (2006) confirm that managers value financial flexibility. In various European countries, regardless of firm size, accounting regulations, legal systems, and public and private ownership, managers appear to prefer rules of thumb over any of the formal capital structure theories. The differences between U.S. and non-U.S. managers, at least concerning capital structure, do not appear to be material.

Summary and Conclusions

The status of our understanding of how managers actually make capital structure decisions does not appear to be anchored by any of the extant academic theories. Despite several decades of theory development and refinement, none of the normative capital structure theories indicating how managers should act seem to fit the survey data. Conversely, observations made in early survey research reviewed in this chapter appear to still hold true today. Scott and Johnson (1982), Stonehill et al. (1986), Pinegar and Wilbricht (1989), Norton (1991), and Kamath (1997) all conclude that financial planning principles primarily guide capital structure decisions. Survey evidence from these researchers and others (even those that do not acknowledge the importance of rules of thumb) suggests that a positive theory, no matter how elegant, is unlikely to capture how managers make capital structure decisions in practice.

At the same time, the understanding of capital structure decisions has come a long way since the 1970s. The comprehensive work by Graham and Harvey (2001) confirms that across a broad spectrum of firms, managers make capital structure decisions that maximize their flexibility. Corporate managers may even act opportunistically when cost-benefit conditions are right. Many practicing managers do not consistently follow any specific academic theory, or at least not one that has already been developed. Almost without exception and despite MM's theory that suggests capital structure is irrelevant, managers must think capital structure is important, because all the surveys confirm that they try to manage their cost of capital.

Miller (1977) provides what is arguably the best explanation of why the connection between normative theory and practice is so tenuous. In his presidential address to the American Finance Association in 1976, Miller says,

> No corporate treasurer's office, controller's staff, or investment banker's research team that I have ever encountered had, or could remotely be

expected to have, enough reliable information about the future course of prices for a firm's securities to convince even a moderately skeptical outside academic observer that the firm's value had indeed been maximized by some specific financial decision or strategy. (p. 272)

Miller goes on to say that economists develop models because

rational behavior models generally lead to better predictions and descriptions at the level of the industry, the market and the whole economy than any alternatives available to them. Their experience, at those levels, moreover, need involve no inconsistency with the heuristic, rule-of-thumb, intuitive kinds of decision making they actually observe in firms. It suggests rather that evolutionary mechanisms are at work to give survival value to those heuristics that are compatible with rational market equilibrium, however far from rational they may appear to be when examined up close and in isolation. (pp. 272–273)

Miller's perspective yields two lessons. First, practice need not conform to theory because every theory is an abstract, logical construct. In the normative economic tradition, theories are designed to suggest how managers should behave and not to describe how they actually behave. When researchers empirically test these theories, their inability to accurately model what is occurring in practice is not surprising. Survey results record that some managers appear to believe they are following the static trade-off and pecking-order models, albeit inconsistently. The signaling and agency cost theories do not fare so well in survey results and may not be able to explain behavior.

Second, variables such as life-cycle stage, size, and economic conditions should clearly play a role in explaining why managers do not follow the theoretical models at any moment. Surveys are, by nature, a cross-section and do not accommodate variation over time. Financial managers frequently report using rules of thumb to make capital structure decisions. At some point, researchers may be able to develop a theory that incorporates a time dimension or to conduct a time-series survey that will resolve the question of which intervening variables are most important. Until that time, the questions of difference in capital structure and whether a firm may enhance its value by changing its capital structure should continue to be the subject of academic research.

References

Armitage, Seth, and Claire Marston. 2008. "Corporate Disclosure, Cost of Capital and Reputation: Evidence from Finance Directors." *British Accounting Review* 40:4, 314–36.

Asquith, Paul, and David Mullins Jr. 1986. "Equity Issues and Offering Dilution." *Journal of Financial Economics* 15:1–2, 61–80.

Bancel, Franck, and Usha R. Mittoo. 2004. "Cross-Country Determinants of Capital Structure Choice: A Survey of European Firms." *Financial Management* 33:4, 103–32.

Barnea, Amir, Robert A. Haugen, and Lemma W. Senbet. 1980. "A Rationale for Debt Maturity Structure and Call Provisions in the Agency Theoretic Framework." *Journal of Finance* 35:5, 1223–34.

Barton, Sydney L., Ned C. Hill, and Shrinivasan Sundaram. 1989. "An Empirical Test of Stakeholder Theory Predictions of Capital Structure." *Financial Management* 18:1, 36–44.

Baskin, Jonathan. 1989. "An Empirical Investigation of the Pecking Order Hypothesis." *Financial Management* 18:1, 26–35.

Beattie, Vivien, Alan Goodacre, and Sarah Jane Thomson. 2006. "Corporate Financing Decisions: UK Survey Evidence." *Journal of Business, Finance and Accounting* 33:9–10, 1042–1434.

Berger, Allen N., Marco A. Espinosa-Vega, W. Scott Frame, and Nathan H. Miller. 2005. "Debt Maturity, Risk and Asymmetric Information." *Journal of Finance* 60:6, 2895–2923.

Brav, Alon, John R. Graham, Campbell R. Harvey, and Roni Michaely. 2005. "Payout Policy in the 21st Century." *Journal of Financial Economics* 77:3, 483–527.

Brealey, Richard A., Stewart C. Myers, and Franklin Allen. 2008. *Principles of Corporate Finance*, 7th ed. New York: McGraw-Hill.

Brigham, Eugene F., and Michael C. Ehrhardt. 2008. *Financial Management: Theory and Practice*, 12th ed. New York: Thomson.

Brounen, Dirk, Abe De Jong, and Kees C.G. Koedijk. 2004. "Corporate Finance in Europe: Confronting Theory with Practice." *Financial Management* 33:4, 71–104.

———. 2006. "Capital Structure Policies in Europe: Survey Evidence." *Journal of Banking and Finance* 30:5, 1409–42.

Burton, Bruce, Christine Helliar, and David Power. 2005. "Practitioner Perspectives on the Seasoned Equity Offering Process in the UK." *British Accounting Review* 37:2, 153–75.

Chang, Chun. 1992. "Capital Structure as an Optimal Contract between Employees and Investors." *Journal of Finance* 47:3, 1141–58.

Chaplinsky, Susan, and Robert S. Harris. 1998. "Capital Structure Theory: A Current Perspective." Darden Business Publishing Case no. UVA-F-1165, Darden Graduate School of Business Administration, University of Virginia.

Cheung, Yin-Wong, and Lilian K. Ng. 1992. "Stock Price Dynamics and Firm Size: An Empirical Examination." *Journal of Finance* 47:5, 1985–97.

Demirgüç-Kunt, Asli, and Vojislav Maksimovic. 1999. "Institutions, Financial Markets and Firm Debt Maturity." *Journal of Financial Economics* 54:3, 295–336.

Fischer, Edwin O., Robert Heinkel, and Josef Zechner. 1989. "Dynamic Capital Structure Choice: Theory and Tests." *Journal of Finance* 44:1, 19–40.

Gitman, Lawrence J., and Vincent A. Mercurio. 1982. "Cost of Capital Techniques Used by Major U.S. Firms: Survey and Analysis of Fortune's 1000." *Financial Management* 11:4, 21–29.

Graham, John R., and Campbell R. Harvey. 2001. "The Theory and Practice of Corporate Finance: Evidence from the Field." *Journal of Financial Economics* 60:2–3, 187–243.

Graham, John R., Campbell R. Harvey, and Shiva Rajgopal. 2006. "Value Destruction and Financial Reporting Decisions." *Financial Analysts Journal* 62:6, 27–39.

Jahera, John S. Jr., and William P. Lloyd. 1991. "Corporate Capital Structure: Further Evidence on Determining Factors." *Journal of Financial and Strategic Decisions* 4:4, 105–15.

Jensen, Michael C., and William H. Meckling. 1976. "Theory of the Firm: Managerial Behavior, Agency Costs and Ownership Structure." *Journal of Financial Economics* 3:4, 305–60.

Kamath, Ravindra R. 1997. "Long-Term Financing Decisions: Views and Practices of Financial Managers of NYSE Firms." *Financial Review* 32:2, 350–56.

La Porta, Rafael, Florencio Lopez-de-Silanes, Andrei Shleifer, and Robert Vishny. 1997. "Legal Determinants of External Finance." *Journal of Finance* 52:3, 1131–52.

Miller, Merton H. 1977. "Debt and Taxes." *Journal of Finance* 32:2, 261–75.

Miller, Merton H., and Kevin Rock. 1985. "Dividend Policy under Asymmetric Information." *Journal of Finance* 40:4, 1031–51.

Modigliani, Franco, and Merton H. Miller. 1958. "The Cost of Capital, Corporate Finance, and the Theory of Investment." *American Economic Review* 48:3, 261–97.

Myers, Stewart C. 1984. "The Capital Structure Puzzle." *Journal of Finance* 39:3, 575–92.

Myers, Stewart C., and N. S. Majluf. 1984. "Corporate Financing and Investment Decisions When Firms Have Information That Investors Do Not Have." *Journal of Financial Economics* 13:2, 187–221.

Norton, Edgar. 1991. "Factors Affecting Capital Structure Decisions." *Financial Review* 26:3, 431–46.

Pinegar, J. Michael, and Lisa Wilbricht. 1989. "What Managers Think of Capital Structure Theory: A Survey." *Financial Management* 18:4, 82–91.

Scott, David F., and Dana J. Johnson. 1982. "Financing Policies and Practices in Large Corporations." *Financial Management* 11:2, 51–59.

Smith, Clifford W. Jr. 1986. "Investment Banking and the Capital Acquisition Process." *Journal of Financial Economics* 15:1–2, 3–25.

Stonehill, Arthur, Theo Beekhuisen, Richard Wright, Lee Remmers, Norman Toy, Antonio Pares, Alan Shapiro, Douglas Egan, and Thomas Bates. 1986. "Financial Goals and Debt Ratio Determinants: A Survey of Practice in Five Countries." *Financial Management* 4:3, 27–41.

VanHorne, James C. 2001. *Financial Management and Policy*, 12th ed. New York: Prentice Hall.

৫ 6

Dividends and Dividend Policy

> The harder we look at the dividend picture, the more it seems
> like a puzzle, with pieces that just don't fit together.
>
> Fischer Black (1976, p. 5)

Introduction

From a strategic perspective, the most important decisions that corporate financial managers make involve capital budgeting, capital structure, and distribution
of profits. Black's (1976) highly referenced comment cited at the beginning
of this chapter provides a useful starting point for considering distributions or
payouts in the form of cash dividends. The questions of why companies pay
dividends, which is a costly administrative exercise, and how investors respond
to such payments have perplexed academics and others for decades and has
resulted in mixed and ambiguous empirical results.

Dividend policy refers to the payout policy that a firm follows in determining
the size and pattern of distributions to shareholders over time. According to
Allen and Michaely (2003), the word *policy* connotes that dividends do not
develop in a random and arbitrary manner and involve some consistency over
time. As a core component of a firm's overall financial policy, dividend policy
consists of a series of decisions about how the firm distributes profits to its
shareholders.

There are three ways firms can distribute cash to shareholders: cash dividends, share repurchases, and special dividends. Historically, the most common
payout mechanism has been to pay regular cash dividends, but the corporate use

of repurchases has shown remarkable growth since the early 1980s. In fact, Dittmar (2008) provides evidence that the annual aggregate volume of share repurchases in the United States surpassed that of dividends for the first time in 2005. Other studies such as Bagwell and Shoven (1989), Dittmar (2000), Grullon and Michaely (2002), and Dittmar and Dittmar (2007) document the general upward trend in repurchases since the approval of Regulation 10b-18 in November 1982. Special dividends, also known as specially designated dividends (SDDs), have traditionally served as a means of distributing cash to shareholders without raising expectations of such payment continuing. Although once fairly common, the decline in the payment of SDDs occurred at about the same time that stock repurchases became a more widespread financial practice. This chapter focuses on cash dividends, while Chapter 7 concentrates on other forms of payment—namely, share repurchases and special dividends, as well as dividend-related issues involving stock dividends and splits, reverse splits, and dividend reinvestment plans.

Approaches to the Study of Dividend Policy

In studying dividend policy, Weigand and Baker (2009) observe that researchers rely mainly on two approaches to identify variables related to dividend decisions and to study the dividend irrelevance hypothesis, which basically states that an issuance of dividends should have little, if any, impact on stock price. The first approach uses economic modeling and has dominated the modern literature on dividend policy. This line of research relies heavily on statistical analysis of published financial data to test various hypotheses about dividend policy. Chiang, Frankfurter, Kosedag, and Wood (2006) believe that such ex post data can explain surface reality but cannot measure motivation. Chiang et al. (p. 78) conclude:

> Yet, ratcheting up the complexity of models, singly applied to a whole universe of stocks will not answer the most intriguing subject of finance: why do shareholders love dividends? Therefore, the cardinal thrust of academic research must turn toward learning about motivation and on what perceptions this motivation is based.

The second approach to studying dividend policy uses survey methodology such as interviews and questionnaires to obtain primary data about dividend policy. Because this approach investigates dividends based on perceptions of various decision makers, it offers a more direct way of gaining an understanding of motivation than the surface reality gleaned from using market data. Tufano (2001) and Graham and Harvey (2001) contend that using different empirical approaches can help validate the results of quantitative studies based on capital markets-based research. As Frankfurter, Kosedag, Schmidt, and Topalov (2002, p. 202) note,

> Our approach differs from traditional dividend research because it is based on the belief that one cannot understand the motivation and perception of people by simply analyzing market data. We believe the only way to understand the dividend enigma is to ascertain people's perceptions of the issue by asking for their candid opinions.

Aggarwal (1993), however, notes that grounds exist for being hesitant to accept the reasons managers give for their actions. As with other types of empiricism, the results of survey research should be evaluated by their plausibility and their explanatory power, not just by the weaknesses of methods used to obtain the results. Thus, insights gained by surveying decision makers—with all the caveats that are reasonable to consider, as discussed in Chapter 2—can augment existing evidence about dividends and dividend policy.

Survey research can offer valuable insights into how corporate managers and others view different aspects of dividend policy. Such studies provide much unique information that complements existing knowledge from traditional analysis of large samples and clinical studies. For example, why do some firms pay dividends and some investors prefer them? Do managers perceive that their firm's distribution policy creates value for shareholders? What factors influence a firm's dividend payout pattern? Do managers' views align with theoretical explanations for why firms do or do not pay dividends? As this chapter documents, the combination of these two approaches (survey and non-survey research) offers a richer and more complete view of dividend policy than a single data source or methodology. As Bruner (2002, p. 50). notes, "The task must be to look for patterns of confirmation across approaches and studies much like one sees an image in a mosaic of stones." Thus, the confirmation of results by different research methods provides stronger evidence of the validity of the results than by using a single research methodology.

Development of Dividend Policy

As Frankfurter and Wood (1997, 2003) and Benrud (2009) discuss, dividend policy has evolved over several centuries. Yet, survey research on dividends dates back only about a half century, when Lintner (1956) laid the foundation for the modern understanding of dividend policy. Survey-based research is particularly valuable when theoretical and other empirical research methods provide insufficient guidance for corporate policymakers, investors, regulators, academics, and others. In this situation, surveys can produce data unavailable from other methods and can lead to an improved understanding of the grey areas where theory meets practice.

Views about dividend policy have changed dramatically over the years. As Weigand and Baker (2009) note, two distinctly different branches of thought emanate from the early literature on corporate distribution policy. One common stream of thought before the 1960s asserts that dividends are an important determinant of firm value. Specifically, the belief was that higher dividend payouts lead to higher stock valuations. For example, Williams (1938) was among the first economists to view stock prices as determined by "intrinsic value" and to articulate the theory of dividend-based valuation. Graham and Dodd (1951), Lintner (1956), and Gordon (1959) provide early arguments that an increase in dividend payout increases a firm's stock price and lowers its cost of equity.

In contrast to this prevailing opinion, Miller and Modigliani (1961; hereafter MM), in a pioneer work, rebelled against the popular sentiment of the times. The purpose of MM was to point out what conditions would need to exist for dividends to be irrelevant. Based on a simplifying set of assumptions involving perfect and frictionless capital markets, MM argued that given a firm's optimal investment policy, its choice of dividend policy is irrelevant for firm value. Consequently, a firm cannot increase its stock price by changing its dividend payout policy. Bernstein (1992, p. 176) notes, however, that the "MM theory was admittedly an abstraction when it was originally presented," and "no one—least of all Modigliani and Miller—would claim that the real world looks like this." Black (1976) largely echoed MM's beliefs and found no convincing explanation for public corporations paying cash dividends to their shareholders. He referred to the practice of paying dividends and the interest of shareholders in receiving dividends as the "dividend puzzle." The controversial conclusion about dividend irrelevance stirred a heated debate that reverberated throughout the finance community for decades. Studies by Black and Scholes (1974), Miller and Scholes (1978, 1982), Miller (1986), and Jose and Stevens (1989), among others, support the dividend irrelevance argument. Blume (1980), Litzenberger and Ramaswamy (1982), and Ang and Peterson (1985), however, argue that stocks with high dividend payouts have higher costs of equity and therefore lower stock prices.

Still others criticize MM's restrictive assumptions involving perfect and frictionless capital markets as unrealistic and offer alternative theories about why corporations pay dividends and why investors want them. For example, Lease, John, Kalay, Loewenstein, and Sarig (2000) partition market imperfections into two groups: the "big three" (taxes, asymmetric information, and agency costs) and the "little three" (transaction costs, flotation expenses, and behavioral considerations). The lack of imperfections is essential for establishing dividend irrelevancy. Thus, Lease et al. (p. 196), based on their analysis of the dividend literature, state, "In conclusion we believe that dividend policy *can* have an impact on shareholder wealth because of various market imperfections."

Despite several decades of research resulting in the emergence of conflicting theoretical models and empirical findings, many questions remain unanswered. Consequently, dividend policy remains one of the greatest enigmas of modern finance. For example, in a survey of chief financial officers (CFOs) of *Fortune* 500 companies, Trahan and Gitman (1995) report that dividend policy is among the top areas these respondents would like to know more about. In reviewing evidence on the dividend puzzle, Baker, Powell, and Veit (2002, p. 255) note that "despite a voluminous amount of research, we still do not have all the answers to the dividend puzzle." In particular, managers are left with general and sometimes conflicting views about whether they can have an optimal dividend payout and which factors are most important in determining that payout. As previously noted, survey research provides some important insights about the mystery that has long surrounded dividends.

Changing View on Dividends

In a recent challenge to dividend irrelevance, DeAngelo and DeAngelo (2006, p. 296) offer a biting attack on the status of the MM propositions and view the MM irrelevance theory as being of "trivial import". Specifically, DeAngelo and DeAngelo (p. 295) criticize the MM irrelevance theory as follows:

> For corporate finance research, a more troubling consequence of the MM irrelevance theorem is that its central lesson—that investment policy alone determines value—has both limited our vision about the importance of payout policy and sent researchers off searching for frictions that would make payout policy matter, while it has mattered all along even in the standard (frictionless) Fisherian model.

Moreover, DeAngelo and DeAngelo question the proof of the irrelevance theory. In a related work, DeAngelo and DeAngelo (2007) challenge MM's contentious conclusion that all feasible payout policies are equally valuable to investors and assert that dividend policy matters. Given that considerable controversy surrounds MM's views, debate is likely to continue in this area for some time to come.

Despite the controversy surrounding Miller and Modigiani's (1961) classic paper, there is no doubt that MM's irrelevance theorems have exerted considerable influence on financial theory. As Ang and Ciccone (2009, p. 110) note regarding MM, "Aside from the issues with the irrelevance proof, their conclusion has little practical value. Dividends clearly do matter".

DeAngelo, DeAngelo, and Skinner (1996, p. 353) comment on the changing nature of dividend policy as follows:

> Taking history as a guide, there is no guarantee that the practices that currently seem of greatest relevance will continue to seem so important even 20 or 30 years from now. A more realistic view is that there is not a single fixed set of payout practices to be explained, but that instead these practices

are in constant flux, so that an important task of corporate finance research is to help identify the factors that share their evolution.

This observation gains particular credence considering the phenomenon of disappearing dividends in the United States at the end of the twentieth century (Fama and French 2001) and the later reappearance of dividends (Julio and Ikenberry 2004).

The objective of this chapter is to review and synthesize the dividend literature that primarily uses survey methodology and to chronicle how perspectives on corporate dividend policy have changed over time. By focusing on those studies that attempt to describe dividend policy in practice, this chapter shows how survey research contributes to the dividend debate and to our understanding of dividend policy.

Given the vast amount of theoretical and empirical research on dividends, this chapter limits its review to some of the more salient theories and evidence. This chapter is not, nor is it meant to be, a comprehensive survey of every study involving dividends and dividend policy. Instead, it seeks to reference a representative set of papers, with the goal of providing a clear and uncluttered summary of the major issues and viewpoints regarding cash dividends. The studies referenced here make important contributions to the literature, but they are not the only ones that do so. Those interested in delving into these topics in greater depth will find a wealth of interesting and relevant research available in Lease et al. (2000); Frankfurter and Wood (2002, 2003); Allen and Michaely (2003); DeAngelo, DeAngelo, and Skinner (2009); and Baker (2009).

The remainder of this chapter has the following organization. The first section focuses on theories, models, and explanations for paying dividends and provides some empirical evidence about each. The next section provides a synthesis of the survey evidence involving dividends and dividend policy. These surveys provide the views from various types of respondents on such issues as whether dividend payout affects firm value and the determinants of a firm's dividend payout policy. Finally, the chapter offers a summary and conclusions.

Theories, Models, and Explanations for Paying Dividends

This section provides an overview of various theoretical explanations for different dividend policies. Even a cursory review of the literature reveals that financial economists have suggested many explanations. However, the finance theory on dividends often begins with the behavior of shareholders. The question of why firms pay dividends has intrigued financial economists since Gordon and Shapiro (1956), Gordon (1963), and Walter (1963), all early proponents of the so-called bird-in-the-hand dividend theory. Yet, serious doubts surfaced about the economic rationality of this theory with the appearance of Miller and

Modigliani's (1961) indifference proposition. Another approach, called residual dividend policy, stems from MM. As discussed previously, MM's dividend irrelevance theory argues that there is no effect from dividends on a firm's stock price.

Researchers also set forth various theories to explain the relevance of dividends to shareholder wealth. Not surprisingly, early explanations of irrelevance focus on major market imperfections or frictions including taxes, asymmetric information, and agency costs. Researchers generally focus on each market imperfection in isolation, but complex interactions could exist among the big three (taxes, asymmetric information, and agency costs) and the little three (transaction costs, flotation expenses, and behavioral considerations) frictions (Lease et al. 2000). Other explanations for why companies pay dividends include behavioral explanations, the firm life-cycle theory of dividends, and the catering theory of dividends. These theories, however, are not necessarily mutually exclusive. In addition to these more mainstream theories, there are also some unconventional explanations for paying dividends. For example, Frankfurter and Lane (1992) contend that dividends are partially a tradition and partially a method to allay investor anxiety.

The issue of whether dividends matter or do not matter has intrigued researchers for several decades. Broadly speaking, academic views on dividend policy consist of two main conceptual positions: the irrelevance position (dividends do not matter) and the relevance position (dividends do matter). The relevance position is dichotomous: one camp contends that increases in dividend payouts increase share price, while the other camp holds the opposite view. As Ang (1987, p. 58) noted more than two decades ago,

> dividend theories do not fit neatly into the relevance vs. irrelevance dichotomy. There are finer shades of irrelevance (or relevance), depending on whether the question concerns the investors, the firms, the market, or the tax authority. Taxes, asymmetric information, agency costs, transformation costs, endogenous financing, and investment decisions may have a role singly or jointly in the determination of observed dividends.

Bird-in-the-Hand Theory

One of the earliest explanations of dividend relevance, predating Miller and Modigliani's (1961) classic dividend irrelevance article, is the bird-in-the-hand theory, also called resolution theory. This explanation is derived from the old saying, "A bird in the hand is worth two in the bush." According to this theory, the bird in the hand refers to dividends that are in hand and the bush refers to uncertainty of the capital gains. Lintner (1956) and Gordon (1959) argue that investors value dividends more than capital gains when making decisions related to stocks. Because dividends are supposedly less risky than capital gains, firms should set a high dividend payout ratio and offer a high dividend yield to maximize stock price. Thus, the bird-in-the hand explanation asserts that paying higher dividends increases firm value because dividends represent a sure thing, while future share price appreciation is uncertain.

Not surprisingly, Miller and Modigliani (1961) hold a different view. They refer to the notion that a high dividend payout ratio will maximize a firm's value as the "bird-in-the-hand fallacy." Bhattacharya (1979) concurs, contending that the reasoning behind the bird-in-the-hand explanation for dividend relevance is misleading. The underlying argument is that the riskiness of project cash flows determines a firm's risk, not how the firm distributes these flows. A firm that increases its dividend payout today will experience an equivalent decrease in its stock's ex-dividend price.

Residual Dividend Theory

According to Miller and Modigliani (1961), firms should pay out as dividends all cash flows after funding all profitable investments (e.g., positive net present value [NPV] projects). Thus, the amount of dividends is simply a residual of a firm's investment decision. In theory, using a residual cash dividend policy serves as a means of optimizing the efficiency of corporate resources. This policy requires that managers be able to accurately forecast cash flows and investment opportunities, which is challenging at best. One drawback of pursuing a pure residual dividend policy is that it can produce highly unstable dividends because dividends are linked to a firm's investment needs. Investors are likely to view a residual dividend policy as unreliable due to the fluctuating dividends. Based on his analysis of the literature, Smith (2009) concludes that firms almost never follow a strict short-run residual dividend policy but instead generally follow a managed payout policy that involves dividend smoothing.

Taxes and Clientele Effects

In Miller and Modigliani's (1961) ideal world of perfect markets without corporate and personal taxes, shareholders should be indifferent to receiving either dividends or capital gains. Yet, investors live in a world with taxes, representing one of the big three market imperfections as discussed by Lease et al. (2000). Not surprisingly, there are numerous tax-effect explanations (see, for example, Miller and Scholes 1978; Litzenberger and Ramaswamy 1980, 1982; Lakonishok and Vermaelen 1983; Masulis and Trueman 1988). Favorable tax treatment on capital gains (a lower capital gains tax rate and deferral of capital gains tax) should cause investors to prefer non-dividend-paying stocks. Therefore, one of the earliest explanations for paying dividends centers on the tax-preference argument, which holds that rational investors prefer firms to retain and to reinvest cash instead of paying dividends when tax rates are higher on dividends than on long-term capital gains. This approach suggests that firms should keep dividend payments low to maximize share price. Brennan (1970) and others develop an optimal dividend policy based on the tax differential between capital gains and dividends. Yet, Brennan's empirical results are mixed. Black and Scholes (1974) find no evidence of this tax effect, while Litzenberger and Ramaswamy (1980) find evidence of a relationship between pretax returns and dividend yield.

Other researchers test the tax-preference explanation for paying or not paying dividends by examining the ex-dividend-date price drop. Favorable capital gains treatment could result in a price drop that is less than the dividend payment and cause investors to prefer non-dividend-paying stocks. As Saadi and Dutta (2009) note, empirical evidence on this matter is voluminous but also inconclusive. For example, early studies by Elton and Gruber (1970b) find an ex-dividend-date price drop that is less than the dividend amount, but Michaely (1991) reports an ex-dividend-date price drop equal to the dividend payment.

Because of varying tax effects, investors may seek out firms whose different dividend policies are appropriate to their particular tax circumstances, resulting in tax-induced clientele effects. Ogden, Jen, and O'Connor (2003, p. 479) define *clientele effects* as "a set of investors who are attracted to the stock of firms that have the dividend policy they prefer, based on their tax or liquidity circumstances." For example, stockholders in high-tax brackets may prefer stock with low dividend payout rates, whereas stockholders in low-tax brackets may prefer high dividend payouts. Elton and Gruber (1970a), Pettit (1977), Fung (1981), Booth and Johnston (1984), and Bajaj and Vijh (1990) provide further discussion of clientele effects.

Other things being equal, stocks with a low payout should attract investors in high-tax brackets, leaving high-payout stock to investors subject to low or zero tax rates. Graham and Kumar (2006) find strong evidence that taxes are important and lead to tax clienteles. In their review of the literature on tax effects, Saadi and Dutta (2009, p. 139) conclude, "The extant theoretical and empirical evidence provide contradictory results involving the impact of taxation on both stock price and dividend policy." Thus, the empirical evidence on the tax-preference explanation of dividends is inconclusive.

Kalay and Michaely (2000, p. 73) offer a possible explanation for why researchers have been unsuccessful in linking the changes in tax laws to changes in the dividend policy of firms:

Our empirical evidence—time-series return variations and no cross-sectional return variations—is not explained by the known tax models.

It could very well be that these empirical findings are somehow related to a more complex theory of tax effects, yet to be developed.

Asymmetric Information and Signaling Theory

A second market imperfection involves information asymmetry. The basis of signaling theory rests on the premise of asymmetric information. The roots of signaling theory trace to the work of Lintner (1956), who shows how stock prices tend to react to changes in dividend rate. Early models developed by Ross (1977), Bhattacharya (1979, 1980), John and Williams (1985), Miller and Rock (1985), Asquith and Mullins (1983, 1986), Bar-Yosef and Huffman (1986), and Ofer and Thakor (1987) assume that managers have access to information that the market does not. Signaling theory says that as insiders, managers choose dividend-payment levels to convey private information about the firm's future prospects to investors, which in turn reduces asymmetries. Managers have an incentive to signal this private information to the investing public when they believe that the current market value of their firm's stock is below its intrinsic value. For example, an increased dividend payment may serve as a credible signal when other firms without favorable inside information cannot mimic the dividend increase without unduly increasing the probability of later incurring a dividend cut or slower growth. In general, the implication of the dividend-signaling hypothesis is that firms that unexpectedly initiate or increase (omit or decrease) cash dividends should experience positive (negative) price reactions. Simply stated, dividend initiations or increases convey good news, while dividend omissions or decreases convey bad news.

Although managers can use dividend actions to convey useful information, dividend changes may not be perfect signals. For example, Easterbrook (1984) notes that dividend increases may be ambiguous signals unless the market can distinguish between growing firms and disinvesting firms, i.e., those lacking investment opportunities.

Empirical tests involving the signaling explanation are voluminous and offer mixed results. Much evidence shows that dividend changes are positively associated with stock returns in the days surrounding the dividend-change announcement (e.g., Lakonishok and Vermaelen 1983; Kalay and Lowenstein 1986). Some studies support the ability of dividends to signal the direction of future profitability or earnings (e.g., Healy and Palepu 1988; Aharony and Dotan 1994; Brook, Charlton, and Hendershott 1998; Nissim and Ziv 2001; Mougoué and Rao 2003), while others report contradictory evidence (e.g., DeAngelo, DeAngelo, and Skinner 1992, 1996, 2004; Jensen and Johnson 1995; Benartzi, Michaely, and Thaler 1997; Li and Zhao 2008). In his review of the empirical evidence involving asymmetric information and signaling theory, Filbeck (2009, p. 174) concludes, "Overall, most empirical evidence tends to support theoretical models regarding the ability of dividend changes to affect share price". Thus, signaling theory may provide at least a partial explanation for the existence of firm dividend policy.

The Agency Explanation

Agency relationships between various claimholders of the firm may offer another explanation for why firms pay dividends. Agency costs represent the third big market imperfection (Lease et al. 2000). There are various agency cost explanations for paying dividends. For example, Easterbook (1984) contends that firms pay dividends to overcome the agency problem stemming from the separation of ownership and control in a firm with diffused ownership. By paying dividends, managers must enter the capital markets more often to raise funds, where they are subjected to scrutiny and the disciplining effects of investment professionals. This monitoring by outside suppliers of capital helps to ensure that managers act in the best interests of shareholders. In exchange for the increased monitoring that the professional investment community and outside suppliers of capital provide, shareholders are willing to accept the higher personal taxes associated with dividends. Thus, as Easterbook notes, dividend payments may serve as a means of monitoring or bonding management performance.

Jensen (1986) makes a similar argument that managers have a self-serving motive to expand the firm beyond its optimal size because the larger size increases resources under their control and leads to higher compensation. Thus, managers could fund suboptimal investments that benefit themselves but diminish shareholder wealth. To counteract this potential overinvestment problem, shareholders might prefer that managers pay dividends to reduce the firm's discretionary free cash flow. Jensen labels this approach to overcoming the overinvestment problem the free cash flow theory. Thus, as Jensen notes, paying dividends can help to overcome the agency problems resulting from the separation of ownership and control in a large firm with diffused ownership.

Allen, Bernardo, and Welch (2000) provide another agency argument for paying dividends. Firms paying dividends attract relatively more institutions when institutional investors are relatively less taxed than individuals, resulting in "ownership clientele" effects. Because institutions tend to be better informed than individuals, they possess a relative advantage in identifying high-quality firms and use this information to help the firm control the agency problem. Compared to individual investors who are dispersed, institutions are more likely to play a larger role in overseeing management.

Empirical evidence on the agency cost explanation for paying dividends is mixed. For example, some studies (e.g., Rozeff 1982; Lang and Litzenberger 1989; Jensen, Solberg, and Zorn 1992; Agrawal and Jayaraman 1994) provide empirical support for these agency explanations for paying dividends. Crutchley and

Hansen (1989) and Moh'd, Perry, and Rimbey (1995) conclude that managers make financial policy trade-offs such as paying dividends to control agency costs. Other studies provide little or no support (e.g., Denis, Denis, and Sarin 1994; Yoon and Starks 1995; Lie 2000). Despite this mixed evidence, Megginson (1996, p. 377) states that "the agency cost model is currently the leading mainstream economic model for explaining observed dividend payouts." In his review of the pertinent literature on agency costs and the free cash flow hypothesis, Mukherjee (2009) also concludes that the cumulative evidence supports the agency cost model as the leading contender for explaining why companies pay dividends.

Behavioral Explanations

Lease et al. (2000) classify behavioral considerations as one of the little three frictions, along with transaction costs and flotation expenses. Although they view these three frictions as relatively minor within the total scheme of frictions, a growing body of literature exists on psychological or sociological explanations for dividend policy relevance. Shefrin and Statman (1984) offer a behavioral framework to explain why some investors want to receive dividends. They base their framework on the theory of self-control developed by Thaler and Shefrin (1981) and the theory of choice under uncertainty described by Kahneman and Tversky (1979). Frankfurter and Lane (1992) describe several other behavioral theories of dividends involving habits, bounded rationality, and implicit contracts.

According to Shefrin and Statman (1984), from a stockholder's perspective, receiving dividends and generating cash from the sale of stock are not perfect substitutes. They contend that many investors prefer specific dividend payouts. As Lease et al. (2000, p. 48) note, "By adjusting their consumption to the level of dividends received, investors substitute the discipline of the firm's dividend policy for the self-control they may lack if they have to routinely sell shares of stock to finance consumption." Shefrin (2009) discusses a formal behavioral model to explain the role that dividends play in decisions about consumption and portfolio selection. The model produces various predictions about the impact of various demographic attributes of investors including age, retirement status, and income on the relationship between consumer expenditures and the preference for dividends. Shefrin (p. 194) states the following:

> In particular, behavioral theory predicts that older, retired households will find dividends more attractive than younger households that are still in the workforce. Moreover, households that have few options for replacing labor income after retirement will find dividends especially attractive. Low-income households are similar to older, retired households. For both

groups, the shadow price of current income is high, and yet both are trying to protect the balances in their asset accounts. In this respect, demand for dividends will be negatively related to income.

Studies by Graham and Kumar (2006) and Baker, Nagel, and Wurgler (2007) lend support to these behavioral predictions. For example, Graham and Kumar find that older households prefer dividend-paying stocks over non-dividend-paying stocks regardless of household income. Younger households with low income exhibit a stronger preference for dividend-paying stocks than households with higher income. They also find that retirement status increases the demand for dividends, which is consistent with the predictions of behavioral dividend theory.

The Firm Life-Cycle Theory of Dividends

Mueller (1972) presents a theory of the firm life cycle and traces the implications of this theory to dividend policy. The underlying premise of the firm life-cycle theory of dividends is that when a firm's product lines mature, its ability to generate cash exceeds its ability to find profitable investment opportunities. At some point, the optimal decision is for the firm to distribute any free cash flow to shareholders as dividends. For a value-maximizing firm, the optimal dividend policy would be to retain all earnings in the rapid growth phase and to pay out 100 percent of the earnings at maturity.

Damodaran (1999) also contends that the pattern of cash dividends generally changes over a firm's life cycle. According to his life-cycle model, companies tend to pay no dividends during the rapid expansion stage, increase dividends during the mature growth stage, and use special dividends or repurchase stock during the declining stage.

Lease et al. (2000) develop a competing frictions model and illustrate how a firm's dividend policy changes as a function of the firm's life cycle (start-up, initial public offering, rapid growth, maturity, and decline). According to this model, management considers each friction or imperfection (taxes, asymmetric information, agency costs, flotation costs, and transaction costs) in isolation and then in combination to arrive at its choice of a "reasonable" dividend policy. The authors exclude behavioral considerations because of the difficulty of incorporating a lack of investor rationality into their model. This model differs only slightly from Damodaran's (1999) dividend life-cycle model.

According to the competing frictions model of Lease et al. (2000), how is dividend policy likely to differ in the start-up versus the decline stage of the dividend life cycle? During a firm's start-up stage, Lease et al. assume that marginal tax rates of equity holders are high. Agency costs are low because the agents and principals are the same. Asymmetric information is extremely high because outsiders understand little about the firm and its prospects. Both flotation and transaction costs are high because access to the capital markets under reasonable terms is impossible. Thus, at this early stage of the firm's life cycle, the implied dividend policy according to the competing frictions model would be for a firm to pay no dividends.

At the decline stage of a firm's life cycle, market erosion and new technology continues to supplant the firm's basic markets. Relative to the maturity stages, taxes paid by equity holders are declining because of institutional and corporate ownership. Agency costs are very high because of the separation of ownership and control. Asymmetric information is modest largely due to continuous following by analysts, and both flotation and transaction costs are low. Under these circumstances, Lease et al.'s (2000) competing frictions model indicates that a firm should pay generous dividends.

Several recent studies directly test the firm life-cycle theory of dividends. For example, Fama and French (2001) investigate the dividend payment behavior of publicly traded U.S. firms in the period from 1926 to 1999. They find that dividend-paying firms have the characteristics of mature firms, but non-dividend-paying firms have the characteristics of young, fast-growing firms. Their study reports a significant relationship between the overall patterns of dividend payment and the firm characteristics associated with a firm's life-cycle stage. Using a sample of publicly traded U.S. firms in the period from 1972 to 2002, DeAngelo, DeAngelo, and Stulz (2006) test the firm life-cycle theory of dividends by relating dividend payment propensity to the mix of retained earnings to contributed capital and find support for the theory. Based on international evidence on the determinants of dividend policy, Denis and Osobov's (2008) findings cast doubt on signaling, clientele, and catering explanations for dividends but support agency-cost-based life-cycle theories.

In their synthesis of the literature on the firm life-cycle theory of dividends, Bulan and Subramanian (2009, p. 211) conclude,

> Overall, the empirical evidence favors the firm life cycle theory of dividends in terms of dividend payment propensity and life cycle characteristics. Firms in the early stages of their life cycles rarely pay dividends, while firms in the mature stage are likely to be dividend payers. Moreover, the decision to pay the first regular cash dividend is usually made contingent on having reached maturity.

The Catering Theory of Dividends

Baker and Wurgler (2004) develop a catering theory of dividends stressing the importance of investor sentiment in dividend policy decisions. This theory posits that managers cater to investor demand for dividends by paying dividends when investors prefer dividend-paying firms and by not paying or reducing dividends when investors prefer non-dividend-paying companies; that is, when the shares of existing dividend-paying firms are trading at a premium relative to those of non-dividend-paying firms, non-dividend-paying firms will initiate dividends. On the other hand, when the shares of dividend-paying firms are trading at a discount, firms will reduce or omit dividends. Baker and Wurgler also assume that investor demand for dividend-paying stocks is uninformed and varies over time.

Various studies using samples of U.S., U.K., European, and cross-country firms examine the catering theory as proposed by Baker and Wurgler (2004) and show mixed results. In their review of the empirical evidence on the catering theory of dividends, deRooji and Renneboog (2009, p. 235) conclude,

> Despite these mixed findings, some general conclusions emerge. First, the announcement effects for dividend initiations are more strongly positive than the announcement effects of dividend increases. Therefore, the catering theory seems to explain dividend initiations better than dividend omissions. Second, because individual firm characteristics still play an important role in determining dividend policy, they should be integrated with investors' sentiment to explain dividend policy. Finally, the validity of the catering theory of dividends is confined not only to countries with strong investor protections but also to those with weaker investor protections.

Recap of Dividend Theories and Explanations

After several decades of empirical evidence on alternative explanations of why firms pay dividends, what do the results of existing studies using secondary data from capital markets and accounting statements show? Lease et al. (2000, p. 179) offer the following observation about the existing dividend policy research:

> We believe that the lack of empirical support for a particular dividend policy theory is the result of problems in quantitatively measuring market frictions and the statistical complications in dealing with the myriad interactive imperfections that likely affect individual firms differentially. In other words, since each firm faces a combination of potentially different market frictions with varying levels of relevance, the optimal dividend policy for each firm *may* be unique. If each firm has a uniquely optimal dividend policy, we should not be surprised that significant statistical generalizations still elude researchers.

Thus, the results are far from conclusive or unanimous as to what theory can best explain the dividend payout. After analyzing close to 200 published papers,

Frankfurter and Wood (2002) conclude that none of the dividend theories is unequivocally verified. In fact, all of these theories and explanations suffer from either a lack of verifiability or contradictory empirical evidence. According to Allen and Michaely (2003), the theories based on agency or signaling are inconsistent with the empirical evidence, and the question of why firms distribute dividends remains a puzzle. Yet, DeAngelo, DeAngelo, and Skinner (2009) express a different conclusion and argue that asymmetric information could provide an explanation for the dividends phenomenon. Thus, managers searching for help in making dividend policy decisions encounter many theories but only limited practical guidance.

The mixed results may stem from many factors, including researchers using different time periods, methodologies, and variables to test each theory. Additionally, the problem partly stems from the difficulty of designing empirical tests to examine the impact of dividend policy on firm value in a macro fashion; that is, researchers typically examine dividend policy using a broad cross-section of firms (macroanalysis) instead of focusing on a single firm (microanalysis). Further, concentrating on only one piece of the dividend puzzle at a time (for example, focusing on a single market imperfection) is unlikely to provide a satisfactory resolution because the dividend puzzle contains many pieces.

There is no clear winner among the competing dividend theories, and no single theory has become the dominant solution to the dividend puzzle. Some empirical support exists for each theory. As the previous discussion of the three big imperfections suggests, the agency costs and asymmetric information (signaling) explanations appear to have more convincing empirical support than the tax-preference explanation. While no theory provides definitive answers, more recent theories involving behavioral considerations, the firm life-cycle theory of dividends, and the catering theory of dividends provide some useful insights but still produce mixed results. Thus, the empirical contest among the various theories continues.

U.S. Survey Evidence on Cash Dividends and Related Issues

The types of theoretical and empirical research just discussed rely on secondary data in which researchers look at firms' dividend payout behavior in indirect ways. In contrast, other researchers have taken a different path to learn about dividend policy. Instead of using data to extract evidence to support or reject various dividend theories and hypotheses, researchers gather information directly from managers and others in order to learn about firm practices and manager perceptions surrounding various dividend policy issues. Despite extensive research, many dividend theories suffer from contradictory empirical evidence. Given the mixed results of the empirical evidence based on secondary data, surveys may help to provide a better understanding of the grey areas between theory and practice.

Given the plethora of surveys involving dividend policy and the fact that some such surveys date back more than 50 years, this section focuses on some of the more noteworthy and representative survey evidence on cash dividends and other dividend issues. This section examines survey evidence involving dividend policy in the United States and orders the surveys chronologically based on the publication date of the research, not on the date the authors conducted the survey, which often is several years earlier.

A caveat is needed when interpreting the results of the following survey studies. The evidence should not be viewed as generally applicable to all time and all firms. Many surveys have limited generality, as the conflicting results so amply demonstrate.

Dividend Surveys Published During the Pre-1980s

This section provides a synthesis of major dividend surveys published during the pre-1980s. The section begins with the seminal study of Lintner (1956).

The Lintner Survey and Model

Lintner's (1956) path-breaking analysis of dividend policy represents one of the earliest and most important studies on dividend policy. From a group of more than 600 exchange-listed and well-established U.S. companies, he carefully selected 28 industrial companies for detailed investigation but did not choose the sample for purposes of drawing statistical conclusions. For each firm, Lintner and his research associate conducted field investigations, typically with two to five senior managers who were involved in the firm's dividend policy. These individuals included presidents, financial vice presidents, treasurers, controllers, and directors. The purpose of these interviews was to investigate their thinking on the determination of dividend policy. Before the interview process began, Lintner identified about 15 factors and characteristics, such as firm size and relative average earnings on capital expenditures, appearing to have an important bearing on dividend payments and policy.

Lintner's (1956) fieldwork provides several observations about dividend policy. First, his respondents view the starting point for most payout decisions as the payout ratio (i.e., dividends as a proportion of earnings). He reports that most firms have long-run target dividend payout ratios. In general, mature firms with stable earnings have a high payout ratio, while growth companies have a low dividend payout.

Second, dividend changes follow a shift in long-term sustainable earnings. Lintner (1956, p. 101) finds evidence that "major changes in earnings or levels of earnings 'out of line' with existing dividend rates were the most important determinants of the firm's dividend decisions." Given that firms tend to have long-run target dividend payout ratios, this leads to a smoothing of dividend payments over time. Smoothing occurs not only because management perceives that stockholders prefer a reasonably stable rate but also because managers need time to determine the permanence of any earnings increases. Thus, changes in dividends only partially adjust to changes in the existing rate of earnings.

Third, Lintner (1956) also finds that managers are more concerned with dividend changes than with the absolute level. Finally, managers do not tend to reverse the change in dividends. Given the perceived investor preference for reasonably stable but growing dividends, management typically seeks to avoid making changes in the firm's dividend rates that it might have to reverse within a year or so. Thus, firms appear to increase dividends only after they are reasonably confident that they can maintain them permanently at the new level. This rationale also helps to explain why managers are hesitant to cut dividends unless they expect the adverse circumstances to persist.

Taken as a whole, these observations suggest that managers view dividends as an active decision variable and that companies have reasonably well-defined standards regarding the speed with which they attempt to move toward adjusting the dividend payout relative to earnings. Also, these corporations tend to make dividend decisions conservatively.

Based on this fieldwork showing the dominant patterns of decision making involving dividends, Lintner (1956) develops a simple behavioral model, often called a partial-adjustment model. Lintner suggests that the following equation describes corporate dividend behavior:

$$\Delta Div_{it} = a_i + c_i \left(Div^*_{it} - Div_{i,t-1} \right) + u_{it}, \tag{1}$$

where

ΔDiv_{it} = the change in dividends,

c_i = the speed of adjustment to the difference between a target dividend payout and last year's payout,

Div^*_{it} = the target dividend payout (i.e., the target payout ratio × current year's profits after taxes),

$Div^*_{i,t-1}$ = last period's dividend payout, and

a_i, u_{it} = a constant and a normally distributed random error term.

This model indicates that the change in a firm's dividend (ΔDiv_{it}) is a function of its target dividend payout (Div^*_{it}) less the previous period's dividend payout ($Div^*_{i,t-1}$)—both of which are in dollar terms—multiplied by a speed of adjustment factor (c_i); that is, dividends per share equal a coefficient times the difference between the target dividend payout (in dollar terms) and lagged dividend per share. Dividend conservatism dictates that the coefficient is less than 1 because it reflects only a partial adjustment.

Lintner (1956) tests his model using regression and finds that the model explains about 85 percent of the year-to-year dividend changes for his sample of companies. Others such as Brittain (1964, 1966), Fama and Babiak (1968), and Bond and Mougoué (1991) reevaluate Lintner's model and conclude that his basic model continues to perform well after making alternative specifications. In a more recent study, Benartzi, Michaely, and Thaler (1997, p. 1032) provide additional supportive evidence when they state that "Lintner's model of dividends remains the best description of the dividend setting process available" Kumar and Lee (2001) indicate that their dynamic model of discrete dividend policy outperforms the basic Lintner (1956) model by a substantial margin.

In summary, Lintner's (1956) classic study suggests that the managers interviewed typically view dividend policy decisions as an important part of their job. They do not follow a residual policy or leave dividends to chance. Instead, they follow a managed dividend policy in which managers tend to stabilize dividend distributions and provide a consistency in the pattern of dividends, as described in Lintner's model. Yet, Lintner's evidence does not permit concluding that the market rewards a managed dividend policy with a higher price; that is, Lintner does not show that dividend policy is consistent with wealth maximization of the shareholders. Further, Lintner's results do not explain why companies pay dividends in the first place. Lintner (p. 100) does note, however, that the managers interviewed generally believe that "unless there are compelling reasons to the contrary, their fiduciary responsibilities and standards of fairness required them to distribute part of any substantial increase in earnings to the stockholders in dividends."

The Harkins and Walsh (1971) Survey

Harkins and Walsh (1971) survey 166 members of the Conference Board panel of senior financial executives to learn their views about dividend policy. They find that those surveyed perceive a conflict between shareholder desires for dividends and managements' need to retain earnings to help fund investment opportunities. To deal with this conflict, the firms they survey choose a compromise policy that partially satisfies the wants and needs of each party. Their evidence shows that the major considerations of managers in making dividend decisions are current earnings and expected earnings, regularity of payment, stability of rate, cash flows and investment opportunities, and stockholder needs and expectations. Additionally, managers consider loan provisions and taxes on excess retained earnings. Of the firms surveyed, about half report having target dividend payout levels. Similar to Lintner's (1956) study, these firms gradually adjust their dividends over some period to reach their target level.

Dividend Surveys Published During the 1980s

With a few notable exceptions previously mentioned, survey research on dividend policy received scant attention until the 1980s. Although the objectives of these studies during the 1980s differ, they often focus on (1) the perceived relationship between dividend policy and value, (2) explanations of dividend relevance, and (3) determinants of dividend policy.

The Baker, Farrelly, and Edelman (1985); Edelman, Farrelly, and Baker (1985); and Farrelly, Baker, and Edelman (1986) Survey of Dividend Policymakers

About thirty years after Lintner's (1956) classic study, Baker, Farrelly, and Edelman (1985); Edelman, Farrelly, and Baker (1985); and Farrelly, Baker, and Edelman (1986) published the results of the most comprehensive dividend survey to date. These authors base all three articles on different aspects of this single survey. The major objectives of the survey are (1) to compare the determinants of dividend policy with Lintner's behavioral model and to assess management's agreement with Lintner's findings, (2) to examine management's perception about theoretical issues such as the relationship between dividend policy and firm value as well as signaling and clientele effects, and (3) to determine whether managers in different industries share similar views about the determinants of dividend policy. In 1983, the authors use a mail survey to contact the chief financial officers (CFOs) of firms listed on the New York Stock Exchange (NYSE) from three industry groups: utilities (150), manufacturing (309), and wholesale/retail (103). The survey yielded 318 usable responses (a 56.6 percent overall response rate) including 147 manufacturing firms, 114 utilities, and 57 wholesale/retail firms, resulting in response rates of 47.6 percent, 76.0 percent, and 55.3 percent, respectively.

The researchers accomplish their first objective of examining how well Lintner's model describes current practice by asking respondents to indicate the importance of each of 15 factors in determining their firm's dividend policy. Using a five-point importance scale, from 0 = no importance to 4 = maximum importance, their evidence shows that all three industry groups list the same four factors among their top rankings. Two of these factors are consistent with Lintner's (1956) findings—namely, the anticipated level of a firm's future earnings and the pattern of past dividends. Although not directly addressed by Lintner, another important factor is the availability of cash. The fourth major determinant is concern about maintaining or increasing stock price. Farrelly, Baker, and Edelman (1986) conclude that the major determinants of dividend payments during the time period studied appear strikingly similar to Lintner's behavioral model developed during the mid-1950s. In particular, respondents express a high concern for dividend continuity.

To examine this study's second objective of investigating CFOs' attitudes about Lintner's (1956) findings and their perceptions of signaling and clientele effects as well as other issues, Baker, Farrelly, and Edelman (1985) pose 18 closed-ended statements about theoretical issues involving corporate dividend policy. Respondents rank each statement on a seven-point scale, from −3 = strongly disagree to +3 = strongly agree, with 0 = no opinion. Of the five statements relating to Lintner's (1956) findings, three are among the four most highly ranked statements: (1) a firm should avoid making changes in its dividend rates that might have to be reversed in a year or so; (2) a firm should strive to maintain an uninterrupted record of dividend payments; and (3) a firm should have a target payout ratio and periodically adjust the payout toward the target. On average, the responding managers express no strong opinions on two other findings associated with Lintner.

Regarding attitudes on various theoretical issues involving corporate dividend policy, the majority of respondents agree that dividend payout affects the price of their firm's common stock. Yet, a substantial percentage of respondents, ranging from about 22 percent for utilities to 42 percent for wholesale/retail firms, offer no opinion about the relationship between dividend policy and value of their corporation.

Overall, the evidence supports dividend relevance. Although the survey does not uncover the exact reasons managers believe in dividend relevance, it does offer evidence that respondents are generally aware of signaling and clientele effects. For example, about half of the respondents perceive that dividend payments provide a "signaling device" of future prospects. Overall, the study finds fairly strong support for using dividends as a signal but mixed support for a series of statements involving the clientele effect.

The final objective of the survey involves determining whether differences in managers' beliefs exist across the three broad industry groups. Edelman, Farrelly, and Baker (1985) use chi-square analysis to test for differences in the responses among the three industry groups. The results show that the opinions of respondents from the high-payout, regulated utilities differ significantly from those of the low-payout, unregulated firms in manufacturing and wholesale/retail. Specifically, the tests show that the responses of the three groups differ significantly at the 0.05 level among eight of the 15 determinants of dividend policy. Further analysis shows that the differences occur primarily as a result of responses from utilities relative to either manufacturing or wholesale/retail.

For example, the respondents from the utilities view various determinants of dividend policy as more important than do respondents from manufacturing and wholesale/retails. Examples of these factors include the concern about maintaining or increasing stock prices, desire to conform to industry dividend practice, and characteristics and requirements of stockholders. On the other hand, respondents from the unregulated firms consider the availability of profitable investment opportunities as more important than respondents from the utilities. Regarding several of these differences, Edelman, Farrelly, and Baker (1985, p. 30) comment,

> There is the possibility that utility dividends have become so automatic and the desire to conform to industry practice so strong that the suggestion to omit or reduce them may not be considered seriously. The threat of possible negative consequences may be too severe. Thus firms may not investigate investment opportunities unless they can "cover" their dividend first.

The chi-square tests in Baker, Farrelly, and Edelman (1985) show significant differences among the three industry groups for nine of the 18 issues. For example, respondents from utility firms more strongly agree that a firm should strive to maintain an uninterrupted record of dividend payments than respondents from nonutilities. These results suggest that managers of regulated firms have a somewhat different view of various dividend issues than managers operating in a more competitive environment. The authors posit that the observed differences may be due to regulation or to other characteristics.

In summary, the results of this comprehensive survey show that the major determinants of dividends are similar to those reported by Lintner (1956). The results support the notion of dividend relevance and signaling as an explanation for this relevance. Additionally, the evidence shows that the views about dividends of managers of utilities sometimes differ from the views of managers of manufacturing and wholesale retail firms.

Kennedy, O'Brien, and Horn's (1987) Survey of Large Public Utilities

Kennedy, O'Brien, and Horn (1987) survey top executives in public utilities (electric power, telecommunications, and motor carriers) in 1983 about their dividend policies. One objective of this study is to determine whether these utilities have a target percentage of earnings that they attempt to pay out in dividends. Their results show that 55 percent of respondents have a formal target dividend payout percentage, but a substantial minority (36 percent) report having no formal or informal payout policy. A second objective is to identify the most important factors influencing the dividend decision. For the electric power and telecommunications industries, the most important factor influencing dividend policy is the desire to avoid a reduction in an established dividend per share. For the motor-carrier industry, the most influential factors relate to earnings.

The authors also find that concern over the market price of common stock is not a strong influence in the dividend decision. Kennedy, O'Brien, and Horn (1987, p. 69) conclude that "our findings indicate that decision-makers in the public utility industry are not convinced that dividend policy is an important factor in stock value." This finding is contrary to evidence provided by another 1983 survey conducted by Edelman, Farrelly, and Baker (1985) in which respondents from the utility industry place "concern about increasing or maintaining stock price" as the second-most highly ranked determinant of dividend policy following the "anticipated level of future earnings."

Baker and Farrelly's (1988) Survey of Dividend Achievers

Baker and Farrelly (1988) investigate the decision-making behavior of dividend achievers, defined as companies having an unbroken record of at least 10 consecutive years of dividend increases (1974 to 1983). Because this study focuses on a group of long-term, dividend-paying firms, the results may not apply generally to all firms. In spite of this, the authors note that focusing on dividend achievers provides a means of examining the perceived impact of clientele effects on a firm's dividend behavior. The study extends the survey research by Baker, Farrelly, and Edelman (1985) and Farrelly, Baker, and Edelman (1986).

Using a pretested questionnaire, Baker and Farrelly (1988) survey 397 CFOs of U.S. and Canadian dividend-achiever firms listed on the NYSE, American Stock Exchange (AMEX), and NASDAQ and obtain a 62 percent response rate. They conduct the survey in 1985. Of the responding firms, slightly fewer than one-half (47.6 percent) are regulated firms, mainly utilities and finance-related companies. The authors provide evidence involving six research questions about the behavior of dividend achievers.

Regarding reasons for paying dividends, the overwhelming reason given by 93.3 percent of respondents is to meet stockholders' expectations for continued dividend growth. As the authors note, this result is consistent with the firms' historical behavior as dividend achievers. Other reasons include maintaining or increasing the stock price from the current level (30.1 percent), attracting new investors/capital (23.2 percent), and following industry norms (8.1 percent). The two most highly ranked reasons for paying dividends may not be independent because failing to maintain dividend payments at historical levels may result in stockholder disappointment and a drop in stock prices (Benesh, Keown, and Pinkerton 1984).

Additionally, Baker and Farrelly (1988) ask the CFOs to indicate the importance of 12 factors in determining their firm's dividend policy by using a five-point scale, from 0 = no importance to 4 = maximum importance. The most highly ranked factor is the sustainability of dividends, closely followed by the anticipated level of future earnings. Third ranked is the pattern of past dividends, followed by the level of current earnings. These findings are similar to those reported in other behavioral studies such as Lintner (1956) and Baker, Farrelly, and Edelman (1985), but dividend achievers place greater emphasis on the importance of dividend stability.

Responses to the remaining research questions yield the following results. Baker and Farrelly (1988) report that almost three-fourths (73.5 percent) of the responding dividend achievers maintain a target payout ratio, but only 34.1 percent divulge this information to shareholders. Most respondents report awareness of dividend announcement effects. In fact, 91.1 percent indicate that they believe a change in the rate of dividends serves as a message from management about the future prospects of their firms. (When referring to the rate of dividends, the authors do not distinguish between dividend payout ratio and the dollar amount of dividends.) On the issue of whether their firms try to conform to an industry norm in terms of the dividend payout ratio, only one-third of the CFOs respond affirmatively. Combined with other results included in the survey, this finding suggests that the desire to conform to industry practice is only a second-order determinant of dividend policy to most dividend achievers.

Finally, the results suggest that regulation does not affect dividend policy behavior in a meaningful way for dividend achievers. This result differs from the belief expressed in the Baker, Farrelly, and Edelman (1985) study. Baker and Farrelly (p. 88) conclude, "Not surprisingly, dividend achievers placed more emphasis on the importance of dividend stability and its perceived impact on stock prices than did respondents in other behavioral studies".

Baker's (1989) Survey of Nondividend Payers

Baker (1989) examines the behavior of a sample of NYSE firms with a long-standing policy of paying no cash dividends. Two conflicting rationales exist for paying no cash dividends. In one scenario, fast-growing firms have less cash available than they need to fund growth and expansion. Thus, decision makers may prefer to retain earnings because using internally generated funds to finance capital expenditures is less expensive than raising external equity and less risky than raising additional debt. This rationale is consistent with a residual dividend policy. In the other scenario, firms do not pay cash dividends because they lack sufficient cash flows due to their poor financial performance and weak condition.

The initial sample consists of 175 NYSE-listed companies that paid no cash dividends over the five-year period from June 1980 through June 1985. Baker (1989) conducted the survey in 1985. Of the 175 questionnaires mailed, the authors received 68 usable questionnaires, giving an overall response rate of 38.9 percent. The survey consists of two major parts: (1) 11 closed-end statements about factors that may influence a firm's policy of no cash dividends and (2) 15 questions designed to elicit managements' opinions about various facets of their firms' dividend policy and to provide a profile of respondents. The most common industry groups represented by the responding firms are manufacturing (52.5 percent), wholesale/retail (13.1 percent), and transportation/utility (11.5 percent).

The survey addresses four major research questions. The first question focuses on the major reasons that some firms pay no cash dividends. Of the 11 factors presented, respondents view availability of cash, availability of profitable investment opportunities, cost of raising external funds, and the level of current earnings as the most important factors influencing a no-cash-dividend policy. A comparison of these results to those of earlier surveys of dividend payers by Farrelly, Baker, and Edelman (1986) and Baker and Farrelly (1988) shows that only availability of cash ranks among the three most highly ranked factors for both sets of studies. An implication of this comparative evidence is that a firm's status of paying or not paying dividends influences the importance that its managers attach to the determinants of dividend policy. The importance that non-dividend payers place on the most highly ranked factors suggests that interaction effects exist among financing, investment, and dividend policy decisions. This finding conflicts with advocates of the neoclassical theory of finance, such as Miller and Modigliani (1961), who show that under ideal conditions involving highly restrictive assumptions, no interaction effects exist among these three types of decisions.

When asked to list the key reason for not paying dividends, the most common response, given by 76.2 percent of the respondents, is growth and expansion through investment and/or reinvestment. Segregating the data into two broad classes based on profitability measures shows that high-profitability firms are more inclined to cite this motive as an important rationale for retaining earnings than low-profitability firms. An implication of this finding is that a firm's financial condition influences its rationale for not paying dividends.

The second research question examines whether policymakers consider shareholders' preferences when setting a policy of paying no cash dividends. The overwhelming majority of the respondents (77.9 percent) perceive that their shareholders prefer capital gains to dividends. Yet, only 46.3 percent indicate that their firm is responsive to its shareholders' dividend preferences, while 41.2 percent perceive that most of their shareholders prefer a no-dividend policy. Based on the responses to three statements about shareholder preferences, Baker (1989) finds only marginal support for the notion that policymakers are responsive to shareholders' preferences.

The third research question examines managements' perceptions of the relationship between a no-cash-dividends policy and common stock prices. The evidence shows mixed results, with 29.8 percent believing that paying no dividends positively affects the price of their firm's stock, while 43.3 percent answer no, and the remaining 26.9 percent indicate "don't know." These results contrast with the findings in Baker, Farrelly, and Edelman (1985) and Baker and Farrelly (1988), who show stronger agreement with the notion that dividend payout affects common stock prices. Thus, Baker (1989) notes that the survey results are inconclusive as to whether managers believe dividends affect share value.

The final research question inquires about whether managers perceive that paying no dividends provides a signal about current and future prospects of a firm. The responses are divided among 43.9 percent "yes," 45.5 percent "no," and 10.6 percent "don't know." Thus, the evidence provides mixed results about signaling effects.

In conclusion, Baker (1989) observes that firms with different dividend schemes—for example, non-dividend-paying firms and dividend achievers—place different degrees of importance on factors influencing dividend policy. Baker (p. 57) notes, "An implication for academicians is that developing a single model to explain the behavior of firms with both normal and unusual dividend policies may prove to be difficult." This observation may help to explain why there is no clear winner among the competing dividend theories despite extensive empirical research.

Farrelly and Baker's (1989) Survey of Institutional Investors

Instead of studying dividend policy from the perspective of the firm as in previous surveys or from the individual's perspectives as examined by Shefrin and

Statman (1984), Farrelly and Baker (1989) survey the views of institutional investors including portfolio managers, investment advisors, and security analysts. They deem the views of institutional investors relevant because of their impact on the market. The authors investigate such issues as dividend patterns, information signaling through dividends, and perceived relationships between dividend and share prices.

Using a pretested survey, Farrelly and Baker (1989) mail the questionnaire to a random sample of 503 members of the Financial Analysts Federation (FAF) in 1985 and receive 130 responses, resulting in a 25.8 percent response rate. Members of the FAF represent proxies of different types of institutional investors. The respondents are highly experienced, with 73.8 percent having more than 10 years of experience in the investment business, and well educated, with 63.1 percent having at least a master's degree.

The study addresses four major questions. The first question involves whether institutional investors believe dividend policy affects stock prices. The survey asks respondents to rank the following three statements based on their level of agreement: (1) dividend policy has no effect on a firm's stock price; (2) an increased dividend increases a firm's stock price; and (3) an increased dividend reduces a firm's stock price. The overwhelming majority of respondents (91.4 percent) rank the second statement most highly; that is, institutional investors see a positive relationship between an increase in dividends and an increase in stock prices. This view seems consistent with survey evidence provided by managers as reported in studies by Baker, Farrelly, and Edelman (1985) and Farrelly, Baker, and Edelman (1986). Thus, institutional investors generally believe that dividends matter, as they affect share price.

In the second research question, Farrelly and Baker (1989) examine whether these institutional investors believe that in general, investors have preferences toward dividends versus capital gains. The survey provides three choices: "preference for dividends," "preference for capital gains," or "value dividends and capital gains equally." The majority of respondents (67.9 percent) rank "preference for capital gains" as their first choice, while 17.7 percent select the "preference for dividends" option. At the time of the survey, the tax treatment of capital gains was more favorable relative to dividends. Thus, the authors speculate that tax consequences play a part in the expressed preference for capital gains. (If the tax treatment of capital gains and dividend income changes, this could change investor preferences.)

The third research question addresses whether institutional investors regard dividends as a better signal of the future profitability of a firm than earnings or cash flow. The results show that only a small percentage of the respondents select dividends. The survey evidence reveals that the majority of respondents (50.4 percent) believe that "past and current earnings" are more useful in predicting future profitability than "past and current cash flows to the firm" (43.3 percent) and "past and current dividends" (3.3 percent). These results may suggest that signals other than dividends can perform the same function in a more effective and less expensive manner.

The fourth research question, which previous survey studies on dividend policy do not address, asks institutional investors about their views on the appropriateness of the level of cash dividends paid by most firms. The results show that institutional investors view the current level of cash dividends paid by most firms as appropriate. In fact, almost 74 percent of the respondents advised companies to retain their current dividend payout ratios.

The final part of the study examines the opinions of institutional investors on 17 closed-ended statements about various dividend policies by using a five-point scale, from −2 = strongly disagree to +2 = strongly agree, with 0 = no opinion. A key finding is that institutional investors show a high level of agreement with statements involving the information content of dividends. For example, the statement with the highest mean ranking is that "sudden shifts in dividend policy cause abrupt changes in stock price." In fact, 87.7 percent of the respondents agree with this statement. These institutional investors also express a high level of agreement (92.6 percent) with the statement that "a firm's industry helps to explain its payout ratio." This finding complements other empirical evidence by McCabe (1979), Michel (1979), and Baker (1988) showing a relationship between industry classification and corporate dividend policy. By contrast, Rozeff (1982) concludes that a firm's industry does not help to explain its dividend payout ratio. Farrelly and Baker (1989) conclude that the opinions of institutional investors about dividends are highly similar to those of dividend policymakers reported by Baker, Farrelly, and Edelman (1985) and Baker and Farrelly (1988).

Dividend Surveys Published During the 1990s

This section discusses various surveys during the 1990s involving dividend policy.

Abrutyn and Turner's (1990) Survey of Taxes and Dividend Policies

The objective of Abrutyn and Turner's (1990) study is to obtain direct evidence on the importance of tax factors in firms' dividend payout decisions and to distinguish between competing theories of how taxes affect dividends. This 1988 survey involves the chief executive officers (CEOs) of 550 of the largest 1,000 corporations in the United States. The authors base their analysis on 163 completed surveys, resulting in a 29.6 percent response rate. Abrutyn and Turner note, however, that the corporations surveyed may not be representative of the general corporate population because they do not test for nonresponse bias.

The analysis of the survey responses casts doubt on the notion that the responding firms base their dividend policy on shareholders' tax rates. The results show that only 42 percent of the firms claim to know their shareholders.

The authors reason that tax laws are unlikely to play an important role in the determination of the payout ratio if managers are unaware of whether dividends will result in large tax liabilities for the firm's shareholders. Thus, firms would be unable to tailor dividend policy to their shareholders' tax status.

Abrutyn and Turner (1990) also investigate managements' views involving four theories of why corporations pay dividends: taxes, signaling, agency cost, and clientele effects. Their results do not provide unambiguous support for any of the four explanations. Of these theories, the signaling explanation receives the highest ranking, with 63 percent of the firms ranking this choice first or second, while the tax clientele hypothesis receives the weakest support. Abrutyn (pp. 495-496) and Turner posit that "empirical investigations attempting to identify the single 'correct' explanation of dividend behavior are unlikely to succeed, since no single explanation is correct for all firms."

Pruitt and Gitman's (1991) Survey on Investment, Financing, and Dividend Decisions

Pruitt and Gitman (1991) provide evidence about the interactions between the investment, financing, and dividend decisions in major U.S. firms. Of primary concern here, however, is their evidence involving dividends. Using a mail questionnaire, the authors survey the highest-ranking financial officer of each of the 1,000 largest U.S. firms in terms of annual sales. The authors conduct the survey in 1988. They receive 114 usable responses, resulting in a response rate of 11.4 percent. Of these surveys, 65 deal with dividend-financing issues.

Using a seven-point scale, Pruitt and Gitman (1991) ask respondents to indicate their degree of agreement with 21 statements about dividend practices in major U.S. firms. The results suggest that respondents do not consider the level of investment expenditures an important influence when establishing dividend policy. Finding that firms report making dividend decisions independently of their investment and financing decisions supports Modigliani and Miller's (1958) separation theory, which asserts that in the presence of perfect capital markets, a firm's value is completely independent of how it finances its productive assets.

Pruitt and Gitman's (1991) survey evidence is consistent with the indirect empirical evidence of Fama (1974) and Smirlock and Marshall (1983), which suggests no relationship between dividend and investment decisions. By contrast, using other nonsurvey evidence, McCabe (1979) finds a strong degree of interdependence between investment and dividend decisions and the financing (fund-raising) decision.

Pruitt and Gitman (1991) find that the respondents agree that the most important influences on the dividends paid by the respondents' firms are current and past years' profits, the year-to-year variability of earnings, the growth in earnings, and the prior year's dividends. These determinants consistent with Lintner's (1956) partial-adjustment model and the survey work of Baker, Farrelly, and Edelman (1985) and Farrelly, Baker, and Edelman (1986). Similar to other

U.S. surveys, the results suggest that respondents attempt to maintain a high degree of consistency in the level of their firms' dividends.

The survey by Pruitt and Gitman (1991) also asks respondents to indicate the variables having the greatest value in predicting their firm's dividend decisions. In rank order, the most important explanatory variables for dividend policy decisions for these respondents are (1) projected net earnings, (2) recently enacted dividend changes, (3) current dividend payout ratio, (4) level of cash flows, and (5) previous earnings levels and capital investment requirements (a tie).

Pruitt and Gitman (1991, p. 428) conclude that

> the dividend decision was found to be made independently of the firm's investment and financing decisions; rather, profits and prior year's dividends appear to act as major influences on current dividend policies. As such, the current research suggests that opinions consistent with the separation principle, originally put forth by Modigliani and Miller in their seminal work, are held by practicing real world financial managers despite significant violations of many of Modigliani and Miller's underlying assumptions.

Baker and Powell's (1999a, 1999b) Survey of NYSE Firms

Baker and Powell (1999a, 1999b) expand and update a previous study by Baker, Farrelly, and Edelman (1985). They investigate the views of corporate managers of major U.S. firms about three topics: (1) the relationship between dividend policy and value; (2) explanations of dividend relevance including the bird-in-the-hand, signaling, tax-preference, and agency explanations; and (3) how firms determine the amount of dividends to pay. They ask respondents to indicate their general opinion about each of 26 closed-ended statements based on a five-point scale, from −2 = definitely don't agree to +2 = definitely agree, and 0 = no opinion.

Their sample consists of U.S. corporations listed on the NYSE that paid a cash dividend in at least one year during the period from 1994 to 1995. As with Baker, Farrelly, and Edelman (1985), Baker and Powell (1999a, 1999b) examine three industry groups: manufacturing, wholesale/retail trade, and utilities. Using a pretested mail questionnaire, they survey CFOs of 603 firms and receive 198 usable responses, a 32.9 percent response rate. Baker and Powell conduct the survey in 1997.

To test for nonresponse bias, they conduct t-tests for differences in means between respondents and nonrespondents on five characteristics (total assets, total sales, market value of equity, dividend payout ratio, and dividend yield). Among the competing dividend theories, there is no clear winner; that is, no single theory is found to be dominant. The authors find no statistically significant differences at the 0.05 level for any of the characteristics by the three industry groups.

Baker and Powell (1999a) address four research issues. In response to the question, "Do corporate managers believe that dividends are relevant?" the authors find that the respondents tend to believe that dividend policy affects firm value and hence view dividends as relevant. For example, 77 percent of respondents from manufacturing firms agree that "a change in dividend policy affects firm value." The evidence shows that at least 87 percent of the respondents for each industry group agree or strongly agree that "a firm's investment, financing, and dividend decisions are interrelated." Therefore, unlike Pruitt and Gitman (1991), evidence from Baker and Powell (1999a) does not support Modigliani and Miller's (1958) separation theory. Also, the respondents hold widely divergent views about whether a firm should view cash dividends as a residual after financing desired investments from earnings. This evidence is contrary to an implication of Miller and Modigliani's (1961) argument that the dividend decision is a residual decision. Thus, the views of these respondents about residual dividend theory are diverse, and the evidence in support of the various theories is inconclusive.

The second research question is, "What explanations of dividends do managers tend to favor?" Of the four explanations for dividend relevance examined in this study, Baker and Powell's (1999a) evidence shows the highest level of agreement with statements involving signaling. Responses to statements involving the bird-in-the-hand, tax-preference, and agency explanations produce mixed or inconsistent results. In general, respondents are often unable to offer an opinion (they neither agree nor disagree) with statements involving these three latter explanations of dividend relevance. For example, the percentage of "no opinion" responses across the three industry groups to the statements involving the tax-preference explanation ranges from 20.4 percent to 57.1 percent.

The third research question is, "How do firms set the amount of dividends that they pay?" The results show that these managers' views on setting dividend payments are generally consistent with those reported by managers interviewed by Lintner (1956), which provides support for his partial-adjustment model. In particular, respondents express a high level of concern for the continuity of dividends. For example, about 85 percent of the respondents agree with the statement that "a firm should avoid changing its regular dividend if that change might have to be reversed in a year or so."

The final research question is, "Do the views of managers about dividend issues differ among different industry groups?" Baker and Powell (1999a) use chi-square analysis to test for significant differences in the level of agreement among the three industry groups, whereas Baker and Powell (1999b) examine differences only between utilities and manufacturing firms. Based on these tests, the responses of the three groups differ significantly at the 0.05 level for only four of the 26 statements. These results suggest that a firm's industry type exerts little influence on managers' views about theoretical and empirical issues involving dividend policy. These findings differ markedly from those reported by

Baker, Farrelly, and Edelman (1985) in which the responses of managers from utilities often differ substantially from those in the manufacturing and whole-sale/retail trade industries. Baker and Powell (1999a) speculate that the greater consistency in responses among the three industry groups may be due to the changing economic and competitive environment for utilities; that is, utilities during the time of the study operate in a more competitive environment than in previous decades. Consequently, the views of managers from different industries may show greater consistency regarding the various explanations for paying dividends.

Dividend Surveys: 2000 to Date

This section reviews the findings of numerous dividend surveys since 2000.

Baker and Powell's (2000) Longitudinal Study

The main purpose of this study is to investigate the views of corporate managers of major U.S. firms about the factors influencing dividend policy. Baker and Powell (1999a, 1999b, 2000) use the same survey instrument and sample of 603 NYSE-listed U.S. firms in all three studies. Baker and Powell (2000) compare the results of their survey conducted in 1997 to the results of a survey conducted in 1983 by Baker, Farrelly, and Edelman (1985) and Farrelly, Baker, and Edelman (1986). Baker and Powell model their survey instrument after the 1983 question-naire to permit comparisons between the two time periods. The Baker and Powell (2000) study expands the topical coverage compared to previous survey research on dividend policy.

Baker and Powell (2000) address three major research questions. The first question is, "What factors are most important in influencing the dividend policy of firms paying cash dividends?" The survey asks managers to indicate the level of importance of 20 factors in setting their firms' dividend policy by using a four-point scale, from 0 = none to 3 = high. Based on 198 responses representing a 32.9 percent response rate, the overall rankings show that the most important determinants of a firm's dividend policy are the levels of current and expected earnings and the pattern or continuity of past dividends. These factors are simi-lar to those identified by Lintner (1956) in his behavioral model of dividends and survey research by Baker, Farrelly, and Edelman (1985); Farrelly, Baker, and Edelman (1986); and Pruitt and Gitman (1991). The next three most highly ranked factors influencing a firm's dividend policy are concern about maintain-ing or increasing stock price, concern that a dividend change may provide a false signal to investors, and stability of cash flows.

The second research question is, "Have these factors changed over time?" In comparing the rankings between the survey conducted in 1983 and 1997, Baker and Powell (2000) find little change in the ranking of the most important factors influencing dividend policy. These findings appear to provide continued support for Lintner's (1956) partial-adjustment model of dividend behavior. Differences in the relative rankings do exist for some lesser-ranked factors across time, but the authors attribute these to changing economic conditions. For example, the economy in 1983 was weaker and the inflation rate was higher compared with 1997. Overall, the evidence suggests that the key determinants of dividend policy have remained remarkably stable over time.

The final research question is, "Do the views of managers about dividend determinants differ between a high payout, regulated industry (utilities), and moderate payout, less regulated industries (manufacturing and wholesale/retail trade)?" Using chi-square tests, Baker and Powell (2000) test for differences in the responses among the three industry groups involving the 20 factors influencing dividend policy. The results show significant differences among the three groups at normal levels for six of the 20 factors (30 percent), none of which are among the five most important determinants of dividend policy. By contrast, Farrelly, Baker, and Edelman (1986) report significant differences in responses among the three industry groups for eight of the 15 factors (53.3 percent). Baker and Powell speculate that these changes may reflect a changing economic environment for utilities, such as the Energy Policy Act of 1992, which made utilities riskier and subject to greater competition than in the past.

In their analysis of dividend practices, Baker and Powell (2000) find that for all firms combined, the CEO (47.5 percent), followed by the CFO (43.9 percent), are the most influential in developing the dividend policy ultimately approved by the board of directors. They also find that the vast majority of firms (73.7 percent) formally reexamine their dividend policy annually. About half (52.5 percent) of the respondents indicate that their firms have an explicit target payout ratio. The three industry groups differ significantly on each of these responses. In response to the question, "How often is your firm unable to take advantage of potentially profitable investment opportunities because of the pressure to pay dividends?" 96.0 percent of the respondents answer "almost never."

Baker and Powell (2000) indicate that their findings have several implications. First, the evidence underscores the importance that managers place on maintaining the continuity of dividends. Thus, the responses of most of the managers surveyed imply the belief that dividend policy affects stock prices. Second, managers indicate concern about the signals that dividend change may provide to investors. The extensive empirical research on the information content of dividends suggest that such concern appears warranted.

The Baker, Veit, and Powell (2001) and Baker, Powell, and Veit (2002) Survey of NASDAQ Firms

The studies by Baker, Veit, and Powell (2001) and Baker, Powell, and Veit (2002) report the results of a 1999 survey of NASDAQ-listed firms. The authors conducted the studies before the bubble involving technology stocks burst. The studies differ from previous U.S. dividend surveys because they focus on the dividend policies of companies trading on NASDAQ rather than on the NYSE. The authors contend that studying how NASDAQ companies make dividend decisions is important because such companies often have different characteristics from those trading on the NYSE, despite the fact that some NASDAQ firms could qualify for NYSE listing.

Their final sample consists of 630 NASDAQ firms from numerous industries that paid eight consecutive quarterly cash dividends during 1996 and 1997. Using a pretested questionnaire based on earlier studies by Baker, Farrelly, and Edelman (1985) and Baker and Powell (2000), Baker, Veit, and Powell (2001, 2002) send a mail survey to the top financial officers of these 630 companies and receive 188 usable responses, giving a response rate of 29.8 percent. Respondents typically hold senior managerial positions, of which the most common are CFO (53.7 percent), followed by vice president of finance (23.4 percent) and chief operating officer/president (10.1 percent). The most common industries represented by the responding firms are finance, insurance, and real estate (Standard Industrial Classification [SIC] 60-67; 24.4 percent); manufacturing (SIC 20-39; 14.9 percent); and transportation, communication, electricity, gas, and sanitary (SIC 40-49; 9.6 percent). Because of the large portion of financial firms, the authors partition the firms into financial and nonfinancial groups to test for industry effects due to different characteristics. Based on the results of three separate tests to investigate nonresponse bias, they conclude that nonresponse bias is small.

The Baker, Veit, and Powell (2001) study has three objectives. The primary objective is to identify the most important factors that U.S. companies trading on NASDAQ use to make dividend policy decisions. Their survey asks respondents to indicate the importance of 22 factors in determining their firm's dividend policy by using a four-point importance scale, from 0 = none to 3 = high. Both the financial and nonfinancial firms rank the same five factors among the most important in influencing dividend policy: pattern of past dividends, stability of earnings, level of current earnings, level of expected future earnings, and concern about affecting the stock price. The authors conclude that the factors that are most important to NASDAQ-listed firms are also important to NYSE-listed firms as reported in previous surveys such as Baker and Powell (2000). Baker, Veit, and Powell (2001, p. 35) conclude, "Our results suggest that many managers are still making dividend decisions consistent with Lintner's (1956) survey results and model."

The second objective of Baker, Veit, and Powell (2001) is to determine whether the factors influencing dividend policy differ by industry type: financial and nonfinancial firms. Although they find a significant relationship between the overall rankings of the financial and nonfinancial firms (a Spearman rank order correlation of 0.81), their chi-square tests reveal that the responses of managers of financial and nonfinancial firms differ significantly on nine of the twenty-two factors, including three of the four most highly ranked factors (stability of earnings, level of current earnings, and level of expected future earnings). Based on these results, Baker, Veit, and Powell (2001, p. 36) conclude,

> Because various market frictions or imperfections may affect firms in different ways, no universal set of factors is likely to be applicable to all firms. That is, the optimal dividend policy for some firms may be unique. Nonetheless, our research, when coupled with other empirical studies and mathematical models, strongly suggests that certain factors emerge as being consistently important over time.

The final objective of this study is to collect and report information about how managers administer dividend policy. The evidence shows that the CEOs (66.5 percent) and CFOs (25.5 percent) who responded to this survey are the most influential individuals in developing their firm's dividend policy. These firms most commonly reexamine their dividend policy on an annual (59.0 percent) or quarterly (36.7 percent) basis. The results show that slightly more than half (50.5 percent) of the respondents report that their firms have an explicit target payout ratio. These results for NASDAQ firms by Baker, Veit, and Powell (2001) are similar to those found for NYSE firms by Baker and Powell (2000).

Baker, Powell, and Veit (2002) survey managers of dividend-paying NASDAQ firms to learn their beliefs about the dividend-setting process and whether dividend policy affects firm value. The authors also examine four common explanations for paying dividends (signaling, tax preference, agency costs, and bird in the hand) plus evidence on the dividend life cycle and residual dividend policy. They ask respondents to indicate their general opinion about each of 27 closed-ended statements using a five-point scale, from −2 = strongly disagree to +2 = strongly agree.

Baker, Powell, and Veit's (2002) evidence shows a high level of agreement with statements supporting Lintner's (1956) behavioral description of the dividend-setting process. In particular, respondents stress the importance of dividend continuity. Additionally, NASDAQ managers widely support statements consistent with the concept that a firm's dividend policy matters; that is, dividend policy affects a firm's value as reflected in share prices, and to a lesser extent, the cost of capital.

Baker, Powell, and Veit (2002) also examine managerial perspectives on the underlying reasons for paying dividends. The authors find the strongest support for the signaling explanation for paying dividends. For example, more than three-quarters (77.7 percent) of the respondents agree that investors generally regard dividend changes as signals about a firm's future prospects. The responses offer little or no support for the tax-preference and agency costs explanations. Most respondents disagree with the bird-in-the-hand explanation for paying dividends. The authors also find that the majority of respondents (57.8 percent) agree that the pattern of cash dividends generally changes over a firm's life cycle, providing support for the dividend life-cycle theory. Their evidence shows mixed support for issues relating to residual dividend policy.

A comparison of the Baker and Powell (1999a, 1999b) studies of NYSE firms and those of Baker, Veit, and Powell (2001) and Baker, Powell, and Veit (2002) of NASDAQ firms reveals several similarities. First, managers of NYSE and NASDAQ firms believe that dividend policy affects firm value. Second, the key determinants of dividend policy are similar between the two groups and include the level of current and expected future dividends and the pattern or continuity of past dividends. Third, respondents from both markets give the strongest support to a signaling explanation for paying dividends.

Brav, Graham, Harvey, and Michaely's (2005) Survey

Brav, Graham, Harvey, and Michaely (2005) survey financial executives and conduct in-depth interviews with 23 other managers to identify the factors that drive dividend and share-repurchase decisions. They receive a 16 percent response rate resulting from 384 surveys from 256 public companies and 128 private companies. This portion of the chapter examines the results from the 166 dividend payers and the 77 nondividend payers.

One issue that Brav et al. (2005) investigate is the relative importance of financing or payout decisions compared to investment decisions. Their survey evidence shows that managers generally make dividend choices simultaneously with or sometimes a bit sooner than investment decisions. Firms tend to first maintain the historic dividend level and then make incremental investment decisions. Responding managers indicate that their firms will pass up some positive NPV investment projects before cutting dividends. In fact, 65 percent of dividend payers in their sample agree that their companies would raise external funds before cutting dividends. The results also show that less than half of the respondents indicate that they view the availability of good investment opportunities as an important factor affecting dividend decisions.

Brav et al. (2005) also benchmark their findings to Lintner (1956). Although the perceived stability of future earnings still affects dividend policy (as in Lintner), their evidence shows that the link between dividends and earnings is weaker. Additionally, they find that managers continue to make dividend decisions conservatively but that the importance of targeting the payout ratio is not as high. Unlike Lintner's findings, Brav et al.'s results indicate that firms use several targets including dividends per share, dividend payout, growth in dividends per share, and dividend yield. Of the responding managers, 45 percent indicate that they are flexible in pursuing their target, while 32 percent view their target as somewhat strict, and another 11 percent say it is very strict. The remaining 12 percent do not view the target as a goal. Dividend payers also tend to smooth dividends from year to year and change dividends in response to permanent changes in earnings.

Another area of interest concerns factors affecting payout policy. Brav et al. (2005) examine management views about several theories on how payout policy may affect firm value. Overall, their results provide little support for the agency, signaling, and clientele hypotheses of payout policy. For example, the executives typically do not view payout policy as a means of self-imposing discipline, which is a tenet of agency theory. Although the pervasive view is that payout conveys information, they conclude that dividends are not a self-imposed cost to signal firm quality or separate a firm from its competitors. Thus, the evidence does not support the signaling models. The survey evidence also indicates that tax considerations play a secondary role. Regarding dividend clienteles, the evidence suggests that responding executives believe retail investors and not institutions, as suggested by Allen, Bernardo, and Welch (2000) in their ownership clientele dividend payout theory, are the most likely investor class to prefer dividends as a form of payout.

Brav et al. (2005) also investigate when and why nonpayers will initiate payout. More than half of the firms indicate that they may never pay dividends. For the remaining firms, the authors find that respondents view having a sustainable increase in earnings and demand by institutional investors as the two most important reasons for initiating dividend payments.

Chiang, Frankfurter, Kosedag, and Wood's (2006) Survey of Professional Investors

Chiang, Frankfurter, Kosedag, and Wood (2006) study the perception of dividends by professional investors, using mutual fund managers as a proxy. They send a pretested survey to a random sample of 1,100 listed mutual funds and receive 122 usable responses, giving them a response rate of 11.1 percent. Their survey instrument consists of 24 statements involving responses on a disagree/agree scale. Of the 24 statements, the responding mutual fund managers express the strongest consensus on the statement, "Stocks that increase dividends send a message of financial strength to the market," with 90 percent of the respondents agreeing with this statement. More than three-quarters (76 percent) of the respondents indicate that they "usually prefer a cash dividend to a stock dividend." The mutual fund managers most strongly disagree with the statement, "We know that dividends adversely affect the value of our holdings."

The authors then use factor analysis and hierarchical grouping to uncover the attitude toward dividends of three distinct groups of professional investors: (A) the more traditional group; (B) the middle-of-the-road group; and (C) the more growth-oriented, aggressive group. Although some uniformly accepted tenets exist across the groups, the greatest differences of perception occur between groups A and C. The traditional group attributes far more importance to dividends than the growth-oriented group. Regarding the statement, "Eliminating the personal income tax on dividends is important to us," about 72 percent of group A respondents agree with this statement compared with about 48 percent of group C respondents. The more growth-oriented group perceives dividends as something needed to pacify the shareholder. Chiang et al. (2006, p. 60) conclude that "none of the academic hypotheses contrived to explain dividend behavior can be supported by empirical evidence."

Chiang et al. (2006) also test to see whether differences in ex-post performance exist between any possible pairing of the three groups. Their results show that how the funds perceive dividends makes no difference in performance.

Baker and Smith's (2006) Survey about Residual Dividend Policy

Baker and Smith (2006) survey 309 sample firms exhibiting behavior consistent with a residual dividend policy and a control group matched on primary SIC code and firm size to learn how firms set their dividend policies. Specifically, they use the Research Insight database to identify firms during the 1990s that have a low standardized free cash flow (FCF). This attribute would be consistent with a firm following a residual dividend policy. The authors calculate standardized FCF by dividing a firm's free cash flow by its then-prevailing market value of equity. Using a pretested survey and multiple mailings during 2001, they send the survey to CEOs and receive 115 usable responses: 67 from the sample firms (21.7 percent response rate) and 48 from the matched firms (15.5 percent response rate). Differences between respondent and nonrespondent firms for the sample and matched group based on 15 firm characteristics are generally insignificant. Hence, the authors conclude that nonresponse bias is small.

Baker and Smith's (2006) survey results focus on three areas: setting a target dividend payout ratio, determinants of dividend policy, and other issues about dividend policy. The results show a significantly larger percentage of the sample compared with matched firms—66.7 percent and 41.0 percent, respectively—use forecasts of earnings (or cash flows) and investment opportunities to set a long-run target dividend payout ratio. This result supports the notion that some firms use a type of residual policy to establish a dividend pattern over the forecast period.

Baker and Smith (2006) also investigate the most important determinants of dividend policy by asking respondents to indicate the importance of each of 16 factors using a four-point importance scale, from 0 = none to 3 = high. The five factors ranked most highly by respondents from both the sample and matched groups are stability of earnings (or cash flows), pattern of past dividends, level of expected future earnings (or cash flows), level of current earnings (or cash flows), and desire to maintain a long-term target dividend payout ratio. A high correlation (r_s = 0.764) exists between the ranks of the 16 factors of the sample and matched firms. When asked to identify the two most important factors in determining their firm's dividend policy, the top-ranked factors are similar to those previously identified. Of particular note is that of the 16 factors identified, at least one respondent viewed each factor (except the cost of raising external funds) among the most important in determining the dividend policy of the responding firm. This finding supports the idiosyncratic view of dividends in which one set of determinants does not fit all firms.

The authors also seek to determine the views of managers about seven key issues involving dividend policy. The majority of both groups agree with four statements: (1) my firm strives to formulate its dividend policy to produce maximum value for its shareholders; (2) my firm strives to maintain an uninterrupted record of dividends; (3) my firm avoids increasing its dividend if it expects to reverse the dividend increase in a year or so; and (4) my firm views its investment, financing, and dividend decisions as interrelated. The respondents, on average, disagree with three statements: (5) my firm's expenditures on new capital investments typically affect its dividend payments; (6) my firm views cash dividends as a residual after funding desired investments from earnings; and (7) my firm often needs additional external financing as a result of paying cash dividends.

Baker and Smith (2006, p. 17) conclude that

> the process for identifying residual dividend payout behavior is neither simple nor obvious. Even firms exhibiting classic residual dividend behavior claim to be giving close attention to the past payment pattern and the market's perception of dividend changes. Thus, during the 1990s the closest most firms came to maintaining a residual policy was a "modified" residual policy. In this case, firms carefully managed their dividend stream. While consistently low free cash flows were an outcome, they were not necessarily a corporate goal.

Brav, Graham, Harvey, and Michaely's (2008) Survey on the 2003 Dividend Tax Cut

Brav, Graham, Harvey, and Michaely(2008) survey more than 7,000 financial decision-making executives during 2005 to determine the effect of the May 2003 dividend tax cut. This tax law reduced the top statutory tax rate on dividend income from more than 38 percent to 15 percent and the top rate on capital gains from 20 percent to 15 percent. Chetty and Saez (2005), among others, document a surge in dividend initiations in the third quarter of 2003, immediately after the tax reduction. Brav et al. base their analysis on 328 responses, consisting of 152 public and 176 private firms, resulting in a 4.7 percent response rate.

Their study focuses on a couple of issues: (1) whether the tax reduction affected payout policy in a first-order or second-order manner and (2) the relative importance of taxes on corporate payout decisions. Brav et al. (2008) find evidence that the tax cut resulted in a temporary surge in dividend initiations, but the overall increase in initiations was part of a long-term trend attributable to first-order factors such as market and firm characteristics other than dividend taxation. Their evidence shows the relative unimportance of dividend tax rates to public firms that already pay dividends. When asked to rank the three most important factors that affect their dividend decisions, the respondents rank the tax rate reduction as less important than the stability of future cash flows, cash holdings, and the historic level of dividends. These respondents roughly regard tax effects as being of similar importance as attracting institutional investors and the availability of profitable investments. The authors also find evidence that press releases only occasionally mention the dividend tax cut as the reason for an initiation. Brav et al. (p. 623) conclude that "taxes are second-order important in dividend decisions." This indicates that taxes are not a primary explanation for paying dividends.

Summary of U.S. Survey Evidence on Cash Dividends and Related Issues

As Table 6.1 shows, survey evidence is available from hundreds of U.S. executives and others involving cash dividends and related dividend issues. Table 6.2 lists the factors affecting dividend decisions. Executives tend to share some commonly held beliefs about the factors that affect dividend policy and tend to use some rules of thumb when making dividend decisions. The evidence suggests that the key determinants that influence dividend policy appear to have remained fairly stable over more than 50 years. Some of the more important and consistent determinants of payout policy include the pattern of past dividends, stability of earnings or cash flows, and the level of current and expected future earnings. Such firm-specific factors appear to be first-order determinants in making dividend decisions.

The survey evidence suggests that firms view a variety of different factors as important in determining their dividend policy. What may be important for one firm may be much less so or unimportant to another. An implication of the finding that firms consider a wide array of factors is that modeling dividend behavior uniformly across firms is difficult, if not impossible, supporting sentiments expressed by Frankfurter and Wood (1997); that is, a one-size-fits-all mentality is unlikely to be universally useful in describing the factors affecting dividend policy.

Based on information contained in Table 6.3, some stylized views emerge based on various conclusions drawn by survey researchers. For example, although the precise impact of dividend policy on value remains a contentious question, managers generally tend to operate as though dividend policy matters. Consistent with Lintner (1956), managers still make dividend decisions conservatively and view stability of dividends as important. To avoid unnecessary surprises, dividend-paying firms strive for a stable and slow-growing stream of dividends. Also, the U.S. evidence suggests that dividend and investment decisions are generally independent.

As Table 6.4 indicates, there is no consensus on the primary explanation for paying dividends. Yet, the survey evidence indicates a pervasive view that payout

TABLE 6.1 U.S. survey evidence on cash dividends

This table shows representative U.S. studies involving regular dividends, the number of usable responses, response rates, and sample characteristics.

Author and date of publication	Usable responses	Response rate (%)	Sample characteristics
Lintner (1956)	28	n/a	Well-established companies having characteristics important to dividend payments and policy
Baker, Farrelly, and Edelman (1985); Edelman, Farrelly, and Baker (1985); Farrelly, Baker, and Edelman (1986)	318	56.6	NYSE-listed firms in three industry groups: manufacturing, wholesale/retail, and utilities
Kennedy, O'Brien, and Horn (1987)	n/a	n/a	Top executives in public utilities (electric power, telecommunications, and motor carriers)
Baker and Farrelly (1988)	246	62.0	U.S. and Canadian companies having an unbroken record of 10 consecutive years of increased dividends from 1974 to 1983
Baker (1989)	68	38.9	U.S. firms listed on the NYSE paying no dividends over a five-year period (1980 to 1985)
Farrelly and Baker (1989)	130	25.8	A random sample of 503 members of the Financial Analysts Association who are mainly portfolio managers, investment advisors, and security analysts
Abrutyn and Turner (1990)	550	29.6	Sample of CEOs of 550 of the largest 1,000 corporations in the United States
Pruitt and Gitman (1991)	114	11.4	Highest-ranking financial officer of each of the 1,000 largest U.S. firms in terms of annual sales

(Continued)

TABLE 6.1 (cont'd) U.S. survey evidence on cash dividends

Author and date of publication	Usable responses	Response rate (%)	Sample characteristics
Baker and Powell (1999a, 1999b, 2000)	198	32.9	U.S. dividend-paying companies listed on the NYSE whose primary business is manufacturing, wholesale/retail, and utilities
Baker, Veit, and Powell (2001); Baker, Powell, and Veit (2002)	162	29.8	Sample of 630 U. S. dividend-paying firms trading on NASDAQ in numerous industries
Brav, Graham, Harvey, and Michaely (2004)	384 plus 23 interviews	16.0	Sample of financial executives from a cross-section of public and private firms coupled with 23 in-depth interviews
Chiang, Frankfurter, Kosedag, and Wood (2006)	122	11.1	A random sample of CFOs of publicly traded mutual funds
Baker and Smith (2006)	115 (67 sample and 48 matched firms)	21.7 sample and 15.5 matched firms	Sample of 309 firms from Research Insight exhibiting behavior consistent with a residual dividend policy and their matched counterparts
Brav, Graham, Harvey, and Michaely (2008)	328	4.7	Sample of about 7,000 financial decision-making executives, most of whom are CFOs

TABLE 6.2 Major determinants of U.S. dividend policy

This table shows the results of representative U.S. studies that seek to identify the most important factors that affect dividend policy.

Author and date of publication	Key determinants found to influence dividend policy
Lintner (1956)	• Major changes in earnings or level of earnings that become "out of line" with existing dividend rates
Hawkins and Walsh (1971)	• Current earnings and future prospects • Continuity or regularity of payment • Stability of rate per share • Cash flow, present cash position, and future needs • Stockholder needs and expectations
Baker, Farrelly, and Edelman (1985); Farrelly, Baker, and Edelman (1986)	• Anticipated level of firm's future earnings • Pattern of past dividends • Availability of cash • Concern about maintaining or increasing stock price
Kennedy, O'Brien, and Horn (1987)	• Avoid a reduction in an established dividend per share (electric power and telecommunications industries) • Earnings (motor carrier industry)
Baker and Farrelly (1988)	• Sustainability of the dividend payout • Anticipated level of future earnings • Pattern of past dividends • Level of current earnings
Baker (1989)	• Availability of profitable investment opportunities • Availability of cash • Cost of raising external funds • Level of current earnings
Pruitt and Gitman (1991)	• Current and past years' profits • Variability of earnings • Growth in earnings • Prior year's dividends
Baker and Powell (1999b, 2000)	• Level of current and expected future earnings • Pattern or continuity of past dividends • Concern about maintaining or increasing the stock price • Concern that a dividend change may provide a false signal to investors • Stability of cash flows
Baker, Veit, and Powell (2001)	• Pattern of past dividends • Stability of earnings • Level of current earnings • Level of expected future earnings • Concern about affecting the stock price

(*Continued*)

TABLE 6.2 (cont'd) Major determinants of U.S. dividend policy

Author and date of publication	Key determinants found to influence dividend policy
Brav, Graham, Harvey, and Michaely (2004)	• Maintain consistency with historic dividend policy • Stability of future earnings • A sustainable change in earnings • Attract institutional investors to purchase stock • Influence institutional shareholders
Baker and Smith (2006)	• Stability of earnings (or cash flows) • Pattern of past dividends • Level of expected future earnings (or cash flows) • Level of current earnings (or cash flows) • Desire to maintain a long-term target dividend payout ratio
Brav, Graham, Harvey, and Michaely (2009)	• Stability of future cash flows • Cash holdings • Historic level of dividends

conveys information, which lends support to the academic signaling models. Thus, regarding the three big market imperfections, the survey results appear more supportive of signaling than of taxes and clientele effects and agency costs. Evidence shows that taxes are a second-order determinant of dividend decisions. Some recent evidence suggests that respondents generally perceive that dividends follow a life cycle. Overall, there does not appear to be a single theoretical model that adequately covers firm dividend behavior, which supports an idiosyncratic theory of dividends.

Non-U.S. Survey Evidence on Cash Dividends and Related Issues

This section examines survey evidence involving dividend policy outside of the United States and orders the surveys by country. The countries are organized alphabetically. If more than one study exists within a country, the surveys are ordered chronologically. This section is not intended to be fully comprehensive but instead discusses representative non-U.S. studies about dividends and how they relate to the various dividend theories.

Australia

Several surveys examine dividend policy in Australia.

TABLE 6.3 Key conclusions of U.S. dividend surveys

This table presents some major conclusions from representative U.S. dividend surveys.

Author and date of publication	Major conclusions
Lintner (1956)	• Firms have a target payout ratio and make periodic partial adjustments to the target over time. • Managers perceive that shareholders prefer stable dividend payments. • Firms have a fiduciary responsibility to shareholders to distribute part of any substantial increase in earnings to the stockholders in dividends.
Harkins and Walsh (1971)	• Firms gradually adjust their dividends over some period to reach their target dividend payout ratio. • Firms follow a compromise policy to partially meet the needs of managers and shareholders.
Baker, Farrelly, and Edelman (1985); Edelman, Farrelly, and Baker (1985); Farrelly, Baker, and Edelman (1986)	• Major determinants of dividend payments in the 1980s resemble those in Lintner's model developed in the mid-1950s. • Dividend policy affects share value. • Managers of utilities have a somewhat different view about dividends than those from manufacturing and wholesale/retail firms.
Kennedy, O'Brien, and Horn (1987)	• The majority of responding large public utilities have a formal target dividend payout percentage. • Major factors influencing dividend policy are avoiding a reduction in an established dividend per share and earnings. • Decision makers in the public utility industry do not view dividend policy as an important determinant of stock value.
Baker and Farrelly (1988)	• The major reason dividend achievers pay dividends is to meet stockholders' expectations for continued dividend growth. • The sustainability of the dividend payout is the most important factor determining dividend policy among dividend achievers. • The majority of dividend achievers maintain a target payout ratio. • Managers are aware of dividend announcement effects. • Industry norms are a secondary factor influencing the dividend payout ratios of dividend achievers. • Regulation does not meaningfully affect dividend policy behavior of dividend achievers.

(Continued)

TABLE 6.3 (cont'd) Key conclusions of U.S. dividend surveys

Author and date of publication	Major conclusions
Baker (1989)	• The most important determinants of non-dividend-paying firms are the availability of profitable investment opportunities and the availability of cash. • Only marginal support exists that companies consider their investors' preferences in deciding to pay no dividends. • Results are inconclusive about managers' views on the relationship between dividend policy and stock prices and the role that dividend policy plays in signaling.
Farrelly and Baker (1989)	• Institutional investors perceive that dividend increases have a positive effect on a firm's stock price. • Institutional investors perceive that investors prefer capital gains to dividends because present tax laws favor capital gains. • Institutional investors accept the existing dividend policy of firms. • Institutional investors generally agree that dividends have an informational content and that industry classification has an effect on dividend policy.
Abrutyn and Turner (1990)	• The survey responses cast doubt on the notion that dividend policy is based on shareholders' tax rates. • The survey results do not provide unambiguous support for any of the four rationales for paying dividends theories (taxes, signaling, agency cost, and clientele effects).
Pruitt and Gitman (1991)	• Dividend decisions are independent of a firm's investment and financing decisions. • Profits and prior year's dividends appear to act as major influences on current dividend policies.
Baker and Powell (1999a, 1999b)	• Most respondents believe that dividend policy affects firm value. • Respondents generally show the highest level of agreement with statements about the signaling explanation of dividend behavior. • Managers' views on setting dividend payments are consistent with those reported by Lintner (1956). • Few statistically significant differences exist among the responses about dividend policy from three industries: manufacturing, wholesale/retail trade, and utilities.
Baker and Powell (2000)	• The most important determinants of a firm's dividend policy are the level of current and expected future earnings and the pattern or continuity of past dividends. • The most important factors influencing dividend policy are highly similar between surveys in 1983 and 1997.

TABLE 6.3 (cont'd) Key conclusions of U.S. dividend surveys

Author and date of publication	Major conclusions
Baker, Powell, and Veit (2002)	• Managers' views on setting dividend payments are consistent with those reported by Lintner (1956). • Most respondents believe that dividend policy affects firm value. • Managers give the strongest support to a signaling explanation for paying dividends.
Brav, Graham, Harvey, and Michaely (2005)	• Managers still make dividend decisions conservatively and are reluctant to cut dividends. • Dividends are sticky, inflexible, and smoothed through time. • The most common target is the level of dividend, followed by the payout ratio and growth in dividends. • Dividend increases are related to permanent, stable earnings. • The tax disadvantage of dividends is of second-order importance. • Dividends convey information.
Chiang, Frankfurter, Kosedag, and Wood (2006)	• Mutual funds consist of three distinct groups regarding their views toward dividends: the more traditional group, which attributes more importance to dividends; the middle-of-the-road group; and the more growth-oriented, aggressive group, which perceives dividends as something needed to pacify the shareholder. • Ex post group performance is not significantly different between each possible pairing of the three groups.
Baker and Smith (2006)	• The most important determinants of dividend policy vary among firms, but among the most highly ranked determinants are the pattern of past dividends, the level and stability of earnings, and desire to maintain a long-term dividend payout ratio. • Firms plan their dividend payments over a longer time horizon than one year. • Few firms follow a "pure" residual dividend policy.
Brav, Graham, Harvey, and Michaely (2009)	• Taxes are only of second-order importance in dividend decisions. • Respondents view the stability of future cash flows, cash holdings, and the historic level of dividends as more important factors affecting dividend policy than tax rates.

TABLE 6.4 U.S. evidence on explanations for paying dividends

This table presents U.S. survey evidence about various theories, hypotheses, and explanations for why firms pay dividends.

Author and Date	Bird-in-the-hand theory	Residual dividends theory	Taxes and clientele effects	Agency theory	Asymmetric information and signaling	Life cycle of dividends
Baker, Farrelly, and Edelman (1985); Farrelly, Baker, and Edelman (1986)			Mixed, depending on industry		Supported	
Baker and Farrelly (1988)					Supported	
Baker (1989)			Inconclusive			
Farrelly and Baker (1989)			Supported		Supported	
Baker and Powell (1999a, 1999b)	Mixed	Mixed	Mixed	Mixed	Supported	Supported
Abrutyn and Turner (1991)			Little support	Some support	Most support	
Baker, Powell, and Veit (2002)	Not supported	Mixed	Little or no support	Little or no support	Supported	Supported
Brav, Graham, Harvey, and Michaely (2005)			Little support	Little support	Little support	
Baker and Smith (2006)		Not supported				
Brav, Graham, Harvey, and Michaely (2009)			Second-order determinant			

Partington's (1984, 1985, 1989) Survey of Large Australian Firms

Partington (1984, 1985, 1989) reports results from a study of dividend policies of Australian firms. All three papers involve firms drawn from the 300 largest firms on the Sydney Stock Exchange in 1980, excluding financial institutions. He received responses from 93 out of 152 firms, giving a response rate of 61.2 percent.

Partington (1984) focuses on firms' use of target payout ratios. His survey results show that about 59 percent of the Australian firms use an explicit target payout ratio and their main objective is to distribute about half the firm's profits as dividends. Of the firms with target payout ratios, slightly more than a third report changing their target during the period from 1965 to 1980. Evidence suggests no industry effect involving the use or magnitude of payout ratios.

Partington (1985) examines the relationship between dividend, investment, and financing decisions. His results show that Australian managers do not follow a residual dividend policy but have specific motives for adopting a different form of policy. Firms usually adopt independent dividend and investment policies but determine external financing on a residual basis; that is, firms set desired levels of dividends and investments. If the firm has insufficient internal funds to meet its needs, it usually meets this shortfall by using debt financing.

In Partington (1989), the focus is on variables influencing dividend policy. He examines and ranks the relative importance of 22 variables in determining cash dividends using a five-point scale ranging from unimportant = 1 to very important = 5. The most important determinants include profitability, share price, and stability of both dividends and earnings. The survey also asks respondents to indicate their level of agreement with 20 statements using a five-point scale, from disagree strongly = 1 to agree strongly = 5. The results show a strong desire for dividend stability, gradually increasing dividends as profits rise and cutting dividends only under exceptional circumstances. Little evidence supports the notion that investment and financing variables or the tax position of shareholders exert a substantial effect on dividend payments.

Canada

Similar to the U.S. and U.K. equity markets, the Canadian equity market is well developed, but its equity market is less liquid than the U.S. market, where average firm size is much greater (Dutta, Jog, and Zhu 2005). Also, Canada and the United States differ in several aspects of corporate governance. For example, unlike the widely diffused ownership of U.S. and U.K. public firms, the ownership of Canadian firms is highly concentrated (Rao and Lee-Sing 1995; Morck, Wolfenzon, and Yeung 2005). In Canada, a small group of families maintains some influence over public officials (Morck, Stangeland, and Yeung 2000). The presence of high ownership concentration (as in Canada) is the norm rather than exception around the world. Many Canadian firms do not pay dividends and use a dual-class share structure. According to La Porta and colleagues (2000), the median dividend payout ratio for Canadian firms (19.78 percent) is one of the lowest payout ratios in their sample of thirty-three countries.

Jog and Srivastava's (1994) Survey of Large Canadian Firms

Jog and Srivastava (1994) provide direct empirical evidence about the financial decision processes followed by large Canadian corporations. Specifically, they attempt to understand the capital expenditure decision-making process, capital budgeting techniques, cost of capital, and dividend policies of these firms. In 1991, they sent a questionnaire to CEOs and CFOs of 582 large Canadian corporations (i.e., Toronto Stock Exchange [TSX] 300 corporations and large foreign-owned and private corporations) and received 133 usable responses, resulting in an overall response rate of 22.9 percent. Thus, the responses are based on the opinions of executives with extensive experience about the finance function of the organization.

Regarding their empirical findings on dividend policy, Jog and Srivastava (1994) report that the factors considered most relevant by Canadian firms in their dividend decisions are the levels of current and expected earnings, availability of cash, the need for investment funds, and the pattern of past dividends. These findings are generally consistent with various U.S. studies including, but not limited to, Lintner (1956); Baker, Farrelly, and Edelman (1985); and Baker, Veit, and Powell (2001). Jog and Srivastava also examine the beliefs held in the marketplace about the possible initial impact of a substantial dividend increase on a firm's stock price. They find, for example, that respondents tend to agree with the contention that the market price will increase as a result of a dividend increase. The majority of respondents, however, disagree with the notion that the stock price will decrease because investors will interpret the increased dividend as reflecting a lack of profitable opportunities. In summary, respondents generally view dividend increases as good news and dividend announcements as an informative signal to outside investors. This evidence is consistent with the signaling arguments for paying dividends.

De Jong, van Dijk, and Veld's (2003) Survey

A study by de Jong, van Dijk, and Veld (2003) examines dividend and share-repurchase policies of Canadian firms. In 1998, they sent a questionnaire to the CFOs or CEOs of the 500 largest nonfinancial Canadian firms listed on the Toronto Stock Exchange (TSX), of which they received 191 usable responses, resulting in a 38.2 percent response rate. The authors collect information on the payout policies, firm characteristics, and shareholder structure using a questionnaire. Respondents generally answer questions on a scale from 1 to 7. Using questionnaires to obtain data, they then use the data in logit models to test different dividend theories.

Their empirical evidence shows that a firm first decides on whether it wants to pay out cash to its shareholders. Next, the firm decides on the form of the payout: dividends, share repurchases, or both. The determining factor of the payout is free cash flow. Both behavioral and tax preferences affect the choice between dividends and repurchases. De Jong, van Dijk, and Veld (2003) find evidence that the payout for Canadian firms with managerial stock option plans is less likely to be dividends. They also find an association between the existence of asymmetric information amongst outsiders and a preference for dividends over share repurchases.

The Baker, Saadi, Dutta, and Gandhi (2007) and Baker, Dutta, and Saadi (2008) Survey of Canadian Dividend Payers

Baker, Saadi, Dutta, and Gandhi (2007) explore the perceptions of Canadian managers with respect to dividend policy and investigate the uniqueness of the Canadian context. Their sample consists of 291 dividend-paying Canadian firms listed on the TSX. They model their survey instrument after those designed by Baker and Powell (2000) and Baker, Veit, and Powell (2001). In 2005, they mailed a survey to CFOs and received 103 usable responses, giving them a 35.4 percent response rate. Tests reveal little concern about potential nonresponse bias.

The survey asks respondents to indicate the level of importance attached to factors influencing dividend policy by managers of TSX-listed firms by using an importance scale, from none = 0 to high = 3. The most highly ranked factors in order of importance are level of expected future earnings, stability of earnings, pattern of past dividends, and level of current earnings. Baker et al. (2007) compare their rankings of factors to those reported by Baker and Powell (2000) for NYSE firms and by Baker, Veit, and Powell (2001) for NASDAQ firms. Although the overall rankings of determinants of dividend policy by managers of Canadian and U.S. firms are highly similar, some differences exist regarding the level of importance of specific factors. Baker et al. (2007, p. 88) conclude, "Overall, the highly concentrated ownership structure and high corporate ownership characteristics of Canadian firms appear to have little impact on how managers of TSX-listed firms perceive the factors influencing dividend policy relative to U.S. managers."

Baker et al. (2007) also examine management views on various dividend issues. Specifically, they ask respondents to indicate their level of agreement with 14 statements partitioned into four areas: the dividend process, dividend patterns, dividend policy and firm value, and residual dividend theory. Their results suggest the following: (1) managers of TSX-listed firms set dividends consistently with the dividend model of Lintner (1956); (2) managers agree that dividends generally follow a smoother path than earnings; (3) managers agree that changes in dividends generally lag behind changes in earnings; (4) most managers perceive that a firm's investment, financing, and dividend decisions are interrelated; and (5) managers offer mixed views of the belief that a firm should view cash dividends as a residual after funding desired investment from earnings.

The authors also examine various dividend theories. Their survey evidence shows that managers of TSX-listed firms express greater support for the signaling and life-cycle explanations for paying dividends than for the bird-in-the-hand, tax-preference/dividend clientele, agency cost, and catering explanations.

Finally, Baker et al. (2007) examine differences between dividend payers and nondividend payers. Their results show that compared with nondividend payers, Canadian dividend-paying firms are significantly larger and more profitable, have greater cash reserves and ownership concentration, and encounter fewer growth opportunities.

Using data from this survey, Baker, Dutta, and Saadi (2008) examine the perceptions of managers of TSX-listed firms to determine whether views differ when partitioned into financial and nonfinancial firms and multinational and domestic firms by repeating the analysis of Baker et al. (2007). Their results suggest the existence of industry effects but weak, if any, multinational operations effects. Although the perceptions of managers from financial versus nonfinancial firms differ on the importance of various factors influencing dividend policy, both groups rank the same four factors as most important: the stability of earnings, the pattern of past dividends, the level of current earnings, and the level of expected future earnings. Both groups rank statements supporting signaling and life cycle the highest among various explanations for dividend relevance. Baker et al. (2008, p. 185) conclude the following:

> Our categorization shows managers of financial versus non-financial firms perceive dividends differently in many respects. This evidence supports the standard practice of treating financial and non-financial firms separately. Thus, partitioning data by industry classification reveals nuances in perceptions that are masked when analyzing the sample as a whole. We conclude that the use of survey data when partitioned by industry can provide insights into the dividend puzzle unavailable by relying solely on market data.

An implication of this conclusion is that using a one-size-fits-all explanation for paying dividends is unlikely to be a successful strategy.

Baker, Chang, Dutta, and Saadi's (2009) Survey of Canadian Nondividend Payers

Using Canadian data, Baker, Chang, Dutta, and Saadi(2009) investigate the factors leading to the decision not to pay cash dividends and manager views on various dividend policy issues. Their sample consists of 538 Canadian firms listed on the TSX that did not pay any cash dividends for at least five years. They mailed a survey in 2005 to the CFOs of each of the 538 firms and received 172 usable responses, a 32.0 percent response rate.

Managers indicate the importance of 18 factors using a five-point importance scale, from 0 = no importance to 4 = maximum importance. Of these factors, the most important determinants influencing a nonpayout policy are as follows: (1) preference to reinvest cash flows instead of paying dividends, (2) state in the firm's life cycle, (3) availability of cash, and (4) level of current earnings. The survey also asks recipients to select the three most important reasons from a set of eight for their firm's decision not to pay dividends. More than 97 percent of respondents select "need of funds for growth and expansion" as the most important reason. Similar to recent U.S. evidence (Brav et al. 2005), taxation is at best a second-order determinant of dividend policy.

Baker et al. (2009) partition their sample into low-growth versus high-growth firms, low-profitability versus high-profitability firms, and widely held versus closely held firms, and then they repeat the analysis. Their findings suggest that factors associated with growth opportunities take a first-order importance for firms not paying dividends, but profitability seems to be a second-order effect on the decision not to pay dividends. The authors find reliable evidence of a control effect. Managers of widely held firms view contractual constraints such as dividend restrictions in debt contracts as the most important reason for firms not paying dividends. By contrast, managers of closely held firms perceive this factor as unimportant. The most important factor for managers of closely held firms is the preference to reinvest cash instead of paying dividends.

The survey asks managers about their views on shareholder preferences and the dividend signaling effect. The results show strong evidence that Canadian firms tailor their dividend to control shareholders' preferences, which supports the catering theory. The results are inconclusive about management views on the relation between dividend policy and stock prices and the role that dividend policy plays in signaling.

Baker et al. (2009) find that firms with smaller size, higher investment opportunities, and lower profitability are less likely to pay dividends. Their empirical results further show that firms typically do not use share repurchases as dividend substitutions in Canada. An implication of these findings is that firm characteristics influence dividend decisions.

China

Li, Yin-feng, Song, and Man-shu (2006) analyze the dividend decision-making policy and the reasons for dividend policy selection in non-state-owned listed companies by using structural equation modeling. In 2003, the authors sent a pretested survey to a sample of general managers, CFOs, and other senior managers from 1,224 listed companies and to a random sample of 3,100 nonlisted firms by using e-mail, regular mail, and other means. Based on the 4,324 firms contacted, they received 670 valid responses, a 15.5 percent response rate. Of these responses, 69 represent non-state-owned-listed companies. The vast majority of these 69 sample firms are in manufacturing (72.5 percent), followed by real estate (14.5 percent), and information technology (10.1). The respondents represent 23 provinces and autonomous regions in China.

Li et al. (2006) draw two main conclusions. First, the dividend policy of non-state-owned listed companies in China is consistent with the Western agency theory for dividends; that is, paying dividends plays a role in reducing agency costs that arise from the owner-manager conflict. Second, of the four motives affecting the dividend decision for non-state-owned companies, the most important is refinancing ability. Other important factors influencing dividend policy are investment opportunities, potential capacity to repay debt obligations, and stock price. Regulations and codes affect most of these important motives for listed companies. The authors also find that the level of earnings is not an important motive influencing dividend policy; that is, companies with more earnings do not necessarily increase their dividend payments.

Germany

Frankfurter, Kosedag, Schmidt, and Topalov (2002) survey CFOs of all publicly listed German firms as of September 2000. The objective of their study is to gain insight into investors' attitudes toward dividends as perceived by chief corporate financial decision makers. They ask respondents to indicate their level of agreement to 26 statements on a continuous range from strongly disagree to strongly agree. They mailed 954 survey forms to the listed firms and received 420 responses, a 44.0 percent response rate.

A key finding is that the majority of German CFOs believe that shareholders like to receive regular dividends, so German firms pay dividends to meet expectations. The majority of respondents (56.7 percent) agree with a statement supporting the irrelevance theory that "dividends have no effect on the inherent value of our stock." Additional evidence also casts doubt on the five rational explanations—tax effects, clientele effect, agency theory, signaling, and social contract (behavioral)—used to explain dividends. Another important finding is that the perceptions of the CFOs are typically consistent with those of Lintner (1956). For example, respondents generally agree with dividend continuity; that is, once a firm starts paying dividends, it should continue to pay them.

Using factor analytical and grouping techniques, Frankfurter et al. (2002) extend their analysis by separating the sample population based on the survey into two distinctly heterogeneous groups and then observe the differences/similarities between the two groups. (Note: The authors characterize the two groups merely by calling them groups A and B.) They find sharp differences between the two groups for the majority of statements. They also explore whether the two groups differ based on seven variables (total assets, insider ownership, ownership by institutions, age, market-to-book ratio, market value of equity, and price-to-earnings ratio). Differences exist between the two groups involving insider ownership, ownership by institutions, age, and market-to-book value. Thus, the perception of dividends and the dividend policy that may be formulated as a result of these seven factors/variables is not universal.

Frankfurter et al. (2002, p. 212) conclude that

> one cannot apply models to explain the value of dividends the same way one can measure, say, barometric pressure at sea level around the globe. The differences may be both intra- and inter-societal, but no current academic hypothesis can be considered valid within a single country or across countries. It is safe to say, therefore, that the manufacture of such models would not withstand Occam's razor.

Occam's razor is a principle stating that "entities should not be multiplied unnecessarily." One interpretation of this principle is that of several acceptable explanations for a phenomenon, the simplest is preferable, provided that it does not contradict the observed facts. An implication of Frankfurter et al's (2002) findings is that developing more complex explanations for paying dividends and applying them across firms or across countries is unlikely to lead to a satisfactory resolution of the dividend puzzle.

India

Several surveys examine dividend policy in India.

Bhat and Pandey's (1993) Study of Managers' Perceptions

Bhat and Pandey (1993) survey finance directors of the *Economic Times* 250 top companies in India. Their study focuses on determinants that managers consider important in deciding their firm's dividend policy. They also seek managers' views on different issues that have implications for dividend policy using a disagreement-agreement scale.

The study results show that determinants of dividend policy include current and expected earnings as well as the pattern of past dividends. Managers do not view liquidity as an important consideration in dividend policy. Indian managers believe that firms strive to maintain an uninterrupted record of dividend payments and avoid making changes in the dividend payment that might have to be reversed. These findings are consistent with those of Lintner (1956) and Baker, Farrelly, and Edelman (1985) in the United States. Bhat and Pandey (1993) find that Indian managers consider dividends as a signaling device, but they do not find any support for the residual dividend hypothesis. Managers do not seem to fully understand the clientele hypothesis. Finally, Indian managers prefer paying dividends, even if companies have profitable investment opportunities. This evidence does not provide any support for the residual dividend theory.

Anand's (2004) Study of Factors Influencing Dividend Policy Decisions

Anand (2004) presents the results of a 2001 survey to identify the factors that CFOs consider in formulating dividend policy in India. His initial sample consists of a large cross-section of 474 private-sector and the top 51 public-sector firms in India based on market capitalization. His survey yields 81 responses, a response rate of 15.4 percent. The survey asks CFOs to indicate their beliefs about 13 questions using a five-point scale, from –2 ("definitely do not agree") to +2 ("definitely agree"), with 0 indicating "no opinion." The author performs no statistical tests to study nonresponse bias but uses factor analytic methodology to analyze the results obtained from the survey questionnaire.

The results of principal components analysis reveal three broad components of dividend policy, which he labels as (1) dynamic-static dividend policy, (2) information signaling, and (3) clientele effect and investors' preference for dividends. According to Anand (2004), the first factor (dynamic-static dividend policy) is static in the sense that firms want to have a stable dividend policy. The policy is also dynamic in that firms want to increase dividends with the increase in the level of sustainable earnings. The second factor (information signaling) means that dividend policy conveys information about the current and future prospects to the less-informed market. Anand interprets the final factor (clientele effect and investors' preference for dividends) as suggesting that certain investors are tax neutral, while others prefer dividends. The payment of dividends helps reduce agency costs.

Anand (2004, p. 14) concludes by stating,

> The results of the present study are consistent with the theory and they are simultaneously revealing as well. The managers of corporate India believe that dividend decisions are important as they provide a signaling mechanism for the future prospects of the firm and thus affect its market value. They do consider the investors' preference for dividends and shareholder profile while designing the dividend policy. They also have a target dividend payout ratio but want to pay stable dividends with growth. Therefore, dividend policy does matter to the CFOs and the investors.

The Netherlands

One survey examines dividend policy of Dutch Consumers.

Dong, Robinson, and Veld's (2005) Survey of Dutch Consumers

Although there is general agreement that investors like dividends, empirical evidence from the individual investors' perspective on why they want dividends is lacking. To fill this gap, Dong, Robinson, and Veld (2005) ask individual investors about their attitude toward dividends. In 2002, they surveyed a voluntary Dutch consumer panel that regularly answers personal surveys on family financial and consumer matters. From a sample of 2,723 household members, they received 2,035 responses. Of the 2,723 household members, only 555 respondents own or previously owned shares in exchange-listed companies and/or investment funds, resulting in a 20.4 percent response rate. Their 32-question survey examines various dividend theories on cash and stock dividends and whether different demographic groups have significantly different attitudes toward the theories.

The following results relate only to cash dividends. Dong, Robinson, and Veld (2005) find that investors have a strong preference for receiving dividends, especially older investors. Investors partly prefer dividends because the cost of cashing in dividends is lower than the cost of selling stock. Apart from older and low-income investors, individual investors do not tend to consume a large part of their dividends. Regarding dividend theories, the results show very strong support for signaling theory but are inconsistent with explanations involving uncertainty resolution (bird in the hand), free cash flow and agency costs (agency theory), taxes, and behavioral finance.

Norway

Limited survey research exists on dividend policy in Norway.

The Baker, Mukherjee, and Paskelian (2006) Survey of Norwegian Firms

Baker, Mukherjee, and Paskelian (2006) survey managers of Norwegian dividend-paying firms listed on the Oslo Stock Exchange about their views on dividend policy. Their study focuses on factors influencing the dividend policies of their firms and theoretical and empirical issues about dividend policy in general. A secondary purpose is to compare the importance that Norwegian and U.S. managers attach to the factors influencing dividend policy. The authors point out that U.S. and Norwegian companies operate under different regulations and tax environments.

Using a sample of 121 firms, Baker, Mukherjee, and Paskelian (2006) conduct their survey in 2004 and receive 33 usable responses, giving them a response rate of 27.3 percent. The survey instrument is similar to that developed by Baker, Farrelly, and Edelman (1985); Farrelly, Baker, and Edelman (1986); and Baker and Powell (1999, 2000). The majority of respondents are either CFOs or CEOs, and the most common industry type is manufacturing (33.3 percent), followed by financial services (15.2 percent). Tests for nonresponse bias show no significant differences between the responding firms and the nonresponding firms on four firm characteristics (total assets, debt ratio, market-to-book ratio, and dividend payout ratio).

Using a four-point importance scale, from 0 = none to 3 = high, the Baker, Mukherjee, and Paskelian (2006) study analyzes the importance of 22 factors influencing dividend policy. The key factors that drive dividend policies of Norwegian firms are the level of current and expected future earnings, stability of earnings, current degree of financial leverage, and liquidity constraints. They find that the relative importance that Norwegian managers attach to earnings as an influence on dividend policy is similar to that previously reported by managers of U.S. firms. No significant correlation exists between the rankings of factors by managers of Norwegian firms and either NYSE or NASDAQ firms. Norwegian managers express mixed views about whether a firm's dividend policy affects firm value. Also, respondents from Norwegian firms express much less agreement about any relation between dividend policy and firm value compared with their U.S. counterparts. In examining the signaling and tax explanations for paying dividends, they find that Norwegian managers favor signaling over the tax-preference explanation.

United Kingdom

Several researchers examine dividend policy in the United Kingdom using survey methodology.

Allen's (1992) Study of Target Payout Ratios and Dividend Policy

Allen (1992) studies the dividend policies of the larger listed British companies and focuses on the sample companies' usage of target payout ratios. In 1990, he sent a mail survey to the finance executives of the 500 largest companies listed on the London International Stock Exchange and appearing in the 1989 *Times* 1000. His sample excludes companies in the banking, finance, and insurance sectors on the grounds that the nature of their industries could condition their financial policies. He receives 67 completed questionnaires, giving a response rate of 13.4 percent.

His results show that about 52.3 percent of respondent firms report using a target payout ratio, which is similar to the 59 percent reported in Partington's (1984) Australian study. Slightly more than half of the firms (51.2 percent) report that they had changed their target payout ratio at least once during the past 10 years. Allen (1992) finds that the target payout ratios range from 9 percent to 75 percent, with a mean of 34 percent.

Allen (1992) also asks respondents to rate a set of eight factors that could conceivably influence their target payout ratios using a five-point Likert scale, where 1 represents not important and 5 corresponds to very important. The results suggest that the two dominant factors influencing target dividend payout ratios are a desire to maintain stable dividends and the firm's recent dividend history. These results are consistent with Lintner's (1956) findings. The third-most important factor is "to signal the management's views of potential future firm performance to the market." Allen notes that the emphasis on the impact of signaling considerations on setting the target payout ratio suggests that dividend changes should lead rather than lag behind earnings changes, which is contrary to the agency costs model of dividends. Allen (p. 18) concludes that

> the picture [which] emerges is one that emphasizes dividend stability, recent dividend payments, and signaling considerations as being predominant. The suggestion is that dividend, financing and investment decisions are

usually independent. This again runs counter to the agency costs model. On balance, the survey results are consistent with an emphasis on the use of dividend payments as a signaling device.

Dhanani's (2005) Study of Views of U.K. Managers on Corporate Dividend Policy

Dhanani (2005) investigates and analyzes the views of U.K. financial managers on the importance and relevance of various theories of dividend policy from their corporate perspective. He also evaluates the extent to which firm characteristics influence corporate managers' views about the various dividend theories. In 2000, he mailed a pretested questionnaire to the firm secretaries of the top 800 London Stock Exchange (LSE) firms and the top 200 Alternative Investment Market (AIM) companies. The AIM is a submarket of the LSE for smaller-growing companies. The questionnaire, consisting of 26 closed-ended statements, asked respondents to indicate their level of disagreement or agreement with each statement from their firms' perspective using a five-point Likert scale, where 1 depicts strongly disagree and 5 depicts strongly agree. The survey yielded 164 completed and useable questionnaires, a 16.4 percent response rate. Tests for nonresponse bias show no differences between various financial characteristics of the early and late respondents.

Dhanani (2005) reports several key findings. First, the results show that dividend policy is important in maximizing shareholder value, refuting the general dividend irrelevance hypothesis. Thus, a firm's dividend can influence one or more of the various capital market imperfections prevalent in the real world. Second, Dhanani finds little support for the hypothesis that a firm's dividend policy can influence its capital structure and/or investment decisions. Further, companies generally refute the residual dividend policy for investment decisions. Third, the evidence supports the role of dividend policy as a relevant signaling mechanism but suggests that U.K. firms make dividend payments for reasons other than resolving principal-agency conflicts (agency theory). Fourth, the results indicate that shareholder requirements are amongst the most important factors that U.K. firms consider when formulating their dividend policies.

Dhanani (2005, p. 1665) offers the following conclusion:

Overall, using a survey approach to capture managerial views of and attitudes to dividend policy, the results of this study support the general hypothesis, in which dividend policy serves to enhance corporate value. Further analysis indicates that managers support the specific hypotheses relating to signaling and ownership structure, in preference to those about capital structure and investment decisions and agency issues. The cross sectional analysis emphasizes the role of corporate characteristics in influencing managerial views in relation to the specific dividend hypotheses; managers' responses differ based on company size, industry sector, growth opportunities, ownership structure and information asymmetry.

Cross-Country Studies

A few survey studies examine dividend policy across various countries.

Frankfurter, Kosedag, Chiang, Collison, Power, Schmidt, So, and Topalov's (2004) Comparative Analysis of Perception of Dividends

Frankfurter, Kosedag, Chiang, Collison, Power, Schmidt, So, and Topalov (2004) study the inter- and intrasocietal differences in the perception of dividends by financial managers in five countries (Germany, Hong Kong, Turkey, the United Kingdom, and the United States). This study is an outgrowth of a pilot study conducted in Germany by Frankfurter et al. (2002). The survey instrument consists of 26 statements relating to existing academic explanations of the dividend phenomenon. The authors score the responses on a scale of 1 = strongly disagree to 5 = strongly agree. The authors send 4,343 survey forms and receive 1,206 usable survey forms, a response rate of 27.8 percent.

Frankfurter et al. (2004) test four hypotheses. The first two hypotheses tested are that there will be differences and similarities in the perception of dividends within a culture (hypothesis 1 involves intrasocietal differences/similarities) and across cultures (hypothesis 2 involves intersocietal differences/similarities) by corporate financial decision makers. The results show that these two hypotheses cannot be rejected. While some perceptions appear similar, many others are nonuniform. An implication of this finding is that positing a theory of why corporations pay dividends that would consistently apply to every country or to a single country could be inappropriate. They reject hypothesis 3, which states that the closer a culture comes to what is generally called a market economy, the more similar the differences and the similarities are regarding the perception of dividends.

Given that hypotheses 1 and 2 cannot be rejected, the authors then test hypothesis 4—that there will be significant inter- and intracultural differences in the accounting and market data of the firms. The authors' analysis of some market/accounting data does not show any categorical and decisive inter- and intracultural differences. Yet, other variables such as age, insider ownership, and market-to-book ratio can adequately separate the two groups across cultures.

In summary, Frankfurter et al. (2004) find that both similarities and dissimilarities in perceptions about dividends exist inter- and intraculturally. Consequently, they conclude that dividend research must take a different track than it has been following so far. The authors suggest that one course of action would to be to conduct field interviews with respondents whose answers deviate most dramatically with respect to prevailing perceptions.

Bancel, Mittoo, and Bhattacharyya's (2005) Survey of Cross-Country Determinants of Payout Policy of European Firms

Bancel, Mittoo, and Bhattacharyya (2005) use a questionnaire to survey managers from 16 European countries in order to examine cross-country determinants of payout policy. These countries are Austria, Belgium, Denmark, Finland, France, Germany, Greece, Ireland, Italy, the Netherlands, Norway, Portugal, Spain, Sweden, Switzerland, and the United Kingdom. Their main goal is to gain insight into two questions. First, are payout policies of European and U.S. firms driven by similar factors? Second, are cross-country differences in managerial views explained primarily by the legal institutions, or do other institutional factors also play a major role? The authors compare European managers' views with those of U.S. managers, as reported in Brav et al. (2005), and across European countries. In 2003, they survey the CFOs of 1,131 predominantly large firms from the *Financial Times European Stock Exchange* pages and receive a total of 93 responses, representing an 8.2 percent response rate. The respondents represent a wide variety of industries including manufacturing (21 percent), financial (21 percent), service (14 percent), and others (34 percent). Almost all respondent firms (99 percent) pay dividends.

The survey asks respondents to rate the importance of 18 factors that determine the respondent firm's decision to pay dividends on a scale of 0 = not important to 4 = very important. An overwhelming majority of respondents (89 percent) consider the factor "stability and level of future earnings" as important in making dividend decisions, followed in importance by a "sustainable change in earnings," which is considered important by 78 percent of the respondents. The survey also asks respondents whether they agree with each of 21 statements involving their firm's dividend decisions. Most respondents agree that they try to avoid reducing dividends (83 percent), that an optimal dividend policy would strike a balance between current dividends and future growth (78 percent), and that they try to maintain a smooth dividend stream from year to year (77 percent).

Bancel, Mittoo, and Bhattacharyya (2005) find that the factors largely driving European managers' views on dividend policy are similar to those of their U.S. peers as reported in Brav et al. (2005). European managers also strongly agree with Lintner's (1956) findings that firms smooth dividends and are reluctant to cut them but follow different dividend targets than a fixed payout ratio. Their cross-country analysis does not support La Porta et al's (2000) view that the quality of the legal system primarily influences dividends. Instead, Bancel, Mittoo, and Bhattacharyya find that a complex interaction of the ownership structure of the firm and the legal and institutional structure of its home country determine dividend policy. These results tend to support an idiosyncratic theory of dividends.

Summary of Non-U.S. Survey Evidence on Cash Dividends and Related Issues

Table 6.5 shows that survey research on dividend policy is a global phenomenon. Table 6.6 provides the most important determinants of dividend policy from

TABLE 6.5 Non-U.S. survey evidence on cash dividends

This table shows representative non-U.S. studies involving cash dividends, the number of usable responses, response rates, and sample characteristics.

Author and date of publication	Usable responses	Response rate (%)	Sample characteristics
Australia			
Partington (1984, 1985, 1989)	93	61.2	Firms listed among the 300 largest firms on the Sydney Stock Exchange Industrial List, excluding financial institutions
Canada			
Jog and Srivastava (1994)	133	22.9	A total of 582 large Canadian firms consisting of TSX-300 corporations and large foreign-owned and private corporations
de Jong, van Dijk, and Veld (2003)	191	38.2	The 500 largest nonfinancial Canadian firms listed on the TSX
Baker, Saadi, Dutta, and Gandhi (2007); Baker, Dutta, and Saadi (2008)	103	35.4	A total of 291 dividend-paying firms listed on the TSX
Baker, Chang, Dutta, and Saadi (2009)	172	32.0	A total of 538 non-dividend-paying Canadian firms listed on the TSX
China			
Li, Yin-feng, Song, and Man-shu (2006)	670	15.5	A total of 69 listed and 601 nonlisted companies from 23 provinces and autonomous regions in China
Germany			
Frankfurter, Kosedag, Schmidt, and Topalov (2002)	420	44.0	A total of 954 firms listed on at least one of the eight stock exchanges in Germany

India			
Ramesh and Pandey (1993)	NA	NA	Top firms in the *Economic Times* 250
Anand (2004)	81	15.4	A cross section of 474 private-sector and the top 51 public-sector firms in India based on market capitalization
The Netherlands			
Dong, Robinson, and Veld (2005)	555	20.4	A Dutch panel of 2,723 household members
Norway			
Baker, Mukherjee, and Paskelian (2006)	33	27.3	A total of 121 firms consisting of a mix of small, medium-size, and large firms listed on the Oslo Stock Exchange
United Kingdom			
Allen (1992)	67	13.4	The 500 largest British listed companies, excluding those in the banking, finance, and insurance sectors
Dhanani (2005)	164	16.4	A total of 800 London Stock Exchange firms and the top 200 Alternative Investment Market firms
Cross-country studies			
Frankfurter, Kosedag, Chiang, Collison, Power, Schmidt, So, and Topalov (2004)	1,206	27.8	A total of about 4,343 firms in five countries
Bancel, Bhattacharyya, and Mittoo (2005)	93	8.2	A total of 1,131 firms from 16 European countries

TABLE 6.6 Major determinants of dividend policy: Non-U.S. firms

This table shows the results of representative non-U.S. studies seeking to identify the most important factors that affect dividend policy.

Author and date of publication	Key determinants found to influence dividend policy
Australia	
Partington (1989)	• Level of profits • Effect of dividend changes upon share price • Maintenance of dividend stability • Stability of earnings
Canada	
Jog and Srivastava (1994)	• The levels of current and expected earnings • Availability of cash • Need for investment funds • Pattern of past dividends
de Jong, van Dijk, and Veld (2003)	• Existence of free cash flow
Baker, Saadi, Dutta, and Gandhi (2007); Baker, Dutta, and Saadi (2008)	• Level of expected future earnings • Stability of earnings • Pattern of past dividends • Level of current earnings
Baker, Chang, Dutta, and Saadi (2009)	• Preference to reinvest cash flows instead of paying dividends • Stage in the firm's life cycle • Availability of cash • Level of current earnings
Li, Yin-feng, Song, and Man-shu (2006)	• Ability to refinance debt • Investment opportunities • Ability to repay existing debt • Stock price
India	
Ramesh and Pandey (2003)	• Current and expected earnings • Pattern of past dividends
Anand (2004)	• Dynamic-static dividend policy • Information signaling • Clientele effect and investors' preference for dividends
Norway	
Baker, Mukherjee, and Paskelian (2006)	• Level of current earnings • Stability of earnings • Current degree of financial leverage • Level of expected future earnings • Liquidity constraints

TABLE 6.6 (cont'd) Major determinants of dividend policy: Non-U.S. firms

Author and date of publication	Key determinants found to influence dividend policy
United Kingdom	
Allen (1992)	• Desire to maintain stable dividends • Company's recent dividend history • Ability to signal the management's views of potential future company performance
Dhanani (2005)	• Shareholder requirements
Cross-country studies	
Bancel, Bhattacharyya, and Mittoo (2005)	• Stability and level of future earnings • A sustainable change in earnings • Desire to pay out a given fraction of earnings in the long run

various non-U.S. studies. Although differences exist among these studies, some commonalities are apparent. For example, the level of current and future earnings, the stability of earnings, and the pattern of past dividends appear to be important determinants in many countries. Comparing the research results in Table 6.2 to those in Table 6.6 reveals many similarities between the determinants of dividend policy among the United States and other countries. Table 6.7 shows the major conclusions drawn from non-U.S. studies on dividend policy. Not surprisingly, the conclusions often differ, given that the focus of these studies varies.

Table 6.8 provides the level of support that non-U.S. surveys find for different theories, hypotheses, and explanations for paying cash dividends. Interpreting these findings requires caution for several reasons, such as the different periods of the studies and the different methods used to analyze the survey results. While no explanation has universal support, signaling theory appears to have the most support based on the non-U.S. studies reviewed. This conclusion is similar to that gleaned from examining the results from Table 6.4 involving the rationale for paying dividends in U.S. studies. The results involving the other big market imperfections (taxes and agency costs) are mixed. Too few studies investigate some newer explanations for dividends such as life-cycle theory and catering theory to draw definitive conclusions. What is apparent is that unanimity does not exist for any of the explanations for paying dividends based on these studies.

TABLE 6.7 Key conclusions of non-U.S. dividend surveys

This table presents some major conclusions from various non-U.S. dividend surveys.

Author and date of publication	Major conclusions
Australia	
Partington (1984, 1985, 1989)	• About 59 percent of firms report using an explicit target payout ratio. • No industry effect appears to influence the use or magnitude of payout targets. • The most important variables influencing dividend policy are profitability, share price, and stability of both dividends and earnings. • Firms usually adopt independent dividend and investment policies and use debt to finance the shortfall when internal funds are insufficient to meet its desired needs.
Canada	
Jog and Srivastava (1994)	• Dividend decisions depend heavily on current and future profitability. • Public firms treat the past pattern of dividends as an important consideration. • Firms view increases in dividends as good news and consider dividend announcements as informative signals to outside investors.
de Jong, van Dijk, and Veld (2003)	• Firms first decide on the payout question and then on the form of the payout (dividends and/or repurchases). • The existence of free cash flow drives the payout decisions. • Factors such as tax and behavioral preferences determine the choice for dividends as the form of payout.
Baker, Saadi, Dutta, and Gandhi (2007)	• The most important determinants of dividends are the level of expected future earnings, stability of earnings, pattern of past dividends, and the level of current earnings. • Managers of TSX-listed firms pay careful attention to their choice of dividend policy. • Managers of TSX-listed firms express the most support for the signaling and life-cycle explanations for paying dividends.
Baker, Dutta, and Saadi (2008)	• The perceptions of managers from financial versus nonfinancial firms differ on the importance of various factors influencing their firm's dividend policy. • There is a weak, if any, multinational operations effect on manager perception of dividends.
Baker, Chang, Dutta, and Saadi (2009)	• The availability of growth opportunities, not profitability, is the main factor leading Canadian firms to pay no dividends. • Canadian firms tailor their dividend policy to meet the preferences of controlling shareholders.

TABLE 6.7 (cont'd) Key conclusions of non-U.S. dividend surveys

Author and date of publication	Major conclusions
China	
Li, Yin-feng, Song, and Man-shu (2006)	• The ability to refinance existing debt is the most important motive affecting the dividend policy decision. • Western agency theory for dividends applies to non-state-owned listed companies in China in which owners impose greater influence on dividend policy than do managers.
Germany	
Frankfurter, Kosedag, Schmidt, and Topalov (2002)	• The vast majority of CFOs of German firms perceive that stockholders like to receive regular dividends. • The majority of respondents believe that dividends have no effect on the inherent value of a firm's stock. • Mixed support exists for the five explanations for paying dividends (tax effects, clientele, agency theory, signaling, and social contract).
India	
Ramesh and Pandey (1993)	• Managers view current and expected earnings as well as the pattern of past dividends as the most important factors influencing dividend policy. • Managers perceive a positive relationship between the payment of dividends and share price. • Managers prefer that Indian companies continuously maintain dividend payments. • Managers consider dividend policy as a signaling device.
Anand (2004)	• Firms have a long-term dividend payout ratio. • Dividend changes follow a shift in long-term sustainable earnings. • Dividends provide a signaling mechanism of future prospects of the firm. • A firm's dividend payout ratio affects the firm's market value. • Dividends subject the firm to the scrutiny of investors.
The Netherlands	
Dong, Robinson, and Veld (2005)	• Investors have a strong preference to receive dividends and partly want dividends because of transaction costs. • Individual investors provide strong confirmation for signaling theories but not explanations involving uncertainty resolution (bird in the hand), agency theory, taxes, and behavioral finance.

(Continued)

TABLE 6.7 (cont'd) Key conclusions of non-U.S. dividend surveys

Author and date of publication	Major conclusions
Norway	
Baker, Mukherjee, and Paskelian (2006)	• No significant correlation exists between the overall rankings of factors that influence dividend policy between Norwegian and U.S. managers. • Norwegian managers express mixed views about whether a firm's dividend policy affects value. • Managers' views provide support for the signaling hypothesis but not the tax-preference explanation.
United Kingdom	
Allen (2002)	• About 52 percent of respondent firms report using a target payout ratio. • The dominant factors influencing target dividend payouts are a desire to maintain stable dividends and the company's recent dividend history. • The evidence supports signaling theory over the agency costs model in explaining why firms pay dividends.
Dhanani (2005)	• Dividend policy serves to enhance corporate market value. • Managers prefer signaling and ownership structure explanations for paying dividends to those about capital structure, investment decisions, and agency issues. • Corporate characteristics influence managerial views about specific dividend hypotheses.
Cross-country studies	
Frankfurter, Kosedag, Chiang, Collison, Power, Schmidt, So, and Topalov (2004)	• Both similarities and dissimilarities involving the perception of dividends exist inter- and intraculturally. • The two groups based on the perception of dividends can be separated based on age, insider ownership, and the market-to-book ratio. • Dividend research must take a different track than it has been following so far.
Bancel, Bhattacharyya, and Mittoo (2005)	• The factors that drive the views of European and U.S. managers' views of dividend policy are similar. • A complex interaction of the firm's ownership structure and the legal and institutional structure of its home country determine dividend policy.

TABLE 6.8 Non-U.S. evidence on explanations for paying dividends

This table presents non-U.S. survey evidence about various explanations for paying dividends.

Author and date	Bird-in-the-hand theory	Residual dividend theory	Taxes and clientele effects	Agency theory	Asymmetric information and signaling	Behavioral theory	Life cycle of dividends	Catering theory
Canada								
Jog and Srivastava (1994)					Supported			
de Jong, van Dijk, and Veld (2003)			Supported					
Baker, Saadi, Dutta, and Gandhi (2007); Baker, Dutta, and Saadi (2008)	Some support	Mixed	Not supported	Not supported	Supported		Supported	Some support
Baker, Chang, Dutta, and Saadi (2009)			Not supported		Inconclusive			Supported
China								
Li, Yin-feng, Song, and Man-shu (2006)				Supported	Not supported			
Germany								
Frankfurter, Kosedag, Schmidt, and Topalov (2002)			Mixed	Mixed	Mixed	Mixed		

(Continued)

TABLE 6.8 (cont'd) Non–U.S. evidence on explanations for paying dividends

Author and date	Bird-in-the-hand theory	Residual dividend theory	Taxes and clientele effects	Agency theory	Asymmetric information and signaling	Behavioral theory	Life cycle of dividends	Catering theory
India								
Ramesh and Pandey (1993)		Not supported			Supported			
Anand (2004)		Not supported	Supported	Supported	Supported			
The Netherlands								
Dong, Robinson, and Veld (2005)	Not supported		Not supported	Not supported	Supported	Not supported		
Norway								
Baker, Mukherjee, and Paskelian (2006)			Not supported		Supported			
United Kingdom								
Allen (1992)				Not supported	Supported			
Dhanani (2005)	Not supported	Not supported	Supported	Not supported	Supported			

Summary and Conclusions

Why firms pay dividends has been one of the important unsolved puzzles in finance. Miller and Modigliani (1961) developed the irrelevance proposition in which dividend policies are equivalent and no policy can increase shareholders' wealth in perfect capital markets. Yet, the dividend irrelevance argument does not explain why many companies develop deliberate payout strategies, as documented by Lintner (1956) and many other researchers. Financial economists have developed many theories to explain dividend payout decisions in imperfect capital markets. Researchers most often test these theories by observing how firms respond to exogenous changes in their environment. In general, such tests have been inconclusive regarding the competing theories of corporate dividend behavior.

As Frankfurter and Wood (2003, p. 167) note, "No theory based on the economic paradigm developed thus far completely explains the persistence of corporate dividend policy." Why has this been the case? An obvious reason is that financial economists have focused on developing universally applicable and mathematically tractable models. Still, the different circumstances facing firms as well as their characteristics (e.g., size, industry, growth opportunities, financial leverage, corporate profitability, information asymmetry, agency costs, ownership structure, and stock exchange status) may influence their views and actions. Consequently, the search for unequivocal empirical evidence to support a single theory of dividends is probably doomed to fail. Consequently, ratcheting up the complexity of models and then applying them to a whole universe of firms is unlikely to resolve the intriguing questions of why companies pay dividends and why investors want dividends.

Empirical evidence on whether dividend policy affects a firm's value offers contradictory advice to corporate managers. Although the field of finance has not yet reached a consensus on the effect of dividend policy on value, managers often pay careful attention to the choice of a dividend policy. Survey research suggests that both institutional and individual investors often perceive that dividend policy matters. This finding may help to explain why firms often devote much time to making and implementing dividend policy decisions. Survey evidence shows little support for a residual dividend policy. The interest in having a properly managed dividend policy apparently stems from the concern about its ability to affect the stock price. Today, academicians and corporate managers alike still debate whether dividend policy matters.

As Baker, Powell, and Veit(2002, p. 256) note,

> While not fully solving the dividend puzzle, theoretical and empirical studies over the past four decades have provided additional puzzle pieces that move us closer in the direction of resolution. In reality, there is probably some truth to all of the explanations of why corporations pay

dividends or repurchase stock at least for some firms. Although evidence shows that fewer corporations are paying dividends, a firm's distribution policy still matters because it can affect shareholder wealth.

The evidence presented in this chapter identifies many factors that *should* be important in establishing a firm's payout policy. Survey results coupled with other empirical studies and mathematical models strongly suggest that certain determinants are consistently important over time in shaping actual policies. The same factors that influence dividend decisions are not equally important to all firms; that is, dividend policy is sensitive to such factors as firm characteristics, corporate governance, and legal environments. Because various factors may affect a firm's dividend decisions in different ways, no universal set of factors is likely to apply to all firms. Thus, universal or one-size-fits-all theories or explanations for why companies pay dividends are too simplistic. As H. L. Mencken, the famous American writer and editor, once remarked, "For every complex problem there is an answer that is clear, simple, and wrong." At this point, how all the pieces fit together to establish an "optimal" policy, or whether such a policy actually exists, is not fully resolved. Although no consensus exists among financial economists on the subject of dividend policy, the popular view is that dividend policy is important, as evidenced by the large amount of money involved and the repeated nature of the dividend payout decision.

Although many criticize surveys for their obvious weaknesses, survey methodology augments the dominant market-based research and helps to validate the results of these quantitative studies by using a different approach. Not surprisingly, survey research on dividends and dividend policy seems to have become more popular in recent years. Despite extensive theorizing and empirical research into the motivations for paying dividends, corporate dividend policy remains one of the more controversial areas in finance. Thus, the dividend puzzle remains one of the most challenging topics in modern finance. This conclusion suggests that researchers may need to develop a new paradigm to deal with the dividend puzzle.

References

Abrutyn, Stephanie, and Robert W. Turner. 1990. "Taxes and Firms' Dividend Policies: Survey Results." *National Tax Journal* 43:4, 491–496.

Aggarwal, Raj. 1993. "Theory and Practice in Finance Education: Or Why We Shouldn't Just Ask Them." *Financial Practice and Education* 3:2, 15–18.

Agrawal, Anup, and Narayanan Jayaraman. 1994. "The Dividend Policies of All-Equity Firms: A Direct Test of the Free Cash Flow Theory." *Managerial and Decision Economics* 15:2, 139–148.

Aharony, Josef, and Amihud Dotan. 1994. "Regular Dividend Announcements and Future Unexpected Earnings: An Empirical Analysis." *Financial Review* 29:1, 125–151.

Allen, D. A. 1992. "Target Payout Ratios and Dividend Policy: British Evidence." *Managerial Finance* 18:1, 9–21.

Allen, Frank, Antonio E. Bernardo, and Ivo Welch. 2000. "The Theory of Dividends Based on Tax Clienteles." *Journal of Finance* 55:6, 2499–2536.

Allen, Franklin, and Roni Michaely. 2003. "Payout Policy." In George M. Constantinides, Milton Harris, and René Stulz (eds.), *Handbook of the Economics of Finance,* vol. 1A, 337–429. Amsterdam: North-Holland-Elsevier.

Anand, Manoj. 2004. "Factors Influencing Dividend Policy Decisions of Corporate India." ICFAI *Journal of Applied Finance* 10:2, 5–16.

Ang, James S. 1987. "Do Dividends Matter? A Review of Corporate Dividend Theories and Evidence." Monograph no. 1987-2, Finance Series in Finance and Economics, Solomon Brothers Center for the Study of Financial Institutions, Graduate School of Business Administration, New York University.

Ang, James S., and Stephen J. Ciccone. 2009. "Dividend Irrelevance Theory." In H. Kent Baker (ed.), *Dividends and Dividend Policy,* 97–113. Hoboken, NJ: John Wiley & Sons.

Ang, James S., and David R. Peterson. 1985. "Return, Risk, and Yield: Evidence from Ex Ante Data." *Journal of Finance* 40:2, 537–548.

Asquith, Paul, and David W. Mullins Jr. 1983. "The Impact of Initiating Dividend Payments of Shareholder Wealth." *Journal of Finance* 56:1, 77–95.

———. 1986. "Signaling with Dividends, Stock Repurchases, and Equity Issues." *Financial Management* 15:3, 27–44.

Bagwell, Laurie Simon, and John B. Shoven. 1989. "Cash Distribution to Shareholders." *Journal of Economic Perspectives* 3:3, 129–140.

Bajaj, Mukesh, and Anand M. Vijh. 1990. "Dividend Clienteles and the Information Content of Dividend Changes." *Journal of Financial Economics* 26:2, 193–219.

Baker, H. Kent. 1988. "The Relationship between Industry Classification and Dividend Policy." *Southern Business Review* 14:1, 1–8.

———. 1989. "Why Companies Pay No Dividends." *Akron Business and Economic Review* 20:2, 48–61.

———. 2009. *Dividends and Dividend Policy.* Hoboken, NJ: John Wiley & Sons.

Baker, H. Kent, Bin Chang, Shantanu Dutta, and Samir Saadi. 2009. "Why Firms Do Not Pay Dividends: The Canadian Experience." Working Paper, Queen's University.

Baker, H. Kent, Shantanu Dutta, and Samir Saadi. 2008. "Impact of Financial and Multinational Operations on Manager Perceptions of Dividends." *Global Finance Journal* 19:2, 171–186.

Baker, H. Kent, and Gail E. Farrelly. 1988. "Dividend Achievers: A Behavioral Perspective." *Akron Business and Economic Review* 19:1, 79–92.

Baker, H. Kent, Gail E. Farrelly, and Richard B. Edelman. 1985. "A Survey of Management Views on Dividend Policy." *Financial Management* 14:3, 78–84.

Baker, H. Kent, Tarun K. Mukherjee, and Ohannes Paskelian. 2006. "How Norwegian Managers View Dividend Policy." *Global Finance Journal* 17:1, 155–176.

Baker, H. Kent, and Gary E. Powell. 1999a. "How Corporate Managers View Dividend Policy." *Quarterly Journal of Business and Economics* 38:2, 17–35.

———. 1999b. "Dividend Policy: Issues in Regulated and Unregulated Firms—A Managerial Perspective." *Managerial Finance* 25:6, 1–20.

———. 2000. "Determinants of Corporate Dividend Policy: A Survey of NYSE Firms." *Financial Practice and Education* 10:1, 29–40.

Baker, H. Kent, Gary E. Powell, and E. Theodore Veit. 2002. "Revisiting the Dividend Puzzle: Do All of the Pieces Now Fit?" *Review of Financial Economics* 11:4, 241–261.

Baker, H. Kent, Samir Saadi, Shantanu Dutta, and Devinder Gandhi. 2007. "The Perception of Dividends by Canadian Managers: New Survey Evidence." *International Journal of Managerial Finance* 3:1, 70–91.

Baker, H. Kent, and David M. Smith. 2006. "In Search of a Residual Dividend Policy." *Review of Financial Economics* 15:1, 1–18.

Baker, H. Kent, E. Theodore Veit, and Gary E. Powell. 2001. "Factors Influencing Dividend Policy Decisions of Nasdaq Firms." *Financial Review* 36:3, 19–38.

———. 2002. "Revisiting Managerial Perspectives on Dividend Policy." *Journal of Economics and Finance* 11:4, 241–261.

Baker, Malcolm, Stefan Nagel, and Jeffrey Wurgler. 2007. "The Effect of Dividends on Consumption." *Brookings Papers on Economic Activity*, 11, 232–291.

Baker, Malcolm, and Jeffrey Wurgler. 2004. "A Catering Theory of Dividends." *Journal of Finance* 59:3, 1125–1165.

Bancel, Franck, Usha R. Mittoo, and Nalinaksha Bhattacharyya. 2005. "Cross-Country Determinants of Payout Policy: A Survey of European Firms." Available at http://ssrn.com/abstract=683111.

Bar-Yosef, Sasson, and Lucy Huffman. 1986. "The Information Content of Dividends: A Signaling Approach." *Journal of Financial and Quantitative Analysis* 21:1, 47–58.

Benartzi, Shlomo, Roni Michaely, and Richard Thaler. 1997. "Do Changes in Dividends Signal the Future or the Past?" *Journal of Finance* 52:3, 1007–1034.

Benesh, Gary, Arthur J. Keown, and John M. Pinkerton. 1984. "An Examination of Market Reaction to Substantial Shifts in Dividend Policy." *Journal of Financial Research* 7:2, 131–142.

Benrud, Eric. 2009. "The Historical Evolution of Dividends." In H. Kent Baker (ed.), *Dividends and Dividend Policy,* 21–34. Hoboken, NJ: John Wiley & Sons.

Bernstein, Peter L. 1992. *Capital Ideas: The Improbable Origins of Modern Wall Street.* New York: Free Press.

Bhat, Ramesh, and I. M Pandey. 1993. "Dividend Decisions: A Study of Managers' Perceptions." Working Paper no. 1082, Indian Institute of Management, Ahmedabad.

Bhattacharya, Sudipto. 1979. "Imperfect Information, Dividend Policy, and 'the Bird in the Hand' Fallacy." *Bell Journal of Economics* 10:1, 259–270.

———. 1980. "Nondissipative Signaling Structures and Dividend Policy." *Quarterly Journal of Economics* 85:1, 1–24.

Black, Fischer. 1976. "The Dividend Puzzle." *Journal of Portfolio Management* 2:2, 3–8.

Black, Fischer, and Myron Scholes. 1974. "The Effects of Dividend Yield and Dividend Policy on Common Stock Prices and Returns." *Journal of Financial Economics* 1:1, 1–22.

Blume, Marshall. 1980. "Stock Return and Dividend Yield: Some More Evidence." *Review of Economics and Statistics* 62:4, 567–577.

Bond, Michael T., and Mbodja Mougoué. 1991. "Corporate Dividend Policy and the Partial Adjustment Model." *Journal of Economics and Business* 43:2, 165–178.

Booth, Laurence D., and D. J. Johnson. 1984. "The Ex-Dividend Day Behavior of Canadian Stock Prices: Tax Changes and Clientele Effects." *Journal of Finance* 39:2, 457–476.

Brav, Alon, John R. Graham, Campbell R. Harvey, and Roni Michaely. 2005. "Payout Policy in the 21st Century." *Journal of Financial Economics* 77:3, 483–527.

———. 2008. "Managerial Response to the May 2003 Dividend Tax Cut." *Financial Management* 37:4, 611–624.

Brennan, Michael. 1970. "Tax Reform and the Stock Market: An Asset Price Approach." *American Economic Review* 23:4, 417–427.

Brittain, John. 1964. "The Tax Structure and Corporate Dividend Policy." *American Economics Review* 54:3, 272–287.

———. 1966. *Corporate Dividend Policy*. Washington, DC: Brookings Institution.

Brook, Yaron, William T. Charlton Jr., and Robert J. Hendershott. 1998. "Do Firms Use Dividends to Signal Large Future Cash Flow Increases?" *Financial Management* 27:3, 46–57.

Bruner, Robert F. 2002. "Does M&A Pay? A Survey of Evidence from the Decision-Maker." *Journal of Applied Finance* 12:1, 48–68.

Bulan, Laarni T., and Naryanan Subramanian. 2009. "The Firm Life Cycle Theory of Dividends." In H. Kent Baker (ed.), *Dividends and Dividend Policy*, 201–13. Hoboken, NJ: John Wiley & Sons.

Chetty, Raj, and Emmanuel Saez. 2005. "Dividend Taxes and Corporate Behavior: Evidence from the 2003 Dividend Tax Cut." *Quarterly Journal of Economics* 120:3, 791–833.

Chiang, Kevin, George M. Frankfurter, Arman Kosedag, and Bob G. Wood Jr. 2006. "The Perception of Dividends by Professional Investors." *Managerial Finance* 32:1, 60–81.

Crutchley, Claire E, and Robert S. Hansen. 1989. "A Test of the Agency Theory of Managerial Ownership, Corporate Leverage, and Corporate Dividends." *Financial Management* 18:4, 36–46.

Damodaran, Aswath. 1999. *Applied Corporate Finance*. New York: John Wiley and Sons.

DeAngelo, Harry, and Linda DeAngelo. 2006. "The Irrelevance of the MM Dividend Irrelevance Theorem." *Journal of Financial Economics* 79:2, 293–315.

———. 2007. "Payout Policy Pedagogy: What Matters and Why?" *European Financial Management* 13:1, 11–27.

DeAngelo, Harry, Linda DeAngelo, and Douglas J. Skinner. 1992. "Dividends and Losses." *Journal of Finance* 47:5, 1837–1864.

———. 1996. "Reversal of Fortune: Dividend Signaling and the Disappearance of Sustained Earnings Growth." *Journal of Financial Economics* 40:3, 341–371.

———. 2004. "Are Dividends Disappearing? Dividend Concentration and the Consolidation of Earnings." *Journal of Financial Economics* 22:3, 425–456.

———. 2009. "Corporate Payout Policy." *Foundations and Trends in Finance* 3:2–3, 95–287.

DeAngelo, Harry, Linda DeAngelo, and René Stulz. 2006. "Dividend Policy and the Earned/Contributed Capital Mix: A Test of the Life-Cycle Theory." *Journal of Financial Economics* 81:2, 227–254.

de Jong, Abe, Ronald van Dijk, and Chris Veld. 2003. "The Dividend and Share Repurchase Policies of Canadian Firms: Empirical Evidence Based on an Alternative Research Design." *International Review of Financial Analysis* 12:4, 349–377.

Denis, David J., Diane K. Denis, and Atulya Sarin. 1994. "The Information Content of Dividend Changes: Cash Flow Signaling, Overinvestment, and Dividend Clienteles." *Journal of Financial and Quantitative Analysis* 29:4, 567–587.

Denis, David J., and Igor Osobov. 2008. "Why Do Firms Pay Dividends? International Evidence on the Determinants of Dividend Policy." *Journal of Financial Economics* 89:1, 62–82.

deRooji, Margot, and Luc Renneboog. 2009. "The Catering Theory of Dividends." In H. Kent Baker (ed.), *Dividends and Dividend Policy*, 215–338. Hoboken, NJ: John Wiley & Sons.

Dhanani, Alpa. 2005. "Corporate Dividend Policy: The Views of British Financial Managers." *Journal of Business Finance and Accounting* 32:7–8, 1625–1672.

Dittmar, Amy. 2000. "Why Do Firms Repurchase Stock?" *Journal of Business* 73:3, 331–355.

———. 2008. "Corporate Cash Policy and How to Manage It with Stock Repurchases." *Journal of Applied Corporate Finance* 20:3, 22–34.

Dittmar, Amy K., and Robert F. Dittmar. 2007. "The Timing of Financing Decisions: An Examination of the Correlation in Financing Waves." *Journal of Financial Economics* 90:1, 59–83.

Dong, Ming, Chris Robinson, and Chris Veld. 2005. "Why Individual Investors Want Dividends." *Journal of Corporate Finance* 12:1, 121–158.

Dutta, Shantanu, Vijay M. Jog, and Phil Zhu. 2005. "Governance and Performance of Restricted Share Firms in Canada." Paper presented at the Northern Finance Association Conference, Vancouver, Canada.

Easterbrook, Frank. H. 1984. "Two Agency-Cost Explanations of Dividends." *American Economic Review* 74:4, 650–659.

Edelman, Richard B., Gail E. Farrelly, and H. Kent Baker. 1985. "Public Utility Dividend Policy: Time for a Change?" *Public Utilities Fortnightly* 115:4, 28–31.

Elton, Edwin J., and Martin J. Gruber. 1970a. "Marginal Stockholder Tax Rates and the Clientele Effect." *Review of Economics and Statistics* 52:2, 68–74.

———. 1970b. "Marginal Shareownership, Voting Power, and Cash Dividend Policy." *Journal of Corporate Finance* 1:1, 33–62.

Fama, Eugene F. 1974. "The Empirical Relationship between the Dividend and Investment Decisions of Firms." *American Economic Review* 64:3, 304–318.

Fama, Eugene F., and Harvey Babiak. 1968. "Dividend Policy: An Empirical Analysis." *Journal of the American Statistical Association* 63:324, 1132–1161.

Fama, Eugene F., and Kenneth R. French. 2001. "Disappearing Dividends: Changing Firm Characteristics or Lower Propensity to Pay?" *Journal of Financial Economics* 60:1, 3–43.

Farrelly, Gail. E., and H. Kent Baker. 1989. "Corporate Dividends: Views of Institutional Investors." *Akron Business and Economic Review* 20:2, 89–100.

Farrelly, Gail E., H. Kent Baker, and Richard B. Edelman. 1986. "Corporate Dividends: Views of the Policy Makers." *Akron Business and Economic Review* 17:4, 62–74.

Filbeck, Greg. 2009. "Asymmetric Information and Signaling Theory." In H. Kent Baker (ed.), *Dividends and Dividend Policy*, 163–177. Hoboken, NJ: John Wiley & Sons.

Frankfurter, George M., Arman Kosedag, Kevin Chiang, David Collison, David M. Power, Hartmut Schmidt, Raymond So, and Mihail Topalov. 2004. "A Comparative Analysis of Perception of Dividends by Financial Managers." *Research in International Business and Finance* 18:1, 73–114.

Frankfurter, George M., Arman Kosedag, Hartmut Schmidt, and Mihail Topalov. 2002. "The Perception of Dividends by Management." *Journal of Psychology and Financial Markets* 3:4, 202–217.

Frankfurter, George M., and William R. Lane. 1992. "The Rationality of Dividends." *International Review of Financial Analysis* 1:2, 115–129.

Frankfurter, George M., and Bob G. Wood Jr. 1997. "The Evolution of Corporate Dividend Policy." *Journal of Financial Education* 23:1, 16–33.

———. 2002. "Dividend Policy Theories and Their Empirical Tests." *International Review of Financial Analysis* 11:2, 111–138.

———. 2003. *Dividend Policy: Theory and Practice.* San Diego: Academic Press.

Fung, William K. H. 1981. "Taxes, Clientele Effect of Dividend and Risk, Return Linearity." *Journal of Banking and Finance* 5:3, 405–424.

Gordon, Myron J. 1959. "Dividends, Earnings and Stock Prices." *Review of Economics and Statistics* 41:2, pt. 1, 99–105.

———. 1963. "Optimal Investment and Financing Policy." *Journal of Finance* 18:2, 264–272.

Gordon, Myron J., and Eli Shapiro. 1956. "Capital Equipment Analysis: The Required Rate of Profit." *Management Science* 3:1, 102–110.

Graham, Benjamin, and David Dodd. 1951. *Security Analysis: Principles and Techniques.* New York: McGraw-Hill.

Graham, John R., and Campbell R. Harvey. 2001. "The Theory and Practice of Corporate Finance: Evidence from the Field." *Journal of Financial Economics* 60:2–3, 187–243.

Graham, John, and Alok Kumar. 2006. "Dividend Preference of Retail Investors: Do Dividend Clienteles Exist?" *Journal of Finance* 6:3, 1305–1336.

Grullon, Gustavo, and Roni Michaely. 2002. "Dividends, Share Repurchases, and the Substitution Hypothesis." *Journal of Finance* 57:4, 1649–1684.

Harkins, Edwin P., and Francis J. Walsh Jr. 1971. *Dividend Policies and Practices.* New York: Conference Board.

Healy, Paul M., and Krishna G. Palepu. 1988. "Earnings Information Conveyed by Dividend Initiations and Omissions." *Journal of Financial Economics* 21:2, 149–175.

Jensen, Gerald R., and James M. Johnson. 1995. "The Dynamics of Corporate Dividend Reductions." *Financial Management* 24:4, 31–51.

Jensen, Gerald R., Donald P. Solberg, and Thomas S. Zorn. 1992. "Simultaneous Determination of Insider Ownership, Debt, and Dividend Policies." *Journal of Financial and Quantitative Analysis* 27:2, 247–264.

Jensen, Michael. 1986. "Agency Costs of Free Cash Flow." *American Economic Review* 76:2, 323–329.

Jog, Vijay M., and Ashwani K. Srivastava. 1994. "Corporate Financial Decision Making in Canada." *Canadian Journal of Administrative Sciences* 11:2, 158–178.

John, Kose, and Joseph Williams. 1985. "Dividends, Dilution, and Taxes: A Signaling Equilibrium." *Journal of Finance* 40:4, 1053–1070.

Jose, Manuel L., and Jerry L. Stevens. 1989. "Capital Market Valuation of Dividend Policy." *Journal of Business Finance & Accounting* 16:6, 651–662.

Julio, Brandon, and David L. Ikenberry. 2004. "Reappearing Dividends." *Journal of Applied Corporate Finance* 16:4, 89–100.

Kahneman, Daniel, and Amos Tversky. 1979. "Prospect Theory: An Analysis of Decision Making under Risk." *Econometrica* 47:2, 262–291.

Kalay, Avner, and Uri Loewenstein. 1986. "The Information Content of the Timing of Dividend Announcements." *Journal of Financial Economics* 16:3, 373–388.

Kalay, Avner, and Roni Michaely. 2000. "Dividends and Taxes: A Re-Examination." *Financial Management* 29:2, 55–75.

Kennedy, William F., Thomas J. O'Brien, and Carl Horn Jr. 1987. "Dividend Policy of Large Public Utilities: Results of a Nationwide Survey of Chief Executives." *Financial Review* 22:3, 69.

Kumar, Praveen, and Bong-Soo Lee. 2001. "Discrete Dividend Policy with Permanent Earnings." *Financial Management* 30:3, 55–76.

Lakonishok, Josef, and Theo Vermaelen. 1983. "Tax Reform and Ex-Dividend Day Behavior." *Journal of Finance* 38:4, 1157–1179.

Lang, Larry H. P., and Robert H. Litzenberger. 1989. "Dividend Announcements: Cash Flow Signaling vs. Free Cash Flow Hypothesis." *Journal of Financial Economics* 24:1, 181–191.

La Porta, Raphael, Florencio Lopez-de-Silanes, Andrei Shleifer, and Robert W. Vishny. 2000. "Agency Problems and Dividend Policies around the World." *Journal of Finance* 55:1, 1–34.

Lease, Ronald C., Kose John, Avner Kalay, Uri Loewenstein, and Oded H. Sarig. 2000. *Dividend Policy: Its Impact on Firm Value.* Boston: Harvard Business School Press.

Li, Kai, and Xinlei Zhao. 2008. "Asymmetric Information and Dividend Policy." *Financial Management* 37:4, 673–694.

Li, Li, Qi Yin-feng, Liu Song, Wang Man-shu. 2006. "What Makes the Dividend Policy Decision and Their Motives for Doing So: An Analysis Based on a Questionnaire Survey of Non-State-Owned Listed Companies in China." Working Paper, NanKai University, People's Republic of China. Available at http://www.ccfr.org.cn/cicf2006/cicf2006paper/20060128200110.pdf.

Lie, Erik. 2000. "Excess Funds and Agency Problems: An Empirical Study of Incremental Cash Disbursements." *Review of Financial Studies* 13:1, 219–248.

Lintner, John. 1956. "Distribution of Incomes of Corporations among Dividends, Retained Earnings and Taxes." *American Economic Review* 46:2, 97–113.

Litzenberger, Robert H., and Krishna Ramaswamy. 1980. "Dividends, Short Selling Restrictions, Tax-Induced Investor Clienteles and Market Equilibrium." *Journal of Finance* 35:2, 469–482.

———. 1982. "The Effects of Dividends on Common Stock Prices: Tax Effects or Information Effects." *Journal of Finance* 37:2, 429–443.

Masulis, Ronald W., and Brett Trueman. 1988. "Corporate Investment and Dividend Decisions under Differential Personal Taxation." *Journal of Financial and Quantitative Analysis* 23:4, 369–386.

McCabe, George M. 1979. "The Empirical Relationship between Investment and Financing: A New Look." *Journal of Financial and Quantitative Analysis* 14:1, 119–135.

Megginson, William. 1996. *Corporate Finance Theory.* Reading, MA: Addison-Wesley.

Michaely, Roni. 1991. "Ex-Dividend Day Stock Price Behavior: The Case of the 1986 Tax Reform Act." *Journal of Finance* 46:3, 845–860.

Michel, Allen. 1979. "Industry Influence on Dividend Policy." *Financial Management* 8:3, 22–26.

Miller, Merton H. 1986. "Behavioral Rationality in Finance: The Case of Dividends." *Journal of Business* 59:4, pt. 2, S451–S468.

Miller, Merton H., and Franco Modigliani. 1961. "Dividend Policy, Growth and the Valuation of Shares." *Journal of Business* 34:4, 411–433.

Miller, Merton H., and Kevin Rock. 1985. "Dividend Policy under Asymmetric Information." *Journal of Finance* 40:4, 1031–1051.

Miller, Merton, and Myron Scholes. 1978. "Dividends and Taxes." *Journal of Financial Economics* 6:4, 333–364.

———. 1982. "Dividends and Taxes: Some Empirical Evidence." *Journal of Political Economy* 90:6, 1118–1141.

Modigliani, Franco, and Merton H. Miller. 1958. "Cost of Capital, Corporation Finance, and the Theory of Investment." *American Economic Review* 48:3, 261–297.

Moh'd, Mahmoud A., Larry G. Perry, and James N. Rimbey. 1995. "An Investigation of the Dynamic Relationship between Agency Theory and Dividend Policy." *Financial Review* 30:2, 367–385.

Morck, Randall K., David A. Stangeland, and Bernard Yeung. 2000. "Inherited Wealth, Corporate Control, and Economic Growth: The Canadian Disease." In Randall K. Morck (ed.), *Concentrated Corporate Ownership,* 319–369. Chicago: University of Chicago Press.

Morck, Randall K., Daniel Wolfenzon, and Bernard Yeung. 2005. "Corporate Governance, Economics Entrenchment, and Growth." *Journal of Economic Literature* 43:3, 655–720.

Mougoué, Mbodja, and Ramesh P. Rao. 2003. "The Information Signaling Hypothesis of Dividends: Evidence from Cointegration and Causality Tests." *Journal of Business Finance and Accounting* 30:3/4, 441–478.

Mueller, Dennis C. 1972. "A Life Cycle Theory of the Firm." *Journal of Industrial Economics* 20:3, 199–219.

Mukherjee, Tarun. 2009. "Agency Costs and the Free Cash Flow Hypothesis." In H. Kent Baker (ed.), *Dividends and Dividend Policy,* 145–161. Hoboken, NJ: John Wiley & Sons.

Nissim, Doron, and Amir Ziv. 2001. "Dividend Changes and Future Profitability." *Journal of Finance* 56:6, 2111–2133.

Ofer, Aharon R., and Anjan V. Thakor. 1987. "A Theory of Stock Price Responses to Alternative Corporate Cash Disbursement Methods: Stock Repurchases and Dividends." *Journal of Finance* 42:2, 365–394.

Ogden, Joseph P., Frank C. Jen, and Philip F. O'Connor. 2003. *Advanced Corporate Finance: Policies and Strategies.* Upper Saddle River, NJ: Prentice Hall.

Partington, Graham H. 1984. "Dividend Policy and Target Payout Ratios." *Accounting and Finance* 24:2, 63–74.

———. 1985. "Dividend Policy and Its Relationship to Investment and Financing Policies: Empirical Evidence." *Journal of Business Finance and Accounting* 12:4, 531–542.

———. 1989. "Variables Influencing Dividend Policy in Australia: Survey Results." *Journal of Business Finance and Accounting* 16:2, 165–182.

Pettit, R. Richardson. 1977. "Taxes, Transaction Costs, and the Clientele Effects of Dividends." *Journal of Financial Economics* 5:3, 419–436.

Pruitt, Stephen W., and Larry J. Gitman. 1991. "The Interactions between the Investment, Financing, and Dividend Decisions of Major U.S. Firms." *Financial Review* 26:3, 209–230.

Rao, P. Someshwar, and Clifton R. Lee-Sing. 1995. "Governance Structure, Corporate Decision-Making and Firm Performance in North America." In Ronald J. Daniels and Randall Morck (eds.), *Corporate Decision-Making in Canada*, Industry Canada Research Series, vol. 5, 43–104. Calgary: University of Calgary Press.

Ross, Stephen A. 1977. "The Determination of Financial Structure: The Incentive-Signaling Approach." *Bell Journal of Economics* 8:1, 23–40.

Rozeff, Michael S. 1982. "Growth, Beta and Agency Costs as Determinants of Dividend Payout Ratios." *Journal of Financial Research* 5:3, 249–258.

Saadi, Samir, and Shantanu Dutta. 2009. "Taxes and Clientele Effects." In H. Kent Baker (ed.), *Dividends and Dividend Policy,* 127–144. Hoboken, NJ: John Wiley & Sons.

Shefrin, Hersh. 2009. "Behavioral Explanations of Dividends." In H. Kent Baker (ed.), *Dividends and Dividend Policy,* 179-199. Hoboken, NJ: John Wiley & Sons.

Shefrin, Hersh, and Meir Statman. 1984. "Explaining Investor Preference for Cash Dividends." *Journal of Financial Economics* 13:2, 253–282.

Smirlock, Michael, and William Marshall. 1983. "An Examination of the Empirical Relationship between the Dividend and Investment Decisions: A Note." *Journal of Finance* 38:5, 1659–1667.

Smith, David M. 2009. "Residual Dividend Policy." In H. Kent Baker (ed.), *Dividends and Dividend Policy*, 115–126. Hoboken, NJ: John Wiley & Sons.

Thaler, Richard, and Hersh Shefrin. 1981. "An Economic Theory of Self Control." *Journal of Political Economy* 89:2, 392–406.

Trahan, Emery A., and Lawrence J. Gitman. 1995. "Bridging the Theory-Practice Gap in Corporate Finance: A Survey of Chief Financial Officers." *Quarterly Review of Economics and Finance* 35:1, 73–87.

Tufano, Peter. 2001. "HBS-JFE Conference Volume: Complementary Research Methods." *Journal of Financial Economics* 60:2–3, 179–195.

Walter, James E. 1963. "Dividend Policy: Its Influence on the Value of the Enterprise." *Journal of Finance* 18:2, 280–291.

Weigand, Robert A., and H. Kent Baker. 2009. "Changing Perspectives on Distribution Policy." *Managerial Finance* 35:6, 479–492.

Williams, John Burr. 1938. *The Theory of Investment Value*. Cambridge, MA: Harvard University Press.

Yoon, Pyung Sig, and Laura T. Starks. 1995. "Signaling, Investment Opportunities, and Dividend Announcements." *Review of Financial Studies* 8:4, 995–1018.

⁓ 7

Share Repurchases, Special Dividends, Stock Splits, and Stock Dividends

> Although dividends and share repurchases are similar in many ways, they are not perfect substitutes. . . . Developing models that describe the choice between paying dividends and repurchasing stock continues to be a fertile area for future research.
>
> Baker, Powell, and Veit (2002, p. 255)

Introduction

The presumed goal of financial management is to create value for stockholders. As discussed in Chapter 6, the finance community has not yet reached a consensus on whether dividend policy affects firm value. Yet, as survey research shows, many firms behave as though dividend policy matters. In addition to distributing regular dividends, some firms also engage in distributing cash to shareholders through share repurchases and specially designated dividends (SDDs). Do these decisions affect shareholder wealth?

Sometimes firms engage in other dividend activities such as issuing a stock split or a stock dividend, each involving the costly process of altering the number of shares in a publicly traded company. A payment involving the issuance of new shares is similar to a stock split because it increases the total number of shares outstanding while lowering the price of each share. Stock dividends are those paid out as additional stock shares of the issuing corporation or another corporation such as its subsidiary corporation. Stock splits and stock dividends are akin to slicing a pie into more pieces without changing the size of the pie. As shown later in this chapter, empirical studies indicate that such transactions often result in puzzling stock market reactions. Survey research helps explain why firms engage in these activities.

Although not examined in this chapter, some companies offer a dividend reinvestment plan (DRIP), which is an equity investment option offered directly by the underlying company. Instead of receiving dividends as cash, participating investors directly invest their dividends in the underlying equity. DRIPs can serve as a low-cost, convenient way for shareholders to invest; however, they also entail certain limitations from the perspective of corporations and investors. Some firms offer another type of direct investing plan called a direct stock purchase plan (DSPP). A DSPP permits investors to buy initial shares directly from the firm or from its transfer agent without commissioned brokers. Baker and Meeks (1990) discuss the evolution of DRIPs. He (2009) provides a detailed discussion of DRIPs and DSPPs, which entails the motives for offering these plans as well as their theories and empirical evidence. Kiymaz (2009) reviews survey studies on DRIPs (e.g., Pettway and Malone 1973; Baker and Seippel 1980, 1981; Fredman and Nichols 1980; Baker and Johnson 1988, 1989; Todd and Domian 1997). Baker, Khan, and Mukherjee (2002) provide a survey study on DSPPs.

Why do firms engage in behavior such as repurchasing shares, paying special dividends, and issuing stock splits and stock dividends? If engaging in these corporate financial decisions results in creating value for shareholders, the answer is simple: managers are doing their jobs to benefit shareholders. If not, why do they undertake these costly actions?

The purpose of this chapter is twofold: (1) to provide an overview of the major theories involving share repurchases, special dividends, stock splits, and stock dividends, and (2) to offer a synthesis of the survey research on these topics. Survey studies provide direct evidence of managerial attitudes and allow an analysis of information not disclosed by companies and not observable through share prices. Because the finance literature is voluminous on these topics, this chapter only highlights some of the more important theoretical and empirical studies. Hence, the chapter provides the theoretical explanations for why firms repurchase their shares, pay special dividends, and engage in stock splits and stock dividends and why managers perceive that they make such decisions. Baker and Powell (2005) provide an overview of share repurchases, special dividends, stock splits, stock dividends, and DRIPs. This chapter, along with others in the book, also attempts to determine whether a gap exists between theory and practice.

The remainder of this chapter is organized as follows. The first section summarizes common explanations for repurchasing stock, followed by a review of the survey research on the topic. The next several sections follow the same format but examine special dividends, stock dividends, and stock splits. Finally, the chapter offers a summary and conclusions.

Share Repurchases

In some countries—notably, the United States, Canada, and the United Kingdom—corporations can buy back their stock in a share repurchase, also called a stock repurchase or share buyback. European firms engage in fewer repurchases compared to their U.S. counterparts (La Porta, Lopez-De-Silanes, Shleifer, and Vishny, 2000; Rau and Vermaelen 2002). With a share repurchase, a corporation distributes cash to existing shareholders in exchange for a fraction of the firm's outstanding equity. The firm can account for these shares either by retiring them or keeping them as treasury stock available for reissuance. Unlike the receipt of cash dividends, shareholders have the option of whether they want to sell their shares back to the firm when a firm engages in a share repurchase. Stockholders generally receive a price above the preannouncement price, and even those who do not sell shares back to the firm theoretically benefit through higher earnings per share (EPS) and stock price.

Methods of Repurchasing Shares

Firms use three main methods for repurchasing shares: (1) open-market share repurchase, (2) fixed-price tender offer, and (3) Dutch auction. Other share repurchase methods are transferable put-rights distributions and target stock repurchases (not discussed in this chapter because of their infrequent practice). In an open-market share repurchase, a firm simply buys back its shares in the market after announcing the buyback to the public. Today, this is the dominant repurchase method, constituting more than 90 percent of all repurchases. In a fixed-price tender offer, a firm offers to buy a portion of its shares at a single purchase price. The firm also indicates the number of shares sought and the duration of the offer. In a Dutch auction share repurchase, a firm specifies a price range for the number of shares within which it will ultimately buy shares. Shareholders are invited to tender their shares at any price within the stated range. The firm compiles these responses, creates a demand curve for the stock, and sets the lowest price at which it can buy the shares sought. The firm pays that price to all investors who tender their shares at or below that price.

Trends in Share Repurchases

Although dividends remain a popular method to distribute cash to shareholders, an increasing number of firms have used repurchases as a distribution method in recent years. This meaningful increase in the use of share repurchases in the

United States started in the 1980s and became meteoric between 1995 and 2005. According to Bierman (2001), the reasons U.S. corporations have increasingly repurchased large amounts of their own common shares are subject to numerous and often conflicting interpretations.

One factor contributing to the trend in share repurchases is the improved regulatory environment resulting from the Securities and Exchange Commission (SEC) adopting Rule 10b-18 in 1982, which provided a "safe harbor" for firms to buy back shares (Grullon and Michaely 2002; Cornell 2009). This regulation coincides with a decreasing proportion of firms paying cash dividends. Researchers including Fama and French (2001) and DeAngelo, DeAngelo, and Skinner (2004) document the disappearing dividends phenomenon at the end of the twentieth century.

Julio and Ikenberry (2004), Chetty and Saez (2005), among others provide evidence of a reversal in the dividend policy of U.S. firms since 2001; that is, the decline in proportion of U.S. corporations paying cash dividends reversed. There is little evidence to show that cash dividends decreased appreciably in the rest of the world (Denis and Osobov 2008). Still others including Wood (2001); Grullon and Michaely (2002); DeAngelo, DeAngelo, and Skinner (2004); and Hsieh and Wang (2007) find a widespread substitution of share repurchases for dividends in both the United States and Europe, especially those firms not among the largest firms. According to Dittmar (2008), the annual aggregate volume of repurchases in the United States surpassed that of dividends for the first time in 2005.

A second factor for the increasing interest in share repurchases during the 1980s involves the economy. Several market crashes, such as those in October 1987 and October 1989, temporarily caused a decline in stock prices. Evidence suggests an inverse relationship between the announcement of repurchases and broader moves in the market. As Netter and Mitchell (1989) find, the number of announcements tends to rise when stock prices fall.

A third explanation for the popularity of share repurchases, especially beginning in the 1990s, is the growing use of stock options to compensate managers and other employees. Studies that examine a link between stock options and the payout policies of firms include Bartov, Krinsky, and Lee (1998); Jolls (1998); Fenn and Liang (2001); Kahle (2002); and Weisbenner (2004).

Firms do not necessarily face the decision of either paying dividends or repurchasing shares. As Grullon and Michaely (2002) report, dividend-paying firms account for almost 90 percent of total dollars spent on repurchases. Given that many firms pay cash dividends and repurchase stock, two related questions remain: (1) Why do firms use share repurchases to distribute cash flows to shareholders? and (2) What factors determine the trade-off between repurchases and dividends?

Regarding why firms buy back their stock, the finance literature proposes many theories, hypotheses, and explanations. Some of the more common explanations involve (1) taxes, (2) signaling and undervaluation, (3) agency costs of free cash flows, (4) capital structure, (5) takeover deterrence, and (6) employee stock options (Hsieh and Wang 2009). The first three explanations are similar to the "big three" market imperfections (taxes, asymmetric information, and agency costs) for paying cash dividends as discussed in Chapter 6. Not surprisingly, most of the early theories attempt to model taxation, signaling, and agency costs of free cash flows. Other possible motives for repurchases exist, such as the wealth transfer hypothesis, which posits a transfer of wealth to nonparticipating from participating (selling) shareholders or from bondholders to nonparticipating stockholders. The next section focuses on the six most popular theories, hypotheses, and explanations.

Regarding the question of what determines a firm's form of payout, papers by Ofer and Thakor (1987), Barclay and Smith (1988), and Brennan and Thakor (1990) attempt to explain and model the trade-off between the two methods. In his review of determinants of corporate payout choices, Cornell (2009) identifies five main reasons firms repurchase shares: (1) taxes, (2) managerial flexibility, (3) management of earnings per share, (4) management of employee stock options, and (5) defense against hostile takeovers. Repurchases offer advantages over paying cash dividends for all of these reasons.

Theories, Models, and Explanations for Repurchasing Shares

This subsection discusses six common motives for repurchasing shares that appear in the finance literature and also reviews selected studies involving each motive. Lease, John, Kalay, Loewenstein, and Sarig (2000), Grullon and Ikenberry (2000), and Baker, Powell, and Veit (2002) discuss various theories explaining why firms buy back their stock.

Taxes

In perfect markets without taxes, dividends and share repurchases are perfect substitutes. In reality, both the tax treatment and tax rates may differ between dividends and share repurchases. In the United States, cash dividends have historically been taxed as ordinary income, whereas gains to stockholders on stock price appreciation resulting from share repurchases have been taxed as capital gains. When the tax rate on capital gains is lower than on ordinary income, share repurchases have a distinct tax advantage over cash dividends. Historically, repurchases have enjoyed favorable tax treatment. The *tax-motivated* or *dividend substitution hypothesis* contends that managers use share repurchases instead of cash dividends to minimize taxes for their stockholders. Thus, tax clienteles may exist due to differences in tax laws and regulations. Yet, the empirical evidence for the tax clientele effect is mixed. For example, a study by Lie and Lie (1999) supports the tax clientele effect, while some but not all of the results from Grinstein and Michaely (2005) support tax clienteles.

In the United States, shifting tax laws have changed the relation between the tax rates on dividends and capital gains. For example, the Tax Reform Act (TRA) of 1986 basically raised the tax rate on capital gains, making share repurchases less attractive than they were but still more attractive than cash dividends. Nonetheless, dividends were still taxed at a higher rate than capital gains as a result of the TRA. Evidence on the response of corporate payout policy to the passage of the TRA reveals mixed results. For example, Bagwell and Shoven (1989) present time-series evidence showing that the aggregate dividend ratio (dividends/net income) has remained stable since the early 1980s, while the aggregate repurchase ratio (repurchases/net income) has increased over time. This pattern is inconsistent with the effectiveness of the TRA. In contrast, Lie and Lie (1999) provide evidence that managers are more likely to distribute cash to shareholders by using stock repurchases if those shareholders have lower tax rates on capital gains than on dividends.

The passage of the Jobs and Growth Tax Relief Reconciliation Act of 2003 equalized the tax rate for dividends and capital gains in the United States at 15 percent. Some argue that the passage of this act encourages firms to pay more dividends. Studies by Julio and Ikenberry (2004) and Amromin, Harrison, and Sharpe (2005) report only limited gains in corporate dividend payouts shortly after the passage of this act. Based on survey evidence, Brav, Graham, Harvey, and Michaely (2008) conclude that the tax rate reduction increased the likelihood of dividend initiation.

Signaling and Undervaluation

The signaling hypothesis is one of the most tested explanations for repurchases. Signaling theory rests on the notion that information asymmetries exist between management and outside investors. These asymmetries provide incentives for firms to announce share repurchase programs to signal managers' private firm information. The *information signaling hypothesis* suggests that managers may use share repurchases to signal that the firm's stock is undervalued (i.e., the existing stock price is below its intrinsic value) or to reveal to the market positive information about the firm's prospects (i.e., future earnings and cash flows). By contrast, the *investment hypothesis* indicates that firms may undertake repurchases because they lack attractive investment opportunities for available net cash flows, which could be viewed as a negative signal. Insufficient investments could be viewed as a negative reason for share repurchase. Thus, the information content of the signal may be ambiguous.

Early signaling models such as those described by Bhattacharya (1979), Miller and Rock (1985), and Williams (1988) consider cash dividends and share repurchases as substitutes. Other models such as those described by Ofer and Thakor (1987), Hausch and Seward (1993), and Chowdhry and Nanda (1994) distinguish between these two payout methods and explain why firms prefer one method over the other as a signaling device. For example, Ofer and Thakor show that managers prefer to use cash dividends as a signal when undervaluation is small but to use repurchases as a signaling device when undervaluation is large. Consequently, repurchases should have greater information content than cash dividends. Still other researchers, such as Vermaelen (1984) and Constantinides and Grundy (1989), propose theories to explain share repurchases alone. As Hsieh and Wang (2009) note, these theoretical papers on the signaling role of share repurchases make different assumptions, but all suggest that managers use share repurchases to convey private information about their firms.

Indirect signaling studies on repurchases form two broad groups. Studies in the first group examine whether firms use repurchases to signal market undervaluation about firms' current performance. Numerous empirical studies report sizable share price reactions to announcements of share repurchase (e.g., Masulis 1980; Dann 1981; Vermaelen 1981; Asquith and Mullins 1986; Lakonishok and Vermaelen 1990; Comment and Jarrell 1991; Ikenberry, Lakonishok, and Vermaelen 1995, 2000; Stephens and Weisbach 1998). These findings of positive announcement returns for repurchasing firms provide evidence consistent with the view that firms are undervalued at the time they announce a repurchase. Prior research also shows a positive correlation between announcement-period returns and both the size of the repurchase program and the amount of the offer premium. Studies in the second group offer mixed evidence about the role of share repurchases in signaling future earnings and profitability. For example, Dann, Masulis, and Mayers (1991); Hertzel and Jain (1991); and Lie (2005) find support for the view that announcements of repurchases convey information about current and future earnings. By contrast, evidence by Nohel and Tarhan (1998) and Grullon and Michaely (2004) is inconsistent with the signaling hypothesis. Overall, the existing studies provide mixed support for the signaling hypothesis.

Agency Costs of Free Cash Flows

The free cash flow (excess funds) hypothesis, developed by Easterbook (1984) and Jensen (1986) and extended by Lang and Litzenberger (1989), asserts that disbursements may mitigate agency problems between managers and shareholders. Their views about the agency effects of dividends can similarly be applied to stock repurchases. Share buybacks provide a way to deal with agency costs of free cash flows associated with managers overinvesting or investing in nonproductive activities such as perquisites and excessive compensation. Free cash flow is the cash flow that remains after a firm undertakes all positive net present value (NPV) projects. Returning extra cash to shareholders as cash dividends or share repurchases might mitigate the conflicts of interest between management and shareholders. As a result, repurchasing shares to reduce cash may serve as a way of disciplining a firm to make efficient decisions. Firms with high levels of excess cash and few investment opportunities may prefer repurchasing shares to increasing cash dividends. Firms can adjust the level of shares they purchase as their free cash flow and their need for internally generated capital fluctuates. Therefore, share buybacks provide firms with greater flexibility compared to cash dividends (Jagannathan, Stephens, and Weisbach 2000). According to the theories of Brennan and Thakor (1990) and Lucas and McDonald (1998), share repurchases are preferable to cash dividends in large cash distributions. They also suggest that larger repurchases convey better news than smaller repurchases or dividends.

In general, empirical evidence supports the free cash flow explanations involving share repurchases (Stephens and Weisback 1998; Dittmar 2000; Lie 2000; Li and McNally 2003; Grullon and Michaely 2004). For example, Grullon and Michaely provide evidence that the market reacts favorably to the announcement of share repurchase programs by companies with declining investment opportunities. Such evidence lends support to the agency cost explanation for repurchases.

Capital Structure

Share repurchase provides managers with a way to change their firm's capital structure. If a firm has a stated optimal or target debt ratio, managers might want to adjust their firm's existing leverage ratios toward the target ratio (e.g., Fama and French 2002; Leary and Roberts 2005; Flannery and Rangan 2006). If managers want to increase financial leverage, they could reduce the number of the firm's shares through repurchases. Using debt-financed stock repurchases would result in even more substantial changes in capital structure (even greater financial leverage) than using cash flows as the source of the repurchase.

According to the *leverage hypothesis*, managers of firms with additional debt capacity may repurchase shares to move the firm toward a more desirable capital structure. A share repurchase using a tender offer can provide a sudden and dramatic change in capital structure. An open-market repurchase program is less drastic because such a program is often smaller in size and spread out over several years.

Several studies investigate the use of share repurchases to change a firm's capital structure. For example, Dittmar (2000) finds that lower-leveraged firms have a greater likelihood of repurchasing shares to increase their leverage ratios than firms with higher leverage ratios. Hovakimian, Opler, and Titman (2001) find that firms tend to use stock repurchases and debt retirements to move their debt ratios toward the targets. These studies lend support to a capital structure motive for repurchasing shares.

Takeover Deterrence

Managers can use share repurchases as an antitakeover mechanism to ward off an unwanted bidder in several ways. First, the announcement of a repurchase may serve as a favorable signal of firm value. Second, a repurchase may increase the cost of purchasing any outstanding shares. Third, repurchases alter the capital structure in the short term by changing the ownership structure of the firm, which in turn may shift the voting power among remaining shareholders. Thus, managers may initiate a repurchase for their own gain, either by reducing the likelihood of a takeover (which reduces the chances that they may lose their jobs) or by increasing management's percentage ownership of the firm (which increases their potential control of voting shares). Various theories and models describe the use of repurchases as a takeover deterrent (e.g., Harris and Raviv 1988; Stulz 1988; Bagnoli, Gordon, and Lipman 1989; Bagwell 1991; Sinha 1991).

The empirical evidence using indirect methods generally supports the notion that some firms use repurchases as a takeover deterrent (e.g., Bradley and Wakeman 1983; Dann and DeAngelo 1983, 1988; Klein and Rosenfeld 1988; Denis 1990; Billett and Xue 2007). Lie and Lie (1999), however, find little support for the notion that firms have an increased likelihood of using tender offer repurchases over special dividends to fend off potential outside threats.

Employee Stock Options

A final explanation for stock repurchases involves a stock option rationale. Hsieh and Wang (2009) suggest three different ways in which the growing popularity of option-based compensation could affect corporate payout policy, especially related to repurchases. First, firms may need to use repurchased shares to fund stock option plans. Thus, the *reissue hypothesis* states that managers may undertake repurchase programs to provide shares for the exercise of stock options, bonuses, or other reissue uses. Kahle (2002) presents strong evidence that firms repurchase shares to fund employees' exercisable options.

Second, firms may want to buy back their stock to offset an increase in common equity resulting from the exercise of stock options and to offset the dilution of EPS resulting from option exercises. Thus, share repurchases may serve as a type of earnings management. Weisbenner (2004) presents evidence that firms granting many options to employees use repurchases to lessen the impact of option exercises on EPS dilution. Other studies including Bens, Nagar, Skinner, and Wong (2003) and Gong, Louis, and Sun (2008) show evidence of a link between earnings management and share repurchases.

Third, a structural change in corporate payouts may result from option grants. Dividend yields decrease the share prices and the corresponding option values in the compensation arrangement. Thus, managers may prefer to use share repurchases instead of cash dividends as the form of payout. Several studies including Lambert, Lanen, and Larcker (1989); Jolls (1998); and Fenn and Liang (2001) support the notion that managers have incentives to substitute repurchases for dividends when managers are heavily compensated with stock options.

Recap of Repurchase Theories and Explanations

The extant literature offers various reasons for share repurchases. The results of empirical studies generally show that firms change their payout policy in response to tax law changes, but the results involving the tax clientele effect are mixed. Recent studies provide mixed evidence for the signaling hypothesis but provide support for the idea that firms use share repurchases as a way to lessen the agency costs of free cash flows. Some support also exists for the capital structure, takeover deterrence, and stock option rationales for repurchasing shares. The evidence suggests a lack of a universally accepted motivation behind repurchases. Thus, different firms are likely to have varying motives for buying back their shares.

Survey Evidence on Share Repurchase

The studies discussed in the previous section are confined to indirect evidence obtained from cross-sectional comparisons of firm characteristics or from event studies of market reaction to repurchase announcements. Such studies are unable to fully reveal the motivation behind a repurchase. Unlike this indirect-evidence literature, survey methods provide direct evidence about managerial attitudes toward possible reasons underlying repurchase decisions. This section reviews a set of survey-based studies involving share repurchases. Powell (2009) also provides a review of the survey evidence on share repurchases.

This section begins by discussing seven U.S. studies, followed by two non-U.S. surveys, and arranges the studies chronologically within the two groups. Reviewing and interpreting the following survey results requires being aware of the limitations of surveys discussed in Chapter 2, such as nonresponse bias and incorrect response bias. Additionally, the studies involve different time periods and samples.

The Baker and Rheinstein (1980) Survey on Odd-Lot Buybacks

Some companies welcome investors who buy only a few shares of their stock, while others view odd-lot shareholders (those who own less than 100 shares) as an expensive nuisance. Baker and Rheinstein (1980) investigate the motives for repurchasing odd-lot holdings of stock. They send a mail survey to the chief financial officers (CFOs) of 78 firms that made odd-lot purchases offers between September 1977 and May 1979 and receive 58 responses, a 73.4 percent response rate.

The authors find that the CFOs indicate cost savings as the most frequent reason for their odd-lot buybacks. The executives also indicate that their firms engage in buying back their shares when they view the stock price as low. The survey results show that buyback firms tend to focus on shareholders who own less than 50 shares because these shareholders are the most uneconomical to service. Baker and Rheinstein's (1980) evidence also shows that about 90 percent of the responding firms offer premiums over the market price, with the most frequent premium being between 11 and 22 percent. They also find that the majority of the sample firms (55.2 percent) leave their offers open for one to two months and another 24.1 percent use a three-to-six-month period.

The Baker, Gallagher, and Morgan (1981) Survey

The purpose of the Baker, Gallagher, and Morgan (1981) study is to identify the reasons for share repurchases and to compare the views of financial managers with theory. The authors survey CFOs of two groups of firms: repurchasers and nonrepurchasers. The repurchase group consists of a random sample of 150 firms listed on the New York Stock Exchange (NYSE) reporting changes in treasury stock between December 1977 and May 1979. The nonrepurchase group consists of a random sample of 150 NYSE firms not on the repurchase list.

Their survey instrument consists of 25 closed-ended statements and six other questions that use either a multiple choice or an open-ended format. The survey questionnaire instructs CFOs to indicate their level of agreement/disagreement with the 25 closed-ended questions by using a seven-point Likert scale, from –3 (strongly disagree) to +3 (strongly agree), with 0 representing no opinion. From their mail questionnaire, Baker, Gallagher, and Morgan (1981) receive 73 usable responses from the repurchase group (48.7 percent response rate) and 63 usable responses from the nonrepurchase group (42.0 percent response rate). They test for nonresponse bias and find no significant differences between the responses of the early and later respondents.

Overall, managers of both groups share similar opinions about share repurchases, as shown by a highly significant Spearman rank order correlation coefficient between the repurchasers and nonrepurchasers. In fact, using chi-square tests, Baker, Gallagher, and Morgan (1981) find that repurchasers and nonrepurchasers differ significantly at the 0.01 on only two of the 25 closed-ended statements. Repurchasers rank two statements most highly: "stock repurchases are a good investment when management feels the firm's stock price is depressed" and "an important reason for repurchasing shares is to provide for stock option privileges or bonuses for employees." The two most highly ranked statements by the nonrepurchasers are "stock repurchases, by increasing the debt ratio, may have a harmful effect on the firm's capital structure" and "stock repurchases can remove a large block of stock overhanging the market." The mean rankings of these two statements by the repurchase group are third and fourth, respectively.

Of the 25 statements, both groups show the greatest disagreement with the statement, "Stock repurchases may be viewed as a substitute for paying dividends." This finding offers strong evidence against the dividend substitution hypothesis. Respondents generally do not agree with statements involving taxes, capital structure, and takeover deterrence motives for share repurchases.

Of the responding firms repurchasing stock, 64.4 percent report using open-market repurchases. No other method amounts to as much as 10 percent of responses. When asked to indicate the major reason underlying their repurchase of stock, respondents give "good investment of excess cash" (34.2 percent) and "use in employee bonus or stock option plans" (34.2 percent) as their most common responses. Of the 73 repurchasers, about 41 percent indicate that they have an ongoing repurchase plan. Their main motives for having such plans are to provide for employee bonus or stock option plans and to make good use of excess cash.

The questionnaire also asks the CFOs whether they regard their repurchase decision as a dividend, investment, or financing decision. The majority (50.7 percent) view repurchases as an investment decision, 15.1 percent as a financing decision, and none as a dividend decision. The second-highest response, at 20.5 percent (a write-in response in the "other" category), is viewing repurchases as a necessity to provide shares for stock options and bonuses.

When asked about their reasons for not repurchasing stock, almost half of the respondents (47.6 percent) indicate that no excess cash is available for repurchases. No other reason amounts to as much as 10 percent of the responses. When queried about the disadvantages of stock repurchases, the top-ranked disadvantage given by both the repurchaser (34.2 percent) and nonrepurchaser (31.7 percent) groups is that buybacks reduce equity capital, which could be detrimental to the firm's capital structure or could impair its debt capacity. Based on their combined responses, both groups view repurchases as disadvantageous because they reduce funds for future growth, dividends, or other investments (14.7 percent) and imply a lack of internal growth or better investment opportunities (14.7 percent).

Overall, the survey evidence provides the most support for the information signaling (undervaluation) and stock option motives (the reissue hypothesis) for repurchasing shares. Baker, Gallagher, and Morgan (1981, p. 246) conclude that "much of the theory underlying stock repurchases is applied in practice . . . . Some gaps between the theory and practice of common stock buyback do exist." However, their questionnaire is unable to fully explain the rationale for this discrepancy.

The Wansley, Lane, and Sarkar (1989) Survey of Share Repurchases and Tender Offer Premiums

The purpose of the Wansley, Lane, and Sarkar (1989) survey is to provide direct evidence of the attitudes of management toward share repurchase and the setting of tender offer premiums in repurchases. In 1987, the authors send a questionnaire to the CFOs of large U.S. corporations as identified in the 1986 *Institutional Investor* annual CFO roster. To ensure a suitably large sample of tender offer repurchasers, they also identify 87 firms from the Merrill Lynch corporate tender offer database for 1983 to 1985. Of the 620 questionnaires mailed, Wansley, Lane, and Sarkar obtain 140 usable responses, a response rate of 22.6 percent. Of these firms, 70.0 percent indicate that they have repurchased shares. The authors find no significant differences in means between repurchasers and nonrepurchasers for various accounting variables (size, growth, investments, dividend payout, and leverage).

The questionnaire consists of 17 statements associated with six reasons for repurchasing shares: (1) dividend substitution hypothesis, (2) leverage hypothesis, (3) reissue hypothesis, (4) investment hypothesis, (5) information signaling hypothesis, and (6) wealth transfer hypothesis. The authors often use multiple statements to represent each hypothesis. The survey instrument also contains 11 statements associated with determinants of premiums in tender offer repurchases. The questionnaire asks respondents to indicate whether they agree or disagree with the statement by using a seven-point scale, from −3 (strongly disagree) to +3 (strongly agree), with 0 as no opinion.

Wansley, Lane, and Sarkar (1989) report only the ranking, but not the percentage response, for each of the 17 statements involving the reasons for repurchasing. Of the six hypotheses for repurchasing stock, both repurchasers and nonrepurchasers express the strongest level of agreement with the information signaling hypothesis; that is, both groups agree that firms repurchase shares because "management felt that the stock was undervalued" and "to signal investors of confidence in the future level of earnings and stock prices." Both of these findings are consistent with the results reported by Baker, Gallagher, and Morgan (1981). The results show some support for the leverage hypothesis but not for negative reasons for repurchasing shares (i.e., dividend substitution and insufficient investments). There is mixed evidence on the wealth transfer hypothesis, which states that repurchases transfer wealth to nonparticipating from participating (selling) shareholders.

Similar to Baker, Gallagher, and Morgan (1981), Wansley, Lane, and Sarkar (1989) find that the two groups share similar rankings on the various statements, as documented by a Spearman rank order correlation coefficient of 0.828, significant at the 0.001 level. Yet, t-tests show significant differences in the degree of agreement/disagreement on six of the 17 statements. Specifically, the two groups differ in their views that firms repurchase shares (1) because the company lacked sufficient investment opportunities to use available cash; (2) to provide shares for dividend reinvestment plans; (3) to reduce the cost of servicing small, odd-lot shareholdings; (4) to provide shares for conversion of other securities; (5) as a substitute for a cash dividend; and (6) to buy out minority shareholders.

Wansley, Lane, and Sarkar (1989) also investigate factors influencing the tender offer premium. They examine three groups: the repurchasing group, the nonrepurchasing group, and those who indicate their firms repurchase shares by a tender offer (as a subset of the repurchasing group). Substantial agreement exists among the CFOs on the effects these factors have on tender offer premiums in repurchases. For example, all three groups indicate the highest level of agreement with four statements on tender offer premiums. Specifically, premiums are larger (1) when the share repurchase is part of a strategy to avoid a takeover, (2) the greater management's confidence is in future earnings and stock prices, (3) the larger the repurchase in percentage of shares outstanding is, and (4) when debt securities are offered (exchange offer) instead of cash.

Based on their survey evidence, Wansley, Lane, and Sarkar (1989, p. 107) conclude,

> These findings cast doubt on several reasons suggested for share repurchase. Indeed, the only motive for which there is significant agreement is to convey management's opinion of the firm's present and future value, results consistent with a positive market reaction to repurchase announcements.

The Tsetsekos, Kaufman, and Gitman (1991) Survey

Tsetsekos, Kaufman, and Gitman (1991) survey CFOs of 1,000 large firms— *Fortune* 500 firms and 500 firms selected from Compustat—to understand the precipitating circumstances and motivations leading to share repurchases. A *precipitating circumstance* refers to a specific event leading to a repurchase, whereas a *motivation* refers to a general reason for engaging in a repurchase. They receive 183 usable questionnaires containing answers to at least half of the questions, an 18.3 percent response rate. The authors use Likert scales to obtain the views of the responding financial executives.

Their results show that the most important precipitating circumstance leading to repurchases is "the low stock price." Respondents typically disagree that firms should implement stock repurchase plans only during periods when stock prices are declining. Unlike Baker, Gallagher, and Morgan (1981), Tsetsekos, Kaufman, and Gitman (1991) find that the most frequently expressed motivation is "the desire to change the capital structure," which supports the leverage hypothesis. Another highly rated motive for share repurchases is to increase the stock price. The majority of responses are also consistent with the signaling hypothesis; that is, respondents generally agree that repurchases serve as a signal to the market that management believes the stock is undervalued.

The authors also ask other questions about repurchases. Unlike Baker, Gallagher, and Morgan (1981), Tsetsekos, Kaufman, and Gitman (1991) find that managers appear to view repurchases as a financing rather than an investment decision. Their evidence also shows that firms finance most repurchases with available cash balances. Additionally, respondents generally disagree that repurchases benefit participating shareholders more than nonparticipating shareholders. This view is inconsistent with the wealth transfer hypothesis. Finally, the respondents tend to agree that firms should not forego profitable capital-spending plans to undertake stock repurchases.

The Baker, Powell, and Veit (2003) Survey of Open-Market Repurchases

Baker, Powell, and Veit (2003) survey top financial executives to learn their views about their firm's share repurchases. To develop their sample, they use a proprietary database developed by Birinyi Associates Inc. consisting of common stock repurchase announcements made primarily by large U.S. firms. The authors select companies that announced new repurchase programs between January 1998 and September 1999. Their final sample consists of 642 U.S. corporations whose shares trade on the NYSE, American Stock Exchange (AMEX), and NASDAQ.

The authors model their questionnaire after Baker, Gallagher, and Morgan (1981); Wansley, Lane, and Sarkar (1989); and Tsetsekos, Kaufman, and Gitman (1991) to improve their ability to make comparisons. Their pretested survey instrument consists of three parts. One part of the questionnaire asks background questions about each firm's most recent share repurchase. Another part of the survey queries managers to rate the level of importance of each of 20 reasons for their firm's most recent common stock repurchase on a four-point scale, from 0 (none) to 3 (high). The final part asks managers to indicate their level of agreement or disagreement with five statements by using a five-point scale, from −2 (strongly disagree) to +2 (strongly agree), with 0 as no opinion. After conducting several mailings in early 2000, Baker, Powell, and Veit (2003) receive 218 usable responses, representing a 34.0 percent response rate.

Baker, Powell, and Veit (2003) use two methods to test for nonresponse bias. First, they compare the responses for firms from the first mailing to those of the second mailing. Using chi-square tests, they find only a few instances of significant differences at the 0.05 level. Second, they conduct t-tests for differences in means between responding and nonresponding firms on five firm characteristics (total assets, net sales, total debt-to-total capital, dividend yield, and price-to-book ratio). No significant differences exist between the responding and nonresponding firms on any of these variables at the 0.05 level. Thus, they conclude that nonresponse bias is likely to be small.

In response to the questions on their most recent repurchase, most (89.8 percent) of the respondents report using an open-market repurchase. This response shows a marked increase from the 64.4 percent of respondents who report using open-market repurchases in Baker, Gallagher, and Morgan (1981). The increase in the use of open-market repurchases is consistent with prior empirical evidence by Barclay and Smith (1988) and Grullon and Ikenberry (2000), among others. Almost three quarters of respondents (74.5 percent) indicate that the most important circumstance that led to the firm's last common stock repurchase was a low (undervalued) stock price. This finding is consistent with the results reported by Tsetsekos, Kaufman, and Gitman (1991). Baker, Powell, and Veit (2003) find that the primary source of funds used to finance the repurchase is available cash balances (71.1 percent), followed by new short-term debt (19.1 percent).

When asked about the reasons for their most recent open-market repurchase, the respondents indicate that the most important motives are as follows: (1) add value to shareholders, (2) acquire stock at a bargain price, (3) increase earnings per share, (4) increase the stock price, and (5) best use of excess cash. At least 60 percent of respondents view these reasons as being of moderate or high importance.

The relatively high ranking that respondents give to the "best use of excess cash" is consistent with the results from Baker, Gallagher, and Morgan (1981). The lowest-ranked reason is to "use the stock as part of a takeover defense strategy;" 89.6 percent of respondents give no importance to this reason. Thus, this evidence does not provide support for the takeover deterrence hypothesis.

Baker, Powell, and Veit (2003) comment that their evidence supports some of the more common reasons for share repurchases cited in the academic literature, especially the undervaluation version of the signaling hypothesis. They note that the relative importance management attaches to several reasons may have changed over the past few decades. In particular, they find fairly low support for three reasons that previous survey studies (Baker, Gallagher, and Morgan 1981; Wansley, Lane, and Sarkar 1989; Tsetsekos, Kaufman, and Gitman 1991) rate highly; namely, to convey positive information possessed by management to the market, to provide for stock option privileges or bonuses for employees, and to remove a large block of stock overhanging the market. On the other hand, the authors find increased support for changing the firm's capital structure and providing a tax-efficient way to distribute funds to shareholders as reasons for repurchasing shares of stock.

Finally, Baker, Powell, and Veit (2003) investigate respondents' opinions about five issues related to share repurchases. One of the more interesting results is that a majority (65.6 percent) agree that the announcement of a common stock repurchase typically leads to an increase in the firm's stock price. This finding is consistent with results from numerous empirical studies (e.g., Masulis 1980; Dann 1981; Vermaelen 1981; Ikenberry, Lakonishok, and Vermaelen 1995; Stephens and Weisbach 1998) that report significant excess returns accompanying share repurchases.

The Baker, Veit, and Powell (2003) Survey of Stock Repurchases and False Signals

Prior survey research provides support for the signaling hypothesis for share repurchases. For example, Wansley, Lane, and Sarkar (1989) find that the second-most important reason cited by managers for repurchasing stock is to signal investors that managers are confident about the company's future. Tsetsekos, Kaufman, and Gitman (1991) report that the third–most important motive that managers give for repurchasing stock is to send a signal (information) to the market. Baker, Veit, and Powell (2003) focus on the signaling motive for repurchases—specifically, whether managers intentionally engage in false signaling.

As previously discussed, research evidence shows that a firm's stock price typically increases when firms announce the repurchase of common stock. Many studies attribute these increases to the signaling effect (e.g., Masulis 1980; Dann 1981; Vermaelen 1981). Although there is an extensive body of literature that involves repurchases, little research exists about their possible legal and ethical concerns. Some firms that announce their intention of repurchasing shares of common stock either repurchase no shares or fewer shares than initially announced.

Because firms have no obligation to carry through with an actual repurchase plan, the number of shares the firm actually repurchases remains in doubt. Although the practice of firms intentionally announcing the repurchase of more shares than they plan to repurchase is technically illegal, the expected increase in the price surrounding the announcement may give firms an incentive to make such false announcements. Evidence indicates that some firms announce share repurchase plans without completing the repurchase (Kracher and Johnson 1997; Kirch, BarNiv, and Zucca 1998; Stephens and Weisbach 1998).

Although Baker, Veit, and Powell (2003) use the same sample of top financial executives and the same questionnaire as Baker, Powell, and Veit (2003), they use different questions from the survey instrument in each study. Their results focus on two areas: (1) the prevalence of repurchasing fewer shares than initially announced and the reasons underlying this practice and (2) the opinions of the respondents about practices used in repurchasing stock. Regarding the first area, the evidence shows that 38.6 percent of respondents believe repurchasing fewer shares than announced is a common practice. When asked if their firms had engaged in this practice between 1995 and the early 2000s, 28.7 percent respond positively. The primary reason reported for repurchasing fewer shares than initially announced is that "the firm is still in the midst of the repurchases program" (26.1 percent), followed by "the stock price rose making the repurchase of shares less attractive than initially anticipated" (16.3 percent). Regarding the views about repurchase practices, managers appear to be unsure about the legality of this activity. Also, they generally believe that the intentional repurchase of fewer shares than announced is unethical, sends a false signal to the market, and damages the firm's credibility with its stockholders. Further, managers believe that firms repurchasing fewer shares than announced should publicly reveal both the reason for not repurchasing all shares and the amount by which the repurchase fell short of the firm's announced intentions.

The Brav, Graham, Harvey, and Michaely (2005) Survey

Brav, Graham, Harvey, and Michaely (2005) ask financial managers about their opinions and motives underlying their firm's payout policies for cash dividends and share repurchases. They administer the survey in 2002 and receive a 16 percent response rate resulting from 384 surveys from 256 public companies and 128 private companies. They also conduct in-depth interviews with an additional 23 financial executives. The authors examine the representativeness of the survey firms relative to the universe of firms listed on the NYSE, AMEX, and NASDAQ based on sales, debt to assets, dividend yield, earnings per share, credit rating, and book to market. The results show that the firms surveyed are larger and have better credit ratings than the typical firms in the population but are representative on the other dimensions (debt to assets, dividend yield, earnings per share, and book to market). The following discussion examines the results from the 167 firms that repurchase their shares.

The questionnaire asks the financial managers to indicate the importance of 23 factors for repurchases by using a five-point scale, from −2 to +2. The repurchasing firms show the highest level of agreement (around 85 percent agree or strongly agree) with two statements: market price of our stock (if our stock is a good investment relative to its true value) and payout decisions convey information about our company to investors. These findings appear to provide strong support for the signaling hypothesis. In fact, Brav et al. (2005) note that both the surveys and interviews reveal a pervasive view that repurchases convey information. Yet, when considering other evidence gleaned from this study, they conclude that this conveyance of information does not appear to be related to signaling in the academic sense. For example, their evidence shows that managers reject the idea that they pay dividends as a costly signal to convey their firm's true worth or to intentionally separate their firm from competitors. Thus, they find little support for the assumptions and resulting predictions of academic signaling theories.

Some of the results from this survey suggest that managers use repurchases to reduce excess cash holdings, which is consistent with Jensen's (1986) free cash flow hypothesis. Overall, the authors find little support for the clientele hypotheses. Although some believe (e.g., Easterbrook 1984; Jensen 1986) that firms can use payouts to self-impose discipline, the survey results show that about 80 percent of the respondents believe that discipline imposed by repurchases is unimportant. Brav et al. (2005) conclude that tax considerations play a secondary role, which is consistent with Julio and Ikenberry (2004). While the results indicate that managers do not view the relation between dividends and repurchases as a one-for-one substitution, the dividend payers generally indicate that at the margin, they would reduce dividend increases to increase repurchases.

Brav et al. (2005) find that the Miller and Modigliani (1961) framework helps to explain repurchase policy. The responding managers believe that operation and investment decisions are more important than share repurchases. Almost 80 percent of managers indicate that they make repurchase decisions after investment decisions. Thus, the authors conclude that managers treat repurchases as the residual cash flow, as implied by Miller and Modigliani. Evidence by Brav et al. shows that many executives view repurchases as more flexible than dividends. Managers use repurchases in an attempt to time the equity market by accelerating repurchases when they believe their stock price is low.

The survey evidence also shows that CFOs are aware of the effect of repurchases on EPS; that is, repurchasing in an attempt to increase EPS is very important. This finding is consistent with Bens, Nagar, Skinner, and Wong (2003). However, Grullon and Ikenberry (2000) contend that the "EPS bump" argument is fundamentally flawed because it effectively assumes that the firm has idle or unproductive assets and that by getting rid of such assets, the firm's productivity (e.g., economic value added or return on capital) increases. This argument is not necessarily true because repurchasing shares with cash or new can affect a firm's ability to generate future earnings.

The de Jong, van Dijk, and Veld (2003) Survey of Canadian Firms

The de Jong, van Dijk, and Veld (2003) study investigates the dividend and share repurchase policies of Canadian firms. The authors note that Canada is the only country besides the United States where share repurchases often occur. Such repurchases are typically in the form of open-market repurchases. Also, in the Canadian market, a large number of firms do not pay dividends (La Porta, Lopez-de-Silanes, Shleifer, and Vishny 2000).

In 1998, de Jong, van Dijk, and Veld (2003) send a questionnaire to either the CFO or chief executive officer (CEO) of the 500 largest nonfinancial Canadian firms listed on the Toronto Stock Exchange and receive 191 usable responses, resulting in a 38.2 percent response rate. Of the responding firms, 35 percent indicate having undertaken a share repurchase within the preceding three years.

The approach of de Jong, van Dijk, and Veld (2003) differs from previous survey studies on repurchases using questionnaires to ask questions about repurchase theories and other issues. Instead of directly reporting the survey results, the authors use questionnaires to obtain firm characteristics and then use logit models to test the different theories using these firm characteristics. They test three models of dividend and share repurchases. The first model treats dividends and share repurchases in isolation. In the second model, dividends and share repurchases influence each other. The third model, a nested logit model, assumes that a firm first decides whether it wants to pay out cash to its shareholders and then decides on the form of payout. Because the authors find the strongest support for the third model, the following discussion focuses on the results of this model.

The results of the third model suggest that the existence of free cash flow drives the payout decision. Confirmation of the free cash flow hypothesis is consistent with earlier empirical research (e.g., Stephens and Weisback 1998; Dittmar 2000; Li and McNally 2003). Tax and behavioral preferences influence the choice of dividends as payout method, whereas tax preferences drive the choice of share repurchases. The evidence also suggests that the payout for firms with managerial options plans is less likely to be dividends than repurchases.

Finally, the results show a large information asymmetry amongst outsiders, which largely confirms the Brennan and Thakor (1990) model. In this model, shareholders have differing amounts of information about the firm's activities. Assuming a fixed cost of collecting information, large shareholders have a greater incentive to become informed about a firm's activities than small shareholders. Thus, share repurchases are associated with a redistribution of wealth from small to large shareholders. Consequently, firms are more likely to pay dividends than to repurchase shares when a large information asymmetry amongst shareholders exists.

The Bancel, Mittoo, and Bhattacharyya (2005) Survey of European Firms

Bancel, Mittoo, and Bhattacharyya (2005) conduct a survey of managers from 16 European countries to examine cross-country determinants of payout policy. They compare the views of European managers with those of U.S. managers in Brav et al. (2005) and across European countries. Unlike in the United States and Canada, some European countries prohibit repurchases. In 2003, the authors conduct two mailings to the CFOs of 1,131 firms drawn from the *Financial Times* European Stock Exchange pages and receive 93 responses, representing an 8.2 percent response rate. The following discussion focuses on the level of importance that managers place on various factors if and when their firms repurchase shares. The respondents rate these determinants of repurchase policy on a scale of 0 (not important) to 4 (very important).

The responding European managers tend to view repurchase as an investment decision rather than a dividend decision, which is similar to evidence reported by Baker, Gallagher, and Morgan (1981) for U.S. managers. Slightly more than 90 percent of the responding managers view the market price of the stock as important or very important in the repurchase decision. Based on non-survey evidence, Brockman and Chung (2001) also find that a firm's stock price affects its repurchase decision. More than three-quarters (77.8 percent) of the respondents view the availability of good investment opportunities as an important or very important factor in repurchase policy. About 64 percent of the respondents believe that "merger and acquisition strategy" (unrelated to take-over deterrence) and "having extra cash/liquid assets" also influence repurchase decisions. A slight majority view "increasing earnings per share" (51.7 percent) and "stability of future earnings" (50.6 percent) as factors influencing repur-chases. Finding that share repurchase is often motivated by the desire to manage earnings corroborates the findings of nonsurvey research such as that of Vafeas, Vlittis, Katranis, and Ockree (2003) and Hribar, Jenkins, and Johnson (2004). The survey evidence also shows that European managers generally view repur-chases as a tool of flexibility rather than a substitute for dividends. Bancel, Mittoo, and Bhattacharyya's (2005) survey results show little support for repur-chase explanations involving agency costs (disciplining the firm to make effi-cient decisions) and stock option plans (offsetting the dilutive effect) and practically no support for personal tax considerations.

Overall, Bancel, Mittoo, and Bhattacharyya (2005) find that the important factors governing share repurchase policy appear highly similar between European managers and their U.S. peers as reported by Brav et al. (2005). Nonetheless, European managers attach less importance than their U.S. coun-terparts to share repurchase programs for increasing EPS (52 percent versus 75 percent, respectively) and for overcoming the dilutive impact of stock option plans (29 percent versus 67 percent, respectively). Finally, their findings support the notion that legal - system variables play a less important role in repurchase policy compared to dividend policy because regulation concerning repurchases varies substantially, even between countries with similar legal systems.

Summary of Survey Evidence on Share Repurchases

Table 7.1 indicates that survey evidence about share repurchases is available from an array of U.S. and non-U.S. studies. Table 7.2 lists some of the major conclusions from survey research on repurchase decisions. Managers' survey responses indicate that they increasingly favor the greater flexibility offered by share repurchases compared to cash dividends. Additionally, strong support exists for the notion that managers repurchase their firm's shares when they view them as undervalued.

Although there is no agreement on the main motive for repurchasing shares, Table 7.3 indicates that some versions of the signaling motive garner more support than others, especially the view that a firm's stock is a good investment relative to its true value. Strong evidence also exists that managers view repurchase decisions as conveying private information about their companies to investors. As Brav et al. (2005) note, managers from their survey believe that repurchases convey at least as much information as dividends. In some instances, firms may even send false signals. Overall, the survey evidence regarding signaling appears stronger than other nonsurvey studies, especially the more recent ones that provide mixed support for the signaling hypothesis. Managerial views about other explanations for share repurchases reveal varying levels of support, which is consistent with other empirical evidence regarding repurchase theories reported earlier in the chapter. Thus, the factors that affect the decisions of some firms to repurchase shares may be unimportant or at least less important to other firms. As with the explanations for why firms pay cash dividends, a one-size-fits-all approach does not appear to be fully satisfactory in explaining why firms repurchase their stock.

Special Dividends

Another means of distributing cash to shareholders besides cash dividends and share repurchases is through a special dividend, also termed a specially designated dividend (SDD). The designation "special" informs shareholders that the firm may not continue to pay the dividend in the future. Over the past 50 years or so, the role that SDDs play in dividend policy has evolved. During the 1950s, almost half of the firms listed on the NYSE paid special dividends. Some firms paid special dividends year after year. In these instances, such payments were precursors to increases in regular dividends. Since the 1980s, the frequency of

TABLE 7.1 Survey evidence on share repurchases

This table shows representative studies involving share repurchases, the number of usable responses, response rates, and sample characteristics.

Author and date of publication	Usable responses	Response rate (%)	Sample characteristics
			A. U.S. studies
Baker and Rheinstein (1980)	58	73.4	CFOs of 78 firms with odd-lot purchase offers between September 1977 and May 1979
Baker, Gallagher, and Morgan (1981)	73 repurchasers, 63 nonrepurchasers	48.7 42.0	CFOs of NYSE-listed firms with a total of 150 repurchases and 150 non-repurchases
Wansley, Lane, and Sarkar (1989)	98 repurchasers, 42 non-repurchasers	22.6	CFOs from 620 large U.S. corporations
Tsetsekos, Kaufman, and Gitman (1991)	183	18.2	Managers of 1,000 firms, consisting of the *Fortune* 500 and 500 firms selected from Compustat
Baker, Powell, and Veit (2003); Baker, Veit, and Powell (2003)	218	34.0	640 top financial executives of primarily large U.S. firms drawn from a proprietary database developed by Birinyi Associates Inc.
Brav, Graham, Harvey, and Michaely (2004)	384 plus 23 interviews	16.c	Sample of financial executives from a cross-section of public and private firms coupled with 23 in-depth interviews
			B. Non-U.S. studies
de Jong, van Dijk, and Veld (2003)	191	38.2	Sample of CFOs and CEOs of the 500 largest nonfinancial Canadian firms listed on the Toronto Stock Exchange
Bancel, Bhattacharyya, and Mittoo (2005)	93	8.2	A total of 1,131 firms from 16 European countries

TABLE 7.2 Key conclusions of share repurchase surveys

This table presents some major conclusions from representative share repurchase surveys.

Author and date of publication	Major conclusions
A. U.S. studies	
Baker and Rheinstein (1980)	• The most important motive for odd-lot buyback is the cost savings, followed by considering the buyback as an investment when the price of the stock is low. • The most common premium offers over the market price is from 11 to 20 percent.
Baker, Gallagher, and Morgan (1981)	• Respondents view share repurchases as a good investment of excess cash and as a means of providing shares for employee bonus or stock option plans. • Respondents do not view share repurchases as a substitute for paying cash dividends.
Wansley, Lane, and Sarkar (1989)	• Respondents believe that managers use share repurchase to signal their confidence in the firm, which management believes is not being incorporated in the stock price. • Managers do not believe that repurchases are a substitute for cash dividends and result from insufficient investments. • Attitudes of repurchasers differ by method of repurchase and industry.
Tsetsekos, Kaufman, and Gitman (1991)	• The responding chief financial executives believe the low stock price is the most important circumstance precipitating share repurchase. • The most frequently expressed motive for share repurchases is the desire to change the capital structure, followed by the desire to increase the stock price. • Evidence is also supportive of the signaling hypothesis.
Baker, Powell, and Veit (2003)	• The responding managers view the low (undervalued) stock price as the most important circumstance that led to the firm's most recent stock repurchase. • The responding managers cite reasons for open-market repurchase that are consistent with the signaling hypothesis—specifically, the undervaluation version of this hypothesis. • Evidence suggests shifts in the importance managers attach to the reasons for repurchasing shares over the past several decades.

(Continued)

TABLE 7.2 (cont'd) Key conclusions of share repurchase surveys

Author and date of publication	Major conclusions
Baker, Veit, and Powell (2003)	• The responding financial executives report that repurchasing fewer shares than announced is a common practice. • Responding managers are uncertain about the legality of this activity. • Respondents believe that the intentional repurchase of fewer shares than announced is unethical, sends a false signal to the market, and damages the firm's credibility with stockholders.
Brav, Graham, Harvey, and Michaely (2004)	• Management views provide little support for agency, signaling, and clientele hypotheses for paying dividends. • Managers generally believe that taxes are not a dominant factor affecting repurchases. • Managers perceive that repurchases provide flexibility and can be used in an attempt to time the equity market or to increase earnings per share.

	B. Non-U.S. studies
de Jong, van Dijk, and Veld (2003)	• The existence of free cash flows drives the payout decision. • Factors such as tax and behavioral preferences lead to dividends as the payout choice, whereas tax preferences drive the choice for repurchases. • The payout for firms with managerial options plans is less likely to be dividends than repurchases. • The existence of asymmetric information amongst outsiders is associated with a preference for dividends over share repurchases.
Bancel, Bhattacharyya, and Mittoo (2005)	• The undervaluation of a firm is a driving force for European managers in repurchasing their shares. • European managers view repurchases as a tool of flexibility rather than a substitute for dividends. • The important factors governing share repurchase policy appear similar between European and U.S. firms.

paying SDDs has waned as the popularity of stock repurchases has increased (DeAngelo, DeAngelo, and Skinner 2000).

Several academic studies show that the announcement of special dividends conveys private information about the firm, which the market typically views as favorable (e.g., Brickley 1983; DeAngelo, DeAngelo, and Skinner 2000). Evidence shows that no significant long-term returns follow special dividends

TABLE 7.3 Survey evidence on explanations for share repurchases

This table presents survey evidence, on average, about various theories, hypotheses, and explanations for share repurchases.

Author and date	Taxes	Signaling and undervaluation	Agency costs/free cash flow	Capital structure	Takeover deterrence	Stock options
A. U.S. studies						
Baker, Gallagher, and Morgan (1981)	Not supported	Supported		Not supported	Not supported	Supported
Wansley, Lane, and Sarkar (1989)	Not supported	Supported		Weak support	Mixed support	Mixed support
Tsetsekos, Kaufman, and Gitman (1991)		Supported		Supported		
Baker, Powell, and Veit (2003)	Some support	Supported	Not supported	Some support	Not supported	Some support
Brav, Graham, Harvey, and Michaely (2004)	Little support	Little support	Little support			
B. Non-U.S. studies						
de Jong, van Dijk, and Veld (2003)	Supported	Supported	Supported			Some support
Bancel, Bhattacharyya, and Mittoo (2005)	Not supported	Supported	Little support			Little support

(Ikenberry, Lakonishok, and Vermaelen 1995; Peyer and Vermaelen 2009). As discussed shortly, the finance literature offers three common explanations for the positive market reaction to announcements of SDDs: (1) an agency cost explanation, (2) a signaling explanation, and (3) wealth transfer explanation.

The market reaction to the announcement of a special dividend payment and an open-market share repurchase is similar, which may initially suggest that they are close substitutes. Several differences exist, however, between these two methods of distributing cash, both in terms of their information content and their tax consequences. First, firms declaring an SDD are obligated to pay the amount of the dividend, whereas firms announcing an open-market repurchase often do not carry through with the repurchase plan. According to Gombola and Liu (2009, p. 319), "The special dividend is a bird in the hand of a cash distribution to shareholders whereas the open-market repurchase announcement is a bird in the bush of a cash distribution that shareholders might never receive." Second, the tax consequences differ between special dividends and stock repurchases depending on the tax regimes in different countries and the year in which the firm distributed the dividend.

Explanations for Special Dividends

There are various rationals for paying special dividends. This section discusses the agency cost, signaling, and wealth transfer explanations.

An Agency Cost Explanation

According to the agency cost explanation, a special dividend may reduce the agency problems associated with generating and holding free cash flow. Distributing free cash flows to shareholders reduces the possibility that management will invest these cash flows inappropriately. Studies by Gombola and Liu (1999) and Lie (2000) provide support for the agency cost explanation. For example, Lie finds that the stock price reaction is positively related to excess funds held by firms for large special dividends but not for small special dividends. Howe, He, and Kao (1992) study the market's reaction to share repurchases and to SDDs. According to the agency theory explanation, firms with a high level of free cash flow and poor investment opportunities should have the strongest positive market reaction to the announcement of SDDs. They use Tobin's Q to measure the firm's level of investment opportunities. Their results show that the market's reaction to share repurchases and SDDs is about the same for both high-Q and low-Q firms. This presents an empirical puzzle: If Jensen's (1986) free cash flow theory applies to dividend changes, it should also apply to these analogous events.

A Signaling Explanation

According to the conditional signaling explanation of the market reaction to SDD announcements, the market interprets this news as a credible signal of a firm's improving its future earnings and cash flows. Nonsurvey studies by Brickley (1983), Jayaraman and Shastri (1988), Shih (1992), Mitra (1997), Chhachhi and Davidson (1997), and Gombola and Liu (1999) provide empirical support for the signaling hypothesis. Crutchley, Hudson, and Jensen (2003) find evidence that firms experience high levels of earnings in the year before the SDD announcement, but earnings generally decline in the year after the announcement. Hence, their results do not support the signaling explanation.

A Wealth Transfer Explanation

The wealth transfer explanation states that special dividends transfer wealth from bondholders to shareholders. The rationale for this explanation is that distribution of cash to stockholders reduces a firm's creditworthiness and lowers its credit rating because the firm has fewer assets available to support the firm's debt. Thus, the value of the firm's debt decreases but is offset by an increase in the value of the firm's equity. A nonsurvey study by Jayaraman and Shastri (1988) does not provide support for a wealth transfer explanation.

Recap of Explanations of Special Dividends

Of the three common explanations for paying special dividends, the strongest empirical support exists for a signaling explanation. Still, an agency cost explanation cannot be ruled out as a factor contributing to the positive market reaction to SDD announcements. The wealth transfer explanation lacks empirical support.

Survey Evidence on Special Dividends

Several survey studies examine special dividends. This section provides a summary of these studies.

The Baker, Mukherjee, and Powell (2005) Survey

In conducting their survey, Baker, Mukherjee, and Powell (2005) identify three main objectives: (1) to identify why firms choose to pay SDDs, (2) to discover why firms choose to use regular dividends or repurchase shares as a means of distributing temporary excess cash instead of paying SDDs, and (3) to learn how managers view various statements about SDDs derived from prior empirical research. They use the Center for Research in Security Prices (CRSP) database to identify firms that paid at least one SDD during the period from 1994 through 2001. Their final sample consists of 343 separate companies (250 NASDAQ, 51 NYSE, and 42 AMEX).

Baker, Mukherjee, and Powell (2005) pretest preliminary versions of their questionnaire among a small group of finance faculty members and master of business administration (MBA) students. The final version of their one-page survey consists of six questions and 14 statements. To respond to each of the 14 statements, the respondents use a five-point scale, from −2 (strongly disagree) to +2 (strongly agree), with 0 as no opinion. The authors send two mailings to the senior executives during 2003. Of the 343 companies surveyed in early 2003, questionnaires from 21 of these firms could not be delivered. The mailings result in 45 usable surveys, representing 14.0 percent of the 322 delivered surveys. The authors test for nonresponse bias by comparing the arithmetic means of five characteristics of responding firms to those of nonresponding firms. The t-test results show no significant difference in means at the 0.05 level for the following characteristics: total assets, net sales, price-to-book ratio, dividend yield, and dividend payout ratio.

The results of an open-ended question show that two reasons given by respondents constitute almost three-quarters of the responses. Responding firms indicate that the primary reasons they distribute excess cash as SDDs are (1) they have strong earnings or cash flows (40.0 percent) and (2) they want to increase, at least temporarily, the yield to shareholders (33.3 percent). The first reason for paying SDDs is consistent with evidence by Brickley (1983) and Crutchley, Hudson, and Jensen (2003) that firms experience unexpectedly high earnings during the year of the SDD announcement.

Another open-ended question asks respondents to state why firms choose to use regular dividends or repurchase shares to distribute temporary excess cash instead of paying a special dividend. The two top motives for initiating or continuing to use dividends are having strong earnings or cash flows (25.8 percent) and serving as a part of standard dividend policy (25.8 percent). The first motive is consistent with evidence by Crutchley, Hudson, and Jensen (2003), who document that firms paying both regular dividends and SDDs have unexpectedly high earnings during the year of the announcement. The major motive for repurchasing shares, mentioned by 34.6 percent of the respondents, is the perception that the shares are undervalued. This finding is consistent with evidence on the relationship between share repurchases and market undervaluation such as that provided by Ikenberry, Lakonishok, and Vermaelen (1995). The second-most important reason for repurchasing shares, given by 28.8 percent of the respondents, is to improve accounting measures of firm performance such as EPS.

Finally, the Baker, Hudson, and Jensen (2005) survey asks managers how they view statements derived from prior empirical research. Of the 14 statements, most respondents (92.9 percent) agree that firms tend to repurchase shares, instead of paying SDDs, when managers believe their firm's current stock is underpriced. Other empirical evidence supports the notion that firms are undervalued at the time they announce a repurchase (e.g., Ikenberry, Lakonishok, and Vermaelen 1995; Stephens and Weisbach 1998). The statement with the second-highest level of agreement (72.5 percent) is that the stock market generally views the announcement of an unexpected SDD as conveying positive information about a firm's short-term (current) earnings. This evidence is consistent with the empirical results reported by Gombola and Liu (1999), Lie (2000), and Crutchley, Hudson, and Jensen (2003). Baker, Mukherjee, and Powell (2004, p. 147) conclude, "Taken as a whole, a major implication of this study is that the results lend support to the signaling explanation for the disbursement of excess funds, but not the free cash flow or wealth transfer explanations."

Summary of Survey Evidence on Special Dividends

The survey evidence on SDDs is very limited. Panel A of Table 7.4 indicates Baker, Mukherjee, and Powell (2005) is the only comprehensive survey on SDDs. Panel A of Table 7.5 and panel A of Table 7.6 indicate that survey evidence lends support to the signaling explanation for SDDs but not to the free cash flow or wealth transfer explanations.

Stock Splits

A stock split is a corporate action in which a firm divides its existing shares into multiple shares; that is, a stock split results in a reduction of the stock's par value and a consequent increase in the number of shares proportionate to the split. Although the number of shares outstanding increases by a specific multiple, the total dollar value of the shares should remain the same compared to presplit amounts. Theoretically, the market price of a stock subject to a stock split should decline in exact proportion to the split ratio, other factors remaining unchanged. For example, if the stock price is $100 a share before a 2-for-1 stock split, the stock price should drop to $50 a share but with twice the number of shares outstanding. Thus, a 2-for-1 stock split is similar in concept to exchanging one $100 bill for two $50 bills. In theory, a stock split results in no real value because shareholders should receive no tangible benefits. Because the proportional ownership does not change, a stock split is analogous to cutting a pie into more but smaller slices.

In practice, empirical evidence shows that the new share price is greater than would be expected by dividing the old share price by the new number of shares. Thus, a stock split appears to be more than a cosmetic accounting change that reduces a stock's par value but instead generates excess returns on the announcement date and ex-date (see, for example, Fama, Fisher, Jensen, and Roll, 1969; Bar-Yosef and Brown 1977; Grinblatt, Masulis, and Titman 1984; Lamoureux and Poon 1987). Given the documented evidence on a wide range of both positive and negative effects associated with stock splits, Easley, O'Hara, and Saar (2001, p. 25) conclude that "stock splits remain one of the most popular and least understood phenomena in equity markets." Thus, stock splits pose a conundrum to finance theorists. These supposed nonevents appear to have real effects. Not surprisingly, much research examines the motives for stock splits and the impact that stock splits have on shareholders' wealth.

TABLE 7.4 Survey evidence on special dividends, stock splits, and stock dividends

This table shows representative studies involving special dividends, stock dividends and stock splits, the number of usable responses, response rates, and sample characteristics.

Author and date of publication	Usable responses	Response rate (%)	Sample characteristics
		A. Special dividends	
Baker, Mukherjee, and Powell (2005)	45	14.0	322 NASDAQ, NYSE, and AMEX firms that paid at least one special dividend during 1994 through 2001
		B. Stock splits	
Dolley (1933)	36	40.9	Eighty-eight firms issuing stock splits over the period from 1922 through 1930
Baker and Gallagher (1980)	63 split group, 64 control group	63.0 split group, 64.0 control group	Two groups: (1) a split group consisting of 100 firms issuing stock splits in 1978 and (2) a control group consisting of 100 randomly selected firms neither issuing stock splits nor stock dividends
Baker and Powell (1993)	136	54.8	NYSE and AMEX firms issuing stock splits of at least 25 percent from 1988 through 1990

C. Stock dividends

Eisemann and Moses (1978)	39 stock dividend payers, 58 nonstock dividend payers	48.8 stock dividend, 65.2 nonstock dividend	Two groups: (1) a stock-payer group consisting of 80 NYSE firms that paid a stock dividend of less than 25 percent in 1974 and (2) a non-stock-dividend-payer group consisting of 89 NYSE firms that did not issue a stock split or a stock dividend during 1970 to 1974
Baker and Phillips (1993)	136	45.5	NYSE, AMEX, and NASDAQ firms that paid at least one stock dividend between 1988 and 1990
Frankfurter and Lane (1998)	127 stock dividend group, 38 control group	34.7 stock dividend, 25.3 nonstock dividend	Two groups: (1) a stock-dividend-paying group consisting of 366 firms that paid at least one stock dividend between 1986 and 1993 and (2) a control group consisting of 150 firms not paying a stock dividend during the same time period

TABLE 7.5 Key conclusions of surveys on special dividends, stock splits, and stock dividends

This table presents some major conclusions from representative surveys on special dividends, stock dividends, and stock splits.

Author and date of publication	Major conclusions
A. Special dividends	
Baker, Mukherjee, and Powell (2005)	• Individual investors should not view cash dividends, share repurchases, and SDDs as perfect substitutes. • Results lend support to the signaling explanation for SDDs but not for the free cash flow or wealth transfer explanations. • Managers perceive that investors should interpret SDDs as conveying positive information about high current performance but not long-run performance.
B. Stock splits	
Dolley (1933)	• Respondents state the primary reason for management to issue a stock split is wider distribution of the firm's shares among stockholders.
Baker and Gallagher (1980)	• Respondents generally agree that stock splits are a useful device to bring the stock into an optimal trading range. • The survey evidence supports the trading range and liquidity hypotheses for issuing stock splits.
Baker and Powell (1993)	• The evidence suggests that the main motive for a stock split is moving the stock price into a better trading range, followed by improving liquidity and signaling optimistic expectations about the future. • The preferred trading range of stock split firms is from $20 to $35 but differs markedly between firms with small (< 2-for-1) versus large (≥ 2-for-1) stock splits.
C. Stock dividends	
Eisemann and Moses (1978)	• Evidence from CFOs of stock-dividend-paying firms offers support for the signaling, liquidity, tax timing, cash substitution, and retained earnings hypotheses. • CFOs of dividend payers indicate that historical company practice, conserving cash, and increasing the yield to stockholders are the most important reasons for issuing a stock dividend. • CFOs of non-stock-dividend firms indicate that high administrative costs and the lack of net change of stockholders' wealth are the most important reasons for not issuing a stock dividend.

TABLE 7.5 (cont'd) Key conclusions of surveys on special dividends, stock splits, and stock dividends

Author and date of publication	Major conclusions
	C. Stock dividends (cont'd)
Baker and Phillips (1993)	• Managers of stock-dividend-paying firms agree that stock dividends have a positive psychological impact on investors receiving them. • The signaling hypothesis for issuing stock dividends receives the most support from stock dividend payers. • The dominant motive for paying stock dividends is to maintain the firm's historical practice. • Managerial views on issues and motives about stock dividends differ little in relation to the firm's trading location or the size of the stock dividend but do differ based on the frequency of stock dividends.
Frankfurter and Lane (1998)	• Responses from managers of firms paying stock dividends provide support for the liquidity, optimal trading range, and signaling explanations for paying dividends. • Both a consensus and a diversity of opinions exist on various benefits and uses of stock dividends for the primary and control groups. • Respondents from both groups perceive that stockholders prefer cash dividends to stock dividends.

Theories, Models, and Explanations for Stock Splits

Corporate managers may view stock splits as more than an arithmetic exercise and may have other reasons for issuing them. The finance literature contains many theories to explain why firms issue stock splits and their real economic effects. The more widely researched hypotheses involve signaling, trading range, liquidity, and tax timing. Baker, Phillips, and Powell (1995), Kiymaz (2009), and Michayluk (2009) provide a review of the stock split literature, including various explanations for stock splits.

The Signaling Hypothesis

According to the signaling hypothesis, also called the information asymmetry hypothesis, managers can use stock splits to convey private information to the market. Given information asymmetry between managers and investors, the

TABLE 7.6 Survey evidence on explanations for special dividends, stock dividends, and stock splits

This table presents survey evidence, on average, about various theories, hypotheses, and explanations for special dividends, stock dividends, and stock splits.

A. Special dividends

Author and date	Signaling	Agency cost	Wealth transfer
Baker, Mukherjee, and Powell (2005)	Supported	Not Supported	Not supported

B. Stock splits

Author and date	Signaling	Trading range	Liquidity
Dolley (1933)			Supported
Baker and Gallagher (1980)		Supported	Supported
Baker and Powell (1993)	Supported	Supported	Supported

C. Stock dividends

Author and date	Signaling	Trading range	Liquidity	Tax timing	Cash substitution	Retained earnings
Eisemann and Moses (1978)[a]	Supported	Mixed support	Supported	Supported	Supported	Supported
Baker and Phillips (1993)	Supported	Some support	Mixed support		Little support	
Frankfurter and Lane (1998)[a]	Supported	Supported	Supported	Not supported	Supported	Mixed support

Responses based on dividend payers only.

former might use stock splits to convey information to the latter. This information typically signals favorable news or optimistic expectations to market participants. This argument requires some cost for false signaling; that is, if there were no costs associated with stock splits, firms would declare splits to realize the benefit of the generally positive price reaction related to the split announcement. Therefore, without costs, separating undervalued from overvalued stocks of firms declaring stock splits would be difficult.

Brennan and Copeland (1988) develop a signaling model in which they view stock splits as a costly but effective signal of a firm's future prospects. Their empirical evidence supports their model. In the Brennan and Hughes (1991) model, higher commissions on stocks with lower prices serve as the cost for issuing the split. Stock splits are costly because of the administrative costs involved in issuing the split and the increased transaction costs to investors. Copeland (1979) and Grinblatt, Masulis, and Titman (1984) also set forth an information signaling argument. Others such as Lamoureux and Poon (1987), McNichols and Dravid (1990), and Szewczyk and Tsetsekos (1993) find at least some evidence supporting the signaling hypothesis. By contrast, Dowen (1990) rejects the information asymmetry hypothesis.

A variant of the information asymmetry hypothesis is the attention-getting hypothesis. Grinblatt, Masulis, and Titman (1984) contend that managers of firms use stock splits to attract attention from institutional investors and financial analysts to trigger a revaluation of their future cash flows. Brennan and Hughes (1991) develop an attention-getting model in which managers with favorable inside information attract the attention of security analysts by announcing stock splits. The positive abnormal returns associated with the release of favorable private information from management via the stock splits supports the attention-getting hypothesis. Ikenberry and Ramnath (2002) find that financial analysts underestimate earnings of split firms, which accounts for the positive abnormal drift of 9 percent in the first year after the stock split.

The Trading Range Hypothesis

According to the optimal or preferred trading range hypothesis, managers use stock splits to lower their firm's share price to a desired range, which makes the stock more affordable to investors. This explanation presumes that shareholders prefer to buy round lots but cannot afford to do so when the share price is high. Lowering the stock price may also broaden the ownership mix of a firm by increasing the number of shareholders and decreasing the institutional ownership of the firm. Opponents contend that fees for odd lots are small and that institutional investors, who buy more stock than individuals, are indifferent to price levels, provided the expected returns are commensurate with the risk.

Both Grinblatt, Masulis, and Titman (1984) and Lakonishok and Lev (1987) propose versions of an optimal trading range hypothesis. Conroy, Harris, and Benet (1990) consider a specific price range to be optimal because stocks in this range are more liquid. McNichols and Dravid (1990) suggest that a firm's desire to keep its stock price in a preferred range may outweigh its desire to signal inside information to investors. Ikenberry, Rankine, and Stice (1996) synthesize both the trading range and the signaling hypotheses into a self-selection hypothesis in which managers not only issue stock splits to realign prices to a lower trading range but also self-select by conditioning the decision to issue a stock split on expected future performance. Evidence by Lakonishok and Lev (1987) and McNichols and Dravid (1990) find support for the trading range hypothesis.

The Liquidity Hypothesis

Closely related to the trading range hypothesis is the liquidity hypothesis. Liu (2006, p. 631) describes liquidity as "the ability to trade large quantities quickly at low cost with less price impact." The liquidity hypothesis suggests that stock splits enhance liquidity by increasing the proportion of shares traded and decreasing bid-ask spreads. Proponents of this view suggest that splitting firms can make shares more attractive to investors by lowering the stock price. By attracting attention, stock splits may affect both the number of trades and the number of stockholders. Increases in these variables may serve to increase a stock's liquidity.

Empirical support on the liquidity hypothesis varies. For example, evidence by Maloney and Mulherin (1992) finds a relationship between changes in liquidity and price increases on the split ex-date. Specifically, they find higher volume, more trades, and increased shareholders after stock splits. Lakonishok and Lev (1987) also find an increase in trading volume in the period around a split. Denis (2003) attempts to disentangle the trading range and liquidity hypotheses from the signaling hypothesis by examining the trading of index stock, which involves no signaling, after a stock split. He attributes the post-split trading differences to liquidity changes. Evidence by Muscarella and Vetsuypens (1996), Kryzanowski and Zhang (1996), and Schultz (2000) lends support to the liquidity hypothesis. By contrast, studies by Copeland (1979); Conroy, Harris, and Benet (1990); Easley, O'Hara, and Saar (2001); and Gray, Smith, and Whaley (2003) indicate that stock splits lower the stock price levels, and instead of improving the stocks' liquidity, they raise their bid-ask spreads. Copeland (1979) and Lamoureux and Poon (1987) find that turnover decreases after stock splits, which leads them to postulate that stock splits induce permanent reductions in liquidity. Murray (1985) and Elgers and Murray (1985) present evidence that stock splits do not increase short-term trading activity. Some of these differences may be attributable to different liquidity measures.

The Tax Option Hypothesis

Both Constantinides (1984) and Lamoureux and Poon (1987) offer a tax option explanation, also called a tax timing hypothesis, for stock splits. According to this hypothesis, stock splits lead to higher volatility, and such volatility has a higher tax option value. A stock with a widely fluctuating price offers its holder an opportunity to realize short-term losses or long-term gains to reestablish short-term tax status. Lamoureux and Poon claim that the announcement effects reported in previous studies are attributable to an increase in the tax option value of splitting stocks. Their empirical results support the tax timing hypothesis. Yet, research by Dammon, Dunn, and Spatt (1989) and Dhatt, Kim, and Mukherji (1997) is inconsistent with the tax timing hypothesis.

Recap of Explanations of Stock Splits

Despite numerous explanations and more than three decades of research, no consensus exists on why managers decide to issue stock splits. Perhaps the most empirical support exists for the signaling hypothesis, but some studies also support the trading range and liquidity hypotheses. These three hypotheses, however, are unlikely to be mutually exclusive. The tax option hypothesis appears to have the least support of the four major hypotheses. Given the mixed evidence on the rationale for initiating stock splits, perhaps survey studies can help to provide additional evidence on why firms split their stock.

Survey Evidence on Stock Splits

Several surveys investigate the motives for issuing stock splits. This section examines the results of those studies.

The Dolley (1933) Survey

Dolley's (1933) objective is to ascertain the general motives for stock splits in the United States. His mail questionnaire asks the managers of 88 corporations a single open-ended question about why firms split their stock. Based on 36 replies, representing a 40.9 percent response rate, he finds that 91.7 percent of respondents indicate that the primary objective is to increase the marketability of the common stock and thus to bring about a wider distribution of the shares. This result is consistent with the essence of this hypothesis. Other reported motives include lowering the dividend rate per share, listing the stock, facilitating sale of stock via stock rights, creating goodwill toward the corporation, and preparing for a proposed merger.

The Baker and Gallagher (1980) Survey

Almost 50 years later, Baker and Gallagher (1980) investigate the rationale for stock splits and compare the reasons corporate managers give for issuing stock splits instead of stock dividends. The sample consists of CFOs of two groups of NYSE-listed firms: 100 companies that issued a stock split of at least 1.25-for-1 during 1978 and 100 randomly selected firms that issued neither stock dividends nor splits during the period from 1974 to 1978. Their mail questionnaire consists of one open-ended question and 18 closed-ended statements asking respondents to agree or disagree with each statement (respondents may also choose to offer no opinion). The response rates for the stock split and control groups are 63 percent and 64 percent, respectively. The authors do not report testing for nonresponse bias.

For the 18 closed-ended statements, the stock split and control groups show the highest level of agreement with the same four statements. The statement with the highest ranking, noted by 98.4 percent of the stock split group and 93.8 percent of the control group, is that stock splits enable small stockholders to buy round lots. The next three most highly ranked statements are (1) stock splits keep a firm's stock price in an optimal price range, (2) stock splits increase the number of shareholders in the firm, and (3) stock splits make stocks more attractive to investors by increasing the number of shares outstanding. Based on chi-square tests, significant differences at the 0.05 level exist between the two groups on seven of the 18 statements. These results show that the stock split group generally agrees more with statements supporting stock splits than the control group and disagrees more with statements that have negative connotations toward splits.

For the stock split group, 65.0 percent of the respondents in the Baker and Gallagher (1980) study indicate that the major reason for having a split is to lower the stock price, which provides a better trading range and attracts small investors. The second-most frequently cited reason (31.7 percent) is that a split increases the number of shares outstanding or liquidity of trading. These views on liquidity are consistent with those reported in an early survey by Dolley (1933). These responses provide support for the preferred or optimal trading range and liquidity hypotheses. The group not engaging in stock splits indicates that they refrain from doing so primarily because their stock price is already in an optimal range (45.0 percent) or is too low (30.0 percent).

The Baker and Powell (1993) Survey

Baker and Powell (1992, 1993) report the responses from a 1991 mail survey to examine managerial motives for issuing stock splits. This study represents an improvement over the previous two studies (Dolley 1933; Baker and Gallagher 1980) because the questionnaire is more comprehensive and the sample includes more firms (both NYSE and AMEX). Baker and Powell also attempt to link their empirical results with certain hypotheses that explain the motivation for stock splits.

Their sample consists of 251 NYSE and AMEX firms issuing stock splits of at least 25 percent between 1988 and 1990. The questionnaire consists of two parts. The first part asks respondents to give their general beliefs on 17 statements about stock splits by using a seven-point scale, from −3 (strongly disagree) to +3 (strongly agree), with 0 as no opinion. The second part of the questionnaire consists of questions about the most recent stock split including motives, along with questions to provide a respondent profile. Of the 248 deliverable questionnaires, they receive 136 completed questionnaires from the two mailings. Baker and Powell (1993) do not test for nonresponse bias.

Of the 17 statements about stock split issues, the three highest ranked statements, based on their means, are (1) a stock split puts a firm's stock price in a preferred trading range (91.2 percent agree), a stock split makes it easier for small stockholders to buy shares in round lots (87.5 percent agree), and (3) a stock split makes shares more attractive to investors by lowering the stock price (93.3 percent agree). Baker and Gallagher (1980) report similar results for comparable questions. A large percentage of respondents also agree that a stock split improves the trading liquidity of a firm's stock (88.2 percent) and conveys favorable information about a firm's future prospects (69.6 percent).

Baker and Powell (1993) also provide evidence about the primary and secondary motives for issuing stock splits. Their results show that the main motive for stock splits is moving the stock price into a better trading range, followed by improving trading liquidity. Other important motives include signaling optimistic managerial expectations about the future and attracting investors. The authors also identify a preferred trading range of stock split firms from \$20 to \$35, but this range differs between firms with small (< 2-for-1) versus large (≥ 2-for-1) stock splits.

Summary of Survey Evidence on Stock Splits

Panel B of Table 7.4 shows that few survey studies examine management motives for stock splits and none of these studies is recent. The survey evidence summarized in Panel B of Table 7.5 suggests strong support for the trading range hypothesis, followed by the liquidity hypothesis. According to Panel B of Table 7.6, the signal explanation that stock splits convey favorable managerial expectations about the future also garners some support. In summary, managers have multiple reasons for engaging in stock splits.

Stock Dividends

A stock dividend is a dividend that a firm pays to its shareholders in the form of additional shares of stock instead of cash. Stock dividends are similar to stock splits but usually create fewer new shares of stock. For example, the NYSE labels distributions resulting in a 25 percent or more increase in shares outstanding as stock splits but defines lesser distributions as stock dividends. With a 10 percent stock dividend, the firm increases its total shares outstanding by 10 percent. Each shareholder receives one new share of stock for each 10 shares now owned. Both stock dividends and stock splits increase the number of shares outstanding and result in each shareholder maintaining the same proportional ownership in the firm. However, they differ in several ways, such as the market response to announcements (Grinblatt, Masulis, and Titman 1984), characteristics of issuing firms (Lakonishok and Lev 1987), and accounting treatment. With a stock dividend, a portion of the retained earnings on a firm's balance sheet transfers to the share accounts and there is no change in par value.

A stock dividend is theoretically a cosmetic change because it does not alter the portion of the company that each shareholder owns or the future cash flows of the firm. Also, such a change should not affect the value of an individual share or the company as a whole. In practice, stock dividends are more than what they seem on the surface. A substantial body of empirical research shows the presence of abnormal changes in stock price at the announcement (e.g., Foster and Vickrey 1978; Woolridge 1983b; Grinblatt, Masulis, and Titman 1984; Lakonishok and Lev 1987) and sometimes at the ex-dividend date (e.g., Woolridge 1983a; Eades, Hess, and Kim 1984). These reactions are puzzling and seem counterintuitive given that a stock dividend simply makes changes in partitioning of equity ownership. Apparently, stock dividends have a favorable psychological impact on investors.

There are two basic questions related to stock dividends: (1) Why do some firms continue to pay stock dividends when they incur real costs in the process? and (2) Why does the market respond favorably, on average, to these distributions? Baker, Phillips, and Powell (1995); Michayluk (2009); and Kiymaz (2009) provide a review of the literature on stock splits.

Theories, Models, and Explanations for Stock Splits

Researchers have long puzzled over why companies pay stock dividends. Therefore, they have advanced various hypotheses to explain this practice. Some of these hypotheses are similar to those for stock splits: the signaling, trading range, liquidity, and tax timing hypotheses. Other explanations for why companies pay stock dividends include the cash substitution and retained earnings hypotheses. These hypotheses are not mutually exclusive.

The Signaling Hypothesis

According to the signaling hypothesis, the announcement of a stock dividend conveys new information to the market. For example, managers could use a stock dividend to signal good news or optimistic expectations to investors about future increases in earnings, cash flows, trading volume, and cash dividends. As company insiders, managers usually have better estimates of a firm's prospects than do outsiders. Grinblatt, Masulis, and Titman (1984) develop several signaling-based explanations for stock dividends. Many empirical studies involving U.S. firms provide at least partial support for the signaling hypothesis (e.g., Foster and Vickrey 1978; Nichols 1981; Woolridge 1983b; Elgers and Murray 1985; Lakonishok and Lev 1987; Doran and Nachtmann 1988; McNichols and

Dravid 1990; Banker, Das, and Datar 1993). Liljeblom (1989) provides support for the signaling hypothesis for Swedish firms.

The Trading Range Hypothesis

The trading range hypothesis indicates that stock dividends help to move a stock into a normal or preferred price range. Theoretically, moving the stock into this range makes the market for trading in the stock wider or deeper by attracting more investors, which increases liquidity. For example, some investors can afford to buy in round lots (multiples of 100 shares) only at a lower price. Empirical results on the trading range hypothesis are mixed. For example, the results of Grinblatt, Masulis, and Titman (1984) and McNichols and Dravid (1990) support the trading range hypothesis. By contrast, Elgers and Murray (1985) report that firms with low stock prices are more inclined to issue small stock distributions. Lakonishok and Lev (1987) conclude that stock price is not a major motive for stock dividends.

The Liquidity Hypothesis

According to the liquidity hypothesis, stock dividends enhance liquidity by creating additional shares that generate greater trading and ownership dispersion of the firm as well as by decreasing bid-ask spreads. Little empirical support exists for this hypothesis. For example, Murray (1985) finds that firms issuing a stock dividend experience both a short-term and long-term decrease in proportional trading volume. They also find that such distributions do not affect the percentage bid-ask spread in the short or long run. Lakonishok and Lev (1987) find that average trading volume for their stock dividend sample is similar to that of their control group in both the pre- and postannouncement period.

The Tax Timing Hypothesis

The tax timing hypothesis of stock dividends involves the tax code. Although cash dividends are immediately taxable to many recipients, shareholders may delay any payments on stock dividends until they sell their shares. Thus, recipients of a stock dividend gain a temporary advantage by deferring taxes into the future. The research evidence on the tax timing hypothesis is mixed. Studies providing at least partial support for the tax timing hypothesis include Eades, Hess, and Kim (1984); Poterba (1986); and Ang, Blackwell, and Megginson (1991). Empirical evidence provided by Long (1978) does not support the tax timing hypothesis.

The Cash Substitution Hypothesis

The cash substitution hypothesis suggests that firms can conserve cash by issuing a stock dividend as a temporary substitute for existing or contemplated cash payments. Firms may need to conserve cash because of limited financial resources resulting from cash flow difficulties or asset expansion. Several studies provide at least partial support for the cash substitution hypothesis including Lakonishok and Lev (1987); Ghosh and Woolridge (1988); and Banker, Das, and Datar (1993). Other evidence does not support this hypothesis. For example, Elgers and Murray (1985) find that a poor cash position is not a factor in the decision to issue stock dividends. Grinblatt, Masulis, and Titman (1984) report the frequent association between the payment of stock dividends and simultaneous or subsequent increases in cash dividends. Similarly, Lakonishok and Lev (1987) provide evidence that firms often increase cash dividends after a stock dividend announcement.

The Retained Earnings Hypothesis

According to the retained earnings hypothesis initially proposed by Barker (1959), stock prices do not fully adjust to a stock dividend on the ex-dividend date. The accounting treatment for stock dividends requires reducing retained earnings and increasing both the common stock and paid-in capital accounts to account for the market value of the additional shares distributed. Therefore, stock dividends provide an assessment of whether a wealth transfer occurs from retained earnings to shareholders, not a signal of future economic activity. Woolridge (1983b); Eades, Hess, and Kim (1984); Grinblatt, Masulis, and Titman (1984); and Dravid (1987) find empirical support for this hypothesis. By contrast, Foster and Vickrey (1978) and Banker, Das, and Datar (1993) do not find empirical evidence supporting the retained earnings hypothesis.

Survey Evidence on Stock Dividends

Survey researchers have also examined why firms issue stock dividends. This section examines results from several surveys.

The Eisemann and Moses (1978) Survey

In 1975, Eisemann and Moses (1978) surveyed CFOs of NYSE firms to learn about their motivations for issuing stock dividends. The sample consists of 80 firms that paid a stock dividend of less than 25 percent in 1974 and 89 firms that did not have a stock split or a stock dividend during the period from 1970 to 1974. Their questionnaire consists of 17 closed-ended questions asking respondents to indicate whether they agree, disagree, or have no opinion about each statement. The questionnaire also contains several open-ended questions to ascertain the respondent's knowledge of the published literature on stock dividends and their attitudes toward it. The authors do not report testing for nonresponse bias.

The responding managers from the dividend and nondividend payers agree that stock dividends increase the number of shareholders (78.9 percent and 60.3 percent, respectively), which supports the liquidity hypothesis. CFOs from both groups agree that stock dividends conserve cash (86.8 percent for dividend payers and 66.7 percent for nondividend payers), thus providing support for the cash substitution hypothesis.

The respondents from the dividend-payers group express mixed views on the statement that stock dividends keep a firm's stock price in an optimal price range (34.2 percent agree, 34.2 percent have no opinion, and 31.6 percent disagree). Most (60.3 percent) of the nondividend payers disagree with the optimal trading range hypothesis. CFOs from both paying (71.1 percent) and nonpaying firms (65.5 percent) believe that stock prices will not fully adjust to occasional stock splits, which lends support to the retained earnings hypothesis. Responses from CFOs, especially from the dividend payers (81.6 percent), support the idea that the use of stock dividends in lieu of cash dividends is attractive to shareholders because shareholders can sell the stock dividends and pay taxes on the gain at the capital gains rate, while cash dividends are taxed at the ordinary income rate. This finding lends support to the tax timing hypothesis.

Finally, the CFOs have differing views on whether stock dividends have information content. The evidence shows that the majority of the dividend payers (63.2 percent) agree that the issuance of stock dividends enables management to express its confidence in the firm to the shareholders, whereas 64.9 percent of the nondividend payers disagree with this statement. Thus, the views of CFOs from stock-dividend-paying firms support the signaling hypothesis, while those from firms not paying stock dividends do not.

When asked why their company issued its most recent stock dividend, the stock dividend payers indicated (in order of importance) historical company practice, to conserve cash, and to increase the yield to stockholders. The two most frequently mentioned reasons by the nondividend payers for not issuing a stock dividend are the high administrative costs and because there is no change in the net position of stockholders.

The Baker and Phillips (1993) Survey

Baker and Phillips (1993) update and expand the Eisemann and Moses (1978) study by investigating NYSE, AMEX, and NASDAQ firms and increasing the sample size. The study's main objective is to provide further evidence about managements' views on issues and motives for distributing stock dividends. Their initial sample consists of 100 NYSE and AMEX firms and 260 NASDAQ firms that paid at least one stock dividend between 1988 and 1990.

The questionnaire consists of three parts. The first part contains 15 closed-ended questions on issues drawn from the finance literature about stock dividends. The questionnaire asks respondents to indicate their level of disagreement or agreement on a seven-point scale, from –3 (strongly disagree) to +3 (strongly agree), with 0 as no opinion. For example, this portion of the survey instrument contains questions involving four hypotheses for issuing stock dividends: the signaling, trading range, liquidity, and cash substitution hypotheses. The second part of the questionnaire contains seven questions about stock dividend decisions, while the third part asks four demographic questions.

In late 1991, Baker and Phillips (1993) mailed their survey to the highest-ranking financial officer of each firm. They subsequently mailed a second questionnaire to nonrespondents. Of the 299 delivered questionnaires, they receive 136 usable responses, giving them a response rate of 45.5 percent. Tests for non-response bias involving 17 financial attributes of the firms suggest that the responding firms represent the broader population of firms declaring stock dividends. An implication of this finding is that nonresponse bias is likely to be small.

Of the 15 statements on stock dividend issues, respondents express the highest agreement (95.0 percent) with the statement that "stock dividends have a positive psychological impact on investors receiving them." Also, 68.3 percent of the respondents agree that "stock prices generally react positively to stock dividend announcements." Such findings are consistent with evidence from empirical studies by Foster and Vickrey (1978); Woolridge (1983a, 1983b); Eades, Hess, and Kim (1984); Grinblatt, Masulis, and Titman (1984); and Lakonishok and Lev (1987).

Of the four hypotheses about stock dividends, the signaling hypothesis receives the most support. The results show that 78.3 percent of respondents agree that stock dividends convey favorable information about the firm's future prospects. More than half (54.6 percent) agree that stock dividends adjust the firm's stock price to a preferred trading range. Respondents have mixed views about statements involving the liquidity hypothesis and show the least support for the cash substitution hypotheses. In fact, the survey shows that a majority of respondents (52.5 percent) disagree with the statement that "stock dividends are a temporary substitute for cash dividends."

In comparing their results to those of Eisemann and Moses (1978), Baker and Phillips (1993) note both similarities and differences in the views of respondents. For example, about 70 percent of both groups agree that stock prices do not fully adjust to an occasional stock dividend. Yet, a much smaller percentage of respondents in the Baker and Phillips study agree that stock dividends are a temporary substitute for cash dividends (40.8 percent versus 86.8 percent, respectively).

The survey also asks respondents to indicate the most important motives for their firm's most recent stock dividend. The questionnaire directs them to select two motives from eight listed or "other" or "don't know." Two motives clearly dominate. The highest-ranked motive is maintaining the firm's historical practice of paying stock dividends, indicated by 42.9 percent of the respondents. Eisemann and Moses (1978) also report that 43.9 percent of respondents indicate historical company practice as the most important reason for issuing a stock dividend. The survey results of Baker and Phillips (1993) indicate that the next most important motive for stock dividends, given by 23.2 percent of the respondents, is signaling optimistic managerial expectations about the future. The third-most highly ranked motive for stock dividends is to increase trading volume.

Overall, the results from the closed-ended and open-ended questions provide different levels of support for the following explanations for paying stock dividends: the signaling motive garners high support, the liquidity hypothesis and the trading range hypothesis have some support, and the cash substitution hypothesis has little support.

Baker and Phillips (1993) partition their samples by trading location, frequency of stock dividends, and size of stock dividends. Their evidence shows that managerial views on issues and motives about stock dividends differ little in relation to the firm's trading location and the size of the stock dividend. They find, however, significant differences between regular and occasional stock dividend payers. For example, compared to those firms occasionally paying a stock dividend, firms regularly paying a stock dividend are more highly motivated by the desire to maintain this historical practice (65.1 percent versus 27.0 percent, respectively).

The Frankfurter and Lane (1998) Survey

Frankfurter and Lane (1998) survey financial managers of publicly traded firms that declared a stock dividend between 1986 and 1993 in order to determine their perceptions about the benefits and limitations of stock dividends. Their initial sample consists of 366 firms selected from the Center for Research in Security Prices (CRSP) database. They also develop a control sample of 150 firms randomly selected from the CRSP files of firms that did not pay a stock dividend during the same time period. Their questionnaire consists of 37 statements asking respondents to indicate their level of agreement or disagreement on a continuous scale, which also includes a neutral response. The authors mail the survey instrument to the highest-ranking financial executive of each firm. Based on two mailings, they receive 127 usable responses from the stock - dividend-paying group (the primary sample) and 38 valid responses from the control sample, resulting in response rates of 37.7 percent and 25.3 percent, respectively. The authors do not report testing for nonresponse bias.

Regarding the motives for using stock dividends, the survey evidence indicates both a consensus on some motives and a diversity of opinion on others. Executives generally agree with the statements implying benefits to increasing the liquidity of their stock (frequency of trading) but disagree on whether stock dividends can accomplish this. Almost two-thirds (64.0 percent) of the stock-dividend-paying group believe that stock dividends enhance liquidity, but less than half (43.4 percent) of the control group share that opinion. Responses from the primary sample support the notion of an optimal trading range and signaling hypotheses, but those in the control group do not. The majority of both groups support the cash substitution hypothesis, but neither group, on average, supports the tax timing hypothesis. The respondents from both the primary and control samples offer mixed perceptions on the retained earnings hypothesis. The authors find no clear support for administrative explanations of stock dividends, such as providing free publicity.

Frankfurter and Lane (1998) find that whether a firm pays stock dividends influences manager opinions. For example, managers of firms that pay stock dividends generally believe that doing so increases firm value, but the majority of the control sample see no such effect. The survey evidence also shows that the frequency with which firms pay stock dividends positively correlates with strong beliefs about stock dividends. Thus, the authors conclude that executives who see benefits to stock dividends are already using them as a strategic tool.

Summary of Survey Evidence on Stock Dividends

Panel C of Table 7.4 lists three surveys that provide managerial views about stock dividends. Panel C of Table 7.5 and Panel C of Table 7.6 summarize evidence about why companies pay stock dividends. Of the six explanations for paying stock dividends (signaling, trading range, liquidity, tax timing, cash substitution, and retained earnings), the signaling hypothesis receives the most consistent support in the three surveys about stock dividends. At least one of the three studies, however, provides support for each of the other five hypotheses. The evidence clearly shows that financial executives hold different views about the benefits, use, and appropriateness of stock dividends as a strategic financial instrument.

Summary and Conclusions

Perhaps the ultimate test of a theory in corporate finance lies not in its formal elegance but in the ability to apply the theoretical concepts to real business problems. As Frankfurter and Lane (1998, p. 37) note, "The usual practice, so far, in academic research has been to derive a theory in the abstract and then hope to find empirical evidence, using market or accounting data and a statistical model, to validate the theory." The finance literature proposes many theories, hypotheses, and explanations for dividend-related decisions including share repurchases, special dividends, stock splits, and stock dividends. Yet, there is a lack of agreement among academic theory, traditional empirical evidence, and options expressed by practitioners regarding all of these dividend policy decisions.

Evidence from survey research provides insights into why firms engage in these dividend-related decisions. This evidence suggests that the responses from survey participants are not haphazard but reflect the heterogeneous nature of the different populations. While no consensus explanation exists for share repurchases, special dividends, stock splits, or stock dividends, the various signaling hypotheses tend to garner more support from survey respondents than do others. Trying to formulate a unified theory of the various explanations is likely to be difficult and potentially unwise. Firms have different characteristics, objectives, and perceptions that influence their behavior on whether they choose to use these financial tools to support a strategy.

References

Amromin, Gene, Paul Harrison, and Steven Sharpe. 2005. "How Did the 2003 Dividend Tax Cut Affect Stock Prices?" *Financial Management* 37:4, 625–646.

Ang, James S., David W. Blackwell, and William L. Megginson. 1991. "The Effects of Taxes on the Relative Valuation of Dividends and Capital Gains: Evidence from Dual-Class British Investment Trusts." *Journal of Finance* 46:1, 383–399.

Asquith, Paul, and David Mullins. 1986. "Signaling with Dividends, Stock Repurchases, and Equity Issues." *Financial Management* 15:3, 27–44.

Bagnoli, Mark, Roger Gordon, and Barton L. Lipman. 1989. "Stock Repurchases as a Takeover Defense." *Review of Financial Studies* 2:3, 423–443.

Bagwell, Laurie S. 1991. "Share Repurchase and Takeover Deterrence." *RAND Journal of Economics* 22:1, 72–88.

Bagwell, Laurie S., and John B. Shoven. 1989. "Cash Distributions to Shareholders." *Journal of Economic Perspectives* 3:3, 129–140.

Baker, H. Kent, and Patricia L. Gallagher. 1980. "Management's View of Stock Splits." *Financial Management* 9:2, 73–77.

Baker, H. Kent, Patricia L. Gallagher, and Karen E. Morgan. 1981. "Management's View of Stock Repurchase Programs." *Journal of Financial Research* 4:3, 233–247.

Baker, H. Kent, and Martha C. Johnson. 1988. "Dividend Reinvestment Plans: A Survey of Current Practices." *Journal of the Midwest Finance Association* 17, 37–49.

———. 1989. "Dividend Reinvestment Plans among Utilities: A Survey of Current Practices." *Midwestern Journal of Business and Economics* 5:3, 55–67.

Baker, H. Kent, Walayet A. Khan, and Tarun K. Mukherjee. 2002. "Direct Investing: The Role of Stock Purchase Plans." *Financial Services Review* 11:1, 47–63.

Baker, H. Kent, and Sue E. Meeks. 1990. "The Evolution of Dividend Reinvestment Plans: 1968–1988." *Southern Business Review* 16:2, 1–22.

Baker, H. Kent, Tarun K. Mukherjee, and Gary E. Powell. 2005. "Distributing Excess Cash: The Role of Specially Designated Dividends." *Financial Services Review* 14:2, 111–131.

Baker, H. Kent, and Aaron L. Phillips. 1993. "Why Companies Issue Stock Dividends." *Financial Practice and Education* 3:2, 29–37.

Baker, H, Kent, Aaron L. Phillips, and Gary E. Powell. 1995. "The Stock Distribution Puzzle: A Synthesis of the Literature on Stock Splits and Stock Dividends." *Financial Practice and Education* 5:1, 24–37.

Baker, H. Kent, and Gary E. Powell. 1992. "Why Companies Issue Stock Splits." *Financial Management*, 21:2, 11.

———. 1993. "Further Evidence on Managerial Motives for Stock Splits." *Quarterly Journal of Business and Economics* 32:3, 20–31.

———. 2005. *Understanding Financial Management: A Practical Guide*. Oxford: Blackwell Publishing.

Baker, H. Kent, Gary E. Powell, and E. Theodore Veit. 2002. "Revisiting the Dividend Puzzle: Do All of the Pieces Now Fit?" *Review of Financial Economics* 11:4, 241–261.

———. 2003. "Why Companies Use Open-Market Repurchases: A Managerial Perspective." *Quarterly Review of Economics and Finance* 43:3, 483–504.

Baker, H. Kent, and Clark Rheinstein. 1980. "Tender Offers to Buy Back Odd-Lot Holdings of Stock." *Harvard Business Review* 58:5, 66–70.

Baker, H. Kent, and William H. Seippel. 1980. "Dividend Reinvestment Plans Win Wide Currency." *Harvard Business Review* 58:6, 182–186.

———. 1981. "The Use of Dividend Reinvestment Plans by Utilities." *Akron Business and Economic Review* 12:1, 24–29.

Baker, H. Kent, E. Theodore Veit, and Gary E. Powell. 2003. "Stock Repurchases and False Signals." *Journal of Applied Business Research* 19:2, 33–46.

Bancel, Franck, Usha R. Mittoo, and Nalinaksha Bhattacharyya. 2005. "Cross-Country Determinants of Payout Policy: A Survey of European Firms." Available at http://ssrn.com/abstract=683111.

Banker, Rajiv D., Somnath Das, and Srikant M. Datar. 1993. "Complementarity of Prior Accounting Information: The Case of Stock Dividend Announcements." *Accounting Review* 68:1, 28–47.

Barclay, Michael J., and Clifford W. Smith Jr. 1988. "Corporate Payout Policy: Cash Dividends versus Open-Market Repurchases." *Journal of Financial Economics* 22:1, 61–81.

Barker, C. Austin. 1959. "Price Changes of Stock-Dividend Shares at Ex-Dividend Dates." *Journal of Finance* 14:3, 373–378.

Bartov, Eli, Itzak Krinsky, and Jason Lee. 1998. "Some Evidence on How Companies Choose between Dividends and Stock Repurchases." *Journal of Applied Corporate Finance* 11:1, 89–96.

Bar-Yosef, Sasson, and Lawrence D. Brown. 1977. "A Reexamination of Stock Splits Using Moving Betas." *Journal of Finance* 32:4, 1069–1080.

Bens, Daniel, Venky Nagar, Douglas J. Skinner, and M. H. Franco Wong. 2003. "Employee Stock Options, EPS Dilution, and Stock Repurchases." *Journal of Accounting and Economics* 36:1–3, 51–90.

Bhattacharya, Sudipto. 1979. "Imperfect Information, Dividend Policy, and 'the Bird in the Hand' Fallacy." *Bell Journal of Economics* 10:1, 259–270.

Bierman, Harold Jr. 2001. *Increasing Shareholder Value: Distribution Policy, a Corporate Finance Challenge*. Boston: Kluwer Academic Publishers.

Billett, Matthew T., and Hui Xue. 2007. "The Takeover Deterrent Effect of Open Market Share Repurchases." *Journal of Finance* 62:4, 1827–1850.

Bradley, Michael, and L. MacDonald Wakeman. 1983. "The Wealth Effects of Targeted Share Repurchases." *Journal of Financial Economics* 11:1, 301–328.

Brav, Alon, John R. Graham, Campbell R. Harvey, and Roni Michaely. 2005. "Payout Policy in the 21st Century." *Journal of Financial Economics* 77:3, 483–527.

———. 2008. "Managerial Response to the May 2003 Dividend Tax Cut." *Financial Management* 37:4, 611–624.

Brennan, Michael, and Anjan Thakor. 1990. "Shareholder Preferences and Dividend Policy." *Journal of Finance* 45:4, 92–1019.

Brennan, Michael J. and Thomas E. Copeland. 1988. "Stock Splits, Stock Prices, and Transaction Costs." *Journal of Financial Economics* 22:1, 83–101.

Brennan, Michael J., and Patricia J. Hughes. 1991. "Stock Prices and the Supply of Information." *Journal of Finance* 46:5, 1665–1691.

Brickley, James A. 1983. "Shareholder Wealth, Information Signaling and the Specially Designated Dividend: An Empirical Study." *Journal of Financial Economics* 12:2, 187–209.

Brockman, Paul, and Dennis Y. Chung. 2001. "Managerial Timing and Corporate Liquidity: Evidence from Actual Share Repurchases." *Journal of Financial Economics* 61:3, 417–448.

Chetty, Ray, and Emmanuel Saez. 2005. "Dividends, Taxes and Corporate Behavior: Evidence from the 2003 Dividend Tax Cut." *Quarterly Journal of Economics* 120:3, 791–833.

Chhachhi, Indudeep S., and Wallace N. Davidson III. 1997. "A Comparison of the Market Reaction to Specially Designated Dividends and Tender Offer Stock Repurchases." *Financial Management* 26:3, 38–96.

Chowdhry, Bhagwan, and Vikram Nanda. 1994. "Repurchase Premia as a Reason for Dividends: A Dynamic Model of Corporate Payout Policies." *Review of Financial Studies* 7:2, 321–350.

Comment, Robert, and Gregg A. Jarrell. 1991. "The Relative Signaling Power of Dutch-Auction and Fixed-Price Self-Tender Offers and Open-Market Share Repurchases." *Journal of Finance* 46:4, 1243–1271.

Conroy, Robert M., Robert S. Harris, and Bruce A. Benet. 1990. "The Effects of Stock Splits on Bid-Ask Spreads." *Journal of Finance* 45:4, 1285–1295.

Constantinides, George M. 1984. "Optimal Stock Trading with Personal Taxes." *Journal of Financial Economics* 13:1, 65–89.

Constantinides, George M., and Bruce D, Grundy. 1989. "Optimal Investment with Stock Repurchases and Financing as Signals." *Review of Financial Studies* 2:4, 445–466.

Copeland, Thomas E. 1979. "Liquidity Changes following Stock Splits." *Journal of Finance* 34:1, 115–141.

Cornell, Bradford. 2009. "Stock Repurchases and Dividends: Trade-Offs and Trends." In H. Kent Baker (ed.), *Dividends and Dividend Policy,* 275–290. Hoboken, NJ: John Wiley & Sons.

Crutchley, Claire E., Carl D. Hudson, and Marlin R. H. Jensen. 2003. "Special Dividends: What Do They Tell Investors about Future Performance?" *Financial Services Review* 12:2, 129–141.

Dammon, Robert M., Kenneth B. Dunn, and Chester S. Spatt. 1989. "A Reexamination of the Value of Tax Options." *Review of Financial Studies* 2:3, 341–372.

Dann, Larry Y. 1981. "Common Stock Repurchases: An Analysis of Returns to Bondholders and Stockholders." *Journal of Financial Economics* 9:2, 113–138.

Dann, Larry Y., and Harry DeAngelo. 1983. "Standstill Agreements, Privately Negotiated Stock Repurchases, and the Market for Corporate Control." *Journal of Financial Economics* 11:1, 275–300.

———. 1988. "Corporate Financial Policy and Corporate Control: A Study of Defensive Adjustments in Asset and Ownership Structure." *Journal of Financial Economics* 20:1, 87–127.

Dann, Larry Y, Ronald W. Masulis, and David Mayers. 1991. "Repurchase Tenders Offers and Earnings Information." *Journal of Accounting and Economics* 14:3, 217–251.

DeAngelo, Harry, Linda DeAngelo, and Douglas J. Skinner. 2000. "Special Dividends and the Evolution of Dividend Signaling." *Journal of Financial Economics* 57:3, 309–354.

———. 2004. "Are Dividends Disappearing? Dividend Concentration and the Consolidation of Earnings." *Journal of Financial Economics* 72:3, 425–456.

de Jong, Abe, Ronald van Dijk, and Chris Veld. 2003. "The Dividend and Share Repurchase Policies of Canadian Firms: Empirical Evidence Based on an Alternative Research Design." *International Review of Financial Analysis* 12:4, 349–377.

Denis, David. 1990. "Defensive Changes in Corporate Payout Policy: Share Repurchase and Special Dividends." *Journal of Finance* 45:5, 1433–1456.

Denis, David J., and Igor Osobov. 2008. "Why Do Firms Pay Dividends? International Evidence on the Determinants of Dividend Policy." *Journal of Financial Economics* 89:1, 62–82.

Denis, Patrick. 2003. "Stock Splits and Liquidity: The Case of the Nasdaq-100 Index Tracking Stock." *Financial Review* 38:3, 415–433.

Dhatt, Manjeet S., Yong H. Kim, and Sandip Mukherji. 1997. "Did the 1986 Tax Reform Act Affect Market Reactions to Stock Splits? A Test of the Tax-Option Hypothesis." *Financial Review* 32:2, 249–271.

Dittmar, Amy K. 2000. "Why Do Firms Repurchase Stock?" *Journal of Business* 73:3, 331–355.

———. 2008. "Corporate Cash Policy and How to Manage It with Stock Repurchases." *Journal of Applied Corporate Finance* 20:3, 22–34.

Dolley, James C. 1933. "Common Stock Split-Ups Motives and Effects." *Harvard Business Review* 12:1, 70–81.

Doran, David T., and Robert Nachtmann. 1988. "The Association of Stock Distribution Announcements and Earnings Performance." *Journal of Accounting, Auditing and Finance* 3:2, 113–132.

Dowen, Richard J. 1990. "The Stock Split and Dividend Effect: Information or Price Pressure?" *Applied Economics* 22:7, 927–932.

Dravid, Ajay R. 1987. "A Note on the Behavior of Stock Returns around Ex-Dates of Stock Distributions." *Journal of Finance* 42:1, 163–168.

Eades, Kenneth M., Patrick J. Hess, and E. Han Kim. 1984. "On Interpreting Security Returns during the Ex-Dividend Period." *Journal of Financial Economics* 13:1, 3–34.

Easley, David, Maureen O'Hara, and Gideon Saar. 2001. "How Stock Splits Affect Trading: A Microstructure Approach." *Journal of Financial and Quantitative Analysis* 36:1, 25–51.

Easterbrook, Frank. H. 1984. "Two Agency-Cost Explanations of Dividends." *American Economic Review* 74:4, 650–659.

Eisemann, Peter C., and Edward A. Moses. 1978. "Stock Dividends: Management's View." *Financial Analysts Journal* 34:4, 77–83.

Elgers, Pieter T., and Dennis Murray. 1985. "Financial Characteristics Related to Managements' Stock Split and Stock Dividend Decisions." *Journal of Business Finance and Accounting* 12:4, 543–551.

Fama, Eugene F., Lawrence Fisher, Michael C. Jensen, and Richard Roll. 1969. "The Adjustment of Stock Prices to New Information." *International Economic Review* 10:1, 1–21.

Fama, Eugene F., and Kenneth R. French. 2001. "Disappearing Dividends: Changing Firm Characteristics or Lower Propensity to Pay?" *Journal of Financial Economics* 60:1, 3–34.

———. 2002. "Testing Trade-Off and Pecking Order Predictions about Dividends and Debt." *Review of Financial Studies* 15:1, 1–33.

Fenn, George W., and Nellie Liang. 2001. "Corporate Payout Policy and Managerial Stock Incentives." *Journal of Financial Economics* 60:1, 45–72.

Flannery, Mark, and Kasturi Rangan. 2006. "Partial Adjustment toward Target Capital Structures." *Journal of Financial Economics* 78:3, 469–506.

Foster, Taylor W. III, and Don Vickrey. 1978. "The Information Content of Stock Dividend Announcements." *Accounting Review* 53:2, 360–370.

Frankfurter, George M., and William R. Lane. 1998. "The Perception of Stock Dividends." *Journal of Investing* 7:2, 32–40.

Fredman, Albert J., and John R. Nichols. 1980. "New Capital Dividend Reinvestment Plans of Electric Utilities." *Public Utilities Fortnightly* 105:5, 119–128.

Ghosh, Chinmoy and J. Randall Woolridge. 1988. "An Analysis of Shareholder Reactions to Dividend Cuts and Omissions." *Journal of Financial Research* 11:4, 281–294.

Gombola, Michael, and Feng-Ying Liu. 1999. "The Signaling Power of Specially Designated Dividends." *Journal of Financial and Quantitative Analysis* 34:3, 409–424.

———. 2009. "Special Dividends." In H. Kent Baker (ed.), *Dividends and Dividend Policy,* 309–323. Hoboken, NJ: John Wiley & Sons.

Gong, Guojin, Henock Louis, and Amy X. Sun. 2008. "Earnings Management and Firm Performance Following Open-Market Repurchases." *Journal of Finance* 63:2, 947–986.

Gray, Stephen F., Tom Smith, and Robert E. Whaley. 2003. "Stock Splits: Implications for Investor Trading Costs." *Journal of Empirical Finance* 10:3, 271–303.

Grinblatt, Mark, Ronald W. Masulis, and Sheridan Titman. 1984. "The Valuation Effects of Stock Splits and Stock Dividends." *Journal of Financial Economics* 13:4, 461–490.

Grinstein, Yaniv, and Roni Michaely. 2005. "Institutional Holdings and Payout Policy." *Journal of Finance* 60:3, 1389–1426.

Grullon, Gustavo, and David Ikenberry. 2000. "What Do We Know about Stock Repurchases?" *Journal of Applied Corporate Finance* 13:1, 31–51.

Grullon, Gustavo, and Roni Michaely. 2002. "Dividends, Share Repurchase and the Substitution Hypothesis." *Journal of Finance* 57:4, 1549–1584.

———. 2004. "The Information Content of Share Repurchase Programs." *Journal of Finance* 59:2, 651–680.

Harris, Milton, and Artur Raviv. 1988. "Corporate Control Contests and Capital Structure." *Journal of Financial Economics* 20:1, 55–86.

Hausch, Donald, and James Seward. 1993. "Signaling with Dividends and Share Repurchases: A Choice between Deterministic and Stochastic Cash Disbursements." *Review of Financial Studies* 6:1, 121–154.

He, Wei. 2009. "Dividend Reinvestment Plans." In H. Kent Baker (ed.), *Dividends and Dividend Policy,* 343–361. Hoboken, NJ: John Wiley & Sons.

Hertzel, Michael, and Prem Jain. 1991. "Earnings and Risk Changes around Stock Repurchase Tender Offers." *Journal of Accounting and Economics* 14:3, 253–274.

Hovakimian, Armen, Tim Opler, and Sheridan Titman. 2001. "The Debt-Equity Choice." *Journal of Financial and Quantitative Analysis* 36:1, 1–24.

Howe, Keith M., Jia He, and G. Wenchi Kao. 1992. "One-Time Cash Flow Announcements and Free Cash Flow Theory: Share Repurchases and Special Dividends." *Journal of Finance* 47:5, 1963–1975.

Hribar, Paul, Nicole Thorne Jenkins, and W. Bruce Johnson. 2004. "Stock Repurchases as an Earnings Management Device." Working paper. Available at http://ssrn.com/abstract=524062.

Hsieh, Jim, and Qinghai Wang. 2007. "Disappearing Dividends and Trends in Corporate Payouts." Working Paper, George Mason University and Georgia Institute of Technology.

———. 2009. "Stock Repurchases: Theory and Evidence," Parts 1 and 2. In H. Kent Baker (ed.), *Dividends and Dividend Policy,* 241–273. Hoboken, NJ: John Wiley & Sons.

Ikenberry, David L., Josef Lakonishok, and Theo Vermaelen. 1995. "Market Underreaction to Open Market Share Repurchases." *Journal of Financial Economics* 39:2–3, 181–208.

———. 2000. "Stock Repurchases in Canada: Performance and Strategic Trading." *Journal of Finance* 55:5, 2373–2397.

Ikenberry, David L., and Sundaresh Ramnath. 2002. "Underreaction to Self-Selected News Events: The Case of Stock Splits." *Review of Financial Studies* 15:2, 489–526.

Ikenberry, David L., Graeme Rankine, and Earl K. Stice. 1996. "What Do Stock Splits Really Signal?" *Journal of Financial and Quantitative Analysis* 31:3, 357–375.

Jagannathan, Murali, Clifford P. Stephens, and Michael S. Weisbach. 2000. "Financial Flexibility and the Choice between Dividends and Stock Repurchases." *Journal of Financial Economics* 57:3, 355–384.

Jayaraman, Narayanan, and Kuldeep Shastri. 1988. "The Valuation Impacts of Specially Designated Dividends." *Journal of Financial and Quantitative Analysis* 23:3, 301–312.

Jensen, Michael. 1986. "Agency Costs of Free Cash Flow." *American Economic Review* 76:2, 323 329.

Jolls, Christine. 1998. "Stock Repurchases and Incentive Compensation." NBER Working Paper no. 6467. Cambridge, MA: National Bureau of Economic Research.

Julio, Brandon, and David L. Ikenberry. 2004. "Reappearing Dividends." *Journal of Applied Corporate Finance* 16:4, 89–100.

Kahle, Kathleen M. 2002. "When a Buyback Isn't a Buyback: Open Market Repurchases and Employee Options." *Journal of Financial Economics* 62:2, 235–261.

Kirch, David P., Ran BarNiv, and Linda J. Zucca. 1998. "Investment Strategies Based on Completion of Open Market Repurchase Programs." *Journal of Financial Statement Analysis* 3:2, 5–14.

Kiymaz, Halil. 2009. "Stock Splits, Stock Dividends, and Dividend Reinvestment Plans." In H. Kent Baker (ed.), *Dividends and Dividend Policy,* 385–403. Hoboken, NJ: John Wiley & Sons.

Klein, April, and James Rosenfeld. 1988. "Targeted Share Repurchases and Top Management Changes." *Journal of Financial Economics* 20:1, 493–506.

Kracher, Beverly, and Robert R. Johnson. 1997. "Repurchase Announcements, Lies and False Signals." *Journal of Business Ethics* 16:15, 1677–1685.

Kryzanowski, Lawrence, and Hao Zhang. 1996. "Trading Patterns of Small and Large Traders around Stock Split Ex-Dates." *Journal of Financial Research* 19:1, 75–90.

Lakonishok, Josef, and Baruch Lev. 1987. "Stock Splits and Stock Dividends: Why, Who, and When." *Journal of Finance* 42:4, 913–932.

Lakonishok, Josepf, and Theo Vermaelen. 1990. "Anomalous Price Behavior around Repurchase Tender Offers." *Journal of Finance* 45:2, 455–477.

Lambert, Richard A., William N. Lanen, and David F. Larcker. 1989. "Executive Stock Option Plans and Corporate Dividend Policy." *Journal of Financial and Quantitative Analysis* 24:4, 409–425.

Lamoureux, Christopher G., and Percy Poon. 1987. "The Market Reaction to Stock Splits." *Journal of Finance* 42:5, 1347–1370.

Lang, Larry H. P., and Robert H. Litzenberger. 1989. "Dividend Announcements: Cash Flow Signaling vs. Free Cash Flow Hypothesis." *Journal of Financial Economics* 24:1, 181–191.

LaPorta, Rafael, Florencio Lopez-De-Silanes, Andrei Shleifer, and Robert Vishny. 2000. "Agency Problems and Dividend Policies around the World." *Journal of Finance* 55:1, 1–33.

Leary, Mark T., and Michael R. Roberts. 2005. "Do Firms Rebalance Their Capital Structures?" *Journal of Finance* 60:6, 2575–2619.

Lease, Ronald C., Kose John, Avner Kalay, Uri Loewenstein, and Oded H. Sarig. 2000. *Dividend Policy: Its Impact on Firm Value.* Boston, MA: Harvard Business School Press.

Li, Kai, and William McNally. 2003. "The Decision to Repurchase, Announcement Returns and Insider Holdings: A Conditional Event Study." *ICFA Journal of Applied Finance* 9:6, 55–70.

Lie, Erik. 2000. "Excess Funds and Agency Problems: An Empirical Study of Incremental Cash Disbursements." *Review of Financial Studies* 13:1, 219–248.

———. 2005. "Operating Performance following Open Market Share Repurchase Announcements." *Journal of Accounting and Economics* 39:4, 411–436.

Lie, Erik, and Heidi J. Lie. 1999. "The Role of Personal Taxes in Corporate Decisions: An Empirical Analysis of Share Repurchases and Dividends." *Journal of Financial and Quantitative Analysis* 34:4, 533–552.

Liljeblom, Eva. 1989. "The Informational Impact of Announcements of Stock Dividends and Stock Splits." *Journal of Business Finance and Accounting* 16:5, 681–698.

Liu, Weiman. 2006. "A Liquidity-Augmented Capital Asset Pricing Model." *Journal of Financial Economics* 82:3, 631–671.

Long, John B. Jr., 1978. "The Market Valuation of Cash Dividends: A Case to Consider." *Journal of Financial Economics* 6:2–3, 235–264.

Lucas, Deborah J., and Robert L. McDonald. 1998. "Shareholder Heterogeneity, Adverse Selection, and Payout Policy." *Journal of Financial and Quantitative Analysis* 33:2, 233–253.

Maloney, Michael T., and J. Harold Mulherin. 1992. "The Effects of Splitting on the Ex: A Microstructure Reconciliation." *Financial Management* 21:4, 44–59.

Masulis, Ronald W. 1980. "Stock Repurchase by Tender Offer: An Analysis of the Causes of Common Stock Prices Changes." *Journal of Finance* 35:2, 305–321.

McNichols, Maureen, and Ajay Dravid. 1990. "Stock Dividends, Stock Splits, and Signaling." *Journal of Finance* 45:3, 857–880.

Michayluk, David. 2009. "Stock Splits, Stock Dividends, and Reverse Stock Splits." In H. Kent Baker (ed.), *Dividends and Dividend Policy,* 325–341. Hoboken, NJ: John Wiley & Sons.

Miller, Merton H., and Franco Modigliani. 1961. "Dividend Policy, Growth and the Valuation of Shares." *Journal of Business* 48:3, 261–297.

Miller, Merton, and Kevin Rock. 1985. "Dividend Policy under Asymmetric Information." *Journal of Finance* 40:4, 1031–1051.

Mitra, Devashis. 1997. "The Information Content of Specially Designated Dividend Announcements." *Mid-Atlantic Journal of Business* 33:1, 37–47.

Murray, Dennis. 1985. "Further Evidence on the Liquidity Effects of Stock Splits and Stock Dividends." *Journal of Financial Research* 8:1, 59–67.

Muscarella, Chris J., and Michael R. Vetsuypens. 1996. "Stock Splits: Signaling or Liquidity? The Case of ADR 'Solo Splits.'" *Journal of Financial Economics* 42:1, 3–26.

Netter, Jeffry M., and Mark L. Mitchell. 1989. "Stock-Repurchase Announcements and Insider Transactions after the October 1987 Stock Market Crash." *Financial Management* 18:3, 84–95.

Nichols, William D. 1981. "Security Price Reaction to Occasional Small Stock Dividends." *Financial Review* 16:1, 54–62.

Nohel, Tom, and Vefa Tarhan. 1998. "Share Repurchases and Firm Performance: New Evidence on the Agency Costs of Free Cash Flow." *Journal of Financial Economics* 49:1, 187–222.

Ofer, Aharon R., and Anjan Thakor. 1987. "A Theory of Stock Price Responses to Alternative Corporate Cash Disbursement Methods: Stock Repurchases and Dividends." *Journal of Finance* 42:2, 365–394.

Pettway, Richard H., and R. Phil Malone. 1973. "Automatic Dividend Reinvestment Plans of Nonfinancial Corporations." *Financial Management* 2:4, 11–18.

Peyer, Urs, and Theo Vermaelen. 2009. "The Nature and Persistence of Buyback Anomalies." *Review of Financial Studies* 22:4, 1693–1745.

Poterba, James M. 1986. "The Market Valuation of Cash Dividends: The Citizens Utilities Case Reconsidered." *Journal of Financial Economics* 15:3, 395–405.

Powell, Gary E. 2009. "Cash Dividends and Stock Repurchases." In H. Kent Baker (ed.), *Dividends and Dividend Policy,* 365–383. Hoboken, NJ: John Wiley & Sons.

Rau, P. Ragnavendra, and Theo Vermaelen. 2002. "Regulation, Taxes, and Share Repurchases in the United Kingdom." *Journal of Business* 75:2, 245–82.

Schultz, Paul. 2000. "Stock Splits, Tick Size, and Sponsorship." *Journal of Finance* 55:1, 429–450.

Shih, Feng-Ying L. 1992. "Dividend Announcements under Varying Market Conditions: The Case of Specially Designated Dividends." *Journal of Economics and Finance* 16:3, 143–152.

Sinha, Sidharth. 1991. "Share Repurchase as a Takeover Defense." *Journal of Financial and Quantitative Analysis* 26:2, 233–244.

Stephens, Clifford, and Michael Weisbach. 1998. "Actual Share Reacquisitions in Open Market Repurchase Programs." *Journal of Finance* 53:1, 313–333.

Stulz, René. 1988. "Managerial Control of Voting Rights: Financing Policies and the Market for Corporate Control." *Journal of Financial Economics* 20:1, 25–54.

Szewczyk, Samuel H., and George P. Tsetsekos. 1993. "The Effect of Managerial Ownership on Stock Split-Induced Abnormal Returns." *Financial Review* 28:3, 351–370.

Todd, Janet M., and Dale L. Domian. 1997. "Participation Rates of Dividend Reinvestment Plans: Differences between Utility and Nonutility Firms." *Review of Financial Economics* 6:2, 121–135.

Tsetsekos, George P. Daniel J. Kaufman, and Lawrence J. Gitman. 1991. "A Survey of Stock Repurchase Motivations and Practices of Major U.S. Corporations." *Journal of Applied Business Research* 7:3, 15–20.

Vafeas, Nikos, Adamos Vlittis, Philippos Katranis, and Kanalis Ockree. 2003. "Earnings Management around Share Repurchases: A Note." *Abacus* 39:2, 262–272.

Vermaelen, Theo. 1981. "Common Stock Repurchases and Market Signaling: An Empirical Study." *Journal of Financial Economics* 9:2, 139–183.

———. 1984. "Repurchase Tender Offers, Signaling, and Managerial Incentives." *Journal of Financial and Quantitative Analysis* 19:2, 163–183.

Wansley, James W., William R. Lane, and Salil Sarkar. 1989. "Managements' View on Share Repurchase and Tender Offer Premiums." *Financial Management* 18:3, 97–110.

Weisbenner, Scott J. 2004. "Corporate Share Repurchases in the 1990s: What Role Do Stock Options Play?" Working Paper, University of Illinois. Available at http://www.business.uiuc.edu/weisbenn/RESEARCH/PAPERS/rp_paper.20041207.pdf.

Williams, John. 1988. "Efficient Signaling with Dividends, Investments, and Stock Repurchases." *Journal of Finance* 43:3, 737–747.

Wood, Adrian. 2001. "Death of the Dividend?" *CFA Europe*, Research Report, December. Available at http://faculty.insead.edu/peyer/FFE/dividends%20CFO%20Europe.pdf.

Woolridge, J. Randall. 1983a. "Ex-Date Stock Price Adjustment to Stock Dividends: A Note." *Journal of Finance* 38:1, 247–255.

———. 1983b. "Stock Dividends as Signals." *Journal of Financial Research* 6:1, 1–12.

8

Risk Management and Derivatives

> As has been made clear by several well-publicized cases of [large] firms experiencing large derivatives losses, companies can use derivatives not only to hedge existing risks, but to create additional or completely new risk exposures. This suggests that the discussion of risk management theories could benefit from closer inspection of actual corporate practices.
>
> Martin Glaum (2002, p. 109)

Introduction

Glaum (2002) eloquently summarizes what academic finance understands and does not understand about why firms use derivatives to hedge. Theory, in this case based on market efficiency and equilibrium, is an essential predicate to empirical research—whether researchers conduct research by analyzing historical accounting data or by surveying corporate decision makers. Because researchers need to test theories against the real world and because empirical research is limited to what firms periodically disclose, survey research is essential to understanding why and how firms use derivatives. This chapter reviews both the theory behind derivatives as a form of risk management and selected surveys that shed light on why and how firms use derivatives.

Risk Management Theory

Firms face business and financial risks that stem from their investment decisions and their use of debt (financial leverage). The theory of corporate finance says firms should invest in those risky projects that offer expected returns greater than their cost of capital. Together and separately, greater business risk and financial leverage make the firm's economic and accounting results more variable. While a firm needs to take risks to earn more than the riskless rate, failing to control risk exposes the firm in such a way that can threaten its existence.

Firms employ natural hedges to control their operating risks by investing in diversified projects and minimize financial risks by balancing their assets and liabilities. Alternatively, firms can use derivatives when natural hedges are impractical or insufficient. Natural and derivative hedges are designed to offset the risk of adverse price changes—typically, the risk of changes in interest rates and currency exchange rates. In either case, financial theory insists that hedging away risk cannot be free—just like a homeowner pays insurance premiums in exchange for security against loss due to fire. While this trade-off might seem like a reasonable financial strategy, theory also says that hedging cannot create value.

Homemade Hedging

Modigliani and Miller's (1958; hereafter MM) theory says that when investors can diversify at no cost, firms should not be able to add value by hedging to control the risks they face. Their theory states that in perfect markets without taxes or bankruptcy costs, investors can create their own hedges—called homemade hedging—in the same way they maintain their own leverage by borrowing or lending or they manage their own dividend policy by selling some of their shares. When investors can diversify at no cost, a firm's (costless) risk management efforts should have no effect on its value. Under these assumptions, the only reasons for firms to hedge are that they are either arbitraging capital market imperfections or avoiding taxes and bankruptcy costs.

Like other MM theories, their purpose is not to describe reality but to highlight those factors that prevent the theory from being descriptively true. For example, not all stakeholders (e.g., managers and insiders) can diversify, and the alternative—homemade hedging—is more difficult than homemade leverage or dividends. A stakeholder could take a currency futures position to hedge some of a firm's translation risk, but it would be difficult for the same stakeholder to balance foreign assets and liabilities with the same precision and at the same available cost as the firm. Furthermore, while investors can measure a public firm's leverage—at least the on-balance sheet leverage—fairly easily, most derivative transactions are not shown on the balance sheet, much less publicly announced, making the calibration of homemade hedges more difficult. Firms may be able to enhance their value through hedging and especially through hedging with derivatives in ways that stakeholders cannot replicate. The post-MM financial theories supporting the use of derivatives, therefore, rely on the firm's information advantage or market imperfections like taxes or bankruptcy costs to make the argument that hedging can enhance the value of the firm.

Smith and Stulz (1985) develop a normative theoretical model that focuses on market imperfections to explore how firms should use hedging to add value. They use this model to investigate how taxes, bankruptcy, and agency costs should affect a firm's hedging policy. In an earlier article, Stulz (1984) uses risk aversion to motivate hedging. As those ideas are incorporated in Smith and Stulz (1985), they are not reviewed separately in this chapter.

Taxes

The Smith and Stulz (1985) model shows that hedging can reduce the variablity of pretax income and, therefore, expected taxes. Consequently, the post-tax value of the firm increases as long as the cost of the hedge does not exceed the tax benefits. Because firms have an incentive to reduce taxable income and preserve their tax preferences, hedging should be more prevalent when tax rates are more progressive and when the tax code awards more tax preferences in the form of tax loss carry forwards, investment tax credits, and the like. Survey research asks risk managers about taxes, although they rarely show up as a concern.

Bankruptcy Costs

Smith and Stulz (1985) extend their model to incorporate bankruptcy costs. Their model implies that because the tax authority is usually the *primus inter pares* claimant in bankruptcy, when hedging lowers the firm's volatility, the probability of bankruptcy also declines. The higher the probability and the greater the costs of bankruptcy, the more likely the firm is to hedge. To the extent that increasing firm size lowers the probability of bankruptcy, this argument implies smaller firms should be more likely to hedge. At the same time, the authors suggest that economies of scale should make hedging less expensive for larger firms that have the financial and human resources to manage a hedging program. Therefore, under Smith and Stulz's model, the propensity to hedge depends on size, either positively or negatively. The influence of bankruptcy costs on hedging is well suited for survey research.

Smith and Stulz (1985) point to two other potential theoretical motivations for hedging related to bankruptcy costs. Hedging transfers wealth from shareholders to bondholders because bondholders benefit most from avoiding bankruptcy, which sets up a potential conflict. The empirical implication is that shareholders will discourage hedging as the probability of financial distress increases. The authors also note that changes in accounting rules that make accounting income more variable would increase the incentive to hedge, especially because shareholders want to avoid triggering bond covenants (which are usually based on accounting numbers). While survey research reports that firms in different countries often use derivatives to actively manage their balance sheets and income statements (e.g., Bodnar, Hayt, and Marston [1996] in the United States; Bensen and Oliver [2004] in Australia; and Alkeback, Hagelin, and Pramborg [2006] in Sweden), no survey evidence overtly indicates that firms alter their hedge ratios in response to a change in accounting rules.

Agency Costs

The form of managerial compensation has implications for hedging. In the Smith and Stulz (1985) model, when managers' compensation is related to the value of the firm and managers are risk averse, they hedge away all the volatility in firm value. This predisposition sets up a conflict with well-diversified shareholders who do not want the manager (their agent) to hedge away the risk of volatility-increasing, return-enhancing projects. When hedging is costly, either because of trading or administrative expenses, well-diversified shareholders have an extra incentive to discourage managers from hedging. Shareholders can offer incentives to the manager for not hedging by making compensation a function only of controllable factors or instituting bonus plans that act like options on the firm's accounting earnings. The flip side of this analysis implies that in closely held firms where stockholders are otherwise poorly diversified, shareholders would prefer that the manager hedge. One empirical implication of the agency cost theory is that firms with better-diversified shareholders and properly incented managers should engage in less hedging.

A variation on the Smith and Stulz (1985) agency cost theory comes from Myers (1977), who characterizes the problem of managers not undertaking risky positive net present value (NPV) projects as underinvestment. In Myers' model, when a firm employs high financial leverage, its bondholders are in a better position than shareholders if the firm files for bankruptcy. Hedging that reduces the volatility of cash flows lessens the likelihood of bankruptcy, so shareholders in firms with more leverage would prefer the firm hedge.

Substitues for Hedging

Nance, Smith, and Smithson (1993) add one more potential explanation for hedging, or the lack thereof. They observe that if firms issue securities like convertible debt and preferred stock that act as close subsites for hedging, or if they have sufficient liquidity to withstand cash flow volatility, their propensity to hedge may be lower.

Cost of Funds and Optimal Hedging

Froot, Scharfstein, and Stein (1993) develop a theory of hedging that is similar to the pecking-order approach to capital structure (see Chapter 5). Froot, Scharfstein, and Stein (p. 1655) acknowledge that "this basic point [that firms follow a pecking-order approach to hedging] seems to have already been recognized in the literature but its implications for optimal hedging strategy have not been fully developed." The authors also critique earlier research as unrealistic when it implies that a firm's optimal strategy is to always be fully hedged. Their model uses the same variability assumption as Smith and Stulz (1985)—namely, that a firm's internal cash flows are variable under any realistic production environment. To counter this volatility, Froot, Scharfstein, and Stein suggest that a firm could reduce the amount of its investment, raise funds externally, or use some combination of those two strategies. Whichever choice the firm makes will be costly. Therefore, the authors argue, when costless hedging decreases cash flow variablity, it increases the value of the firm. Froot, Scharfstein, and Stein provide only two direct empirical implications of their model. First, because their model implies that firms will use hedging to maintain investment programs without recourse to external funds, they expect firms with high research and development (R&D) expenditures to hedge to protect the integrity of ongoing research programs. Second, their model implies very highly levered firms will hedge more because their cost of external funds would be higher than for less-levered firms.

Hedging and Firm Value

Whether because of market imperfections or investors' difficulty in diversifying, empirical research has uncovered some evidence that hedging does enhance firm value. Using financial statement data for 372 of the 1990 *Fortune* 500 nonfinancial firms, Géczy, Minton, and Schrand (1997) find a statistically significantly positive association between growth opportunities and currency hedging, where growth opportunities are measured by the ratio of R&D expenditures to sales.

Howton and Perfect (1998) sample 451 *Fortune* 500 and Standard and Poor's 500 (FSP) firms and 461 randomly selected firms by using financial data from 1994. They find that the use of derivatives is more widespread in the FSP firms (61 percent) than in the randomly selected firms (36 percent). They also report differences between the two samples in the average values of many of their explanatory variables: the random sample has statistically significantly smaller median market value, lower interest coverage, higher leverage, and is more liquid than the FSP firms. Using the combined sample, they test the theoretical models previously discussed for tax effects, the likelihood and costs of bankruptcy, substitutes for derivatives, and leverage. Howton and Perfect find that the FSP firms use derivatives to avoid the costs of financial distress (p-value = 0.011) and taxes (p-value = 0.001). They also find that liquidity is inversely related to derivatives use (p-value = 0.016). Interestingly, the results for the randomly selected sample of firms are not related to any of the theoretical variables. Howton and Perfect do not address this result other than to suggest that further research is required.

In an empirical study of derivatives in 116 New Zealand firms using 1994 accounting disclosures, Berkman and Bradbury (1996) find that the use of derivatives is positively associated with size, leverage, tax losses, insider ownership, growth options, and the payout ratio. Short-term asset growth, the proportion of foreign assets, and alternative financial instruments (e.g., issuing convertible debt and preferred stock) are not associated with the use of derivatives. This study confirms almost all the theoretical predictions extant at the time of the research. Given the lack of support for many of these predictions in subsequent research and the fact that accounting disclosures cannot differentiate between derivatives used for hedging or speculation, the generality of these results is questionable.

Allayannis and Weston (2001) test the association between derivatives hedging and firm value in 720 U.S. nonfinancial firms from 1990 through 1995. Measuring firm value with Tobin's Q, they find that firms using currency derivatives to hedge their exposures have an almost 5 percent higher value than firms that face the same exposure but do not hedge. Their results are invariant to size, profitability, leverage, growth opportunities, ability to access financial markets, geographic and industrial diversification, credit quality, industry classification, and time.

Several studies that look more closely at the results of risk management question these conclusions. Tufano (1996) investigates risk management in U.S. and Canadian gold mining firms. Using accounting disclosures of the firms' use of forward contracts, swaps, options, and other derivatives, Tufano finds that over 85 percent of the 48 firms in the industry use some form of derivative to manage gold price risk. His purpose is to test the theories to see which offer the best explanation for the considerable variation in the amount of risk these firms hedge. Using variables that represent financial distress, disruption of investment opportunities, cost of external financing (firm size), tax savings, officers' and directors' share ownership (risk aversion), and alternative financing policies, Tufano regresses the extent of risk management activity against lagged values of these variables.

Tufano (1996) finds that only one of these variables explains a statistically significant amount of the variation in risk management: managerial ownership. The author acknowledges that the results of his study cannot distinguish between cause and effect—that is, whether stock-based managerial compensation drives risk management or firms with more risk management attract managers who are willing to invest in the company. In any case, firms with managers who have more wealth invested in the firm tend to manage more gold price risk than managers with significant stock options who appear to use derivatives to take risk or, at a minimum, not hedge away their firm's entire exposure as Smith and Stulz (1985) predict.

Taking risk can also add value, according to a study by Adam and Fernando (2006). These researchers investigate the hedging activities of 92 North American gold mining firms from 1989 to 1999. The authors observe that an increase in value can come either from market imperfections or from the reward for taking risk in currency markets. Using detailed data on these firms' derivative positions, they find that gold mining firms speculate as often as they hedge. Furthermore, Adam and

Fernando suggest that gold mining firms are not unique and that managers in other industries often vary the size of their defensive hedges based on their prospective market forecast. That suggestion is consistent with selective hedging, an industry phrase adopted by Stulz (1996) to describe these speculative strategies.

Selective Hedging

Under Stulz's definition, selective hedging is different than hedging away a selected portion of the risk exposure. Selective hedging is varying the hedge based on the manager's price change forecasts or market view. While the phrase "selective hedging" is easily confused with a strategy of hedging a selected portion of the firm's risk exposure, Stulz and the subsequent literature use a very different interpretation. A classic hedging example will help clarify how the phrase "selective hedging" is used. A firm with a foreign currency receivable might decide to hedge possible exchange rate changes with a short exchange rate futures contracts position until the receivable is due to protect the domestic (functional) currency value of the expected cash inflow. The number of contracts would be calculated to protect all or some portion of the face value of the receivable. This classic strategy might maintain the initial position until settlement or may modify the number of contracts to roll the hedge forward or to compensate for changes in the basis. Selective hedging has a different motive. While a selective hedge might take the same opening position as the classic hedge, selective hedging then varies the number of contracts based on the direction the manager thinks exchange rates will move. The purpose of a selective hedging strategy is profit—not protection—and is tantamount to speculation.

If firms sometimes use derivatives in this manner to speculate, then authors who assume hedging is the only motive, like Smith and Stulz (1985), will not explain firm behavior. For example, Stulz (1996) argues that financial managers often have to predict the course of their product markets, so to assume these managers do not occasionally bet on their view of the future of financial asset prices would be unrealistic. Stulz (p. 11) says that "despite the spread of the doctrine of efficient markets, the world remains full of corporate executives who are convinced of their own ability to predict future interest rates, exchange rates, and commodity prices." Stulz suggests selective hedges are logically defensible when firms can reasonably expect to exploit their specialized knowledge of the market. While most nonfinancial firms are unlikely to have any systematic advantage in the highly liquid foreign exchange and interest rate markets, Stulz notes companies occasionally have unique information about commodity markets that would allow them to earn speculative profits. According to Stulz, the downside of selective hedging is that the firm may think it has an information advantage when, in fact, it does not.

Survey Research

Whether firms are using derivatives to exploit market imperfections or to pursue the reward for bearing risk in the underlying financial or commodity markets, derivatives use is widespread, as the survey research reviewed next substantiates. Empirical research became an easier and more popular approach in 1994 when U.S. firms were required to expand their derivatives disclosure by the Statement of Financial Accounting Standards (SFAS) Number 119, Disclosure about Derivative Financial Instruments and Fair Value of Financial Instruments. Yet, survey research continues to provide valuable insights into managers' motivations and objectives—information that is unavailable in mandated financial statement disclosures.

Although the purpose of this chapter is to review survey evidence that helps differentiate the various theories that attempt to explain the connection between firm value and derivatives use, interested readers may want to consult related nonsurvey research such as Jalilvand (1999), who finds that managerial risk aversion and ownership concentration are not related to derivatives use in Canadian nonfinancial firms; Goldberg, Godwin, Kim, and Tritschler (1998), who document the positive relationship between derivatives use by U.S. nonfinancial firms and multinationality, variance of accounting return on assets, growth opportunities, size, and debt levels; Bali, Hume, and Martell (2007), who use U.S. nonfinancial firms from 1995 through 2001 and find that derivatives hedging is more related to nonfinancial and economic factors than a firm's rate of return; Francis, Hasan, and Hunter (2008), who attribute the lack of an observed currency risk premium in 36 U.S. industries to methodological problems rather than the prevalence of hedging; and Koonce, Lipe, and McAnally (2008), who use behavioral experiments to investigate how investors respond to firms' derivative use after the fact.

When a firm has both natural and derivative hedges, measuring the extent to which the firm is hedged can be difficult. Smith and Stulz (1985) define hedging in relative terms by using two firms with the same set of projects and capital structure. If the correlation of the first firm's value with respect to an economic indicator variable is less than the correlation of the second firm's value with that same economic indicator variable, then the first firm is more hedged. These authors, therefore, define hedging in terms of reducing the covariance of the firm's market value and a set of economic variables, whether the hedge is natural or uses derivatives. While this definition works well in the development of their theoretical model, it is not easily employed in survey research. As this chapter documents, in a survey context firms often report that they are fully hedged when they actually protect less than half of their exposure. Survey researchers also have difficulty designing questions that enable firms to explain how they coordinate their natural and derivative hedges, making the interpretation of the responses challenging. Despite these challenges, survey research has much to say about which of the various theories provides the best explanation of observed firm hedging behavior and motivation.

Surveys of U.S. Firms

Most survey research tests at least three of the theoretical models. Nance, Smith, and Smithson (1993, p. 268), for example, say their survey of chief executive officers (CEOs) of the *Fortune* 500 and Standard & Poor's 400 firms in 1986 "test[s] these [three] hypotheses explaining corporate hedging policy and offer[s] empirical evidence on the relative importance of these corporate hedging motives."

Nance, Smith, and Smithson's (1993) sample is robust, with 169 useable responses, a response rate of 31.6 percent. The sample includes 104 firms that used financial hedges in 1986 (62 percent) and 65 firms that did not (38 percent). The authors track which firms respond and can therefore collect financial statement information. The sample appears to be relatively free of response bias based on the authors' analysis of 12 variables measuring size, debt coverage, tax rate, investment opportunities, and financial policies.

Nance, Smith, and Smithson (1993) only analyze derivatives use, taking natural hedges as given. The theoretical framework in which they investigate these hedges is the empirical predictions generated by the Smith and Stulz (1985) model. This model predicts that hedging should be a positive function of the following:

1. Taxes: measured by income tax progressivity and tax-preference items (i.e., firms in the progressive tax-rate range and with more tax preferences should hedge more)
2. Costs of bankruptcy: measured by the inverse of size (i.e., small firms should hedge more) and leverage
3. Agency costs: measured by leverage and growth opportunities (i.e., firms with higher leverage and more growth opportunities should hedge more)

Nance, Smith, and Smithson also argue that firms with sufficient liquidity, a low dividend payout, convertible debt, or preferred stock have less need for derivatives hedging.

Nance, Smith, and Smithson (1993) gather data on taxes (tax-loss carryforwards, investment tax credits, the range of the firm's pretax income in the progressive region of the tax schedule), size (measured by the book value of debt plus the market value of equity in 1986), leverage (three-year average of the ratio of the book value of debt to size and the three-year average ratio of earnings before interest and taxes [EBIT] to interest expense), and investment opportunities (1986 ratio of R&D spending to size and book to market value). They admit the survey results on a univariate basis are difficult to interpret because of correlations like those between size, tax rate progressivity, and financial distress. Therefore, they turn to a multivariate logistic regression (logit) analysis.

In Nance, Smith, and Smithson's (1993) logit, the binary dependent variable represents the firms that use financial derivatives (coded as 1) and those that do not (coded as 0). With 12 explanatory variables and only 65 observations in the group that does not use derivatives, the explanatory power of the regression using the entire data set is understandably low. Despite the observed multicolinearity, the authors employ multiple logistic regressions with subsets of the variables (which they call restricted logit regressions), employing one variable to represent each of the groups: taxes, leverage, size, growth opportunities, and hedging alternatives. This approach provides insight into the data at the cost of ignoring the potential explanatory power of the omitted colinear variables.

Nance, Smith, and Smithson (1993, pp. 275–279) summarize their results as follows:

> The results of the restricted logit regressions suggest that a firm is more likely to hedge if it has more investment tax credits (5–7% probability value), if more of the range of the firm's income is in the progressive region of the tax schedule (11–16% probability value), if the firm is larger (< 1–31% probability value), if the firm has more growth options (i.e., if the firm has higher R&D expenditures [6–21% probability value]), and if the firm has higher dividend payout (1% probability value).

The authors do not find the expected relationship between hedging and leverage. They suggest that perhaps the correlation between leverage and investment opportunities makes leverage redundant. At the same time, the confounding correlation between size and the tax variables suggests that the relationship is not as strong as the logistic regression results might otherwise suggest.

Nance, Smithson, and Smith (1993) provide a useful summary of prior corroborating survey research, adapted here in Table 8.1.

Of the six surveys summarized in Table 8.1, only Nance, Smithson, and Smith investigate the tax hypothesis. While firms appear to hedge to manage their tax liability, only investment tax credits (annotated by "Yes**" in Table 8.1) are statistically significant, while tax-loss carry-forwards and tax rate progressivity are not. The overall evidence for the tax effect is weak, and the authors comment that even the significant investment tax credit results could be due to a cross-correlation with firm size.

Each of the six studies in Table 8.1 examines the probability of financial distress as a hedging determinant. In all studies, the postive sign shows that firms potentially facing financial distress hedge more, as expected, and in three of these studies, this variable is statistically significant. Firm size is negatively related to financial distress and positively related to economies of scale. The five surveys

TABLE 8.1 Comparison of results across six surveys of corporate hedging policies

This table reproduces Table 4 from Nance, Smith, and Smithson (1993). "Yes" ("No") indicates that the sign of the relation between hedgers and nonhedgers reflected in the means (or by the regression coefficient, if estimated) is as predicted (opposite of predicted) by theory, while a dash (—) indicates that the hypothesis was not examined. A single asterisk (*) indicates that the difference in means is statistically significant at the 0.05 level. The purpose of this table is to display the theoretical hypotheses tested by Nance et. al. and compare their results to the findings of five previous surveys of derivative use published between 1984 and 1990.

Received theory suggests a firm is more likely to hedge	Booth, Smith and Stolz (1984) Use of interest rate futures by 238 financial institutions in western United States	Block and Gallagher (1986) Use of interest rate futures by 193 of Fortune 500 firms	Houston and Mueller (1988) Hedging via financial instruments by 48 firms	Wall and Pringle (1989) Examination of 250 swap users	Mayers and Smith (1990) Use of reinsurance by 1,276 insurance companies	Nance, Smith and Smithson (1993) Use of hedging instruments by 169 of Fortune 500 firms
To reduce expected tax liabilities if. . .						
the firm has more tax-loss carry-forwards	—	—	—	—	—	No
the firm has more (investment) tax credits	—	—	—	—	—	Yes**
more of the range of the firm's pretax income is in the convex region of the tax schedule	—	—	—	—	—	Yes
To reduce expected costs associated with financial distress if. . .						
the probability that the firm will encounter financial distress is higher	Yes**	Yes	Yes**	Yes	Yes**	Yes

the costs of financial distress are high—that is, if the firm is small	—	—	—	—	Yes**	—
Due to information scale economies if. . .						
the firm is large	Yes**	Yes**	Yes	Yes	—	Yes**
To reduce agency costs if the firm. . .						
has more growth options in its investment opportunity set	—	—	—	—	—	Yes**
If the firm is not currently using alternatives to hedging—that is, if the firm. . .						
issues less convertible debt	—	—	—	—	—	No
issues less preferred stock	—	—	—	—	—	Yes
has liquid assets	—	—	—	—	—	Yes**
has higher dividends	—	—	—	—	—	Yes**
Due to risk aversion if the firm. . .						
is owned by ill-diversified investors	—	—	—	—	Yes**	—

Source: Nance, Smith, and Smithson (1993, pp. 282–283).

that investigate scale economies in large firms all find that large firms hedge more, and three find size to be statistically significant. These results suggest that the influence of economies of scale is more powerful than the threat of bankruptcy.

The only study in Table 8.1 that specifically looks for a small-firm effect is Mayers and Smith (1990; shown in the last row of Table 8.1), who find small insurance companies hedge more than large insurance companies. These results are also consistent with the theory that risk aversion among ill-diversified investors provides an incentive to hedge. Nance, Smithson, and Smith (1993) suggest that the Mayers and Smith results might not be generalizable because of unique aspects of the insurance industry, like capital regulation.

The Dolde Survey

Dolde (1993) surveys risk management practices of *Fortune* 500 companies, which includes both financial and nonfinancial firms. Curiously, Dolde does not specify when the the survey was administered. The purposes of this study are to characterize the *Fortune* 500 firms' derivative use, to determine whether financial risk management enhances shareholder wealth, and to discover whether these firms hedge or speculate with derivatives. Of the 244 firms responding to the survey, 85 percent report using derivatives—a larger proportion than the 62 percent reported by Nance, Smithson, and Smith (1993).

Dolde's (1993) results are relevant to several theoretical issues involving size, what firms hedge, and whether they hedge or speculate. The derivative users are larger than the nonusers. The results, however, show that small firms hedge more of their exposure, as the theory suggests. When asked whether they have a financial market forecast (termed "market view" in this and most other research), almost 90 percent of the respondents report that they do. Of these companies, the smaller companies hedge more of their foreign exchange and interest rate risk than larger companies. When firms do not have a market view, the difference in derivatives use between large and small companies almost disappears. Dolde (pp. 34-35) interprets these results by saying, "These findings thus point to a potential reconciliation of opposing ideas about firm size and financial risk management. Scale economies appear to tilt the use of risk management products toward larger firms. But, among firms that have surmounted the initial investment barrier, more complete hedgers tend to be smaller firms, perhaps reflecting their higher expected costs of financial distress."

When Dolde (1993) investigates what these firms hedge, he finds that they report difficulty in measuring the risks they face. Whether firms target foreign exchange, interest rate, or cash flow risk, they appear to be using selective hedging. The author finds that only 16 percent of these firms fully hedge even when they have a market view and 22 percent fully hedge when they do not have a market view. The amount of risk the other 78 percent of the firms are willing to hedge depends on the downside potential, their market view, and their confidence in that view. According to the author, firms balance the potential speculative gain against the desired stability of their cash flows. Dolde (p. 41) states that "firms adopting blended strategies often cite a hierarchy of objectives: first and foremost is to insure against large losses; second is to benefit from anticipated market movements if possible. Such selective hedging is more common at larger than smaller firms—and, properly so, given larger companies' greater capacity to self-insure" (p. 41).

The Wharton Surveys

The most cited survey research in the use of derivatives is the Wharton series (Bodnar et al. 1995; Bodnar, Hayt, and Marston 1996, 1998). The authors' objective is to combine firm-specific characteristics with survey results. This is research in a descriptive-positivist vein in that it focuses on cataloging the way the respondents use derivatives rather than utilizing the prescriptive-normative approach of Nance, Smithson, and Smith (1993), who base their investigation on theoretical motivations. The models of Smith and Stulz (1985) and Froot, Scharfstein, and Stein (1993) are available to these authors, but they do not reference any theoretical models. Still, some of their results are relevant to these models.

The target for this series of surveys is the random sample of publicly traded nonfinancial firms originally selected from the 1993 Compustat database and stratified by industry, resulting in 2,000 firms (Bodnar et al. 1995). Table 8.2 summarizes the responses to these surveys.

By monitoring the firms that responded to all three surveys, the authors find that while the derivatives users are mostly unchanged from their two previous surveys, these same firms tend to have larger derivative positions. According to Bodnar, Hayt, and Marston (1998, p. 71), "A significant proportion of derivatives users is finding derivatives helpful enough that they are choosing to increase their usage," but their survey does not provide the respondents the opportunity to explain whether their increased derivatives use comes from derivatives being helpful, as the authors surmise, or from other plausible explanations such as a changing economic environment or increasing familiarity over time. As a result, the authors' interpretation of their findings is not the only possibility.

The survey questions do not touch on taxes, bankruptcy, or agency costs directly. They do, however, reveal that size is an important factor in derivatives usage: 83 percent of the large firms, 45 percent of the medium-sized firms, and 12 percent of the small firms use some form of hedging. Bodnar, Hayt, and Marston (1998, p. 71) mention that this result is "suggestive of an economies-to-scale argument for derivative use, with large firms better able to bear the fixed cost of derivatives use compared to small firms," similar to the findings of other surveys (see Table 8.1). Finding that size is important supports both the bankruptcy and agency cost theoretical motivations for hedging. Even so, this support

TABLE 8.2 Wharton survey response rates and derivatives usage

This table displays the date, sample, response rate and derivatives use for the three Wharton surveys (Bodnar, Hayt, Marston, and Smithson, 1995; Bodnar, Hayt, and Marston, 1996, 1998). The table shows that the bulk of the sample has remained essentially unchanged with the exception of the addition of 154 companies in 1995 that are carried forward to 1998. This table traces the constitution of the sample over the three surveys and shows that the percentage of these firms using derivatives increases from 35 percent in 1994 to 50 percent in 1998.

Survey	Date mailed	Sample	Number of responses and the response rate	Respondents using derivatives (%)
1994	November 1994	2,000 nonfinancial firms listed on Compustat	530 26.5%	35
1995	October 1995	1994 sample plus remaining 154 *Fortune* 500 companies	350 16.2%	41
1998	October 1997 and March 1998	1994 sample plus remaining 154 *Fortune* 500 companies (now 1,928 firms)	399 20.7%	50

may be subject to qualification because the authors also find that large and medium-sized firms are net-revenue exposed, while small firms are predominantly expense exposed. If large firms hedge more than small firms, perhaps it is because they are protecting revenues rather than because they enjoy scale economies. The authors' results cannot differentiate between these two potential causes.

The Wharton surveys also provide an indirect test of the bankruptcy motivation for hedging. In the 1994 and 1995 surveys, the authors investigate why the responding firms hedge. In 1994, Bodnar et al. (1995, p. 113) ask, "If, in Question 4, you indicated that your firm uses derivatives to hedge, please indicate what the firm is trying to achieve with the hedge. Rank by placing a 1 by the most important, a 2 by the next most important, a 3 by the least important item, or a 0 if not at all important." The choices are minimize fluctuations in quarterly accounting earnings, minimize the fluctuations in real cash flows, and protect the appearance of the balance sheet.

In 1995, Bodnar, Hayt, and Marston (1996, p. 129) ask, "If you use derivatives to hedge, please indicate what the firm is trying to manage with the hedge. (Rank each reason: 1–most important, . . . 4–least important; X–if not at all important/not a consideration)." The choices are volatility in accounting earnings, volatility in cash flows, balance sheet accounts or ratios, and market value of the firm. The 1998 survey does not include this question. Table 8.3 shows the results.

Table 8.3 shows the frequency with which repondents choose the reasons for hedging provided in the survey. Despite the similarities between the 1994 and 1995 samples, these two surveys show a dramatic increase in the percentage of firms reporting that they use derivatives to dampen earnings volatility—from 28 percent to 42 percent. Managing either earnings or cash flows is most consistent with the bankruptcy theory's explanation of hedging, as firms could be managing cash flows to avoid the costs of financial distress or managing earnings to avoid triggering bond covenants. The authors do not provide cross-tabulations with leverage, R&D expense, or the presence of derivative substitutes that would allow investigation of alternative explanations.

One aspect of the Bodnar results does pertain to part of the Froot, Scharfstein, and Stein (1993) theoretical development, which finds that using options is often necessary to reach a value-optimizing hedge. Of the 200 derivative-using firms in the 1998 sample, 68 percent use options. Of these firms, 44 percent use foreign exchange options, while 28 percent use interest rate and commodity options.

TABLE 8.3 Reasons firms hedge

This table displays the percentage of firms in the sample selecting as their most important reason for hedging from among the reasons provided in the survey. The first three reasons are provided in 1994 and the fourth is added in 1995. This comparison shows some dramatic differences between the two surveys. While earnings and cash flows are virtually tied as the most important reason for the 1995 respondents, minimizing cash flow fluctuations is the first choice by almost 2.5-to-1 in 1994. The 1995 sample, however, includes the 1994 sample plus 154 new firms. Moreover, the questions appear to be phrased slightly differently (e.g., in 1995 "quarterly" is omitted from the response about accounting earnings and "real" is omitted from the response about cash flows). The authors make no comments on these differences. The purpose of this table is to show that most firms report they are using derivatives to manage either earnings or cash flows and to relate those beliefs to the hedging theories.

Reason for hedging	1994 survey Percentage of firms ranking as most important	1995 survey Percentage of firms ranking as most important
Minimize fluctuations in quarterly accounting earnings	28	42
Minimize fluctuations in real cash flows	67	49
Protect the appearance of the balance sheet	5	1
Hedge the market value of the firm	Not asked	8

Source: Table adapted from Bodnar, Hayt, Marston, and Smithson (1995, p. 108) and Bodnar, Hayt and Marston (1996, p. 129).

The authors note that option usage increases with firm size, which is consistent the economy of scale argument.

An important aspect of the Froot, Scharfstein, and Stein (1993) theory is how much of their exposures firms hedge. Survey questions about exposure management shed light on the argument about whether financial managers who report they use derivatives to hedge actually reduce risk or take risk to follow their market view. Each of the Bodnar surveys conducted between 1994 and 1998 ask firms whether their view of the financial markets alters their hedging strategy.

Table 8.4 shows that in 1994, firms typically hedged 50 percent of their risk or less across all seven exposures. At least one-third of the respondents reduce funding costs by arbitraging the markets or by taking a view either frequently or sometimes. These responses are describing selective hedging. This same question does not appear on the 1995 or 1998 surveys, but Tables 8.5 and 8.6 show the responses to a smilar question about the respondents' market views. In both of these surveys, a much larger percentage report implementing their market view in both their foreign exchange and interest rate hedges. While Froot, Scharfstein, and Stein (1993) do not descibe these strategies as speculation, when these firms hedge less than 100 percent of their exposure and use derivatives to try to profit

TABLE 8.4 Percentage of firms indicating how they use derivatives, 1994 Wharton survey (Bodnar et al. 1995)

This panel shows that hedging contractual commitments (80 percent) and anticipated transactions less than 12 months out (77 percent) are the two most frequently cited uses of derivatives. For at least one-third of the responding firms, their use of derivatives is in response to their market forecast, either through arbitrage (33 percent either frequently or sometimes) by taking a view of market trends (43 percent either frequently or sometimes). These selective hedges indicate these firms are not always using derivatives to hedge away risk.

How often does your firm use derivatives to. . .	Percentage of firms responding		
	Frequently	Sometimes	Total
reduce funding costs by arbitraging the markets?	5	28	33
reduce funding costs by taking a view?	9	34	43
hedge the balance sheet?	22	22	44
hedge foreign dividends?	25	20	45
hedge contractual commitments?	45	35	80
hedge anticipated transactions (≤ 12 months)?	46	31	77
hedge anticipated transactions (≥ 12 months)?	15	35	50
hedge economic/competitive exposure?	16	24	40

TABLE 8.5 Percentage of firms indicating how they use derivatives, 1995 Wharton survey (Bodnar, Hayt, and Marston 1996)

The question asked in 1994 shown in Table 8.4 is not repeated in the 1995 survey. Instead, a question about market views is asked, as shown in this table, which demonstrates that the percentage of the same responding firms (the 1994 sample is resurveyed in 1995) either frequently or sometimes use derivatives more often to reflect their market view. For example, 72 percent of these firms alter the timing of their hedges to reflect their market view of exchange rates and 70 percent do so with their view of interest rates. Only 43 percent of the firms responding to the 1994 survey indicate they use derivatives in an attempt to profit from their market forecasts. In 1995, 39 percent and 36 percent actively take positions in the foreign exchange and interest rate markets, respectively. This approach to using derivatives reflects selective hedging (or speculation) and is a higher percentage than the percentage of firms that use derivatives to reflect their market forecast in Table 8.4. The purpose of this table is to reinforce the observation that firms do not always use derivatives to hedge away risk.

	Percentage of firms responding		
	Frequently	Sometimes	Total
How often does your market view of exchange rates cause you to. . .			
alter the timing of hedges?	11	61	72
alter the size of hedges?	12	48	60
actively take positions?	6	33	39
How often does your market view of interest rates cause you to. . .			
alter the timing of hedges?	8	62	70
alter the size of hedges?	4	51	55
actively take positions?	3	33	36

from their market forecasts, they are not using derivatives exclusively to avoid risk, as Smith and Stulz (1985) assume, but are, in fact, selectively hedging.

Finally, Bodnar, Hayt, and Marston (1998) ask the nonderivative users why they do not use derivatives. The respondents report either that their exposures are too small (60 percent), that they can manage their exposures with natural hedges (14 percent), or that the costs exceed the benefits (13 percent). These results suggest that nonusers are aware of the opportunity to use derivatives and have solid reasons not to. Unfortunately, the authors do not explore whether these firms also use preferred stock or convertible bonds or have sufficient liquidity or a low dividend payout, which would have shed light on the Nance, Smithson, and Smith (1993) conjecture that some firms use these substitutes for derivatives.

TABLE 8.6 Percentage of firms indicating how they use derivatives, 1998 Wharton survey (Bodnar, Hayt, and Marston 1998)

The 1998 Wharton survey repeats the question asked in 1995, as shown in Table 8.5. Compared to the 1995 survey in Table 8.5, using substantially the same sample, a substantial percentage of these firms continue to use derivatives to reflect their market forecasts, if at a slightly lower rate than in 1995. For example, in Table 8.5, 72 percent alter the timing of their hedges to reflect their market view, while only 59 percent indicate they do so in response to the 1998 survey. While the frequencies decline somewhat, a substantial percentage of these firms are using selective hedges.

	Percentage of firms responding		
	Frequently	Sometimes	Total
How often does your market view of exchange rates cause you to. . .			
alter the timing of hedges?	10	49	59
alter the size of hedges?	10	51	61
actively take positions?	6	26	32
How often does your market view of interest rates cause you to. . .			
alter the timing of hedges?	6	60	66
alter the size of hedges?	5	54	60
actively take positions?	4	37	41

While the three Wharton surveys provide some useful details about the hedging programs of the sample firms not available in other surveys, the lack of a theoretical framework makes these surveys less helpful in discerning why firms hedge. Perhaps that missing framework is why, despite a closing promise in Bodnar, Hayt, and Marston (1998) to revisit the firms in a fourth survey, this study has yet to appear. These surveys, however, do provide a basis for comparison, as researchers in other countries have replicated these studies since their publication. A later section of this chapter reviews these studies.

The Treasury Management Association Survey

Phillips (1995) provides a practice-oriented survey that appears about the same time as the Wharton surveys. Phillips (p. 115) sends this survey to members of the Treasury Management Association (TMA) to "assess on a wider basis than previously reported the extent of derivatives practices among treasury professionals." Of the 3,480 firms contacted in late 1994, respondents returned 657 surveys, giving a response rate of 18.9 percent.

Derivatives use is widespread in this sample, with 63 percent of respondents reporting their use. The firms using derivatives cover the size spectrum:

Annual sales	Percentage of sample
Over $10 billion in sales	7.7
Between $1 billion and $10 billion	25.5
Between $1 billion and $250 million	30.6
Under $250 million	25.3

(10.8 percent of the sample did not report their sales.)

Although Phillips (1995) does not provide any tests for statistical significance, he states that the responses indicate a positive relationship between firm size and hedging. Partitioning results by the four size categories shows that what Froot, Scharfstein, and Stein (1993) identified as substitutes for derivatives hedges (convertible callable, putable bonds, and preferred stock) are by far the most frequent funding strategy, regardless of size. Table 8.7 shows these results and the frequencies of the other strategies stratified by size.

TABLE 8.7 Derivative strategies for funding choices by organization size

This table shows the frequencies of funding choice among derivative strategies, stratified by organization size. Size is based on sales and divided into four categories: over $10 billion, between $10 billion and $1 billion, between $1 billion and $250 million, and under $250 million. Derivative types are classified as derivative substitutes (e.g., convertible bonds and preferred stock, callable and putable bonds), asset-backed securities (e.g., securitized receivables, interest only and principal only strips, and collateralized mortgage obligations, and structured securities (e.g., capped and minimax floating rate notes). The purpose of this table is to show that derivative substitutes are the most popular, regardless of firm size.

Derivative type	Size measured by sales ($)				
	Under $250 million	$250 million to $1 billion	$1 billion to $10 billion	Over $10 billion	Total frequency
Derivative substitute	22	37	63	25	147
Asset backed	21	22	23	7	73
Structured security	6	12	5	0	23

Source: Table adapted from Phillips (1995, p. 122).

For the firms using derivatives, Phillips (1995) reports that 67 percent use callable bonds for financing. Firms across the size categories use this heding instrument most frequently. He also says that 76 percent of the firms with less than $250 million in sales select their derivative investments from derivative subsitutes and asset-backed securities. The responses are not available by firm size for any of the risk-hedging strategies. Despite this lack of detail, this survey highlights the importance of alternative securities to a hedging program and can be interpreted as broadly supportive of the positive relationship between size and hedging. Phillips (p. 123) says in his conclusion that "derivative usage for both managing financial risk and obtaining funding, while widespread across organizations of different sizes, increases with the size of the organization."

Probably because of increased disclosure mandated by SFAS 119 in 1994 and the inherent difficulties of survey research, empirical research on derivatives use takes over at this point. Survey research outside the United States, however, continues to provide valuable insights into the questions posed by theory.

Surveys of Non-U.S. firms

Much of the survey research conducted with firms outside the United States is of the descriptive-positivist variety. Several surveys compare their findings to the Wharton surveys and provide a contrast between European and U.S. results.

European Surveys

Bodnar, de Jong, and Macrae (2003) follow the Wharton surveys with a comparable survey of Dutch firms. They assemble a matched U.S. and Dutch sample. For the U.S. firms, they use the responses received by Bodnar, Hayt, and Marston (1998) but exclude the 154 *Fortune* 500 firms added to the survey sample in 1995 (see Table 8.2 for details). They translate the questionnaire into Dutch and survey all 167 listed nonfinancial Dutch firms. They receive 84 responses, a response rate of 50 percent, but reduce the sample to better match the U.S. sample. They eliminate 102 U.S. companies because no Dutch company has the same two-digit Standard Industrial Classification (SIC) code. They also eliminate two U.S. firms with annual turnover (sales revenue) of more than $63 billion. The matched sample then has 267 U.S. and 84 Dutch firms. As reported by the authors, the resulting sample appears reasonably well balanced in terms of firm size and industrial sector.

Following the Wharton surveys, Bodnar, de Jong, and Macrae (2003) state their two-fold purpose as (1) to investigate derivatives use in the Netherlands as part of an effort to understand hedging in various countries and (2) to use the Dutch results to draw inferences about how derivatives usage varies with the institutional and informational environment. They say that because Dutch firms are like firms across Europe, their comparisons are generalizable to both the U.S. and Europe.

Bodnar, de Jong, and Macrae (2003) also acknowledge the theoretical foundations established by Stulz (1984); Smith and Stulz (1985); and Froot, Scharfstein, and Stein (1993), crediting them with establishing that through hedging, firms can enhance their value by decreasing taxes, the threat of bankruptcy, and agency costs. They also recognize the argument that hedging can reduce the investment-financing dilemma brought on by variable cash flows. Finally, Bodnar, de Jong, and Macrae (p. 274) say that if the benefits of hedging exceed the cost, "then derivatives use will be a shareholder-value enhancing activity." Despite these encouraging words, the authors provide little in the way of analysis that might help settle some of the theoretical debate. Their results do offer some evidence, however, about the frequency and motivation for hedging in the two countries.

The census results are not remarkable. In their unweighted sample, more Dutch firms (60 percent) use derivatives to hedge than U.S. firms (44 percent). The authors attribute this difference to the greater degree of openness in the Netherlands. However, about the same percentage of large firms use derivatives (82 percent in the United States and 88 percent in the Netherlands). Nevertheless, firm size does matter, with smaller Dutch firms hedging less, similar to their U.S. counterparts.

From a theoretical point of view, the most interesting question that Bodnar, de Jong, and Macrae (2003) ask is, "If you use derivatives to hedge, please indicate what the firm is trying to manage with the hedge," followed by the possible responses: volatility in accounting earnings, volatility in cash flows, or balance sheet accounts or ratios. As previously noted, the 1997 Warton survey does not ask this question, so the authors take the U.S. responses from the 1995 survey. Again, the authors make no comments about the different responses received to a very similar question in the 1994 Wharton survey. Bodnar, de Jong, and Macrae are also silent about the use of derivatives to hedge variations in market value response that appears on the 1995 Wharton survey, but apparently they do not include this question in the Dutch version. Finally, in a curious twist and without comment, they use different percentages for the U.S. responses than reported in the 1995 survey from which they draw their comparative data; that is, in the Bodnar et al. 1995 study, the percentage of respondents choosing each response is calculated as a percentage of all those offering that response. In the 2003 study, however, Bodnar et al. calculate the percentage of all those ranking each response as most important. While the conclusions are unaltered, these differences are surprising, especially because the two studies have one author in common. Tables 8.8 and 8.9 show the results.

Table 8.8 shows the U.S. results (Bodnar, Hayt, and Marston 1996, p. 129). Table 8.9 shows the Dutch results (Bodnar, de Jong, and Macrae 2003, p. 281). The conclusion of the 2003 study is that the Dutch firms consider managing cash flow volatility as "most important" more often than U.S. firms, who more

TABLE 8.8 What firms report they are trying to manage when they hedge: U.S. firms

The cells in Table 8.8 contain U.S. firms' responses to the question, "If you use derivatives to hedge, please indicate what the firm is trying to manage with the hedge." In each cell, the response frequency is at the top (i.e., 59 firms select volatility in accounting earnings as the most important thing the firm is trying to hedge). Below the frequency are the row percentage (on the left) and the column percentage (on the right). For example, volatility in accounting earnings is selected as most important by 44 percent of the 135 firms responding. Of the 141 firms responding with a most important reason for hedging, 42 percent select volatility in accounting earnings (the column percentage). The authors report the column percentage in Bodnar, Hayt, and Marston (1996) and the row percentage in Bodnar, de Jong, and Macrae (2003). The purpose of this table is to display how respondents rank the potential reasons for hedging. The table shows that regardless of how the frequencies are analyzed, volatility in cash flows and accounting earnings are about equal in importance. Managing balance sheet accounts and ratios and the market value of the firm are universally unimportant. Table 8.3 repeats the "most important" column percentages.

	Most important (1)		Second-most important (2)		Third-most important (3)		Least important (4)		Not at all important or not considered		Row total
Volatility in accounting earnings	59		50		14		3		9		135
	44%	42%	37%	41%	10%	15%	2%	3%	7%	12%	
Volatility in cash flows	70		41		18		4		6		139
	50%	49%	29%	33%	13%	19%	3%	4%	4%	8%	
Balance sheet accounts or ratios	1		14		33		50		29		127
	1%	1%	11%	11%	13%	35%	39%	54%	23%	38%	
Market value of the firm	11		18		30		36		32		127
	9%	8%	14%	15%	24%	32%	28%	39%	25%	42%	
Column total	141		123		95		93		76		

Source: Adapted from Bodnar, Hayt, and Marston (1996).
Note: Each entry shows a frequency followed by row percentage (left) and column percentage (right).

TABLE 8.9 What firms report they are trying to manage when they hedge: Dutch firms

The cells in Table 8.9 contain Dutch firms' responses to the question, "If you use derivatives to hedge, please indicate what the firm is trying to manage with the hedge." In each cell, the row percentage is recorded and these entries are comparable with the row percentages for the U.S. firms shown in Table 8.8. Despite the authors' construction of a sample that matches U.S. and Dutch firms on industry and size, these results are unmatched and unweighted. The purpose of this table is to show that more Dutch firms (60 percent) than U.S. firms (50 percent) respond that their most important use of hedges is to manage their cash flow volatility and that fewer Dutch firms (33 percent) than U.S. firms (44 percent) report that hedging their accounting earnings is their most important use of hedging.[a]

	Most important (%)	Second-most important (%)	Least important[a] (%)	Not at all important or not considered (%)
Volatility in accounting earnings	33	31	13	23
Volatility in cash flows	60	21	10	10
Balance sheet accounts or ratios	8	26	45	21

Source: Adapted from Bodnar, de Jong, and Macrae (2003).

[a]The least important frequency results in Table 8.9 are comparable to the sum of the third-most important and least important results in Table 8.8.

frequently report that managing accounting earnings is most important. Bodnar, de Jong, and Macrae (2003, p. 282) also note that neither group of respondents considers managing balance sheet accounts or ratios as important. Bodnar, de Jong, and Macrae emphasize that "the difference is consistent with the fact that shareholder concerns are more important in the USA than they are in the Netherlands," and "this [difference] is consistent with the view that US firms are more shareholder-oriented while Dutch firms are more stakeholder-oriented."

Difficulty exists in determining whether the differences between the U.S. and Dutch responses are due to the institutional and informational environments, as the authors claim, to the difference in the time period (1994 in the United States versus 1998 in the Netherlands), or to the unmatched and unweighted sample used in this analysis. Bodnar, de Jong, and Macrae (2003) do not offer any cross-tabulations that would allow an inference about the influence of the difference in relative size and industry composition that they claim is a major advantage of their analysis.

Alkeback, Hagelin, and Pramborg (2006) provide another replication of the Bodnar, Hayt, and Marston (1998) survey, this time in Sweden. The authors survey Swedish nonfinancial firms' use of derivatives in 2003. Their purpose is to compare derivatives use over time by using the earlier Alkeback and Hagelin

(1999) survey and to benchmark against the Wharton survey. They send the Bodnar, Hayt, and Marston (1998) survey to 261 Swedish firms and recieve 134 responses, a response rate of 51 percent. Of these respondents, 59 percent report using derivatives—slightly higher than the 1999 survey results. Alkeback, Hagelin, and Pramborg do not find other differences with the earlier surveys that are of interest here.

When Alkeback, Hagelin, and Pramborg (2006) ask the firms using derivatives to rank the three goals—controlling volatility in accounting earnings, controlling volatility of cash flows, and managing balance sheet accounts— the firms' primary objective is to minimize the volatility in balance sheet accounts. This response is different from the U.S. firms, who are more likely to see managing cash flows as most important. The authors say that these firms appear to be hedging appearances rather than economic cash flows. When asked whether the firms impose their view of the market on their hedging strategy, 28 percent of the respondents report that they are more aggressive (hedge a smaller percentage of their exposure) when they expect favorable markets. The authors do not find a significant difference in this behavior between large and small firms. While these results suggest the Swedish firms are more conservative than their U.S. counterparts, a significant portion are using derivatives to selectively hedge.

Loderer and Pichler (2000) add an important perspective on risk management in their survey of 165 Swiss firms in 1996. They receive 96 responses, a response rate of 29 percent. According to the authors' analysis, the responses contain more large firms relative to all listed Swiss firms with higher-than-average exposure to currency risk. Loderer and Pichler suggest that these biases actually help their study, as these firms should be more likely to have a more sophisticated approach to risk management. The purpose of their survey is to examine risk management policies of Swiss industrial firms. They expect these firms to monitor their currency risk and hedge it with derivatives. Their survey shows that these firms, while claiming to manage currency risk, actually do not know their own exposure. Less than 40 percent of the sample can quantify their exposure to currency risk, even though most of the sample reports using derivatives.

Loderer and Pichler (2000) suspect that these Swiss firms may be managing their currency exposure with natural hedges, which the authors term "on-balance sheet" hedging. The authors suggest that in the presence of effective natural hedges, these firms may have little need to know their short-term currency exposures; that is, after establishing natural hedges, these firms may react to market conditions by adjusting these hedges rather than entering into derivative contracts. The authors point out that strategies such as changing foreign prices, marketing less price-sensitive products, moving production out of Switzerland, or revising the base currency of employment contracts are common in Switzerland and can substitute for derivative hedging. Still, Loderer and Pichler (p. 320) admit to being puzzled because managing transaction exposure should help firms "better calibrate their on-balance sheet hedges."

When Loderer and Pichler (2000) ask whether the firm's view of the currency markets influences their use of derivatives, 68 percent of the firms in the sample report that they have a view and act on it when deciding how much of their currency exposure to hedge. Although the authors are unwilling to label these activities as speculation, these firms do appear to be using selective hedges.

Loderer and Pichler (2000) add another piece to the puzzle of interpreting survey research. Almost no other authors think to ask whether the firms are hedging calculated risks. Other researchers, whether doing theoretical or empirical work, assume that if a firm is using derivatives, it is doing so to avoid risk and with careful controls. This assumption is reasonable, given the well-publicized debacles experienced by Mettalgesellschaft in 1993 and Daimler-Benz in 1995. Stulz (1996) provides a brief description of how these companies lost huge sums when their risk management efforts failed. If, however, firms do not know their exposure, the task of interpreting their derivatives use as evidence of their conservative financial management is difficult. Thus, Loderer and Pichler provide additional support for the hypothesis that firms use derivatives both to hedge and to speculate, even if unknowingly.

Glaum (2002) surveys German nonfinancial firms in late 1998 and early 1999. The author's primary contribution to the question of how firms approach hedging is his observations on the tendency of firms to selectively hedge (i.e., the imposition of the risk manager's market view on the extent of the hedge). Adam and Fernando (2006) also observe this tendency with gold firms, and Stulz (1996) identifies this as a motive for using derivatives, as previously discussed.

Glaum (2002) sends his survey to 154 nonfinancial German firms and receives 74 responses (a response rate of 48 percent). The author does not provide information on the representativeness of this sample except to say that the responding firms are among the larger firms in the sample. Of the responding firms, 89 percent report using derivatives, with the most prevalent use being foreign exchange forward contracts.

Glaum (2002, p. 117) observes, "A large majority of these firms (88%) indicated that they use derivatives only for hedging purposes. However, closer inspection of these companies' risk management practices suggests such firms cannot unambiguously be characterized as hedgers." More than half of these firms report using selective hedges. One-third have a policy of hedging a fixed percentage of their exposure, leaving the remainder to be hedged or not, depending on the firm's exchange rate forecast. Two-thirds of these firms give their managers complete discretion as to whether to hedge and by how much. Glaum suggests when firms report that they use derivatives only to hedge and also vary their derivative positions to reflect their market forecast are, in fact, using selective hedging, which Stulz (1996) characterizes as practically the same as speculation.

Marshall (2000) surveys the foreign exchange risk practices of very large multinational companies in the United Kindgom, the United States, and Asia Pacific to determine if there are international differences in attitudes that influence those practices. The author sends questionnaires to the 200 largest (based on sales reported in 1998) U.K., U.S., and Asia Pacific multinational companies in July 1998 for a total size sample of 600 and receives 185 usable responses, a 30 percent response rate. The respondents indicate foreign exchange risk is an important part of their business risk. In answering a question about the relative degree of importance of foreign exchange risk to business risk by using a scale of least important, marginally important, equally important, significantly important, or most important, 87 percent of the Asia Pacific firms rank foreign exchange risk as equally or significantly important, while 66 percent of the U.K. firms and 56 percent of the U.S. firms provide a similar ranking. Marshall proceeds to analyze these regional differences.

Marshall (2000) does not base his analysis on any specific theory that seeks to explain these firms' motivations for hedging. Instead, Marshall (p. 198) couches his analysis by saying that a "general lack of a comprehensive framework . . . for managing and hedging currency exposures would imply that companies would adopt a variety of methods". While Smith and Stulz (1985) and Froot, Scharfstein, and Stein (1993) might disagree with Marshall's analysis that their work does not produce a theoretical framework, some relevant evidence is available within Marshall's survey results.

For example, although Marshall (2000) surveys only the largest firms in each region, considerable size variation exists. Specifically, the average sales for U.K., U.S., and Asia Pacific companies are £3.5 billion, £10.9 billion, and £1.4 billion, respectively. He classifies derivative hedges as external and natural hedges as internal (no external contracts). Marshall finds that the larger firms (dominated by U.S. multinational companies) are statistically significantly less likely (p-value = 0.04) to use either internal or external hedges to manage currency translation exposure. This result is invariant to the degree of internationalization (percentage of overseas business) or industry sector. He finds no significant differences due to size in the importance of transaction or economic exposure. In contrast to the survey results of U.S. firms summarized in Table 8.1, size in this sample does not appear to have much influence on the decision to hedge. Given that all these firms are the largest worldwide, these results should not be viewed as definitive contrary evidence on either the theory or other empirical research.

Other Surveys in Australasia

Benson and Oliver (2004) conduct a survey of derivative use by Australian firms. They conduct their survey in 2000 and target the top-listed domestic companies. The authors send the survey to 429 companies and receive 100 responses, resulting in a 23 percent response rate. The responding firms are relatively large and appear to be representative of the distribution of Australian industry sectors. Of these firms, 76 percent report using derivatives.

The results of this survey are consistent with previous surveys in the United States and elsewhere. Benson and Oliver (2004) provide the respondents with 19 possible reasons for using derivatives. The three most often cited reasons are hedging cash flows, hedging accounting earnings, and improving the value of the firm. Far down the list are avoiding financial distress (ranked ninth) and reducing taxation (ranked eighteenth).

Benson and Oliver (2004) also report on their analysis of how much exposure the derivatives-using firms hedge. Tables 8.10 and 8.11 shows the results.

Tables 8.10 and 8.11 demonstrate that few of the respondents hedge away all their exposure. Other researchers in other countries also find firms using selective hedges.

Sheedy (2006) investigates risk management in Hong Kong and Singapore. Her students interview 131 firms by using the 1998 Wharton survey's questions. The Singapore and Hong Kong interviews occur in 1998 and 2000, respectively. The author reports that derivative use is more common in these two countries (78 percent) than in the Bodnar, Hayt, and Marston (1998) study of U.S. firms (50 percent). Firms in Hong Kong and Singapore are also more likely to use derivatives to manage foreign exchange risk (76 percent versus 90 percent) than U.S. firms and less likely (17 percent versus 54 percent) to hedge commodity price risk.

When Sheedy (2006) compares the percentage of exposures these firms hedge, she also finds differences with the U.S. results. Whereas 54 percent of

TABLE 8.10 Amount of exposure being hedged with derivatives

Table 8.10 compares the risks the derivative-using firms report they face with the amount of that exposure they would typically hedge. Each cell represents the count of firms hedging the amount of exposure indicated in the column heading. For example, eight firms report hedging 25 percent or less of their foreign exchange exposure. Note that a few more firms (63) hedge interest rate risk than hedge their foreign exchange risk (58).

Exposure	Percentage of exposure hedged					
	1% to 25%	26% to 50%	51% to 75%	76% to 99%	100%	Total count
Foreign exchange	8	11	12	22	5	58
Interest rate	12	18	23	10	0	63
Commodity price	6	5	8	7	3	29
Other	3	1	1	2	1	8

Source: Adapted from Benson and Oliver (2004).

TABLE 8.11 Actual amount of exposure being hedged by firms using derivative

Table 8.11 is derived from Table 8.10 and shows how much of the risks that firms using derivatives actually hedge. The purpose of tables 8.10 and 8.11 is to demonstrate that firms do not routinely hedge away all their exposure. In fact, a substantial portion hedge less than 50 percent of their exposure

Exposure	Amount of exposure hedged	
	50% or less	More than 50%
Foreign exchange	33	67
Interest rate	48	52
Commodity price	38	62
Other	50	50

Source: Adapted from Benson and Oliver (2004).

U.S. firms report that they hedge about half or less of their balance sheet exposure, 46 percent of Sheedy's sample hedge away the same amount of their similar exposure. In interpreting these results, Sheedy (p. 93) says, "Hedging intensity is much greater in Asia than in the USA." She reports that this difference is statistically significant at the 5 percent level. However, the magnitude of the difference (54 percent versus 46 percent) does not appear to be economically significant. If 46 percent of the sample firms in Hong Kong and Singapore are hedging less than 50 percent of their foreign exchange exposure, they cannot really be said to be avoiding risk. Sheedy also reports that her sample firms are much more likely to base their derivative strategies on their market views. This result does not hold, however, when she corrects for the subsidiaries of U.S. firms included in the sample. Nevertheless, these firms do not appear to be fully hedged, at least not in the spirit of the Smith and Stulz (1985) theory.

Kim and Sung (2005) are interested in exploring the theoretical hedging models. These authors use the 304 responses to a 2002 survey conducted by the Korea Financial Supervisory Service of 2,941 firms. This study achieves a response rate of 10.3 percent. Despite promised anonymity, the authors uncovered the identity of 223 firms, reducing the usable response rate to 7.5 percent. This survey covers small and medium-sized firms and provides a direct measure of foreign exchange hedging rather than an undifferentiated mixture of hedging and speculation.

Kim and Sung (2005) explore the factors that influence foreign exchange hedging. They define size as the logarithm of assets at book value expressed in won as of December 2001. They use firm size as a proxy for the cost of hedging or economy of scale. According to this theory, the cost of hedging in terms of personnel and computer systems, as well as counterparty risk, should be lower for larger firms. Therefore, larger firms should engage in more hedging. Kim and Sung measure leverage as the debt-to-equity ratio, saying firms with higher leverage should have a higher propensity to hedge to avoid the costs of financial distress. They use liquidity (quick ratio) and profitability (earnings before the ratio of taxes to book assets) to measure the substitution effect cited by Froot, Scharfstein, and Stein (1993). Firms with better liquidity and profitability are less likely to hedge. Finally, growth opportunities, represented by sales growth (three-year compound annual sales growth), should be positively associated with hedging based on the Myers (1977) and Froot, Scharfstein, and Stein (1993) argument that firms should hedge to maintain their investment programs.

The results of the Kim and Sung (2005) survey show that firm size is a statistically significantly positive (p-value = 0.01) determinant of hedging. None of the variables measuring leverage, liquidity, profitability, or sales growth are significant. Kim and Sung also find larger firms are much more likely to use external (derivatives) hedging than internal (natural) hedging. Both of these results support the economies of scale theory.

Kim and Sung (2005) partition their sample into public and private firms. Among the public-firm respondents, size is still significant; however, a dummy variable representing export sales also becomes important in identifying the firms that hedge their foreign exchange risk. In contrast, private firms continue to show only size as a hedging determinant. The larger public or private firms hedge more.

While these results support the economies of scale theory but none of the other theories, Kim and Sung (2005) note that the environment may make their results less generalizable. Following the Asian crisis, which reached its peak in 1997, the Korean government intervened in the currency market to peg the currency. Individual Korean firms, which almost all price in U.S. dollars, therefore had almost no incentive to enter into foreign exchange derivative contracts. Kim and Sung (p. 284) summarize by saying, "With little benefit from hedging, consideration of cost becomes the dominant factor in making risk management decisions. Among all the factors influencing foreign exchange risk management, we find that firm size, which is a proxy for hedging cost or economies of scale, is the single most important factor." Because these firms have no reasons to hedge, the question of hedging or speculation does not apply.

Summary and Conclusions

Hedging is designed to reduce volatility and avoid downside risk. Under the perfect market and complete information assumptions of MM, investors will costlessly diversify or use homemade hedging, so firms cannot use either natural or derivative hedges to enhance their value. Researchers, therefore, identify the following six exceptions that enable hedging to reduce the volatility of the firm and add value.

Taxes

Reducing the variablity of pretax income reduces expected taxes, increasing the posttax value of the firm. The more progressive the tax schedule, the more firms should hedge. For most of recent U.S. history, tax rates have been progressive only for relatively low taxable incomes (less than $100,000 in 2007), so taxes should be a motivation to hedge only for small firms.

Bankruptcy

Reducing cash flow variability reduces the probability of bankruptcy. The propensity to hedge, therefore, depends on both the chance and cost of financial distress. To the extent that small firms have a greater risk of bankruptcy, smaller firms should hedge more. Furthermore, hedging to steer clear of financial distress can transfer wealth from shareholders to bondholders, because bondholders benefit more than shareholders from avoiding bankruptcy. The implication is that shareholders will discourage hedging as the probability of financial distress increases.

Agency Costs

When managers are risk averse and their compensation is related to the value of the firm, they have an incentive to hedge away all the volatility in firm value. Shareholders would prefer that managers not hedge away all risk because they recognize that return and risk are related. The form of managerial compensation and ownership, therefore, should affect how much risk a firm hedges. The greater the portion of management's wealth invested in the firm, the greater management's incentive to hedge. Managers paid with stock options have much less incentive to hedge. Additionally, the greater the firm's leverage, the greater their potential cash flow volatility, so agency cost considerations should make hedging more prevalent in firms with more leverage.

Cost of External Funds

When internal funds are less costly than external funds, the theory suggests firms should hedge cash flow volatility to avoid reducing investment. Firms with higher R&D spending should hedge more.

Economies of Scale

Larger firms are presumedly better able to absorb the administrative cost of establishing a derivatives program. They are also better credit risks as counterparties and should be able to execute hedging transactions more cheaply. Large firms, therefore, should be observed to hedge more often than small firms.

Information Advantage

Firms might use derivatives not to hedge but to arbitrage market opportunities when they have a market information advantage. While foreign exchange and interest rate markets are highly informationally efficient, firms could occasionally have valuable private information. Firms, therefore, might use derivatives occasionally to speculate and not violate the theory. Firms that routinely use selective hedges, however, would not be acting in accordance with theory.

Research Challenges

Four factors challenge the ability of researchers to investigate these theoretical implications: the definition of hedging, the relationship between natural and derivative hedges, hedging substitutes, and the propensity of firms to use selective hedging.

The Definition of Hedging

Most survey and empirical researchers recognize that hedging can be difficult to define and measure. Survey researchers do not often cite the Smith and Stulz (1985) definition of hedging. Yet, when they investigate the theoretical implications of corporate financial policies, they implicitly assume corporations want to reduce the covariance of the value of the firm with one or more economic variables. To reduce these covariances, firms can employ both natural and derivative hedges.

The Relationship between Natural and Derivative Hedges and Substitutes

Survey research almost always focuses exclusively on derivatives, even though the firms' derivatives use should be directly related to the availability and flexibility of their natural hedges. Only a few surveys ask about securities that might be a substitute for derivatives hedging. For example, Phillips (1995) asks about convertible bonds and preferred stock and Nance, Smithson, and Smith (1993) ask about preferred stock, liquid assets, and dividends. These securities are not obvious natural hedges like financing foreign assets with foreign liabilities, even though they can be just as effective. Thus, because most survey researchers do not include these alternatives when they ask respondents about the amount of risk covered by their firm's hedges, they may not be seeing the whole picture.

Even more confounding is Loderer and Pichler's (2000) finding that many firms using derivatives do not even calculate their exposures. If firms are not tracking the effect of their natural hedges, they may not be able to accurately describe how and why they use derivatives and, therefore, their description may bear little meaningful relationship to their actual derivative positions. Furthermore, many survey researchers find that financial managers often use their view of financial markets to establish or alter their derivatives positions. If firms are unaware of their risk and define hedging as using their forecast of financial markets to guide their use of derivatives, their responses to survey questions about hedging could be quite muddled. Certainly, the theories that attempt to explain derivative hedging do not contemplate firms using these instruments to speculate in search of profits.

Selective Hedging

Evidence of selective hedging—using derivatives for profit rather than risk reduction—appears in many surveys. This evidence comes from both the U.S. and non-U.S. surveys. Dolde (1993); Bodnar et al. (1995); Bodnar, Hayt, and Marston (1996, 1998); Loderer and Pichler (2000); Glaum (2002); Benson and Oliver (2004); Sheedy (2006); and Alkeback, Hagelin, and Pramborg (2006) all find that many firms use their view of currency and interest rate markets to set and adjust their financial hedges. For example, Loderer and Pichler suggest that firms are only partially hedged, either because they do not calibrate the financial and operating risks they face or because they assume that their natural hedges will protect against major losses.

Implications of the Theories

One way to review the theoretical inference of survey research is to look at each theory from the perspective of its empirical implications. For example, the tax and bankruptcy arguments suggest small firms should hedge more of their exposure. The economies of scale argument suggests large firms should hedge more. Given the survey results reviewed here, larger firms invariably use derivatives more often, so economies of scale would appear to be a better explanation than taxes or bankruptcy costs. At the same time, Dolde (1993) finds that small firms hedge more of their exposure, which is consistent with the bankruptcy explanation. Furthermore, results such as those of Bodnar et al. (1995) and

Bodnar et al. (1996) suggest that firms use derivatives to manage their cash flow volatility, as they should if they are concerned about avoiding financial distress.

The agency cost argument suggests leveraged firms should use more derivatives. Here, the evidence by Nance, Smithson, and Smith (1993); Kim and Sung (2005); and others is against the proposition, as leverage does not usually show up as an important motivation for hedging in survey responses. Perhaps, as Nance, Smithson, and Smith (1993) suggest, the high correlations between size, bankruptcy, and leverage makes finding a separate leverage effect difficult.

Finally, survey findings that firms with heavy R&D expenditures are also active derivatives users would support the cost of funds argument. Unfortunately, although Nance, Smithson, and Smith (1993) find evidence that R&D expenditures are postively associated with derivatives use, they are the only ones to investigate this theory.

A comprehensive summary of the state of the theory is that large firms use derivatives more either because they enjoy economies of scale or because they are less concerned about taxes or bankruptcy costs. Taxes and managerial compensation have much less explanatory power. Conclusions such as these, however, face two challenges.

First, even though more firms report that they hedge fluctuations in cash flows than report that they hedge reported earnings, somewhere between a third and a half of the firms report that earnings are their most important hedging target (see Bodnar, de Jong, and Macrae 2003; Benson and Oliver 2004; and Tables 8.8 and 8.9), except in Sweden (Alkeback, Hagelin, and Pramborg 2006), where more than half the firms report using derivatives to manage their balance sheet. If firms are manging appearances rather than real cash flows, rational economic theories cannot easily explain their motives.

Second, the theories assume firms will use derivatives to hedge away risk. In fact, many surveys suggest firms use derivatives selectively, guided by their market view. These firms are using derivatives and other positions in an attempt to profit from their market forecasts, in violation of the theories' common assumption that the purpose of hedging is to reduce, not increase, risk.

Implications of Survey Research

As Glaum (2002) predicts, risk mangement theories have benefited from survey research. The picture that emerges is much more complex than the simplified world the theoretical assumptions create. Many firms are concerned about reducing volatility and believe that controlling that risk is important. Most firms appear to use a blend of natural and derivatives hedges as part of their risk management strategy. Other firms, perhaps incented by the evolution of the treasury function as a profit center, expect to profit from their views of the financial and commodity markets with derivatives. The bulk of survey research suggests that many firms employ selective hedges, protecting against major risks and occasionally using derivatives in an attempt to profit from their financial market forecasts. Given the well-publicized losses attributed to derivatives (Mettalgesellschaft in 1993, Daimler-Benz and Barings Bank in 1995, Long-Term Capital Management in 2000, and AIG in 2008, to name a few), this evidence would seem to imply that even experienced financial managers do not always use derivatives to control risk, even when that is their intention. When less-sophisticated corporate treasurers enter into these transactions, there is no guarantee that their derivatives positions accurately reflect their intentions. With this complex world, there is little question as to why theoretical, empirical, and survey researchers cannot sort through all the various countervailing factors. Even so, survey research into derivatives use deepens our understanding of how and why these instruments should be of value.

References

Adam, Tim R., and Chitru S. Fernando. 2006. "Hedging, Speculation, and Shareholder Value." *Journal of Financial Economics* 81:2, 283–309.

Alkeback, Per, and Niclas Hagelin. 1999. "Derivative Usage by Nonfinancial Firms in Sweden with an International Comparison." *Journal of International Financial Management and Accounting* 10:2, 105–120.

Alkeback, Per, Niclas Hagelin, and Bengt Pramborg. 2006. "Derivative Usage by Non-Financial Firms in Sweden 1996 and 2003: What Has Changed?" *Managerial Finance* 32:2, 101–114.

Allayannis, George, and James P. Weston. 2001. "The Use of Foreign Currency Derivatives and Firm Market Value." *Review of Financial Studies* 14:1, 243–276.

Bali, Turna G., Susan R. Hume, and Terrence F. Martell. 2007. "A New Look at Hedging with Derivatives: Will Firms Reduce Market Risk Exposure?" *Journal of Futures Markets* 27:11, 1053–1083.

Benson, Karen, and Barry Oliver. 2004. "Management Motivation for Using Financial Derivatives in Australia." *Australian Journal of Management* 29:2, 225–242.

Berkman, Henk, and Michael E. Bradbury. 1996. "Empirical Evidence on the Corporate Use of Derivatives." *Financial Management* 25:2, 5–13.

Block, Stanley R., and Timothy J. Gallagher. 1986. "The Use of Interest Rate Futures and Options by Corporate Financial Managers." *Financial Management* 15:3, 73–78.

Bodnar, Gordon M., Abe de Jong, and Victor Macrae. 2003. "The Impact of Institutional Differences of Derivatives Usage: A Comparative Study of US and Dutch Firms." *European Financial Management* 9:3, 271–297.

Bodnar, Gordon M., Gregory S. Hayt, and Richard C. Marston. 1996. "1995 Wharton Survey of Derivatives Usage by US Non-Financial Firms." *Financial Management* 25:4, 113–133.

———. 1998. "1998 Wharton Survey of Financial Risk Management by US Non-Financial Firms." *Financial Management* 27:4, 70–91.

Bodnar, Gordon M., Gregory S. Hayt, Richard C. Marston, and Charles W. Smithson. 1995. "Wharton Survey of Derivatives Usage by US Non-Financial Firms." *Financial Management* 24:2, 104–114.

Booth, James R., Richard L. Smith, and Richard W. Stolz. 1984. "The Use of Interest Rate Futures by Financial Institutions." *Journal of Bank Research* 15:1, 15–20.

Dolde, Walter. 1993. "The Trajectory of Corporate Risk Management." *Journal of Applied Corporate Finance* 6:3, 33–41.

Francis, Bill B., Iftekhar Hasan, and Delroy M. Hunter. 2008. "Can Hedging Tell the Full Story? Reconciling Differences in United States Aggregate- and Industry-Level Exchange Rate Risk Premium." *Journal of Financial Economics* 90:2, 169–196.

Froot, Kenneth A., David S. Scharfstein, and Jeremy C. Stein. 1993. "Risk Management: Coordinating Corporate Investment and Financing Policies." *Journal of Finance* 48:5, 1629–1658.

Géczy, Christopher, Bernadette A. Minton, and Catherine Schrand. 1997. "Why Firms Use Currency Derivatives." *Journal of Finance* 52:4, 1323–1354.

Glaum, Martin. 2002. "The Determinants of Selective Exchange Risk Management: Evidence from German Non-Financial Firms." *Journal of Applied Corporate Finance* 14:4, 108–121.

Goldberg, Stephen R., Joseph H. Godwin, Myung-Sun Kim, and Charles A. Tritschler. 1998. "On the Determinants of Corporate Usage of Financial Derivatives." *Journal of International Financial Management and Accounting* 9:2, 132–166.

Houston, Carol O., and Gerhard G. Mueller. 1988. "Foreign Exchange Rate Hedging and SFAS No. 52: Relatives or Strangers?" *Accounting Horizons* 2:4, 50–57.

Howton, Shawn D., and Steven B. Perfect. 1998. "Currency and Interest-Rate Derivatives Use in US Firms." *Financial Management* 27:4, 111–121.

Jalilvand, Abolhassan A. 1999. "Why Firms Use Derivatives: Evidence from Canada." *Canadian Journal of Administrative Sciences* 16:3, 213–228.

Kim, Woochan, and Taeyoon Sung. 2005. "What Makes Firms Manage FX Risk?" *Emerging Markets Review* 6:3, 263–288.

Koonce, Lisa, Marlys G. Lipe, and Mary L. McAnally. 2008. "Investor Reactions to Derivative Use and Outcomes." *Review of Accounting Studies* 13:4, 571–597.

Loderer, Claudio, and Karl Pichler. 2000. "Firms, Do You Know Your Currency Risk Exposure? Survey Results." *Journal of Empirical Finance* 7:3–4, 317–344.

Marshall, Andrew P. 2000. "Foreign Exchange Risk Management in U.K., USA and Asia Pacific Multinational Companies." *Journal of Multinational Financial Management* 10:2, 185–211.

Mayers, David, and Clifford W. Smith Jr. 1990. "On the Corporate Demand for Insurance: Evidence from the Reinsurance Market." *Journal of Business* 63:1, 19–40.

Modigliani, Franco, and Merton H. Miller. 1958. "The Cost of Capital, Corporate Finance, and the Theory of Investment." *American Economic Review* 48:3, 261–297.

Myers, Stewart C. 1977. "The Determinants of Corporate Borrowing." *Journal of Financial Economics* 5:2, 147–175.

Nance, Deana R., Clifford W. Smith Jr., and Charles W. Smithson. 1993. "On the Determinants of Corporate Hedging." *Journal of Finance* 48:1, 267–284.

Phillips, Aaron L. 1995. "1995 Derivatives Practices and Instruments Survey." *Financial Mangement* 24:2, 115–125.

Sheedy, Elizabeth. 2006. "Corporate Risk Management in Hong Kong and Singapore." *Managerial Finance* 32:2, 89–100.

Smith, Clifford W., and René M. Stulz. 1985. "The Determinants of Firms' Hedging Policies." *Journal of Financial and Quantitative Analysis* 20:4, 391–405.

Stulz, René. 1984. "Optimal Hedging Policies." *Journal of Finance* 32:1, 127–140.

———. 1996. "Rethinking Risk Management." *Journal of Applied Corporate Finance* 9:3, 8–24.

Tufano, Peter. 1996. "Who Manages Risk? An Empirical Examination of Risk Management Practices in the Gold Mining Industry." *Journal of Finance* 51:4, 1097–1137.

Wall, Larry D., and John J. Pringle. 1989. "Alternative Explanations of Interest Rate Swaps: A Theoretical and Empirical Analysis." *Financial Management* 18:2, 59–73.

9

State of the Art: Do Theory and Practice Actually Meet?

> Well, it may be all right in practice, but it will never work in theory.
>
> Warren Buffett

Introduction: Theory and Practice

The philosophy of social science research suggests that in advanced fields such as financial economics, theories should be developed first and then tested to determine whether their conclusions are supported. Theorists make assumptions and use closely reasoned, logical arguments to reach meaningful conclusions. Logical arguments in finance are usually conjunctive—structured such that if the first assumption is true *and* the second assumption is true *and* the third assumption is true, then the conclusions are true. Elegant and useful theories present just the necessary and sufficient assumptions for their conclusions to be true. In a conjunctive structure, each assumption is a necessary condition and the set is sufficient. These economic and financial theories can be classified as either normative or positive.

Normative theories use logic to imply what *should* be done, and positive theories describe the logic of what *is* done. John Neville Keynes is usually associated with the normative approach and Milton Friedman with the positive. Friedman (1953) and Boland (1979) provide more discussion of normative and positive theories and their role in contemporary economics. Most financial theories are normative and deal with complicated phenomena. Their assumptions are often unrealistic, typically stripping away real-world attributes such as taxes, transaction costs, the passage of time, and so on. Many contemporary theorists agree with Friedman that testing the truth or falsity of assumptions is not important as long as the effect of the economic actors' behavior is the same as if they followed the assumptions. The question of whether a theory's consistency with practice is a valid test is far more controversial. For example, André Gide, the French author and 1947 Nobel Prize laureate, contends, "No theory is good unless one uses it to go beyond."

In Friedman's view, acceptable positive theories are consistent with practice by construction. Many financial researchers who develop normative theories would disagree with the notion that their theory is invalid if it does not match practice. Perhaps they would argue that financial practice is misinformed and firms would be better off if they adopted the theoretically correct approach. Over the years, financial practice has adopted several normative theories. For example, such theories start with the value of a stock as the discounted value of expected future dividends (Williams 1938), then move through duration as a measure of bond risk (Macaulay 1938) and into diversification and beta as investment management tools (Markowitz 1959; Sharpe 1964). Despite these success stories, many theories are inconsistent with practice. One of the main goals of applied as opposed to theoretical research is to explore the interface between theory and practice.

Empirical research bases its findings on direct or indirect observation as its test of reality. Because indirect financial research relies on objective data, such as stock prices and accounting values, and direct research more on gathering subjective data, such as the attitudes and beliefs of financial managers, the benefits of using indirect research to test theory are clear. With objective data, indirect researchers can explore what firms do rather than relying on what they say they do. Because markets are an important arbitrator in finance, indirect researchers can also observe how markets react to firms' financial management decisions without being filtered through financial executives' perceptions.

Because most phenomena interesting enough to study are not directly observable, indirect research can only support inferences and is difficult to generalize. For example, capital structure is a practical decision for every firm's financial executive and plays an important role in the theory of the firm. Financial theory says that each firm has an optimal capital structure and the firm should move toward that mix of debt and equity when raising external capital. Indirect researchers can gather data on changes in firm value that follow changes in capital structure. This research, however, cannot reveal whether the financial executives have an optimal structure in mind as a goal. Survey research, on the other hand, is ideally suited to gathering those kinds of insights.

Surveys can investigate the validity of theory and compliment empirical research by exploring why theory either does or does not match practice; that is, only survey research can ask financial executives whether they are pursuing an optimal capital structure. Yet, survey results can be ambiguous. If surveys find that financial executives do not believe their firms have optimal capital structures, at least two explanations are plausible. First, firms do not have optimal capital structures because of possible flaws in the theory. Second, firms do have optimal capital structures, but practice lags behind theory and financial executives have not accepted capital structure theory as valid. In this case, practice will conform to theory over time. Unfortunately, only longitudinal repeated surveys can unambiguously distinguish between these two possibilities—and surveys can never be replicated exactly. Despite these difficulties, evidence of the gradual acceptance of theory is one way in which survey research validates theory.

Surveys can also aid indirect research. Many times, researchers using indirect methods have too many alternative variables from which to choose when representing their theoretical constructs. Although the primary objective of survey research is rarely to discriminate between instrumental variables in statistical analysis, survey research can provide helpful directions. Another often unintended side benefit of survey research is to uncover problems theorists should solve.

Throughout the chapters in this book, relevant theories are discussed before the survey results. Surveys without theoretical precedents are a poor research strategy—much like the Cheshire Cat's advice to Alice in Lewis Carroll's *Alice's Adventures in Wonderland:* if you don't know where you are going, any road will get you there. Therefore, Chapters 3 through 8 begin with financial theory and then turn to surveys for confirmatory evidence. Except in unusual circumstances, the discussion of statistical techniques or methods is beyond the scope of this book.

Financial theories such as the theory of optimal capital structure are strongly normative, describing what firms ought to do. The assumptions that predicate these theories are typically unrealistic. Even so, highly unrealistic assumptions can often produce clearer implications for practice. Other financial theories are less prescriptive, such as the theory of the cost of capital, and rely on logical argument to make the case for the theoretically correct weighted average cost of capital (WACC). Because surveys often involve different questions, diverse populations and samples, and varied response rates, the evidence surveys bring to bear on theory may be disjointed. While this book attempts to avoid speculation, the results of survey research must be connected and interpreted to provide insights on the status of important financial theories. Those insights often require considering disparate surveys that are rarely repeated. Yet, linking the insights gained from these surveys is a useful way to define the unique contribution of survey research to financial management.

The following overview presents key observations from the previous chapters. Regarding Chapters 3 through 8, this discussion attempts to summarize which of the theories, hypotheses, and explanations presented therein find the greatest support in practice. This discussion focuses on the links between theory and practice as shown by direct evidence acquired through survey research but also comments on empirical results from more traditional studies that provide indirect evidence.

Conducting Survey Research

Survey research has both benefits and limitations. Two of its most important attributes are the ability to produce data unavailable from other sources and to suggest new avenues for future research. Providing direct evidence about the attitudes, beliefs, and behaviors of corporate managers and others can provide valuable insights that complement other types of empirical research. The data accumulated from surveys in corporate finance can serve as a basis for launching other studies to help understand the perceptions and possible motivations of executives who make strategic decisions involving investment, financing, and dividend policy.

Despite these attributes, interpreting the results of surveys requires caution because of potential biases and measurement problems. For example, non-response bias is a common concern. Another potential limitation of surveys is that respondents may not provide truthful answers either because they are hesitant to reveal their firm's strategies or are unaware of those strategies. Respondents may also answer the survey as they believe the researchers want the questions to be answered. Survey researchers can overcome or at least mitigate these and other limitations by developing and executing an effective plan. Chapter 2 provides guidance in how to produce credible survey results. Those interested in conducting survey research and publishing their results in high-quality outlets should be mindful of the importance attached to the originality and rigor of their work.

Capital Budgeting

Capital budgeting describes the process by which firms select investments in capital goods. These decisions involve forecasts of both costs and benefits and are typically large enough to have significant consequences for the firm and its stakeholders.

Financial theory suggests a number of techniques to help managers assemble and process the cost-benefit information needed to make sound decisions. Financial theory's major contribution to the finance discipline is to point out that the cost of capital used to finance a project and the timing of the cash flows are as important as the cost of the physical assets. Chapter 3 discusses five major topics in capital budgeting: project evaluation methods, risk evaluation and adjustment, capital rationing, hurdle rates, and postaudits.

Project Evaluation Methods

Financial theory contends that a firm's WACC should be used as a discount rate to equate present and future costs and benefits. This approach says firms should use discounted cash flow (DCF) methods instead of methods that fail to properly account for the cost of capital or the passage of time. Despite the long history of theoretically correct discounted methods, surveys show that nondiscounted methods remain popular among financial managers.

What is reasonably clear from the surveys conducted between 1960 and 2002 is the increase in the percentage of firms that use a DCF approach. Tables 3.1, 3.2, and 3.3 in Chapter 3, despite the wide variation in samples and questionnaires, suggest that the theory has made substantial inroads into being adopted in practice. Survey researchers such as Kim and Ulferts (1996) agree that DCF techniques have become much more widely accepted in the past 40 years. Graham and Harvey (2001) provide some explanation and support for this trend when they report that large firms and firms with chief executive officers (CEOs) who hold a master of business administration (MBA) degree are more likely to use a DCF approach, and small firms with CEOs without an MBA are more likely to use alternative methods. Recent surveys of executives outside the United States (e.g., Kester, Chang, Echanis, Haikal, Isa, Skully, Tsui, and Wang, 1999; Brounen, de Jong, and Koedijk 2004) also find that the DCF approach is the most popular, again with larger firms being more likely to use the theoretically correct DCF approach.

Risk Evaluation and Adjustment

Most of the capital budgeting components (e.g., cash flows) are uncertain. Understandably, financial theory says that risk should be recognized in every capital investment analysis. Once an analyst has measured project risk, theory suggests that when project risk differs from firm risk, firms should adjust the project's discount rate or cash flows to reflect the risk.

Table 3.7 in Chapter 3 traces the survey history of financial practice regarding risk in capital budgeting. From 1975 to 2000, these results suggest that firms recognize risk when they analyze capital projects. These approaches to risk adjustment are consistent with financial theory, as most surveys report that either adjusting discount rates or cash flows is the most popular method for accommodating risk.

Despite this support for theory, Gitman and Vandenberg (2000) find that less than half of the responding firms use one of these methods. Over time, the preferred alternative to the two theoretical methods is the payback period method. Despite many differences in samples and questionnaires, the survey results from non-U.S. companies appear consistent with the U.S. findings.

Capital Rationing

Financial theory says that firms should adopt all positive net present value (NPV) investment opportunities without regard to the source of capital. In practice, managers may reject positive-NPV projects to avoid issuing stock and diluting ownership, to control estimation bias that causes projects to be analyzed optimistically, and to avoid operational bottlenecks. The first practice is contrary to theory, while the second two are reasonable exceptions that recognize realistic constraints.

The trend among firms appears to be away from capital rationing. Table 3.13 in Chapter 3 suggests that between Robichek and McDonald's 1966 survey and Gitman and Vandenberg's 2000 research, the popularity of capital rationing declined.

Mukherjee and Hingorani (1999) report that their respondents tend to cite reluctance to issue external financing and avoiding estimation bias as their primary motivations for rationing capital. The first rationale is inconsistent with theory, while the second may be a reasonable exception to theory. Other studies that survey firms outside the United States report similar responses. This research unfortunately does not answer the question of whether theory prevails and does not support a trend.

Hurdle Rates

To be theoretically correct, firms should use their WACC adjusted for risk as their hurdle rate when accepting or rejecting projects. The evidence suggests a trend toward broader acceptance of WACC. The strongest evidence comes from two pairs of similar surveys: (1) Schall, Sundem, and Geijsbeek (1978) and Payne, Heath, and Gale (1999) and (2) Gitman and Mercurio (1982) and Gitman and Vandenberg (2000). Both pairs are separated in time and use similar samples and questionnaires. Based on the first two studies, the evidence shows the percentage of firms using the WACC as their hurdle rate rises from 46 percent to 64 percent during the 21-year period. Data from the second two studies show that the percentage of firms using the cost of the specific source of project financing as a hurdle rate declines from 17 percent to 8 percent over the 19-year period. Non-U.S. firms report using the WACC as a hurdle rate less frequently than U.S. firms, but the trend toward using the WACC is similar.

Postaudits

Estimation bias and the difficulty of making accurate cash flow forecasts suggest that postaudits might be useful tools to improve firms' capital budgeting process. In contrast to other areas, earlier surveys show a wider use of postaudits than more recent research. Survey evidence reveals that over a 20 to 30 year period, the percentage of firms that report using postaudits falls from more than 80 percent (Klammer 1972; Scapens and Sale 1981) to less than 50 percent (Gitman and Vandenberg 2000). Gitman and Vandenberg suggest that the decline could actually be a validation of earlier postaudits, indicating that firms have learned to make better decisions. The truth of their conjecture is difficult to determine.

Cash Flows

Another topic in capital budgeting that typically pits theory against practice concerns the appropriate measure of cash flows generated by capital projects. Theory says that incremental cash flows should be the measure of a project's contribution to the firm. In practice, managers use accounting measures that use accounting depreciation (rather than the appropriate tax deduction for depreciation), incorporate interest expense (which incorrectly double-counts the cost of debt), and ignore the working-capital requirements of the project.

The results of Kim, Crick, and Farragher (1984) show that more than 59 percent of U.S. respondents and 63 percent of non-U.S. respondents report that they measure benefits in terms of cash flow. These authors conclude that this evidence is consistent with finance theory and an improvement over the findings of Stonehill and Nathanson (1968), who report that only 48 percent of surveyed firms measure projects in terms of cash flow.

Cost of Capital

Chapter 4 reviews the theory and survey research related to the cost of capital, which involves the cost of a firm's sources of long-term financing. Financial theory says that firms should calculate their cost of capital using the weighted average cost of their capital components using target weights, that they should use the marginal component costs (adjusted for tax benefits as appropriate), and that they should use multiple risk-adjusted costs of capital for projects whose risks differ from the normal or average risk of the firm. Theory says that firms should use market values rather than book values in determining their cost of capital because capital investment analysis, one of the primary purposes of calculating the cost of capital, is forward-looking and balance sheet values reflect historical—not current—costs.

Survey research generally supports the financial theory. In early survey-based studies, both Pflomn (1963) and Christy (1966) report that few survey respondents use any form of WACC. Both surveys confirm that even though the theory was available for use, firms did not widely accept it. Data from later surveys such as Gitman and Mercurio (1982) show, however, that 42 percent of the survey respondents report using the theoretically correct WACC. In a similar study,

Gitman and Vandenberg (2000) find that 50 percent of their respondents use the appropriate WACC. In these same surveys, however, the percentage of respondents using the theoretically incorrect measures of specific financing source or book-value weights drops modestly, from 33 percent in 1982 to 28 percent in 2000.

The two Gitman surveys provide evidence that most firms exclude some sources of capital in their calculations. For example, the Gitman and Vandenberg (2000) study finds that 35 percent of firms with capital leases and 21 percent of firms with preferred stock outstanding exclude these sources from their WACC calculation.

The overall conclusion from survey research into the cost of capital seems to be that practice grows much closer to theory between the 1960s and 1980s, with more firms adopting the theoretically correct WACC approach. The adoption is far from universal, however, with about a third of the firms using book values or project-specific costs that are theoretically incorrect. The adoption percentages are a little more favorable toward theory by 2000. Even so, many firms appear to omit sources of capital and a substantial percentage continues to use approaches that are inconsistent with theory. Surveys conducted of firms domiciled outside the United States show similar percentages. Using Stonehill and Nathanson's (1968) survey as a benchmark, the results presented by Stanley and Block (1984) and Arnold and Hatzopoulos (2000) suggest the trend among multinational and non-U.S. firms appears to be toward a wider acceptance of theory.

Other topics important to this theory including cost of capital components, suitable multiple hurdle rates, and calculations of the WACC with appropriate frequency are covered by many of the same surveys and reach similar conclusions. Given that many financial executives believe that appearances are important, that the market for their firm's stock is informationally inefficient, and that investors are subject to behavioral biases, discovering that theory has failed to find more converts is not surprising. Even so, cost of capital seems to be an area where survey research confirms theory has had a substantial impact on practice.

Capital Structure and Financing Decisions

A firm's capital structure reflects how a firm finances its activities through some combination of long-term liabilities and shareholders' equity. Modigliani and Miller (1958) propose a normative theory of capital structure where, under stringent assumptions of perfect information and no taxes or bankruptcy costs, a firm's capital structure is irrelevant. This theory says that capital structure does not matter because shareholders can make their own leverage. Under this theory's bankruptcy assumption, firms can fail, but this does not involve any cost to them. Therefore, bankruptcy is not a concern. The tax assumption removes the tax benefits of debt. Of course, these are not realistic assumptions but are necessary and sufficient for the irrelevance conclusion to hold, thereby focusing attention on the conditions that make capital structure important.

Capital structure theory has a stronger normative structure when compared to the theory supporting the weighted average cost of capital. By relaxing unrealistic assumptions, theorists can demonstrate that with tax deductibility of interest on debt and with costly bankruptcy, every firm should maintain a capital structure that balances the tax advantages of debt against the threat of bankruptcy. The "should" is what gives this theory its strong normative flavor. The most consistent result across decades of survey research is that a majority of firms use financial rules of thumb rather than any of the variations of the theory.

The original capital structure theory is elegant but untestable. Therefore, to design empirical tests, researchers have to specify how taxes and bankruptcy costs matter to the firm. These specifications include the following:

- Static trade-off models, where firms maintain an optimal capital structure in the face of bankruptcy costs and taxes
- Pecking-order models, where managers have a preference for internal financing because the market undervalues the firm's equity
- Signaling models, where managers use capital structure changes to indicate their belief in the future of the firm
- Agency cost models, where debt is used to control managers' perquisites
- Neutral mutation models, where capital structure decisions are products of vestigial habit

Theorists proposed each of these models because earlier versions had been difficult to justify in the face of inconsistent empirical tests.

Survey research, on the other hand, pursues the question of how financial managers make decisions about their capital structures. From Pinegar and Wilbricht (1989) to Kamath (1997) to Graham and Harvey (2001), one result stands out: more firms use financial rules of thumb (labeled financial flexibility in many surveys) than any one of the theoretical models. This contradiction poses many challenges when the survey researchers interpret their results.

A prime example is Graham and Harvey (2001), who characterize their results as unsupportive of any of the capital structure theories. In classic normative style, the authors suggest that capital structure theorists may be correct, but firms ignore their advice. If this suggestion is true, an informationally efficient market would ensure that these firms had higher costs of capital than firms that followed the theorists' models. In time, these firms would become less competitive and eventually disappear. This conclusion puts the authors in a somewhat awkward position because their sample favors large and successful firms (42 percent of the firms in their sample have annual sales of more than $1 billion) and their respondents consistently rank financial flexibility as the most important determinant of capital structure. To their credit, Graham and Harvey also suggest that the theories may be flawed and that alternate theories need to be developed. Perhaps because their finding that financial rules of thumb are the most common approach to managing capital structure does not fit with their theoretical paradigm or because developing a theory was not their purpose, neither they nor any of the other survey researchers suggest how financial rules of thumb might be the basis for a theory.

Survey research on capital structure outside the United States must adjust for the variation in institutional arrangements among jurisdictions. Nevertheless, many of these surveys replicate Graham and Harvey's (2001) survey with minor local adaptations. The results consistently show that financial flexibility ranks above all other alternatives in helping the respondents make their capital structure decisions.

Despite several decades of developing and refining capital structure theory, none of the normative theories indicating how managers should act fits the survey data. Instead, financial rules of thumb seem to be the first choice of many financial managers. As Merton Miller observed (1977), capital markets are opaque and the task of pursuing an optimal capital structure is daunting. A rational response is to stick to rules of thumb, especially if they have proven sufficient over time.

Dividends and Dividend Policy

As Baker, Powell, and Veit (2002, p. 242) note, "Despite exhaustive theoretical and empirical analysis to explain their pervasive presence, dividends remain one of the thorniest puzzles in corporate finance". As repeatedly discussed throughout this book, corporate financial managers should strive to make decisions that lead to maximizing the wealth of shareholders as reflected in the firm's stock price. On the surface, paying cash dividends may seem to be a logical way to increase shareholder wealth unless the firm can reinvest earnings back in the business to benefit shareholders. The decision of whether to pay or retain earnings is often a puzzling decision because it involves many conflicting forces. Much debate exists about the role, if any, of dividend decisions in share prices. Financial executives, investors, investment analysts, and academic researchers continue to be at odds over the connection between dividends and firm value.

Beginning with Miller and Modigliani (1961), academic theorists show that dividends are irrelevant to the value of the firm, assuming various highly restrictive assumptions. For example, such assumptions include that markets have perfect information and lack structural impediments such as taxes and that firms hold their investment policy constant. The purpose of Miller and Modigliani's theory is not to describe the world as it is but rather to identify the necessary and sufficient conditions for dividends to be irrelevant. If dividends *are* relevant, therefore, it must be because one or more of the assumptions does not hold.

To explain why firms pay dividends, most theories of dividends relax one or more of Modigliani and Miller's (1961) assumptions of perfect information, frictionless markets, and investment policy as the only factor driving value. The "big three" imperfections are taxes, information asymmetry (signaling), and agency costs. Not surprisingly, researchers developed and tested theories involving these imperfections. Others devised behavioral explanations for paying dividends, while still others concocted theories involving the firm life cycle and catering.

Despite decades of empirical evidence on alternative explanations for why firms pay dividends, the results are mixed for studies using secondary data from capital markets and accounting statements. In short, there is no clear winner. Whether this widespread failure of empirical research rests with variable misspecification, tests that lack statistical power, or a misunderstanding of the corporate mindset, theorists cannot fully explain why firms behave as they do.

Survey research based on the views of financial executives and others provides useful insights on how and why firms make their dividend decisions. Although Lintner (1956) was successful with his partial-adjustment model in explaining how firms pay dividends, his research does not explain why they do it or how investors view dividends. Since Lintner's seminal work, survey researchers have examined various theoretical explanations for paying dividends. Results from both the U.S. and non-U.S. surveys show that no single theoretical model adequately explains corporate dividend behavior. Although no consensus exists on the primary explanation for paying dividends, signaling models appear to garner the most support. Survey studies also reveal that certain factors such as the level of current and future earnings, the stability of earnings, and the pattern of past dividends appear to be important determinants of dividend policy in many countries.

Perhaps the most reasonable explanation for why direct and indirect empirical research has failed to solve the dividend puzzle is that researchers are looking for a simple, unified solution. As if guided by Occam's razor, they have constructed models that avoid complexity. Occam's razor, while prizing simplicity, also insists that every simple explanation be consistent with the facts. Research has reached the point where simplicity may have to give some ground to complexity. Firms face different circumstances and have different characteristics, which may influence their views and behavior. Financial economists will probably have to develop and study models that incorporate companies' idiosyncrasies before finance can give more practical advice on dividend policies based on something other than a rule of thumb; that is, they may need to veer from a one-size-fits-all model to one offering a more customized fit. Baker, Powell, and Veit (2002, p. 257) state this view somewhat differently:

> Our view is that researchers have identified all the key pieces of the dividend puzzle but need to focus their attention on developing firm-specific

dividend models. If this puzzle were a jigsaw puzzle, different firms use different combinations of puzzle pieces to form different pictures of the firm. This results because each firm has different characteristics, managers, and stockholders. One firm may focus on puzzle pieces that together form an Andrew Wyeth–like picture of the firm and another firm may select puzzle pieces that form a Pablo Picasso–like picture of the firm. Is one of them correct and the other incorrect? Not necessarily. Each policy may be appropriate for each firm. Conversely, both firms may possibly need a Wyeth-like structure in which case the value of the Picasso-like firm is lower than necessary.

Share Repurchases, Special Dividends, Stock Splits, and Stock Dividends

Instead of paying regular cash dividends, some firms distribute cash to shareholders in the form of share repurchases and special dividends. A frequent question examined in the finance literature concerns the motives for these different distribution methods. Financial economists offer various explanations for repurchasing shares of which the most common involve taxes, signaling and undervaluation, agency costs of free cash flows, capital structure, takeover deterrence, and stock options. Empirical evidence from nonsurvey research suggests some support for each of these explanations. Thus, there is no universally accepted motivation behind repurchases.

The survey evidence on share repurchases involves U.S., Canadian, and European firms. Overall, the results show that managers favor the flexibility of repurchases to cash dividends and buy their firm's stock when they view it as undervalued. Additionally, managers view buybacks as conveying private information about their firms to investors. Although no unanimous agreement exists on the most important motive for repurchasing shares, managers give the greatest support to the signaling motive.

The finance literature offers several theoretical models that propose to explain why firms pay special dividends including the signaling, agency cost of free cash flow, and wealth transfer explanations. The strongest empirical support goes to the signaling explanation; that is, special dividends convey information to investors. Although little survey evidence exists on special dividends, the results lend support to the signaling explanation for disbursing excess funds but not the other two explanations.

Some firms also engage in stock distributions in the form of stock splits and stock dividends. Theoretically, both forms of distribution are purely cosmetic accounting changes that should not change a firm's economic value. In practice, stock distributions are more than what they seem on the surface. In practice, empirical evidence indicates that the new share price is greater than would be expected by dividing the old share price by the new number of shares.

Of the common explanations for stock splits, the most empirical support exists for the signaling hypothesis. The trading range and liquidity hypotheses receive some support, and the tax option hypothesis gets the least. By contrast, the survey evidence suggests greater support for the trading range and liquidity hypotheses than the signaling explanation. For stock dividends, empirical evidence lends support to the signaling hypothesis, provides mixed support for the trading range, tax timing, cash substitution, and retained earnings hypotheses, and offers little support for the liquidity hypothesis. Of the six explanations for paying stock dividends, the results of managerial surveys appear to provide the most support for signaling.

Overall, both the indirect and direct empirical results do not produce a clear winner for explaining share repurchases, special dividends, stock splits, or stock dividends. What appears to be consistent among all of these decisions is that they affect share price and hence affect shareholder value. The underlying reason this occurs still requires additional research.

Risk Management and Derivatives

Financial theory says if the market is informationally efficient and if investors can diversify away unsystematic risk without incurring costs, firms cannot add value by hedging the risks they face. When firms incur costs to hedge, the theory implies, they reduce their value because their investors are apprised of both the hedge and its costs. As Glaum (2002) points out, explanations for risk management hedging practice must rely on market imperfections not accounted for by the theory. These imperfections include costly and asymmetric information and financial managers or shareholders who cannot diversify. By exploiting these imperfections, firms can create value by hedging their risks. These hedges can be natural, as when foreign assets are financed with foreign liabilities, or derivative, as when a firm takes a long position in foreign currency futures to guarantee an exchange rate.

Smith and Stulz's (1985) normative model anchors most other theories in this area. Their analysis suggests that hedging is more beneficial with higher marginal tax rates, as the threat of bankruptcy increases, and with poorly diversified managers and shareholders. Other theorists add that securities such as convertible bonds and preferred stock are close substitutes for derivatives and should be considered when measuring a firm's hedge.

Indirect research into how firms use derivatives really begins after 1994 when the Financial Accounting Standards Board issued the Statement of Financial Accounting Standards (SFAS) Number 119, Disclosure about Derivative

Financial Instruments and Fair Value of Financial Instruments, which requires firms to expand their derivative disclosure. Following SFAS 119, researchers could measure firms' derivative positions periodically, and much of the research in this area is empirical. Despite the disadvantage of being limited to subjective data, survey research since 1995 has added considerably to the understanding of how and why firms use derivatives.

Surveys consistently report that more than half of the firms responding to surveys use derivatives. While the percentage varies with the survey, by the early 1990s, reported derivatives usage varies between 60 percent (Nance, Smith, and Smithson 1993) and 85 percent (Dolde 1993). Furthermore, "selective hedging" appears to be the norm. Stulz (1996) originates this term to describe firms that report they hedge but only in light of their market view and rarely all their exposure. Selective hedging is not the risk management strategy the theorists are modeling and is a polite way of describing speculation, which most financial executives would be reluctant to report in a survey. Stulz (p. 11) says, "Despite the spread of the doctrine of efficient markets [which would make hedging irrelevant], the world remains full of corporate executives who are convinced of their own ability to predict future interest rates, exchange rates, and commodity prices." Dolde finds that 78 percent of his respondents hedge selectively and are well aware of the potential to gain from this activity. The Bodnar series of surveys (Bodnar, Hayt, and Marston 1996, 1998; Bodnar et al. 1995) reports that firms typically hedge less than 50 percent of their exposure.

Surveys of non-U.S. firms reveal even more about the nature of hedging. Many surveys of firms outside the United States use the same questionnaire as the Bodnar surveys. They find, like their U.S. counterparts, that a majority of firms report using derivatives. Also like the U.S. firms, hedging away their risk exposure does not appear to be their goal. Glaum (2002, p. 117) observes, "A large majority of these [German] firms (88%) indicated that they use derivatives only for hedging purposes. However, closer inspection of the companies' risk management practices suggests such firms cannot unambiguously be characterized as hedgers." Even more revealing are Loderer and Pichler's (2000) results. In a survey of large Swiss firms, they find a majority of respondents report using derivatives to manage currency exposure, much like other studies. When the authors ask the respondents to quantify their currency risk, less than 40 percent of the sample can do so. The central assumption of the theory—that firms want to hedge away risk to add value—may be incorrect. When firms decide how much to hedge based on their view of the market, they are not hedging in the theoretical sense. Furthermore, if these firms do not calculate and monitor their risk exposure, then taking risk in search of trading profit is a more likely explanation for their behavior.

Surveys also reveal other reasons for using derivatives. As reported in Chapter 8, between a third and a half of U.S. and non-U.S. survey respondents say they use derivatives to manage reported earnings. If firms are managing appearances rather than economically relevant risk exposures, their behavior will not correspond to any normative economic theory based on risk reduction.

The real world is more byzantine than the theories allow, and financial executives' motives are more complex. Given the well-publicized financial meltdowns like those of Metallgesellschaft, Orange County, Sears Roebuck, Proctor & Gamble, Daiwa and Barings, and Long-Term Capital Management, to name a few, what financial executive would admit to using derivatives to speculate? Even so, the bulk of survey research suggests that many firms recognize their natural hedges, strive to protect against major risks, and occasionally use selective hedges to bet on their view of financial markets.

Given that experts (and several economic Nobel prize winners) were behind some of the most spectacular financial failures in recent history, basing indirect research on companies' accounting reports of their derivative positions is probably incomplete because such reports may not be fully reliable. Survey researchers have a better chance of finding out why firms behave as they do because they can ask them. Getting an honest and knowledgable answer remains a potential problem. Even though academics' theoretical understanding has not advanced much in the past several decades, survey research has identified some promising avenues for future development.

Summary and Conclusions

As previously noted, Graham (2004, p. 40) comments that "survey research is by no means the standard academic approach these days; in fact it's sometimes looked down on in academic circles as 'unscientific'." This view is undeserved. As the chapters in this book show, survey research has made many valuable contributions that have advanced the understanding of how corporate finance works in the real world. Without survey research's reality check, many elegant, but incorrect, financial management theories would go unchallenged.

The purpose of research in corporate finance is to help managers looking for guidance in making capital budgeting decisions, calculating the cost of capital, designing their capital structure, and making dividend policy decisions. Some authors suggest that theories should trump practice, such as Graham and Harvey (2001, p. 233) when they say, "Alternatively, perhaps the theories are valid descriptions of what firms should do—but corporations ignore the theoretical advice." Most academics, however, believe that when practice is inconsistent with theory, the theory needs revising. That is not to say that theory cannot be useful. Any theoretical explanation of real-world phenomena that is consistent with the facts and helps managers either predict or understand is a valuable addition to management practice. The ultimate test of any financial theory is whether it makes firms better off.

At the most fundamental level, theory describes what companies should do, indirect research describes what companies actually do, and direct research reports what companies say they do and why they do it. All three are necessary for progress in financial practice.

References

Arnold, Glen C., and Panos D. Hatzopoulos. 2000. "The Theory-Practice Gap in Capital Budgeting: Evidence from the United Kingdom." *Journal of Business Finance and Accounting* 27:5–6, 603–626.

Baker, H. Kent, Gary E. Powell, and E. Theodore Veit. 2002. "Revisiting the Dividend Puzzle: Do All of the Pieces Now Fit?" *Review of Financial Economics* 11:4, 241–261.

Bodnar, Gordon M., Gregory S. Hayt, and Richard C. Marston. 1996. "1995 Wharton Survey of Derivatives Usage by US Non-Financial Firms." *Financial Management* 25:4, 113–133.

———. 1998. "1998 Wharton Survey of Financial Risk Management by US Non-Financial Firms." *Financial Management* 27:4, 70–91.

Bodnar, Gordon M., Gregory S. Hayt, Richard C. Marston, and Charles W. Smithson. 1995. "Wharton Survey of Derivatives Usage by US Non-Financial Firms." *Financial Management* 24:2, 104–114.

Boland, Lawrence A. 1979. "A Critique of Friedman's Critics." *Journal of Economic Literature* 17:2, 503–522.

Brounen, Dirk, Abe de Jong, and Kees Koedijk. 2004. "Corporate Finance in Europe: Confronting Theory with Practice." *Financial Management* 33:4, 71–101.

Christy, George A. 1966. *Capital Budgeting: Current Practices and their Efficiency.* Eugene: Bureau of Business and Economic Research, University of Oregon.

Dolde, Walter. 1993. "The Trajectory of Corporate Risk Management." *Journal of Applied Corporate Finance* 6:3, 33–41.

Friedman, Milton. 1953. "The Methodology of Positive Economics." In *Essays in Positive Economics,* 3–43. Chicago: University of Chicago Press.

Gitman, Lawrence J., and Vincent A. Mercurio. 1982. "Cost of Capital Techniques Used by Major U.S. Firms: Survey and Analysis of Fortune's 1000." *Financial Management* 11:4, 21–30.

Gitman, Lawrence J., and Pieter A. Vandenberg. 2000. "Cost of Capital Techniques Used by Major U.S. Firms: 1997 vs. 1980." *Financial Practice and Education* 10:2, 53–68.

Glaum, Martin. 2002. "The Determinants of Selective Exchange Risk Management: Evidence from German Non-Financial Firms." *Journal of Applied Corporate Finance* 14:4, 108–121.

Graham, John R. 2004. "Roundtable on Corporate Disclosure." *Journal of Applied Corporate Finance* 16:4, 338–362.

Graham, John R., and Campbell R. Harvey. 2001. "The Theory and Practice of Corporate Finance: Evidence from the Field." *Journal of Financial Economics* 60:2–3, 187–243.

Kamath, Ravindra R. 1997. "Long-Term Financing Decisions: Views and Practices of Financial Managers of NYSE Firms." *Financial Review* 32:2, 350–356.

Kester, George W., Rosita P. Chang, Erlinda S. Echanis, Shalahuddin Haikal, Mansor Md. Isa, Michael T. Skully, Kai-Chong Tsui, and Chi-Jeng Wang. 1999. "Capital Budgeting Practices in the Asia-Pacific Region: Australia, Hong Kong, Indonesia, Malaysia, Philippines and Singapore." *Financial Practice and Education* 9:1, 25–33.

Kim, Suk H., Trevor Crick, and Edward J. Farragher. 1984. "Foreign Capital Budgeting Practices Used by the U.S. and Non-U.S. Multinational Companies." *Engineering Economist* 29:3, 2–10.

Kim, Suk H., and Gregory Ulferts. 1996. "A Summary of Multinational Capital Budgeting Studies." *Managerial Finance* 22:1, 75–88.

Klammer, Thomas. 1972. "Empirical Evidence of the Adoption of Sophisticated Capital Budgeting Techniques." *Journal of Business* 45:3, 387–398.

Lintner, John. 1956. "Distribution of Incomes of Corporations among Dividends, Retained Earnings and Taxes." *American Economic Review* 46:2, 97–113.

Loderer, Claudio, and Karl Pichler. 2000. "Firms, Do You Know Your Currency Risk Exposure? Survey Results." *Journal of Empirical Finance* 7:3–4, 317–344.

Macaulay, Frederick R. 1938. *Some Theoretical Problems Suggested by the Movements of Interest Rates, Bond Yields, and Stock Prices in the United States since 1856.* New York: National Bureau of Economic Research.

Markowitz, Harry. 1959. *Portfolio Selection-Efficient Diversification of Investments.* New Haven, CT: Yale University Press.

Miller, Merton H. 1977. "Debt and Taxes." *Journal of Finance* 32:2, 261–275.

Miller, Merton H., and Franco Modigliani. 1961. "Dividend Policy, Growth and the Valuation of Shares." *Journal of Business* 34:4, 411–433.

Modigliani, Franco, and Merton H. Miller. 1958. "The Cost of Capital, Corporate Finance, and the Theory of Investment." *American Economic Review* 48:3, 261–297.

Mukherjee, Tarun K., and Vineeta L. Hingorani. 1999. "Capital-Rationing Decisions of Fortune 500 Firms: A Survey." *Financial Practice and Education* Spring/Summer 9:1, 7–15.

Nance, Deana R., Clifford W. Smith Jr., and Charles W. Smithson. 1993. "On the Determinants of Corporate Hedging." *Journal of Finance* 48:1, 267–284.

Payne, Janet D., Will Carrington Heath, and Lewis R. Gale. 1999. "Comparative Financial Practice in the US and Canada: Capital Budgeting and Risk Assessment Techniques." *Financial Practice and Education* 9:1, 16–24.

Pflomn, Norman P. 1963. *Managing Capital Expenditures.* New York: National Industrial Conference Board.

Pinegar, J. Michael, and Lisa Wilbricht. 1989. "What Managers Think of Capital Structure Theory: A Survey." *Financial Management* 18:4, 82–91.

Robichek, Alexander A., and John G. McDonald. 1966. "Financial Management in Transition, Long Range Planning Service." Report no. 268. Menlo Park, CA: Stanford Research Institute.

Scapens, Robert W., and J. Timothy Sale. 1981. "Performance Measurement and Formal Capital Expenditure Controls in Divisionalized Companies." *Journal of Business Finance and Accounting* 8:3, 389–419.

Schall, Lawrence D., Gary L. Sundem, and William R. Geijsbeek Jr. 1978. "Survey and Analysis of Capital Budgeting Methods." *Journal of Finance* 33:1, 281–287.

Sharpe, William F. 1964. "Capital Asset Prices: A Theory of Capital Market Equilibrium under Conditions of Risk." *Journal of Finance* 19:3, 425–442.

Smith, Clifford W., and René M. Stulz. 1985. "The Determinants of Firms' Hedging Policies." *Journal of Financial and Quantitative Analysis* 20:4, 391–405.

Stanley, Majorie T., and Stanley B. Block. 1984. "A Survey of Multinational Capital Budgeting." *Financial Review* 19:1, 36–54.

Stonehill, Arthur, and Leonard Nathanson. 1968. "Capital Budgeting and the Multinational Corporation." *California Management Review* 10:4, 39–52.

Stulz, René. 1996. "Rethinking Risk Management." *Journal of Applied Corporate Finance* 9:3, 8–24.

Williams, John Burr. 1938. *The Theory of Investment Value*. Cambridge, MA: Harvard University Press.

Author Index

Content Index